ONE HUNDRED FIFTY YEARS OF JAPANESE FOREIGN RELATIONS

ONE HUNDRED FIFTY YEARS OF JAPANESE FOREIGN RELATIONS

From 1868 to 2018

HATANO Sumio

A project of The Society for Promotion of Japanese Diplomacy

Translated by Carl Freire, Terry Gallagher, and Tom Kain

Editorial supervision by HAMAOKA Takayuki

Japan Publishing Industry Foundation for Culture

Note to Readers
This book follows the Hepburn system of romanization. In general, Japanese names are given in Japanese order (surname first). Macrons are used in people's and place names, except very common place names such as "Tokyo." Chinese and Korean names are also given in traditional order (surname first), except for individuals with names widely known in Western order (e.g., "Wellington Koo"). With the English reader in mind, some of the sidebar articles and charts from the original have been omitted or replaced.

One Hundred Fifty Years of Japanese Foreign Relations: From 1868 to 2018
by Hatano Sumio.
A project of The Society for Promotion of Japanese Diplomacy.
Translated by Carl Freire, Terry Gallagher, and Tom Kain.
Editorial supervision by Hamaoka Takayuki.

Published by
Japan Publishing Industry Foundation for Culture (JPIC)
2-2-30 Kanda-Jinbocho, Chiyoda-ku, Tokyo 101-0051, Japan

First English edition: August 2022

Originally published in Japanese under the title *Nihon gaikō no 150 nen: Bakumatsu Ishin kara Heisei made* by Nihon Gaikō Kyōkai (The Society for Promotion of Japanese Diplomacy) in 2019.
English publishing rights arranged with The Society for Promotion of Japanese Diplomacy.

Book design: Miki Kazuhiko, Ampersand Works
Jacket and cover illustration: "First Landing at Gorahama," an illustration from Commodore M. C. Perry's *Narrative of the Expedition of an American Squadron to the China Seas and Japan, Performed in the Years 1852, 1853, and 1854.* (Courtesy of International Research Center for Japanese Studies)

Printed in Japan
softcover ISBN 978-4-86658-173-6
ebook (ePub) ISBN 978-4-86658-185-9
https://www.jpic.or.jp/

Preface to the English Edition

Since the establishment of the Ministry of Foreign Affairs in 1869, Japanese diplomacy has been aimed at improving the country's international standing through an emphasis on cooperation with the West. It has been buffeted by relations with East Asia and the constant wars and conflicts there, as well as by the wild fluctuations in domestic politics. However, Japanese diplomacy was reborn after World War II with a new focus on international cooperation, and it has maintained that approach to this day.

The focus on international cooperation is distinguished by its emphasis on flexible adaptation to changes in the international situation. Japanese diplomacy avoids setting topics for international discussion or engaging in molding the international order or the rules of the game. In that sense, it has no grand strategy. Rather, its diplomatic strategies are designed around what is "feasible" more than on what is "desirable" in the context of diplomatic objectives and principles, with international relations as they actually exist taken as a given. Originality and ingenuity are at the forefront in this paradigm, with Japan sometimes demonstrating a capacity for strategic action and sometimes pragmatic adaptability.

Since the end of the Cold War, based on Japan's awareness of itself as an "economic superpower," Japanese diplomatic policies have shown signs of changing in the direction of a "proactive diplomacy" that plays a greater role in shaping the international order.

The present volume provides an overview of the aforementioned changes in Japanese diplomacy as it traces its 150-year history. Two distinctive features of this work are that it covers the final fifteen years of the Tokugawa shogunate that laid the foundations for Japanese diplomacy, and that it also includes, in "column" sidebar articles, portraits of the foreign ministers and diplomatic officials who have supported the country's diplomacy.

The Japanese edition upon which this English translation is based was published in 2019. The plan for that volume grew out of a suggestion from Ikeura Yasuhiro, the then-president of the Society for Promotion of Japanese Diplomacy.

It is to President Ikeura—who did not live to see this English edition published—that this volume is dedicated.

Finally, I would like to thank Hamaoka Takayuki, Kobayashi Hiroyuki, Suzuki Shō, Tani Kazushi, and Liu Yingwu for their patience and their confidence in this volume. I would like to offer special thanks to Mr. Hamaoka for his dedicated assistance.

Hatano Sumio
Professor Emeritus
University of Tsukuba

March 2022

Contents

CHAPTER 1

Bakufu Diplomacy and the Opening of Japan

1-1. Depiction of the challenges faced aboard the *Kanrin Maru*

TIMELINE

1853 (Kaei 6)

July 8 Commodore Matthew C. Perry's squadron arrives at Uraga

July 14 Perry makes landfall at Kurihama, delivers personal letter from US president Millard Fillmore

August 5 Senior Councillor Abe Masahiro solicits daimyo opinions on response to the US diplomatic message

August 22 Russian squadron commanded by Vice-Admiral Yevfimiy Putyatin arrives at Nagasaki

1854 (Kaei 7/Ansei 1)

March 31 Japan-US Amity Treaty (Kanagawa Treaty) signed in Kanagawa

October 14 Anglo-Japanese Friendship Treaty signed in Nagasaki

1856 (Ansei 3)

January 30 Signing of Dutch-Japan Treaty of Peace and Amity

August 21 US consul general to Japan Townsend Harris arrives at Shimoda

October 23 British army invades Guangzhou (the Arrow War, a.k.a. the Second Opium War)

1857 (Ansei 4)

June 26 Signing of convention between Japan and US

December 7 Harris travels to Edo Castle, presents shogun with a diplomatic message from the president

1858 (Ansei 5)

March 23 Senior Councillor Hotta Masayoshi visits palace to seek imperial sanction for commercial treaty

July 29 Signing of Japan-US Treaty of Amity and Commerce

October 9 Japan signs treaty of amity and commerce with France, following three others agreed with the UK, the Netherlands, and Russia; this completes the so-called Ansei Five-Power Treaties

October 13 Ansei Purge begins

1859 (Ansei 6)

July 2 Ports of Kanagawa and Hakodate opened to foreign trade

1860 (Ansei 7/Man'en 1)

February 4 Bakufu mission to US departs Shinagawa aboard warship *Kanrin Maru*

1861 (Man'en 2/Bunkyū 1)

January 15 Henry Heusken, interpreter for US envoy, assassinated by Satsuma domain warriors

January 24 Signing of Japan-Prussia Treaty of Amity and Commerce

March 13 Rusian corvette *Posadnik* arrives at Tsushima (Tsushima Incident)

1862 (Bunkyū 2)

February 13 Members of Mito's Rōshi Corps attack Senior Councillor Andō Nobumasa at Edo Castle's Sakashita Gate

September 14 Satsuma domain retainers kill and wound British subjects at Namamugi, Kanagawa (Namamugi Incident, a.k.a. the Richardson Affair)

1863 (Bunkyū 3)

June 25 Chōshū domain shells US, and later French and Dutch vessels in the Straits of Shimonoseki (Shimonoseki Shellings Incident)

August 15	British squadron battles with Satsuma domain at Kagoshima Harbor (Anglo-Satsuma War)
September 30	*Kōbu gattai* (unity of court and bakufu) faction carries out coup d'état at the court ("8.18 Disturbance")

1864 (Bunkyū 4/Genji 1)

August 19	Chōshū domain soldiers fight bakufu army (Kinmon Incident, a.k.a. Hamaguri Gate Rebellion)
August 24	Court gives Hitotsubashi Yoshinobu (Keiki) orders for punitive attack on Chōshū (First Chōshū Expedition)
September 5–8	Combined squadron of British, American, French, and Dutch ships battles with Chōshū domain in the Straits of Shimonoseki (Shimonoseki Incident, a.k.a. Shimonoseki War)
October 22	Accord signed between representatives of four powers and bakufu on reparations for Shimonoseki Incident

1865 (Genji 2/Keiō 1)

November 4	Representatives of four powers demand prompt opening of Hyōgo to foreign vessels and imperially sanctioned treaties
November 9	Shogun visits imperial palace, receives sanction for second punitive expedition to Chōshū
November 22	Emperor Kōmei sanctions treaties, but does not authorize opening of Hyōgo (Kobe) port

1866 (Keiō 2)

March 7	With Sakamoto Ryōma as mediator, Kido Takayoshi et al. form the Satsuma-Chōshū alliance with Saigō Takamori
June 25	Senior Councillor Mizuno Tadakiyo signs Tariff Convention with the four powers
July 18	Second Chōshū Expedition (a.k.a. Summer War) begins
August 29	Shogun Tokugawa Iemochi dies
September 28	Following the death of Iemochi, Yoshinobu (Keiki) pronounced head of the main Tokugawa family branch
October 10	Bakufu and Chōshū domain agree to a cease-fire

1867 (Keiō 3)

January 10	Tokugawa Yoshinobu becomes shogun
January 30	Emperor Kōmei dies
February 13	Prince Mutsuhito ascends to the throne
March 18	Provisional agreement on Karafuto (Japan-Russia Sakhalin Joint Habitation Treaty) signed
July 23	Gotō Shōjirō et al. meet with Saigo and Ōkubo Toshimichi, conclude secret Satsuma-Tosa agreement on returning political power to the emperor (*taisei hōkan*)
October 15	Ōkubo Toshimichi et al. meet with the lord of Chōshū domain and his son, enter secret agreement to attack the bakufu
October 29	Gotō Shōjirō et al. submit Yamauchi Toyoshige's written petition to Senior Councillor Itakura Katsukiyo on returning political power to the emperor
November 8	Iwakura Tomomi hand-delivers to Ōkubo an imperial rescript addressed to the lord of the Satsuma domain and his son on felling the bakufu
November 9	Shogun Tokugawa Yoshinobu formally announces the restoration of imperial rule to the court
November 10	Imperial court hands Yoshinobu a written proclamation from the emperor sanctioning the return of political power to the emperor

1 The Difficulties of Opening Japan: Barriers to Free Trade

The Black Ships Appear

On July 8, 1853 (Kaei 6), the US East India Squadron commander Commodore Matthew C. Perry led his flotilla of four warships to the entrance of Edo Bay just off Uraga. The first people to make contact with Perry's squadron were Nakajima Saburōsuke, a police official (*yoriki*) attached to the office of the Uraga magistrate (*bugyō*), and Hori Tatsunosuke, who had been serving as a Dutch interpreter. As the pair drew closer to Perry's flagship, the *Susquehanna*, they were told by the ship's interpreter that the commodore would meet only with the top-ranked official from the magistrate's office. Despite this, they somehow still managed to get on board. Perry, through his adjutant, asked the Japanese to decide on who could officially receive a diplomatic message addressed to the shogun from US president Millard Fillmore. The Japanese responded that Nagasaki was where their country handled foreign relations issues and requested that Perry

1-2. Commodore Matthew C. Perry

1-3. "A North American: Portrait of Perry" (woodblock print by unknown artist)

1-4. *First Landing at Gorahama* (print by Wilhelm Heine/Eliphalet M. Brown Jr.)

and his flotilla sail there. However, the squadron determinedly chose not to respond.

On July 9, Nakajima again went to the *Susquehanna*. Offering the explanation that this was a matter of national law, and to act against those laws would be unacceptable, he refused to accept the message. In other words, for Japan the question was a matter of Japanese law. Furthermore, Nakajima said the bakufu had spent several days discussing the matter, and even after they had decided provisionally to accept the message, they said they would deliver a response to it at Nagasaki. Shocked by news of the Opium War, the bakufu had withdrawn the 1825 Edict to Repel Foreign Vessels and instead changed to a policy of supplying them with fuel, water, and food supplies. However, they had done so because receiving visitors from foreign countries was restricted to Nagasaki. Now, however, Perry did not yield on hand-delivering the diplomatic message to the bakufu, and on the following day he sent part of his squadron sailing into Edo Bay itself.

The Uraga magistrate, Toda Ujiyoshi, sent an inquiry to the bakufu on how to respond. The bakufu already had considerably detailed information about Perry's visit in advance through the Dutch trading house in Nagasaki, but they had not considered any particular response other than to

1-5. The delivery of the letter from the US president to the magistrate of Uraga

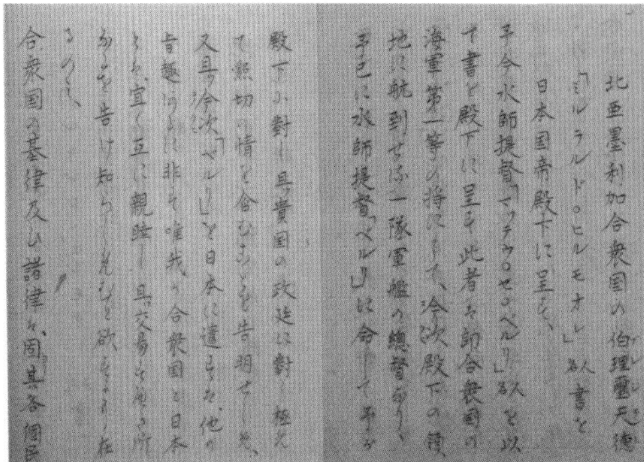

北亜墨利加合衆国の伯理璽天徳
「ミルラルド○ヒルモオレ」以書を
日本国帝殿下に呈す。
予今水師提督「マツチウ○セ○ペルリ」なる人を以
て書を殿下に呈す。此者は即合衆国の
海軍第一等の将にして、今次殿下の領
地に航到せる一隊軍艦の総督なり。
予已に水師提督「ペルリ」に命じて予か
殿下に対し、且貴国の政廷に対し、極て
て親切の情を合はふことを告明せしめ、
又且今次「ペルリ」を日本に遣すは、他の
旨趣あるに非ず、唯我か合衆国と日本
とは宜く互に親睦し、且交易を施す所
あらんを告け知らしめんと欲するに在
るのみ。
合衆国の基律及ひ諸律令、同其各国民

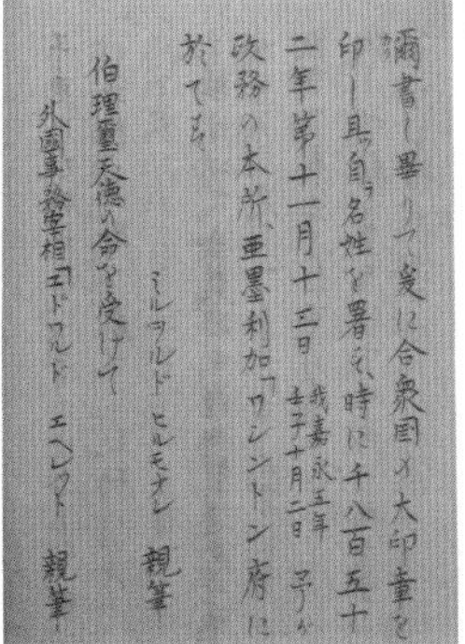

爾書し畢りて、爰に合衆国の大印章を
印し、且自ら名姓を署す。時に千八百五十
二年第十一月十三日 我嘉永五年壬子十月二日 予か
政務の太所、亜墨利加「ワシントン」府に
於てす。
ミルラルド ヒルモオレ 親筆
伯理璽天徳の命を受けて
外国事務宰相「エドワルド エヘレット」 親筆

1-6. Diplomatic message from President Fillmore

1-7. The USS *Susquehanna*

send the ships away. In fact, while the bakufu was consciously aware of the crisis posed by foreign vessels pressing in on Japan's home waters, its defense policies were wholly inadequate.

The top official in the bakufu was Abe Masahiro. He had been promoted from his position as leader of the Fukuyama domain in Bingo province, and before he was thirty, he had attained the status of head of the Senior Council (*rōjū shuza*). Mindful of Qing China's defeat in the Opium War, Abe realized that it would be impossible to commence hostilities without adequate defensive preparations. Accordingly, he directed Toda to receive the message at Kurihama.

On July 14, at the sound of a signal gun, Perry disembarked at Kurihama with a little over 300 soldiers and met with Toda and his men at a temporary structure erected for the meeting. The magistrate silently received the diplomatic message and handed Perry a rolled-up note by way of receipt. The note said that receiving visitors from foreign countries was meant to be handled at Nagasaki, and that this message was being received here in Kurihama in departure from national law. Accordingly, the bakufu now wanted Perry to leave without delay. Perry said that he would depart from the waters off Uraga in a few days, but he planned to return the following spring. On July 17, the squadron left Uraga for the Ryūkyūs and set up a coaling station at Naha (the present-day capital of Okinawa), heedless of the wishes of the Ryūkyū monarch.

Playing for Time as Policy

The United States sent Perry on his mission to Japan for two reasons. One was that American trade with China had increased after the Opium War, and in the US Congress there was a growing desire to open maritime routes across the Pacific. For this reason, the United States was focused on the importance of Japan as a way station. The other reason was to provide shelter for shipwrecked sailors from whaling vessels whose ships had foundered while conducting operations in the North Pacific.

Perry—who had worked hard to boost US naval power—had come up with a plan years before to take a flotilla of larger steam-powered warships around the Cape of Good Hope on an expedition to Japan, and presented it to the secretary of the navy. The steamships of the day were one of the great fruits of the nineteenth-century Industrial Revolution. However, they were not fuel efficient, and required frequent port calls and supplies of coal, fuel, and water. Accordingly, he had the thought that, should negotiations with the bakufu fail, the Ryūkyū and Ogasawara (Bonin) Islands could provide alternative sites.

It was not the US government's intention to forcibly open Japan backed by pressure from the squadron. President Fillmore's message even explicitly said, "I have particularly charged Commodore Perry to abstain from every act which could possibly disturb the tranquility of your imperial majesty's dominions." Perry was urged to be prudent. In the US system, the right to declare war rested with Congress; rash military actions were naturally

The Shapers of Bakufu Diplomacy

Diplomats from the Shōheizaka Gakumonjo

The new Meiji government retained many of the treaties that the bakufu regime had signed with Western nations. However, these existing agreements often included unfair terms such as unilateral consular jurisdiction. While scholars have continued to criticize the bakufu administration for a do-nothing, plan-nothing approach that ended up binding Japan to a host of unequal treaties, recent studies have reexamined bakufu diplomacy in a different light. Despite having a weak military relative to the Western powers, the country managed to achieve an incremental opening and maintain the independence of Edo Japan via international treaties in the face of unrelenting pressure from the West, which never escalated into armed conflict. That, observers argue, is no mere coincidence—it was the product of the skill with which the "enlightenment faction" (*kaimei-ha*) officials recruited by the bakufu administration went about their diplomatic negotiations.

Of Japan's first five foreign magistrates (*gaikoku bugyō*)—namely, Iwase Tadanari, Nagai Naoyuki, Mizuno Tadanori, Inoue Kiyonao, and Hori Toshihiro—four (all, that is, except for Inoue) had passed the *gakumon ginmi* (civil-service examinations) at the Shōheizaka Gakumonjo at the former site of Yushima Temple in Tokyo's Bunkyō Ward. Originally a private academy run by the Hayashi clan of Confucian scholars, the Shōheizaka Gakumonjo dated all the way back to Hayashi Razan, a tutor and advisor to the first four shoguns of the Tokugawa bakufu. It opened as a *gakumonjo* (place of learning) under direct bakufu control in 1797 with the objective of establishing Neo-Confucianism as Japan's "official education."

Research has shown how the Confucianists at the Gakumonjo played roles in shaping late-Tokugawa bakufu diplomacy by handling paperwork in classical Chinese—compiling documents, conducting case research, translating diplomatic credentials, and writing official replies. Makabe Jin also argues, in *Tokugawa kōki no gakumon to seiji* (Scholarship and politics in the late Tokugawa period), that they did more than simply flaunt the fruits of their timeworn Neo-Confucianist educations. Boasting virtual libraries of book knowledge, retentive memories, and expertise in foreign know-how, the Confucianists fostered the brand of intellectual flexibility and negotiation skills that the bakufu relied on in navigating the volatile, turbulent environment on the international scene. Among those powerful, influential minds was Hayashi Akira (Hayashi Fukusai; 1800–59), who served as the plenipotentiary representing the bakufu when Perry's fleet steamed into Edo Bay.

The collapse of the bakufu sealed the unlucky fate of many Gakumonjo graduates, as their status as Tokugawa retainers and their fierce loyalty to the main branch of the Tokugawa family naturally drew a political line between them and the Meiji government. Several products of the Gakumonjo still managed to flourish on the diplomatic front after the Meiji Restoration, however: Tanabe Taichi, Miyamoto Okazu, and future foreign minister Enomoto Takeaki are a few examples. Foreign Minister Terashima Munenori was also a pupil of Koga Kindō. (The Japanese term for "foreign minister" from 1869 to 1885 was "*gaimukyō*," a title equivalent to "lord of foreign affairs"; for simplicity's sake, however, this text uses "minister" instead of "lord" when referring to the "*-kyō*" designation.)

restricted. On the other hand, to provide for unexpected situations, it was acknowledged that Perry had a certain amount of latitude. In fact, Perry's words and actions in Edo Bay were quite aggressive.

President Fillmore's letter had requested the humane treatment of shipwrecked sailors and supplies of coal and provisions for ships that found themselves wrecked on Japan's shores. However, the most important part was the fact that if Japan updated its "old laws" (meaning its *sakoku* policy of isolation) and consented to "foreign trade," then the United States would like to embark on such trade "between the two countries [that] would be extremely beneficial to both." To decide on how to respond, Abe had the message translated into Japanese by a team led by Hayashi Fukusai, rector of the bakufu-operated academy Shōheizaka Gakumonjo. Abe then circulated this among the daimyo—including the *tozama* ("outside") daimyo who were kept at a distance by the Tokugawa shoguns—and the shogun's direct retainers and solicited their opinions. Most supported retaining

Tanabe Taichi (1831–1915)

Touted as one of the Gakumonjo's best and brightest, Tanabe Taichi (pen name: Renshū) won the favor of Mizuno Tadanori and eventually accompanied Mizuno on an expedition to claim the Ogasawara (Bonin) Islands in 1861. Three years later, Tanabe found himself on his way to France as part of the second Japanese mission to Europe under Ikeda Nagaoki, whose task was to reclose the port of Yokohama and return Japan to *sakoku* (closed) status. The mission ended in failure. Having come to the realization that Japan would be foolish to close Yokohama off again, Ikeda headed back to Japan without permission—and the consequences were swift. He was removed from his post and given a punishment; Tanabe, too, was placed under house arrest for 100 days. In 1867, however, Tanabe received another opportunity to head abroad, this time as a member of Tokugawa Akitake's delegation to the Paris Exposition. Under the new Meiji government, Tanabe became a junior secretary of the Ministry of Foreign Affairs in 1870 and served as the chief secretary of the Iwakura Mission to Europe the following year. In 1874, he visited Qing China, accompanying Ōkubo Toshimichi, to help deal with the repercussions of the Taiwan Expedition. Tanabe's service also included a stint as the interim chargé d'affaires (the acting head of a legation) to Qing China, a role that he assumed in 1881, and membership in the House of Peers, starting in 1890. As a member of the bakufu's Gaikoku-kata (akin to a ministry of foreign affairs), meanwhile, Tanabe had played a pivotal role in compiling the *Tsūshin zenran* (Collected diplomatic correspondence), a valuable historical compendium of bakufu diplomacy. In 1898 he also published *Bakumatsu gaikō-dan* (Accounts of diplomacy during the last years of the bakufu), which comprised a selection of articles that had appeared in the *Yomiuri Shimbun*.

1-8. Tanabe Taichi

Miyamoto Okazu (1836–1916)

Miyamoto Okazu, like his father before him, was a student at the Gakumonjo. At the time of the bakufu's downfall, Miyamoto was on the front lines of the regime's international negotiations, serving as an administrator in charge of numerous officials at the Kanagawa Magistrate's Office. He maintained his influence after the Meiji Restoration, too, earning an appointment as an agent in foreign relations and commerce for the diplomatic service and—when the government formally established the Ministry of Foreign Affairs in 1869—became one of the few top officials at the ministerial headquarters. Although he made his way up the ranks from junior secretary to senior secretary, Miyamoto never served on any prolonged assignments overseas; his duties largely involved receiving foreign guests of honor, such as hosting General Ulysses S. Grant during the former US president's sojourn in Japan, and overseeing investigations into the issue of Karafuto (Sakhalin). He also applied his extensive background in Sinology in a variety of initiatives, from assisting plenipotentiary Kuroda Kiyotaka on a visit to Korea after the Ganghwa Island incident to engaging in Sino-Japanese negotiations concerning territorial disputes over the Ryūkyūs and, in 1881, negotiating trade regulations between Japan and Korea as an assistant to Hanabusa Yoshimoto. Miyamoto later went on to serve in the House of Peers, nominated by the cabinet.

the isolation policy by rejecting the letter outright. Other opinions included what might be termed a "passive opening" that entailed avoiding a military confrontation and keeping the response to the requests down to the bare minimum, as well as a more "active opening" favored by only a few. Regardless of opinion, the one point raised in common among all was the need to strengthen Japan's military strength (coastal defenses).

In order to build upon that unifying force and handle this difficult situation, the bakufu appointed the Mito domain's Tokugawa Nariaki—who enjoyed the confidence of the powerful domains for his hard-line *jōi* ("expel the barbarians") stance—to serve as its advisor on coastal defense. Based on a written report from Nariaki, in November 1853 the bakufu issued an order to all domains. Owing to inadequate defensive preparations, the bakufu would try to play for time and not give Perry a formal response when he returned, and it appealed to the domains to strengthen their defensive measures. This was aimed at maintaining the isolation policy: attempt to procrastinate and play for time on answering, build up a military force all the while, and in the end reject the trade overtures. The bakufu made a range of other decisions. These included lifting the ban on building large vessels, placing orders for Western-style vessels from foreign countries, and building a fort in Edo Bay and outfitting it with cannons. It also put Hayashi Fukusai in charge of dealing with the United States and made ready for Perry's return.

Informed parties had already been debating the pros and cons of opening foreign trade prior to Perry's arrival. Various reasons for rejecting trade were offered, including the economic chaos that would result from an influx of useless goods and an outflow of necessities; the issue of fair play, which meant that if they started trading with one country, they would have to trade with others as well; and the question of whether Japan, a minor power, could maintain a self-sufficient economy.

The Signing of the Japan-US Amity Treaty

Perry's squadron showed up in Edo Bay again in February 1854. He had received information that the Russian admiral Yevfimiy Putyatin had come to Nagasaki, and so returned ahead of schedule to not lose the initiative in negotiations with the Japanese. The squadron set anchor off Yokohama and asked to hold talks in Edo, but the bakufu finally decided that the negotiations would take place in Yokohama instead. The talks began on March 8. There were many points on which the bakufu yielded and ceded to the demands presented by the resolute Perry. Even so, the bakufu remained quite opposed to opening any ports outside of Nagasaki.

In its response to Fillmore's message, the bakufu acceded to providing coal, fuel, and water, as well as assistance for shipwrecked vessels, but it postponed the question of opening ports for five years, and during the interim directed visitors to Nagasaki. However, Perry demanded the opening of the ports at Kagoshima (Kyushu), Matsumae (Hokkaido), Naha (Ryūkyūs), and Uraga as well. Hayashi, who had full powers to represent the bakufu, rejected Uraga, proposing Shimoda (in present-day Shizuoka) in its place. As to Naha, he said that because

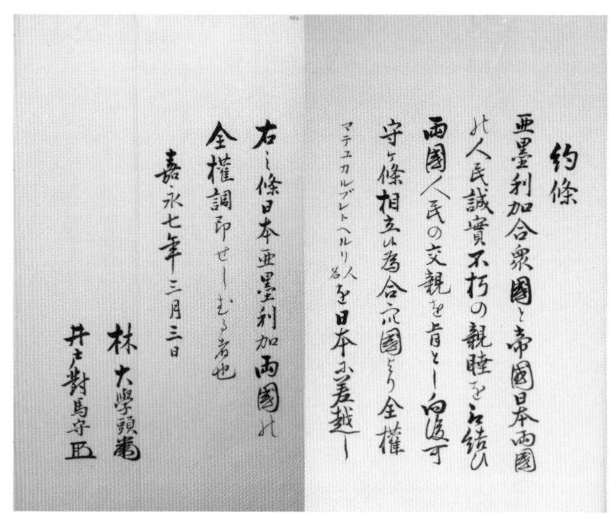
約條
亜墨利加合衆國と帝國日本両國
の人民誠實不朽の親睦を取結ひ
両國人民の交親を旨とし向後可
守ヶ條相立ル為合衆國より全權
マテユカルブレトヘルリ人名を日本に差越し
右之條日本亜墨利加両國の
全權調印せしむる者也
嘉永七年三月三日
林大學頭
井戸對馬守

1-9. Japan-US Amity Treaty (copy of signed treaty)

this was "on the outskirts of the Japanese political system," negotiations about it would be difficult. He also said that the bakufu could not arbitrarily decide about Matsumae since it was the territory of its daimyo. Since Perry spoke of his intention to go to the Matsumae domain and speak directly with the lord there, the bakufu allowed for the opening of the port of Hakodate. Nevertheless, it did not accede to the request for the opening of trade.

Perry highlighted the unjust treatment accorded to shipwrecked sailors, and pushed for a change to a policy that he regarded as one that disregarded human life. Hayashi countered with a discourse on the universality of the moral code of Confucian cultures about the respect for human life.

The Japan-US Peace and Amity Treaty that was signed at the end of March 1854 established that the ports of Shimoda and Hakodate would be opened; ships that visited those ports would be provided with necessities such as fuel, water, and coal (Article 2); and shipwrecked sailors would be repatriated (Article 3). Furthermore, whereas private trading in goods was forbidden (Article 8), the provision of necessary supplies was authorized based on their value in gold and silver, and a *ketsubōsho* (supply shop) was opened in Shimoda; its purveyor was to be under the authority of the Shimoda magistrate. This business conducted through the *ketsubōsho* could be interpreted as—however slightly—de facto foreign trade.

Furthermore, the Peace and Amity treaty opened the door for the first time to a Western country other than the Netherlands and promised that the United States would be unilaterally granted most-favored-nation treatment.[1] After this, the bakufu would sign similar peace and amity treaties with the United Kingdom, Russia, and the Netherlands, but it did not allow for the freedom of commercial activities (i.e., free trade).

Perry used the Ryūkyūs as a base when negotiating with the bakufu. Once the Peace and Amity Treaty was signed, he returned there, and in July 1854 he signed a similar treaty with the kingdom of the Ryūkyūs.

The Repercussions of the Crimean War

The United Kingdom and Russia were embroiled in the Crimean War (1854–56) at this time, which had an impact on actions that the European powers undertook in the "Far East." In September 1854, Rear Admiral Sir James Stirling of the UK Royal Navy's East Indies and China Station arrived in Nagasaki leading a flotilla of four ships. He sought to keep the activities of Russian warships in Far Eastern waters in check, to maintain Japan's neutrality in the United Kingdom's war with Russia, and to obtain access to Japanese ports. While the Nagasaki magistrate Mizuno Tadanori rejected these requests at first, he agreed to a Japanese-Anglo compact that October, based on the negotiations over a peace and amity treaty with the United States. The Anglo-Japanese Friendship Treaty would allow British ships to dock at Nagasaki and Hakodate. It would also grant most-favored-nation treatment to the United Kingdom, but, once again, this did not include trade relations. In 1855, Stirling returned to Nagasaki for the ratification of the Anglo-Japanese Friendship Treaty. However, while Stirling in his response did talk about opening the path toward trade, it postponed actual negotiations.

The Crimean War also had an impact on Putyatin's actions. The standoff between the United Kingdom and Russia in the Far East would persist even after the war, with the so-called Tsushima Incident of 1861 (a.k.a. the *Posadnik* Incident) serving as one such example.

Incidentally, after the United Kingdom and Qing China concluded the Treaty of Nanking

1 Most-favored-nation treatment is a provision in treaties concluded with another country. This provision would say, for example, that if Japan granted to any other nation more favorable terms than those given to the United States, those terms would automatically be applicable to the United States as well.

The Treaty of Friendship and Commerce between the United States and "Lew Chew"

Having made one unsuccessful stop in the Ryūkyūs to secure a commercial treaty in May 1853, Perry and his fleet returned to the islands after signing the Japan-US Amity Treaty with the bakufu and then proceeded to conclude the "Treaty of Friendship between the United States and Lew Chew" (a rendering of "Ryūkyū") with the Ryūkyū Kingdom in July 1854. The document articulates terms that the Ryūkyū Kingdom had been forced to accept since Perry's first arrival, such as provisions permitting free trade in the Ryūkyū market and the establishment of coaling stations.

The Ryūkyū Kingdom also signed nearly identical treaties of amity with France and the Netherlands. The fact that the countries' agreements with the Ryūkyū Kingdom were separate from the corresponding agreements with the bakufu attests to the Ryūkyūs' position within Japan's isolationist framework: it remained a *gaihan*—a domain outside the Japanese political system—subordinate to both Japan and China. After the establishment of the Ryūkyū domain in 1872, the Ministry of Foreign Affairs kept the treaty of friendship between the United States and the Ryūkyū Kingdom and other agreements in place.

(Nanjing) in 1842, the Netherlands had counseled the bakufu to open trade relations, but the bakufu did not accede.

The Dutch Trading House in 1852

In 1852, Jan Donker Curtius had been dispatched as chief Dutch trade negotiator, but his attempts to negotiate a commercial treaty had been rejected by the bakufu. The Dutch-Japan Treaty of Peace and Amity would eventually be concluded in January 1856, but trade remained limited to the existing trade post in Dejima (where Japanese merchants would bid for imported goods). The (Supplementary) Treaty of Commerce and Navigation between the Netherlands and Japan that was concluded in October 1857 did little more than expand the trading post in Dejima, but it was the first treaty with a Western power to include provisions for trade. The bakufu also concluded a Supplementary Treaty between Japan and Russia with similar content. Neither Curtius nor US consul general Townsend Harris recognized these supplementary treaties as commercial treaties.

Having concluded peace and amity treaties with the Western powers, the bakufu closed ranks around Senior Councillor Abe Masahiro and the Council of Elders and worked to strengthen its power by gathering the daimyo together, including the *tozama* ("outside") daimyo. However, the fact that the bakufu reported to the imperial court on its negotiations with foreign countries and sought daimyo opinions resulted in the increased authority of the court, contrary to the bakufu's agenda, and the daimyo strengthening their capacity to make themselves heard. Above all, the voices of certain daimyo speaking out against bakufu governance—particularly Shimazu Nariakira of Satsuma (Kagoshima), Yamauchi Toyoshige of Tosa (Kōchi), Date Munenari of Uwajima (Ehime), and Matsudaira Yoshinaga of Fukui—were becoming more powerful.

Putyatin Arrives: The Treaty of Peace and Amity between Japan and Russia

In late August 1853, one month after Perry's squadron departed, the commander of Imperial Russian naval forces in the Pacific, Vice Admiral Yevfimiy Putyatin, arrived at Nagasaki with a flotilla of four warships. Similar to Perry, his purpose was to negotiate about commencing trade, and also to discuss border problems. However, as Russia was increasingly wary about the United Kingdom after the latter had won the Opium War, another objective was to increase its own influence in East Asia.

Putyatin's flotilla departed from Portsmouth in the United Kingdom in January 1853, passed through Singapore, and arrived in Hong Kong in late June. There, he learned that Perry's squadron was in waters around the Ryūkyūs and headed for Japan. Putyatin hurriedly left Hong Kong, and after struggling through a typhoon, made a port call at Chichijima in the Ogasawara (Bonin) Islands in early August. There, he received additional instructions from another Russian vessel that had arrived ahead of him. Just after Putyatin had departed, German physician Philipp von Siebold contacted the Russian government to explain that the ships should go to Nagasaki rather than Edo to negotiate with Japan. Via the other vessel, the Russian government conveyed this information to Putyatin, along with their additional instructions that touched on the border negotiations. These outlined the Russian position as being that the Chishima Islands (also called the Kuril/Kurile Islands) belonged to Russia through to the island of Urup at the southernmost end (from the Japanese perspective, Japan's territory would therefore extend to the northernmost tip of Etorofu Island).

While Perry had led a large squadron of steamships, Putyatin's consisted of antiquated sailing vessels. However, in contrast to Perry's haughty attitude, Putyatin's gentlemanly comportment charmed the person charged with handling the negotiations in Nagasaki. Abe Masahiro had proposed trying to partner with Russia to counter the United States, but Tokugawa Nariaki rejected this. His skepticism arose from the concern that the United States and Russia themselves might be in collusion.

The Nagasaki magistrate, who was in charge of the talks, refused to receive a letter intended for the bakufu's senior councillors or to meet with Putyatin, on the grounds that he needed permission from the bakufu. In response to an urgent message received from Nagasaki, the bakufu accepted the letter that Putyatin brought but used the pretext that shogun Tokugawa Ieyoshi had passed away in late July to state that it would reply at some later date, and asked the Russians to leave in the meantime. However, Putyatin did not hear of this until late October. The bakufu sought to play for time with its response, but Putyatin called their bluff and said he would not leave Japan until he received a definite answer. Accordingly, in mid-November the bakufu decided to dispatch Tsutsui Masanori and Kawaji Toshiakira as its plenipotentiaries. The pair finally arrived in Nagasaki at the end of December, and formal negotiations began in January 1854.

1-10. Yevfimiy Putyatin

Putyatin emphasized that no country had ever fallen because of trade, but rather had seen increased prosperity as a result of it. Tsutsui and Kawaji countered that Japan's reluctance to engage in foreign commerce arose from its lack of experience in such practices, and claimed that they would need several years to prepare. At the end of January, Putyatin presented them with a draft treaty his government had prepared and—having received a promise that Russia would be given precedence when Japan opened—left Nagasaki for the time being. Putyatin had grown to trust the Japanese style of receiving a visitor with the utmost decorum. Similarly, in their correspondence to the bakufu reporting on the results of the negotiations, Tsutsui and Kawaji said that Putyatin was a person worthy of trust.

Negotiations in Shimoda and the Treaty between Japan and Russia

After he left Nagasaki, Putyatin transferred his flagship to the *Diana*, which was a state-of-the-art sailing vessel at the time. A year later, he headed back to Japan, and in early December 1854, put in at Shimoda. In even starker contrast to Perry's steamship squadron, this time Putyatin came into negotiations with just his single frigate. For Japan, Tsutsui and Kawaji again served as plenipotentiaries, and the negotiations began in late December.

On December 23, the day after the first round of talks had been completed, Shimoda was struck by the massive Ansei-Tōkai earthquake and tsunami. The *Diana* incurred major damage, and so the negotiations were put on hold.

The talks resumed in January 1855. The biggest issue was trade. Putyatin pressed to establish trade relations. Kawaji and Tsutsui allowed for the opening of the ports at Hakodate, Shimoda, and Nagasaki, but—noting that such privileges had not been granted to the United States, either—did not accede to trade. Talks on the border issue were also rough going, but a compromise was reached on Karafuto (Sakhalin), with Putyatin's proposal to leave it unpartitioned. Demarcating the border was not a matter to be handled at Putyatin's individual discretion. The Russian government had ordered Putyatin to regard Sakhalin as Russian territory. With respect to the Kuril Islands, depending on how negotiations went, he had the latitude to concede to establishing a national border between Urup and Etorofu (Iturup).

In February 1855, the negotiators signed the Treaty of Peace and Amity between Japan and Russia. The treaty affirmed that all the islands in the Kuril chain from Etorofu to the south were Japanese territory, and those from Urup to the north were Russian. It also established that Sakhalin would remain unpartitioned. (One of the reasons the sides could not demarcate a border in Sakhalin was that, having lost his flagship to the Ansei Tōkai earthquake and with the Crimean War crisis pressing, Putyatin had to quickly return to Russia.) Furthermore, the treaty opened the ports of Shimoda, Hakodate, and Nagasaki; allowed for Russia to establish consulates in Shimoda and Hakodate; and accorded Russia most-favored-nation treatment. In terms of provisions regarding jurisdiction (which had not been included in the Japan-US Amity Treaty), the treaty stipulated that when a Russian in Japan broke Japanese law or a Japanese in Russia broke Russian law, that person would be punished in accordance with their home country's law. In other words, it established bilateral consular jurisdiction.

1-11. Yokoi Shōnan

Before entering into the negotiations with Russia, Kawaji had received a letter from his close friend, the scholar Yokoi Shōnan, outlining Yokoi's opinions about dealing with the foreign visitors. Yokoi

The Ansei-Tōkai Earthquake and Putyatin

The Ansei-Tōkai earthquake hit Shimoda on December 23, 1854. The jolt, with a magnitude of 8.4, created a tsunami that left 90 percent of the over 850 homes in the area either destroyed or partially collapsed. Also feeling the effects of the earthquake was Yevfimiy Putyatin's fleet, which suffered one death and several injuries. Despite the losses to his crew, Putyatin still made landfall that very evening, asked after Kawaji Toshiakira's health, and offered to have Russian doctors care for the wounded.

The tsunami dealt severe blows to the *Diana*, the flagship that Putyatin was on when the earthquake struck. Although the crew attempted to steer the vessel toward the village of Heda (now a part of the city of Numazu) on Suruga Bay, the damage proved too catastrophic. As the *Diana* began to sink, local Japanese residents headed out in droves to help rescue the sailors, bring them ashore, and provide them with food, lodging, and clothing.

Putyatin had succeeded in signing an amity treaty with Japan, but he now also had to find a way to get roughly 500 stranded crew members from the sunken *Diana* home to Russia. Eventually, he came up with an idea: starting essentially from scratch, he would launch an effort to build a new small vessel that could transport the crew to the Russian Far East. Luck was in Putyatin's favor, as the location in Heda was ideal for shipbuilding, and a group of Japanese shipwrights and smithies was willing to pitch in. The effort came to fruition in April 1855, when the workers completed a two-masted schooner measuring argued that the *sakoku* policy contravened the logic of "the common good for heaven and earth" and that it would compromise Japan's credibility in the world. On the other hand, he also held that trade should be conducted only with those countries that were true to their word and that establishing connections with those that were not trustworthy would eventually be contrary to the national interest. Taking Yokoi's suggestions to heart, Kawaji directly asked whether Russia was a country that valued truthfulness. He badgered the Russians and was tough in his negotiations, wondering whether the talk that Russia was a "merciless country" that would simply steal another country's territory was true or not, and whether Russia was a country that respected truthfulness, in which case it should also listen to Japan's reasoning.

According to novelist Ivan Goncharov, who also took part in the Nagasaki negotiations, Kawaji frequently would skillfully tear down whatever points the Russian side was making, and the Russians admired his great intellect and wisdom.

Harris and the Japan-US Treaty of Amity and Commerce

It was not until 1857 that the bakufu looked more favorably on trade and contemplated shifting to

1-12. *The Russian Putyatin Mission* (painting by Kishi Magodayū)

25 meters long and 7 meters wide. Putyatin named the ship *Heda*, a nod to the community. The ship, featuring a type of keel that no Japanese vessel had ever used, also gave the bakufu a new model that it quickly applied in constructing several other ships in the *Heda* mold. The original *Heda* set off for Nikolayevsk with roughly fifty men aboard, reaching shore safely at the end of May.

The rest of the stranded crew waited and waited for a neutral vessel to dock at Shimoda and provide them passage home. In July, more than two months after the completion of the *Heda*, a German ship arrived. The men boarded the vessel—only to see it fall into the hands of the naval forces of the United Kingdom, a member of the alliance opposing Russia in the Crimean War (1854–56). For Putyatin, the Crimean War was a conflict that restricted him severely.

Putyatin went on to receive the Grand Cordon of the Order of the Rising Sun from the Meiji government in 1881 on the recommendation of Yanagiwara Sakimitsu, Japan's second resident envoy to Russia. Of all the foreign officials to have engaged in treaty negotiations with Japan in the waning stages of the Edo period, Putyatin was the only one to receive the Grand Cordon of the Order of the Rising Sun—an honor that recognized his contributions to Russo-Japanese negotiations, his role in fostering Western-style shipbuilding in Japan through the *Heda* effort, and his generosity in helping numerous Japanese students pursue studies in Russia and assisting the personnel at the new Japanese legation in Russia in finding their footing. Putyatin's assistant on the expedition to Japan, Konstantin Posyet, also received an official decoration from the Meiji government.

1-13. A model of the *Heda*

1-14. Townsend Harris goes to Edo

open the country up. In October of the previous year, the bakufu had learned through the Netherlands' Jan Donker Curtius that an English flotilla was bringing a trade delegation to Japan. Through the Nagasaki magistrate, Curtius urged the bakufu to sign a commercial treaty. This news, combined with word of the outbreak of the Arrow War (also called the Second Opium War; 1856–60) pitting the United Kingdom and France on one side against Qing China on the other, would eventually strengthen the determination of Hotta Masayoshi—who had taken over as top official in the bakufu's Senior Council following Abe's death in August 1857—to encourage the bakufu to open the country and engage in trade. There was a real threat that, having defeated Qing China, the British and French fleets would then attack Japan.

In autumn 1856, Townsend Harris had arrived in Japan to take up his post as the US consul general. This was in accordance with the terms of the Japan-US Amity Treaty, and Harris opened his consulate in Shimoda. Harris's orders were to conclude a trade treaty with Japan, and so his intention was to go to Edo to obtain an audience with the shogun and deliver a letter from the US president on that matter. The bakufu continually refused to allow Harris to go to Edo, and it took more than a year for Harris to get his meeting. The bakufu knew that it could not avoid allowing Harris to make the trip to Edo, but pretended to be taking opposition into consideration until it felt that the time was right.

Harris finally received his permission, and in December 1857, accompanied by his interpreter Henry Heusken, he went to Edo for an audience with the shogun Tokugawa Iesada, at which he delivered his letter from President Franklin Pierce. Harris had already entered negotiations with the Shimoda magistrate Inoue Kiyonao and, in June 1857, concluded a treaty (the Convention of Shimoda) between the United States and Japan. This convention opened the port of Nagasaki to US vessels, granted Americans permission to live in Shimoda and Hakodate, allowed for American silver dollars to be exchanged at equal weights with Japanese silver currency, and furthermore stipulated unilateral consular jurisdiction.[2] These terms would also all be incorporated into the Japan-US Treaty of Amity and Commerce of the following year.

Following his audience with the shogun, Harris then met with Hotta and his delegation and

2 Unilateral consular jurisdiction: A clause whereby, on Japanese territory, the consul of a foreigner's country is recognized as having the right to put their nation's citizens on trial (consular jurisdiction), but Japan renounces its right to do the same to those foreign citizens.

Harris (1804–78) and Alcock (1809–97)

1-15. Townsend Harris

New York native Townsend Harris made extensive trading voyages throughout the Pacific and Indian Oceans. Over the course of his travels, he developed an eager determination to connect with Japan and made it his personal mission to sign a free-trade agreement with the country. He persuaded then US president Franklin Pierce to assign him that task and, in August 1856, set foot in Japan as the first US consul general in the country under the Japan-US Amity Treaty.

This initiated a string of new developments in the Japan-US relationship. After opening the US consulate at Gyokusenji Temple in Shimoda, Harris began to emphasize the importance of free trade and international law. He knew that he would need to convince Japan's leadership in order to effect his vision, so he asked the bakufu government for an official audience with the shogun. One year later, in December 1857, Harris got his wish and met with the administration in Edo. Addressing a group that included Head Senior Councillor Hotta Masayoshi, he explained that Japan would need to sign free-trade agreements—especially to ward off the threat of potential attacks by British and French fleets. That was enough to get the bakufu administration to the negotiating table. After fourteen meetings, the sides finally agreed on the Japan-US Treaty of Amity and Commerce—but the Imperial Court declined to give the accord its official sanction. Harris applied even more pressure to secure authorization and ultimately succeeded in bringing the signing to fruition in July 1858. He went on to earn a promotion, becoming envoy to Japan, and established a residence at Zenpukuji Temple in the Azabu area of Edo before returning to the United States in 1862.

With the American Civil War redirecting the US government's attention from international matters to domestic strife, the United Kingdom assumed a leading role in directing the Western powers' policy stance on Japan. At the helm was Rutherford Alcock, who had earlier served at the British consulate in Canton (China). He arrived in Japan in June 1859 as consul general, and became British minister to Japan that fall. Alcock encountered several challenges, however; in July 1861, for example, he narrowly escaped an attack by the Mito *rōshi* (a group of lordless samurai from the Mito domain) on the British legation at Tōzenji Temple. He returned home in 1862 to spend more than a year away from Japan, making his way back in the spring of 1864. Months later, with the Chōshū domain firing on foreign ships in order to "expel the barbarians," Alcock was instrumental in implementing a hard-line "Bombardment of Shimonoseki" attack on the Chōshū battery by a combined squadron of ships representing the United Kingdom, the Netherlands, France, and the United States. Because Alcock had not received official authorization from the British authorities for dispatching naval forces to Shimonoseki, however, he was ordered to return home at the end of the year. The British government eventually consented to the Shimonoseki expedition, and Alcock resumed foreign service as minister to Qing China in 1865.

proposed that a trade treaty be concluded. In particular, he sought the right for the United States to station an envoy, free trade between the two countries, and access to additional ports. On this occasion, Harris launched into a long speech. He spoke of the threat to Japan when the British and French naval squadrons that had defeated Qing China in the Arrow War arrived there. He pointed out that, unlike other countries, the United States had no territory in Asia, and spoke of the possibilities for wealth and power should Japan also participate in the development of trade among the nations.

Hotta had been searching for some way to open Japan on favorable terms. He sent an official from the bakufu's "enlightenment faction" (*kaimei-ha*) to Harris and asked about dealings among Western nations, in particular the role of envoys. Harris responded that such dealings were done in accordance with "the universal law among the nations"; that is, international law. This set of common rules among Western nations was separate from the laws internal to each. Thus, the bakufu learned that the posting of envoys was done in accordance with the arrangements of international law.

What Is an "Unequal Treaty"?

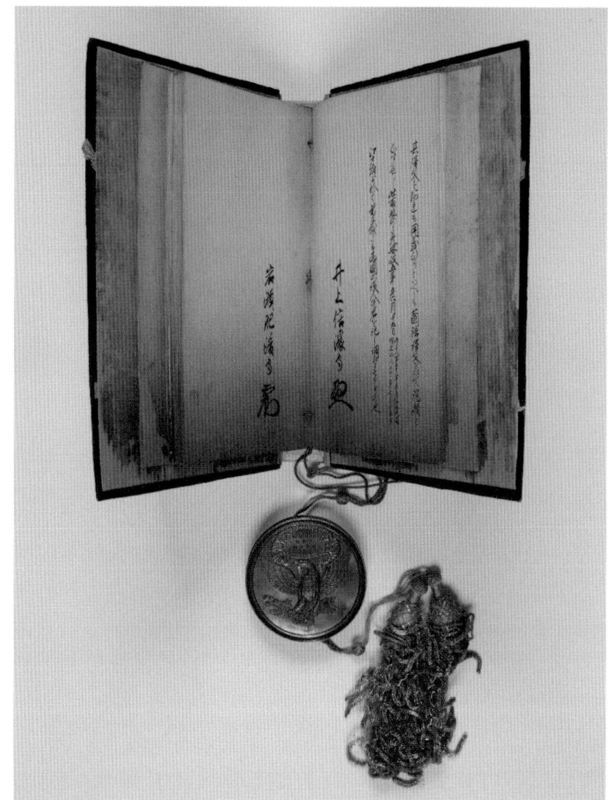

1-16. Japan-US Treaty of Amity and Commerce

Inoue Kiyonao and Iwase Tadanari were assigned full authority to negotiate a commercial treaty with the United States, and they began their work in January 1858. Back in October 1857, the bakufu had concluded its first commercial treaty with the Netherlands (the so-called Supplementary Dutch-Japan Treaty), and furthermore also signed a similar document with Russia. Now, on top of setting down commercial provisions similar to those found in these two existing treaties and opening the port of Yokohama, Inoue and Iwase sought to take Harris's wishes into consideration and allow for the stationing of diplomatic envoys. Harris, however, rejected using the two treaties as the basis for negotiations. Instead, he offered a draft treaty that would call for the exchange of diplomatic officials (envoys) with each set residing in the capital cities; the opening of six ports and cities, including Osaka, Edo, and Kyoto; the right to travel freely around Japan; and the launch of free trade. The bakufu's plenipotentiary delegation led by Inoue and Iwase stressed the uneasiness in popular sentiment in Japan and called for a gradual approach, but Harris argued that only by accepting the US draft could Japan avoid conflict with the West (meaning the United Kingdom and France) and strengthen itself.

As to free trade—the point on which Harris placed his greatest emphasis—it was already an established policy that the bakufu would decide which ports were to be opened. The biggest problem was the exact ports. The Japanese side rejected Osaka and Kyoto, but ultimately allowed for the ports of Hyōgo (Kobe), Kanagawa (Yokohama), Hakodate, Nagasaki, and Niigata to be opened. The cities that would be opened for commerce (though leasing land was forbidden) were Edo and Osaka. Harris pressed for freedom of travel and trade in Japan, but as a rule, the bakufu restricted the movements of foreigners to within a 40 square kilometer radius of the open ports. Naturally, trade was also restricted to those foreign settlements.

The Japan-US Treaty of Amity and Commerce that was eventually agreed to (it would be signed in July 1858) also stipulated unilateral consular jurisdiction. From the perspective of a sovereign nation, the presence of unilateral consular jurisdiction clearly made this an unequal treaty, but the bakufu's concern over this point was low. It was something they accepted from their perspective that it would mitigate the burdens of any hearings in which a foreign defendant was involved. In the Japan-Russia treaty, Putyatin had also recognized Japan's consular jurisdiction, but the bakufu did not attempt to retain this bilateral characteristic in all of its treaties. It also did not have a deep understanding of the most-favored-nation treatment that Russia had bilaterally acknowledged, so there was no opposition to the unilateral treatment.

Foreign-Settlement Trade

The bakufu opened the ports of Nagasaki, Shimoda, and Hakodate in accordance with the 1854 Japan-US Amity Treaty and similar conventions with the United Kingdom, Russia, and the Netherlands, but the agreements permitted only a limited scope for trade to foreign vessels—they did not include provisions allowing for direct free trade with private citizens. With the conclusion of the Ansei Five-Power Treaties, however, came a transformative change on the trading front: the government opened the ports of Kanagawa, Nagasaki, Hakodate, Niigata, and Hyōgo and also designated Edo and Osaka as open markets. The open ports allowed foreigners to establish permanent residence, lease land, and purchase buildings; the open markets applied tighter restrictions, permitting stays for the purposes of commercial trading only. The government also allowed foreign individuals free passage within a 10-*ri* (roughly 40-kilometer) area around each open port.

The open ports bustled with "foreign-settlement trade," or transactions between foreign merchants and Japanese *urikomi-shō* (local selling agents) and *hikitori-shō* (local buying agents). The *urikomi-shō* served as go-betweens, selling exports to foreign merchants on consignment from producers and shippers. The *hikitori-shō*, on the other hand, would buy imports from foreign merchants and then resell the items to general traders. While a form of "free trade" in name, the transactional framework of the *urikomi-shō* and *hikitori-shō* amounted to a type of monopolistic trading by both sides. The setup may have drawn protests from countries subscribing to free-trade principles, but it also helped Japan stave off an infiltration of foreign capital looking to corner the Japanese market with production and distribution bases on the ground. The basic practices of foreign-settlement trade continued for a considerable stretch of time, even after the treaty revisions of 1899 officially did away with the system. When Japanese merchants replaced their foreign counterparts in the trading arenas, the *urikomi-shō* and *hikitori-shō* still retained their dominant, market-controlling positions until trading companies and production plants began making more and more direct transactions, thereby weakening the hold of the monopoly.

2 The Upsurge of the "Expel the Barbarians" Movement: The Quest for National Unification

The Issue of Imperially Sanctioned Treaties and the Ansei Five-Power Treaties

Abe Masahiro died in August 1857. Hotta Masayoshi, who had become the central figure in the new Senior Council, wanted the daimyo to understand the need to sign the treaties; he also went to Kyoto himself in February 1858 to meet with Emperor Kōmei twice to get his sanction for the treaties. However, the court held that an opening of the country accompanied by trade would be harmful to the domestic and international order, and withheld its permission.

The issue of imperial sanction would become intertwined with the problem of who would succeed the thirteenth shogun, Tokugawa Iesada, influencing the domestic political situation. Iesada was sickly and had no children. Powerful daimyo such as Shimazu Nariakira from Satsuma and bakufu bureaucrats from the enlightenment faction favored Mito domain lord Tokugawa Nariaki's son, Hitotsubashi (later Tokugawa) Yoshinobu—also known as Keiki—despite his youth. The daimyo who comprised the "Hitotsubashi faction" endorsed signing the treaties. Opposed to them were the *fudai* (hereditary vassal) daimyo and the shogun's direct retainers (the "flag men," or *hatamoto*), who argued that the bakufu should take the lead in policy matters related to the foreign powers. They believed that the shogun's successor should be "of the blood," and so, even though he was just a child, they favored Tokugawa Yoshitomi (Iemochi), the lord of the Kii (Kishū) domain, who was a direct descendent of the first Tokugawa shogun, Ieyasu. One of the most prominent figures among those advocates was *fudai* daimyo Ii Naosuke, the foremost lord of the Hikone domain.

In June 1858, Iesada appointed Ii to be chief minister (*tairō*). The chief minister was the highest-placed person within the bakufu whenever a change of shogun or political instability was expected. Ii then dismissed those senior councillors who, like Hotta, had been allied with the Hitotsubashi faction. Ii wanted to regain control of the situation by adopting the line indicated by the court of rejecting signing the treaty, and so in his parleys with Harris, as a preliminary measure, he postponed the date for signing the accord. Meanwhile, Iesada firmed up his intention to designate Tokugawa Yoshitomi (Iemochi) to succeed him as the fourteenth shogun, and made those wishes known to Ii.

Harris's demands to conclude a treaty became all the more urgent. Finally, that July, Iwase Tadanari and Inoue Kiyonao would—on Ii's approval—sign the Japan-US Treaty of Amity and Commerce aboard an American vessel anchored in Edo Bay. Tokugawa Nariaki and Matsudaira Yoshinaga met with Ii and censured him for allowing the treaty to be signed without imperial sanction. They also recommended that Yoshitomi—who had informally been selected as Iesada's successor—be withdrawn as a candidate to be the fourteenth shogun, and that Hitotsubashi Yoshinobu (Keiki) be selected instead. However, it was announced that Yoshitomi was to succeed, and that Nariaki and Yoshinaga were put under house arrest by Ii.

Upon hearing that the officials had signed the treaty, the court castigated them for having done so. It then issued a secret edict (*Bogo no mitchoku*) declaring that the punishment meted out to Nariaki and his partners was unreasonable, and distributed it among Mito domain retainers and bakufu bureaucrats. The edict's content was unusual in that, through

Tokugawa Yoshinobu (1837–1913)

Yoshinobu (also pronounced Keiki), the son of Tokugawa Nariaki, became head of the Hitotsubashi house in 1847 at just ten years of age. In 1862, he became the shogunate's guardian (*kōken-shoku*) on an imperial order and began propelling reforms to the shogunate administration along *kōbu gattai* (unity of court and bakufu) lines. Three years later, in 1865, Yoshinobu successfully secured an imperial sanction for the pending treaty with the diplomatic agents of the four Western powers (the UK, the United States, France, and the Netherlands), keeping the port of Hyōgo closed. Yoshinobu eventually became shogun in 1867 and, without ever relocating from Kyoto, led Oguri Tadamasa and other pro-France officials in initiating a massive administrative overhaul to modernize the government along Western models and bolster the nation's military strength.

In 1867, Yoshinobu declared the restoration of political power to the emperor (*taisei hōkan*) in line with the *kōgi seitai* concept (government deliberations through open discussion) and resigned as shogun, expecting that he would preside over a governing council of clan representatives upon stepping down. The transition did not transpire as Yoshinobu had envisioned it, however, as the factions opposing the bakufu quickly launched a coup to restore imperial rule and barred Yoshinobu from serving in any of the three senior ranks under the new regime (*sōsai*, *gijō*, and *san'yo*; roughly equivalent to director-general, peer, and councillor). After the so-called Kogosho Conference (Kogosho Kaigi), a meeting of the incoming regime, he was officially stripped of his titles and ordered to forfeit the land in his possession.

1-17. Tokugawa Yoshinobu (Keiki)

Yoshinobu responded by sending Tokugawa troops against the Satsuma-Chōshū anti-bakufu forces (the it, the court was criticizing the bakufu. The court was indignant that the treaty had been signed, and refused to accept that the bakufu had done so on its own. Finally, however, in December 1858 it issued a written proclamation to the effect that it would accept the signing, but with the condition that Japan would return to a closed state in the near future.

Ii was anxious about the disruptions to bakufu government created by the succession issue, the matter of gaining imperial sanction for treaties, and the eventual proclamation that the court would issue. In an attempt to restore order, he issued severe punishments in the name of the emperor to sixty-nine individuals, including nobles (*kuge*) connected to the Hitotsubashi faction in the court, as well as certain daimyo and their retainers (this was later called the Ansei Purge). The three influential daimyo Tokugawa Yoshinobu (Keiki), Matsudaira Yoshinaga, and Tokugawa Nariaki were forbidden to visit Edo Castle, among other punishments. However, the Hitotsubashi faction would not give up on its hopes for Keiki to be named Iesada's successor.

As part of the purge, death penalties were issued for such individuals tied to the secret edict as Yoshida Shōin from Chōshū and Hashimoto Sanai from Echizen. In accordance with Matsudaira Yoshinaga's wishes, Hashimoto had prevailed on the court about the need to sign the treaties and approve the succession of Yoshinobu (Keiki). Kawaji Toshiakira, Iwase Tadanari, and Nagai Naoyuki (Naomune) were all ordered to retire from active life, or were dismissed from their respective posts. In 1860, a group of warriors from the Mito domain who had received the most severe punishments would assassinate Chief Minister Ii near the Sakurada gate of Edo Castle (the Sakuradamon Incident).

In any case, following on from the Japan-US Treaty of Amity and Commerce, the bakufu would go on to conclude similar treaties with the Netherlands, Russia, the United Kingdom, and France (the Ansei Five-Power Treaties). With this, Japan would formally begin to conduct trade with the West. After the Japan-US Treaty of Amity and

---

Battle of Toba–Fushimi). After three days of fighting, Yoshinobu realized that he was waging a losing battle and fled Osaka Castle for Edo. Placing himself under voluntary confinement for fear of retribution, he professed his allegiance to the new government and made five-year-old Tokugawa Iesato the head of the main branch of the Tokugawa family. Yoshinobu's house arrest came to an end in 1869, after which he relocated to Suruga. He later moved back to Tokyo and, in 1902, received the title of prince (*kōshaku*).

Tokugawa Nariaki (1800–60)

Lord of the Mito domain and a prominent force in the *sonnō jōi* ("revere the emperor, expel the barbarians") faction, Tokugawa Nariaki held substantial sway in shaping diplomatic and coastal-defense responses when Abe Masahiro enlisted his help to navigate the deadlock stemming from Perry's arrival in 1853.

1-18. Tokugawa Nariaki

Nariaki's work on concluding the Japan-US Amity Treaty proved frustrating. While he was willing to include provisions for supplying American ships with fuel and water, he took a hard line in opposition to allowing communications and commercial activity—a stance that fell out of alignment with those among the bakufu cabinet officials and coastal-defense leaders pushing to open the country, prompting Nariaki to resign as a bakufu advisor in 1854. After being reappointed to the same position in 1855, Nariaki objected to the idea of Harris having an official audience with the shogun, and also led the "Hitotsubashi faction" calling for Yoshinobu to succeed Iesada as the next shogun. Furthermore, after he attempted to hold Chief Minister Ii Naosuke responsible for his role in the issues surrounding the imperial sanction for the treaty, Ii had Nariaki placed under house arrest in 1858.

The Mission to the United States and the *Kanrin Maru*

After the signing of the Japan-US Treaty of Amity and Commerce, the bakufu sent a mission to the United States to exchange the instruments of ratification for the agreement. Foreign magistrates Iwase Tadanari and Mizuno Tadanori proposed holding the official exchange in Washington, saying that it was the bakufu's wish to do so, and Harris agreed to the idea. The mission thus set off, a three-man delegation—fellow foreign magistrate Shinmi Masaoki serving as the ambassador, Muragaki Norimasa the vice-ambassador, and Oguri Tadamasa the *metsuke* (an inspector-type role, ranking under the *bugyō* magistrate)—along with a crew of seventy-four. The group departed Yokohama aboard the USS *Powhatan* in February 1860. Absent from the group were Iwase and Mizuno, the officials behind the organization of the meeting, whose careers had fallen victim to the repercussions of the Ansei Purge.

The USS *Powhatan* did not make the voyage alone, however. It was escorted by the *Kanrin Maru*, a wooden ship that Japan had ordered from the Netherlands. Naval magistrate (*gunkan bugyō*) Kimura Yoshitake entrusted the *Kanrin Maru* to a young, inexperienced crew. Serving as captain was Katsu Rintarō (also known as Kaishū), who then occupied a low rung on the leadership ladder. Also aboard was Fukuzawa Yukichi, a young samurai from the Nakatsu domain who had been in Edo studying English. The *Kanrin Maru* endured a rough, storm-tossed voyage across the Pacific, eventually reaching San Francisco in March 1860 to complete its forty-three-day journey. The USS *Powhatan* arrived twelve days later, and, leaving the battered *Kanrin Maru* behind, made its way through the Panama Canal and reached Washington in mid-May. The Japanese mission exchanged the instruments of ratification at an official meeting with US secretary of state Lewis Cass and President James Buchanan, after which the members visited the Smithsonian Institution and other prominent locations in Washington, and then embarked on a veritable world tour aboard the USS *Niagara*: sailing around the Cape of Good Hope, crossing the Indian Ocean, and visiting European colonies in Indonesia and Hong Kong before returning to the Port of Yokohama in November. The *Kanrin Maru*, meanwhile, underwent repairs in San Francisco and then made its way back to Shinagawa in June 1860.

Fukuzawa's autobiography, *Fukuō jiden*, includes a proud recollection of the *Kanrin Maru*'s voyage. "The Japanese people made a trans-Pacific crossing without help from foreign experts," Fukuzawa wrote. "I think we can without undue pride boast before the world of this courage

Commerce was signed, in February 1860, Japan dispatched a mission to the United States in order to exchange instruments of ratification. However, the fact that the bakufu had signed such commercial treaties without official court sanction served to stir up anti-bakufu sentiment among powerful daimyo. The problem of imperial sanction for treaties was not over yet.

The Pros and Cons of Opening Trade

"Free trade" as established in the Ansei Five-Power Treaties was restricted to the foreign settlements in the open ports. For that reason, demands on the part of those foreign countries to have areas elsewhere in Japan also opened to them grew stronger. That said, trade restricted to the foreign settlements worked to prevent the entry of foreign merchants into the domestic market. But for the bakufu, accepting free trade was a major decision. This was certainly no coincidence. Rather, it was a product of the bargaining strength of the more enlightened bakufu officials who had been appointed to their posts by the bakufu.

For example, five bakufu officials—Iwase Tadanari, Nagai Naoyuki, Mizuno Tadanori, Inoue Kiyonao, and Hori Toshihiro—and such individuals as Tsutsui Masanori and Kawaji Toshiakira had major parts to play in 1858 as magistrates of foreign affairs (*gaikoku bugyō*). Iwase held that the profits to be earned from trade would serve as the foundation for the "rich nation, strong army" (*fukoku kyōhei*), and saw this as a favorable opportunity for reviving the bakufu's grip on power. Iwase was involved in all of the Ansei Five-Power Treaties. Harris would later write, "Envoys Inoue and Iwase and skill." While the memory may have fanned Fukuzawa's Japanese pride, the group actually traversed the Pacific with the help of Lieutenant John Brooke and nine other American sailors.

Another passenger aboard the *Kanrin Maru* was Nakahama Manjirō (also known as John Manjirō), who served as the lead interpreter for the expedition. Originally a fisherman from Tosa, Nakahama suddenly found himself bound for the United States one fateful day when his boat was wrecked and an American whaling ship stopped to rescue him. He made his way stateside and went on to spend the next ten years there. Upon his eventual return to Japan, Nakahama served in an official capacity in Tosa until the bakufu summoned him to Edo when Perry's ships arrived. Nakahama later made a return to the United States aboard the *Kanrin Maru* and, after the Meiji Restoration, continued to teach English. He died in 1898.

1-19. Members of the 1860 mission to the United States visit the Washington Navy Yard

1-20. Gold watch with likeness (not visible in photograph) of President Buchanan

combed through article after article meticulously weighing their merits and demerits, and it was not unusual for me to be somewhat at a loss as to what to say. . . . It is Japan's good fortune to have such plenipotentiaries to depend on."

Trade with Western countries would commence in earnest in 1859 through the foreign settlements at the ports of Kanagawa, Nagasaki, and Hakodate, with the overwhelming bulk of the business being conducted at Yokohama (Kanagawa). Exports from Japan were mainly of raw silk and tea, while imports focused on woolen fabrics, cotton fabrics, and firearms and other weapons. The dramatic increase in exports of raw silk and tea that occurred almost instantly after trade began created chaos in the domestic economy, and postponing the opening of cities and ports became an issue for the bakufu.

In 1866, under the lead of the UK's representative Harry Parkes, the bakufu would conclude a supplementary convention on tariffs with the United Kingdom, the United States, France, and the Netherlands. This convention revised the sections of the Ansei Five-Power Treaties that had to do with customs duties, which were set at 5 percent for exports and 20 percent on average for imports. Specifically, the tariffs on imports were set to 5 percent across the board, giving the foreign powers an advantage. The revisions also changed the ad valorem duty tied to commodity prices to a specific duty tied to quantities. For that reason, it became profitable to import large quantities of the same item, particularly in the case of expensive commodities. This convention stimulated free trade.

The Shapers of Bakufu Diplomacy

Iwase Tadanari (1818–61) and Nagai Naoyuki (1816–91)

Best friends ever since their days at the Gakumonjo, Iwase Tadanari and Nagai Naoyuki made an impression on many—including Abe Masahiro, who tagged the pair as bakufu prodigies. Iwase passed the 1843 *gakumon ginmi* (civil-service examinations) and began serving under shogun Tokugawa Iesada. He then became a *metsuke* (inspector) in 1854, a role in which he focused on diplomatic affairs. It was in the *metsuke* capacity that Iwase handled dealings with Townsend Harris upon the new US consul general's arrival in Japan in the summer of 1856, doing everything in his power to arrange a formal audience with the shogun. Iwase also joined Inoue Kiyonao in negotiating additional treaties with the Netherlands and Russia, embracing the idea of an autonomous opening of Japan, and was firm in his belief that trade profits would be the core driver of Japan's pursuit of financial and military strength. With that experience under his belt, Iwase was involved in the signing of the Japan-US Treaty of Amity and Commerce and all the other Ansei treaties. That involvement included accompanying Senior Councillor Hotta Masayoshi to Kyoto to secure imperial sanction for the Japan-US Treaty of Amity and Commerce and then advising on Ii Naosuke's decision to sign the treaty without imperial sanction. Iwase would later be demoted from his position due to his affiliation with the Hitotsubashi faction during the debate over shogunal succession. He was ultimately dismissed from service altogether in 1859, shortly before his death.

1-21. Iwase Tadanari

Nagai, having previously served as a finance magistrate (*kanjō bugyō*), joined Mizuno and Iwase in becoming Japan's first foreign magistrates in 1858. Although his political leanings would jeopardize his career during the Ansei Purge, Nagai was a key player in the handling of the Chōshū expeditions and one of Tokugawa Yoshinobu's most trusted confidants. In addition to assisting the likes of senior councillors Itakura Katsukiyo and Ogasawara Nagamichi with the bakufu's political affairs, he also consulted with Yoshinobu on writing the declaration finalizing the restoration of political power to the emperor. When the effort to give the emperor back his political power crumbled in the face of a coup seeking a restoration of imperial rule (*ōsei fukko*) before a meeting of the feudal lords could even convene, Nagai found himself swimming against a powerful tide. He continued to reject and oppose the new regime through the end of the Boshin War, a stance that earned him life imprisonment under the Meiji government. Nagai proceeded to immerse himself in Dutch books and reading. He eventually received a pardon and went on to take various roles, including serving as a commissioner (*goyōgakari*) for the Hokkaido Development Commission. After retiring, Nagai built a *shidō* (small hall) to enshrine the departed soul of his dear friend Iwase Tadanari, whom he continued to honor until his own death.

Kawaji Toshiakira (1801–68) and Inoue Kiyonao (1809–68)

Kawaji Toshiakira and Inoue Kiyonao were brothers born to a low-ranking official in the magistrate's office (*daikansho*) in Bungo Province in eastern Kyushu and later adopted by different families. Growing up under stern parenting, the two brothers remained serious, diligent workers as they rose through the government ranks, maintained an extraordinarily loyal devotion to the Tokugawa clan, and won the favor of Senior Councillor Abe Masahiro. Inoue played a role in negotiating with Townsend Harris in 1856, then served as Shimoda magistrate, and later assisted Iwase Tadanari in the negotiations for the Japan-US Treaty of Amity and Commerce.

1-22. Kawaji Toshiakira

Kawaji also played a vital role in *bakumatsu* (late Edo period) diplomacy. At the age of seventeen, he sat for Gakumonjo examinations. While he failed the *gakumon ginmi* (civil-service examinations), he managed to pass the arithmetic examination and secured a position as an accounting officer (*kanjō shutsuyaku*). He went on to become a finance magistrate (*kanjō bugyō*) in 1852, joining Tsutsui Masanori in negotiating the Treaty of Peace and Amity between Japan and Russia (Treaty of Shimoda). Kawaji evidently made a significant impression on the Russian side; Ivan Goncharov, a member of the Russian retinue, recalled that "Kawaji was extremely intelligent. . . . Each and every one of his words, each look in his eyes, each gesture hinted at his sound judgment, keen insight, wit, and skill." In 1858, Kawaji and Iwase accompanied Hotta Masayoshi to the imperial court in an unsuccessful attempt to receive official sanction for the treaty with the United States. The Ansei Purge would disrupt the careers of both brothers, however, with Inoue receiving a demotion and Kawaji losing his official position altogether. Inoue died just before the fall of Edo, while Kawaji returned to service as a foreign magistrate before committing suicide upon the surrender of Edo Castle.

Mizuno Tadanori (1815–68)

Promoted from *hatamoto* (direct retainer of the shogunate) to Nishinomaru (Edo Castle's west compound) *metsuke* (inspector) by Senior Councillor Abe Masahiro in 1844, Mizuno Tadanori went on to become an Uraga magistrate in 1852 and a Nagasaki magistrate in 1853. His career included work on numerous negotiations, such as assisting in talks with Yevfimiy Putyatin's Russian contingent and discussions on the Anglo-Japanese Friendship Treaty in 1854. Four years later, in 1858, Mizuno became a foreign magistrate and helped negotiate treaties of amity and commerce with both the United Kingdom and France; he also handled the opening of the Port of Yokohama. In addition to being an adept negotiator, Mizuno was savvy in currency-related matters. He formulated a proposal advocating the minting of Ansei *nishu-gin* (silver coins) to prevent an outflow of gold coins due to an imbalance in the domestic and foreign prices of gold and silver, but vehement opposition by foreign powers made the issue non-negotiable. Mizuno would relinquish his official post in 1859 due to suggestions that he should take responsibility for the killing of a Russian military officer—the first officially recorded murder of a foreigner on Japanese soil—but went on to resume service as a foreign magistrate in 1861. He also led the expedition to claim the Ogasawara (Bonin) Islands, where he conducted survey work that proved the islands to be Japanese territory. Due to his opposition to the *kōbu gattai* philosophy promoting unity of court and bakufu, in 1862 Mizuno was demoted to Hakodate magistrate, a position from which he quickly resigned. Committed to improving the shogunate administration through reform initiatives, Mizuno joined Oguri Tadamasa in calling for a continued resistance by Tokugawa Yoshinobu's camp against the new government's army leading up to, and shortly after, the surrender of Edo Castle. Mizuno advocated continuing the resistance, but his counsel was not heeded. He withdrew to the Musashi-Tama area, where he soon died of illness, apparently consumed with bitterness and grief. Mizuno, along with Iwase and Oguri, is now known as one of the "three heroes of the *bakumatsu*."

1-23. Mizuno Tadanori

Tsutsui Masanori (1778–1859)

After making his way through the Gakumonjo, where he was a standout student, Tsutsui Masanori became a Nagasaki magistrate in 1817. He worked tirelessly to expand trade between Japan and the Netherlands, and also spent a full two decades in the position of Edo municipal magistrate—a key post in the bakufu administration. Tsutsui weathered the difficulties of the Tenpō Reforms, after which he became a Confucian scholar at the Gakumonjo in 1845 and advised Abe Masahiro on foreign policy. When the East India Squadron (led by US commander James Biddle) and Danish warships arrived in Japan demanding that the country open up for trade, Tsutsui formulated a moderate, peaceable response: Japan would refuse to trade with any nation other than the Dutch, citing its intent to maintain a self-sufficient economic structure, but would agree to provide the incoming vessels with fuel, water, and food, thereby staving off armed conflict. Despite the stance he took on the US and Danish overtures, Tsutsui showed his understanding that trade that would benefit the people through the exchange of scarce resources was rooted in the Western Christian notion of salvation.

1-24. Tsutsui Masanori

In 1854, Tsutsui assumed two leadership roles: *ōmetsuke* (chief inspector) and *kaibō-gakari* (coastal-defense officer). Aligning his stance with proponents of opening of the country, particularly Iwase and other coastal-defense inspectors, Tsutsui served as the chief plenipotentiary for the talks with Yevfimiy Putyatin's Russian delegation and, with Kawaji, negotiated the Treaty of Peace and Amity between Japan and Russia (Treaty of Shimoda). He also played a substantial role in securing Harris an audience with the shogun (in order to present an official letter on behalf of US president Franklin Pierce), which proved to be a significant policy reversal. Restarting the "Joseon missions" from Korea to Japan was another objective that Tsutsui worked to pursue, but the effort fell through with the eventual collapse of the bakufu.

Parkes (1828–85) and Satow (1843–1929)

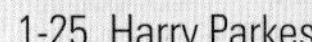

1-25. Harry Parkes

1-26. Ernest Satow

Rutherford Alcock's successor was Harry Parkes, who arrived in Yokohama in July 1865 to take over as the British minister and consul general in Japan. A scrupulous type, Parkes worked to protect British citizens in Japan, made free trade a key priority, and, due to his focus on liberalizing trade, often butted heads with Minister Léon Roches of France. He assumed a wait-and-see approach on the direction Japan's domestic affairs would take at the end of the Edo period, but when the Satsuma and Chōshū domains began embracing the idea of foreign trade, he quickly aligned himself with the anti-shogunate camp. In 1866, Parkes successfully negotiated to bring import tariff rates down to 5 percent across the board (*kaizei yakusho,* a supplementary convention on trade tariffs) as the debate over whether to open the Port of Hyōgo simmered. At the same time, he also objected to the bakufu's plan to monopolize trade, and forced the administration to revise its policy. By quickly moving to recognize the legitimacy of the new Meiji government, Parkes lodged a foothold in the contemporary political discourse—a position from which he fought hard against projects and policies that would put the British side at a disadvantage, and showed little interest in any treaty revisions.

One effort that did command Parkes's interest, however, was propelling Japan's Westernization; he exercised his influence to help bring foreign advisors to Japan and place them in capacities where they could provide meaningful assistance. As the United Kingdom jostled with Russia for position in the Far East, Parkes also looked to help the United Kingdom establish a stronger relationship with Japan by advising the Japanese government on its territorial disputes with the Russians. After completing his service in Japan, Parkes went on to become the British minister to Qing China in 1883, but died two years later.

During Parkes's tenure, the United Kingdom's central policy on Japan went from supporting the bakufu administration to backing the rebels in the southwestern domains. A key player in shaping that shift was a young diplomat named Ernest Satow. Thanks to his fluent command of Japanese, Satow forged close ties with the anti-shogunate resistance that had rooted itself in the southwest and offered Saigō Takamori his assistance. In the spring of 1866, a series of three articles by Satow appeared in the *Japan Times* under the title "Eikoku sakuron" (British policy). The commentaries verbalized Satow's aim to foster support for the anti-shogunate cause, explaining that the shogun (to whom Satow simply referred as *taikun* [tycoon]) was little more than the country's top daimyo; the true head of state, he argued, was the emperor. In addition to writing *A Diplomat in Japan,* a record of his stay in Japan, Satow also penned several classics in the field of diplomatic theory.

"Kōbu Gattai" and the Rise of the Movement to Expel the Barbarians

After Ii's death, senior councillors Andō Nobumasa and Kuze Hirochika became key players in bakufu government. To achieve their goal of restoring the bakufu's waning authority, the pair embarked on a policy aimed at achieving a "unity of court and bakufu" (*kōbu gattai*) that would bring it closer to the imperial court. The objective of this unity of court (*kō*) and military (*bu*) was to present an image of integration with the court led by the emperor, thereby strengthening the bakufu. Satsuma's Shimazu Hisamitsu (younger brother of Shimazu Nariakira), in particular, came up with the idea of suspending the punishments for the Hitotsubashi faction members, and instead appointing them to important posts in the bakufu and at the court. With Nagai Uta's "crossing the seas" policy (*kōkai enryaku saku*) in mind, Shimazu began his own efforts in 1861. This policy basically argued that setting an objective for Japan to actively go abroad,

The *Posadnik* Incident (Tsushima Incident)

Since the Edo period, Tsushima had been a key island in the context of bakufu operations. The administration had entrusted the island's ruling Sō clan with a variety of key tasks, such as receiving Korean missions and handling trade with Korea. In April 1861, the *Posadnik*, a Russian warship, temporarily seized Tsushima on the pretense of conducting repairs on the vessel. The bakufu responded by sending foreign magistrate Oguri Tadamasa in to negotiate a withdrawal of the Russian contingent, which was claiming the island for itself. Hakodate magistrate Muragaki Norimasa also demanded that the Russian consul order the ship to leave Tsushima, but the *Posadnik* stayed put—and the crew decided to entrench its position. The Russian forces started building a stronghold on the island, and soldiers even began to loot the islanders' property and attack local residents.

The standoff eventually ended when British minister Rutherford Alcock arranged for a British ship to rush to the island, prompting the *Posadnik* to withdraw. The United Kingdom apparently had a keen interest in Tsushima as well; records suggest that the British were planning to occupy the island, and they were ready to fight Russia for possession. Since the Crimean War, in fact, Tsushima had been a symbolic battleground for Russo-British enmity. For Japan, meanwhile, Russia's arrival on Tsushima fanned concerns that Russia might advance southward from Karafuto (Sakhalin) and into the Korean Peninsula by way of Tsushima.

rather than just waiting for foreign vessels to come, would itself also make it possible for the court and the bakufu to come together. The court, also being in favor of such an outcome, accepted Shimazu's efforts. The effort was given concrete form by easing the punishments imposed on the Hitotsubashi faction daimyo, and by the marriage of Emperor Kōmei's sister Kazunomiya to shogun Tokugawa Iemochi. As a measure to calm the chaos in the economy that had developed after the opening to foreign trade, the proposal to postpone opening cities and ports was also a part of this movement to unify the court and bakufu.

However, in the end this unification drive would encourage the rise of the "revere the emperor, expel the barbarians" (*sonnō jōi*) movement among the lower samurai in the middling to lower levels of the warrior class in Satsuma and Chōshū. Those two domains would tilt toward more radical anti-foreign sentiment. In February 1862, Andō was assaulted by warriors from among the Mito domain's *roshi*, or lordless samurai (the Sakashita Gate Incident). He resigned his position as senior councillor soon thereafter, and Kuze was also dismissed. Furthermore, the Chōshū domain—where debate over "revere the emperor, expel the barbarians" sentiment was rife—established connections with extremist nobles, and worked to influence the imperial court. By December 1862, the bakufu found itself obliged to order the domains to take steps toward expelling the foreigners. The bakufu had no real intention of driving foreigners away, but in 1863 the Chōshū domain began shelling foreign vessels passing through the Straits of Shimonoseki, and blockading the straits (Shimonoseki Shellings Incident).

Foreign vessels coming to Japan would call first at Nagasaki, after which they would travel by way of the straits through the Seto Inland Sea to get to Yokohama, so a blockade was a serious matter for them. With the United Kingdom's minister, Rutherford Alcock, taking the lead, the United Kingdom, France, the United States, and the Netherlands asked the bakufu to halt Chōshū's hostile activities. However, the bakufu's attitude was ambiguous, and so in July 1864 the four powers decided to mount an attack mission to Shimonoseki (Shimonoseki Campaign). Itō Shunsuke (Hirobumi) and Inoue Monta (Kaoru), two men who had been studying in the United Kingdom, hurried home and asked

Alcock to hold off on military action. The pair also sent a warning to the lord of Chōshū in an effort to avert a clash, but two months later in September a combined fleet of the four powers destroyed the gun battery in Shimonoseki and occupied the area. Chōshū was defeated, and with this, the blockade of the Straits was lifted. The United Kingdom demanded an enormous sum of reparations from the bakufu, the payment of which would extend into the years of the successor Meiji government.

Furthermore, when Alcock was replaced by Harry Parkes as the United Kingdom's envoy, representatives of the four powers would set to work pushing for the port at Hyōgo to be opened, and

The Issue of Procrastination in Opening Markets and Ports and the Japanese Mission to Europe

After the death of Chief Minister Ii Naosuke, Andō Nobumasa became a central force in the bakufu administration. Judging that it would be impossible to open the markets and ports in Edo, Osaka, Hyōgo, and Niigata by the dates specified in the Ansei Five-Power Treaties, Andō asked British consul general (and later envoy) Alcock for permission to delay the openings. Behind Andō's appeal were two motivating factors. The opening of trade relations was bound to trigger political and economic confusion that would take time to settle. Meanwhile, as a firm believer in *kōbu gattai* (unity of court and bakufu), Andō also saw the delay as a way to appease the imperial court and thereby bring the shogunate and the emperor into closer alignment.

Alcock suggested that Japanese representatives meet with the respective treaty signatories. The bakufu responded by assembling a thirty-eight-member mission, with finance magistrate Takenouchi Yasunori serving as chief ambassador. The group set off for Europe aboard a British warship in January 1862 and eventually reached the United Kingdom by way of France. That June, the Japanese contingent convinced the British government to an agreement under which the markets and ports in Niigata, Hyōgo, Edo, and Osaka would remain closed for five years (from January 1863 on), but the three other ports would remain open, adhering strictly to the treaty provisions. Having secured a compromise in London, the mission then visited the Netherlands, Prussia, Russia, France, and Portugal and reached similar agreements, and then made its way back to Japan in January 1863. The one signatory that the yearlong mission did not negotiate a delay with was the United States, which eventually assented to the same terms as its European counterparts in February 1864.

The 1862–63 Japanese mission to Europe not only covered the largest geographical scope of any *bakumatsu*-era foreign mission, but also brought Japan into closer contact with the cultures, goods, and domestic affairs of European nations, giving the voyage a transformative legacy. A pivotal figure was Fukuzawa Yukichi, who penned *Seiyō jijō* (Conditions in the West) on what he saw and experienced during the trip to Europe with the mission. Among other Embassy members were the likes of Fukuchi Gen'ichirō and Terashima Munenori (Matsuki Kōan).

Passports at the End of the Edo Period

In 1866, the Tokugawa bakufu began allowing Japanese citizens to travel abroad for the purposes of study or commerce. The administration thus began issuing its first passports. The image here shows the passport for an individual by the name of "Kamekichi," who was apparently an acrobat of some kind. Each passport from the *bakumatsu* (late Edo) period included an official passport number, the traveler's name and age, and even a brief description of his or her appearance: Kamekichi had "small eyes," for instance.

1-27. A *bakumatsu*-era passport

obtaining imperial sanction for the treaties. Amid the turmoil in the bakufu government, the powers kept their warships offshore of Hyōgo to put pressure on the bakufu. In November 1865, the powers presented the shogun with an ultimatum to press for imperial sanction of the treaties. Emperor Kōmei and some of the court nobles were still opposed to issuing the sanction. However, representing the bakufu's interests in a meeting at the imperial court, Tokugawa Yoshinobu prevailed on them by saying that Kyoto would be burned to the ground if war broke out. And so, finally, the treaties received imperial approval. While the emperor still did not sanction opening the port at Hyōgo, the problem that had existed since 1858 was finally settled, and the Ansei Five-Power Treaties were now deemed legitimate domestically as well.

1-28. The occupation of the Shimonoseki battery

The Bunkyū Mission to Europe

The Ansei Five-Power Treaties stipulated that Japan would open the ports of Hyōgo and Niigata and allow foreign-settlement trade in the markets of Edo and Osaka, but the bakufu asked the treaty signatories for permission to delay the openings until Japan's political and economic circumstances could stabilize. British consul general (and later envoy) Alcock argued that the demands ran counter to the purpose of the treaties, but he suggested that Japan's best course of action would be to dispatch an official delegation to Europe and negotiate directly with the countries party to the agreements. Taking part in the mission were several notable individuals, including Fukuzawa Yukichi, Fukuchi Gen'ichirō, and Terashima Munenori (Matsuki Kōan).

1-29. Fukuzawa Yukichi

1-30. Fukuchi Gen'ichirō

Repercussions of the Anglo-Satsuma War

Meanwhile, in September 1862 an incident occurred in which a group of four British merchants who encountered the procession of Shimazu Hisamitsu as he was traveling from Edo to Kyoto were attacked by Satsuma retainers. One man was killed and the others were injured (Namamugi Incident, a.k.a. the Richardson Affair). The incident was a chance occurrence, but in retaliation the British sent a fleet into Kagoshima Bay and, in August 1863, the Anglo-Satsuma War (commonly known as the Bombardment of Kagoshima) began. Satsuma put up a good fight, but realized that it was up against a mighty military power. Lower samurai such as Saigō Takamori and Ōkubo Toshimichi now held the real power in domainal politics, and Satsuma was becoming more inclined toward overthrowing the bakufu. Chōshū, too, had learned of the might of Western weaponry through the Battle of Shimonoseki, and its warriors were acutely aware of the need to build up its military strength. Chōshū would also change tack from anti-foreign sentiment to working toward overthrowing the bakufu and establishing a new government. Central to that movement were such lower samurai as Takasugi Shinsaku and Katsura Kogorō (Kido Takayoshi).

For an influential domain seeking to have a bigger voice in national politics, an extreme anti-foreign movement was now only an impediment. In Satsuma, Shimazu now worked to eliminate the extremists in the domain. In 1863, Emperor Kōmei swept the imperial court (in Kyoto) clean of Chōshū political influence and of such extremist nobles as Sanjō Sanetomi and Sawa Nobuyoshi (the "8.18 Disturbance" of September 30, sometimes referred to as the "Satsuma-Aizu coup d'état"). Thus, by the second half of 1863, the extreme anti-foreign elements were in retreat. Based on the recommendations of Shimazu, a reform of the imperial court was carried out with a council of advisory lords (*chōgi san'yo*)—which included representatives of the leading domains other than Chōshū, as well as Tokugawa Yoshinobu—to provide counsel to the court. The advisory council lasted for only three months amid conflicts between Yoshinobu and Shimazu over foreign policy, among other problems, but from the perspective of placating both the court and the bakufu, it represented the success of the movement to unify the two.

As part of this effort to mollify an imperial court where anti-foreign sentiment was strong, the bakufu came up with a plan to close Yokohama Port in place of a blanket expulsion of foreigners. In February, the bakufu dispatched a delegation led by Ikeda Nagaoki to negotiate the closure, but it failed.

Occupation of the Ogasawara Islands

The Ogasawara (Bonin) Islands—named for Ogasawara Sadayori, the man who supposedly discovered the chain in 1593—were a long-neglected territory. With the bakufu paying little attention to this archipelago, which lies some 1,000 kilometers south of Tokyo, the location had seen plenty of traffic from the outside: not only did British and American whaling ships land there on occasion, but settlers from Hawaii, the United States, and Europe had made the islands their new home. After opening Japan's ports, bakufu representatives found descriptions in Matthew Perry's documentation of his expedition to Japan indicating that, before sailing into Yokohama Bay, Perry had signed an agreement with the people of Chichijima (one of the Ogasawara Islands) to build a coaling station on the island. The administration was alarmed; they knew that foreign influence over the islands could be highly problematic.

In January 1862, the bakufu sent foreign magistrate Mizuno Tadanori and Tanabe Taichi, along with Nakahama Manjirō and other interpreters, to the Ogasawara Islands aboard the *Kanrin Maru* (which had recently returned from the Japanese mission to the United States). The group arrived in mid-January, assembled the foreign immigrants on the Ogasawara Islands to sign written oaths, and issued land-title certificates to the immigrants who signed. A bakufu government office also went up in the Ōgiura area of Chichijima,

In summer 1864, Chōshū—persuaded by hardliners worked up over the Ikedaya Incident (in which the bakufu's specially selected Shinsengumi police force attacked a gathering of the so-called *shishi*, or "men of high purpose," from Chōshū)—moved aggressively on Kyoto with a large army. However, the bakufu and Satsuma worked together to repel the Chōshū forces, resulting in Chōshū now being regarded as "rebels against the imperial government" (Kinmon Incident, a.k.a. Hamaguri Gate Rebellion). The court gave Yoshinobu command authority over the Kinai region (the territories in the vicinity of Kyoto under direct imperial rule), and thus he established a sort of political authority independent of the Senior Council in Edo. This cooperative relationship between the court and the bakufu was also sustained through the First Chōshū Expedition, a punitive military expedition carried out by the bakufu from August 1864 through January 1865.

The United Kingdom and France: Rapprochement between Satsuma and Chōshū

In May 1865, in order to carry out the Second Chōshū Expedition, shogun Tokugawa Iemochi (formerly Yoshitomi) went to Osaka at the head of a large army, and put together a punitive force that would bring together all of the *fudai* daimyo

as did a stone monument to the "new development of the Ogasawara Islands." Upon receiving a report of the group's efforts, the bakufu notified its foreign counterparts of its plans to redevelop Ogasawara and then sent thirty-eight Hachijōjima islanders in to settle there that August.

The following year, however, the bakufu abruptly aborted its settlement plan and ordered the settlers to be sent home. Behind that development were myriad factors, including strained relations with the United Kingdom stemming from the Namamugi Incident and ensuing friction over reparations; the bakufu's fears that the United Kingdom might move to attack Chichijima; the attempted assassination and subsequent withdrawal of Senior Councillor Andō Nobumasa, who had been one of the most enthusiastic supporters of Ogasawara development; the ousting of Mizuno; and the financial difficulties that limited the bakufu's activities.

1-31. First view of the Ogasawara Islands

After the Japanese presence vanished, the Ogasawara Islands essentially operated under self-government, with American settlers taking the administrative lead. The transition from the bakufu to the Meiji regime brought little change in Japan's stance on the islands; in the greater scheme of the contemporary border disputes, the solitary, far-flung Ogasawara archipelago sat low on the new government's list of priorities. However, the 1874 Taiwan Expedition gave the Japanese government an opportunity to assert its legitimacy in governing the "terra nullius" (land deemed unoccupied or uninhabited) of Taiwan as a "civilized nation" under international law—a powerful statement to the nations of Europe and Qing China. Coming off that development, the government took a renewed interest in the Ogasawara Islands: it could follow the same logic in asserting its control. In November 1875, the Meiji government dispatched the *Meiji Maru* to transport a mission to the islands for a survey of the area. Roughly one year later, in October 1876, Foreign Minister Terashima Munenori declared the Ogasawara Islands to be Japanese territory in the "Ogasawara Rules," which he sent to representatives of various foreign countries in accordance with international law.

Ikeda Nagaoki (1837–79) and the Second Japanese Mission to Europe

Ikeda Nagaoki became a *metsuke* in 1862 and then rose to the position of Kyoto City magistrate and foreign magistrate in 1863. At the time, the bakufu was looking for a way to appease the emperor through a compromise on closing the country. The imperial court advocated exclusionism, favoring a complete closure of the country's borders. That stance ran contrary to the bakufu's approach, however, so the shogunate attempted to find a middle ground by proposing the closure of the Port of Yokohama. However, that idea was met with fierce opposition from the prevailing Western powers. The bakufu thus decided to dispatch a mission to Europe with the express task of shutting off traffic to the Port of Yokohama; Ikeda was named chief ambassador. The expedition set off in February 1864 and eventually arrived in Paris, where the Ikeda Mission had an audience with Napoleon III and began negotiating with the French minister of foreign affairs. The French side told the group that they would offer support if the bakufu needed help suppressing the anti-opening sentiment at home, although they sought several concessions in exchange: compensation for the damage to the French warship that the Chōshū domain had fired on in the Straits of Shimonoseki, for example, and three free ports within Japan, including the Port of Yokohama. Eventually, in June 1864, the Ikeda Mission signed the Agreement of Paris—an arrangement under which the Japanese government would guarantee French ships free passage through the Straits of Shimonoseki, pay for the Chōshū domain's damages to the French navy, and reduce the tariff rates on imports. Upon returning to Japan in August 1864, the Ikeda Mission proposed making a policy shift toward opening the country and reforming the domestic political structure. The bakufu administration, however, refused to ratify the Agreement of Paris and decided to punish members of the group, stripping Ikeda of his official status. Ikeda would return to service as a naval magistrate in 1867, but he resigned after just five months in the position.

1-32. Ikeda Nagaoki (Chōhatsu)

against the rebel domain. However, Satsuma domain under Saigō Takamori was unenthusiastic, seeing little justification for punitive action. Satsuma had been moving toward a rapprochement with Chōshū, and in March 1866 Saigō and Chōshū's Kido Takayoshi met in Kyoto to conclude an alliance between their two domains. This was facilitated and brokered by Sakamoto Ryōma and Nakaoka Shintarō of Tosa domain. Through this pact, Satsuma promised to provide rearguard support to secure Kyoto and Osaka in the event of war between the bakufu and Chōshū. It served to solidify Satsuma and Chōshū's positions as powers seeking to overthrow the bakufu. In July 1866, the bakufu ordered that the punitive Second Chōshū Expedition be carried out with the large battalion of forces that had been assembled in Osaka. However, Satsuma refused to send troops for this war with Chōshū (also known as the Summer War). Chōshū mobilized the Kiheitai (Irregular Militia) and other forces and swept away the bakufu army on the field of combat. With the shogunate already on the defensive, shogun Iemochi suddenly died, and the bakufu ceased hostilities.

While the Satsuma-Chōshū Alliance had been concluded between low-ranking samurai of the two domains, it had an enormous impact that extended to other domains. The lower-ranking warriors involved were able to influence domainal politics on the basis of the pact and the lords of their domains acquiesced to those moves.

Minister Parkes of the United Kingdom welcomed the Satsuma-Chōshū rapprochement, and even played a certain role in the pact itself. Parkes had been critical of the bakufu for its efforts to monopolize the benefits of trade. He was worried

The Question of the Opening of the Port of Hyōgo

In April 1865, the United Kingdom approached Japan with a proposal: in exchange for a reduction of the amount of reparations for the Shimonoseki Bombardment, the bakufu would open up the Port of Hyōgo in January 1866, secure imperial sanction for the Ansei Five-Power Treaties, and reduce tariffs on British imports. The British were hoping to speed up the opening of the Port of Hyōgo, which had been delayed, and finalize the treaties via imperial sanction, which also had yet to materialize. The United Kingdom, France, the United States, and the Netherlands sent ships to Japan under the command of British minister Parkes to pressure the bakufu into accepting the demands. Senior councillors, including Abe Masato, recommended that the bakufu approve the opening of the port, but the government's response broke down when Yoshinobu, then in control of Kyoto, called a meeting of the court council and dismissed two of the senior councillors for attempting to open Hyōgo without imperial sanction. Furious at what had transpired, shogun (Tokugawa) Iemochi submitted his resignation and threatened to return to Edo.

In late November, Yoshinobu persuaded Iemochi to go back to Kyoto and convene a meeting of the imperial court, which resolved to sanction the treaties—but did not approve the opening of the Port of Hyōgo. The Satsuma domain, seeing a predicament that could weaken the bakufu's position, attempted to use the Hyōgo issue as an anti-shogunate tactic. Yoshinobu, however, evaded the opposition's tactics by making the opening a non-issue: in May 1867, he met with representatives of the four countries at Osaka Castle, told the attendees that he had secured supreme authority over the entire nation, and announced that he would open the Port of Hyōgo as scheduled. Yoshinobu then met with officials from Satsuma, Echizen, Tosa, and Uwajima at Nijō Castle in June. After discussing a punishment for the Chōshū domain and the opening of the Port of Hyōgo, the attendees decided to assign the Chōshū situation top priority and address the port problem later—but that was merely a formal distinction. For all intents and purposes, the group had settled on pursuing both issues simultaneously, rendering Satsuma's scheme a failure. Yoshinobu called a meeting of the imperial court in late June, gave the Chōshū domain a lenient punishment, and had the imperial court authorize the opening of the Port of Hyōgo as a *chōshi* (an order representing the will of the imperial court). It was a victory for Yoshinobu, who had successfully thwarted Satsuma's attempt to debilitate the shogunate via political means, and the plan to open the Port of Hyōgo in January 1868 was confirmed.

that a defeat for Chōshū—which was the most powerful force opposed to the bakufu—would provide an opportunity for the bakufu to once again reunite the country. With Satsuma and Chōshū having become more positive toward trade with foreign countries, he counted on the two domains to join together in insurrection against the bakufu.

The bakufu, meanwhile, adopted a pro-France position. Léon Roches, who was appointed France's minister to Japan in April 1864, made a point of getting close to the bakufu. At the time, France was in the final stages of its own industrial revolution, and was aggressively seeking to develop its foreign presence through increased trade and other measures. The conflict between Satsuma and Chōshū and the bakufu mirrored the tug-of-war between France, which hoped to increase its influence on Japan by supporting the bakufu, and the United Kingdom, which sought free trade. Within the bakufu, a group of pro-France officials seeking to reform the bakufu government with French assistance was on the rise. Finance magistrate Oguri Tadamasa (Kōzukenosuke) and foreign relations magistrate Kurimoto Kon were at the center of this. By the end of 1864, this cohort held sway, and the bakufu embarked on such moves as putting together a professional bureaucracy and reforming the Senior Council system.

Léon Roches (1809–1901)

Léon Roches, France's second minister in Japan, provided the bakufu with plenty of support in direct opposition to the British policy. To fortify the bakufu's military strength, Roches offered aid by mediating the provision of weapons, munitions, and warships, along with the construction of the Yokosuka Ironworks. He also advised the sitting shogun, Yoshinobu, on implementing internal reforms, establishing a standing army, and encouraging the development of new industry. Seeing promise in Roches's suggestions, the bakufu invited a group of French military advisors to come to Japan and help train its army. The momentum that Roches had helped initiate would come to an abrupt halt, however, when the French government made a policy about-face, abandoned its pro-bakufu stance, and ordered Roches to return home. Roches remained determined to see his support for the bakufu through despite the shifting discourse in France, even urging Yoshinobu to reclaim the shogunate's authority amid the restoration of imperial rule, until ultimately leaving Japan in June 1868.

The End of Bakufu Governance: The Stirrings of a New Nation

From 1865 to 1866, a situation developed in which there were three competing ideas for a new administration. The first was that of the bakufu, which, with French support, sought to cement its power and reunify the country under Tokugawa Yoshinobu. The second was that favored by Satsuma and Chōshū, which recognized the need for "imperial authority" and "reverence for the emperor" and sought the bakufu's overthrow through military force. The third was the concept of restoring political power to the emperor favored by the Tosa domain, which incorporated the spirit of the "unity of court and bakufu" movement.

Sakamoto Ryōma and Gotō Shōjirō of Tosa were keenly aware of the need to unite Japan under the emperor and reform the country's feudal system in order to stand up to the great powers of the West. In July 1867, the pair departed Nagasaki and headed for Kyoto by sea. The document that Sakamoto wrote while on that vessel was known as the "Eight-Point Plan" (*Senchū hassaku*, literally "Eight theses from aboard a ship"). Premised on the return of political power to the emperor, he offered a concept for what essentially was a legislature-centered polity (*kōgi seitai*) that would create a nation based on a constitutional monarchy. It called for such measures as creating a unified state centered on the imperial court, establishing a legislature, reforming how "relations with foreign countries" were handled, and creating an imperial army under the new government.

Saigō and Ōkubo of Satsuma persisted in their calls for overthrowing the bakufu through force of arms, but Tosa's Gotō negotiated with them to push through a Satsuma-Tosa alliance. The Tosa-Satsuma pact envisioned a return of political power to the emperor whereby the bakufu would return political authority to the imperial court, and a legislature-centered polity would be established with a permanent council whose membership would involve all of the daimyo—not just those who volunteered to establish a legislature. For Sakamoto and Gotō, this was the best way to avoid Satsuma and Chōshū working to overthrow the bakufu by military means. Pro-bakufu elements opposed to these schemes aimed at returning political power to the emperor, and in December 1867, they sent assassins to Sakamoto's lodgings in Kyoto and killed him.

1-33. Sakamoto Ryōma

In late October, the Tosa domain had

The Shapers of Bakufu Diplomacy

Oguri Tadamasa (1827–68) and Kurimoto Kon (1822–97)

1-34. Oguri Tadamasa

The son of a *hatamoto* (direct retainer of the shogunate), Oguri Tadamasa, later known as Oguri Kōzukenosuke, was one of the three plenipotentiary members (the *metsuke*) of the 1860 Japanese mission to the United States. The group visited the US Mint in Philadelphia, where Oguri used balance scales and a *soroban* (Japanese abacus) that he had brought from Japan to determine the exact difference in gold content between Japanese and American coins—and used his findings to argue that the prevailing exchange rate was unfair. The US contingent, though impressed with Oguri's acumen, refused to revise the existing treaty.

Upon returning home, Oguri served as a foreign magistrate and occupied several other key positions. A core focus for him in his official capacities was the effort to modernize the bakufu military. In 1866, he enlisted the help of French military advisors to train the bakufu's forces and give the administration more muscle in battling the opposition. It was one of the bold, sweeping moves that characterized Oguri's push for modernization, an industrial and social course of action that Ōkuma Shigenobu would later say the Meiji government "copied" in implementing its own modernization campaign. Oguri's initiatives did not always enjoy support; the construction of the Yokosuka Ironworks, which took place during his time as a financial magistrate, drew considerable criticism for its funding woes. Even when the bakufu folded, however, Oguri pressed on in spearheading the facility's construction—a project he saw as vital to the nation's development—despite foreign loans falling into arrears.

An important ally in the effort to build the ironworks was Kurimoto Kon, also known as Kurimoto Joun. A product of the Gakumonjo, where he studied for four years, Kurimoto moved to Ezo (now Hokkaido) in 1858 and later worked for the Hakodate magistrate, overseeing several successful projects including the construction of a hospital in Hakodate and a medicinal herb garden in Nanae. He relocated to Yokohama in 1865, where he provided Oguri with support on the ironworks project and held a foreign magistrate post for a time. Kurimoto maintained a pro-bakufu stance when he traveled to France as a member of Tokugawa Akitake's delegation to the Paris Exposition, but the demise of the shogunate brought him back to Japan. After the Meiji Restoration, Kurimoto established a career in journalism, writing for the *Yūbin Hōchi Shimbun* newspaper and other publications.

Oguri, meanwhile, met with a much different fate. In January 1868, he tried to convince Tokugawa Yoshinobu to engage the new government's forces in armed combat—but Yoshinobu would have none of it. Frustrated, Oguri fled to Jōshū and sought seclusion as a farmer. When he was found by the Meiji government's army, he was executed without even being interrogated.

Oguri's ironworks project came to fruition, as the Meiji government sustained the effort and eventually completed what would become the Yokosuka Shipyards in 1871. After Japan's victory in the Naval Battle of the Sea of Japan (Battle of Tsushima) in 1905, Admiral Tōgō Heihachirō sent Oguri's family a letter saying that the shipyards had played an integral role in the triumph. The first dock at the Yokosuka Shipyards is still in operation today, serving as a dry dock for the US naval base in Yokosuka (officially Commander Fleet Activities Yokosuka).

submitted a petition to return political power to the emperor. This plan would create a coalition government by returning, for the time being, political power from the shogun to the court and then creating a council of all of the domains—led by the Tokugawa—which would be subordinate to the court. On November 8, Yoshinobu assembled the chief vassals of all domains valued at 100,000 *koku* or more (a *koku* being the amount of rice sufficient to feed one person for a year) at Nijō Castle in Kyoto. After deliberations, the following day he presented his opinion to the court of the restoration of imperial rule. Yoshinobu had surrendered political power in name, but essentially his aim was to convene a conference of all the lords, get support from a plurality of the daimyo, and retain the seat of power. The court accepted Yoshinobu's petition, and confirmed that he would retain his position as shogun.

However, under the guidance of Saigō and Ōkubo, the anti-bakufu factions in both Satsuma and Chōshū linked up with the powerful court noble Iwakura Tomomi. Having obtained a secret rescript to overthrow the bakufu from the emperor (Emperor Kōmei had died in January 1867, and was replaced by the sixteen-year-old Mutsuhito as Emperor Meiji), the two domains now dispatched an anti-bakufu force to accomplish that task. With warriors from the anti-bakufu forces guarding the Imperial Palace in Kyoto, on January 3, 1868 the court issued a proclamation declaring the return of imperial rule (*Ōsei fukko no daigōrei*). This development has been described as the *Ōsei fukko* coup d'état, in the sense that—in contrast to Yoshinobu's announcement on restoring political power to the emperor—the anti-bakufu faction had managed an overthrow that did away with the bakufu in the name of the emperor. Yoshinobu was stripped of his position as shogun, and a new government comprising court nobles, the daimyo of influential domains, and their retainers was formed under the young emperor. This marked the end of the Tokugawa bakufu, which had ruled for more than 260 years.

That evening, with the emperor in attendance, the so-called Kogosho Conference was held at the Imperial Palace in Kyoto. At this event—the first to convene participants from the three senior ranks (*sōsai*, *gijō*, and *san'yo*)—Yoshinobu was ordered to surrender his official position and his domains. Yoshinobu left Nijō Castle and withdrew to Osaka Castle, where he made his plans to recover his position.

Averting Civil War: The Boshin War

In January 1868, the army of the former bakufu, led by Yoshinobu, marched from Osaka toward Kyoto. However, in a battle conducted around Toba and Fushimi, on Kyoto's outskirts, they were defeated by the pro-court forces (i.e., the new government's army). The new government already had western Japan in its grasp, and now it sought to militarily take down the former government's forces around Edo. Prince Arisugawa Taruhito was put in command of the Eastern Expedition and sent to Edo. In March, he ordered his advance guard to launch an all-out assault on the city. Meanwhile, as a result of negotiations in April between Tokugawa representative Katsu Kaishū and Satsuma's Saigō Takamori, an agreement was reached whereby

The Paris Exposition

On the invitation of Napoleon III, the bakufu sent a delegation led by Tokugawa Akitake to exhibit numerous ukiyo-e woodblock prints and other pieces of artwork at the 1867 Paris Exposition. The twenty-six-member group, which included a young Shibusawa Eiichi (then a vassal of the shogunate), remained in Europe into the following year to absorb the milieu of Western industry and economy. The event also spurred rival domains into action. On hearing about the exposition from Godai Tomoatsu, who was in Europe at the time, the Satsuma domain decided to participate independently. The Nabeshima domain in Saga then followed suit. With the bakufu, the Satsuma domain, and the Nabeshima domain all showcasing items under the banner of "Japan," the Paris Exposition provided a captivating—if unusually disjointed—introduction to Japanese culture.

1-35. Tokugawa Akitake

The Boshin War and the *Stonewall*

Of all the factors that steered the outcome of the Boshin War, the declarations of neutrality by the Western powers were pivotal. The bakufu had arranged for the purchase of the *Stonewall* (*Kōtetsukan*)—a state-of-the-art armored ship—from the United States before the war. As the United States had declared itself neutral in the conflict, however, it could not release the vessel. That roadblock remained in place until the Aizu domain fell in November 1868 and Western nations lifted their declarations of neutrality, recognizing the new Meiji government as a legitimate regime. The *Stonewall* could now change hands—the recipient, however, was not the crumbling bakufu but rather the new Meiji government, which deployed the warship in its attack on Goryōkaku in June 1869. Enomoto Takeaki had mustered a sizable fleet of former bakufu warships in Hakodate for the shogunate, fortifying an apparent naval advantage, but the *Stonewall* helped turn the tide and secure victory for the nascent imperial government. Incidentally, the negotiator responsible for landing the delivery of the *Stonewall* for the imperial side was none other than former Kaientai (a trading company and private navy) member Mutsu Munemitsu, who would go on to have an illustrious career in the Meiji government.

Yoshinobu would be confined to Mito, Edo Castle would be surrendered, and the pro-bakufu forces would turn over their warships and weapons. With this, Edo Castle fell with no loss of life.

Fighting would continue between the new government's army and an alliance of northeastern domains that were dissatisfied with the new regime. Finally, in October 1868, Sendai domain—a leader of that alliance, known as the Ōuetsu Reppan Dōmei—surrendered. The alliance collapsed, and shortly thereafter the last leading site of resistance, Aizu-Wakamatsu Castle, fell. Around this time, the deputy commander of the navy of the former bakufu, Enomoto Takeaki, led a flotilla of eight ships out of Edo Bay and set off for Ezo, the island of Hokkaido. In January 1869, he put the region under his control. However, the new government had received state-of-the-art ironclads from the United States, giving it superiority in naval strength. In June 1869, Enomoto's forces were defeated in the Battle of Goryōkaku (Hakodate War) and the Boshin War was thus brought to an end. The Boshin War could have led to a civil war partitioning Japan in two. Had that been the case, it would have opened the way for foreign military intervention, and a repeat of what had happened to the Qing court in China. Wariness about this put a check on the actions of both the new government and its bakufu (Tokugawa) predecessor.

The European powers likewise did not want this internal conflict to expand. British minister Parkes—at the request of Katsu Kaishū—lodged his strong opposition to Saigō and an attack on Edo. Much of this was rooted in the United Kingdom's realization that a civil war would impede trade.

CHAPTER 2

The Age of "Elder Statesmen Diplomacy"

2-1. From left to right, front row: Itō Hirobumi, Ōkuma Shigenobu, Nakai Hiromu. Back row: Inoue Kaoru, Kuse Jisaku

TIMELINE

1868 (Keiō 4/Meiji 1)

January 3 Proclamation of the Restoration of Imperial Rule issued

January 27 Boshin War begins (fighting between the former bakufu's army and a Satsuma-Chōshū force around Toba and Fushimi near Kyoto)

February 4 Foreigners attacked by samurai from Bizen domain (Kobe Incident)

February 8 New government declares its establishment to representatives of six countries

February 13 New government notifies countries that it will continue to honor treaties signed during bakufu regime

March 8 Tosa-domain soldiers kill French sailors (Sakai Incident); Tosa soldiers executed as punishment and indemnity paid

April 5 Saigō Takamori and Katsu Kaishū start negotiating the surrender of Edo Castle; negotiations completed following day

April 6 Emperor assembles courtiers and nobles to present the Charter Oath of Five Articles

May 3 Edo Castle surrenders; Tokugawa Yoshinobu withdraws to Mito

May 22 UK envoy Harry Parkes presents credentials from Queen Victoria to the emperor

June 11 Constitution of 1868 (the "Seitaisho") promulgated; Bureau of Foreign Affairs (Gaikokukan) established in Osaka (moved shortly thereafter to Kyoto), Date Munenari appointed as first director (*chiji*)

September 3 Imperial edict promulgated changing the name "Edo" to "Tokyo"

October 23 Era name changed from Keiō to Meiji; practice of assigning one era name per emperor established

1869 (Meiji 2)

March 2 Lords of the four domains of Satsuma, Chōshū, Tosa, and Hizen return their lands and people to the emperor

June 27 Boshin War ends

August 15 Staff Ordinance (Shikinryo) promulgated; Ministry of Foreign Affairs established, with Sawa Nobuyoshi appointed first foreign minister

1870 (Meiji 3)

November 24 Three-tier system for foreign postings (top level, medium level, and low level) established; Samejima Naonobu sent to Europe as chargé d'affaires and first overseas diplomat

1871 (Meiji 4)

January 31 Ministry of Foreign Affairs moved to Kasumigaseki

August 29 Imperial edict on abolishing domains and establishing prefectures (domain governors dismissed, governors of three urban prefectures appointed)

September 13 Japan-China Friendship and Trade Treaty signed in Tianjin

December 23 Diplomatic mission headed by Iwakura Tomomi as plenipotentiary departs by ship from Yokohama, returns to Japan September 13, 1873

1872 (Meiji 5)

March 8 Consulate established in Shanghai, with Shinagawa Tadamichi appointed consul (*ryōji*)

April 5 Ministry of Military Affairs abolished, Army Ministry and Navy Ministry established

November 4 Post of "consul" (*benmushi*) abolished; replaced by "minister" (*kōshi*)

December 5 Ambassador Iwakura has audience with Queen Victoria

December 9 Use of lunar calendar ended, switch to Gregorian (solar) calendar (Meiji 5.12.3 becomes Meiji 6.1.1)

1873 (Meiji 6)

January 9 Garrisons stationed in Nagoya and Hiroshima, resulting in six military districts nationwide

January 10 Conscription Ordinance established

August 17 Council of State decides to dispatch Saigō Takamori to Korea (Joseon)

October 24–25 Emperor indefinitely postpones the dispatch of any envoy to Korea; Saigō Takamori, Soejima Taneomi, Itagaki Taisuke, and Gotō Shōjirō resign their positions as councillors (*sangi*) (Political Upheaval of 1873)

1874 (Meiji 7)

February 6 Japan decides to dispatch troops to Taiwan (expedition led by Saigō Tsugumichi (Jūdō) lands in Taiwan on May 22)

April 4 Saigō Tsugumichi appointed governor-general of the Taiwan Aboriginal Affairs Bureau (*Taiwan banchi jimu totoku*)

October 31 Agreement between Japan and China regarding Taiwan signed in Peking (Beijing)

1875 (Meiji 8)

May 7 Signing of Treaty for the Exchange of Sakhalin for the Kurile Islands (Treaty of Saint Petersburg)

September 20 Gunboat *Un'yō* battles with troops garrisoning Ganghwa Island off Korean coast (Ganghwa Island Incident)

1876 (Meiji 9)

February 26 Signing of Japan-Korea Treaty of Amity (Japan-Korea Treaty of 1876)

1877 (Meiji 10)

January 30	Seinan War (Satsuma Rebellion) breaks out
February 22	Army of Saigō Takamori surrounds Kumamoto Castle
April 15	Government army led by Kuroda Kiyotaka enters Kumamoto Castle
September 24	Saigō Takamori and followers commit suicide at Shiroyama, ending Seinan War

1878 (Meiji 11)

February 20	British merchant John Hartley prosecuted for opium smuggling; acquitted by British consular court (Hartley Incident)
July 25	Signing of Japan-US Commercial Treaty (Yoshida-Evarts Treaty)

1879 (Meiji 12)

March 11	Promulgation issued abolishing the Ryūkyū domain and replacing it with Okinawa Prefecture
July 3–August 10	Former US president Ulysses S. Grant visits Japan by way of Qing China while on world tour; holds talks with emperor at Hama-Rikyū Palace in Tokyo

1881 (Meiji 14)

October 11	Imperial Council (Gozen Kaigi) settles on guidelines regarding constitutional system of government, dismissal of Ōkuma Shigenobu, etc. (Political Upheaval of 1881)

1882 (Meiji 15)

July 23	Korean soldiers rise up in Gyeongseong (Seoul), Japanese legation attacked (Imo Incident)
August 30	Japan-Korea Treaty of 1882 (Treaty of Chemulpo) signed to resolve Imo Incident

1883 (Meiji 16)

July 25	Signing of Japan-Korea Trade Charter
August 3	Itō Hirobumi and entourage return from visit to western Europe to study constitutions

1884 (Meiji 17)

June 23	Sino-French War begins
December 4	Pro-Japan faction launches coup d'état in Gyeongseong, suppressed by Qing China force after two days (Gapsin Coup)

1885 (Meiji 18)

January 9	Signing of Treaty of Hanseong (Japan-Korea Treaty of 1885)
April 15	British squadron occupies Geomun Island at southern tip of Korean Peninsula to curb Russia (Geomun Island Incident, a.k.a. Port Hamilton Incident) (withdraws in 1887)
April 18	Japan and China sign the Tianjin Convention
December 22	Cabinet system inaugurated; first Itō Hirobumi cabinet formed

1886 (Meiji 19)

May 1	First meeting held at the Ministry of Foreign Affairs on issue of treaty revision
October 24	British merchant ship *Normanton* sinks in open seas off Kumano, Wakayama (*Normanton* Incident)

1887 (Meiji 20)

April 22	At 26th meeting on treaty revision, Anglo-German proposal on court jurisdiction accepted pending amendment
July 29	Notification that treaty revision meetings to be postponed indefinitely until Japan compiles legal codes

1888 (Meiji 21)

April 30	Kuroda Kiyotaka cabinet formed
November 30	Signing of Japan-Mexico Treaty of Amity, Commerce and Navigation (first equal treaty)

1889 (Meiji 22)

February 11	Constitution of Imperial Japan (Meiji Constitution) promulgated
February 12	Prime Minister Kuroda delivers lecture on "transcendentalism"
October 18	Negotiations on treaty revision postponed owing to an attack on Foreign Minister Ōkuma Shigenobu
December 24	First Yamagata Aritomo cabinet formed

1890 (Meiji 23)

November 25	First regular session of Imperial Diet convened
December 6	Prime Minister Yamagata Aritomo in a policy address emphasizes "line of sovereignty" and "line of interest"

1891 (Meiji 24)

March 29	Russian czar Alexander III orders construction of Trans-Siberian Railway (railroad completed in September 1904)
May 6	Fisrst Matsukata Masayoshi Cabinet formed
May 11	Ōtsu Incident occurs

1892 (Meiji 25)

August 8	Second Itō Cabinet formed

1894 (Meiji 26)

July 16	Anglo-Japanese Treaty of Commerce and Navigation signed; new "Mutsu Treaties" with the US, Italy, Russia, and Germany implemented in 1899 (restoration of Japan's legal rights)

1 Creating a New Government

The Legitimacy of the New Government

The first task for the Restoration government was to win recognition as the legitimate government representing the country from the Western powers with which the bakufu had established diplomatic relations. This was because the new government was established following a coup d'état by the monarchy (imperial court) which now held political power in place of the bakufu. In January 1868 (Keiō 3.12), Tokugawa Yoshinobu had met with envoys of the regime's five treaty partners at Osaka Castle. There, he explained to them the situation regarding the bakufu's proposal to return power to the emperor (*taisei hōkan*), and excoriated the violence associated with the restoration of imperial rule. He then went on to say that, until Japan established a polity rooted in the "public opinion of the entire country," it was his responsibility to respect the treaties in place with each country and conduct relations (*kōsai*) (i.e., diplomacy) with them. When the Battle of Toba-Fushimi broke out between the pro-shogunate forces and Restoration forces, the bakufu requested that the foreign delegations in Japan not supply weapons or warships to the Satsuma domain, which was at the core of the Restoration regime. From the perspective of international law, the new regime was regarded as a hostile group rebelling against the bakufu. In that sense, there was legitimacy to Yoshinobu's complaint; conversely, the Restoration regime agonized over the notification of the regime change to foreign countries.

On February 4, 1868 (Keiō 4.1.11), an incident occurred at the newly opened port city of Kobe in which a group of foreigners who had cut across a procession of samurai from the Bizen domain was attacked by one of the samurai (Kobe Incident). Parkes saw here a chance to steer the policies of the new government toward opening the country to the world. He contacted the British and French warships in the harbor and got them to send landing parties to mount an attack on the Bizen samurai. The foreign powers then seized Japanese vessels in the harbor and occupied central Kobe. Upon hearing the news of these developments, the new government in Kyoto hastily dispatched Mutsu Munemitsu and Nakai Hiroshi (Hiromu) to the scene. When Mutsu and Nakai reported on the seriousness of the situation, Higashikuze Michitomi—the advisor (*san'yo*) in charge of business related to foreign countries—set out for Kobe together with Iwashita Michihira, Terashima Munenori, and Itō Hirobumi as imperial envoys on February 6. Meeting representatives of the six powers with ships in the harbor on February 8, he read out an imperial rescript that declared the

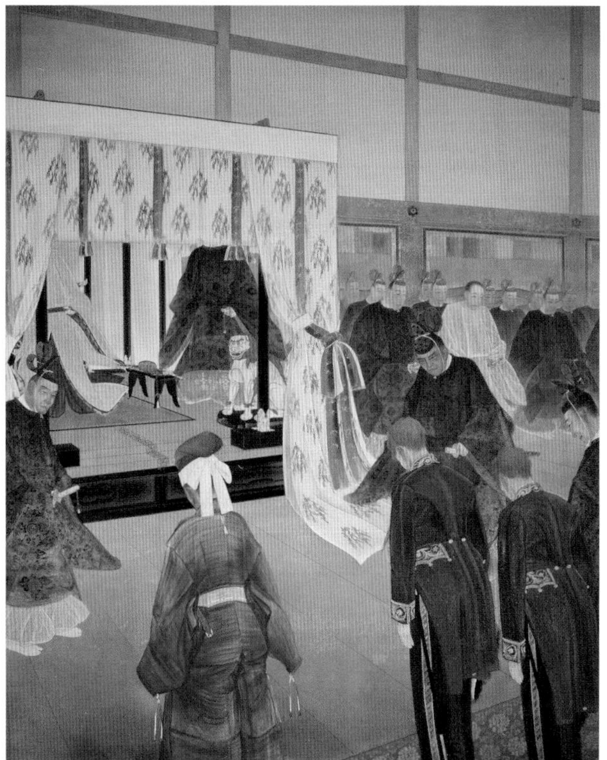

2-2. *The Emperor Receives Foreign Ministers* (painting by Hiroshima Kōho)

"restoration of imperial rule of old" (*ōsei fukko*). The rescript explained that Emperor Meiji himself was in charge of "both domestic and foreign political affairs, and that interactions with foreign countries were not the business of the shogun but rather would be carried out in the name of the emperor based on "international law among the nations."

On February 10, the Restoration government released its first foreign policy statement, "Proclamation on the Opening of the Country through Peace and Amity." Directed at a domestic audience, it declared that relations with other nations would be handled addressing the "law of the whole world" (i.e., international law). When the new,

The Diplomats of Satsuma

The Satsuma domain produced a bevy of diplomatic talent during the early Meiji era. Joining Kuroda Kiyotaka and Nishi Tokujirō (both with strong ties to the Boshin War and noted elsewhere), Terashima Munenori was one of the most prominent examples of a Satsuma native who went on to flourish in the new Meiji government as a councillor and foreign minister. Others include Mori Arinori, Samejima Naonobu, Yoshida Kiyonari, and Ueno Kagenori, all of whom were integral to forging the Meiji administration's first diplomatic ties with the West on the ground in Europe and the United States. The profiles below cover Terashima, Mori, and Samejima, but Yoshida (1845–91) also merits mention. One of the "Satsuma students" (samurai from the Satsuma domain sent to study abroad), along with Mori and Samejima, Yoshida took a position in the Ministry of Finance upon returning to Japan. In 1874, he became the Japanese envoy in the United States and helped Terashima negotiate treaty revisions and eventually sign what would be the Yoshida-Evarts Treaty. Ueno (1844–88), meanwhile, built a reputation as one of Satsuma's top talents and created the opportunity for Terashima to serve in the nascent government administration. Besides being Terashima's right-hand man, Ueno also went on to become Japan's envoy in the United Kingdom and a *gaimu taifu* (equivalent to a deputy minister in the Ministry of Foreign Affairs).

Terashima Munenori (1832–93)

Born in the Satsuma domain, Terashima Munenori was adopted by his uncle Matsuki Muneyasu and took the name Matsuki Kōan. After studying Dutch-style medicine in Edo with financial support from the domain, he became court physician to Shimazu Nariakira. His extraordinary talent impressed observers—so much so, in fact, that he earned himself a place on the bakufu's first mission to Europe in 1862. Terashima began to develop a strong interest in the United Kingdom, not so much as a source of Western knowledge but rather as a model of civilization, and eventually set foot in the country himself in 1865 as a member of the Satsuma domain's mission to the United Kingdom, along with other notable names like Godai Tomoatsu. Terashima's two voyages provided unique insights into Western systems of government, a perspective that led him to conclude that the only way for feudal lords to swear allegiance to the emperor would be to require the return of their land and the people to the imperial court. He submitted an official petition advocating that course of action in November 1867, predating Kido Takayoshi's petition for *hanseki hōkan* (order to return the domains to the emperor). The night before the coup aiming to restore imperial rule, Terashima met with Ōkubo Toshimichi and others to lay the groundwork for a lasting connection.

2-3. Terashima Munenori

Terashima also served as Japan's negotiator in the Meiji government's first diplomatic dispute, which arose in the wake of the Kobe Incident. Sitting down with Harry Parkes and Ernest Satow, Terashima navigated the arduous, touch-and-go discussions to reach a compromise—and, in the process, established himself as a reputable diplomat. His career took him to Yokohama, where he took charge of diplomatic affairs, replacing the Kanagawa magistrate, in March 1868. In that position, he helped arrange the purchase of minting machinery and implementation of the infrastructure for connecting Tokyo and Yokohama by telegraph.

In April 1872, Terashima became an envoy extraordinary and senior minister (*dai-benmushi*; he would become minister plenipotentiary [*zenken kōshi*] in October), took up a post in London, and, as part of his duties, provided the Iwakura Mission's visits to the United States and the United Kingdom with support. He then took over for Soejima court-centered administration was established in Kyoto under the restoration of imperial rule proclamation, many people were very surprised, because they had believed that Japan would return to a closed state that exluded foreigners.

In the meantime, the Kobe Incident was brought to a close with the samurai who had injured the foreigners being ordered to commit ritual suicide. However, in order to make everyone in Japan aware that there would be no return to the anti-foreign, closed-country state of affairs, it was also necessary to gain the trust and approval of foreign governments as quickly as possible.

On February 13, 1868, the Restoration government notified the treaty powers that it would continue to honor the treaties signed during the

Taneomi as councillor and foreign minister the following October, assuming a central presence in the Ōkubo administration. The position presented Terashima with several challenging problems to address. The aftereffects of the *María Luz* Incident—a concern that had been simmering since Soejima's time in office—were still lingering, so Terashima worked with envoy to Russia Enomoto Takeaki to settle the matter. In negotiating treaty revisions, meanwhile, Terashima stuck to Japan's existing policy of not granting foreigners freedom to move throughout the interior unless they abided by Japanese law. At the request of the Ministry of Finance, he also worked to recover Japan's tariff autonomy. Terashima went into the negotiations with a determination to limit the scope of the talks with the United States, which proved to be a fruitful decision. Making smoother progress with a clear, singular goal, the two sides eventually agreed to restore most of Japan's tariff autonomy through the Yoshida-Evarts Treaty in July 1878. Wary of making Japan's relations with the United States appear too prominent, Terashima also engaged the United Kingdom, Germany, and France in negotiations.

The talks with the United Kingdom proved frustrating. While the British side was receptive to the idea of adjusting the agreed tariff rates, they refused to restore Japan's tariff autonomy out of concerns that doing so might encourage protectionism. The 1877 Seinan War (Satsuma Rebellion) put Japan's financial standing on thin ice, creating the need for more revenue. For the Ministry of Finance, the solution was clear: revise the extant tariff rates to boost tax yields. Terashima, however, never attempted to restrict the negotiations with trading partners to tariff-rate modifications. In response, Ōkuma Shigenobu and the higher-ups at the Ministry of Finance moved to coordinate with Japan's resident envoys in the United Kingdom, France, and Germany and wrest diplomatic control over the negotiations away from Terashima. The acquittal of John Hartley, a suspected opium smuggler from the United Kingdom, only amplified the growing public calls for the Japanese government to reclaim its legal rights. In September 1879, Terashima admitted that he had been mistaken in focusing exclusively on tariff autonomy and resigned from his position as foreign minister. With a reputation for remaining calm, never resentful when shamed or indignant when insulted, Terashima is remembered as having possessed a level-headed, intellectual sincerity but lacking the qualities of strong leadership.

Samejima Naonobu (1845–80) and Mori Arinori (1847–89)

2-4. Samejima Naonobu

2-5. Mori Arinori

Samejima Naonobu and Mori Arinori joined the group of students (which also included Yoshida Kiyonari and Godai Tomoatsu) sent from the Satsuma domain to the United Kingdom for further schooling in 1865—and they would remain lifelong friends. They headed back to Japan when they heard about the restoration of imperial rule. Samejima became senior secretary of foreign affairs in 1870. That same year, the government named him chargé d'affaires to Europe (that is, the United Kingdom, France, and Prussia). On his arrival in London in February 1871, however, the British government refused to recognize him as a diplomatic representative. He headed for Paris, where he opened a Japanese diplomatic mission. Mori, meanwhile, was named Japan's first resident envoy to the United States at around the same time that Samejima began his service in Europe. His work in Washington began in 1871. When the Iwakura Mission arrived in the United States, Mori urged the group to pursue treaty-revision negotiations. The American government refused, however, and Mori decided to step down from his position bakufu's regime. They did so in order to stress that the new government was a legitimate one that respected international law. Furthermore, on February 29, the six lords—those of Echizen and Aki joining Satsuma, Chōshū, Tosa, and Hizen—presented to the new government a proposal that the representatives of the foreign powers be given an audience with the emperor. The lords explained that the parties handling diplomacy needed to make efforts to disabuse the populace of their misconceptions about foreigners. Arranging for an audience with the emperor as soon as possible with representatives of those countries was part of that effort, and news of the meeting was to be proclaimed at home and abroad as soon as possible. Responding to this proposal, on March 7 Date Munenari and

---

when the talks came to a standstill. He returned to Japan in 1873 and formed the Meirokusha (an academic society) with old friends including Katō Hiroyuki, Nishi Amane, and Fukuzawa Yukichi. Mori wrote several contributions to the group's journal, the *Meiroku zasshi* (an academic journal). In his writings, he criticized the government's weakness in addressing the issue of giving foreigners freedom to move throughout the interior, and argued that allowing the major world powers to "disrespect" Japan would endanger the country's independence. In addition, he lambasted the government for relying on a decidedly Japanese style of "persuasion" diplomacy—attempting to win other countries over by explaining Japan's side of things and appealing to "personal" considerations—which he believed would invite the contempt of other nations. For Mori, the best approach was the "international approach" of negotiating on a level playing field with arguments rooted in reason and principle. After becoming Japan's resident envoy to Qing China in 1875, Mori sat down with Li Hongzhang to argue for Korea's independence as a sovereign nation and for keeping the tributary relationship between Qing China and Korea in check, and was able to make some headway on both fronts.

Samejima began undergoing treatment in Paris for tuberculosis in 1874 and returned to Japan the following year, transitioning into a role as a *gaimu taifu* (a deputy minister in the Ministry of Foreign Affairs). Despite his ill health, he threw himself into learning the ways of diplomacy and compiling a guide for Japanese diplomats. When treaty-revision negotiations with the United States started up in 1877, Foreign Minister Terashima set his sights on initiating simultaneous talks on treaty revisions with the United Kingdom, France, and Germany. He needed expertise on Europe to guide the negotiations in the right direction, and Samejima fit the bill. Terashima thus sent Samejima back to Europe to serve as Japan's representative in France for a second time. Arriving in Paris in March 1878, Samejima attempted to convince the French to amend the treaties, reasoning that tariff autonomy would not only benefit Japan's domestic industries but would also help promote trade on an international scale. Unfortunately, things would take a tragic turn just two years later. In December 1880, Samejima's tuberculosis worsened. When Samejima sank into critical condition, Mori rushed to Paris from London to care for his dear friend—but the disease proved fatal. Mori was at Samejima's bedside when he died. Samejima's funeral at Montparnasse Cemetery was attended by a proxy representing the French president, along with ambassadors and ministers from around the world who came to mourn a diplomat who died at just thirty-five years of age.

Mori began serving as Japan's resident envoy to the United Kingdom in 1879. While he worked under Foreign Minister Inoue on treaty-revision talks with the United Kingdom—Japan's biggest challenge in the effort to secure equal treaties—Mori made the acquaintance of Herbert Spencer and several other preeminent thinkers and cultural figures. The experience fostered a keen interest in national education, which led Mori to begin exploring educational systems in the West. He also discussed his views with Itō Hirobumi, who was in Vienna doing constitutional research. Mori eventually resigned from the Ministry of Foreign Affairs in 1884, after the negotiations with the British had made sufficient progress, and worked his way into his dream position at the Ministry of Education with a recommendation from Itō. In 1885, Itō became prime minister and selected Mori to be his minister of education. Mori seized the leadership opportunity and worked to formulate a variety of educational reforms, including the imperial university establishment ordinance. His career would come to a sudden end when he was fatally stabbed by an ultranationalist who accused him of not following the proper religious protocols. The attack came on the very day of the promulgation of the Meiji Constitution. Researchers still debate whether or not Mori was a Christian.

Higashikuze met in Osaka with the representatives of foreign countries to announce that the government would be establishing a Bureau of Foreign Affairs that would handle relations with other countries and respond to demands for an audience with the emperor.

Immediately thereafter, the so-called Sakai Incident occurred, in which Tosa samurai clashed with French sailors at the port of Sakai. There was a gunfight that left eleven French sailors dead. The facts of the incident are unclear, but French envoy Léon Roches declared it a barbarous act unworthy of a civilized nation. He demanded punishment for the Tosa samurai, reparations, and apologies from the lord of the domain and from Japan's diplomatic representatives. Coming at a time when the Boshin War was underway, it would not have been difficult for a harsh punishment of the parties involved to accidentally stir up the smoldering anti-foreign sentiment. In the end, the new government accepted the French request and issued punishments for twenty Tosa samurai. However, taking French concerns into account, the lives of nine of them were spared. The executions thus were limited to the same number (eleven) as the French sailors who had been killed.

The settling of the Sakai Incident opened the door to representatives of other countries receiving an imperial audience. Starting on March 23, the emperor had audiences with foreign envoys including Roches from France and Dirk de Graeff van Polsbroek of the Netherlands. Harry Parkes of the United Kingdom also headed for the palace in Kyoto in the company of Gotō Shōjirō, but en route the pair were attacked by samurai and barely escaped with their lives. However, the new government's

"Foreign Employees" in Meiji Japan: The *Oyatoi Gaikokujin*

For the Meiji government, leveraging foreign expertise was critical to the push toward modernization. Between 1868 and 1899, the administration employed as many as 2,300 foreign advisors in fields as diverse as the military, science and technology, industry, finance and economy, diplomacy, education, and the arts. The number of official "government employees" from foreign countries began to grow in the 1870s, as the situation in Japan gradually stabilized, and topped 500 at its peak in 1874 and 1875; Ōkubo Toshimichi alone hired over 200 of these *oyatoi gaikokujin* in his time as home minister. While they brought over more and more advisors from overseas, Meiji government officials made sure to define their hires as "advisors" and "assistants"—they never gave *oyatoi gaikokujin* free rein to make any policy decisions of their own volition, ensuring that the process of Japan's modernization would be an independent, voluntary one.

Oyatoi in the Diplomatic Sphere

With the exception of honorary posts, no foreigners were hired during the bakufu era to serve as diplomatic officials such as commissioners. In the Meiji era, however, the Ministry of Foreign Affairs employed foreigners to work at the ministry and diplomatic offices abroad under fixed contracts. Foreigners also found employment as temporary staffers for specific projects (treaty revisions, for example), language teachers, and translators, although few details are known.

Japan's first foreign hire in the diplomatic sphere was most likely a Frenchman by the name of Paul Flury-Hérard. When the bakufu administration was in full embrace of its pro-France policy, then minister Roches suggested that the bakufu set up an outpost in Paris to help procure building materials for the Yokosuka Ironworks and establish a supply of state-of-the-art weaponry. Flury-Hérard signed on with the outpost in 1866 and aided in Japan's showing at the Paris Exposition the following year.

American Henry W. Denison is a prime example of an *oyatoi gaikokujin* at the Ministry of Foreign Affairs. After coming to Japan in 1869 and working at the US consulate for a decade, he eventually took an *oyatoi* position at the ministry in 1880 and spent the majority of his professional life advising the foreign minister in that capacity until his death in 1914—but the scope of his duties stretched beyond simply consulting. As the Tripartite

2-6. Henry Willard Denison

speedy response to this attack satisfied Parkes, and he was granted an imperial audience on March 26. With those measures taken, Parkes presented his letter of credentials from Queen Victoria to the emperor on May 22. This act signified that the United Kingdom, as a representative of the foreign delegations, recognized the Restoration government as legitimate.

The Transition from Bureau of Foreign Affairs to Ministry of Foreign Affairs

The new Meiji government needed to obtain the support of a majority of domains for it to become stable. On April 6, 1868, the emperor invited the court nobles and all the lords to be presented with the Charter Oath of Five Articles that would serve as the basic guidelines for state affairs. The first article reads, "Deliberative assemblies shall be widely established and all matters decided by public discussion." Roughly 500 court nobles, lords, and chief vassals of each domain swore to and signed the Charter Oath. The proposal for the oath came from advisor (*san'yo*) Yuri Kimimasa. A comrade of Sakamoto Ryōma, Yuri displayed his talent in the fiscal reforms he undertook for the Echizen domain as a disciple of Yokoi Shōnan. Yuri's "Five Articles of National Policy" (*Kokuze goshō*) draft was revised by two other advisors, Fukuoka Takachika and Kido Takayoshi. Article four, "Evil customs of the past shall be broken off and everything shall be based upon the just laws of nature," was added by Kido. It carried the same meaning as that emphasized regarding "the law of the whole world" in a "Proclamation on the Opening of the Country through Peace and Amity." As such, it was regarded as a

Intervention unfolded, for example, the ailing Foreign Minister Mutsu had Denison draft a response to Germany, France, and Russia. The debate over the Anglo-Japanese Alliance also thrust Denison into an important role, as then foreign minister Komura Jutarō asked him to help win the support of elder statesman Inoue Kaoru. In terms of diplomatic policy, Denison was often a player in key decisions.

The first *oyatoi gaikokujin* at a diplomatic office abroad was Charles Lanman, whom Mori Arinori (Japan's first US envoy) hired in 1871. Although Lanman was originally a writer by trade, his close connections in Washington gave Japan a means of influencing lawmakers to help bring a favorable resolution to the Japanese government's attempts to recover reparations from the Shimonoseki Incident. Lanman and his wife Adeline also cared for Tsuda Umeko and Yoshimasu Ryōko, two of the five girls who made the trip with the Iwakura Mission, in an arrangement that Mori helped put together.

In October 1867, shortly before the restoration of political power to the emperor, the bakufu delegated its consular duties in San Francisco to a man named Charles W. Brooks. For years, Brooks had been providing Japanese traders with commercial assistance in San Francisco and performing de facto consular roles at no charge, and it was the US government that pushed for his consular nomination. He had even helped take care of the *Kanrin Maru* crew in 1860. Even after the Meiji government took shape, Brooks continued to act in that same consular capacity at his own expense. When Itō Hirobumi traveled to the US and became aware of the situation, it seems that he urged the Meiji government to provide Brooks with financial compensation. Brooks accompanied the Iwakura Mission back to Japan and even had an official audience with the emperor in 1873, a meeting that testified to the high esteem in which the Meiji administration held him.

The Ministry of Foreign Affairs also hired international-law advisors, the first of whom was E. Peshine Smith, then a legal advisor to the US Department of State. The Ministry of Finance under the Ōkuma administration was looking for experts in commercial law, tax law, and marine customs administration. Seeing Smith as an ideal fit for that role, envoy to the US Mori Arinori negotiated with the State Department to let Japan employ their advisor. Smith made his way to Japan in 1871 and soon found himself counseling the Meiji administration on Japan's first-ever international trial, the case stemming from the *María Luz* Incident. Guiding the Ministry of Foreign Affairs through the proceedings from start to finish, Smith helped Japan score a victory in the Russian czar's eventual arbitration ruling before returning to the United States in 1876.

promise that international law would be respected.

Next, on June 11 the government promulgated the so-called Constitution of 1868 (the Seitaisho). This created a Council of State (Dajōkan) system that copied the imperial court-based political framework that dated back to the Nara period (710–794). The system of "Three Offices" (*sōsai*, *gijō*, and *san'yo*) that had been established immediately after the new government was created was now abolished. The basic governing structure that replaced it concentrated authority in the Council of State, which comprised seven departments; separated executive, legislative, and judicial powers; and allowed for election (albeit internal to the government) of government officials. In the legislative body known as the Giseikan, a mechanism had been created for eliciting the "public opinion" (*kōgi yoron*) of the domains. That said, the Giseikan would be dispensed with almost immediately after its creation. The objective of establishing a powerful centralized administrative framework had come to take precedence over "public opinion."

Under this constitution, the Bureau of Foreign Affairs (Gaikokukan) was to be based in Osaka (it was moved shortly thereafter to Kyoto). It was to have jurisdiction over business related to diplomacy, trade, development projects, and territorial affairs. However, the authority to conclude treaties and make decisions over going to war was to reside with the Giseikan. Hence, the authority of the Bureau of Foreign Affairs was limited. Date Munenari became its first director, but soon after his appointment he tendered his resignation. The recurrence of an illness was the reason given, but in fact it was because he was fed up with the haughty attitude assumed by United Kingdom envoy Harry

"Foreign Employees" in Meiji Japan: The *Oyatoi Gaikokujin*

Alexander von Siebold and the Tragedy of Durham Stevens

Alexander von Siebold, the eldest son of Philipp von Siebold, first came to Japan with his father in 1859 at the age of twelve. His career as an *oyatoi gaikokujin* began eleven years later, as he landed a position at the Ministry of Popular Affairs in 1870. Following a stint at the Ministry of Finance, where he began in 1875, von Siebold eventually moved on to the Japanese legation in Berlin on the recommendation of minister to Germany Aoki Shūzō in 1878. Aoki had taken notice of von Siebold's talents, meeting him at the 1873 Vienna World's Fair and when he accompanied Vice-Finance Minister Matsukata Masayoshi on a tour through Europe.

A key *oyatoi gaikokujin* at Japan's legation in France was Frederic Marshall. Initially hired to be a secretary to Samejima Naonobu, Japan's first envoy to France, Marshall spent a full seventeen years gathering information and interpreting for numerous envoys—and his assets, from his Europe-spanning information network to his intelligence-gathering skills and dogged dedication, earned him a sterling reputation. When it came to assisting with treaty-revision negotiations, Marshall had to live up to almost excessive expectations; the Meiji government enlisted his help not only in getting a reluctant United Kingdom to appreciate Japan's position, but also in cutting off the United Kingdom from Germany, France, and the other continental nations at the negotiating table.

2-7. Alexander von Siebold

In his years as foreign minister, Inoue Kaoru amassed a selection of the best and the brightest *oyatoi gaikokujin* from diplomatic missions abroad to work at his disposal in Tokyo. In addition to von Siebold, the group in Tokyo also included Durham Stevens, who had entered Envoy Terashima's service at the US diplomatic office in 1882. Together, von Siebold and Stevens were present at every single treaty-revision conference—a total of twenty-seven gatherings from 1886 on—as part of Japan's official commission. Even when the meetings went on an indefinite hiatus, Inoue gave von Siebold and Stevens a secret directive to keep reaching out to prominent Western politicians, government officials, and newspapers to make the Japanese government's position as clear as possible, exchange opinions, and report back to him with all the details.

Stevens continued gathering intelligence and working to influence American public opinion at Japan's diplomatic office in the United States, but von Siebold operated as a free

Parkes. For his part, a succession of incidents had made Parkes believe there was fierce lingering anti-foreign sentiment, and this strengthened his distrust of the new government.

Date had received a majority of votes in the government's official election process and was once again selected to be director of the Bureau of Foreign Affairs. However, he refused to retract his intention to resign, and was succeeded by Sawa Nobuyoshi, who was both a court noble and an advisor (*san'yo*).

The new government (the Council of State) would relocate to Tokyo after the Boshin War; it was preceded there by the Bureau of Foreign Affairs. On August 15, 1869, the government promulgated a Staff Ordinance. As part of this, it established a Ministry of Foreign Affairs. The ordinance created a hierarchy of administrative posts such as *taifu* and *shōfu*, with the foreign minister at its head. Sawa was appointed the first foreign minister, while the position of *taifu*—analogous to that of vice-foreign minister—went to Terashima Munenori. In January 1871, the ministry would be relocated to the former Kuroda estate, where the Ministry of Popular Affairs had been previously, in Tokyo's Kasumigaseki neighborhood. It is from this time that the term "Kasumigaseki diplomacy" emerged.

Following the establishment of the Ministry of Foreign Affairs, in November 1870 a system for foreign envoys was set in place that would post "ministers" (*benmushi*) of three different grades (*dai*, *chū*, and *shō*—equivalent to "envoy extraordinary and minister plenipotentiary," "minister resident," and "chargé d'affaires") to foreign countries. First, it was decided to send Senior Secretary Samejima Naonobu to Europe (the United Kingdom, France, and Prussia) as a chargé d'affaires. This made him

---

agent of sorts—without any official ties to any diplomatic office, he moved from country to country across Europe, secretly gathering information and manipulating opinion. He even had the clearance to telegraph his information to Japan's foreign minister and vice-ministers at will. Von Siebold also assisted envoy to Germany Inoue Katsunosuke with influencing public opinion and manipulating newspaper reportage prior to the Russo-Japanese War, and remained active in Europe until his death in Italy in 1911. Von Siebold provided Tokyo with regular reports on the European political climate, but the Meiji government's dependence on "Von Siebold intelligence" waned as Japan expanded the scope of its continental diplomatic offices.

Stevens continued to serve as an advisor under several Japanese envoys to the United States, but his role shifted away from his previous negotiation work on treaty revisions; now, he was simply assisting envoys in their negotiations with the United States on customs and immigration-related matters. In December 1904, after the onset of the Russo-Japanese War, Stevens was reassigned from Washington to Keijō (Gyeongseong, which corresponds to present-day Seoul) to advise Korea on diplomatic concerns as Japan looked to make the country a protectorate. The Japanese government then ordered Stevens back to Washington in March 1908. Upon arriving in San Francisco on his way to Washington, Stevens gave an interview with a local newspaper on Japan's policy toward Korea. He told the reporter that Korea would reap enormous benefits from Japanese protection, championing Japan's cause—remarks that quickly stirred the ire of Koreans in San Francisco. Furious at the article's provocative implications, several Koreans confronted Stevens and shot him. A few days later, he was dead.

The *oyatoi gaikokujin* would play a diminishing role on the diplomatic stage as a clearer path to treaty revisions began to emerge in the latter half of the Meiji period. To put it the other way around, the treaty revisions were what most of the foreign advisors at the Ministry of Foreign Affairs had been hired for in the first place.

The "*o*" at the start of the phrase "*oyatoi gaikokujin*" was an honorific connoting that the advisors were in the distinguished employ of the emperor's government. The significance of that honor was particularly apparent in the treatment of official "government employees," who received audiences with the emperor, official decorations, gratuities, and other special benefits. The government awarded three *oyatoi gaikokujin* the First Order of Merit for their services in diplomacy: Denison, von Siebold, and Stevens.

Japan's first diplomatic representative. Traveling by way of France, Samejima arrived in London in February 1871. However, the United Kingdom did not recognize him as Japan's diplomatic representative due to his age (he was twenty-five) and rank, so he proceeded to begin work on opening a diplomatic office in Paris instead. That summer, Samejima hired a British secretary named Frederic Marshall, who was well informed about European affairs and diplomacy, and began engaging in his duties at a temporary diplomatic office. Marshall would work devotedly for no less than seventeen years for successive envoys based out of the Paris Legation.

2-8. The first Ministry of Foreign Affairs building

At the same time as Samejima, Mori Arinori was appointed to serve as chargé d'affaires in the United States. He arrived in Washington in January 1871. Mori also hired a personal secretary, in his case the American Charles Lanman. Making the most of Lanman's expansive personal network, Mori would use the Japanese legation as a stage for conducting a wide range of "cultural diplomacy."

In April 1872, former vice-foreign minister Terashima Munenori arrived in the United Kingdom to take up his new post as envoy extraordinary and

The Diplomats of Satsuma

Ōkubo Toshimichi (1830–78)

Ōkubo Toshimichi, a native of the Satsuma domain, was a fervent adherent of the *sonnō jōi* ("revere the emperor, expel the barbarians") movement. Under the wing of Shimazu Hisamitsu, Ōkubo worked to shift domain policy from the *jōi* policy (opposition to opening Japan) to the *kōbu gattai* approach: one that sought the unification of the imperial court and the bakufu, thereby creating a framework by which Japan could open its borders. Joining forces with the like-minded Iwakura Tomomi, a court noble, Ōkubo pushed ahead with his *kōbu gattai* vision. The passionate proponents of *sonnō jōi* proved too strong an opposition, however, sapping the momentum of the *kōbu gattai* cause. Ōkubo decided to leave the Kyoto political scene in the hands of Saigō Takamori. He then redirected his focus to internal Satsuma affairs and the *fukoku kyōhei* ("enrich the country, strengthen the armed forces") policy, which he fostered by purchasing warships from the United Kingdom, sending students to study in the United Kingdom, and engaging in trade with countries across Europe. Having united the domain on a solid foundation, Ōkubo headed back to Kyoto to help forge the Satsuma-Chōshū Alliance. He collaborated with Iwakura and Saigō on readying the alliance for military action against the bakufu, but the shogun attempted to preempt military conflict by surrendering his authority to the emperor. Despite the conciliatory move by the bakufu, the anti-bakufu alliance went ahead with the coup to restore imperial rule and thus culminate a bloodless revolution—one that Ōkubo had been instrumental in staging.

2-9. Ōkubo Toshimichi

Ōkubo assumed a central role in the new Meiji government and quickly got to work, implementing diplomatic measures to give the regime a stronger international footing, ordering the return of land and people from feudal lords to the emperor in hopes of achieving better centralization, and abolishing domains in favor of prefectures. He also took part in the Iwakura Mission. Upon returning to Japan, where political debate surrounding the *seikanron*—the dispatch of a punitive expedition to Korea—was simmering, Ōkubo took a strong stand against the advocates of an invasion and successfully argued for giving top priority to domestic minister plenipotentiary in that country. This move came at the suggestion of Foreign Minister Soejima Taneomi, who expected Terashima to play a key role in negotiations over treaty revision in Europe. Terashima was now Japan's third diplomatic representative, following Samejima and Mori. The United Kingdom was also satisfied with his appointment. Terashima arrived in Washington in June. He traveled together with Ōkubo Toshimichi and Itō Hirobumi, who had temporarily separated from the Iwakura Mission (discussed below) so they could return to Japan to obtain commissions of plenipotentiary powers. He finally arrived in London that August, where he was given an audience with Queen Victoria at which he presented his credentials. More than one year had passed since the British government had rejected Samejima as chargé d'affaires. This was Terashima's first audience as an envoy.

In October 1872, the Japanese term *benmushi* ("minister") would be formally replaced by the term *kōshi*, but with the same three grades: envoy extraordinary and minister plenipotentiary, minister resident, and chargé d'affaires. The Japanese titles of Samejima in Paris and Mori in Washington would thus change, but their status as chargé d'affaires would remain the same; the office organization would now also feature secretaries ranked from first to third. With this, Japan's modern diplomatic structure took another step forward. As of 1874, Japan had established legations in eight cities: Washington, London, Paris, Saint Petersburg, Vienna, Berlin, Rome, and Peking (Beijing). Furthermore, Japan had also opened a consulate in Shanghai in January 1872, with Shinagawa Tadamichi appointed as consul (*ryōji*).

---

security. When the new government met with its first political crisis, the *Meiji roku-nen no seihen* (Political Upheaval of 1873), Ōkubo immediately established the Home Affairs Ministry, made himself the first home minister, and took it upon himself to see the country through the strife. A year later, in 1874, Ōkubo had to contend with another crisis: the Saga Rebellion led by Etō Shinpei. Despite being a civil official, Ōkubo took command of the Meiji armed forces and headed to Saga himself to snuff out the unrest almost as soon as it had erupted.

Another pivotal event that took place in 1874 was the Taiwan Expedition, which put Japan at the negotiating table with Qing China. Ōkubo made his way to Peking (Beijing) and helped secure the Qing authorities' agreement to pay Japan an indemnity of 500,000 Kuping taels, thereby heading off the risk of open hostilities between the two and bringing the talks to a conclusion.

Ōkubo also came up with the conceptual basis for the new government's central bureaucracy, made up of ten separate ministries. Firm in his belief that the government needed to put the right people in the right positions, he made quick work of assigning promising personnel to official positions. His decisions to make Ōkuma Shigenobu the finance minister and Itō Hirobumi the industry minister proved wise, as the two leaders helped drive the growth of new industry and propel the opening of the country. The projects that the administration undertook were ambitious, and Ōkubo acted accordingly: he brought in legions of *oyatoi gaikokujin* ("foreign employees"), including more than two hundred foreign experts in civil engineering alone.

Ōkubo's tendency to handle thorny domestic and international issues unaided earned him a reputation for being an autocrat. The democratic faction, pointing to Ōkubo's despotic streak, argued that the real power of the Meiji government was in the grip of a small, exclusive cadre of officials, characterizing it as "*yūshi sensei*," or clique despotism. For Ōkubo, there was no course to follow in diplomatic relations at a time of nation-building other than to restrain hard-line foreign policies, put in place a central government system, and prioritize domestic affairs to promote new industry. Although he staked out a dominant position and often exercised his power at will, Ōkubo was an honorable man; he had no assets and died in debt. Along with Saigō and Kido Takayoshi, Ōkubo stands in history as one of the "three great nobles of the Restoration." The successors to that honored trio include Itō Hirobumi, who inherited Ōkubo's political power, and Yamagata Aritomo, who took command of Saigō's army.

The Return of Domains to the Emperor and the Replacement of Domains with Prefectures

In October 1868, the new government changed the era name from Keiō to Meiji and established the practice of assigning one era name to the reign of an emperor. The government also changed the name of Edo to Tokyo, meaning "eastern capital." In March 1869, Emperor Meiji made a formal visit to Tokyo, and the government itself relocated there from Kyoto.

The first step toward centralizing administrative power was breaking up the power of the domains. Under the feudal system with daimyo as autonomous rulers of their domains, Japan was split up into nearly 300 separate domains led by individual daimyo and lords. To steer the country toward unification, it was necessary to formally return the domain registers (*hanseki hōkan*). In practice, this meant that the feudal lords would return authority over the territories and people under their control to the emperor. In March 1869, the lords of the four domains of Satsuma, Chōshū, Tosa, and Hizen jointly signed a petition to the new government to be allowed to return their registers to the emperor. The other domains followed suit. The central government then appointed the lords to be the governors of their former domains. Their formers retainers were now all treated as "warrior" (*shizoku*) class regardless of the size of their former fiefs, while the daimyo and court nobles all formed the new peerage (*kazoku*). The return of the domain registers was also meant to impress upon the common people the absolute authority of an emperor who, until then, had been a presence that was of little relevance to them.

Two years later, in April 1871, the domains of Satsuma, Chōshū, and Tosa presented a combined force of samurai approximately 8,000 strong to the new government (the imperial court) to serve as an imperial guard. This force became the first army corps under the government's direct authority, and they were quickly incorporated into the new Ministry of Military Affairs. Yamagata Aritomo, who had come back from his fact-finding mission to Europe, was appointed vice-minister. At the same time, the government also established four garrison districts around the country—Tokyo, Osaka, Chinzei (Kyushu), and Tōhoku (northeastern Japan)—that pulled together the troops under its direct control. These forces under government authority would exercise their power in handling such crises as the Saga Rebellion (1874), the Hagi Rebellion (1876), and the Seinan War (a.k.a. the Satsuma Rebellion; 1877).

The reason this military strength was needed can be traced back to August 1871, when the government had abolished the domains and established prefectures in their stead. Under this new system, the government had dismissed all of the domain governors. Local administration was now to be handled through prefectural governors (*chiji* and *kenrei*) appointed by the government. In this case, the wishes of the former domain lords were ignored. Instead, three leaders from Satsuma and Chōshū—Ōkubo Toshimichi, Saigō Takamori, and Kido Takayoshi—put the emperor's authority to use and forced the change through. Foreseeing a major backlash, Saigō was resolved to go as far as using military force to suppress opposition. However, the effort miraculously succeeded. Kido, who had been passionate about making the change, wrote in his diary that the promulgation would "lay the foundations that should allow us to hold our own against the nations of the world." For Japan to be ranked with the Western powers, it needed to establish a strong, centralized state. The structure that divided the country up into autonomous, daimyo-ruled domains was a hindrance to that goal; its elimination was therefore necessary.

Be that as it may, how was it possible that, just three and a half years after it had been formed, the new government achieved this "miracle" of taking back the authority of the domains that had persisted for more than 250 years and concentrating it at the center? There were three crucial reasons behind this. First, in the dying years of the Tokugawa regime, many domains were being driven into bankruptcy, and they had lost the capacity for autonomous fiscal management. Second, while the country may have been divided up into autonomous domains, there was a strong perception among the lords that they themselves were part of a "family bureaucracy" (officials in the service of their liege) headed by a member of the Tokugawa family. Finally, there was growing concern among the domains that, in the absence of a centralized government, it would not be possible to resist Western pressure to open the country.

The Iwakura Mission and Setbacks on Treaty Revision

In December 1871, not long after prefectures had replaced the domains, a diplomatic mission with Minister of the Right (Vice-Minister of State) Iwakura Tomomi serving as the ambassador (plenipotentiary) set sail from Yokohama. Several senior figures in the new government, including Ōkubo Toshimichi, Kido Takayoshi, and Itō Hirobumi, were along as vice-ambassadors. Between the forty-six people who were formal members of the delegation and the fifty-nine who were set to study abroad, more than one hundred people traveled as part of the mission. Three of the men who would be entrusted with overseeing the government in their absence—Saigō Takamori, Itagaki Taisuke, and Sanjō Sanetomi (who was, in effect, the prime minister)—were opposed to the inclusion of Kido and Ōkubo. Aided by the stabilization of the political situation that had resulted from the successful replacement of domains with prefectures, however, the determination of those two men to be included carried the day. Initially the plan was for the mission to last ten and a half months; in fact, the trip was extended for more than a year, and the mission did not return to Japan until September 1873.

One of the mission's objectives was to get a sense of how to revise the Ansei Five-Power Treaties. The treaties stipulated that it would become possible to negotiate any revisions beginning in 1872. However, the new government had only just set up a post to handle treaty revision and begun looking into the nature of such revisions in 1871. For Iwakura and Vice-Foreign Minister Terashima Munenori, the mission's work would therefore be limited to discussing objectives and desires for revision, aiming to lay the groundwork for proper treaty revision in the future.

The first country on the itinerary was the United States. There, the mission was helped by the warm welcome they received. Itō and Mori Arinori (who had just assumed his position as chargé d'affaires) stressed the benefits of signing a revised treaty in the United States, even if some compromises had to be made. Ambassador Iwakura and his team were swayed and commenced negotiations. Secretary of State Hamilton Fish also had a positive attitude toward negotiating a revision, but he pointed out that a preliminary agreement would invite confusion. Accordingly, Ōkubo and Itō temporarily returned to Japan to ask for the plenipotentiary powers needed to sign the documents. Meanwhile, the delegation was also conscious of the fact that repealing consular jurisdiction would be difficult, and so they sought to restore tariff autonomy and the right to establish administrative regulations concerning foreign commerce and activities in Japan. However, the US side did not recognize these as problems. Rather, they wanted Japan to increase the number of open ports, open its interior to foreigners, and eliminate export duties.

The caretaker government in Tokyo was aware of the disadvantages that would come of applying most-favored-nation treatment to the United States, in that any concessions by Japan would also have to be applied in equal measure to the European

The Diplomats of Chōshū

Kido Takayoshi (1833–77)

Born to a family of doctors in the Chōshū domain, Kido Takayoshi was adopted into the Katsura family at the age of eight and was thence known as Katsura Kogorō. The young Katsura traveled to Edo for his education, aiming to study military training and techniques, but he began to feel drawn to Yoshida Shōin, whose influence led him to join the *sonnō jōi* ("revere the emperor, expel the barbarians") movement. In the wake of the 1864 Hamaguri Gate Rebellion (Kinmon Incident), the bakufu thwarted an attempted insurrection by the Chōshū domain. The ensuing First Chōshū Expedition, a retaliatory measure by the shogunate, resulted in the Chōshū domain pledging fealty to the bakufu. Katsura was expelled by the bakufu and went into hiding. His ally Takasugi Shinsaku went into exile. After Takasugi returned to the domain and regained control of the domain administration from the sitting bakufu-loyalist faction, Katsura made his return in April 1865. Building on the political foundation that Takasugi had laid, Kido (who had abandoned his Katsura name for the new moniker Kido Jun'ichirō) formed the Satsuma-Chōshū Alliance with Satsuma leader Saigō Takamori in 1866 to unify the anti-bakufu cause ahead of the Second Chōshū Expedition.

2-10. Kido Takayoshi

Kido then went on to join Ōkubo Toshimichi and Iwakura Tomomi in leading the coup to restore imperial rule, after which he became one of the leaders (*chōshi* [official] and *san'yō* [imperial advisor]) in the new Meiji government. He also helped draft the Charter Oath of Five Articles. The first article in the document's initial draft began with the statement, "Councils of feudal lords shall be established," a phrasing that Fukuoka Takachika and his fellow advocates of the *kōgi-seitairon* (parliamentary-regime theory) favored. It was apparently Kido who reworded the phrase to read, "Deliberative assemblies shall be widely established," to show that the new government, which had neither an army nor a defined territory under its direct control, would not root its power on the existing structure of a feudal union but rather would embody the concept of a centralized, consolidated state body.

In 1868 and 1869, Kido (now going by the first name Takayoshi) championed the first calls in administration circles for a punitive expedition to Korea. The aim in Kido's mind was not expressly to wage an attack against Korea; instead, he was hoping to use the initiative as an impetus to create an army under the direct control of the imperial court to suppress the domestic opposition that would arise when the government moved to implement its *hanseki hōkan* directive requiring domains to return their land and people to the emperor. Kido was one of the first leaders to understand that the new government would need to do away with the domain system altogether—reclaiming jurisdiction over

powers as well (to ensure equality of treatment). They thought that the wiser course of action would be to hold an international conference in Europe with the United States also in attendance. However, the United States did not agree.

Immediately after Ōkubo and Itō returned to Washington with their commissions of plenipotentiary powers, Ambassador Iwakura notified Secretary of State Fish that they were halting negotiations. The mission then headed to Europe. In London, the mission was joined by Terashima Munenori, who had arrived ahead of them as an envoy extraordinary and minister plenipotentiary. In late October, the delegation held talks with Foreign Secretary Lord Granville of the United Kingdom. The British side pressed strongly for opening Japan's interior to foreigners and for permission to conduct coastal trade. However, citing such issues as nonpayment of rent for the land at the foreign settlement in Kobe, Terashima and Iwakura countered that it was of crucial importance that foreigners be required to abide by Japanese law if they were given permission to move about freely in the interior.

The mission finally had an audience with Queen Victoria in December 1872, and then moved on to the European continent. Traveling from country to country, they had audiences with the president of France, the emperors of Belgium and the Netherlands, and the German kaiser. In France, land and inhabitants, along with establishing prefectures to replace the domain structure—if it wanted to avoid the inter-domain strife of a fractured nation and establish a truly centralized state.

While the new government indeed got its own army, Kido, Ōkubo, and Saigō clashed over how to organize the force. The leaders eventually settled on combining groups of soldiers from the Satsuma, Chōshū, and Tosa domains into a directly controlled force (government troops). That set the stage for the abolition of domains and the establishment of prefectures, which took place in August 1871. In the immediate aftermath of the initiative, Kido penned a diary entry: "We may say that the foundation for a structure which will enable us to face the nations of the world on a basis of equality for the first time has been established." Kido knew that ranking with the Western powers would require a strong, centralized state to replace the decentralized feudalism of the past.

After the implementation of the *haihan chiken* policy came the Iwakura Mission, on which Kido served as a vice-ambassador. Kido's return to Japan thrust him right back into the political fray. With the debate over sending a punitive expedition to Korea swirling at a heated pitch, Kido joined Ōkubo and Itō Hirobumi in arguing for a focus on domestic affairs over the insistent pleas for military action coming from Saigō, Etō Shinpei, Itagaki Taisuke, and others. The impasse eventually resulted in a victory for Kido and the anti-war camp, with Saigō and his fellow allies resigning en masse (Political Upheaval of 1873). Kido also opposed the Taiwan Expedition that Ōkubo and Saigō Tsugumichi had proposed, resigning from the Councillors in protest. The fallout had drawn clear lines between differing viewpoints. Itō decided to step in and mediate the situation by organizing the 1875 Osaka Conference, where Kido met with Ōkubo and agreed to return to government service with Itagaki on the condition that the government would soften its authoritarian stance and expand the rights of the people. However, Kido would die two years later, during the Seinan War (Satsuma Rebellion), at his residence in Kyoto.

One of Kido's strongest allies in government during the prime of his career was Ōkuma Shigenobu. "Kido was of a genius mind in every aspect and spoke with a refined eloquence," Ōkuma wrote, "and he was a man of honesty, resolve, and sincerity through and through." While he was certainly open-minded, quick to grasp concepts, and well respected among his peers, Kido lacked the outstanding action-taking faculties that set Ōkubo apart. After completing his service as a vice-ambassador on the Iwakura Mission and returning home, he became unwell, and no longer had the spirit of the man who had driven the *haihan chiken* initiative just a few years prior. Both Saigō and Ōkubo met with violent deaths, in 1877 and 1878, thus bringing to an end the era of the "three great nobles of the Restoration."

the mission again was asked to open the Japanese interior. The French also brought up the issue of the persecution of Christians in Urakami (Nagasaki), and demanded that freedom of belief be recognized.

In the end, the Iwakura Mission sidestepped negotiations over treaty revisions and limited themselves to expressing their wishes. They uniformly demanded the right for foreigners to travel within Japan's interior and guarantees for freedom of belief. In particular, the mission received strong remonstrances regarding the persecution of Christians. It sent word back to the caretaker government advising that the ban on Christianity be lifted; as a result, in February 1873 the edict that prohibited Christianity was rescinded. However, this was not

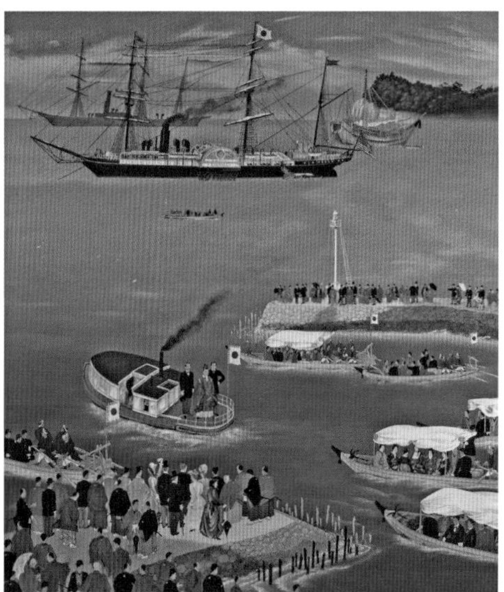

2-11. *The Iwakura Mission to America and Europe* (painting by Yamaguchi Hōshun)

The Iwakura Mission and Japanese Students Abroad

The Iwakura Mission was more than a diplomatic venture. Also aboard the vessel bound for San Francisco were roughly fifty government-funded students, including Kaneko Kentarō (a descendant of a Fukuoka-based samurai family), who would later help draft the Meiji Constitution; Dan Takuma, the founder of the Mitsui zaibatsu; Nakae Chōmin (born Nakae Tokusuke to a Kochi-based samurai family), who led the Freedom and People's Rights Movement and authored the famous *Sansuijin keirin mondō* (A discourse by three drunkards on government); and Makino Nobuaki, Ōkubo Toshimichi's second son. The passenger list was a veritable who's who of the makers of modern Japan.

Among the government-funded students were five girls: Tsuda Umeko, Yamakawa Sutematsu, Ueda Tei, Nagai Shigeko, and Yoshimasu Ryōko. Tsuda was just six at the time, making her the youngest participant; the four other girls were all in their teens. After the mission arrived in the United States, it was none other than Mori Arinori—Japan's first envoy to the US—who coordinated the living arrangements for the girls. Tsuda and Yoshimasu stayed with the family of Charles Lanman, who was then Mori's personal secretary. Tsuda made her way back to Japan in 1882 and subsequently embarked on a distinguished career. After serving in a variety of positions, including as Itō Hirobumi's interpreter, she would later go on to found the Joshi Eigaku Juku (the predecessor of Tsuda University) in 1900 and devote the remainder of her life to women's education. Yamakawa was the younger sister of Yamakawa Kenjirō, an Aizu domain native who was Japan's first PhD in physics. She had experienced the siege of Aizu Castle firsthand, having been confined in the castle; then the Iwakura Mission took her to the United States, where she studied international politics. She later became the second wife of Army Minister Ōyama Iwao and rose to prominence in Rokumeikan society; her admirers fondly called her the "flower of the Rokumeikan." Ueda became the mother of foreign-literature scholar and poet Ueda Bin, while Nagai wed Uryū Sotokichi.

Most of the government-funded students sent overseas to study were eager to learn, but some were chosen despite a lack of interest or capacities because of maneuvering by ministries, or people having connections with political leaders, leading to an increasing number of them not reaping any benefits. One of the objectives of the Iwakura Mission was therefore to monitor the academic performance of the students going overseas, and, as a result, government-funded

Lifting the Ban on Christianity

The Ansei Five-Power Treaties (1858) granted freedom of religion to foreigners in foreign settlements, which brought in streams of missionaries—but Japan's official ban on Christianity prevented foreign missionaries from doing missionary work outside the settlements. After the bakufu collapsed, the new Meiji government kept the ban on Christianity in place. When it came to light in January 1870 that there was a community of hidden Christians in Urakami, Nagasaki, the government detained and exiled more than 3,000 of the clandestine believers to domains across the country. The move spurred protests from envoys in Japan, sparking a diplomatic dispute. Meiji leaders argued that their actions were meant to punish the Urakami Christians not for religious reasons but for anti-government activity and interference in domestic affairs, asserting that the Christians had been working to undermine the credibility of the government with the protection of the foreign missionaries. The government also argued that by worshipping the Christian god, the Christians were rejecting traditional Shinto and Buddhist beliefs and, by extension, refusing to recognize the divinity of the emperor—a national belief. Imari Prefecture (later part of Saga Prefecture) moved to arrest the Christians in its jurisdiction in December 1871, just prior to the departure of the Iwakura Mission. The delegation thus left the Port of Yokohama with the troublesome cloud of the Christianity question hanging overhead.

Sure enough, representatives from virtually every country that the Iwakura Mission visited demanded that Japan find a solution to the Urakami *kirishitan* ("Christian") issue and lift its ban on Christianity. The pressure prompted Iwakura to telegraph the Japanese government in February 1873 with a request to remove the *kōsatsu* (public notices on wooden signboards) proclaiming the prohibition of Christianity, and the government followed through by ordering their removal by means of a Dajōkan Fukoku (Grand Council Proclamation). In March, overseas study was temporarily suspended in 1873.

An exhaustive collection of information on the Iwakura Mission is available at "The Iwakura Mission: Tracking 150 People Who Crossed the Oceans," a special online exhibit by the Japan Center for Asian Historical Records that uses related resources to trace the mission's itinerary, places visited, and fact-finding tours.

2-12. Iwakura Mission, from left to right: Kido Takayoshi, Yamaguchi Masuka, Iwakura Tomomi, Itō Hirobumi, and Ōkubo Toshimichi

the government freed the Nagasaki Christians that it had exiled to various locations and restored their official status as Urakami residents. In effect, however, the removal of the *kōsatsu* was more a tacit approval of Christianity than a lifting of the ban on the faith.

The Meiji Constitution may have recognized the freedom of religion as a prerequisite for establishing a modern state, but this was limited to freedom of thought, on the premise that the emperor was "sacred and inviolable." In order to uphold emperor worship but still ensure nominal freedom of religion, the Meiji government needed to find a way to deny the religious nature of Shinto. They did so by positioning Shinto as a "state ritual," not a "religion," with the emperor in the role of presiding over the rituals at the court.

a total lifting of the ban, but rather a "tacit consent" to worship.

A Lesson from Bismarck and Its Effects

In March 1873, Prussian chancellor Otto von Bismarck delivered a speech at a reception for the Iwakura Mission. The gist of his message was that a strong country will respect international law if it is seen as being in its own interests, but will overrule international law with military power when respecting it is seen as being against its own interests. Weaker countries depend on international law to protect their right to autonomy, but they are helpless in the face of the power of stronger countries. The chancellor's words brought home for the mission the idea that international relations were governed not by international law, but rather by the theory of the survival of the fittest; therefore, becoming a strong country was a prerequisite for treaty revision.

Among the purposes of the Iwakura Mission was to study Western institutions, as well as Western culture and civilization. Members of the entourage visited government facilities, factories, schools, and cultural institutions as part of their mission. The circumstances of those various activities are outlined in the *Tokumei zenken taishi Bei-Ō kairan jikki* (A true account of the tour in America and Europe of the Special Mission) compiled by Kume Kunitake. It was Samejima Naonobu, in particular, who did all the groundwork in organizing the visits efficiently in Europe, having asked each country to provide the facilities and information in accordance with diplomatic custom and etiquette.

Ultimately, the varied information had wide-ranging benefits back in Japan for the building of a modern state. For example, Ōkubo Toshimichi argued in an 1874 memorandum on the promotion of industry that the prosperity of the United Kingdom—an island nation just like Japan—was due to that government's protection of industry. He declared that government protection and promotion of private industry was the very thing that Japan needed. Also, in an opinion paper on the constitutional system of government, he argued that the British system drew out spontaneous efforts by the British people and provided support for a strong country. He put forward the so-called British model as the image of a state that Japan should aim to become. Thus, Ōkubo would strongly promote domestic industry based on his stance that internal affairs should take precedence.

Even if the Iwakura Mission achieved these sorts of results, the fact remains its tour of the West was too long. The caretaker government broke with the promises it made to the mission's members, and moved to carry out a variety of new reforms such as introducing a new educational system, building

The Chinese Hegemony (Hua-Yi Distinction) and International Law

International relations in East Asia bore almost no resemblance to those in Europe, where diplomacy rested on the premise of sovereign nations on an equal footing. The dominant international order in East Asia from the seventeenth century onward was the Chinese "Hua-Yi distinction," which put China at the center of everything. Under that framework, China's neighbors subordinated themselves to China and paid China tribute in recognition of the country's superiority; in exchange, China agreed to offer the countries protection. The system was a hierarchical order that defined relationships clearly. It originally formed around a relationship framework where the extent to which Chinese "virtue" had influenced (been assimilated by) the people in a given country determined the country's position in the structure; there was no exclusionist, territorial element in play. While the order of the Hua-Yi distinction included Korea and the Ryūkyūs, Japan maintained its independence from the Edo period onward due to its closed borders.

After the signing of the Treaty of Tientsin (now known as Tianjin) in 1858 and the Convention of Peking in 1860, however, the Hua-Yi distinction became increasingly ambiguous. The countries that had paid tribute to China became European colonies in some cases or fell under the jurisdiction of other countries, as was the case with the Ryūkyūs becoming a Japanese territory in 1879. By the 1880s, in fact, the system had faded to such a shadow of its past state that Korea was the only nation still paying tribute to China. The two sides saw the balance of the relationship differently. China, set on preserving its hierarchical dominance, saw Korea in a "subordinate" position, first and foremost, but was willing to grant the country autonomy in foreign diplomacy. Korea, meanwhile, saw its subordination to China as secondary to its autonomy and proceeded to sign numerous treaties with the West.

The tribute system was not the only framework governing China's relations with other countries. There was also a "vassal system," in which a delegation from a neighboring nation would visit China on an official mission representing its leader and seek China's recognition of their leader as "king"; China would then send its own mission to make the approval of the nation's leader official. Whereas the tribute system involved international trade by envoys, the vassal system was free of any transactions—the relationships were essentially symbolic. The composite power structure may be referred to as a "tributary-vassal system," considering that some countries were technically both tributaries and vassals of China. The tribute system offers one hypothesis for understanding East Asian international relations on the basis of the Hua-Yi distinction.

In Europe, a different perception of international order emerged. The Peace of Westphalia (1648) established the principles of mutual recognition of national sovereignty and non-interference, planting the seeds for what would become the structure of "international law." When European nations began encroaching into Asia via military means, however, the Hua-Yi distinction was eroded by European international law, while the existing principles of national sovereignty and non-interference were lost, morphing into a three-layered order. To clarify, the power structure put the "civilized nations" of the West at the top, "semi-civilized nations" (barbarian nations) like China and Japan in the middle, and the "uncivilized nations" of Southeast Asia and elsewhere at the bottom. Within that structure, a "semi-civilized nation" maintained its national sovereignty but only to a limited extent, leaving it susceptible to unequal treaties. An "uncivilized nation," meanwhile, had no sovereignty to speak of—even if it had its own political system—and was thus deemed a "terra nullius," a land without any established ruling authority.

railroads, and implementing military conscription. There were hints of a split within the government over the appropriateness of these policies. In January 1873 Prime Minister Sanjō Sanetomi urged Ōkubo and Kido Takayoshi to return as quickly as possible, and they set forth for Japan separately.

That September, just as the Iwakura Mission had returned home, the caretaker government was confronted with three international issues. The first was over the opening of Korea, the second was Russia's southward advance in Karafuto (Sakhalin), and the third was the dispatch of the Taiwan Expedition. Hard-line positions, including disputes over troop dispatches, assumed greater prominence in the face of these three external crises. What lay behind this were the feelings of dissatisfaction among former feudal retainers who had lost their jobs and been stripped of their special privileges as retainers when domains were replaced by prefectures. They no longer had an outlet to display the mettle they had shown as "men of high purpose" in opposing the bakufu as a sign of their loyalty to the emperor.

2 Adjusting Relations with Neighboring Countries: Responding to External Crises

The Start of Sino-Japanese Relations: The Japan-China Friendship and Trade Treaty

Until the final years of the Tokugawa regime, Japan and Qing China had engaged in conventional trade limited to the port of Nagasaki, without any official arrangements in place. However, during the closing years of the bakufu, Chinese merchants traveled to various places around Japan as agents for Western merchants. As seafood started to be transported to Shanghai and other destinations, it became apparent that it would no longer be possible to handle the business by carrying out trade only through Nagasaki. Japan also needed an entry to the trade system centered on Shanghai. Thus, starting in 1870, plenipotentiary Date Munenari (with Yanagiwara Sakimitsu as his assistant) and his Qing China counterpart Li Hongzhang entered into negotiations. The Japan-China Friendship and Trade Treaty was concluded in September 1871.

This treaty of amity and commerce was a unique one, established on equal terms. It confirmed the details of the commercial treaties that each party had concluded with the Western powers, and recognized one another's consular jurisdiction and agreements on tariffs. The style of the treaty, however, was based on a Sinocentric perspective (the Hua-Yi distinction; see sidebar on page 68 for details) that was particular to East Asian countries. For example, the preamble avoids the use of such honorific titles as "the emperor of Japan" and "the Qing emperor." This was done out of consideration for Qing China's insistence that the use of the character for emperor (皇) should be reserved for use by the Qing emperor. Furthermore, Article 1 of the treaty stipulates, "In all that regards the territorial possessions of either country the two Governments shall treat each other with proper courtesy, without the slightest infringement or encroachment on either side, to the end that there may be for evermore peace between them undisturbed." This established the mutual inviolability of their respective territories. But for Qing China, the words "territorial possessions" referred to its tributary states (countries such as Korea and the Ryūkyūs). The Qing interpreted this as something that Japan was forced to accept. In short, it saw both Korea and the Ryūkyū Kingdom as Chinese territory, as they paid tribute to China. On this basis, China argued that for Japan to turn the Ryūkyūs into a domain or a prefecture would be a treaty violation. Japan did not accept such an interpretation, and in any case the use of classical Chinese as the official text for the treaty gave rise to contradictory interpretations.

In any event, the Japanese side asked to postpone ratification in order to revise the treaty and the trade charter appended to it. This was because the wording of Article 2 carried the suggestion of an offensive and defensive alliance, which would invite backlash from the West. Furthermore, Japan's rules on trade differed from Qing China's, and so adjustments would be necessary. However, the Qing refused to make any revisions before ratification, and so in April 1873 the two sides exchanged an instrument of ratification bringing the treaty into force.

Seikanron and Its Political Context

In the face of military pressure from the West, both Japan and Qing China made moves toward opening their respective countries by opening ports. Korea still remained a closed country, however. In particular, the uncompromising anti-foreign policies during the regency of Daewongun ("prince of the great court") Yi Ha-eung (1863–73) impeded the country's opening. Symbolic of this was the *General Sherman* incident of 1866. A US merchant vessel called the SS *General Sherman* traveled up the Taedong River and anchored near Pyongyang seeking to initiate trade. The Korean side responded by turning down the request to allow either trade or the request of a missionary on board to proselytize, and asked the vessel to leave. When the *General Sherman* did not comply, it was set on fire and all the crew killed. The Daewongun, displeased with the now-open Japan, also notified it of a ban on travel between the two countries.

Amid these circumstances, in early 1869 the new Japanese government sent an emissary from the Tsushima domain to Busan (Pusan). The emissary carried a letter conveying to the Joseon court news of the restoration of imperial rule and updates on Japan's diplomatic relations. Korean government officials were shocked to see the earlier-mentioned character heretofore used for the Chinese emperor now applied to the Japanese emperor in the letter, and they refused to accept it. Under the Hua-Yi distinction, as a tributary state of China, Korea held that only the emperor of China was entitled to use that character in the context of external relations. Negotiations between Japan and Korea came to an impasse; furthermore, Korea shut off all modes of intercourse including the Waegwan ("Japan House") that the Tsushima domain had established in Busan.

In response to these measures, the hard-line position arguing that the use of military force in Korea was inevitable grew ever more powerful within the new Japanese government. This view, termed *seikanron*, had a variety of motivations. Proponents argued that Japan and Korea should join together in order to resist the West, and that Korea should be compelled to do so with military force if necessary. The argument that stirring up an external crisis would solidify domestic unity was also influential. Further boosting calls for a punitive expedition were those who held that the Korean Peninsula should pledge allegiance to the Japanese emperor. Now that imperial rule had been reinstated, the argument went, Korea should be a tributary state and "show every courtesy as expected of a vassal serving his monarch."

In an August 1873 letter he sent to Itagaki Taisuke, Saigō Takamori proposed that he himself go to Korea, and that if the Koreans could be provoked as a result, then the situation could be turned into war. If justification for war were thus obtained, it would accomplish the aim of a "strategy to divert the feelings of those ardently seeking insurrection at home to an external issue and rouse the nation." In Saigō's view, the bakufu had fallen because it had avoided going to war over anti-foreign sentiment.

As a consequence, Japan's noble spirit of independence had been whittled away. He believed those "men of high purpose" who had opposed the bakufu as a sign of their loyalty to the emperor needed a suitable venue for action.

At an August 1873 meeting of the Council of State, Itagaki put forth the idea of dispatching warships. Saigō replied that, since there was little pretext for war with Korea, he was prepared to serve as an envoy to handle negotiations himself, and to find himself compelled to bombard them due to provocation. The council took note of Saigō's suggestion, and decided to dispatch him as a special envoy to Korea to press it to open up to the world. Vehemently opposed to the dispatch of a special envoy, due to misgivings that it would lead to the use of military force, were the three members of the just-completed Iwakura Mission: Iwakura Tomomi, Ōkubo Toshimichi, and Kido Takayoshi. They had been shocked at the disparity in national strength between Japan and the Western powers. They argued that building up Japan should take precedence over getting involved with Korea.

Ōkubo stayed informed about world trends. He was on the alert for Russian and British intervention in Korea, and warned against any impetuous Korean expedition. In particular, he pointed out that Russia had sent troops to Sakhalin—which it regarded as a "land of mixed residence" with joint habitation by subjects of both countries—and furthermore showed it had the impetus to advance further south. If Japan were to embark on a Korea expedition, he argued, it would give Russia a pretext for dispatching its own troops, and not only Sakhalin or Korea, but even Hokkaido could be in danger. Ōkubo's warning of the Russian threat was a foreshadowing of the Treaty for the Exchange of Sakhalin for the Kurile Islands (Treaty of Saint Petersburg) that would eventually serve as a security guarantee.

The debate over the Korea expedition went on for more than a month. Finally, in October, the returnee group took advantage of Prime Minister Sanjō Sanetomi's "mental agitation" and—with Iwakura acting in his place—overturned the Council of State decision and forced a halt to the special envoy dispatch. In protest, the five councillors who had favored the punitive expedition (Saigō, Etō Shinpei, Itagaki, Soejima Taneomi, and Gotō Shōjirō) resigned their positions en masse (Political Upheaval of 1873). Only four councillors remained: Ōkubo, Kido, Ōkuma Shigenobu, and Ōki Takatō.

After discussions with Itō Hirobumi, Ōkubo implemented his long-cherished project of enacting a joint-appointment structure that would allow someone to be both a councillor and a minister of state. Each councillor would concurrently serve as a minister heading one ministry or another in an attempt to strengthen the running of the government's administration. Ōkuma was to serve concurrently as minister of finance, Itō as minister of industry, and Terashima Munenori as foreign minister. Ōkubo would head the newly established Ministry of Home Affairs, which would supervise all domestic affairs.

The Japan-Korea Treaty of Amity

At the end of 1873, King Gojong and Queen Myeongseong (Min), along with her clan, ousted the Daewongun regent to assume power in Korea. They displayed a readiness to embark on returning to normal relations with Japan. This was noted in Japan, and the government dispatched Foreign Ministry official Moriyama Shigeru to Busan. The first official talks between Japan and Korea to be held since the Meiji Restoration took place in September 1874. However, the use of the Chinese character for "emperor" in Japan's documents again became an issue. Moriyama was adamant about Japan's justification for the usage, and asked that warships be dispatched to break the impasse.

The following September, the government dispatched three warships to conduct military reconnaissance in Korean waters. As part of this mission, the gunboat *Un'yō* (under the command of Inoue Yoshika) was ordered to survey the Korean coast. It intentionally and without warning drew close to Ganghwa Island and provoked an attack from the shore batteries there (Ganghwa Island Incident). The *Un'yo* prevailed in the engagement. However, the Meiji government received a report that the Korean side had deliberately fired on the vessel, and, in an attempt to resolve the issue, sent Kuroda Kiyotaka and Inoue Kaoru to Korea as plenipotentiaries. Before dispatching the pair, Mori Arinori was sent to Peking (Beijing) as a resident envoy in order to sound out Qing China's stance toward Korea. While Li Hongzhang did not acknowledge Korea's independence as such, there was the sense from Mori's negotiations that China was holding back on its suzerainty over Korea, and that the talks would prove favorable for Japan. Based on this, Kuroda's mission, which had been to open Korea (i.e., to conclude a treaty) through persistent peaceful negotiations, instead turned to coercion applied by the presence of warships.

The Japan-Korea Treaty of Amity was signed with the Korean government at Ganghwa in February 1876. Its preamble avoided the use of the honorific titles for the two parties' respective heads of state ("the emperor of Great Japan" and "the king of Korea") in favor of forms that put them on equal terms ("Great Japan" and "Great Korea"). Mindful of Korea's position that it was a tributary nation to the Qing court, the treaty avoided the use of characters for the Japanese emperor that would imply superiority to the Korean monarch.

Article 1 read, "Chosen [Korea], being an independent state, enjoys the same sovereign rights as does Japan." Japan took this to mean that they were equally independent countries.

Korea also agreed, in another article, to open two other ports beyond Busan, and elsewhere in the document it agreed that Japan had unilateral consular jurisdiction over its own citizens. This article in fact fulfilled the wishes of the Korean side, since they did not imagine that their own people would leave the country. The talk of most-favored-nation treatment that was in the Japanese proposal was eliminated, since Korea had no intention of concluding treaties with any other country. Later, the Japan-Korea Treaty of Amity would be seen as the model for the "unequal treaties" that Japan imposed on Korea, but at the time the Korean government had little sense of it being unequal.

On the other hand, numerous issues remained. These included the stationing of diplomatic envoys permanently in one another's capital cities, allowing travel within the interior, determining the locations of open treaty ports, and setting tariffs on the import and export of rice. Negotiations would continue afterward on these points, eventually resulting, in July 1883, in the Japan-Korea Trade Charter. Senior Secretary Miyamoto Okazu took the initiative in the negotiations, and pointed out the discrepancy in how the Japanese and classical Chinese text could be interpreted.

The Taiwan Expedition

In December 1871, two years before the Korea expedition debate developed, the Mudan incident occurred, in which fifty-four Ryūkyūans shipwrecked on Taiwan were killed by indigenous Taiwanese. When the details of the incident were conveyed to the central government from Kagoshima Prefecture the following summer, Foreign Minister Soejima Taneomi came up with a plan to conquer and subjugate Taiwan. In spring 1873, Soejima and Yanagiwara Sakimitsu went to Qing China to solicit that government's view on the matter. The Qing responded that the Taiwanese natives were "people outside their jurisdiction," and that Qing China's rule did not extend there. The Japanese side took "people outside their jurisdiction" to mean that Taiwan was a "terra nullius" under international law, and consequently saw no problem with dispatching troops there.

This issue would be temporarily shelved because Japan had become enmeshed domestically in the *sei-kanron* debate, but when Soejima and others left public office with the political upheaval of 1873, it again came to the surface. Ōkubo and his allies tried to redirect the heated enthusiasm for an expedition to Korea toward Taiwan, which they thought would offer less resistance. A further rationale was that dispatching troops in the name of the Ryūkyū people would be a way to show to everyone that the Ryūkyūs were under Japanese rule.

2-13. Leaders of the Japanese expeditionary force with Taiwanese aborigines

In April 1874, Saigō Tsugumichi (Takamori's younger brother) became governor-general for Taiwan Aboriginal Affairs (*Taiwan ban-chi jimu*), and a bureau was established with Ōkuma Shigenobu as its director. Saigō then moved forward with preparations for military action. A punitive expedition made up of samurai recruited from around Kyushu was also put together. However, US envoy John Bingham and British envoy Harry Parkes opposed the troop dispatch. Furthermore, Kido Takayoshi, who had disagreed with the talk of a Korea expedition, said that to dispatch troops to Taiwan now would be contradictory. He was so strongly against it that he resigned his position as councillor and left the government. Prime Minister Sanjō Sanetomi was forced to put a halt to the troop dispatch. However, Saigō forcefully pushed the expedition through. He landed in southern Taiwan in late May, and brought the area under his forces' control. Only twelve Japanese soldiers died in fighting, but more than five hundred would die from malaria, which was endemic to the region.

The Taiwan Expedition delivered a shock to the Qing government. They felt as though the Japan-China Friendship and Trade Treaty—which had established that neither signee would encroach on the other's territory—had been violated. The Qing strongly protested to Japan, and marshaled more than 10,000 troops in Taiwan's south. Japan, too, made provisions for a breakdown in negotiations, and Ōkuma took the lead in preparing for a war with China. In an attempt to avert an outbreak of hostilities, in September 1874 Ōkubo himself set out for Peking (Beijing). After difficult negotiations, at the end of October the two parties finally concluded the Engagement between Japan and China Respecting Formosa (the Beijing Agreement). Under the terms of this agreement, Japan's troop dispatch was justified as a "noble deed to protect its own." Japan would withdraw its troops on the condition that China would pay compensation to the families of the shipwrecked Japanese who had been murdered by Taiwanese aboriginals. Ōkubo's negotiating abilities staved off a crisis that could have led to war.

The Occupation of the Ryūkyūs

Since the start of the seventeenth century, the Ryūkyū Kingdom had been under the control of the Satsuma domain. At the same time, since the days of the Ming dynasty (1368–1644), the kingdom had had a tribute relationship with China, and its rulers were considered Chinese vassals. These relationships had continued under the Qing. Consequently, the Ryūkyūs had "dual affiliations" with both Satsuma and Qing China. Now, though, Japan made the claim that its Taiwan Expedition had put an end to those dual affiliations, and the Qing acknowledged that the Ryūkyūs were now under Japanese jurisdiction. In a sequence of events termed "the Ryūkyū *shobun*," or the annexation of the Ryūkyūs, Japan ordered an end to the vassal and tribute relationships with China in 1875, and in 1879 it went on to end the domain status the Ryūkyūs had held only since 1872, and created Okinawa Prefecture. The Qing government repeatedly protested against these unilateral measures by Japan, but the latter regarded these steps as an issue of internal affairs and persistently ignored China's objections. As a consequence, bilateral relations cooled. Because Qing China was then in the middle of a border conflict with Russia in the Ili region of Xinjiang, it could not adopt an uncompromising stance toward Japan out of the fear that this would push the latter closer to Russia.

In July 1879, former US president Ulysses S. Grant visited Japan by way of China while on a world tour. The Chinese had asked Grant to mediate the Ryūkyū problem, and in the end, Grant advised the Japanese that the islands be partitioned. Based on this recommendation, the following year the two sides conducted negotiations in Peking (Beijing), where the Japanese side offered a proposal along those lines. Specifically, the proposal would revise the Japan-China Friendship and Trade Treaty, and in exchange for China granting Japan most-favored-nation treatment and the right to do business inland, the main island of Okinawa would be regarded as Japan's territory, the islands of Miyako and Yaeyama would be ceded to China, and the Ryūkyū Kingdom would be reestablished. By autumn 1880, negotiations had reached an agreement in line with the Japanese proposal, but Li Hongzhang shifted his position to one of opposition and refused to sign. Indignant, the Japanese negotiator Inoue Kowashi returned home that November. The reason Li Hongzhang changed his position was not because of any Chinese territorial ambitions, but because the loss of the Ryūkyū Kingdom would be a blow to Qing China's honor. This made Japan's possession of the Ryūkyūs a fait accompli and led to the First Sino-Japanese War.

"The Northern Threat" and the Treaty for the Exchange of Sakhalin for the Kurile Islands

From its early years, the new Meiji government was concerned about any possible Russian advance into Sakhalin. No boundaries had been established for Sakhalin under the Treaty of Amity between Japan and Russia of 1855. In 1867, the bakufu dispatched Koide Hozumi as its plenipotentiary to establish a formal boundary. However, his efforts were unsuccessful. Instead, Japan and Russia concluded a provisional agreement on Sakhalin that would allow free movement of one another's nationals ("mixed residence") throughout the island. However, the only Japanese who lived there were temporary residents like officials and merchants present during the summer months only. Russia, meanwhile, saw the island as a defense outpost for its Primorsky Krai maritime province, and was also enthusiastic about developing it. Aside from the area around Aniva Bay, Sakhalin in real terms was a Russian possession.

Following the Restoration, the Japanese government decided in June 1868 that it would allow people to migrate to Sakhalin and settle there. Three hundred people landed at the Sakhalin village of Kushunkotan (modern-day Korsakov). However, due to the bitter cold and being forbidden to live clustered together, many of the settlers starved or froze to death.

In August 1869, there occurred an incident in which Russian troops seized Hakkotomari (part of Korsakov) and built a barracked encampment. Senior Secretary Maruyama Sakura held talks with the Russians in Hakkotomari, but the situation went unresolved. A similar incident occurred again the following year. Maruyama was acutely aware that, without military backing, any talks would be a waste of time, so he adopted a hard-line stance.

Meanwhile, the United Kingdom's Harry Parkes brought up the dangers of the Japanese government clinging to Sakhalin. Parkes was wary of the possibility that Russia's policy of advancing southward would reach Hokkaido. Based on the reality that Sakhalin was de facto Russian territory, he counseled the new Japanese government to relinquish its territorial rights under conditions such as concessions over financial guarantees. This talk of abandoning Sakhalin attracted the interest of Hokkaido Development Commission vice-chairman Kuroda Kiyotaka, among others. However, the government was still expecting the US to mediate the dispute, and seemed slow to come to a decision. Amid these developments, Kuroda made an inspection trip of Sakhalin. He speculated that the "mixed residence" situation could be maintained for three years, and was discouraged by the spread of Russian influence there. For a time, he was inclined toward dispatching troops to the region. However, this was because acting on a Sakhalin crisis would stop Saigō Takamori from pushing for a Korea expedition; in truth, he was inclined to relinquish Sakhalin.

In 1872, Foreign Minister Soejima Taneomi proposed to Russia that Japan purchase the entire island, but Russia did not accept the suggestion. In 1874, faced with the prospect of serious negotiations with Russia, the decision was made to relinquish Sakhalin, and all Japanese living there were ordered to pull out. When Soejima withdrew from government due to the conflict over the Korea expedition, his successor as foreign minister, Terashima Munenori, appointed Enomoto Takeaki to serve as resident envoy to Russia and tasked him with handling negotiations. In June 1874, having gone to Russia, Enomoto first sought to have the mixed-residence arrangement for Sakhalin dissolved. In response, the Russians stressed that possession of the whole of Sakhalin should serve as the basis for talks. Enomoto asked that Japan be ceded part of the Chishima (Kuril) Islands as compensation. Thus, negotiations unfolded based on Kuroda's call to relinquish Sakhalin.

In May 1875, the two countries signed the Treaty for the Exchange of Sakhalin for the Kurile Islands. The treaty established that all of Sakhalin would be Russian territory, and that the Sōya Strait (La Pérouse Strait) would be the border between the two countries. It also established that Russia would hand over to Japan all rights to the eighteen islands of the Kuril Islands, and that the strait between Cape Lopatka on the Kamchatka Peninsula and Shumshu Island would be the border between the two countries.

During the final stage of these negotiations, Russia recognized even Onekotan as Japanese territory, but held the line at Paramushir and any point north of that. Still, in the end, it conceded. One interpretation of the situation from the Russian point of view was that, if Japan were regarded as possessing all of the Kuril Islands, it would no longer be possible for Russian vessels to head out to the high seas from Vladivostok without passing through Japanese territorial waters. In spite of this, it conceded the point on the advice of Yevfimiy Putyatin. In any event, while from a territorial perspective Japan made some significant compromises, it cut any conflict with Russia at the root, reaping a major benefit in terms of security guarantees. Having secured the safety of the area to the north, the new government could now concentrate on developing Hokkaido with Kuroda, Ōkubo's trusted man, in charge.

Enomoto Takeaki (1836–1908) and Kuroda Kiyotaka (1840–1900)

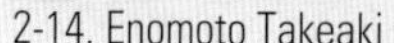

2-14. Enomoto Takeaki

2-15. Kuroda Kiyotaka

Kuroda Kiyotaka hailed from the Satsuma domain, while Enomoto was a *bakushin* (faithful follower of the Tokugawa shogunate) from Edo. Enomoto studied at the Shōheizaka Gakumonjo, found a position as a naval trainee for the bakufu, and later headed to the Netherlands for additional studies in 1861. After returning to Japan, he became a naval magistrate. In 1868, following the Meiji Restoration, the nascent government's military ordered all bakufu-owned warships to be handed over. Enomoto, however, had no intention of acquiescing to the demand. He sailed the entirety of the bakufu's remaining naval forces off to Hokkaido, where he occupied Hakodate, commandeered control of the Matsumae area, and entrenched himself in the Goryōkaku fort (the Battle of Hakodate). On the other side of the battle lines, directing the new government's army in the attack on Goryōkaku, was Kuroda. Enomoto refused to surrender despite the tide of the conflict swinging in favor of the imperial forces. That prompted Kuroda to send Enomoto a letter pleading with him not to commit ritual suicide. If Enomoto lived, Kuroda wrote, it would ensure that his comrades lived, too. Enomoto was swayed by this, and chose the path of surrender. With Enomoto's knowledge of naval engineering, his years studying in the Netherlands, and his knowledge and experience in military systems, law, and engineering, Kuroda viewed him as necessary for the new government, and made every effort to save his life. Kuroda threatened to go off and become a priest if Enomoto was executed, even going as far as shaving his head. Enomoto eventually received a special pardon from the Meiji government in 1872 and, two years later, relocated to Saint Petersburg as Japan's first envoy to Russia.

After signing the Treaty for the Exchange of Sakhalin for the Kurile Islands, Enomoto became navy minister in 1880, assumed the position of minister to Qing China in 1882, and proceeded to help plenipotentiary Itō Hirobumi forge the Tientsin Convention (now known as the Tianjin Convention) between Japan and Qing China. His career

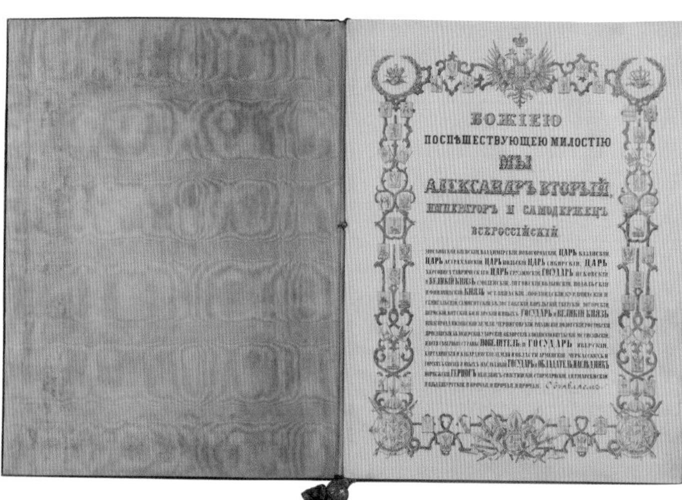

БОЖІЕЮ
ПОСПѢШЕСТВУЮЩЕЮ МИЛОСТІЮ
МЫ
АЛЕКСАНДРЪ ВТОРЫЙ,
ИМПЕРАТОРЪ И САМОДЕРЖЕЦЪ
ВСЕРОССІЙСКІЙ

2-16. Treaty for the Exchange of Sakhalin for the Kurile Islands (instrument of ratification)

2-17. Borders based on the Treaty for the Exchange of Sakhalin for the Kurile Islands (1875)

also included serving as minister of communications and minister of education before taking over from Foreign Minister Aoki Shūzō—who had resigned in the aftermath of the Ōtsu Incident—in 1891. The government probably appointed Enomoto as Aoki's replacement because of his long relationship and good standing with Russia, whose attitudes toward Japan had grown increasingly bitter after the Ōtsu Incident.

Kuroda Kiyotaka also took on prominent roles in the new administration. After serving as a *daijō* (senior secretary) in both foreign affairs and military affairs, he became a deputy of the Hokkaido Development Commission (Kaitaku Jikan) in 1870 and made a voyage to the United States the following year. Returning home with Horace Capron, whom he had recruited to serve as a development advisor, Kuroda took charge of the Hokkaido development effort as acting secretary of the initiative. In 1873, he spoke out in favor of abandoning Karafuto (Sakhalin) and instead focusing on the development of Hokkaido. That November, he proposed to mobilized a group of young, able-bodied men from the Tōhoku region to settle in Hokkaido, cultivate the land, establish a security framework, and defend the area in case of an emergency: it was all part of Kuroda's "*tondenhei*" vision, in which a group of "farmer-soldiers" was responsible for both reclaiming and protecting Hokkaido. The concept came to fruition with the official establishment of the *tondenhei* system in 1874, the year that Kuroda was appointed councillor and director of the Development Commission. When the Ganghwa Island Incident erupted in 1875, Kuroda led a fleet of warships on a mission to Korea, demanded that Korea open up trade channels with Japan, and effected the signing of the Japan-Korea Treaty of Amity.

While Kuroda rose to become the leader of the Satsuma group following the death of Ōkubo Toshimichi, his heavy drinking habits and other issues began to tarnish his reputation. He was embroiled in the 1881 "Hokkaido development assets scandal," for example, drawing criticism for attempting to sell off land assets to friends at egregiously low prices. The next year, with the disbanding of the Hokkaido Development Commission, he withdrew to a much less visible role as a cabinet advisor. He then spent time in Qing China, Europe, and the United States before making his way back to Japan in 1887, when he became minister of agriculture and commerce. A year in that leadership position gave way to an even loftier post: he became the second prime minister of Japan, holding office from early 1888 to late 1889. As soon as the government promulgated its imperial constitution in February 1889, Kuroda declared his advocacy for the concept of "transcendentalism." His time as prime minister came to an end not long thereafter, however, as the uproar surrounding Foreign Minister Ōkuma Shigenobu's inability to break deadlocked treaty-revision negotiations, as well as an attempt on Ōkuma's life, created so much pressure that Kuroda had no choice but to resign.

3 The Korean Peninsula and Japanese Diplomacy

The Imo Incident

In early 1880, Queen Myeongseong (Min) and the people she had brought into the government brushed aside the anti-foreign policies of the Daewongun (King Gojong's father) to implement a pro-Japan policy. They invited military advisors from Japan to help them set about creating a modern, Western-style military force known as the Beolgyegoon. The Japanese government, which supported Korean independence, believed the country could be moved in a pro-Japan direction by advancing the modernizing "enlightenment" policies favored by the Min clan regime. However, the influx of Japanese goods and merchants produced by the opening of Korean ports put pressure on the lives of the populace to an extent that brought to mind the 1592 invasion of the peninsula by Toyotomi Hideyoshi.

In late July 1882, soldiers from the former army who had grown increasingly dissatisfied by the Japanese-style military reforms and their treatment instigated a riot that also drew support from the Hanseong (Seoul) populace. The riot was further abetted by the Daewongun, who had been looking for an opportunity to stage a comeback. The

Hanabusa Yoshimoto (1842–1917)

The son of a retainer in the Okayama domain, Hanabusa Yoshimoto was taught Confucianism (the Four Books and Five Classics) at a domain school and later also studied Dutch literature and artillery science. Drawing on his education, Hanabusa led the construction of a coastal artillery battery for Osaka on the orders of the domain. In 1867, he left to study in Europe and the United States, securing a position in the Ministry of Foreign Affairs upon his return in 1869. His diplomatic career centered on Korea (Joseon): he was dispatched to Korea as an officer of foreign affairs in 1872 and stationed there as a diplomatic officer beginning in 1876. When Korea eventually allowed foreign diplomats to establish official residences in 1880, Hanabusa became the first Japanese envoy to Korea—and also the first foreign envoy to have an audience with the Korean king. As the resident Japanese envoy, Hanabusa worked to fulfill requests from the Korean government, such as bringing over Japanese military advisors to instruct local troops. Several years prior, he had also assisted with the preliminary negotiations for the Japan-China Friendship and Trade Treaty and talks with Korea on an amity treaty. Hanabusa had helped Japan navigate the *María Luz* Incident by assisting Foreign Minister Soejima, representing Japan in its negotiations to secure Russia's participation as a neutral arbiter, and then joining Enomoto Takeaki, Japan's envoy to Russia, in securing a victory in the ensuing arbitration.

2-18. Hanabusa Yoshimoto

Hanabusa's time in Korea would take a dramatic turn, however, with the attacks on the Japanese legation during the 1882 Imo Incident. After managing to escape the legation and return safely to Japan, Hanabusa headed back to Korea with military backing, reestablished his post in the country, and helped conclude the Japan-Korea Treaty of 1882. In his post-Korea career, Hanabusa occupied a variety of positions, such as envoy to Russia in 1883, vice-minister in the Ministry of Agriculture and Commerce, vice-minister in the Imperial Household Ministry, privy councillor, and head of the Japanese Red Cross Society.

uprising grew and rioters forced their way into the royal palace, where they killed a senior statesman from the Min clan faction. The rioters also stormed the dwellings of her relatives as well as the Japanese legation. Minister Resident Hanabusa Yoshimoto narrowly escaped to Incheon and eventually fled to Nagasaki aboard a British warship. The Min clan regime collapsed, and the Daewongun once again seized power.

Minister Hanabusa was instructed to call for an apology and reparations from the Korean government, and also to demand that Japan receive the right to station troops in Korea and to increase its holdings in the open ports. Hanabusa traveled to Hanseong with several warships and a small infantry contingent. He began talks with the Daewongun, but in the end he confronted the latter with a note containing Japan's demands and withdrew to Incheon. However, in late August Li Hongzhang stepped in. China took the view that the Daewongun—whom they saw as a subject of the Qing emperor—was an insurrectionist. Li rushed Chinese troops to Hanseong, seized the Daewongun, and confined him in Tianjin. Thus, the Min clan was restored to power under the protection of the Qing army, which also suppressed the uprising.

The Japanese government accepted a letter of apology from its Korean counterpart, and the two sides reopened negotiations offshore from Incheon aboard the Japanese ironclad *Kongō*. These talks resulted in the signing of the Japan-Korea Treaty of 1882 (Treaty of Chemulpo) at the end of August. Japan secured reparations, along with the right to station troops to protect its legation. Qing China at the time was experiencing strained relations with France over Annam (Vietnam), and so it did not intervene in the negotiating process lest relations with Japan worsen. However, after the treaty was concluded, the Qing government stationed a military and government official named Yuan Shikai and a brigade of troops in Korea, and worked to nurture pro-China elements there. At the same time, the China-Korea Treaty of 1882 had won the Chinese the right to travel about the Korean interior, as well as consular jurisdiction. China was also able to establish concessions in Wonsan, Busan, and Incheon. The suzerain-subordinate relationship between China and Korea was strengthened in substance to one between the ruler and the ruled. King Gojong and the Min clan would come to depend on Qing China in domestic and foreign affairs.

The Gapsin Coup

For the Japanese government, the Imo Incident was evidence of the Qing's suzerainty over Korea. Still, Japan had to steer clear of any armed conflict with China. Foreign Minister Inoue appointed the scholar and diplomat Takezoe Shin'ichirō to serve as Japan's envoy to Korea. Takezoe had already had some interactions with Li Hongzhang, and he was to attempt to stave off any conflict with China while working to stabilize Korea's status as an independent country.

Meanwhile, in Korea a standoff was developing between the Min clan regime, with its heightened dependence on China, and the young bureaucrats of the so-called Enlightenment faction such as Park Yeonghyo and Kim Okgyun, who were becoming increasingly confrontational. The latter stepped up their contacts with Japan as a counterweight to the Qing as they sought to reform and modernize state affairs. Park and Kim visited Japan in October 1882 as their country's representatives for the purpose of delivering an official apology for the Imo Incident. They stayed in Japan through the end of the year, meeting with Fukuzawa Yukichi and other figures from the political and business establishments. After returning to Korea, they arranged to send around four dozen youths to Japan as students.

Meanwhile, the Enlightenment faction was also in contact with Minister Takezoe as they made plans to overthrow the Min clan regime. Finally, on December 4, 1884, they staged a coup d'état. They seized the opportunity presented by the fact that the Qing government had withdrawn half of its forces stationed in Korea to deal with the war that had begun between it and France. Kim Okgyun and his conspirators seized the royal palace and took the king into custody. They then asked Minister Takezoe to assign Japanese troops to the palace's defense, to which Takezoe agreed. The following day, the conspirators formed a new government. The coup d'état appeared to have been a success.

In response to an urgent message from court officials, however, on December 6, Chinese resident-general Yuan Shikai mobilized his garrison in Korea. They overcame the small force defending the Japanese legation and set fire to the buildings. The conspirators pleaded with Takezoe to move the king to Incheon and wait there for Japanese relief forces, but Takezoe did not respond. The Enlightenment faction was left on its own. The coup d'état launched by a minority faction of Korean elites had depended on support from Japanese forces, and it ended in failure. Kim and Park were obliged to exile themselves to Japan, and Minister Takezoe escaped Hanseong to take refuge in Incheon.

The Japanese government saw the situation as quite grave, and they sent Foreign Minister Inoue to Hanseong to handle negotiations. The Korean government saw the Enlightenment faction and Takezoe as having conspired together and questioned Takezoe's role in the incident. Japan sidestepped the issue of responsibility, and eventually in January 1885 the Treaty of Hanseong (the Japan-Korea Treaty of 1885) was concluded, in which the Korean government issued an apology and paid compensation to the Japanese victims of the incident.

That said, in the course of the coup attempt, Chinese troops had fired shots at the Japanese legation and injured Japanese citizens, and this needed to be resolved. In Japan, the government's involvement with the coup attempt was concealed; news reports only mentioned that there had been an attack by Chinese forces, and that Japanese residents in Korea had been killed or wounded. This served to suddenly worsen anti-Qing opinion. Fukuzawa Yukichi fanned the flames further with articles in *Jiji Shinpō* advocating an attack on China. Encouraged by public opinion and anticipating that talks with China would be difficult, the government—with the mediation of Harry Parkes, who was now the United Kingdom's minister to the Qing—decided in February 1885 to dispatch Itō Hirobumi to negotiate with Li Hongzhang.

In their talks, both parties agreed to withdraw their respective forces from Korea. However, Li stressed that, as suzerain, China would dispatch troops if some future upheaval were to occur. In the end, they agreed that both countries would send troops in such a case. The Tianjin Convention, concluded in April 1885, firstly agreed that both countries would withdraw their troops from Korea within four months; and secondly, that neither would send troops to Korea in the event of another internal disturbance without advance notification; furthermore, any troops sent would be withdrawn immediately after the disturbance had been suppressed. The Tianjin Convention would provide the justification for Japan and China to dispatch troops in response to the Donghak Peasant Revolution of 1894.

Japan and China faced the possibility of confrontation as a result of the Imo and Gapsin incidents, but the crises were brought under control through the efforts of Foreign Minister Inoue and of Itō, who would become prime minister in December 1885. The political leadership was bent on avoiding a clash with China so they could pour their energies instead into getting the unequal treaties with the Western powers revised.

Trilateral relations among Japan, China, and Korea changed through the two political disturbances. The pro-Japan faction in Korea experienced a major setback, and the avenue that this faction provided Japan to make inroads into Korea was closed off. Meanwhile, the suzerain-subordinate relationship between China and Korea deepened, and in the wake of the Gapsin Coup, King Gojong seemed poised to move closer toward Russia. In April 1885, Russia's rival, the United Kingdom, had used its gunboats to take control of Geomun Island off the southern tip of the Korean Peninsula (the Geomun Island incident, a.k.a. the Port Hamilton incident). Accordingly, to forestall any machinations by King Gojong, Inoue proposed to China a reform plan that would become the template for Korea's later internal reform efforts. The aim was to create a channel for collaboration with China so that Korea could carry out reforms under Qing guidance while blocking any Russian efforts to intervene. However, for Japan there was some significance to preventing Qing China from monopolizing its suzerainty over Korea. Li rejected this, and on his own he dispatched Yuan to Hanseong to launch an internal reform program. Furthermore, Li obtained a guarantee from Russia that it would not occupy Korean territory, and with this forced the United Kingdom to withdraw its forces from Geomun Island.

Even though relations between Japan and China may have worsened, Japan decided to support Korea's efforts to be an independent state, although it meant avoiding a comprehensive conclusion to the bilateral standoff. Even if Japan stepped into Korea through sheer force, the danger of becoming embroiled in the conflict between Russia and the United Kingdom remained.

Yamagata Aritomo and the Effort to Keep Korea Neutral

The leaders of the new government, who had won the argument over the subjugation of Korea, shared the belief that, rather than having control over it, it would be more beneficial for both Japan and Qing China for Korea to exist as an independent country. Ōkubo Toshimichi argued that any Korea expedition would be of no advantage to Japan, in light of the financial burden, the possibility of British or Russian intervention, and unremitting resistance on the part of the Koreans. Viewed from a different perspective, Korea signing treaties with the Western powers as an independent country would help stabilize the balance of power in East Asia while ensuring Japan's security. In an 1882 opinion paper on Korea policy, Inoue Kowashi argued that Korea's independence needed to be preserved and Russia's southward advances kept in check in order to maintain the balance of power in Asia. He suggested creating a trilateral alliance between Japan, China, and Korea, but given the difficulty of achieving this under the circumstances, he advocated a multinational effort to jointly guarantee Korean neutrality. A similar stance on Korean neutrality can also be seen in an opinion paper by Yamagata Aritomo.

In the 1888 paper he wrote on military affairs, Yamagata noted that construction of the Trans-Siberian Railway (begun 1891, completed 1904) put Korea in the path of Russia's advances. This meant that there was an increased danger of Korea becoming the setting for a war between the United Kingdom and Russia. In light of this threat, Yamagata argued that Japan should strengthen its military readiness alongside its diplomatic maneuvers. "Japan's policy should be to sever China's relationship with Korea completely and make Korea into an autonomous, independent state. By doing so, we can rid ourselves of the worry that one of the great powers of Europe might take advantage of the situation and occupy Korea." In short, he called for Japanese diplomatic maneuverings to sever Korea from its subordinate-suzerain relationship with China and help it to stand on its own as an autonomous and independent state in international society. In particular, Japan should stave off a Russian occupation of Korea.

Two years later, in December 1890, Yamagata delivered a policy speech to the first session of the Imperial Diet. He argued that in order for Japan to maintain its independence as one country among all the nations of the world, it would need to not only preserve a "cordon of sovereignty" (i.e., the Japanese homeland) but also go farther and safeguard a "cordon of interest" (i.e., the Korean Peninsula) as well. Safeguarding a cordon of interest meant guaranteeing Korea's independence.

2-19. "Fishing" (cartoon by Georges Ferdinand Bigot). The implication of the sketch is that, should Japan and China quarrel over Korea, Russia would be the one to benefit.

The goal of Yamagata's speech was to win the Diet's approval for enhancing the readiness of Japan's army and navy. The government had been operating under straitened financial circumstances due to the Seinan War. Following the Imo Incident, it had already begun to focus seriously on Japan's military preparedness, but the work of building up the military strength needed to defend this "cordon of interest" was yet to come. For that matter, the project of developing a naval force to counter the modernized Beiyang Fleet that was the pride of China had only just begun. Yamagata thought that using diplomatic means to get the countries involved to pledge to guarantee Korea's independence and neutrality would serve the purpose of ensuring Japan's security.

In the end, the opportunity to implement a plan to neutralize Korea never arrived. The Tianjin Convention—with its mutual ban on stationing troops in Korea—provided the foundation for Japan-China relations and just managed to ensure Korean independence. However, owing to chaos in internal Korean politics and deepening Chinese intervention in Korea, this agreement, too, was now at risk. It was under these circumstances that a proposal to work with China to reform Korean internal politics emerged within the Japanese government to take the place of the neutralization idea.

Foreign-Settlement Trade and the Question of Opening Up the Interior

The Ansei Five-Power Treaties (treaties of amity and commerce) prohibited foreigners from traveling beyond 10 *ri* (equivalent to roughly 40 kilometers) from any open port. When free trade began in 1859, therefore, the only places where transactions could take place were around the newly opened ports in Kanagawa (or, more accurately, Yokohama to the south), Nagasaki, and Hakodate. At the open markets in Edo and Osaka, foreigners could only be present for trade. Foreigners at the open ports, on the other hand, were free to establish permanent residence, lease land, and purchase and build buildings. This government-sanctioned "foreign settlement" system, which Japan had modeled after Qing China's "concessions," remained in place until the treaties underwent revisions in 1899.

Trading at open ports (foreign settlements) was something of a monopoly. The only parties who could deal in exports were *urikomi-shō* (local selling agents), who sold raw silk, tea, and other items from Japanese producers on consignment; imports, meanwhile, were the domain of *hikitori-shō* (local buying agents), who would buy products from foreign merchants and then resell them at a profit. Crucial in shaping and propelling "foreign-settlement trade" was Yokohama. Accounting for more than half the total foreign-settlement area in Japan, Yokohama grew to rival Hong Kong and Shanghai as one of the world's leading hubs of international trade. One of the most prominent foreign firms in the Yokohama trading game was Jardine Matheson, a Scottish conglomerate.

As time went on, however, the dominating presence of *urikomi-shō* and *hikitori-shō* gave foreign-settlement trade a monopolistic quality—and foreign merchants began to object to treaty provisions that confined their trading outlets to foreign settlements. These types of commercial needs led to calls for the opening of the interior (*naichi zakkyo*, or "mixed residence outside foreign settlements"), which came up repeatedly during the treaty-revision negotiations. Qing China had already opened its interior and allowed foreigners to travel freely throughout the empire via the 1858 Treaty of Tientsin (now known as the Treaty of Tianjin).

In August 1874, Foreign Minister Terashima Munenori decided to permit foreigners with passports issued by their respective governments' diplomatic offices to travel freely within Japan, but the move had minimal impact. The Meiji government largely stood its ground on the issue, never going through with a complete opening of its domestic territory or permitting foreigners to own real estate, and that refusal ended up having diplomatic ramifications. During the talks surrounding revisions to the existing treaties with foreign counterparts, the *naichi zakkyo* issue turned out to be one of Japan's biggest bargaining chips. Not kowtowing to demands for a full opening prevented a rapid influx of foreign products and foreign capital, which may have helped Japan spare its domestic market from potentially devastating blows.

4 Putting the Finishing Touches on Independence

The Issue of Treaty Revisions

While the new Japanese government continued to honor the treaties that the bakufu had signed, it also concluded new treaties with several powers, including Sweden-Norway, Spain, the Northern German Confederation, and Austria-Hungary. The Treaty of Amity and Commerce signed between Japan and Austria-Hungary in October 1869 stood out as a particularly clear example of the unequal treaties. It made ever more plain the rights of Japan's counterpart and exhaustively laid out points that were unfavorable to Japan. It also codified and inserted the practices that had arisen after Japan's opening. Moreover, by making it possible for other countries to share equally through most-favored-nation treatment, the agreement lay the foundation for a succession of other unequal treaties.

The Meiji government rapidly understood which parts of these treaties were unequal, and set out to

The *María Luz* Incident

In July 1872, the *María Luz*, a Peruvian ship en route to Peru with a cargo of indentured laborers ("coolies" in the contemporary parlance) from Qing China, stopped in Yokohama for repairs after a severe storm. While the ship was anchored at the port, one of the Chinese laborers (Mo Hing) escaped from the vessel and approached a nearby British warship, claiming that he and his fellow passengers were being abused. The British government deemed the *María Luz* a "slave ship" and asked Japan to rescue the passengers. Determining the incident to fall within Japan's legal jurisdiction, Foreign Minister Soejima Taneomi headed up an investigation and subsequently ordered the *María Luz* to remain in port and allow the Qing Chinese passengers to disembark. The Japanese government also held court to resolve the incident. With Kanagawa governor Ōe Taku presiding, the court ordered the laborers freed. Even though *María Luz* captain Ricardo Herreira was found not guilty of any wrongdoing, he challenged the decision in an appeal, seeking to fulfill the indentured immigrants' contract. However, the court ruled the contracts null and void. In the wake of the ruling, Herreira abandoned the *María Luz* and fled home to Peru, while the Japanese government delivered the 230 laborers back to Qing China. The incident seemed to have reached a conclusion—but the Peruvian government had more to say. Through a minister plenipotentiary to Japan, Peru called the legality of the Japanese court's decision into question, sought reparations, and demanded an official apology from Japan. The ensuing negotiations between Japan and Peru stalled, leading the Japanese government to request that Alexander II of Russia arbitrate the issue. The new foreign minister, Terashima, who had replaced Soejima, took over the case for the Japanese side.

Representatives of Japan and Peru headed to Russia for the international arbitration. In May 1875, the Russian czar found that Japan's actions had not violated general international law or any treaties, and Japan was thus under no obligation to pay Peru any reparations. It was a resounding, outright victory for Japan. Not only did the ruling represent the Japanese government's first victory in international arbitration, but it also demonstrated the legitimacy of Japan's legal action on a global stage—and spurred several members of the international community to ban the trafficking and trade of slaves. Japan also addressed its own issues on that front. The Peruvian representatives had argued that Japan had no place criticizing enslavement when it, too, openly practiced human trafficking in its treatment of geisha and prostitutes. This prompted the government to abolish the indentured servitude of geisha. The successful outcome of the arbitration was the result of the contributions of American advisor Erasmus Peshine Smith, who advised on the drafting of Japan's official response, and the skills at the negotiating table of Japan's envoy to Russia Enomoto Takeaki. Some studies also draw connections between Japan's victory and the Treaty for the Exchange of Sakhalin for the Kurile Islands, signed just prior to the arbitration verdict, along with Russo-Japanese territorial negotiations.

Rokumeikan Diplomacy

At the end of 1880, Foreign Minister Inoue Kaoru commissioned Josiah Conder, a British architect, to build a state guest house that would give Japan a fitting venue for gatherings among distinguished foreign guests and members of high society. Construction on the facility began soon thereafter and was eventually completed in November 1883. The venue, the Rokumeikan ("Deer-Cry Pavilion"), was located in Tokyo's Kōjimachi-ku (next to the eventual site of the Imperial Hotel). For Inoue and Itō Hirobumi, who were busy trying to develop Japan's national legislative system, the Rokumeikan served a diplomatic purpose: by impressing visitors with the image of Japan as a civilized, modernizing nation where popular sensibilities echoed the manners and customs of the West, the Rokumeikan could bolster Japan's position in its efforts to revise existing treaties with its international counterparts. Inoue and Itō were fixtures at the Rokumeikan's various events, which included balls, soirees, masquerades, bazaars, and other functions for high-ranking officials and guests of distinction.

The Rokumeikan's name was apparently the brainchild of Nakai Hiroshi (Hiromu), chief secretary in the Ministry of Industry and the first husband of Inoue's wife Takeko. He took his inspiration from an ode in the *Shijing* (Book of songs), a Chinese classic, called "Lu Ming." The work describes how deer call to one other when they find food, gathering to eat together rather than alone, an image that officials agreed would befit a place for international gatherings.

In his seminal *Gakumon no susume* (An encouragement of learning), Fukuzawa Yukichi discussed the outer and inner dimensions of modernization. "The civilization of a country should not be evaluated in terms of its external forms. Schools, industry, army and navy, are merely external forms of civilization," he wrote. "In short, if people lack [the] spirit of independence, the outward forms of modern civilization are ultimately useless." Fukuzawa's argument voiced a sound, reasoned position that true "civilization" grows out of a spirit of independence and self-respect, not merely a "form" of modernity. Still, there was also criticism of a Europeanization policy that placed "form" first.

At the forefront of that criticism was Tokutomi Sohō, who had established the Min'yūsha publishing company and launched publication of the general-interest magazine *Kokumin no tomo* (The nation's friend) in 1887. Tokutomi found kindred spirits in the minds behind the publisher Seikyōsha and its publication *Nihonjin* (Japanese), founded in 1888: Shiga Shigetaka, Miyake Setsurei, and Sugiura Jūgō. These voices formed a chorus lambasting what they saw as trifling commotion surrounding the Rokumeikan, Japan's approach to the treaty revisions, and the country's fixation on Europeanization. For these outspoken critics advocating a type of nationalistic conservatism, the key point of contention was not the foreign element. Rather than stressing an anti-foreign brand of nationalism, the "nationalists," as many called them, actually espoused a new nationalism in reaction to the radical pursuit of Europeanization.

After Inoue's resignation, Rokumeikan diplomacy fell into decline. The Rokumeikan itself underwent a repurposing, serving as the Kazoku Kaikan (Peers' Club) until it was destroyed in 1940. Despite the Rokumeikan's demise, however, Japan's Europeanization policy impelled the creation of the Rōmaji-kai (a society to promote the romanization of the Japanese language) and the development of the Theater Reform Movement (*engeki kairyō undō*). In addition to having a wide-ranging impact on cultural history, the quest for European standards also accelerated the Westernization of everyday life for the average Japanese citizen.

Some observers have posited that Rokumeikan diplomacy was a fusion of Itō's aristocratic tastes and Inoue's diplomatic tactics, and this may very well have been the case. Itō's aspirations to create a House of Peers, along with his creation of the "noble" designation via the Peerage Act in 1884, certainly point to his interest in the concept of "nobility." For Itō, then, the Rokumeikan and Kazoku Kaikan may have served as a sort of training ground for nobles in the making.

2-20. "A Glimpse of Dignitaries Dancing" (woodblock print by Yōshū Chikanobu)

revise the troublesome parts. First, there was the system of consular jurisdiction by which, if a foreigner in Japan became a suspect in a crime, the consul of that person's home country had jurisdiction over bringing them to justice. Second was the loss of the right to set and revise tariffs. In Japan, levying any customs duties beyond the agreed tariffs was not permitted. Even so, while the Japan-US Treaty of Amity and Commerce had allowed an import tariff of around 20 percent on average, the four powers (led by the British, who were joined by France, the Netherlands, and the United States) signed a supplementary Tariff Convention with Japan in 1866. This reduced the agreed tariff in principle to 5 percent. Third, most-favored-nation treatment was a one-sided feature that laid all obligations on Japan alone. Any treaty power could enjoy whatever rights Japan had granted to the other powers, but Japan did not have reciprocal rights.

There were, however, restrictions on the privileges of the treaty powers and their citizens. They had the rights to reside and do business only in the open ports (Kanagawa/Yokohama, Hyōgo/Kobe, Hakodate, Niigata, and Nagasaki) and open markets (Edo and Osaka). As a rule, doing business or residing anywhere else was not permitted. This is why many countries' representatives were vocal about wanting Japan to open its interior. However, Japan had concluded it would be difficult to open the interior to foreigners who were not bound by Japanese law or customs and might cause problems.

Consular jurisdiction would also apply in the event that a foreigner committed an infraction of general Japanese administrative regulations in the context of the treaty's application. Furthermore, such administrative regulations could only be applied to foreigners through consular jurisdiction. Even when it came to establishing administrative regulations, they had to be negotiated with the various countries' consuls and envoys. These negotiations to revise the treaties were not so much driven by the desire to repeal the unequal treaties per se, as by wanting to eliminate unfairness in operating administrative regulations and to regain the right to establish these administrative regulations, and so were conducted in earnest to that end.

(1) The Terashima Years (1873–79): Recovering Tariff Autonomy

When Soejima Taneomi resigned as foreign minister following the political upheaval of October 1873, he was succeeded by Terashima Munenori. Terashima would address the delayed payment of reparations demanded of Japan after the 1864 Shimonoseki Campaign. Furthermore, travel through Japan's interior would be permitted only for those foreigners who held a passport issued by their country.

More than legal rights, Terashima's goal was to restore Japan's right to tariff autonomy (taxation rights) and its right to formulate rules governing trade. This was because government finances were strained after the Seinan War, and Finance Minister Ōkuma Shigenobu wanted the agreed tariffs to be raised as soon as possible. Under the Japan-US Commercial Treaty (Yoshida-Evarts Treaty) that Minister Yoshida Kiyonari signed in Washington in July 1878, Japan was granted tariff autonomy and the right to establish regulations on trade. In return for the restoration of tariff autonomy, the agreed tariffs (export taxes) were to be abolished and new ports opened to foreign trade.

Harry Parkes, envoy of the United Kingdom, was critical of Japan having arbitrarily concluded this treaty without informing the other treaty powers. Terashima responded by sending the text of the treaty to the British, French, and German governments in Japan, and instructed that individual talks should be held with each. The British were wary that restoring Japan's tariff autonomy would lead to protected trade, and so they rejected the treaty on the grounds of protecting free trade. The French and Germans accepted only the raising of tariffs

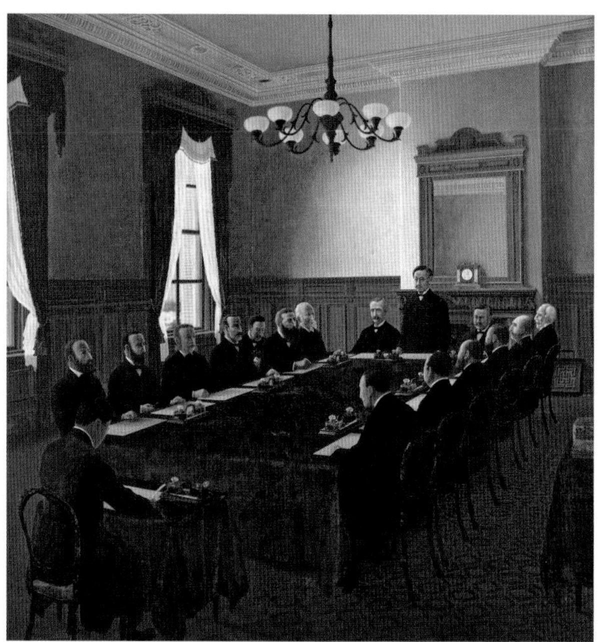

2-21. *Conference on the Revision of Treaties* (painting by Ueno Kōichi of the 1882 joint conference chaired by Inoue)

as a means to supplement Japan's revenues, but did not accede to the restoration of its tariff autonomy. In the end, because the Japan-US treaty included a clause stating that it would go into effect only after similar agreements had been reached with the other treaty powers, the treaty never went into force.

The United Kingdom responded to Terashima's calls for separate negotiations with each power in Tokyo by proposing that joint negotiations on revision with all the treaty powers take place in Europe. As a result, Terashima's proposal foundered. Around this time, over the course of 1877 and 1878, the Hartley Incident occurred, in which a British merchant named John Hartley was revealed to have twice smuggled opium into Japan. When the British consul delivered a verdict of "not guilty" in the first instance (though the verdict was "guilty" in the second), the Japanese populace was outraged by this example of the high-handed behavior of foreigners, and public opinion held that any treaty revisions that did not restore to Japan its legal rights would be meaningless. There was also much criticism of Terashima within the government, and in September 1879, he resigned.

(2) The Inoue Years (1879–87): The Rokumeikan and Opening Inland Japan to Foreigners

Terashima's successor as foreign minister, Inoue Kaoru, worked hard to emphasize Japan's standing as a "civilized nation"—symbolized by the Western-style Rokumeikan built in Tokyo to accommodate foreign guests of the government—in order to create an environment amenable to treaty revision. Speaking at the Rokumeikan in October 1884, Inoue said: "This is the policy that we should pursue. My only wish is to make Japan into a Western-style civilized nation in East Asia, with a standing equal to nations of the West."

Inoue's policy on negotiations was not aimed at restoring Japan's legal and tariff autonomy all at once. He angled to restore some legal rights at first by getting administrative regulations over such matters as ports, hunting, and quarantines to apply to foreigners. His strategy was to wait for the development of a court system before seeking full restoration of Japan's rights. As to taxation rights, he sought to replace the existing agreed tariffs with increased tariffs restricted to certain essential imported goods. The Ministry of Foreign Affairs

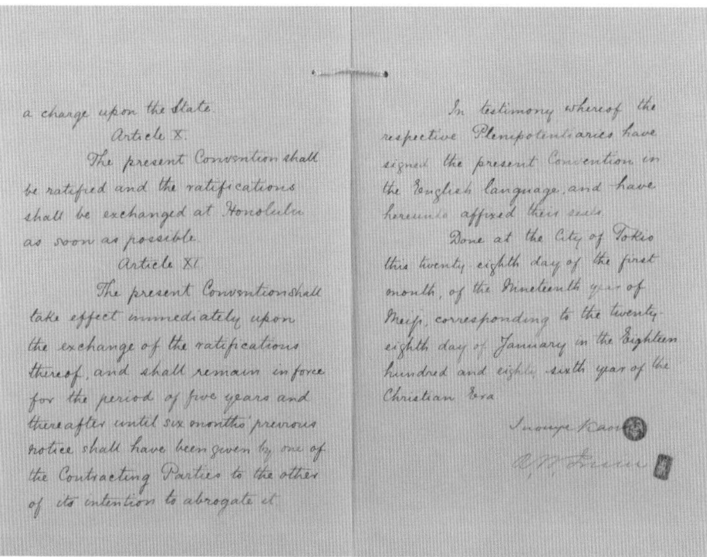

a charge upon the State.

Article X.

The present Convention shall be ratified and the ratifications shall be exchanged at Honolulu as soon as possible.

Article XI.

The present Convention shall take effect immediately upon the exchange of the ratifications thereof, and shall remain in force for the period of five years and thereafter until six months' previous notice shall have been given by one of the Contracting Parties to the other of its intention to abrogate it.

In testimony whereof the respective Plenipotentiaries have signed the present Convention in the English language, and have hereunto affixed their seals.

Done at the City of Tokio this twenty eighth day of the first month, of the Nineteenth year of Meiji, corresponding to the twenty-eighth day of January in the Eighteen hundred and eighty sixth year of the Christian Era.

Inouye Kaoru

2-22. Japan-Hawaii Immigration Convention of 1886 (signed treaty)

The *Normanton* Incident

On the evening of October 24, 1886, the *Normanton*, a British freighter bound for Kobe, ran aground in a storm off Katsuura in the Kumano Sea and began to sink. Captain John Drake and his twenty-six-man crew escaped the wreck in lifeboats and eventually drifted ashore in Kushimoto and the Sue Inlet, but the twenty-five Japanese passengers who had been aboard the *Normanton* were nowhere to be found, and were assumed to have drowned in the ship's hold. The British consulate in Kobe conducted a marine-accident inquiry in early November and accepted the statements of the captain and crew, declaring the sailors innocent of any negligent wrongdoing. That set off a firestorm in major newspapers, including the *Tokyo Nichi Nichi Shimbun* and *Jiji Shinpō*, with indignant writers launching diatribes on the crew's discriminatory treatment of the vessel's Japanese passengers. After receiving a report on the circumstances of the incident and surveying the public outcry for uncompromising action that the consulate's ruling had provoked, the Japanese government (specifically Foreign Minister Inoue) brought charges of murder against Captain Drake in the name of the governor of Hyōgo Prefecture to the British consulate on November 13. After a preliminary examination, the court relocated to the British consulate in Yokohama. On December 8, the court found the captain guilty of dereliction of duty and sentenced him to three months in prison. While the verdict quieted the public furor over the incident to some degree, the tragedy of the *Normanton*'s Japanese passengers was a frequent point of reference in campaign speeches, inspired songs, and even formed the narratives of picture-card shows (*kamishibai*), lodging itself in Japan's collective memory as a lasting reminder of wrongful consular jurisdiction.

2-23. "The *Normanton* Incident" (cartoon by Georges Ferdinand Bigot)

and the Ministry of Justice hired a large number of foreign specialists, and preparations moved forward on putting together legal codes for civil and commercial law.

Inoue sent his proposals for revised treaties to each of the treaty powers, but they would not readily accept changes to administrative rights; each held fast to their vested interests. The United Kingdom, in particular, opposed the Inoue draft, which it saw not as a revision, but as an attempt to scrap the old treaty and create a new one. Beginning in 1882, a joint conference on treaty revision chaired by Inoue, with representatives of all the powers concerned, met twenty-one times in Tokyo. However, the conference stood at an impasse over the issues of raising tariffs and restoring Japan's administrative rights. Within Japan, too, there was no consensus over the matter of opening Japan's interior to foreigners. As a way to break the deadlock, Inoue declared in April 1882 that so long as foreigners abided by Japanese law, the country's interior would be open to them; in effect, this would restore Japan's legal rights, annulling consular jurisdiction. Inoue's plan would allow foreigners to own property in addition to being permitted to conduct trade and travel. However, the detailed proposal about how this was to be implemented met with strong opposition from both the United Kingdom's envoy Harry Parkes and Inoue Kowashi at home, among others.

At the May 1886 conference on treaty revision held at the Japanese Ministry of Foreign Affairs, the United Kingdom and Germany offered a joint proposal in place of Inoue's that would ensure that foreigners would abide by Japanese law in exchange for opening Japan's interior. The Japanese responded favorably to the proposal, which served as the basis for subsequent negotiations. The essentials of the Anglo-German draft agreed to in April 1887 came down to (1) opening Japan's interior within an agreed timeframe, (2) compiling a Western-style legal code and communicating it in advance to all countries, and (3) restoring legal rights to Japan. The latter point contained a caveat, however, that a certain number of foreigners would participate in judgments in hearings related to litigation in which a foreigner was either a plaintiff or a defendant.

If the conference had concluded on this note, then the treaty powers would likely have signed. However, the Anglo-German draft leaked out to the public, and it suddenly became a political issue. Furthermore, Gustave Boissonade—a French legal scholar working for the Ministry of Justice—criticized the proposal, saying it would sign away Japan's sovereignty to the foreign powers. There was also strong dissent within the government, fueled by bitter memories of the *Normanton* Incident that had occurred the previous year (see sidebar on page 87), which brought popular criticism as well. The treaty revision conference was indefinitely postponed in July, and in September Inoue resigned as foreign minister.

(3) The Ōkuma Years (1888–89): The Issue of Appointing Foreign Justices

Ōkuma Shigenobu was appointed foreign minister in February 1888. To mollify domestic opposition, Ōkuma sought to restrict the use of foreign jurists to Supreme Court (Daishin'in) cases, and to have the provisions regarding foreign jurists removed from the treaty texts themselves and placed instead in a written declaration. Similarly, the compilation of legal codes and the notification obligation would also be announced in a written declaration. On the matter of tariff autonomy, Ōkuma's new treaty proposal followed in the footsteps of Inoue's draft. Japan approached the United States, Germany, and Russia individually on these proposals, and by August 1889 each had signed off (they were not ratified). The United Kingdom—which had asked that the Supreme Court with its foreign jurist participants be granted the power to engage in fact-finding—was leaning toward signing. However, on April 19, 1889, the draft treaty between Japan and the United States was reproduced in the pages of the *Times* of London, and public opposition to foreign judges still being allowed to participate in Japanese legal affairs grew. Critics protested that, as with the Inoue draft, employing foreign jurists would detract from the independence of Japan's judicial powers, and that it also infringed on the Meiji Constitution, which was already in force by this time.

2-24. Ōkuma Shigenobu

2-25. *Promulgation of the Constitution* (painting by Wada Eisaku)

In October 1889, Ōkuma was attacked by a young follower of the nationalist Gen'yōsha (Dark Ocean Society) and gravely wounded. The government decided to postpone revision negotiations, and in late December Ōkuma resigned. Around the same time, the Yamagata Aritomo cabinet took office and Vice-Foreign Minister Aoki Shūzō became foreign minister.

(4) The Aoki Years (1889–91): Creating the Imperial Diet and Revision Negotiations

One of the objectives of the Meiji government had been to get the treaties revised on its own before creating the Imperial Diet, because it expected opposition forces to constrain the government's diplomatic efforts through that body. Stymied on that front, Foreign Minister Aoki Shūzō now adopted an approach of focusing on the United Kingdom as the object of negotiations. Furthermore, unlike with the Inoue and Ōkuma proposals, he sought to achieve a more complete restoration of Japan's legal rights, without any compromises. He anticipated the effort to be even more difficult, but the negotiations with the United Kingdom were unexpectedly smooth. The crucial reason for this was the creation of the Imperial Diet (a legislative branch) in February 1889 through promulgation of the Constitution of Imperial Japan. Aoki's

Aoki Shūzō (1844–1914)

Aoki Shūzō, the son of a village physician in the Chōshū domain (Nagato Province), studied medicine at the Meirinkan (a domain school) and Nagasaki before heading to Prussia to pursue further studies on the recommendation of fellow Chōshū native Kido Takayoshi. The goal was not to hone his skills in medicine, however—he headed abroad to learn politics and law. In January 1873, with another endorsement from Kido, Aoki secured a position with the Japanese legation in Berlin. He then went on to become Japan's minister to Germany the following year, staying there until 1885—more than a decade. His marriage to the daughter of a Prussian aristocrat only deepened his affection for his adopted home.

Aoki began serving as foreign undersecretary (vice-minister) under Foreign Minister Inoue Kaoru in December 1885 and would remain in the same position under subsequent foreign minister Ōkuma Shigenobu, pouring his energies into treaty-revision negotiations. In December 1889, after the attack on Ōkuma, Aoki became foreign minister in the first Yamagata cabinet with the enthusiastic endorsement of the "Chōshū group" (Inoue, Yamagata Aritomo, and others). Aoki was the first career diplomat to become foreign minister.

During the treaty-revision negotiations, Japan's talks with the UK were the biggest hurdle of all, and Aoki made them his top priority. The chances of persuading the British side to approve the changes appeared to be remote, but Aoki took advantage of developments at home in his attempts to win the United Kingdom over. He emphasized that the promulgation of the Meiji Constitution in February 1889 solidified Japan's foundation as a state governed by the rule of law, and also noted that, with the Imperial Diet's first meeting looming the following year, the only agreement that the government would be able to sign was the revised treaty, which the Diet was sure to support. As Russia was openly preparing for a southern advance, a development that worried the British, Aoki knew that the United Kingdom would be eager to push the revision negotiations forward. Aoki's adept handling of the situation helped soften the British position and moved the negotiations forward, earning him a reappointment as foreign minister in the ensuing Matsukata Masayoshi administration. His career in that leadership capacity would come to a frustrating end shortly thereafter, however, when the Ōtsu Incident in May 1891—an assassination attempt on Czarevitch (heir apparent) Nicholas Alexandrovich of Russia by a Japanese police officer—forced him to resign (see sidebar on page 91).

2-26. Aoki Shūzō

hard-line stance carried the implicit message that, keeping in mind the advantages of a constitutional system, a revised treaty could only be concluded with the approval of the new legislature.

His proposal discontinued the appointment of foreign jurists to the Supreme Court and made no promises about compiling a legal code or communicating it to foreign powers in advance. The United Kingdom, chiefly concerned with protecting its citizens residing in Japan from laws and regulations that the new legislative branch might establish, came to accept the elimination or easing of provisions that would agitate the legislative branch. Also, creating the Imperial Diet had made it impossible for foreign consuls and envoys to interfere with the formulation of laws and regulations. Additionally, once Japan's interior was opened, the United Kingdom requested that the right of foreigners to lease land in perpetuity in the foreign settlements be replaced with the right to own land outright.

The Anglo-Russian rivalry in East Asia mentioned earlier had also contributed to this softening of the British stance. The United Kingdom had occupied Geomun Island off the southern tip of the Korean Peninsula in 1885 to keep Russia in check (they withdrew in 1887), and in 1891 Russia embarked on building the Trans-Siberian Railway. Tensions between the United Kingdom and Russia led the former to adopt a more compromising attitude toward its relations with Japan.

In January 1892, Aoki headed back to Germany in his third stint as Japan's resident envoy. He took on a concurrent role the following year, coupling his duties in Germany with an envoy appointment to the United Kingdom, where he handled Japanese-British negotiations in London under Foreign Minister Mutsu. The talks posed significant challenges, however. A change in the British political guard and pressure for a stronger stance on foreign policy at home altered the dynamics of the revision negotiation considerably. Aoki headed into the talks with the intention to play hardball, given the tones of the political climate in Japan, but the resulting pushback from the British led him to seek the Japanese government's help in keeping the hard-line diplomacy faction in check. In the spring of 1894, the government decided to put Aoki in charge of securing a quick signing of the treaties as attacks from the Mintō ("people's parties") during the sixth Diet session and fragile Qing-Japanese relations turned up the political heat in Japan. Aoki answered the call with aplomb. Working closely with Mutsu, he provided the government with an accurate picture of the conditions at the negotiating table, found common ground with his British counterparts, and helped the sides finalize the Anglo-Japanese Treaty of Commerce and Navigation just before the Sino-Japanese War broke out.

Recalling the revision negotiations, Aoki wrote that the biggest challenge in the entire process was "changing permanent leases for foreigners into ownership rights." It was the United Kingdom's wish to obtain the right for foreigners to own land rather than hold leases, but Mutsu had also come to regret denying foreigners land ownership based on the conventional wisdom that this would prove dangerous. As a result of not approving land ownership by foreigners, Japan would not be able to collect land taxes and taxes on residences except for the low rents agreed on in the Ansei period, leading to a major revenue shortfall. Aoki had shown foresight on these matters, although he was unable to challenge Mutsu.

Aoki once again assumed the title of foreign minister as part of the second Yamagata cabinet in 1898. The eruption of the Boxer Rebellion in 1900 presented Aoki with an important diplomatic situation to navigate, and he steered cabinet discussions toward dispatching troops to China. When Russia refused to withdraw after the conflict subsided, Aoki took a hard-line position against Russia. Aoki later went on to serve as the first official ambassador to the United States in 1906, but his decision to challenge US president Theodore Roosevelt and other top American officials in an uncompromising stand on immigration issues—all without any official instructions from Tokyo—earned him a one-way ticket back to Japan.

An avid reader of Western literature and a lifelong lover of learning, Aoki relished the art of the debate and rarely backed down from any argument. In the sphere of Meiji-era diplomacy, those qualities may have been exactly what Japan needed.

The Ōtsu Incident and Foreign Minister Aoki

The Ōtsu Incident was a failed assassination attempt on Czarevitch (heir apparent) Nicholas Alexandrovich of Russia (later Czar Nicholas II) on May 11, 1891, in Ōtsu, Shiga. The perpetrator was a police officer named Tsuda Sanzō, who was on duty escorting Nicholas. Tsuda swung a sword at the czarevitch's head, cutting his forehead but not endangering his life. The government pressured the Supreme Court of Judicature (Dai-shin'in) in late May to try Tsuda under Article 116 of the Criminal Code—a provision stipulating the death penalty for anyone inflicting harm on the emperor or crown prince—but the court dismissed the government's request, instead sentencing Tsuda to life imprisonment. Considering the circumstances in context, observers would later see the ruling as a demonstration of Japan's judicial independence and an example of state governance under the rule of law. In its immediate aftermath, however, the incident left a sizable wake. Anxieties that the attack would push Russo-Japanese relations over the edge gripped the nation; a woman even announced that she would take her own life as an act of contrition for the assassination attempt. Emperor Meiji paid the czarevitch a visit to inquire after his health.

The Ōtsu Incident came shortly after another tense moment between Japan and Russia—a "prelude" of sorts to the incident. The year prior, a coach carrying the Japanese emperor had passed in front of the Russian legation in Tokyo. Eager to catch a glimpse of the procession, the Russian minister's wife and legation staff looked down from the building's second-story window. On the pretext that it was disrespectful to look down on the emperor, several students began hurling rocks at the building. The rock-throwing incident sparked concerns in certain circles, with many worrying that the fallout could complicate Czarevitch Nicholas's already planned visit to Japan. The Russian envoy to Japan asked Foreign Minister Aoki Shūzō to make an emergency revision to the Criminal Code so that the government could take legal action, and Aoki gave the envoy his word that any attack on the crown prince would be tantamount to an attack on a member of the Japanese imperial family. When the Dai-shin'in later sentenced Tsuda to life imprisonment for that exact offense, the Russian foreign minister told Enomoto Takeaki (Aoki's successor as foreign minister) that it would have been better for Japan to sentence Tsuda to death and then have the Russian emperor plead with the Japanese emperor to reduce Tsuda's sentence to life imprisonment. Despite this, the Russian government openly declared its full satisfaction with Japan's actions, bringing the incident to a close.

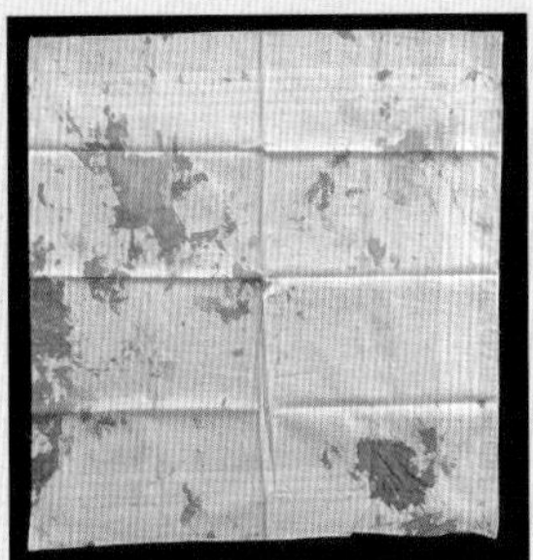

2-27. The sword used in the Ōtsu Incident; a handkerchief stained with Czar Nicholas's blood

It looked as though the Anglo-Japanese negotiations were drawing to a close, but Aoki was forced to resign in May 1891 in the wake of the difficulties presented by the Ōtsu Incident (see sidebar on this page). His successor as foreign minister, Enomoto Takeaki (1891–92), with the assistance of then president of the Privy Council Itō Hirobumi, formed an investigative commission on the issue of treaty revision with the goal of coordinating opinions within the government. However, the effort was unsuccessful, and with the mass resignation of the Matsukata cabinet in August 1892, Enomoto stepped down.

(5) The Mutsu Years (1892–96): The Argument for Strict Treaty Enforcement and the Restoration of Legal Rights

In August 1892, Itō Hirobumi formed his second cabinet and appointed his trusted colleague Mutsu Munemitsu to the position of foreign minister. Mutsu's revision proposal was not much different from Aoki Shūzō's. However, on the matter of tariff autonomy, it called for agreeing on certain import tariffs on major commodities coming from France, Germany, the United Kingdom, and the United States, and restoring tariff autonomy to Japan on all other items. It also differed from the Aoki proposal in that it would not allow foreigners to own land once Japan's interior was opened, though the perpetual leases held on land in the foreign settlements would be maintained.

Mutsu left negotiations with the United Kingdom up to Aoki, who was to be stationed in Germany, but before he could start negotiations in London, he was hindered by the "Argument for Strict Treaty Enforcement" of the strong foreign policy faction (*Taigai-kō*). This faction held that foreigners should be dealt with according to the letter of the treaties currently in force, making them painfully aware of how inconvenient and unfavorable the current treaties were to them, while working to conduct more profitable negotiations on revision. Elements opposed to opening Japan's interior also joined up over this strict enforcement approach; as a result, the strong foreign policy faction held more than half the seats in the House of Representatives. The Itō cabinet formed an alliance with the Liberal Party to oppose this faction.

As the strict treaty enforcement movement gained influence, there were frequent instances of violence against foreigners. Under the circumstances, the United Kingdom responded negatively to Aoki's approaches, and the talks in London were put on hold temporarily. In December 1893, the strong foreign policy faction introduced a proposal to the fifth session of the Imperial Diet on the matter of strict treaty enforcement. Mutsu responded by pressing the Diet to reflect on the fact that if such enforcement attempts were carried out, the one-sided treaties would remain in place, and, if anything, it was the Japanese people who would lose out. Itō and Mutsu repeatedly adjourned the session, and at the year's end the House of Representatives was dissolved. The rivalry between the government's supporters and the strong foreign policy faction continued, and in the sixth Imperial Diet session, a proposal rebuking the government's diplomatic efforts was adopted. The Itō cabinet was driven into the difficult position of dissolving the

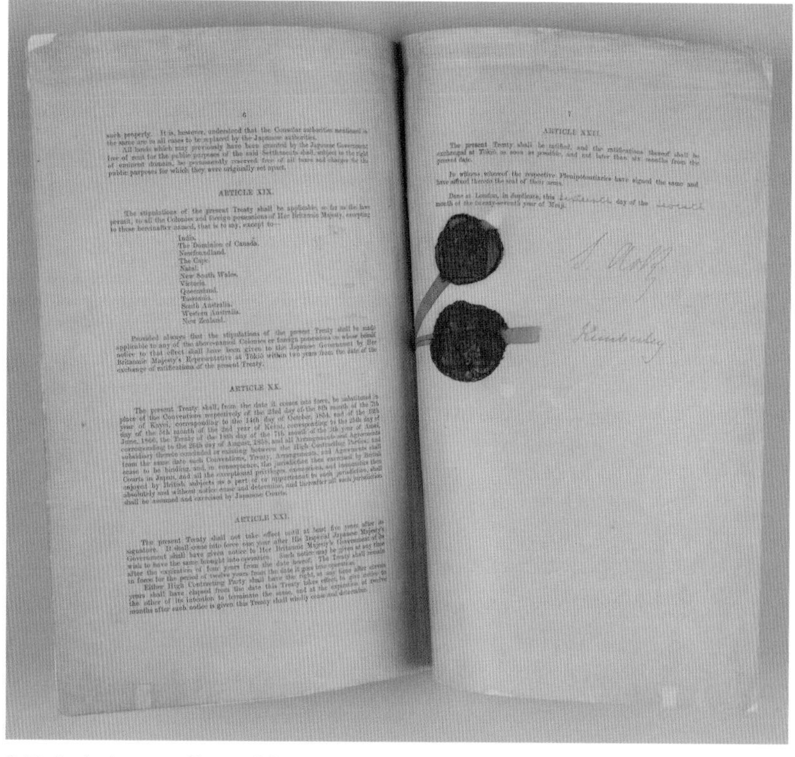

2-28. Anglo-Japanese Treaty of Commerce and Navigation

Itō Hirobumi (1841–1909) and Inoue Kaoru (1836–1915)

Two sons of the Chōshū domain, Itō Hirobumi and Inoue Kaoru, left enormous legacies on Japanese history. Itō studied at Yoshida Shōin's Shōkasonjuku Academy, and Inoue was educated at the Meirinkan, the domain school in Hagi. While both eagerly took up the *sonnō jōi* ("revere the emperor, expel the barbarians") cause, it was a clandestine trip to the United Kingdom in 1863 that forged a lifelong bond between the pair. Inoue, five years Itō's senior, is believed to have extended the invitation to head abroad together. Seeing the overwhelming power of Western civilization firsthand in London, Itō and Inoue began to embrace the idea of an "open Japan" and hurried back home as soon as they got wind of the Chōshū domain's intent to execute its plan to expel the foreigners. They tried in vain to dissuade the domain from engaging a combined fleet of ships from four Western powers, but they did succeed in negotiating an accord to end the conflict. With that, the two set to work to steer the Chōshū domain toward a policy supporting Japan's opening and bolstered the effort to bring the shogunate down.

After the Meiji Restoration, Itō and Inoue served as councillors and held a succession of other posts in the new government. Itō was one of the lead ambassadors on the Iwakura Mission, for example. While the mission was away, Inoue embarked on innovative policies, including land tax reform and the promotion of new industries under the guidance of the Ministry of Finance, following the abolition of domains and creation of prefectures.

Inoue staked out a leading position in the camp favoring a priority on domestic security, but clashes with the government's more conservative faction prompted him to resign from the Ministry of Finance along with Shibusawa Eiichi in 1873.

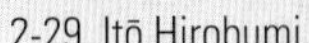

2-29. Itō Hirobumi

2-30. Inoue Kaoru

The Designers of Japan's Constitutional State

After returning from the Iwakura Mission, Itō joined Ōkubo Toshimichi in opposing Saigō Takamori's *seikanron* push to invade Korea. What Itō saw as most vital to Japan's success was not military conquest but rather new industrial growth, a vision he used to chart a path toward establishing Japan as an industry-driven nation. Ōkubo's assassination in 1878 left a chasm in the leadership structure, and Itō—just thirty-six at the time—became Ōkubo's de facto heir. Itō thus took over as home minister, with close friend Inoue and fellow "Chōshū group" stalwart Yamagata Aritomo providing political support.

A few years later, Itō joined others in ousting Ōkuma

House yet again, but around this time the First Sino-Japanese War broke out and the situation changed completely.

Meanwhile, in the talks taking place in London, Japan's proposal of granting foreigners the same treatment as Japanese in the country's interior, along with the authority to establish laws restricting the rights of those foreigners when necessary, was accepted. However, the right of foreigners to own property was denied to the end. On the matter of tariff autonomy, the United Kingdom called for refined sugar to be included among the items subject to the agreed tariff. Japan, constrained by its war with China and wanting to hasten the signing of the treaty, agreed to the proposal conditionally. The Anglo-Japanese Treaty of Commerce and Navigation was finally signed in July 1894, and would come into force five years later. In addition, since the new treaty included a clause on most-favored-nation treatment, new treaties would also be concluded with the United States, Italy, Russia, and Germany. This series of so-called Mutsu

Shigenobu from power via the *Meiji jūyo-nen no seihen* (Political Upheaval of 1881). Ōkuma had been urging the creation of a parliamentary body as quickly as possible, a stance that irked many in the political sphere, along with other factors that spurred a revolt. Itō then convinced Emperor Meiji to declare that a parliamentary government would be established in ten years' time. With a timeframe now in place, Itō traveled to Europe with Itō Miyoji and Saionji Kinmochi to study constitutions. The experience proved significant. Though he had initially envisioned Japan's constitution following the British model, Itō's exposure to the ideas of Lorenz von Stein opened his eyes to what he saw as a more apt approach: building a constitutional model that would align with Japan's historical experience around the concept of constitutional monarchy, a monarchical sovereignty checked by legislative and executive branches.

Itō eventually became Japan's first prime minister upon the introduction of the cabinet system in 1885 and began pouring his energies into establishing the country's new constitutional system. In August 1892, he formed his second cabinet, naming Mutsu Munemitsu foreign minister and making Inoue his deputy prime minister. Having solidified his administration, he then set out to cement Japan's constitutional monarchy and bring the ongoing treaty revisions to a conclusion. That November, however, Itō suffered an injury in a carriage accident, and Inoue (home minister and deputy to Itō) stepped in to serve as the interim prime minister until Itō eventually returned in February 1893. In the events surrounding the Sino-Japanese War, Itō sent Home Minister Inoue to Korea to work on internal reforms—which partially formed the basis of Japan's justification for war—and also backed Mutsu's concessionary stances in negotiating postwar terms of peace and the Tripartite Intervention.

The Anglo-Japanese Alliance (1902) was another dynamic in play during Itō's time. While the Katsura Tarō cabinet eagerly attempted to forge a pact with the United Kingdom, Itō anticipated that an alliance would encounter substantial challenges and thus advocated a *Nichi-Ro kyōshō* (Russo-Japanese agreement) as a complementary measure.

Itō's negotiations with Russia may have been unsuccessful, but they gave impetus to the formation of the Anglo-Japanese Alliance. In January 1898, Itō put together his third cabinet as prime minister with the help of Inoue (tapped this time as minister of finance) and others—but ended up dissolving it less than six months later. He later embarked on a long tour through Europe and, after the Russo-Japanese War, began to work toward eliminating the military regime in Manchuria and guiding Korea through a modernization of its domestic affairs in the official capacity of resident-general. Before he could fulfill these visions, however, he was assassinated by Korean nationalist An Junggeun in 1909.

Itō handled the bulk of the key diplomatic issues facing the Meiji government, centering his focus on international cooperation and keeping a careful watch on Russia's moves. While he often found himself a target of criticism from hard-liners in the Diet and the court of public opinion, Itō remained steadfast on policy. He was a solid fixture in the upper echelons of Japanese government for a full twenty years, from the assassination of Ōkubo to the dissolution of his third cabinet in 1898. That political longevity was a product of Itō's cheerful, lively character, one that allowed him to win the confidence of Emperor Meiji and coordinate with the Satsuma political heavyweights.

"Western Principles" and Japan's Korea Policy

After making his way back into government in 1875, Inoue Kaoru became foreign minister in 1879 and remained in that position for eight years. During this time, he worked to forge an international agreement in which the Japanese interior

treaties would also come into force in 1899, leading to the complete restoration of Japan's legal rights.

(6) The Komura Years (1908–11): Complete Restoration of Tariff Autonomy

The Mutsu treaties did not obtain complete tariff autonomy for Japan. The agreed maximum tariff rates of around 15 percent remained in place for many essential imports such as wool and steel. Since the agreed tariff rate was a specific tax, even if Japan was forced to pay higher import prices due to rising costs, it could not increase the amount of import duties. It also offered no protection to Japanese industries that were still on a growth curve. Accordingly, with the Mutsu treaties coming to term in April 1910, then foreign minister Komura Jutarō submitted a new treaty proposal to the United Kingdom. Komura argued that if, while would be opened to foreigners in exchange for the revocation of consular jurisdiction, which was one of the core components of the treaty revisions.

German doctor Erwin von Bälz wrote in his diary that Inoue had "flawlessly assimilated himself to European culture and the European mode of life." Inoue often used the term *Taisei-shugi*, or the "principles of the 'West,'" which referred to the essence of Western Europe. Based on the premise that the treaty revisions rested on a complete adoption of Western principles as a model of civilization, Inoue saw the socializing at the Rokumeikan, into which he had poured all his energy, as the manifestation of this. In his determination to immerse Japan in the ways of Western civilization, Inoue pursued what he called "*kokumin kyōka*" (educating the people) by working to popularize novels, plays, art, music, and *rōmaji* (Japanese written in Latin script), encouraging citizens to wear Western clothing and eat meat, and driving various social reforms.

In his time as foreign minister (through 1887), Inoue not only had to tackle treaty revisions but also needed to deal with instability on the Korean Peninsula. Evading conflict with Qing China after the 1884 Gapsin Coup, Inoue went to Korea in person to negotiate and sign the Treaty of Hanseong (Japan-Korea Treaty of 1885). In October 1894, he resigned as home minister to become Japan's envoy to Korea at Itō's behest and begin modernizing Korea through an overhaul of its domestic administration. Inoue shared Itō's basic outlook on handling Korea. Instead of controlling the country, the two believed that helping Korea stand on its own as an independent nation would benefit both Japan and Qing China. Breaking Korea out of Qing China's sphere of influence for a more stable, independent existence was Inoue's chief aim.

Although Inoue was the only elder statesman in the "domain clique" (*hanbatsu*) who never had the opportunity to form a cabinet, he exhibited no fixation on becoming prime minister. Rather, he spent most of his political career in prominent supporting roles. After Ōkubo's assassination, he served in multiple councillor positions (industry minister and foreign minister), received appointments in three of Itō's four cabinets, and continued to provide Itō with support during Japan's treaty revisions and efforts on Korean issues. Inoue's diplomatic initiatives often went unfinished, but judging his career on his personal achievements alone would be misguided. Inoue's true value lay in his unwavering support of his close, like-minded friend Itō, who relied on him for valuable advice in handling affairs both domestic and international.

Inoue also possessed shrewd financial acumen that allowed him to thrive as vice-finance minister and finance minister proper. His influence remained intact as he transitioned into the role of a *genrō* (retired elder statesman), too. Making use of his connections in the business world, especially in the Mitsui zaibatsu, Inoue helped negotiate foreign loans during the Russo-Japanese War and paved economic inroads for Japanese enterprises into Manchuria and Korea. Inoue also saw China as a fertile business opportunity for Japan after the eruption of World War I, which he called the "divine aid of the new Taishō era," and helped shape the terms of the Twenty-One Demands. He was, however, critical of the strong-arming tactics of then foreign minister Katō Takaaki.

On a personal level, Inoue was gregarious, talkative, and obliging—but his assertive nature and quick temper were in sharp contrast to the more patient and accommodating Itō; these traits may have hurt his chances to ascend to the premiership.

abiding by fixed tax rates as a general rule, Japan could exceptionally use reciprocal tariffs, then it would have no choice but to grant the United Kingdom, as a believer in free trade, most-favored-nation treatment. The UK requested that, since they were offering very generous terms for Japanese goods based on the principle of free trade, Japan should also set agreed tariff rates for staple exports from the United Kingdom.

Japan countered that an agreed tariff-based treaty with a nation like the United Kingdom that stressed free trade would force it into a continuation of a unilateral treaty, and would not achieve the objective of restoring tariff autonomy, and negotiations came to a temporary halt. However, given the fears that any collapse in negotiations would have a negative effect on the workings of an Anglo-Japanese alliance, both sides became more conciliatory in their positions. Agreement was reached that tariff rates would be set for some imports from the

United Kingdom to Japan, and no tariffs would be imposed on certain Japanese exports to the United Kingdom. Thus, by assigning obligations to both parties, Japan achieved tariff autonomy. The new Anglo-Japanese Treaty of Commerce and Navigation was signed in April 1911. This was followed in succession by the signing of new commercial and navigation treaties with France, Germany, and the United States. Hence, nearly half a century after the signing of the Japan-United States Treaty of Amity and Commerce, Japan finally managed to do away with all of the unequal treaties.

The Real Significance of Treaty Revision

The issue of treaty revision has been understood as one in which Japan made an effort as a whole to achieve equal standing with the Western powers by revising the unequal treaties that had been concluded in the late days of the bakufu and early days of the Meiji Restoration, infringing on Japanese sovereignty and putting it in an unfavorable position. From today's perspective, the Ansei Five-Power Treaties certainly contained three points of unfairness: unilateral consular jurisdiction, most-favored-nation treatment, and the agreed tariffs. However, viewed in terms of the realities of the 1860s and 1870s, is it appropriate to regard the treaty structure they set up as "unfair" in its entirety?

Why were these unequal treaties necessary in the first place? The most important objectives of these treaties were to establish free trade and obtain the maximum amount of profit out of such trade. The Western powers of the nineteenth century were seeking to create a global capitalist market with free trade as its pillar, and the treaties were a product of their effort to impose this vision on the countries of Asia, including Japan. The United Kingdom's minister to Japan, Rutherford Alcock, said, "We are constantly searching for the next new market. . . . Our first step is to close in on the market that [these countries] offer by means of treaty." This thinking was used to justify the imposition of such treaties by force. The treaties in such situations would have to be unequal ones. This was because it was believed that the legal systems and social order of East Asian countries—which were not seen as "civilized nations" in the European sense—would be impediments to the cross-border movement of people, goods, and capital from "civilized" nations. The unequal treaties would compensate for this. Above all, the consular jurisdiction system was introduced as a mechanism for guaranteeing the security of life, property, and business dealings of their citizens and eliminating friction under existing local legal systems.

Taking consular jurisdiction as an example, certainly the conditions that Japan accepted under the Ansei Five-Power Treaties (with the exception of the treaty with Russia) imposed unilateral obligations on Japan. Should some conflict arise on Japanese soil between a local and a foreigner, the foreigner who had been accused by the local would be judged by the consul of the foreigner's country, based on that country's laws. In contrast, a Japanese person accused of some transgression in a Western country would have to submit to that country's courts. The Japanese consul in that country would have no jurisdiction over the matter. Thus, consular jurisdiction was clearly unequal, except in the sense that, when it came to jurisdiction for matters on Japanese soil, foreign defendants would be judged by their country's consul and Japanese defendants would be judged in Japanese courts. At the time the treaties were signed, it was unimaginable that any Japanese who were not government officials would travel abroad. Accordingly, the officials who signed these treaties had no sense that consular jurisdiction was unfavorable to the Japanese.

Nonetheless, touting the principles of "friendly foreign relations" and "holding out against the world," the Meiji government sought, in international recognition, a basis for its own existence as a state, aiming for Japan to become a nation that could stand shoulder-to-shoulder with its Western counterparts. It viewed treaty revision as a national issue that went beyond the problem of the advantages and disadvantages in the treaties themselves.

Enacting the Constitution of Imperial Japan

Among the various reforms undertaken as part of the Meiji Restoration, the one that clearly laid the foundations for subsequent political and economic modernization was the abolition of the domains and establishment of prefectures (1871). Fukuzawa Yukichi argued, "Abolishing the domains in a single stroke is what will put the entire nation on an equal footing. It will give government ordinances a new standing, and bring uniformity to all national affairs, whether they be military or financial concerns." The imperial edict that established the prefectures touted "hold out against the world"—in the sense of the nation being its own master in international society—as the national objective. The matter of being able to "hold out against the world" that had been a restoration-era concern—along with the concept of public discourse as taken up in the Charter Oath of Five Articles—would finally be achieved two decades later with treaty revision and the enactment of a constitution.

The Constitution of Imperial Japan promulgated in 1889 was distinguished by its powerful prerogatives for the emperor. Going from the principle that a constitutional system lies in its stipulation, by law, of the rights of the rulers and the ruled, this document did not adequately protect the rights of the ruled. The Japanese people were given rights for the first time by this constitution, and these were within the bounds of law. Meanwhile, the constitution did not offer a framework by which the emperor could directly wield those powerful prerogatives; that ability was left in the hands of state institutions and divided among them. All state institutions were seen as being linked directly to the emperor, and the function they performed was to assist (counsel) him. Above all, the supreme command maintained a high degree of independence when it came to matters of "command prerogatives" regarding campaign planning and chain of command. This was an institutional factor that would upset uniform administration of state affairs from the inside.

Putting in place this kind of high-level separation of power in line with the ideals of the restoration meant avoiding the reappearance of absolute power such as the bakufu's, and a parliamentary cabinet system that would underpin the Diet would in turn serve to eliminate party politics. For Itō Hirobumi and the other founders of the Meiji Restoration (the elder statesmen), it was still too soon for Japan to have British-style party politics like those that Ōkuma Shigenobu advocated. It took thirty years from the 1890 establishment of the Imperial Diet for political parties to come to play a central role in running the country in place of the "domain clique" (*hanbatsu*).

CHAPTER 3

The Mutsu and Komura Periods:
The First Sino-Japanese War and the Russo-Japanese War

3-1. *Declaration of War with Russia* (painting by Yoshida Shigeru)

TIMELINE

1894 (Meiji 27)

June 16	Foreign Minister Mutsu proposes to Chinese government that Japan and China work together to reform Korean domestic politics
July 16	Signing of Anglo-Japanese Treaty of Commerce and Navigation (abolishes consular jurisdiction, ending extraterritoriality)
July 23	Japanese army captures Korean royal palace, disarms forces there
July 25	Japanese fleet attacks Chinese warships near Pungdo Island off Korea's western coast (Battle of Pungdo)
August 1	Both Japan and China declare war

1895 (Meiji 28)

January 14	Japan decides to incorporate Senkaku (Diaoyu) Islands into Okinawa Prefecture
April 17	Japan and China sign peace treaty (Treaty of Shimonoseki)
April 23	Russia, France, and Germany stage the Tripartite Intervention
May 10	Japan decides to return Liaodong Peninsula to China
June 8	Signing of Treaty on Commerce and Navigation between Japan and Russia
October 8	Resident minister to Korea Miura Gorō and his cohorts stage coup in support of the Daewongun; Queen Myeongseong assassinated (Eulmi Incident)

1896 (Meiji 29)

May 14	Komura-Weber Memorandum over Korea signed
June 3	Signing of Sino-Russian (Li-Lobanov) secret treaty
June 9	Yamagata-Lobanov Agreement on Korea reached
July 21	Signing of Japan-China Treaty of Commerce and Navigation
September 18	Second Matsukata cabinet formed

1897 (Meiji 30)

June 16	US annexes Hawaii (Treaty of Annexation signed)

1898 (Meiji 31)

January 12	Third Itō cabinet formed
March 6	Germany leases Kiautschou (Jiaozhou) Bay on China's Shandong Peninsula (returned to China in 1922)
March 27	Russia leases Lushun (Port Arthur) and Dalian from China; also acquires rights to construct railroad to South Manchuria
April 22/24	Japan and China exchange notes on the non-concession of Fujian Province (Fujian Non-Alienation Agreement)
April 25	Spanish-American War breaks out
April 25	Japan and Russia sign Nishi-Rosen Agreement concerning Korea in Tokyo
June 11	China's Emperor Guangxu issues proclamation on law reform and self-strengthening (Hundred Days' Reform, through September 23)
June 30	First Ōkuma Shigenobu cabinet (Ōkuma-Itagaki cabinet) formed
November 8	Second Yamagata cabinet formed

1899 (Meiji 32)

May 18–July 29	First Hague International Peace Conference held
September 6	US issues Open Door Note (declaration by Secretary of State John Hay)
November 16	France leases Guangzhou (Canton) Bay from China (returned to China in 1946)

1900 (Meiji 33)

May 19	*Gunbu daijin geneki bukan-sei* (system allowing only active-duty officers to serve as army and navy ministers in the cabinet) enacted
June 15	In response to China's Boxer rebels encircling foreign legations in the country, Japan decides to dispatch military force (Boxer Rebellion)
June 21	Empress Dowager Cixi declares war on Western powers
August 14	Japanese army enters Beijing's fortifications as member of Eight-Nation coalition
October 19	Fourth Itō cabinet formed

1901 (Meiji 34)

June 2	First Katsura Tarō cabinet formed
September 7	Boxer Protocol (Peking Protocol) signed with Chinese government

1902 (Meiji 35)

January 30 First Anglo-Japanese Alliance signed in London

1903 (Meiji 36)

June 23 Imperial Council decides to negotiate with Russia regarding Manchurian and Korean issues

1904 (Meiji 37)

February 4 Imperial Council ends talks with Russia and decides to declare war

February 10 Declaration of war issued to Russia (start of Russo-Japanese War)

February 23 Signing of the Protocol between Japan and Korea

August 22 Signing of Japan-Korea Agreement

1905 (Meiji 38)

January 1 Russian forces at Lushun surrender

January 22 "Bloody Sunday" incident occurs in Russia

March 1 Battle of Mukden (through March 10)

May 27–28 Battle of Tsushima

June 9 US president Theodore Roosevelt urges Japan and Russia to make peace

July 29 Katsura-Taft Agreement

August 10 Portsmouth Peace Conference (through September 5)

August 12 Signing of Second Anglo-Japanese Alliance

September 5 Signing of Japan-Russia Treaty of Peace (Treaty of Portsmouth)

September 5 Hibiya Incendiary incident (Hibiya Riots) occurs

November 17 Signing of Japan-Korea Treaty of 1905

December 22 Treaty and Additional Agreement between Japan and China Relating to Manchuria signed

1906 (Meiji 39)

January 7 First Saionji Kinmochi cabinet formed

May 22 Conference held to discuss the Manchuria issue

November 26 South Manchuria Railway Company ("Mantetsu") founded

1907 (Meiji 40)

April 19 "Imperial Defense Policy," and similar guidelines enacted

June 10 Signing of Franco-Japanese Treaty of 1907

June 15 Second Hague International Peace Conference held (through October 18)

June 25 Hague secret emissary affair (arrival of emissaries)

July 24 Signing of Japan-Korea Agreement of 1907

July 30 Signing of Russo-Japanese Agreement of 1907

November 16 Gentlemen's Agreement of 1907 between Japan and US reached (eleven notes exchanged until March 25, 1908)

1908 (Meiji 41)

February 5 *Tatsumaru* Incident (China seizes Japanese vessel *Dai-ni Tatsumaru* on grounds of arms smuggling; movement arises locally to boycott Japanese goods)

May 5 Signing of Convention of Arbitration of May 5, 1908, between Japan and the US

July 14 Second Katsura cabinet formed

September 10 Documents delineating the Russo-Japanese border on Karafuto (Sakhalin) promulgated

November 30 Signing of Root-Takahira Agreement (exchange of notes)

1909 (Meiji 42)

September 4 Signing of five-item accord on Manchuria between Japan and China

October 2 US and UK sign agreement with Chinese government to build Chinchow–Aigun (Jinzhou–Aihun) railroad

October 26 Itō Hirobumi assassinated in Harbin

November 6 US secretary of state Philander C. Knox proposes to UK to make the Manchurian Railroad neutral territory (Japan and Russia signal their disapproval in January 1910)

1910 (Meiji 43)

July 4 Signing of Russo-Japanese Agreement of 1910

August 22 Signing of Japan-Korea Treaty of 1910 (Japan-Korea Annexation Treaty)

November 10 UK, France, Russia, and Germany put together alliance to provide railway infrastructure loan to China as equal participants

1911 (Meiji 44)

February 21 Japan and US sign new Treaty of Commerce and Navigation (first to confirm tariff autonomy for Japan)

July 13 Signing of Third Anglo-Japanese Alliance

August 30 Second Saionji Kinmochi cabinet formed

October 10 Chinese (Xinhai) Revolution (Wuchang Uprising) breaks out

1 Mutsu Diplomacy and the First Sino-Japanese War

The Donghak Peasant Revolution and the Start of Hostilities between Japan and China

As the 1890s began, both modernization and anti-Chinese policies in Korea met with crucial setbacks due to the country's financial difficulties, and the impoverishment of the countryside grew all the more severe. Owing to this domestic situation, in spring 1894 the peasant rebellion that had erupted in Jeolla Province began to spread. It had spread throughout all provinces by the end of May, and the Korean monarch asked China to send in troops. Known as the Donghak Peasant Revolution, this uprising would produce an enormous change in Sino-Japanese relations, since both nations had withdrawn the troops they had stationed in Korea after the agreement reached at the Tianjin Convention in 1885.

On June 2, 1894, the second Itō Hirobumi–led cabinet decided that—based on the counsel of Foreign Minister Mutsu Munemitsu and under the Japan-Korea Treaty of 1882—Japan would dispatch troops to Korea to protect its legation and citizens residing in the country. On June 5, an imperial decision led to the establishment of a wartime Imperial General Headquarters to oversee total control of Japan's land and sea forces. The headquarters was situated in Tokyo's Miyakezaka district, though in September it was transferred to Hiroshima. In any event, with this move the armed forces were put on a wartime footing. On June 7, Japan and China notified one another in accordance with the Tianjin Convention that they were dispatching troops. The army landed part of its Fifth Division at Incheon, and the Qing government likewise landed some of its forces at Asan.

However, when envoy Ōtori Keisuke arrived in Hanseong at the head of an army on June 10, he learned that that capital was at peace. The peasant forces that had been at war with the government troops had heard that Japan and China were dispatching their own expeditions and so they withdrew. The Chinese forces stayed in Asan and did not advance to Hanseong. Naturally, the Chinese resident-general Yuan Shikai—dispatched by the Qing government—and the Korean government asked Japan to withdraw its troops. Ōtori hastily telegraphed Mutsu to say that the dispatch of reinforcements was unjustifiable, but the first expeditionary force was already on its way and could not be stopped.

On June 16, Itō's cabinet decided it would propose that Japan and China work jointly to reform Korea's domestic political situation, and in the event that China did not agree, Japan would station troops there on its own. One of the Japanese government's goals was to keep Russia from making its own moves into Korea. Foreign Minister Mutsu made the request to the Qing government. However, China refused on the basis that the domestic unrest had already been quelled and Korean

3-2. "News from Korea: An Account of a Skirmish" (woodblock print by unknown artist)

domestic affairs were a matter for Korea to handle for itself. China having already withdrawn its own forces, Japan should also be withdrawing its troops to comply with the Tianjin Convention.

On June 23, the Japanese government sent a note breaking off talks on the grounds that Japan would handle domestic reforms in Korea itself. This meant that a military confrontation was now just a matter of time. On July 20, Minister Ōtori issued a final note that demanded, among other things, the dissolution of China's suzerain relationship with Korea. The note set July 23 as the deadline for a response. The Japanese army then went on to seize the royal palace. They toppled the Min clan regime and set up a new regime under the Daewongun in its place. The Japanese army justified itself by saying it had no choice but to seize the royal palace on the grounds that Korean forces had fired on them. However, in fact it was an act that Minister Ōtori had carefully planned in advance with the army. On July 25, Japanese and Chinese ships engaged with one another near Pungdo Island off Korea's western coast, and Japan followed up by issuing a declaration of war to the Qing government on August 1.

During the final stage of negotiations between Japan and Korea, the Koreans pointed out that Japan had lost its justification for dispatching troops, as the Donghak Peasant Revolution had already been quelled. Accordingly, the line of reasoning presented in the imperial rescript declaring war was that China was obstructing Korea's efforts at internal reform aimed at achieving Korean

Mutsu Munemitsu (1844–97)

In *Hikawa seiwa* (Quiet talks at the Hikawa mansion), Katsu Kaishū praised Mutsu Munemitsu as "talented"—but also touched on Mutsu's potentially volatile nature. "Mutsu is the type of man who will give his all if he feels that his superior is competent," Katsu wrote, "but will become a malcontent firebrand and stamp out any ruler who does not measure up." Luckily, Itō Hirobumi played the "superior" role to perfection. In fact, Mutsu might never have found the success he did if not for Itō.

Born to a feudal retainer of Wakayama domain, Mutsu broke from his domain and headed for Edo when his father lost his official position. He then quickly relocated to Kyoto, where he studied at Katsu Kaishū's naval academy and impressed Sakamoto Ryōma with his abilities. That helped him land a position in Sakamoto's Kaientai (a private navy and trading company). After the Battle of Toba-Fushimi, Mutsu stole away to Osaka, met with British envoy Parkes to discuss Japan's post-Restoration diplomatic strategy, and then reported the details to Iwakura Tomomi. "There is no way forward but furthering the opening of the country," Mutsu explained. Iwakura agreed; to facilitate progress on that front, he named Mutsu a *goyōgakari* (official) in the Foreign Affairs Office. Shortly after assuming his post, Mutsu accompanied Higashikuze Michitomi to brief the foreign diplomatic corps on the circumstances surrounding the restoration of imperial rule, and pledged that the new government would maintain the bakufu's diplomatic ties.

3-3. Mutsu Munemitsu

Mutsu continued a steady climb up the ranks as an "enlightened bureaucrat" (*kaimei-ha kanryō*) and eventually began crossing paths with Itō Hirobumi, Inoue Kaoru, and Kido Takayoshi. That trajectory veered off course, however, when Mutsu was arrested on suspicion of plotting to overthrow the government and was imprisoned for crimes against the state. He received amnesty and left prison in 1883, after which Itō and Inoue arranged for him to pursue studies in Europe. In addition to studying international law and British politics in London, Mutsu also attended lectures by Lorenz von Stein in Vienna on a referral from Itō and earned the admiration of Saionji Kinmochi (then Japan's envoy in Austria) for his dogged academic drive. After returning to Japan, Mutsu headed up the preparations for the effort to revise Japan's treaties with foreign powers in 1886, and became Japan's resident envoy to the United States in 1888. Working on orders from Foreign Minister Ōkuma Shigenobu, he succeeded in securing the Treaty of Friendship and Commerce between Mexico and Japan, an independence. Until the outbreak of hostilities, the argument laid out by the Japanese government for keeping Korea neutral and maintaining its independence, based on cooperation with China and a multi-national guarantee, had not been mere posturing. Japanese newspapers, too, noticeably adopted a discourse that contrasted Japan's position with China's, presenting Japan as promoting reform and China as rejecting it.

When it came to public opinion serving as a justification for going to war, the story of Kim Okgyun also had considerable repercussions for how it symbolized Chinese "barbarism." Kim had fled to Japan after the 1884 coup and was living in Tokyo. However, in late March 1894 he was lured to Shanghai, where he was murdered by an assassin sent by the Min clan regime. His body was then sent to Korea aboard a Chinese warship. Kim's supporter Fukuzawa Yukichi argued that the significance of the war was that it would be a "conflict between those working to promote the progress of civilization and enlightenment and those trying to block such progress."

On the other hand, Foreign Minister Mutsu levelheadedly noted in his memoir *Kenkenroku* that "whether the issue is reforming Korean domestic politics or China's suzerain authority over Korea, if we go back to the start, in the final analysis this war is the product of a struggle for power between Japan and China that is being settled in Korea." For the players in this warmongering diplomacy, war was just part of the struggle for power within the imperialistic nation.

---

equal treaty stipulating that Japan would open its interior to Mexicans in exchange for the elimination of consular jurisdiction.

Mutsu returned to Japan in 1890 and ran in the first election for Japan's new House of Representatives, winning a seat representing Wakayama. Yamagata Aritomo picked Mutsu to serve in his first cabinet as minister of agriculture and commerce, but the appointment hit a snag when Yamagata submitted his cabinet petition for imperial approval—the emperor balked when he learned that Mutsu had been imprisoned. Yamagata pushed for his man, saying that Mutsu had paid his dues and making a clear, urgent case for his selection. "Mutsu will likely align himself with the opposition and obstruct the government unless we place him in the cabinet," Yamagata argued. "Making him a cabinet member and using his skills for our own purposes is actually in the better interests of the country." The appeal was successful, and Mutsu became the first cabinet official to hold a seat in the House of Representatives. As minister of agriculture and commerce, Mutsu took note of a promising talent: Hara Takashi, then secretariat director at the Ministry of Agriculture and Commerce, who would go on to become Japan's prime minister in 1918. "I was never satisfied," the argument-loving Mutsu said, "with people who lacked the backbone to voice their own opinions without reserve and engage in debate." In that sense, Hara certainly met Mutsu's approval.

In 1892, Itō Hirobumi assembled his second cabinet and tapped Mutsu to serve as foreign minister—a position that the latter had long aspired to. Tasked with spearheading treaty revisions in his new leadership post, Mutsu named Hayashi Tadasu his deputy and Hara the head of the Bureau of Trade; together, they made a formidable team capable of achieving Itō's treaty objectives. Mutsu proceeded to stand with Itō, weathering attacks from the diplomatic hard-liners in the Diet, and restored consular jurisdiction. Although he was unable to prevent the Sino-Japanese War from breaking out, Mutsu strove to contain the conflict and keep the other countries out of the fray by seeking a quick peace and immediately acceding to the Tripartite Intervention. Mutsu's health began to deteriorate around the time of the peace negotiations, however. As he underwent treatment in Ōiso, he dictated an account of Japanese diplomacy spanning his experiences from the onset of the First Sino-Japanese War to the Tripartite Intervention. The resulting volume, *Kenkenroku* (A diplomatic record of the Sino-Japanese War), would not see the light of day until thirty-four years later. In 1907, a bronze statue of Mutsu was installed at the Ministry of Foreign Affairs. The memorial took shape at the urging of Hara, who remembered Mutsu as the man whose work transformed Japanese diplomacy and "put Japan on equal footing with its counterparts across the globe."

The First Sino-Japanese War and the Treaty of Shimonoseki

When hostilities broke out between Japan and China, the diplomatic hard-liners within the Diet who had been critical of the government on the issue of treaty revision shifted their position to one that supported the government. They saw this as a "crusade" aimed at helping Japan's neighbor Korea. At the seventh session of the Imperial Diet held in Hiroshima, an appeal for enormous temporary military expenditures and war bonds was unanimously approved in no time at all. The populace likewise enthusiastically supported going to war, and they purchased war bonds in droves.

For its war with China, Japan's strategy was to go north along the Korean Peninsula by land. The Third Division, under the Yamagata Aritomo–led First Army Corps, landed at Incheon, and the September 1894 Battle of Pyongyang resulted in an overwhelming victory for the Japanese army in the conflict on the Korean Peninsula. The Battle of the Yellow Sea in the same year saw Japan's Combined Fleet challenge China's Beiyang Fleet to a decisive naval clash. The Japanese fleet drove its Chinese foes from Lushun (Port Arthur) to Weihaiwei and almost totally wiped them out.

The Japanese army then crossed the Yalu River to invade Manchuria. In November, the newly organized Second Army Corps (under Ōyama Iwao) stormed the fortifications at Lushun forcing a surrender. At the same time, following a US offer to mediate peace talks, after Lushun fell, Japan pushed forward with preparations to conduct a decisive battle at Zhili, near Beijing, aiming for a more favorable military position in negotiations. However, before Japan could follow through, the Qing government made moves toward peace. In early 1895, Li Hongzhang came to Japan as a plenipotentiary and met with Itō and Mutsu to negotiate. The Japanese side wanted to conclude a peace agreement as quickly as possible so that the Western powers would not have a chance to intervene. This resulted in the two sides signing the Treaty of Shimonoseki in April 1895.

The first article of the treaty clearly stated, "China recognizes definitively the full and complete independence and autonomy of Korea." This was significant for the recognition by an international treaty that Korea was not a tributary state of China, and also that the traditional "Sino-barbarian distinction" (that is, the "Hua-Yi" distinction, as the Chinese tributary system was known) had collapsed. Korea had been regarded as an independent state in the 1876 Japan-Korea Treaty of Amity, but it still held the status of tributary state in its relations

3-4. "The Occupation of Port Arthur by Japanese Forces" (woodblock print by Yōsai Nobukazu)

3-5. "The Japanese Naval Attack on Weihaiwei" (woodblock print by unknown artist)

3-6. *Peace Conference at Shimonoseki* (painting by Nagatochi Hideta)

with China. Separating itself from its status as a tributary state opened the door for the establishment, in 1897, of the "Empire of Korea."

The second and third articles of the Treaty of Shimonoseki laid out the fact that Taiwan and the Liaodong Peninsula would now be ceded to Japan. For Japan, annexation of Taiwan marked its first acquisition of an overseas territory (i.e., a colony). There was considerable debate in Japan over the merits and demerits of annexing Taiwan, but arguments highlighting the resources Japan could obtain ultimately carried the day. Japan created the position of governor-general for Taiwan, and appointed Kabayama Sukenori—the admiral who had fought so valiantly in the Battle of the Yalu River—to be the first holder of that post. However, shortly after Japan and China made peace, the Qing bureaucrats who had been administering Taiwan fomented a war of resistance that drew in civilians on the island. In May 1895, the Republic of Formosa, presided over by former Qing governor-general Tang Jingsong, issued a declaration of independence. The Qing officials still present in Taiwan subsequently returned to the Chinese mainland, but resistance by people from Taiwan continued.

Article 4 of the Treaty of Shimonoseki called for China to pay an enormous sum in indemnities amounting to 200 million taels (roughly 7.5 million kilograms) of silver. These funds served as financial resources for Japanese infrastructure projects, such as the construction of state-operated ironworks. Some would also eventually provide the capital for the 1897 shift to the gold standard, which had long been called for by Finance Minister Matsukata Masayoshi as evidence that Japan was a leading nation.

The subsequent articles are supplementary, but nonetheless important. First, they established a two-year grace period for inhabitants of the ceded territories (Taiwan and the Liaodong Peninsula) to dispose of their assets, and guaranteed them the right to move to another country if they desired. In accordance with international practice, this granted residents of a colonized region the option to choose their nationality.

In any case, the clause under the Treaty of Shimonoseki that discussed the "Treaties, Conventions, and Regulations now subsisting between China and the European Powers" incorporated the provision that Japan and China would conclude a new treaty. It made it possible for Japan to arrange a treaty with Qing China on equal terms with treaties made with the West. As a result, in place of the equal Japan-China Friendship and Trade Treaty signed in 1871, in 1896 the two parties signed the Japan-China Treaty of Commerce and Navigation, which was more favorable to Japan. With this, Japan obtained treatment on par with the Western powers with respect to the exercise of unilateral consular jurisdiction, preferential treatment on taxation measures, and the opening for trade of

Chinese cities including Chongqing, Shashi, and Suzhou. This preserved free trade within China and freedom of employment within open ports for Japanese. By getting its own treaties revised and then signing an unequal treaty with China, Japan drew closer to becoming one of the powers that dominated East Asia. The abolition or revision of the unequal treaties it had been forced to sign then became the main objective of the Republic of China as it sought to restore its sovereign rights.

The Tripartite Intervention and Mutsu's Decision

Japan's unexpected victory drew the attention of the Western powers. However, China made it evident that it did not want their mediation, and so until the war's end the powers refrained from any vigorous intervention or intercession. In revising its treaty with Japan in July 1894, on the eve of the conflict, the United Kingdom restored to Japan its legal rights through the new Anglo-Japanese Treaty of Commerce and Navigation, signaling its tacit acceptance of the war to come.

For Russia, maintaining the status quo in Korea was fundamental to preserving the security of its Far East (Primorsky Krai). Accordingly, even after both Japan and China had dispatched their troops, its policy was to partner with the other powers to encourage the two countries to cease hostilities as soon as possible. Furthermore, when the Japanese army crossed over from Korea into Manchuria, Russia worked hard to secure cooperation from the United Kingdom, France, and Germany in preparing for the demands that Japan would submit for peace negotiations. When Japan offered its peace proposal in early April 1895, Russia encouraged the United Kingdom, France, and Germany to join it in advising Japan to abandon its claims on the Liaodong Peninsula. France and Germany agreed, but the United Kingdom declined, viewing Japan as a more likely candidate than China to serve as a power that could stand up to the expansion of Russian influence in the Far East.

In mid-April, Russian leadership considered whether it should advise Japan to abandon the Liaodong Peninsula without support from the United Kingdom, or if it should recognize Japan's annexation of the peninsula and instead also claim reparations from China and Korea. Eventually, hoping to acquire an advantage in the expected competition to partition China, Russia decided that, even if it had to use military force, Japan should be prevented from occupying the Liaodong Peninsula.

For the Qing government, the status of the Liaodong Peninsula was a question of vital importance. It is said that Li Hongzhang signed the treaty with Japan after he was informed that it would be possible to recover the peninsula through international intervention. As expected, on April 23 the French, German, and Russian envoys to Japan carried out the so-called Tripartite Intervention and pressured the Japanese government to relinquish the Liaodong Peninsula. The Itō cabinet immediately arranged for an Imperial Council to study three possibilities. One, Japan could reject the proposal; two, Japan could call for a conference of the various powers involved; or three, Japan could return the Liaodong Peninsula. The Imperial Council tentatively approved of option two. However, Mutsu—who was on his sickbed and could not attend the conference in person—opined that choosing option two would only lead to another intervention on the part of the Western powers, and instead strongly supported option three. The Itō cabinet quickly decided to follow the Mutsu proposal, and told the Russians, French, and Germans that it would accept their recommendation.

Mutsu to a certain degree had already anticipated international intervention even during the conflict, and had received advance warning from the Germans, among others. However, accepting the Tripartite Intervention was a real predicament for him. Later, he wrote his true feelings in his

Kenkenroku: "I want to believe that anyone under these circumstances would have found that this was the only strategy possible."

The Aftermath of the First Sino-Japanese War: Korea and Russo-Japanese Relations

After war broke out between Japan and Qing China, Japan dispatched Inoue Kaoru to serve as its minister to Korea. He helped to replace the Daewongun with an Enlightenment faction around Park Yeonghyo and Kim Hongjip in an unsuccessful bid to reform Korean domestic politics. Meanwhile, having been excluded from the core of Korean domestic politics, Queen Myeongseong sought to join with Russia to increase her influence and keep Japan contained. Lieutenant General Miura Gorō, who succeeded Inoue as minister, backed the Daewongun and tried to put in place a pro-Japan government. On October 7, 1895, he instigated a coup d'état, using the Japanese security forces and some elements of the Korean army to storm the royal palace. They killed the queen and installed a new government under Kim Hongjip (the Eulmi Incident). Kim's antagonist, King Gojong, asked

Nishi Tokujirō (1847–1912) and Motono Ichirō (1862–1918): The "Russia Experts"

Satsuma-domain native Nishi Tokujirō sailed to Russia in 1870 to further his studies and then went on to Europe, assuming the secretary position at the Japanese legation in France. After returning to Japan, he became the country's Russian envoy in 1886 and helped anchor Japanese diplomacy over a tumultuous ten-year period—one that included the First Sino-Japanese War, the Tripartite Intervention, and the Russo-Japanese War. He then served as foreign minister in the second Matsukata cabinet and the third Itō cabinet, signing the Nishi-Rosen Agreement in 1898 under Itō. In 1899 he received an appointment as Japan's envoy to Qing China. Amid the Boxer Rebellion, which erupted shortly after he took his new post, he worked with Komura Jutarō to protect Japanese citizens and to deal with incidents through a series of multinational negotiations before relinquishing his envoy position to Komura in 1901 and retiring from service.

Nishi's mastery of Russian (in addition to French) gave him a reputation as a "Russia expert" around the Ministry of Foreign Affairs, but he was not the only one. Motono Ichirō, a Saga domain native, was another. The eldest son of Motono Morimichi, who himself had been a junior secretary at the Ministry of Foreign Affairs, Ichirō studied in France at the University of Lyon, where he obtained a doctorate in law. His time at the Ministry of Foreign Affairs started in 1890 with a stint as an official translator—and for much of the remainder of his career, from 1896 to roughly twenty years later, he was posted to Europe. For the lion's share of that time abroad he was in Russia, where he served as ambassador from 1907 to 1916 and helped orchestrate four pacts between Japan and Russia behind the scenes. Motono rose to the position of foreign minister in November 1916 as part of the Terauchi cabinet, but his closeness to the House of Romanov may have affected his judgment to some degree. When the October Revolution began in 1917, Motono underestimated the ensuing spread of Bolshevik power and argued for military intervention against the revolution (the Siberian Expedition). He died just weeks after the Japanese government declared its support for the Siberian Expedition.

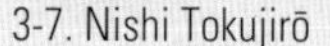

3-7. Nishi Tokujirō

3-8. Motono Ichirō

Russia to send troops, but Russia did not respond, wanting to avoid provoking Japan. Finally, in February 1896, King Gojong left the palace and took refuge in the Russian legation. From there he swept away the Japan-supported administration of Kim Hongjip and established a new pro-Russian regime (the Agwan Pacheon incident, or Gojong's asylum bid). King Gojong returned to the royal palace one year later. Thereupon, he took the title of Emperor Gojong and declared the founding of the Korean Empire. He also deepened the country's ties with Russia by getting the latter to dispatch troops to Korea and appointing Russians as financial advisors to his government. This was a major setback for Japanese influence in Korea, and Russo-Japanese relations also cooled.

To repair the deteriorating Japan-Russia relationship, Japan's envoy to Korea, Komura Jutarō, and Russia's representative, Karl Ivanovich Weber, negotiated a memorandum in May 1896 that led, the following month, to the signing of the Yamagata-Lobanov Agreement. Under instructions from Prime Minister Itō, who was keen to repair ties with Russia, Yamagata Aritomo reached this agreement with Russian foreign minister Alexei Lobanov-Rostovsky while attending the coronation ceremony for Czar Nicholas II. The agreement recognized that Japan and Russia had the same degree of rights in Korea, such as the right to station the same number of troops in the country. Furthermore, with an eye toward leasing Lushun (Port Arthur) and Dalian, in February 1898 Russian envoy to Japan Roman Romanovich Rosen and Japanese foreign minister Nishi Tokujirō concluded the Nishi-Rosen Agreement. This agreement recognized Russia's right to lease Lushun and Dalian, while Russia pledged not to interfere with Japanese commercial and industrial development efforts in Korea. Both parties also promised not to interfere with Korean domestic politics. In addition, Foreign Minister Nishi proposed exchanging Manchuria and Korea—which would have been a way for Japan to secure Korea completely—but the Russian side did not accept. In any case, these agreements were of a provisional nature, and therefore did not provide a stable foundation for Russo-Japanese relations.

2 The Period under Foreign Minister Komura: Changes in China and the Anglo-Japanese Alliance

Conflicts over Partitioning Territory and the Open Door Note

Following China's defeat in the First Sino-Japanese War, it faced merciless encroachment by the Western powers. First, in May 1896, Russia's Lobanov concluded a secret treaty with China's Li Hongzhang, pledging that China and Russia would jointly respond to any Japanese threat. While the agreement in fact lacked teeth, as compensation for signing, Russia acquired the right to build and operate the Chinese Eastern Railway. Work on the railway began the following year. Beginning from a point along the Trans-Siberian Railway, the Chinese Eastern Railway would cut across Chinese territory (Manchuria) and stretch to Russia's maritime provinces. With it, Russia secured a direct route to Vladivostok rather than skirting around the border between Russia and China. Furthermore, in March 1898, Russia used the Tripartite Intervention to force China to lease the Liaodong Peninsula that the latter had just gotten back from

The Open Door Notes and the United States

In the waning years of the nineteenth century, major global powers looked to expand their reach into China. In 1898 and 1899, the likes of Germany, the United Kingdom, France, and Russia sought from the Qing administration the rights to lease harbor cities, build railroads, mine, and pursue a host of other interests that would allow them to establish spheres of influence and interest in the region. The United States, meanwhile, followed a slightly different path. After the American Civil War, which took the US government's attention away from pursuing its interests in Asia, it secured the Philippines as a result of the Spanish-American War and annexed Hawaii (both in 1898), providing a convenient base of operations for entry to Asia. The US government was determined to keep the other colonial superpowers from dividing China among themselves and leaving the United States on the outside looking in. US secretary of state John Hay thus sent the "First Open Door Note" to six major powers (the United Kingdom, Germany, Russia, France, Italy, and Japan) in September and November 1899. The note asked the recipients to guarantee each other equal privileges in matters of trade and sea transport within their respective spheres of influence.The six nations each assented to the proposal on the condition that the other parties would also give their consent. The text of the First Open Door Note communicated its purport in discreet, measured diction, but the motivations behind the note were strong: the United States wanted to stop other powers from dividing up China.

When the events of the Boxer Rebellion eventually prompted the foreign powers to declare war on Qing China in 1900, the division and dissolution of the Chinese state appeared imminent. Sensing that the "open doors" in China might be closing, Hay sent representatives of eleven countries the Second Open Door Note—a unilateral declaration by the United States demonstratively asserting China's territorial and administrative integrity and effectively denying the powers' spheres of influence—in July 1900.

The principles of the open-door policy, equal opportunity, and territorial integrity not only formed the core of American policy on China thereafter but also set the ground rules for any nation looking to make its way into China, as the Nine-Power Treaty (a February 1922 agreement on China) spelled out the principles in official terms. While the Nine-Power Treaty stipulated that the signatories would not assert their "superiority of rights" with respect to commercial or economic development in China, the agreement actually aimed to contain Japan's attempts to expand its influence and establish exclusionary interests. Japan thus found itself facing a diplomatic dilemma, one that lasted through its eventual war with the United States: reconciling its strategy of achieving a dominant position in China with complying with the open-door principles of the Nine-Power Treaty.

Japan. Russia thus obtained the right to build a southern branch of the Chinese Eastern Railway that would connect the major hub city of Harbin to Lushun and Dalian on the peninsula.

To balance out Russia, the United Kingdom leased Weihaiwei from China that July. It had also leased the Kowloon Peninsula and placed it under its governor-general in Hong Kong in June. Germany—using the pretext that German missionaries had been murdered on the Shandong Peninsula—leased Kiautschou (Jiaozhou) Bay and Tsingtao (Qingdao) in March 1898, and won the rights to build the Qingdao-Jinan railway and operate mining concessions along the tracks. France, taking cues from Germany and Russia, leased Guangzhouwan (the Bay of Canton).

Leased territories were different from concessions in that the leasing country had the right to govern the territory, pass legislation, and administer justice. It also had sovereign rights, such as the right to station troops in the territory. Essentially, the leases had the same effect as ceding the territory to the leasing country. However, they had expiration dates. In the event that the lease came to term or the leasing country abandoned the territory, the sovereignty of the lessor country would be completely restored. Accordingly, it was normal to set up a long expiration date on the leases. The leases on all of the aforementioned territories were for ninety-nine years. One could say that the twenty-five-year lease that Russia had on Liaodong Peninsula was extremely unusual, but it

3-9. The Peking Protocol

seems that Russia hurried getting the lease to forestall the United Kingdom, which had set its sights on Lushun.

In March 1898, in order to preserve the security of its new territory, Taiwan, and to solidify its foothold on future moves to the Asian mainland, Japan asked that China neither concede nor lease Fujian Province and its coastal strip to any country. Since China had agreed to this through an exchange of diplomatic notes, Fujian fell within Japan's sphere of influence by default. Japan also took a page from the European powers and demanded the right to build railroads in Fujian Province, but China turned this down. Rather, it limited itself to an oral promise that it would first consult with Japan in the event that a railroad was to be built in the province.

Meanwhile, the United States had become increasingly wary of the various powers' moves to encroach on China. Between September and November 1899, Secretary of State John Hay issued his series of Open Door Notes (notices regarding keeping China's doors open to trade) to the governments of the United Kingdom, Germany, Japan, Russia, Italy, and France. Each of these six countries agreed in principle, provided that all of the countries concerned agreed.

The powers' interest in the Chinese market was not limited to the profits that could be earned from trade. They were also becoming interested in investing in constructing railroads, developing mines, and building factories. For example, the United Kingdom—which controlled trade with China—had until then made the open door the basis for financial and import-export activities, but, as the interest of foreign powers shifted to building railroads and developing mining as security for their loans, it also looked to secure such rights.

The concept of international trade centering around China had spread around the world as the twentieth century began. In his 1900 work *The Problem of Asia*, American naval strategist Alfred T. Mahan wrote that the powers were no longer satisfied by merely competing over free trade, concluding, "Thus, competition becomes conflict, the instrument of which is not commercial emulation, but military power—land or sea." The dispute among the great powers over China would have to play out, regardless of the means.

The Boxer Rebellion and the Peking Protocol

The surge of encroachments into China by the powers resulted in two popular movements. One was the "law revision and self-strengthening" reform movement (the Hundred Days' Reform) undertaken by such younger officials as Kang Youwei and Liang Qichao, who modeled it on the Meiji Restoration. It differed from previous movements like the Westernization Movement (1861–95) that overemphasized the introduction of Western technologies. However, there was a strong backlash from conservative elements that led to the Guangxu emperor being placed in confinement, and the movement collapsed after around three months.

3-10. The United Kingdom stirs conflict between Japan and Russia (cartoon by Georges Ferdinand Bigot)

The other movement was the xenophobic drive led by the Boxers under the slogan, "Support the Qing, exterminate the foreigners." By the turn of the century, the Boxers had become more of a force, and they were besieging the Western powers' legations in Peking (Beijing). Taking advantage of this situation, the Qing government issued a declaration of war against the powers. The besieged legations requested help from their governments, and eight countries (Austria-Hungary, the United Kingdom, France, Germany, Italy, Japan, Russia, and the United States) jointly decided to dispatch troops. In fact, however, only Russia and Japan were able to dispatch troops in large numbers, and it was Japan that played the major role in suppressing the Boxers.

The Peking Protocol (Final Protocol on the Boxer Rebellion) that was concluded between the Qing government and the Western powers in 1901, stipulated that China had to pay reparations totaling about 2.5 times the amount agreed to under the Japan-China agreement (Japan's share was 7.7 percent). Aside from reparations, the protocol also recognized the right of the Western powers to garrison their legations in Peking. The share for Japan in all of this was relatively small, although the Japanese army had played a major role not only in the actual hostilities but also in protecting each country's resident foreigners. In the end, however, Japan had gained admission to the "imperialism club."

After the Boxer Rebellion was quashed, most of the European powers withdrew their troops. However, Russia—which had dispatched a force of more than 150,000 troops to Manchuria—did not. Russia's occupation of Manchuria was seen as a threat by the other powers. In 1901, the United States issued another round of Open Door Notes that emphasized respecting Chinese territorial integrity. The United Kingdom, too, took this situation seriously. It abandoned its policy of "splendid isolation" and began working through alliances and agreements to block Russian expansion. It also started looking for measures that would impede Russian interests in China. In October 1900, the United Kingdom signed an agreement with Germany as a means of putting a check on Russia. Moreover, this would open the way to a triple alliance between the United Kingdom, Germany, and Japan.

The "Man-Kan Kōkan" (The Exchange of Manchuria for Korea) Doctrine

A triple alliance between Japan, the United Kingdom, and Germany became increasingly realistic, as the proposal delivered to Japan's minister to the UK Hayashi Tadasu in April 1901 contained, as its first clause, a recognition of Japan's freedom of action in Korea. In an opinion addressed to Prime Minister Itō Hirobumi, Yamagata Aritomo wrote that, for the moment, the Western powers were trying to maintain equilibrium with their advocacy for preserving the integrity of China. A triple alliance would serve that purpose, and could also block Russia's southern advance.

At the peak of the Boxer Rebellion, Japan's minister to the Qing, Komura Jutarō, reported to Foreign Minister Aoki Shūzō that, in his view, both Japan and Russia should maintain their freedom of action in Korea and Manchuria, respectively, while also guaranteeing that they each would be able to do business within the other's sphere of influence. Based on Japan's objective of securing Korea, this was known as the "Man-Kan Kōkan" (literally, "Manchuria for Korea trade") doctrine: Japan would recognize Russia's free hand in Manchuria, and Russia would acknowledge Japan's free hand in Korea. Foreign Minister Aoki supported the idea, and the proposal was promptly offered to Russia, but Russia was unenthusiastic. In Japan, ideas about how to secure Korea by having Japan and Russia trade freedom of action in Manchuria for the same in Korea were held through the end of 1901 among the "elder statesmen" (*genrō*) who formed Japan's top leadership.

Minister Hayashi in London resumed talks in July 1901, immediately after the first Katsura Tarō cabinet was formed. Hayashi was charged with sounding out the United Kingdom's position while hinting at an agreement with Russia. However, the scope and nature of any alliance remained vague. Also, the Japanese government was not totally unified on the solution to the Korea problem. On the one hand, all the principals were in agreement that establishing Japan's right of control over Korea was of primary importance, but when it came to what to do about the related Russian question, they had not settled on whether Japan should sign an agreement with Russia or negotiate with Russia after forming an alliance with the United Kingdom. Accordingly, in mid-September, three of the elder statesmen—Itō, Inoue Kaoru, and Yamagata—exchanged a series of opinion notes with Prime Minister Katsura. Regardless of the proposal, they all agreed that negotiations with Russia were necessary, and so it was agreed that Itō would travel there. Concurrently, Japan continued to hold talks with the United Kingdom about an alliance.

In the meantime, Komura Jutarō, who had played a role in responding to the Boxer Rebellion as Japan's minister to the Qing government, had returned from China. In late September 1901 he was appointed foreign minister while Itō traveled to Russia. At this point, among the elder statesmen, the Man-Kan Kōkan doctrine still formed the basis for diplomatic talks with Russia.

The Anglo-Japanese Alliance: The "Marrow" of Japanese Diplomacy

By November 1901, negotiations about an Anglo-Japanese alliance were proceeding based on a detailed draft presented by British foreign secretary Lord Lansdowne. Katsura Tarō and Komura Jutarō, under pressure to leave their options open, asked Itō Hirobumi for his views. Itō, who was in Paris preparing to visit Russia, offered two opinions on the matters at hand. One was that there was danger in excluding Germany from any alliance, as it could be driven toward Russia and France, which could lead to a repeat of the Tripartite Intervention. Two, merely preventing annexation of Korea by some other country was insufficient; Japan needed to stipulate its freedom to act there. These views were incorporated into Japan's alliance proposal. Inoue Kaoru was particularly concerned about the issue raised by Itō's first point, and assumed that Germany would join in after the alliance with the United Kingdom was formalized.

The Anglo-Japanese Alliance

The United Kingdom, wary of Russia's refusal to withdraw troops from Manchuria after the Boxer Rebellion, abandoned its "Splendid Isolation" policy and began looking for ways to hinder Russian expansion via alliances and agreements. For the United Kingdom, however, the standoff with Russia went beyond the Far East and had a global significance encompassing West Asia and Europe. To help check Russian advances, seeking an alliance with Germany would also be a viable option. The initial proposal for the Anglo-Japanese Alliance also included Germany as a third player, demonstrating that the British conceived the agreement as part of a global diplomatic strategy against Russia.

The gist of the January 1902 Anglo-Japanese Alliance came down to three basic points. The two parties to the pact were each to mutually recognize each other's interests in China and Korea (Article 1), maintain a strict neutrality and work to prevent other powers from joining in hostilities if either party were to become involved in a war in defense of its interests (Article 2), and come to its ally's assistance and conduct war in common should another power enter hostilities against that party (Article 3). If Japan and Russia were to go to war, for example, the United Kingdom would maintain its neutrality; the United Kingdom would need to come to Japan's aid only if a nation friendly to Russia—France, for example—were to enter the fray. The terms of the agreement thus forged a "defensive alliance" between the two countries.

Article 4 stipulated that neither party was to enter into a separate arrangement with another power to the "prejudice of the interests" of the other party without prior consultation. This provision was included in anticipation of a Russo-Japanese Agreement after the Anglo-Japanese Alliance took effect. Essentially, the purpose of Article 4 was to convince the major powers that Russo-Japanese negotiations would take place within a scope that would not conflict with the Anglo-Japanese Alliance. Article 5 provided for mutual communication in the event that Japanese or British interests were in jeopardy. Article 6, the final article in the agreement, set the term of the alliance to five years and required the parties to notify one another a year in advance in order to terminate it.

The First Anglo-Japanese Alliance also included an exchange of notes establishing a framework for peacetime cooperation between the Japanese and British navies. Under the terms of the exchange of notes, naval officials from both countries began holding regular deliberations in May 1902 to share information and offer each other

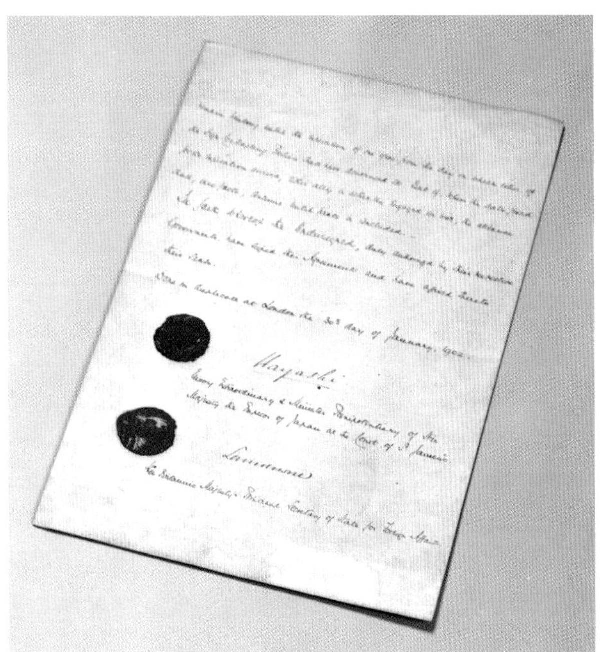

3-11. First Anglo-Japanese Alliance (signed treaty)

While making sure that the negotiations over an Anglo-Japanese alliance were continuing, Itō also engaged in preparatory talks based on the idea that Russia would agree to the Manchuria-Korea trade-off. The preliminary negotiations deadlocked over a Russian proposal that would restrict Japan's free hand in Korea while leaving Russia free to act in Manchuria, and were suspended in late December. Itō returned to Japan the following February after the Anglo-Japanese Alliance had been formalized.

The emphasis placed on the Anglo-Japanese Alliance by Prime Minister Katsura, Komura, Yamagata Aritomo, and Japan's former envoy to the UK Katō Takaaki was not incompatible with the comparable emphasis being put on reaching an agreement with Russia by Itō, Inoue, and Matsukata Masayoshi. With the Russian threat extending technical support. The sides also discussed plans for military strategies against Russia.

Japan and the United Kingdom renewed their alliance agreement in August 1905 during the Portsmouth Peace Conference. The terms had three key features. First, the agreement extended the applicable scope of the alliance to India in order to preserve peace in both East Asia and India, to protect the territorial rights of both parties, and to defend their special interests in the area; the larger reach of the alliance also included Qing China, where the signatories were to uphold the country's independence, respect its territorial integrity, and ensure equal opportunity for all nations there. Second, the 1905 agreement stipulated that if either party were to be involved in a war, the other party would come to the immediate assistance of its ally, conduct the war in common, and make peace in mutual agreement (Article 2). Whereas the First Anglo-Japanese Alliance was decidedly defensive, the new agreement established an "offensive and defensive alliance." Finally, the United Kingdom acknowledged Japan's paramount interests in Korea and recognized Japan's rights to take measures of guidance and protection in the country. This agreement would remain in force for ten years.

In July 1911, before the second alliance's ten-year period of validity had expired, Japan and the United Kingdom signed their third Anglo-Japanese Alliance. The reason for this was that the United States was no longer a potential target of coordinated Anglo-Japanese action, having recently signed a general arbitration treaty with the United Kingdom, thus eliminating any possibility of war between the two countries. The updated agreement also did away with all references to Korea in the Second Anglo-Japanese Alliance, as Japan had annexed Korea in 1910. The parties agreed that the alliance would remain in force until 1921, ten years from the date of its signing.

For the United Kingdom, the Anglo-Japanese Alliance was an element of a larger, global policy. For Japan, on the other hand, the agreement had a more direct significance: it allowed the country to keep Korea secure and Russia in check. The alliance's pertinent, initial significance for the Japanese side would soon begin to fade, however, as the aftermath of the Russo-Japanese War saw a network of alliances and agreements—the Russo-Japanese Agreement, the Franco-Japanese Treaty, and the Anglo-Russian Convention, to name a few—take shape in quick succession.

to the Korean Peninsula, both sides agreed that securing Korea was essential to guarantee Japan's security. Both the Anglo-Japanese Alliance and an agreement with Russia were aimed at this. In other words, there was consensus on pushing for an agreement with Russia, using the pressure of the Anglo-Japanese Alliance, in order to bring about the Manchuria-Korea exchange that would secure Korea once and for all.

In a report addressed to Foreign Minister Komura on the particulars of the conclusion of the Anglo-Japanese Alliance, Japan's resident envoy to the UK Hayashi Tadasu criticized Itō for how he and Tsuzuki Keiroku (Inoue's son-in-law and vice-minister for foreign affairs under Aoki Shūzō) sought to promote achieving an agreement with Russia while hindering the work toward the alliance with the United Kingdom. This presentation of affairs in later years became one of the factors behind the commonly held view that an Anglo-Japanese Alliance and a Russo-Japanese Agreement represented an either-or proposition.

The Anglo-Japanese Alliance signed in January 1902 stated that if either Japan or the United Kingdom went to war, the other party would remain neutral. It also said that if one or the other was attacked by a third country, then the other would join in to help against that third country as an ally. Essentially, it would prevent some third country from joining in on Russia's side should Japan and Russia go to war. The Anglo-Japanese Alliance would be revised twice, but in any case, it provided the "marrow" for Japanese diplomacy for twenty years.

Hayashi Tadasu (1850–1913)

Born to a doctor practicing Western medicine in the Sakura domain, Hayashi Tadasu was adopted by bakufu physician Hayashi Dōkai. He later studied in the United Kingdom, one of several students sent abroad by the Tokugawa shogunate. Upon returning home in 1868, Hayashi fought with Enomoto Takeaki's forces in the Battle of Hakodate—a losing effort that resulted in his capture by the Meiji government's imperial troops. After his release in 1871, Hayashi landed a position in the Kanagawa prefectural government (upon the recommendation of Mutsu Munemitsu) and later earned a spot on the Iwakura Mission. His subsequent government service included a stint as chief secretary at the Ministry of Industry and an extended period as vice-minister in the Ministry of Foreign Affairs, which he began in 1891 under Foreign Minister Enomoto. Hayashi remained second in command when Mutsu, whom Hayashi remembered as "the best friend he ever had," took over as foreign minister in 1892. In April 1895, he became painfully aware of the need to forge alliances with European powers after receiving directly, by hand, notice of the Tripartite Intervention. The most promising prospective allies in Hayashi's view were Russia, France, and especially the United Kingdom. In addition to pushing for an Anglo-Japanese alliance, he also argued for a Russo-Japanese alliance in 1898 during his time as Russian envoy, seeing both as being possible.

3-12. Hayashi Tadasu

Hayashi began serving as Japan's minister in the United Kingdom in 1900 under Foreign Minister Komura Jutarō.

Komura Jutarō (1855–1911)

Reigning Supreme in Kasumigaseki (1901–11)

In June 1901, Komura Jutarō became foreign minister in Katsura Tarō's first cabinet. For the next decade—over seven years in total as foreign minister (1901–06 and 1908–11) and roughly three years as vice-minister—Komura would reign over Kasumigaseki's late-Meiji political landscape and lay the foundation for imperial diplomacy.

Komura's life began in the Obi domain, a small section of the province of Hyūga (now Miyazaki Prefecture). His schooling took him to Nagasaki, where he studied English and Western knowledge, and then on to the Daigaku Nankō, and later to Harvard Law School as one of the first students to study abroad on a scholarship from the Ministry of Education. He returned home and first worked for the Ministry of Justice, after which a recommendation from former Daigaku Nankō classmate Sugiura Jūgō earned him a position in the Ministry of Foreign Affairs at the age of twenty-nine. Komura spent the next ten years or so working in the ministry's Communications Bureau and Translation Bureau. He also helped set up a new system of diplomats and consuls that was the brainchild of Hara Takashi, then director-general of the Trade Bureau. It was a bit of a turbulent phrase in Komura's life: he found himself saddled with considerable debt due to his father's business misadventures, but he also seized opportunities to involve himself in Sugiura's nationalist organization, the Nippon Club.

3-13. Komura Jutarō

The Translation Bureau eventually ceased operations as a result of institutional reforms. In 1893, Komura was transferred to Qing China, but soon returned to Japan at the outbreak of the First Sino-Japanese War to serve as the director-general of the Political Affairs Bureau. After the murder of Queen Myeongseong, the Japanese government dispatched Komura to Korea to handle the aftermath of the incident, and he stayed on to serve as Japan's envoy. To allay the strain that the queen's murder had placed on Russo-Japanese relations, Komura drew up the Komura-Weber Memorandum—an arrangement that gave Japan and Russia joint supervision of Korea's domestic administration—in 1896. He then served as vice-minister for foreign affairs under three foreign ministers (Saionji Kinmochi, Ōkuma Shigenobu, and Nishi Tokujirō), beginning in 1898, and also served in a succession of envoy positions: to the United States, Russia, and Qing China, where he demonstrated his diplomatic acuity during the Boxer

The following March, Baron Hermann von Eckardstein (the German chargé d'affaires in the United Kingdom) floated a proposal for an alliance among Japan, the United Kingdom, and Germany to help establish a balance of power in East Asia. There followed preliminary negotiations in London between Hayashi and British foreign secretary Lansdowne and other officials. Hinting at Japan's proximity to Russia, Hayashi convinced the British side that an alliance would be the right path to take. As the talks progressed and the government's position had to be clarified, Hayashi was dispatched by the Japanese government to Paris in November 1901 to convince and get the approval of elder statesman (*genrō*) Itō Hirobumi. The Anglo-Japanese Alliance was signed in London in January 1902 (see sidebar on pages 114–115). Hayashi would then become Japan's first official ambassador to the United Kingdom in 1905, when the local legation was upgraded to a full-fledged embassy. Having adopted a pro-British stance in the Russo-Japanese War, Hayashi worked to negotiate the second Anglo-Japanese Alliance. In May 1906, he rose to the position of foreign minister in the Saionji Kinmochi cabinet with endorsements from Yamagata Aritomo and Inoue Kaoru. In that leadership role, Hayashi concluded the Franco-Japanese Treaty and Russo-Japanese Treaty—two additional pieces in a growing, multilateral network of agreements that he worked to build around the Anglo-Japanese Alliance. During his two-year tenure at the helm of the Ministry of Foreign Affairs, he also received valuable support from Komura, who had been appointed Japan's ambassador to the United Kingdom. As Fukuzawa Yukichi observed, Hayashi was a scholarly type, often aloof and detached from the ways of the world—a personality that stood in stark contrast to the more businesslike, practical-minded Komura. Neither Hayashi nor Komura would get to see the future of the alliance network they forged together, however; Komura died in 1911, while Hayashi passed away in 1913.

Rebellion. As Japan's envoy to Russia at the time, Komura proposed dispatching troops to Qing China in numbers that would rival the contingents from other countries to ensure that the major powers would not be able to leave Japan out of joint cooperative action. The proposal won over the Yamagata Aritomo cabinet, which decided to pour in approximately 8,000 Japanese troops—nearly half the number of the Eight-Nation Alliance's total forces. Additionally, tales are told of how, as envoy to Qing China, he took up the challenge of negotiating in Beijing to resolve issues, scurrying around like a rat, barely a meter and a half tall, as he led the negotiations.

Komura's time in Russia stoked his concerns about Russia making a southward push into Manchuria and Korea, and these worries shaped his course of action when he became foreign minister in September 1901. Working with Katsura Tarō, Komura began exploring diplomatic routes to an Anglo-Japanese Alliance that would deter Russia's advances. Informal talks with the United Kingdom about a potential pact had already begun under Foreign Minister Katō Takaaki, but Komura was in Beijing when envoy to the UK Hayashi Tadasu first reported to the Katsura cabinet on the possibility of an alliance, leaving him unable to take part in the government's decision-making process. After taking over for Katō as foreign minister, however, Komura was in a position to oversee the effort. He gave Hayashi the authority to resume the negotiations, which ultimately culminated in the signing of the Anglo-Japanese Alliance in 1902. In Komura's eyes, the alliance was a means of impelling Russia to withdraw its troops from Manchuria—something it had refused to do even after the end of the Boxer Rebellion—and an essential tool for securing Japan's control over Korea. The Anglo-Japanese Alliance quickly appeared to have at least some of the impact that Komura had envisioned: in April 1902, Russia and China signed an agreement under which Russia would gradually pull its forces out of Manchuria and return the territory to Qing China.

However, Russia did not hold up its end of the bargain: the Russian troops stayed put. At the Imperial Council (Gozen Kaigi) in June 1903, Komura argued that preventing foreign domination of Korea was "part of the imperial legacy." He also said that Japan's best line of attack in its negotiations with Russia would be to assert its interests in Korea and attempt to limit Russia's interests in Manchuria to rail operations and other similar assets. Komura headed into the negotiations with Roman Rosen, the Russian representative. During the talks, Russia proposed restricting Japan's "dominant interests" in Korea to commerce and industry and making Korean territory north of the 39th parallel a neutral zone. The Japanese side fired back with a counterproposal that included military assistance and advice in the scope of Japan's interests in Korea and the creation of a neutral zone on the Manchuria-Korea border. Russia refused to budge.

Seeing no favorable end in sight, Komura decided to forego further negotiations and pursue a resolution through military action.

Laying the Foundation for Imperial Diplomacy

After the war with Russia, Japan strengthened its hold over Korea through the Japan-Korea Protocol of 1904 and the Japan-Korea Agreement (August 1904), while seeking recognition from the United Kingdom to make Korea a protectorate through the renewal of the Anglo-Japanese Alliance (the Second Anglo-Japanese Alliance). The renewed agreement was an "offensive and defensive alliance," stipulating that if either party were to be involved in a war, the other party would come to its immediate assistance. The agreement was to remain in force for ten years.

At the peace conference mediated by US president Theodore Roosevelt in August 1905, Komura's focal point was securing reparations from Russia, but Russian plenipotentiary Witte obstinately rejected the idea of paying reparations or ceding territory. Concluding that a compromise was unlikely, Komura advised the Japanese government to break off the negotiations. However, the Japanese government decided that prolonging the war would be next to impossible, considering the limits on its capacities, and instructed Komura to abandon the demand for reparations and settle for the territory of Karafuto (Sakhalin) south of the 50th parallel. The fact that the peace agreement contained no terms guaranteeing reparations for Japan incensed parts of the Japanese population, stirring a movement against the treaty and sparking the Hibiya Incendiary Incident.

The Treaty of Portsmouth gave Japan control over Korea, Russia's lease of the Liaodong Peninsula, and rights to the South Manchuria Railway. Assuming that the provisions of the Treaty of Portsmouth, the Anglo-Japanese Alliance, and the signing of the Taft-Katsura Agreement in July amounted to tacit approval of these interests from Russia, the United Kingdom, and the United States, Japan began its initiative to make Korea an official protectorate via the conclusion of the Japan-Korea Treaty (signed in November 1905).

Komura was determined to keep foreign powers from meddling in Japan's interests in Korea. When American rail baron Edward H. Harriman proposed joint ownership of the Manchurian Railway, for example, Komura rebuffed the offer and forced Harriman to rescind the provisional contract. He also visited Beijing in December 1905 to sign the "Treaty and Additional Agreement between Japan and China Relating to Manchuria" (i.e., the Sino-Japanese Treaty on Manchuria) based on the terms of the Treaty of Portsmouth, securing

The Outbreak of the Russo-Japanese War

It appeared that the Anglo-Japanese Alliance might pressure Russia to withdraw troops from Manchuria. In April 1902, Russia and the Qing government signed a treaty on returning Manchuria to the Qing, in which Russia pledged to pull its troops out in three phases. However, while Russia did carry out the first troop withdrawal, it did not keep its April 1903 deadline for the second withdrawal. Furthermore, after Russia had submitted its withdrawal conditions to the Qing government, its relations with Japan once again grew tense. Within Russia itself, there was a conflict between moderates and hard-liners. The moderates called for a staged troop withdrawal that would not stir up other countries, while the hard-liners had in mind to use this opportunity to put Manchuria and Mongolia under Russian control. The Qing-Russia agreement on returning Manchuria was in line with the moderate position advocated by the foreign and finance ministers. However, hard-liners close to the czar had regained their influence, and because they advocated halting the troop withdrawals, the second round did not happen. In August 1903, hard-liner Admiral Yevgeni Ivanovich Alekseyev was appointed governor-general of Russia's Far East and the diplomats stationed in Japan and China were put under his command.

Negotiations between Japan and Russia began the next month with talks between Foreign Minister Komura Jutarō and Roman Romanovich Rosen, Russia's minister to Japan. Russia's position was

Qing China's recognition of the Manchurian interests that Japan had obtained from Russia.

Although Komura stepped down from his position as minister for foreign affairs in the Katsura cabinet's mass resignation in January 1906, he resumed the post in August 1908 as part of the second Katsura cabinet. The new Katsura administration's foreign policy strategy had two key components: putting the Anglo-Japanese Alliance at the core of Japanese diplomacy—the "marrow" of Japan's international relations—and "maintaining the current state of Manchuria in perpetuity" as a grounding for its policy on Qing China. The stance represented a departure from the preceding Saionji administration's diplomatic policy, one where Foreign Minster Hayashi appeared to welcome an open-door policy. When Komura reclaimed his leadership role, however, he set out to maintain Japan's sole dominion, at least in southern Manchuria, on a permanent basis.

Under the terms of the Second Russo-Japanese Agreement (the Russo-Japanese Agreement of 1910, secret article 5), Japan and Russia promised to collaborate and offer mutual aid to protect each other's special interests in Manchuria. The agreement also brought Japan another step closer to its annexation of Korea and established a united Russo-Japanese front to prevent the United States from encroaching into Manchuria. The Second Russo-Japanese Agreement formed a trinity of Japanese policy, in a sense, harmonizing with the Imperial Defense Policy of 1907 and the Katsura cabinet's foreign policy strategy. Japan's initiative to take control of Korea had gained traction with the creation of the 1909 "Basic Policy on Korea." Formulated under Komura's supervision, the document explained that Japan's imperial policy on Korea was to "establish Japan's power on the Korean Peninsula" and that Japan was "naturally in the position to make its presence patently clear." With the diplomatic developments that followed in 1910, Japan officially moved to bring that vision of Korean annexation to fruition. Komura also managed to restore Japan's tariff autonomy, the final hurdle in the treaty-revision process, in 1911 before succumbing to pulmonary tuberculosis that November.

Komura's diplomatic achievements were instrumental in laying the groundwork for Japan's advance into continental Asia after the Russo-Japanese War, but the exclusivity of Japan's core interests remained shaky. That uncertainty left Japan confronting the serious—and confounding—question of how to go about dealing with the United States, which maintained a tenacious commitment to an open-door policy.

premised on its continued occupation of Manchuria; it sought to uncouple the Manchuria issue from the talks and debate only the Korea issue. Japan's position, however, was founded on the Man-Kan Kōkan doctrine, and it sought an agreement that included the Manchuria issue. Japan's Army General Staff anticipated that, if no satisfactory agreement were reached in the negotiations with Russia, war would begin before the Trans-Siberian Railway had reached its full transportation capacity. Except for one section that detoured around Lake Baikal, the Trans-Siberian Railway was fully operational.

Russia acknowledged Japan's dominant interests in Korea, but it demanded that Korean territory not be used for military purposes and that a militarily neutral zone be established in Korea's north. Russia's argument was that, while Russia still had influence over Korea, Japan had no such influence over Manchuria; therefore, Japan and Russia's status vis-à-vis Manchuria and Korea could not be discussed in the same terms.

On the basis of the Man-Kan Kōkan doctrine, Japan sought to preserve complete freedom of action for itself in Korea. In January 1904, it presented its own final proposal that excised the provisions for a ban on military activity in Korea and for establishing a neutral zone, while adding a stipulation about the territorial integrity of Manchuria. Russia postponed its response. Japan's elder statesmen, who had been guarded about going to war, were now forced to recognize that Russia had given up hope of achieving a diplomatic solution. At an extraordinary cabinet meeting and Imperial Council meeting held on February 4, it was decided to halt negotiations. For its part, although Russia had rejected the demand for Manchuria's territorial integrity at the end of January, it agreed at a special conference to excise the provision establishing a neutral zone; however, the news did not get to Rosen in Tokyo.

The war began at midnight on February 8 with a surprise attack launched by the Combined Fleet on the Russian squadron anchored in the harbor at Lushun. Around the same time, advance troops landed at Incheon, and entered Hanseong (Seoul) on February 9. In the imperial edict, dated February 10, offering the pretext for declaring war, the Meiji emperor said, "The independence of Korea is essential to the safety of our realm," and stated that the "integrity of Korea" was now being threatened by Russia. This was an era in which the safety of another country could be regarded as a "vital interest" and therefore a reason for going to war. It was truly the age of imperialism.

3-14. *The Surrender of Port Arthur* (painting by Arai Rokuo)

The Russo-Japanese War and the Second Anglo-Japanese Alliance

When its troops entered Hanseong, the Japanese government asked Korea for the right to use Korean territory for military purposes in order to protect Korea's independence and maintain its territorial integrity. The Korean side agreed, and the Japan-Korea Protocol of 1904 was signed. The protocol stated that Japan would wage the war to guarantee Korea's independence and territorial integrity, as well as the safety of the Korean's imperial house. Within the Japanese government, however, plans were underway to turn Korea into a protectorate, under which all of the important functions of state—such as those tied to military, diplomatic, and financial affairs—would be placed under Japanese administration. In August 1904, as a first step in this direction, the Japan-Korea Agreement of 1904 was signed; this document required Korea's diplomacy and finances to be overseen by Japanese advisors.

For its part, the Qing government's stance on the Russo-Japanese War was delicate. In the end, it decided to adopt a neutral position and keep an eye on how the war developed. That said, it also wound up allowing the Japanese army to fight on Chinese territory (Manchuria).

Engagements on Chinese territory began with the landing of Japanese troops on the Liaodong Peninsula in May 1904. The Japanese army crossed the Yalu River and advanced into Manchuria. That September, it defeated Russian forces in the Battle of Liaoyang, but it suffered severe losses. The army also paid a terrible price in the attack on 203 Hill at Port Arthur, but in January 1905 it finally overcame the Russian forces.

In February 1905, at a time when the Japanese populace was stirred up over the victory at Lushun, Japan held a celebration to commemorate the third anniversary of the Anglo-Japanese Alliance. In concluding his remarks made at the event, Komura Jutarō expressed his hope that ties between the two countries would continue to strengthen. Word of this quickly reached the United Kingdom, where it was warmly welcomed. Japanese envoy Hayashi Tadasu and Foreign Secretary Lansdowne began unofficial talks in late March with the result in August that—even as the Portsmouth Peace Conference was underway—a second Anglo-Japanese Alliance treaty was signed. The scope of this treaty expanded to include India, while the nature of the alliance changed from a purely defensive one to one that included both offense and defense. The second treaty would more explicitly spell out the terms of military cooperation, grounded in the "Imperial Defense Policy" (see sidebar on pages 124–25) that envisioned Russia as Japan's primary hypothetical foe.

A War of Attrition: Financing the War Effort

In March 1905, the Japanese army scored another victory in the Battle of Mukden. However, both armies suffered major losses. At sea, the Japanese navy also prevailed in the Battle of the Yalu River (Battle of the Yellow Sea), delivering a major blow to the Russian fleet that was using Vladivostok as its base of operations. Having lost its Pacific Fleet, Russia dispatched its Baltic Fleet to join the Third Pacific Squadron and head toward the Sea of Japan. For a time, the exact whereabouts of this flotilla were unclear. Opinion in the Japanese navy was divided on whether the Russian vessels would pass through the Tsushima Straits or the Tsugaru Straits. Admiral Tōgō Heihachirō, at the head of the Combined Fleet, believed it was headed for Tsushima, and stayed on alert. It was there at the end of May that his forces caught up with the Baltic Fleet. They engaged in battle and delivered a devastating blow. At this stage, Japan's victory became inevitable.

The battles of the two nations' armed forces resulted in enormous losses of personnel and munitions. The numbers of Japanese dead and wounded from the land battles far exceeded any predictions, reaching 59,000 in the Battle of Port Arthur, and 70,000 in the Battle of Mukden. Russian losses were even higher. Due to the severity of the losses, Chief of the Manchuria Army General Staff Kodama Gentarō returned to Japan after the Battle of Mukden and asked the government to

3-15. *The Scene of the Bridge on* Mikasa (painting by Tōjō Shōtarō)

make peace as soon as possible. There was also the matter of how much the war cost. Initially, based on the fact that the First Sino-Japanese War had cost 220 million yen, the Japanese government estimated that the cost of a war with Russia would be around 500 million yen. The actual cost ended up being more than 1.9 billion yen. The expenses were covered by increasing taxes and issuing government bonds at home and abroad, ramping up the foreign bonds to 800 million yen. Floating such a large amount in foreign bonds was not easy. To handle this important task, the government dispatched Bank of Japan deputy governor (later governor) Takahashi Korekiyo to the West. Fortunately, the loan flotations were better received than expected in the United Kingdom and the United States, and Japan secured the funds to cover its war costs.

3-16. Japan-Russia Treaty of Peace (Treaty of Portsmouth) instrument of ratification

Russo-Japanese Peace Talks and Establishing a Korea Protectorate

In the early stages of the war, elder statesman Itō Hirobumi specially dispatched Kaneko Kentarō—who had a close personal relationship with US president Theodore Roosevelt—to search for opportunities for peace. There were moves among the Western powers to mediate peace talks, but in 1904 neither Japan nor Russia could entertain peace. With the fall of Lushun in 1905 and the annihilation of the Russian Pacific Fleet, the social unrest already evident in Russia—as symbolized by the Bloody Sunday events of that January 22—had spread, and Russia's ally France pushed it toward making peace. However, Russia assembled a mighty army in the vicinity of Harbin and looked for an opportunity to strike back.

Knowing that Russia's traditional military strategy was to lure its enemy deep into the interior and decimate it in a single blow, the Japanese military was in favor of seizing a favorable moment to strike peace. The military was already reaching its limits in terms of arms, ammunition, and troop reinforcements. Chief of Army General Staff Yamagata Aritomo in March 1905 told the leaders in Tokyo that, based on the situation on the ground, he did not expect Russia to make any offer of peace on its own. He urged them instead to find the right moment to call for peace.

The cabinet meeting held in April after the Battle of Mukden decided on three absolute conditions for peace: Japan's free hand in Korea, the withdrawal of both countries' forces from Manchuria, and the lease of the Liaodong Peninsula and transfer to Japanese hands of the Chinese Eastern Railway's southern branch. It also settled on four "desired" conditions: reparations for war costs, the handing over of Russian naval vessels that had fled to neutral ports, the cession of Karafuto (Sakhalin), and the granting of the right to fish in waters near Russia's maritime provinces. The previous July, Foreign Minister Komura Jutarō had written an opinion paper to Prime Minister Katsura Tarō presenting bullish peace conditions topped by reparations for war costs, but one year later these had been downgraded to desired conditions. This spoke to the severity of the war situation. At the end of April 1905, a formal request was made to President Roosevelt to provide "amicable mediation." Roosevelt had hopes for Japan as a power that would check Russia's advance into East Asia, and was favorable to mediating.

Roosevelt made approaches to Russia through European monarchs and heads of state. Germany's Kaiser Wilhelm II had opposed any peace effort, but Roosevelt convinced him to change his position. This led Czar Nicholas II to view American mediation more favorably, and so the road to peace was opened. Serving as Japan's plenipotentiaries to the peace conference were Foreign Minister Komura and Takahira Kogorō. Their Russian

Kaneko Kentarō (1853–1942)

Growing up in the family of a feudal retainer of the Fukuoka domain, Kaneko Kentarō started his education at the Shūyūkan domain school when he was eleven years old. During his subsequent studies in Tokyo, he went from Chinese studies to a broader curriculum of Western learning. Kaneko eventually went to the United States as part of the Iwakura Mission, along with fellow Fukuoka native Dan Takuma. He remained there, graduating from a high school in Boston and enrolling at Harvard Law School in 1876, where he shared lodgings for a year with Komura Jutarō—a Ministry of Education scholarship student who had started at the law school a year earlier.

After returning to Japan, Kaneko became a Genrō-in (Chamber of Elders) secretary in 1884 and began drafting Japan's new constitution as part of the Bureau for the Study of Constitutional Systems. The bureau operated under the direction of Itō Hirobumi, who took a liking to Kaneko and named him secretary to the prime minister in the first Itō cabinet. In 1889, Kaneko made his way back to the United States for an investigative survey into how the legislative assembly operated. It was then that he made the acquaintance of fellow Harvard alumnus Theodore Roosevelt. In the ensuing stages of Kaneko's career, he became an executive secretary of the House of Peers in 1890, then a peer himself, and later a minister in both the third and fourth Itō cabinets (first as minister of agriculture and commerce, then as minister of justice). During his years in these numerous high-ranking positions, Kaneko helped write the Constitution of the Empire of Japan and was made a baron for his contribution.

When the Russo-Japanese War started, Itō (then president of the Privy Council) charged Kaneko with two pressing, clandestine missions in the United States. One was to secretly ask President Roosevelt for his assistance in mediating a Russo-Japanese peace agreement when the time was right. The other was to improve Japan's image in the US popular consciousness—making Japan's war objectives clear to the general US public, working to quell the fears of a "Yellow Peril" that had set in since the First Sino-Japanese War, and making US views toward Japan less hostile. Kaneko arrived in the United States in March 1904 and promptly paid Roosevelt several visits with envoy Takahira Kogorō. During their meetings, Kaneko explained the reasons for and objectives of Japan's war with Russia, discussed measures to hold the "Yellow Peril" in check, and even gave Roosevelt a copy of Nitobe Inazō's *Bushido: The Soul of Japan*. On June 7, 1904, Kaneko attended a White House luncheon and relayed the Japanese government's hopes that Roosevelt would conciliate the Russo-Japanese peace process. According to diplomatic documents, Roosevelt was obliging to the proposal. "The time is not yet ripe," Roosevelt stated, "but if a suitable opportunity should present itself, I do not decline to take the trouble to mediate on behalf of Japan."

3-17. Kaneko Kentarō

It would be another year before Roosevelt mediated the peace treaty, and in the meantime, Kaneko relocated from Washington to New York and began a fervent effort to cultivate favorable attitudes toward Japan: from giving lectures in major cities on the East Coast to penning essays on various topics, he strove to make good on the mission that Itō had entrusted him with. All in all, his contributions toward making the Russo-Japanese War a success for Japan earned him another new title (viscount) in 1907, after he returned to Japan. He also became the first chairman of the America-Japan Society, a Tokyo-based consortium of leading figures from the two countries, in 1917. Several years later, however, he resigned from the position out of frustration at the US Congress's decision to pass the 1924 Immigration Act, which contained anti-Japanese provisions.

3-18. Portsmouth Peace Conference

counterparts were former finance minister Sergei Witte and former envoy to Japan Rosen.

Meanwhile, in July 1905—a delicate moment in which the war was in a cease-fire state—US secretary of war William Howard Taft led a delegation to Japan, where he met with Prime Minister Katsura Tarō in Tokyo. The pair exchanged a memorandum known as the Katsura-Taft Agreement—a secret agreement between two executive-branch leaders that was not formally released. In it, Katsura said that Japan had no designs on the Philippines, while Taft said Japan's establishment of a protectorate in Korea would contribute to "peace in the East." Japan's quest for a free hand in Korea in the peace talks with Russia and US wariness about Japanese designs on the Philippines were congruent matters.

The Portsmouth Peace Conference between Russia and Japan began on August 10. Russia rejected the first three of the four "desired" conditions in Japan's proposal as affronts to Russia's dignity. Given that Japanese forces were occupying Sakhalin at the time, Plenipotentiary Witte sounded out Saint Petersburg on ceding it to Japan. However, Nicholas II was firm on the issues of

Imperial Defense Policy

The April 1907 "Imperial Defense Policy" outlined the basic vision for Japan's security policy (national defense policy) as a facet of its military strategy after the Russo-Japanese War. Passed by the Board of Marshals and Fleet Admirals (the highest advisory body to the emperor on military matters) and subsequently sanctioned by Emperor Meiji, the document started out as the brainchild of Field Marshal Yamagata Aritomo. Army and navy leaders then began drafting Yamagata's concepts into a concrete plan, but the product underwent numerous revisions due to administrative concerns. Seeing potential issues with the plan's financial and diplomatic implications, Prime Minister Saionji Kinmochi consulted the emperor, whose input resulted in substantial modifications. This could therefore be called a comprehensive national strategy.

The aim of the Imperial Defense Policy was to protect and expand the "interests implanted in Manchuria and Korea" that Japan had gained via the Russo-Japanese War. Another point was to safeguard and build on those continental interests not by taking a "defensive" stance to protect the Japanese mainland, but rather by adopting an "offensive" game plan premised on armed conflict on

Yamagata Aritomo (1838–1922) and Katsura Tarō (1847–1913)

Leading Military Politicians from Chōshū

Both Yamagata Aritomo and Katsura Tarō were natives of the Chōshū domain and subscribers to the exclusionist *jōi* philosophy. At Shōkasonjuku Academy, Yamagata studied under Yoshida Shōin—the man he would call his lifelong mentor. In 1864, Yamagata was part of the fight against the combined squadron of ships from four Western powers. Witnessing the West's might in person gave Yamagata a keen awareness of how desperately Japan's weaponry and military systems needed an overhaul, prompting him to abandon his strident anti-foreign sentiment and instead support the opening of Japan. He went on to steer the Chōshū domain toward taking up the anti-bakufu cause and led the Kiheitai (Chōshū's volunteer militia) in its clash with the Aizu domain during the Boshin War. Yamagata later sailed to Europe in 1869 to survey the military structures in use and, after returning home, took up the slain the continent. The most likely threat to Japan's continental interests was Russia—and the document verbalized that awareness, ranking Russia ahead of the United States, Germany, and France in a list of "hypothetical future enemies." Even the Japanese navy, which tended to focus its energies on strategizing against the United States, agreed with making Russia the number-one hypothetical enemy.

The Imperial Defense Policy also stipulated the logistical requirements of an offensive strategy. The army, which considered Russia its hypothetical enemy, requested at least twenty-five divisions in peacetime (and fifty divisions in wartime)—eight more than the seventeen divisions that had been in place at the end of the Russo-Japanese War. The navy, meanwhile, considered the United States its top "imagined" enemy and requested a fleet of eight battleships and eight cruisers (an "Eight-Eight Fleet") in the event that a conflict broke out. The logistical targets were long-term objectives, however, and the Imperial Defense Policy did not specify a timeframe for the necessary expansions in light of prospective budgetary limitations.

The national defense policy also touched on diplomacy. "In addition to maintaining the Anglo-Japanese Alliance, Japan must also work to ensure that other countries do not form their own alliances." The aim was to keep the Anglo-Japanese alliance intact and stop countries whose interests were not aligned with Japan's from forming their own alliances.

As world affairs shifted and the national-defense environment evolved, so did the Imperial Defense Policy. In its first revision in 1918, shortly before the end of World War I, the document listed Japan's top three "imagined enemies" with Russia at the top, the United States second, and China third. The second revision (1923) positioned the United States as the top hypothetical adversary, followed by the Soviet Union and then China. After the Manchurian Incident came a third revision (1936) in which the army and navy jointly designated the Soviet Union and the United States atop the list of potential enemies, followed by China and the United Kingdom in a tie.

In the interim, the target for the required troop strength was revised downward in the 1920s, and the navy also saw its Eight-Eight Fleet target as difficult to sustain, leading to a change in direction away from these plans. The Imperial Defense Policy thus played a clear role in containing Japan's military buildup, but with the eruption of the Second Sino-Japanese War in 1937, it lost much of its substance.

Ōmura Masujirō's dying wish to implement military reforms as Japan's first army minister. Driving efforts to introduce a conscription system, establish a general staff office, and formulate the Imperial Rescript to Soldiers and Sailors, Yamagata literally set the foundation for the Japanese army.

Katsura, ten years Yamagata's junior, was also active in support roles on the front lines of the Boshin War. After the Restoration, he made frequent voyages to Germany with a focus on studying military administration. In addition to driving a variety of reforms, including the creation of a general staff office, Katsura served in the First Sino-Japanese War and eventually became army minister—a position he would occupy in four separate cabinets, including Yamagata's administration, beginning in 1898. Katsura served for more than thirty years in the army, but it was more as a military administrator than as a commander that he earned Yamagata's trust.

Yamagata was cautious about using military force to settle issues on the international stage, preferring to concentrate instead on cultivating Japan's national strength at home. He opposed the *seikanron* (punitive expedition to Korea) doctrine, for example, and demanded that Japan promptly pull its troops out of the Taiwan Expedition to avert a potential war with Qing China. During his first period as prime minister (1889–91), Yamagata expressed his defensive-leaning ideas in a policy speech to the first-ever meeting of the Imperial Diet in 1890. The address, asserting that protecting Japan's "sovereignty line" (the Japanese mainland) would entail defending its "interest line" (the Korean Peninsula), emphasized the need for military preparedness—not, however, to invade Korea, but rather to neutralize it.

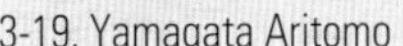

3-19. Yamagata Aritomo

3-20. Katsura Tarō

Yamagata adopted an appeasement policy toward Russia during the Tripartite Intervention and Russia's subsequent push into Korea. The 1896 Yamagata-Lobanov Agreement was Yamagata's attempt to establish a balance of power between Japan and Russia in Korea. During his second tenure as prime minister (1898–1900), Yamagata promoted the Anglo-Japanese Alliance, warning against a Russian advance in Manchuria and Korea following the Boxer Rebellion, and agreeing with Itō Hirobumi and Katsura in supporting the "Man-Kan-Kōkan" policy (exchanging Manchuria for Korea). He recognized that war with Russia would follow if Russia maintained its unyielding stance, but, as general chief of staff, he was apprehensive about committing the country's resources and looked for an early peace after the Battle of Mukden.

The Legacy of the "Second Generation" Cabinets: Katsura and Komura

After the resignation of the Yamagata administration, Katsura Tarō formed a cabinet in 1901. This marked the first time a member of the "second generation," not a member of the elder statesmen, had risen to power. The Japanese public may have derided what many considered a "second-rate" regime whose days were numbered from the start, but the Katsura cabinet managed to remain together for an impressive four years and eight months. Katsura struck bargains and partnerships with the Rikken Seiyūkai (also known simply as the Seiyūkai), the political party of Itō Hirobumi and Hara Takashi, to strengthen the administration's political base. From the end of the Russo-Japanese War to 1913, Katsura would alternate with Saionji Kinmochi in leading the government. During the so-called Katsura-Saionji era, Japanese politics gradually stabilized.

Backed by Yamagata and Itō, Katsura set out to conclude the Anglo-Japanese Alliance and deal with the international impact of the Russo-Japanese War in his first administration, putting trusted ally Komura Jutarō in charge of the Ministry of Foreign Affairs. Korea was a prime concern for Katsura, who sought to make the country an official protectorate and to ensure international approval for this. He took the initiative in the renewal of the Anglo-Japanese Alliance, the signing of the Taft-Katsura Agreement, and, in 1909, a resolution to push Korean annexation forward, but the dominant theme shaping Katsura's first premiership was actually the need to establish an adequate financial base for waging war. To ready the country for the possibility that the Russo-Japanese War might drag on, Katsura worked to raise taxes to secure military funding and expand the military, and solicited foreign loans. During his third time in office as prime minister, which began in late December 1912, Katsura doubled as minister of finance and turned his attention to repaying the foreign loans from the Russo-Japanese War and dealing with the postwar outflow of coin currency. He enlisted the assistance of Inoue Kaoru and

ceding territory and war-cost reparations, and he rejected them. Japan, which eventually covered its war costs by issuing national bonds, was strongly committed to obtaining reparations.

Komura saw the demands for reparations and territorial concessions (Liaodong Peninsula and Sakhalin) as matters involving Japan's honor, and in late August he sent a telegram to the government in Tokyo, urging it to break off negotiations. However, both the cabinet and Imperial Council decided that peace must be achieved even if it meant abandoning the two demands. Japan had already lost the reserves of power to continue the war.

As this was happening, Roosevelt asked the Japanese side not to insist on reparations, while he pushed Russia to cede the southern half of Sakhalin (already held in its entirety by Japan). The combatants accepted this mediation proposal, and on September 5 signed the Japan-Russia Treaty of Peace (Treaty of Portsmouth).

What Did Peace between Russia and Japan Produce?

Although it had made noticeable concessions, such as abandoning its quest for reparations, Japan did achieve its most important objectives with the peace treaty: eliminating Russian influence from the Korean Peninsula and guaranteeing lasting security there. Article 2 of the treaty stated that Russia recognized Japan's paramount interests in Korea, and would not obstruct measures for guidance, protection, and control of Korea that Japan might take. Furthermore, Russia was to (1)

Matsukata Masayoshi, who helped him force through a tight budget and administrative streamlining measures.

As the First Movement to Protect Constitutional Government began to gain momentum, Katsura decided to establish a new political party and stepped down as prime minister, but as he worked with the likes of Gotō Shinpei and Katō Takaaki to establish the Rikken Dōshikai (Association of Allies of Constitutional Government), he fell ill and died in the fall of 1913. Katsura's move to establish his own political party drew a contrast with Yamagata's aversion to party politics. This was due to the prevalent hard-line foreign policy parties frequently thwarting his domestic and foreign policies in the Diet. Some even posit that Yamagata may have instituted the controversial rule allowing only active-duty officers to serve as army and navy ministers in the cabinet in order to prevent party politicians from recklessly thrusting Japan into wars.

Yamagata as an Elder Statesman

As Japan's highest-ranking elder statesman after the death of Itō Hirobumi in 1909, Yamagata exerted enormous, sustained political influence on the domestic and international policies of the "second generation." The events of the 1911 Xinhai Revolution put the Qing dynasty on the verge of collapse, which Yamagata feared would be calamitous. He thus advocated providing support to the administration of Yuan Shikai in order to stabilize China. During the First World War, while advocating cooperation with China in the anticipation of a "white peril" based on his theory of a racial warfare between "whites" and "yellows," he strongly criticized Foreign Minister Katō's anti-Chinese stance, such as the Twenty-One Demands, as well as his propensity for ignoring the elder statesmen. Yamagata made a committed effort to bring the Fourth Russo-Japanese Agreement to fruition and stated his approval for a joint Japanese-US Siberian Expedition, but his inclinations toward those measures were not so much a demonstration of specific allegiances as part of a larger objective to keep Czarist Russia's war with Germany going in hopes of eventually fragmenting the white race. When the Czarist regime ultimately crumbled, he professed his support for the Hara cabinet's decision to withdraw troops from Siberia. He died shortly thereafter.

Generously supportive of those he took under his wing, Yamagata stood by the bureaucrats and military personnel he saw promise in and appointed them to key positions, as he did with Katsura. That style led to the development of a "Yamagata circle" in government—and stood in contrast to the approach of Itō, who, despite being one of Yamagata's closest confidants, was averse to the idea of political coteries and took little interest in forming tight personal networks.

transfer to Japan, with the consent of the Chinese government, the lease to the Liaodong Peninsula (Lushun, Dalian, and adjacent waters) and all rights and privileges connected to that lease (Article 5); (2) transfer to Japan, with the consent of the Chinese government, control of the railway between Changchun and Lushun, including all the branch lines, as well as all the associated rights, privileges, properties, and coal mines (Article 6); and (3) cede to Japan the southern half of Sakhalin (Article 9).

The twenty-five-year lease on the Liaodong Peninsula was set to expire in 1923, while the rights to build and operate the railway between Changchun and Lushun were set to expire in 1939 (formally, the Qing government had the right to buy back the tracks thirty-six years after they were completed in 1903). These rights had been handed over from treaties between Russia and Qing China.

For Japan, the Russo-Japanese War had been a victory by only a small margin, and the way it ended precluded any amicable Russo-Japanese relationship in the aftermath. The Japanese army had mobilized more than 900,000 troops, including reservists. The fact that it was able to endure the fierce fighting on the Chinese mainland was arguably owed to the all-out push by a Japanese public that vigorously met its obligations to pay taxes and be conscripted. Between emergency special taxes, levies for relief expenses, appeals for donations, subscriptions for treasury bonds, and other measures, the populace was able to get a real sense in their daily lives that they had a stake in the war. On September 5, 1905, when people learned that their government had been unable to obtain reparations in the peace talks, there was an uprising in Tokyo's Hibiya district (later called the Hibiya Incendiary Incident, or the Hibiya Riots). This response to the outcome of a war that had been proactively supported by the public, and which had left 200,000 people dead or injured, was the manifestation of the despair of people who felt they had been trampled on by the government.

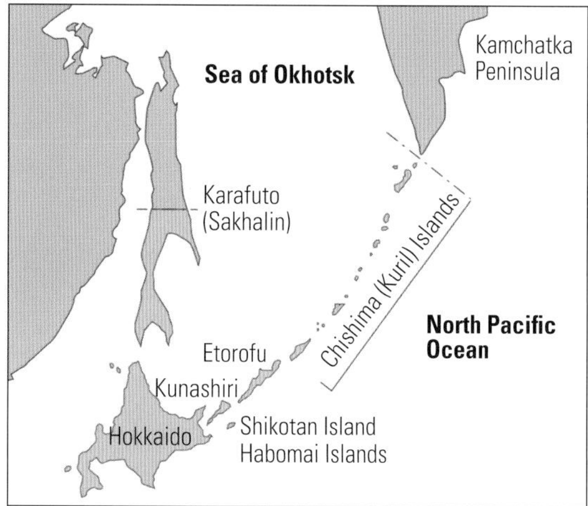

3-21. Borders based on the Treaty of Portsmouth (1905)

3-22. *Demarcation of Saghalin [Sakhalin] Frontier* (painting by Yasuda Minoru)

3 International Relations after the Russo-Japanese War: The Russo-Japanese Agreement and the Annexation of Korea

Itō Hirobumi and the Administration of Manchuria

Central to the rights and interests in Manchuria that Japan inherited from Russia were the lease on Liaodong Peninsula (Lushun and Dalian) and the right to operate the southern branches of the Chinese Eastern Railway. These positioned Japan strategically to become a "continental state." As stipulated by the Treaty of Portsmouth, both Japan and Russia were to withdraw their troops from all of Manchuria outside of the Liaodong Peninsula leasehold by April 1907. Until that time, however, the areas in question were under military rule by the forces that held them. Economic activities by foreigners were restricted, which was criticized by the United Kingdom and the United States as being contrary to the principles of the open-door policy. Sensing a crisis, Itō Hirobumi (now serving as resident-general of Korea) in February 1906 and again that May brought together government and military leaders for conferences to discuss the Manchuria issue. At the May conference that took place after Prime Minister Saionji Kinmochi had gone on an inspection tour of Manchuria, the chief of Army General Staff, General Kodama, suggested entrusting sovereignty over Manchuria to a single entity and putting together a new agency to supervise everything. Itō was fiercely critical in his response: "From my perspective, General

The Hague International Peace Conferences

The Napoleonic Wars implicated civilians in war like never before, and the unprecedented nature of the conflicts spawned the entirely new concepts of "people's wars" and "total war"—realities so tragic and devastating that they fostered an anti-war sentiment among the politicians and thinkers of the mid-nineteenth century. People began voicing the need for certain rules to govern war. The growing calls eventually culminated in an international consensus via the First Hague Peace Conference of 1899. Proposed by Russian Czar Nicholas II, the gathering brought nations together for diplomatic negotiations on the conduct of warfare. In attendance were twenty-six nations, most of which were European, as well as an East Asian contingent from Japan (represented by envoy Motono Ichirō) and Qing China. The attendees adopted three treaties (including the Convention for the Pacific Settlement of International Disputes and the Convention respecting the Laws and Customs of War on Land) and three declarations (one of which prohibited the use of poisonous gases). Japan signed all six of the agreements and ratified them in 1900. The Convention for the Pacific Settlement of International Disputes resulted in the creation of the Permanent Court of Arbitration, which was to resolve disputes in cases where the opposing parties agreed to referral to arbitration.

The Second Hague Peace Conference, which ran from June to October 1907, was called at the suggestion of US president Theodore Roosevelt and the official request of Czar Nicholas II. The conference drew forty-four countries, comprising the majority of nations in the world at the time. Japan was present again, with Satō Aimaro serving as envoy extraordinary and minister plenipotentiary. In all, the Second Hague Peace Conference produced thirteen treaties: expanded and revised versions of the Convention for the Pacific Settlement of International Disputes and the Convention respecting the Laws and Customs of War on Land, along with conventions stipulating matters relative to the opening of hostilities, the rights and duties of neutral powers in cases of war, and the position of merchant ships in cases of war. Japan signed all the treaties except for Convention (XII) Relative to the Creation of an International Prize Court, which failed to pass, and ratified the agreements in 1911. The Russo-Japanese War was the first war to be subject to the rules governing land wars and other conventions that came out of the Hague Peace Conferences.

While the two Hague Peace Conferences were never intended to deny or limit countries' rights to resort to war, they espoused a revolutionary vision of international society in the twentieth century. That outlook found expression in the attendees' work in outlining systems for peaceful resolution to offer recourse to conflict in peacetime, establishing rules of engagement, making international arbitration court a permanent fixture rather than an ad hoc arrangement for isolated conflicts, and producing numerous agreements on restricting instruments of war in the interest of humane conduct. The fact that even Qing China and Turkey, both subject to unequal treaties at the time, engaged in the discussions on an equal footing with their counterparts was no mere coincidence—their involvement spoke to the growing influence of the United States in world politics.

3-23. Peace Palace, the Hague

3-24. Tapestries in the Japanese Room of the Peace Palace

Kodama and others are fundamentally mistaken about Japan's status in Manchuria. Manchuria is, purely and simply, Chinese territory." Itō was fully in agreement with pulling out the troops as soon as possible and arranging for an "open door" for commercial interests.

The position of governor-general of Kwantung was to be restructured as a peacetime institution, and martial rule would come to an end. In place of the martial-rule offices, a consulate general was opened in Mukden, and Hagiwara Moriichi was appointed the first consul general. Japan's forces on the ground and back in the homeland were more concerned about the Russian threat than British and American demands for an open door in Manchuria, and they argued for continued military rule. This was incompatible with the view of the Ministry of Foreign Affairs, which considered the defense of Japan's rights and interests based on the rights granted by treaty to be fundamental. This conflict would have a lasting effect.

In August 1906, Japan called Lushun and Dalian the "Kwantung Leased Territory." It appointed a Kwantung governor-general to administer the area, and opened Dalian as a free port. With regard to management of the Chinese Eastern Railway's southern branches, Japan established the South Manchuria Railway Company (known informally as Mantetsu) that November, and appointed Gotō Shinpei—who had already proven himself as Taiwan's civil governor—to be its first president.

Gotō argued that supporting the transfer of immigrants and technology from Japan, as well as economic development, was necessary in order to consolidate control over Manchuria as a stronghold in the event of another conflict with Russia. Yamagata Aritomo was of a similar mind. In a 1909 opinion paper, he argued that it would not be possible to part with "a trophy of war captured with a 2-billion-yen fortune and more than 200,000 casualties." Given that circumstance, he said, until the Qing government demanded its return, Japan should establish an outstanding record in its administration of Manchuria. This would provide a rationale for demanding massive compensation.

The reasoning here was that Manchuria was not to be annexed like Korea, but rather left open to the Western powers for trade, investment, and commerce. In addition, Japan would build up a good track record in its administration of Manchuria, particularly with the South Manchuria Railway. Being unwavering in this would also be effective in Japan's own future moves on the Asian mainland and to counter the Russian threat. This also tied in to the train of thought that its own interests would be protected by concluding an agreement with Russia.

In practice, however, protecting and developing Japanese rights and interests in Manchuria (actually, South Manchuria) while also maintaining an open door there was difficult to achieve. The United States in particular continued to cast a suspicious eye on Japan. In March 1908, a US State Department official wrote in a memorandum, "If Japan continues with its current Manchuria policy, it will be to the great detriment of the US policy to protect the territorial integrity of China, and will deal a severe blow to the principles of an open door and equal opportunity in China."

Establishing Manchurian Rights and Interests

According to the Treaty of Portsmouth, Russia's rights and interests in Manchuria were to have been ceded to Japan with the consent of the Qing government. Toward that end, Japan and the Qing government began negotiations in November 1905, with Foreign Minister Komura Jutarō serving as a special plenipotentiary. The talks were hard going, since Japan wanted to get the Chinese to recognize as many rights and interests as possible beyond those stipulated in the Treaty of Portsmouth, while the Qing government sought to block the effort.

In particular, there was disagreement over two issues related to railroad building: the transfer of two military railways that the Japanese army had laid to conduct the war with Russia—the An-Feng Line (from Andong to Fengtian) and Hsin-Feng Line (Hsinmin to Fengtian)—and the laying of a third railway, the Chi-Chang Line (Chi-lin to Changchun). Eventually, it was agreed that the An-Feng Line would be sold to China fifteen years after it had been refurbished; the Hsin-Feng Line would be sold to China outright (with China borrowing from Japan to cover a portion of the costs); and China would handle construction of the Chi-Chang Line (with China borrowing from Japan to cover half of the costs). As to the issue of stationing guards to protect the railways, China requested that the troops be withdrawn within a year, after which it would station its own troops. In the end, Japan agreed it would take the same steps that Russia had.

The main text of the Treaty and Additional Agreement between Japan and China Relating to Manchuria signed in December 1905 comprised three articles. In them, Japan pledged to withdraw its troops from Chinese territory, while China consented to transfer all rights held by Russia to Japan as stipulated in the Treaty of Portsmouth, and to recognize the lease of the Liaodong Peninsula and ownership of the railway between Changchun and Lushun. Aside from this, the two countries also concluded numerous adjunct and undisclosed agreements, such as China's promise to forbid construction of railway lines parallel to those of the South Manchuria Railway.

However, as of 1908 the arrangements agreed to under the 1905 treaty and undisclosed adjunct agreements still had not yielded any practical effects. Accordingly, Komura—who had retained his appointment as foreign minister under the third Katsura cabinet—decided to negotiate over the railroad, mining, and Jiandao (Chientao) issues en bloc. The Jiandao issue referred to an ongoing border dispute between China and Korea that began in the mid-1800s over the possession of the Jiandao region in northern Korea. Given that Japan had seized the right to conduct diplomacy for Korea under the Japan-Korea Treaty of 1905, the dispute over jurisdiction over Jiandao that had been between China and Korea was now one between China and Japan.

Japan's resident envoy to China, Ijūin Hikokichi, was put in charge of the negotiations. In August 1909, he issued a memorandum on the refurbishing of the An-Feng Line. The following month, he and Qing representatives signed the China-Japan agreement concerning Jiandao (on issues including the residence status of Koreans in Jiandao) and the five-point China-Japan agreement on Manchuria (on handling railroads, on Japan's mining rights at the mines in Fushun and Yantai, and on the Sino-Japanese joint operation of mines along the railway lines). With these, the Treaty and Additional Agreement between Japan and China Relating to Manchuria finally came into full effect.

The Russo-Japanese Agreement

After the Russo-Japanese War, the sense that Russia was a threat still remained within the army. However, it was necessary for Japan to work together with Russia to keep Chinese nationalism in check and to retain the rights that Japan had obtained in Manchuria. This was the view of Yamagata Aritomo. Postwar Russia likewise wanted to avoid another conflict with Japan owing to pressures on the nation's finances and domestic social unrest. When former envoy to Japan Alexander Izvolsky was appointed foreign minister in May 1906, he simultaneously worked to improve relations with the United Kingdom to counter Germany (leading to the signing of the Anglo-Russian Convention in August 1907) while also seeking ways to improve ties with Japan in order to maintain peace in the Far East. Starting in early 1907, Izvolsky began negotiations with Japan's resident envoy to Russia, Motono Ichirō, to fine-tune the relationship.

In parallel with these negotiations with Russia, Japan was also negotiating with France over a flotation of public debt. France sounded out the disposition of its ally Russia on this Japanese public debt offering, which Russia rejected after scrutiny of the plan. On hearing this, Motono worked to dispel Russia's concerns, and succeeded. The negotiations that had begun the previous autumn between Japan's envoy to France Kurino Shin'ichirō and French foreign minister Stéphen Pichon now moved forward. The Franco-Japanese Treaty signed in June 1907 addressed the protection of China's territorial integrity, the preservation of the local status quo, and the mutual affirmation of the two parties' spheres of influence in the Chinese province of Fujian and Indochina. The Franco-Japanese Treaty also helped to encourage negotiations between Russia and Japan, leading to the signing of the Russo-Japanese Agreement of 1907 at the end of July.

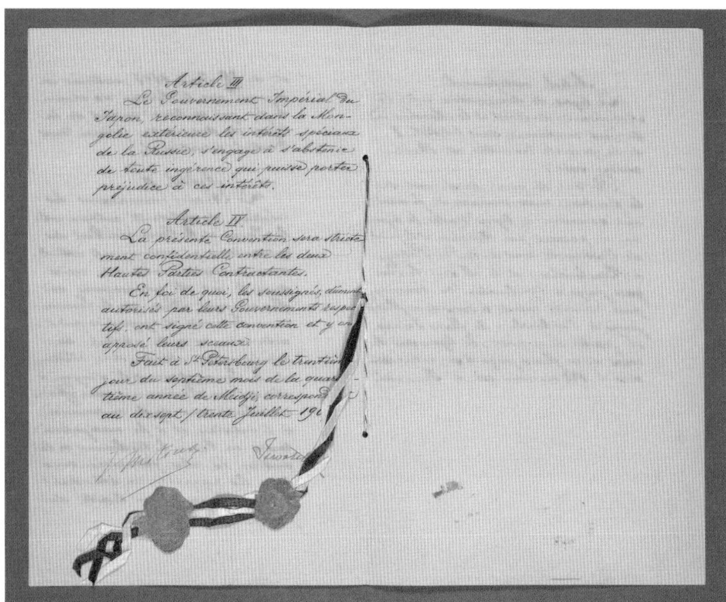
Article III
Le Gouvernement Impérial du Japon, reconnaissant dans la Mongolie extérieure les intérêts spéciaux de la Russie, s'engage à s'abstenir de toute ingérence qui puisse porter préjudice à ces intérêts.

Article IV
La présente Convention sera strictement confidentielle entre les deux Hautes Parties Contractantes.

En foi de quoi, les soussignés, dûment autorisés par leurs Gouvernements respectifs, ont signé cette convention et y on apposé leurs sceaux.

Fait à St. Pétersbourg le trentième jour du septième mois de la quar tième année de Meidji, correspond au dix sept / trente Juillet 190

3-25. Russo-Japanese Agreement of 1907 (signed treaty)

The latter agreement signaled that the two parties mutually affirmed the independence of China, its territorial integrity, and the equality of opportunity in commercial activities there. In addition, under the terms of secret codicils, they affirmed their respective spheres of influence (southern Manchuria for Japan, and northern Manchuria for Russia). Furthermore, the 1907 Russo-Japanese Agreement affirmed that Japan acknowledged Russia's special status in Outer Mongolia, while Russia in exchange deferred to Japan's predominance in Korea. Simply put, this agreement was aimed at coordinating the rights of the two nations involved in East Asia, and at preventing any conflict. It would not lead to an offensive and defensive alliance like the one between Japan and the United Kingdom. The details of the Russo-Japanese Agreement, including its secret codicils, were passed on to the United Kingdom and France, and they were welcomed by both. The longstanding negotiations continued, and eventually resulted in the conclusion of an agreement on connecting local railway lines to the Manchurian Railroad, as well as the Treaty of Commerce and Navigation between Russia and Japan of 1907 and the Russian-Japanese Fisheries Convention of 1907.

For Japan, the 1907 Russo-Japanese Agreement meant that its freedom of action in South Manchuria was assured and that a repeat of the war with Russia had been avoided. The agreement provided the diplomatic framework that would define bilateral relations for the next decade or so.

As to Korea (which was already on the way to becoming a protectorate), Japan aimed to avoid Russian intervention by concluding yet another agreement (the Japan-Korea Agreement of 1907) in July, just before the Russo-Japanese Agreement of 1907 was formalized. For Russia, the Japan-Korea Agreement strengthened the security of its rights and interests in the Far East; this would encourage its advance into the Balkan Peninsula.

Kurino Shin'ichirō (1851–1937)

Kurino Shin'ichirō was the son of a master spearman in the Chikuzen Kuroda domain. He went to study in the United States earlier than Komura Jutarō, and returned before him, in 1881, taking a job at the Ministry of Foreign Affairs, investigating the Imo Incident and Gapsin Coup. He started working on treaty revisions in 1885, but disagreements with Vice-Minister for Foreign Affairs Aoki Shūzō led to his transfer to the Ministry of Communications in 1886; he remained there until 1890. He then returned to the Ministry of Foreign Affairs and headed up the Political Affairs Bureau. In 1894, Foreign Minister Mutsu Munemitsu selected Kurino to serve as Japan's envoy to the United States. Kurino set about negotiating treaty revisions, eventually signing the new Japanese Treaty of Commerce and Navigation before being named envoy to France in 1897.

In July 1900, just as Katō Takaaki, Komura, and Hayashi Tadasu (Japan's minister to the UK) agreed on a doctrine of "Kasumigaseki diplomacy" that would leverage the Anglo-Japanese Alliance to mount a hard-line stance on relations with Russia, Kurino in Paris wrote a bold endorsement of a pact with Russia, embarrassing elder statesmen Itō Hirobumi and Inoue Kaoru. In addition to calling the British diplomatic tactics surrounding the Hokushin Incident (in which Japan came to the aid of the United Kingdom to suppress the Boxer Rebellion) an "attempt to use Japan to its own advantage," Kurino also told Prime Minister Itō in October 1900 that a war between Japan and Russia would be a battle of attrition that would wear both sides down, allowing the United Kingdom and Germany to "enjoy the good fishing in troubled waters." When Kurino made his way home in January 1901, Katsura Tarō and Komura persuaded him to become Japan's envoy to Russia. He left in November; on a stopover in Paris, he met Itō, who had returned from Russia, and was told that the Anglo-Japanese Alliance was going ahead. Kurino was indignant and tried to decline the Russian minister position, but Komura would not accept his resignation. He finally assumed his duties in Russia in February 1902 and began working to mend Japan's relations with Russia, but the Japanese government would not budge from its hard-line position. In the end, he found himself in February 1904 having to inform the Russian government that Japan would be severing its diplomatic ties. After the Russo-Japanese War, Kurino served as Japan's ambassador to France until 1911, in which capacity he helped realize the Franco-Japanese Treaty and revise trade agreements.

3-26. Kurino Shin'ichirō

"Dollar Diplomacy" and the Russo-Japanese Agreement of 1910

E. H. Harriman was an American rail baron who had become interested in administering railways overseas after Russia had ceded the southern branches of the Chinese Eastern Railway to Japan under the Treaty of Portsmouth. He proposed to the Japanese government that he should invest in the South Manchuria Railway and become its joint operator. Aware of the Japanese government's financial straits, Prime Minister Katsura had finalized a preliminary agreement (in the form of a memorandum) to accept the proposal in October 1905. However, Foreign Minister Komura saw the South Manchuria Railway as the key component of Japan's administration of Manchuria and opposed any joint administration, so he canceled the Harriman memorandum.

Rather than objecting to Japan having excessive economic rights and interests in Manchuria, US president Theodore Roosevelt expected that Japan would cooperate in preserving the territorial integrity of China and maintaining an economic open door there. Those expectations were reflected in the Root-Takahira Agreement of 1908, which mutually affirmed preserving the status quo in the Pacific region, as well as freedom of trade, and recognized the economic open-door policy, equality of opportunity, and territorial integrity with respect to China.

The Roosevelt administration had prioritized cooperation with Japan. However, Philander Knox, secretary of state in the subsequent Taft administration, grew concerned in the latter half of 1909 that Japan and Russia were building a sphere of influence in Manchuria through their control of the railways. He sought to reverse this by neutralizing the railways in Manchuria and developing the plans for a Chinchow–Aigun (Jinzhou–Aihun) railroad branch. The plan consisted of providing the Chinese government with consortium loans to make it buy back the railroads held by Japan and Russia, and have those railroads under international control until the debt had been repaid. To move that plan forward, international loans would be used to build a Chin-Ai Line that ran from Chinchow in southern Manchuria to Aigun (Aihun) in northern Manchuria. This was to be used as leverage in forging an agreement that would move Manchuria away from Japanese or Russian influence toward a more neutral status. However, Japan and Russia alike saw any plan to neutralize the Manchurian Railroad as a threat to their respective positions and special interests in Manchuria. This would practically render the Root-Takahira Agreement null and void. Former foreign minister Hayashi Tadasu is said to have been as shocked by the proposal as he had been at the Tripartite Intervention.

In January 1910, with both Japan and Russia objecting to Knox's neutralization plan, Russia approached Japan about writing a new treaty that would go beyond the earlier Russo-Japanese Agreement. Japan responded right away, and that July the two concluded the Russo-Japanese Agreement of 1910. Using the limits that had already been set down with the Agreement of 1907 to define "spheres of influence," each party agreed to accept free movement within the other's respective spheres of influence. The new agreement better clarified the positions that South Manchuria was in the Japanese sphere of influence, while North Manchuria was in Russia's. In an accompanying secret treaty, the two parties also agreed to take joint action in the event that their mutual "special interests" were threatened. This made the 1910 arrangement more proactive than the 1907 treaty. Foreign Minister Komura welcomed the new treaty as one that would eliminate sources of any future conflict between Japan and Russia, and as "an agreement that would offer the most effective guarantees for preserving peace in the East."

3-27. "People, the Exhausted Horse" (cartoon by unknown artist). The implication is that the Japanese people will be unable to bear the cost of additional military action.

Since Japan had recognized North Manchuria as being within the Russian sphere of influence, its next direction of advance would be toward Inner Mongolia. Arrangements had to be made with Russia, which already had Outer Mongolia within its sphere of influence. The opportunity to do so would arrive with the collapse of the Qing regime in the 1911 Chinese (Xinhai) Revolution.

The Annexation of Korea: The Significance of Turning Korea into a Protected Territory

Under strong Japanese pressure, Emperor Gojong had relinquished Korea's right to conduct its own diplomacy. In 1907, however, he dispatched secret emissaries to the Second Hague International Peace Conference. The emissaries pleaded with the international community to render the Japan-Korea Treaty of 1905 invalid. The emissaries were not allowed to attend the conference, so they worked to raise awareness of their case outside by other means, such as publishing written protests in the newspapers. Japan reacted sharply to news of the Hague secret emissary affair. It forced Emperor Gojong to abdicate the throne, and with the Japan-Korea Agreement of 1907 Japan completely took over the reins of power in Korea.

Arguments in favor of annexing Korea gathered force in Japan; in July 1909, the cabinet decided that Japan would carry out the annexation at "a suitable time." However, this did not mean that Japan was aiming toward annexing Korea immediately. It attached great importance to conforming to international law, and was cautious in its handling of the matter. Resident-General Itō Hirobumi had been seeking political and economic reform in Korea to establish its autonomy, and he was unenthusiastic about total annexation. But in October 1909, while on a trip to Harbin, Itō was assassinated by an independence activist, An Junggeun. The following August, Resident-General Terauchi Masatake and Prime Minister Lee Wanyong signed the Japan-Korea Annexation Treaty. This came one month after the Russo-Japanese Agreement of 1910 had been signed, and the premise was that Japan would consult Russia, against whom it had fought over control of Korea, about the annexation before going ahead.

The Annexation Treaty stipulated, "His Majesty the Emperor of Korea makes the complete and permanent cession to His Majesty the Emperor of Japan of all rights of sovereignty over the whole of Korea" (Article 1) in order "to assure permanent peace in the Extreme East" (preamble). "Peace" on the Korean Peninsula had been Japan's objective ever since the dying years of the bakufu, and with an annexation, this had now been achieved.

The process that led to the annexation of Korea

The Hague Secret Emissary Affair

At the Second Hague Peace Conference in 1907, "secret emissaries" from Korea unsuccessfully attempted to take part in the gathering and then claimed from outside the venue that the Japan-Korea Treaty of 1905 was invalid. Korea had not received an invitation to the 1899 First Hague Peace Conference or the 1907 Second Hague Conference, so Emperor Gojong dispatched a secret mission to the second gathering with directives to sign the Convention for the Pacific Settlement of International Disputes as a signatory nation in order to bring the conflict between Japan and Korea before the Permanent Court of Arbitration—a potential legal path to rendering the Japan-Korea Treaty null and void. The prospects of the court actually hearing the case were essentially nonexistent, as both countries needed to agree to such a hearing, but Japan was already on its guard. Suspecting that secret emissaries from Korea might appear at the conference, the Japanese government had repeatedly asked its Russian counterpart to make sure that Korea would not be invited.

It thus came as quite a shock to the Japanese contingent when the secret emissaries did, in fact, show up. The Japanese government demanded that the Korean emperor abdicate the throne and pressed Korea to accept the Japan-Korea Agreement of 1907. In a secret memorandum outlining the terms of the agreement, Japan stipulated that it would appoint Japanese officials to serve as Korea's attorney general and chief justice of the Korean supreme court, disband the Korean army, seize police authority, and appoint Japanese officials to the country's central and local administrative bodies.

In addition to fomenting distrust in the arbitration system as a means of peaceful conflict resolution, the Hague secret emissary affair also heightened concerns about countries using arbitration to further their own agendas. Coming out of the incident, Japan took a more cautious stance on arbitration-related treaties.

3-28. Ōkuma and Resident-General of Korea Itō

differed from the colonialization process under Western imperialism. As had been the case with the Katsura-Taft Agreement, Japan pushed toward creating the protectorate by working assiduously to secure international approval while conforming to international law. Annexation was not simply a matter of increasing Japan's control over Korea; it was also a means of preemptively excluding any intervention by a third country in Korea.

Having established its dominance over Korea through the Russo-Japanese War, Japan used the interests it had gained from Russia in southern Manchuria to administer the region, mainly through the Manchuria railway, hoping to validate its Manchurian interests through successful management. However, the foundation for those Manchuria interests was unstable. Of the interests acquired from Russia through the Treaty of Portsmouth, the lease on Lushun and Dalian would expire in 1923, and the right to operate the South Manchuria Railway would expire in 1939. Accordingly, one of Japan's most important diplomatic issues was getting these rights extended.

Japan's Manchuria rights and interests were

Prisoners of War and the Japanese Red Cross

The Sino-Japanese War, the Russo-Japanese War, and Conforming to International Law

Emperor Meiji's August 1894 imperial rescript declaring war on China contained a passage referring to adherence to international law. This was a rare instance in world history of a sovereign explicitly instructing the military to conform to international law. Shortly after the hostilities broke out, Army Minister Ōyama Iwao echoed the emperor's directive, invoking Japan's membership in the Geneva Convention to remind his troops that they were to "aid the injured and sick in accordance with civilized law, care for surrendering captives, and act with benevolence, regardless of how brutal or evil the enemy may be." Every division leader heading into battle received orders from the army minister to provide the injured and sick with proper care and protect prisoners of war (POWs).

The Geneva Convention was the "First Red Cross Treaty" of 1864, an agreement that the International Committee of the Red Cross (ICRC) proposed "for the Amelioration of the Condition of the Wounded and Sick in Armies in the Field." Japan became a signatory in 1886 (as well as the subsequent revisions to the treaty in 1906 and 1929, which Japan joined in 1908 and 1934, respectively). Qing China was not a signatory at the time of the Sino-Japanese War, however, which meant that the Japanese side alone was bound to uphold the terms of the convention and was prohibited from retaliating against whatever atrocities the Chinese side might commit. The allusion to "civilized law" was likely a very intentional one, part of a conscious attempt to earn Japan international recognition as one of the world's "civilized nations." Ōyama, having observed the Franco-Prussian War as a *kansen-bukan* (foreign official observing war operations) in 1870, spent the next three years in France studying military systems and later, as army minister, poured his energies into making Japan a member of the Geneva Convention. Upon Japan's signing of the convention, Ōyama distributed a document titled "Interpretation of the Red Cross Treaty" to all of the officers and soldiers in his command so that the army as a whole would gain an understanding of the agreement's stipulations.

The imbalance of the playing field between China and Japan was not lost on international law scholar Ariga Nagao. In light of the fact that Japanese forces banned all looting, cared for sick and wounded soldiers, treated POWs also insufficient in terms of international recognition. In all of the treaties Japan had in place—the second Anglo-Japanese Alliance treaty concluded during the Russo-Japanese War, the Treaty and Additional Agreement between Japan and China Relating to Manchuria signed after that war, the Franco-Japanese Treaty of 1907, the Russo-Japanese Agreement, and the Root-Takahira Agreement, among others—only Qing China and Russia had clearly acknowledged Japan's Manchuria rights and interests by treaty. In particular, the US open-door policy on China was becoming even more burdensome, and was making it increasingly difficult for Japan to achieve its objectives of defending and expanding its rights and interests in Manchuria. It was against this backdrop that the Chinese Revolution took place in 1911.

4 Japanese Immigration to the United States and the Gentlemen's Agreement

The immigration restrictions in the western United States were initially targeted at Chinese people. The numbers of Chinese immigrants had been continually increasing since the mid-1800s. At first, they were welcomed for working low-wage jobs that white Americans did not want to do. Before long, however, the view took hold that they were competing with whites for jobs, and violent expulsion movements arose in many places. In 1882, the US Congress passed the Chinese Exclusion Act, which

hospitably, and strove to embody the spirit of international law and civilized customs through and through, while the Chinese forces committed repeated atrocities in complete disregard of international law, Ariga concluded that "the most important feature of the [Sino-Japanese] war was that one of the warring sides strove to uphold the laws and customs of war while the other did not."

During the Sino-Japanese War, the Japanese Red Cross (originally the Hakuaisha [Philanthropy Society] until it changed its name in 1887) was extremely active. The first wave of relief sent 120 Red Cross relief workers to Korea, initiating a campaign that would dispatch a total of more than 1,400 personnel and provide care to over 100,000 sick and injured. The Japanese Red Cross also played an important role at home, as the organization's hospitals treated as many as 1,500 POW patients in Japan.

3-29. Citizens listening to a performance by German prisoners of war (POW Camp in Bandō, Tokushima Prefecture)

The Russo-Japanese War was the first war subject to the 1899 Hague Peace Conference's Convention respecting the Laws and Customs of War on Land, which stipulated that POWs "must be humanely treated" and prohibited prisoner abuse by member countries. Japan had already ratified the convention in 1900. The purport of the agreement played into many facets prohibited the immigration of Chinese laborers (merchants, etc., were excluded). Initially, the Act was set to expire in ten years, but it was extended into perpetuity by subsequent legislation.

In the wake of the ban on Chinese immigration, the number of Japanese immigrants rose. More than 1,000 Japanese emigrated to the United States each year of the final decade of the 1800s, and more than 10,000 did so in 1900. It was around this time that another exclusion movement, directed toward Japanese immigrants, arose. In California, which had become home to many Japanese immigrants, a movement arose to pass legislation to drive out Japanese laborers. Starting in 1895, the Japanese government intermittently imposed measures to regulate emigration of its own accord, but was unable to dampen people's enthusiasm for emigrating. Moreover, when the United States annexed the Hawaiian Islands in 1898, the number of immigrants heading to the United States via Hawaii rose sharply. In 1899, there were 35,000 Japanese on the US mainland, and by 1908—after the Russo-Japanese War—there were more than 100,000.

Japanese immigration became a diplomatic issue in 1906. In April of that year, in the wake of the San Francisco earthquake and fire, the city's Board of Education in October adopted a measure that banned Japanese children from attending public schools on the grounds that there was a shortage of facilities. They would instead have to attend the city's segregated Oriental School. This segregation of Japanese children—there were fewer than a hundred of them in the city—may be characterized as racial discrimination. San Francisco Consul General Ueno Suesaburō worked hard to get the problem resolved. However, neither he nor the state

Prisoners of War and the Japanese Red Cross

of Japan's war approach: not only did the February 1904 imperial rescript declaring war stipulate that Japan's forces were to use "all the means within the limits of the law of nations" to avoid making errors in judgment (just as the rescript for the Sino-Japanese War had articulated an imperial order to observe international law), but each field army was accompanied by two scholars of international law.

The Russo-Japanese War produced POWs in numbers that dwarfed those of the Sino-Japanese War. Japan operated a total of twenty-nine POW camps across Japan, from Hirosaki (in the northern reaches of Japan) to Kumamoto (at the southwest tip of Japan) to accommodate upward of 79,000 Russian prisoners. The injured and sick numbered more than 600,000, over 100,000 of whom were given emergency care by the Japanese Red Cross. Amid the events of the Hokushin Incident (Boxer Rebellion), the Japanese Red Cross also dispatched 490 personnel to locations both at home and overseas and tended to nearly 20,000 patients. The organization's efforts garnered praise at a meeting of the ICRC. In many ways, it was the work of the Japanese Red Cross that solidified Japan's standing as a "model nation" for the observance of international law.

POW Camps and the Japan-Germany Relationship: The First Performance of Beethoven's Ninth Symphony in Japan

In 1914, following Japan's clash with Germany at the port of Tsingtao on the Shandong Peninsula in World War I, roughly 4,700 German POWs (officers and soldiers) were transported to twelve (later sixteen) POW camps in locations such as Kurume (Fukuoka), Kumamoto, Tokyo, and Himeji (Hyōgo). The last camp to open was the Bandō Prisoner of War Camp (in what is now Naruto, Tokushima Prefecture), in April 1917. The Bandō Camp director, Colonel Matsue Toyohisa, gave POWs a considerable amount of independence and created numerous opportunities for prisoners to connect with the local community, and was said to be held in high regard by the prisoners. On June 1, 1918, POW Hermann Hansen conducted an orchestra at the Bandō Camp in the first performance of Beethoven's Ninth Symphony in Japan. Music and art were big parts of camp life in Bandō and other locations as well. Musicians at Japan's largest camp in Kurume, which accommodated over 1,300 POWs, performed more times than the Bandō orchestra did, and even played the Ninth for an audience in town. Sports were another medium of exchange. In January 1919, for example, a team of prisoners at the governor could find a solution. Meanwhile, Foreign Minister Hayashi Tadasu sent a letter of protest to Secretary of State Root via Japan's ambassador to the United States Aoki Shūzō.

President Roosevelt viewed the situation seriously. In his special message to Congress delivered in December 1906, he showed he was willing to actively step in with his comments indicating that it would be unacceptable for the United States' historically friendly relations with Japan to be spoiled by any one state. However, the notion that the federal government would actively intervene served only to harden the attitudes of the governor and the Board of Education. The local newspapers and press also stirred up antagonism toward the federal government, with the result that anti-Japanese elements talked frequently about "the outbreak of war with Japan" and "the threat of war."

The US government thought that banning Japanese immigration would settle the matter while also putting a check on the anti-Japanese movement. Accordingly, it sounded out the Japanese government on a bill to ban the intermigration of laborers. However, in substance the proposed legislation was discriminatory in that it would exclude only Japanese immigrants, and the Japanese government simply could not accept it.

While these difficult negotiations were going on, Roosevelt—having gotten their understanding that the federal government would have exclusive authority over immigration issues—promised San Francisco city officials that effective limits would be imposed on Japanese immigration and in turn got them to withdraw the discriminatory measures. In the end, Japanese children would be allowed to go back to their old schools so long as they were under

Ninoshima POW camp in Hiroshima Bay faced off against a joint team of players from Hiroshima Higher Normal School and other institutions for a soccer "friendly." The camp even organized a *baumkuchen* (German cake) sale at the Hiroshima Prefectural Commercial Exhibition Hall (now the A-Bomb Dome). Exchange activities continued until the camps shut down, with POW repatriation beginning in late 1919 and most camps closing in April 1920.

Out of World War I grew a deepening appreciation of humanitarianism. The development of international humanitarian law in Europe after the war, for example, testifies to that spirit. Continuing its active role, the Japanese Red Cross also contributed to relief work during the Siberian Expedition by housing isolated Czech patients and answering the Ministry of Foreign Affairs' call to rescue Polish orphans stranded in Vladivostok. However, the Japanese government did not ratify the 1929 Geneva Convention Relative to the Treatment of Prisoners of War due to opposition from the military. The rationale behind not ratifying the agreement—which Japan had actually signed, initially—was that endorsing it would put Japan at a disadvantage because the idea of surrender was so foreign to Japanese troops. Imperial soldiers were taught not to become prisoners of war, which may not have been the case for the soldiers of other countries. The convention was reciprocal in form, but Japan saw the provisions as unfair: Japan would need to care for the POWs it captured, but other countries would not face that same obligation because there would be no Japanese prisoners—surrender was simply unthinkable for the imperial troops. On a conceptual level, that refusal to surrender became an anomaly in the international context; Japanese norms and global standards started to deviate from each other. By the 1930s, the Japanese army had regressed considerably in terms of education in humanitarianism and international law.

The war years also created havoc for the Japanese Red Cross, which faced severe restrictions on its capacity for action, but the underlying commitment to providing relief via international cooperation remained intact and sustained the organization through to renewed prosperity after World War II.

sixteen years of age and possessed a certain level of English proficiency. Furthermore, to show that the measures were not directed toward Japanese alone, they were to be applied to all non-US citizens. The San Francisco Board of Education withdrew its decision to segregate Japanese children. In addition, while the US government guaranteed that Japanese could emigrate freely to Hawaii, the Japanese government promised to restrict emigration to the US mainland to 500 persons per year.

Around this time, the US government had asked Japan to voluntarily restrict overseas travel as a way to discourage various state governments from imposing harsh anti-immigration laws. The Japanese government was more concerned about guaranteeing that Japanese residing in the United States would be treated like citizens of other countries than in eliminating racial discrimination. Accordingly, it responded by imposing certain voluntary restraints.

Between November 1907 and February 1908, Foreign Minister Hayashi and US ambassador to Japan Thomas O'Brien exchanged eleven notes and memoranda that collectively created the so-called Gentlemen's Agreement. The Gentlemen's Agreement in essence called for Japan to restrict emigration. Aside from laborers who were returning to the United States, the parents, wives, or children of Japanese already in the United States, students, merchants, and people who fell into other specific categories, Japan would voluntarily ban all new emigration to the United States (excepting Hawaii).

The Gentlemen's Agreement between the two national governments did not take the form of a treaty for two reasons. For one, it would have been difficult for the United States to get the Congress to agree to such a treaty. Secondly, for the Japanese government, a treaty agreeing to voluntary restriction of emigration would smack of an unequal treaty. A non-treaty agreement was thus the best solution for both parties under the circumstances. However, the fact that it was not a formal treaty between governments would later reignite immigration-related diplomatic issues. In February 1908, Japan also came to a Gentlemen's Agreement with Canada (Hayashi-Lemieux Agreement). The idea of voluntary restraints would be a through-line for policies on emigration to North America until the Gentlemen's Agreement was unilaterally voided by the United States with passage of the Immigration Act of 1924.

CHAPTER 4

Political Movements in China and Japanese Diplomacy

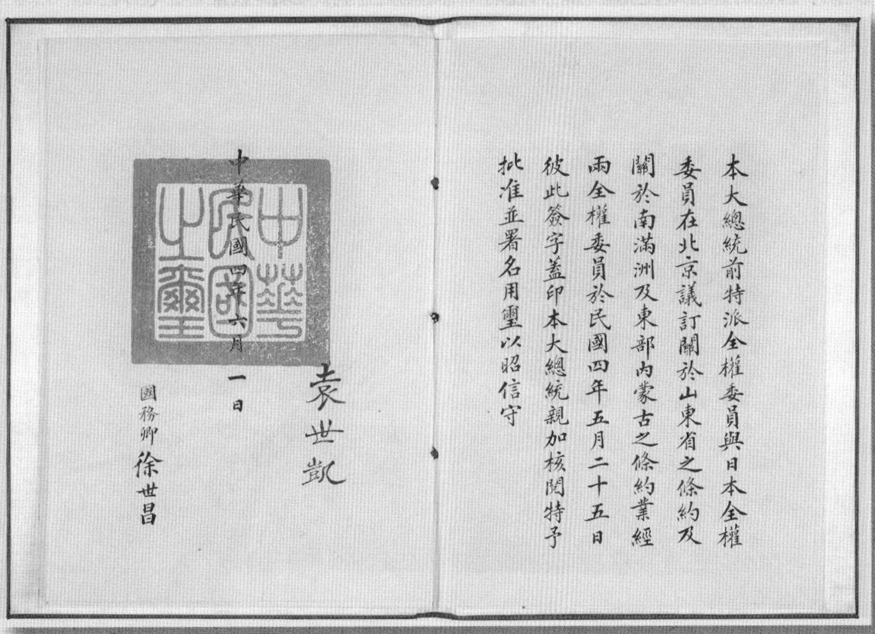
本大總統前特派全權委員與日本全權
委員在北京議訂關於山東省之條約及
關於南滿洲及東部內蒙古之條約業經
兩全權委員於民國四年五月二十五日
彼此簽字蓋印本大總統親加核閱特予
批准並署名用璽以昭信守

中華民國四年六月一日
袁世凱
國務卿 徐世昌

4-1. Treaties related to South Manchuria and eastern Inner Mongolia (instruments of ratification)

TIMELINE

1912 (Meiji 45/Taishō 1)

January 1 Sun Wen (Sun Yat-sen) declares founding of Republic of China

February 12 Qing regime collapses

March 10 Yuan Shikai appointed provisional president of Republic of China

June 18 Six-Power Consortium formed (including Japan and Russia)

July 8 Signing of Russo-Japanese Agreement of 1912

July 30 Emperor Meiji dies; Crown Prince Yoshihito assumes the throne; era name changed to Taishō

November 22 Army Minister Uehara demands that cabinet add two army divisions in Korea

December 21 Third Katsura cabinet formed

1913 (Taishō 2)

February 20 First Yamamoto Gonnohyōe cabinet formed

March 4 Woodrow Wilson takes office as president of the US

March 19 US banks withdraw from Six-Power Consortium

May 19 Anti-Japanese California Alien Land Law of 1913 passed

June 13 *Gunbu daijin geneki bukan-sei* (system allowing only active-duty officers to serve as army and navy ministers in the cabinet) revised

July 12 Second Chinese Revolution carried out by Sun Wen

October 6 Yuan Shikai installed as president; Japan officially recognizes the Republic of China (Beijing government)

1914 (Taishō 3)

January 23 Shimada Saburō investigates government over Siemens Scandal

April 16 Second Ōkuma cabinet formed

July 28 Outbreak of World War I

August 23 Japan declares war on Germany

1915 (Taishō 4)

January 18 Japan submits Twenty-One Demands to China

May 7 Japanese minister Hioki Eki submits ultimatum on Twenty-One Demands

May 9 Chinese government accepts Twenty-One Demands ("day of national disgrace")

May 13 US warns that it will not accept infringements on either Chinese territorial integrity or its open-door policy (second Bryan Note)

May 25 Japan and China sign a series of treaties related to Shandong Province, South Manchuria, and eastern Inner Mongolia

December 25 Third Chinese Revolution erupts

1916 (Taishō 5)

March 7 Ōkuma cabinet decides policy opposing Yuan Shikai's regime

June 6 Yuan Shikai dies

July 3 Signing of Fourth Russo-Japanese Agreement ("Secret" Russo-Japanese alliance)

October 9 Cabinet of Terauchi Masatake formed

1917 (Taishō 6)

January 20 Japan starts to issue Nishihara loans (through September 1918)

March 12 February Revolution takes place in Russia

March 27 Japan approves recognizing interim Russian government

April 6 United States declares war on Germany

May 11 America-Japan Society founded

June 6 Ad Hoc Advisory Council on Foreign Relations established

August 14 Republic of China enters World War I with declaration of war on Germany

November 2 Lansing-Ishii Agreement signed (exchange of notes)

November 7 October Revolution takes place in Russia; Soviet government established

1 The Yuan Shikai Regime and Japan

The Impact of the Chinese Revolution

In China under Qing rule, there had been repeated attempts to overthrow the Qing government since before the Russo-Japanese War. Finally, an uprising that took place on October 10, 1911, in Wuchang (present-day Wuhan) succeeded. The waves of revolution spread, and one after another all of the provinces south of the Yangtze River issued declarations of independence or secession from the Qing dynasty. In late December, the revolutionary forces brought together representatives from each province, and in January 1912, they formed the provisional government of the Republic of China in Nanjing, electing Sun Wen (Sun Yat-sen) as its president.

Meanwhile, the Qing court in the north attempted to regain control of the situation by restoring the secluded Yuan Shikai as prime minister on November 1, 1911. The United Kingdom, which had many interests mainly across the Yangtze River delta, responded positively to the revolution. In mid-December, it stepped in to mediate between the northern and southern factions. The talks were mediated by British minister John Jordan. The United Kingdom proceeded on the assumption that the Qing-court faction in the north favoring Yuan would gain control of the situation rather than the southern revolutionary forces, which were a hodgepodge with neither financial strength nor a stable political power base. If the Qing court rallied its forces with Yuan at its lead, then the Revolutionary Alliance would be inclined to compromise with him. Yuan had skillfully picked up on the United Kingdom's interests. In order to achieve his own ambitions to seize power, he promptly abandoned the effort to support Qing rule and pursued control through a constitutional republic in accordance with British expectations.

Meanwhile, in late November 1911, the recently installed second Saionji cabinet—while coordinating with the other powers concerned—affirmed in a meeting that it would wait for the right situation to develop in order to achieve a "fundamental solution to the Manchuria problem." However, at the end of that month, Saionji—heeding the views of his minister to the Qing Ijūin Hikokichi and Foreign Minister Uchida Yasuya (Kōsai)—shifted his policy toward coordinating with the British on achieving a cease-fire between the northern and southern factions and mediating a peace aimed at putting a constitutional monarchy into place. This was for two reasons. First, it was hoped that support for a constitutional monarchy would prove favorable in solving the Manchuria problem. Second, the establishment

Yamaza Enjirō (1866–1914) and Ijūin Hikokichi (1864–1924)

A native of the Fukuoka domain, Yamaza Enjirō joined the Ministry of Foreign Affairs in 1892 and spent the ensuing years in a variety of locations—Korea, several places in China, and London. He then served as the director-general of the Bureau of Political Affairs from 1901 to 1906, during which time he helped implement Komura Jutarō's diplomatic policies. After another stint in London, Yamaza toured China in the wake of the 1911 Chinese (Xinhai) Revolution. Seeing the country firsthand and meeting with key officials to discuss the situation, Yamaza began to take a critical view of sending the Japanese military onto the continent. He was appointed Japan's minister in the Republic of China in 1913, but died suddenly of a heart attack the following May, unable to use his political talent for governance in the country. Although Yamaza tended to be viewed as a hard-line diplomat, given his association with the Fukuoka-based nationalist Gen'yōsha (Dark Ocean Society) and his close relationships with members of other conservative groups like Konoe Atsumaro's Tōa Dōbunkai (East Asia Common Culture Society) and the Tai-Ro Dōshikai (Anti-Russia of a republican government would conflict with Japan's monarchical system, and the Saionji government feared this as a negative influence.

However, the United Kingdom rejected the Japanese proposal and was already mapping out its own north-south peace. Yuan also deferred to the United Kingdom. The Saionji cabinet had no choice but to keep pace with this situation as it developed in China. As the month ended, it gave up on the constitutional monarchy, backed off on the idea of a joint intervention with the United Kingdom, and returned to its course of watching and waiting. Seeing that the United Kingdom ignored Japan and took independent action led some in Japan to voice doubts about the significance of the Anglo-Japanese alliance.

In the end, the post-revolution chaos was brought under control as Yuan wished. Xuantong (Puyi), the last Qing emperor, abdicated; after Sun Wen's letter of resignation was received in March 1912, Yuan was made president of the Provisional Republic of China. This marked the start of the Yuan era.

The Emergence of "Manchurian and Mongolian Interests"

The Chinese Revolution presented an opportunity for Japan to change its China policy, which had been limited to maintaining and bolstering Japan's interests in Manchuria. At a cabinet meeting held in October 1911, Foreign Minister Uchida Yasuya first proposed a policy that, in addition to preserving Japan's interests in Manchuria, would get world powers to recognize Japan's dominant bargaining position and "expansion of its rights" in China

League), along with his broad-minded personality, there was also a careful side to him that made him excel at diplomatic affairs. Komura saw Yamaza as one of his potential successors, alongside Ijūin.

Ijūin Hikokichi, born in the Satsuma domain (now Kagoshima Prefecture), joined the Ministry of Foreign Affairs in 1890, at the same time as Ishii Kikujirō. After holding a variety of positions, including consul general in Tientsin, he became Japan's minister to Qing China in 1908. The 1911 Chinese Revolution put Ijūin opposite a new regime, the Yuan Shikai administration, which he urged to adopt a constitutional monarchy as part of Foreign Minister Uchida Yasuya's policy of cooperating with the United Kingdom. When Yuan instituted a republic with British support, Ijūin offered to step down from his position, but Uchida, worried about jeopardizing diplomatic relations with China, did not allow it. Ijūin thus continued his diplomatic efforts on the premise that the major powers would be working together, and managed to make Japan part of the Six-Power Consortium. Ijūin was finally relieved of his duties in 1913, with Yamaza taking over as envoy to the Republic of China. He became Japanese ambassador to Italy in 1916 and served as a plenipotentiary in the Japanese delegation at the Paris Peace Conference. He was impressed by the unrelenting propaganda war waged

4-2. Yamaza Enjirō

4-3. Ijūin Hikokichi

by the Chinese delegation in Paris, and on his return home, he poured his energy into bolstering Japan's information and propaganda framework as part of the Hara Takashi cabinet. When the Ministry of Foreign Affairs Information Department was created in 1921, he became its first director. In 1923, Prime Minister Yamamoto Gonnohyōe appointed Ijūin foreign minister in his second cabinet, but he only served for three months, as the cabinet resigned en masse at the end of that year. He was taken ill three months later and died suddenly. Yamaza and Ijūin, who had both served long stints in Korea and China and were well regarded there, had been considered possible successors to Komura.

Saionji Kinmochi (1849–1940)

Saionji Kinmochi was born in Kyoto to the Tokudaiji *kuge* (noble) family and later adopted into the Saionji family, another *kuge* house. Strong-minded and bright from a young age, Saionji enrolled at the Kaiseisho (Institute for Western Studies) in 1870. Before long, he was off to study in France, where he befriended writer and political thinker Nakae Chōmin. Saionji returned to Japan at the age of thirty and founded the *Tōyō Jiyū Shimbun* (Oriental Free Press) with Nakae and Matsuda Masahisa, heading the newspaper for a short stint before stepping down. In 1881, an introduction from Iwakura Tomomi landed Saionji a role as an assistant to members of the Sanji-in (Legislative Advisory Council) under Itō Hirobumi. Impressed by Saionji's legal acumen and aptitude, Itō brought him along on his European trip to study constitutional systems in 1882. Saionji would later head back to Europe as a minister in 1884 and strike up a friendship with Mutsu Munemitsu, who was in Vienna studying under Lorenz von Stein.

Upon returning to Japan in 1891, Saionji harnessed his knowledge of French law in furthering enhancements to Japan's systems for civil law and commercial law. He made his cabinet debut in 1894, as minister of education in the second Itō cabinet. He also ended up taking over as foreign minister for an ailing Mutsu and overseeing Japan's diplomatic affairs in the aftermath of the Sino-Japanese War until the Itō cabinet resigned en masse in 1896. Four years later, Saionji joined Itō's new Rikken Seiyūkai (Association of Friends of Constitutional Government) along with Hara Takashi. His connections with Itō would remain strong. When the Itō cabinet folded in May 1901, for example, Saionji stepped in to serve as acting prime minister until the Katsura Tarō cabinet officially took shape. Saionji's position as a successor to Itō continued to solidify in 1903, when Itō stepped aside as president of the Seiyūkai and Saionji assumed the role. He then went on to serve several stints as Japan's prime minister after the Russo-Japanese War, alternating with Katsura Tarō as one half of the "Katsura-Saionji" era of political leadership.

4-4. Saionji Kinmochi

In 1906, during his first tenure as prime minister, Saionji drew on Itō's support to plot a roadmap for terminating Japan's military rule in Manchuria—which had triggered international protests—and opening up local operations. Saionji's first premiership also included efforts to build relationships with major global powers that would allow Japan to secure its Manchurian interests under the relevant treaties and maintain an upper hand in Korea, using the Anglo-Japanese alliance and the Russo-Japanese agreement as strategic cornerstones. When the Imperial Defense Policy and its noticeably military-influenced plans emerged in 1907, Saionji also worked to curtail the push for unilateral

proper. However, the Saionji cabinet was unable to finalize a new China policy.

Japan had a variety of connections, public and private, to both the Revolutionary Alliance and the Qing court. In the early stages of the revolution, the government put these connections to work. It secretly provided arms and funds (in the form of loans) to the Qing government in response to a request from the court, demanding in return a change in the Qing's attitude toward Japan and recognition of Japan's status in Manchuria. On the other hand, it also tacitly accepted the actions of the likes of soldiers, merchants, and Japanese political activists operating in mainland China who were providing support to the Revolutionary Alliance by such means as furnishing arms via trading companies. While the army had repeatedly explored plans for large-scale troop dispatches, these were cast aside, as coordinating with other powers was considered preferable to a solo military offensive. This indecision over dealing with the revolution hindered the creation of a unified China policy.

That said, the 1911 revolution offered the opportunity to introduce the new concept of "Manchurian and Mongolian interests" (*Man-Mō ken'eki*). In November 1911, taking advantage of the revolution's outbreak, Outer Mongolia declared its independence from Qing China with Russian support. This meant that, in addition to settling on a border that would divide the existing Manchuria into north and south, Japan and Russia needed to determine whose sphere of influence Inner Mongolia lay militarization out of concern for international diplomacy and state finances. The Katsura-Saionji era lost some of its luster in its waning years as Katsura Tarō and the Seiyūkai's Hara began to command a larger presence on the political stage, and it became clear to Saionji that trying to keep staking out political power would be futile. In late 1912, Saionji dissolved his second cabinet over disagreements surrounding the issue of creating two additional army divisions, left the leadership of the Seiyūkai in Hara's hands, and withdrew from the political spotlight to Kyoto for a full three years. While he may have removed himself from the country's day-to-day administration, Saionji still wielded considerable influence. As an elder statesman, Saionji had a big hand in selecting candidates for the premiership after the mass resignation of the third Katsura cabinet.

Saionji's political philosophy also shaped the composition of cabinets well after his departure from the scene, particularly after the Terauchi Masatake cabinet resigned in September 1918. Holding the British model of two-party politics as the ideal to aspire to, Saionji led the elder statesmen in working to shape Japan's first real partisan cabinet under the Hara administration.

Saionji was appointed to lead the Japanese delegation to the Paris Peace Conference in November 1918 and began attending meetings of the Supreme War Council the following spring, but he never made any statement whatsoever at the gatherings. By that time, his French had grown quite rusty and was inadequate to make Japan's presence known on the international stage. On his return from Paris, he took to spending most of the year at his villa in Okitsu, Shizuoka Prefecture. He would use messengers to gather the information he needed so that he could exercise political influence remotely. With the death of Yamagata Aritomo in 1922, Saionji found himself the highest-ranking elder statesman, and used this status to help inculcate party politics through recommendations for selecting the prime minister. He also held a powerful influence over Imperial Household Minister (and later Lord Keeper of the Privy Seal) Makino Nobuaki, whose proximity to Emperor Shōwa gave Saionji considerable control of the court. As Sino-Japanese conflict intensified in the aftermath of the Manchurian Incident, Saionji recommended Ugaki Kazushige and Konoe Fumimaro for the premiership in hopes that they would keep the military in check and resolve the matter.

Around the time that Japan recognized the statehood of Manchukuo, Saionji stated, "Itō and the rest of us don't hold a narrow vision of wanting Japan to be the leader of Asia or creating a Monroe Doctrine for Asia, but rather have aimed to establish Japan as part of the global community." A strong, able leader with the type of "insight" that Saionji hoped for would not emerge in Japan's wartime years, however.

under. The two governments began negotiations in early 1912, resulting in the secret Russo-Japanese Agreement of 1912, which divided Inner Mongolia into eastern and western halves along a meridian running through Beijing and acknowledged the two countries' respective special interests.

The Japanese sphere of influence was established as "South Manchuria and eastern Inner Mongolia" (Man-Mō), leading to the emergence, in 1913, of the concept of "Manchurian and Mongolian interests." While the 1912 Russo-Japanese Agreement was completely secret, both the United Kingdom and France were notified of its contents. As a result, those two countries, as well as Russia, recognized South Manchuria and eastern Inner Mongolia as being within Japan's sphere of influence. However, international recognition of Japan's Manchurian and Mongolian interests was nebulous at best. Japan's interests and rights (particularly with respect to eastern Inner Mongolia) also were not firmed up by treaty with China. As a consequence, the foundation for Japan's rights and interests was fragile.

International Consortia and the North-South Conflict

Even after this, the Taft administration pursued a strategy whereby international assistance in running the South Manchuria Railway and domestic development would be financed by an international consortium, and American banks would participate. With their significant holdings and interests in

What Were the Manchurian and Mongolian Special Interests?

"Manchuria-Mongolia" ("*Man-Mō*" in Japanese), a geographic zone encompassing special Japanese interests, refers to southern Manchuria and eastern Inner Mongolia—although there were actually no interests in the area that Japan called "eastern Inner Mongolia." The inclusion of the Mongolian element was, in essence, a rhetorical device that signified nothing of substance. Japan had actually offered up its only vested interests in the region—the Taonan-Rehe route—upon the formation of the new Four-Power Consortium in China. As a result, the special interests that Japan held under treaty terms extended no further than southern Manchuria; "Manchuria-Mongolia" was an overstatement. From the beginning, however, Japan maintained unilaterally that its Manchurian-Mongolian interests were grounded in rights that were not only part of the Sino-Japanese treaties after the Russo-Japanese War, but were also heavily dependent on special historical and politico-economic relationships. Therefore, since the fait accompli and practices were based on regional agreements with only vague legal grounding, it was extremely difficult for Japan to make a convincing case for its special interests to the international community.

For example, Japan based its argument for excluding all of its interests in Manchuria and Mongolia from the scope of the new Four-Power Consortium on its assumption that the United Kingdom, the United States, Russia, and France had already recognized those interests—but there were no actual treaty provisions corroborating that premise. Even the Treaty Respecting South Manchuria and Eastern Inner Mongolia, which had its grounding in the Twenty-One Demands, was opaque in its legitimacy. The United States voiced no objections to the agreement initially, but it later adopted an all-out nonrecognition policy concerning every provision in the Japan-China treaties of 1915. The Lansing-Ishii Agreement did nothing more than acknowledge that Japan had "special interests" in China, based on the premise that there were special relationships between nations with mutual land borders. The Russo-Japanese agreements

Manchuria, both Japan and Russia objected to the concept of creating a Four-Power Consortium. As the United Kingdom and France were also giving signs of support for the Japanese and Russian positions, the United States called for including Japan and Russia in the consortium rather than excluding them. Since Japan had delayed loans related to concessions in central and southern mainland China before the British curbs and China's move to recover its rights, it accepted the request of the consortium, even as it remained mindful of its special rights in Manchuria. As a result, it joined to make a Six-Power Consortium in March 1912, designating the

4-5. Headquarters of the South Manchuria Railway Company

Uchida Yasuya (Kōsai) (1865–1936)

Uchida Yasuya spent a total of over seven years leading the Ministry of Foreign Affairs in five separate cabinets between the late Meiji to the early Shōwa eras. Born in Yatsushiro, in the province of Higo (now Kumamoto Prefecture), Uchida graduated from the faculty of law at Tokyo Imperial University in 1887 and then joined the Ministry of Foreign Affairs. He was transferred to the United States, where Mutsu Munemitsu was stationed as minister, in 1888. When Mutsu became Japan's minister of agriculture and commerce in 1889, Uchida moved to the ministry with him, and there he met his lifelong friend Hara Takashi. Two years later, Uchida returned to the Ministry of Foreign Affairs—once again under Mutsu, who had become vice-minister. In 1893, Uchida assumed a post in London and worked on the signing of the Anglo-Japanese Treaty of Commerce and Navigation. He was then posted to Qing China in 1895. After his return to Japan, he served in several leadership positions, such as heading up the Trade Bureau and the Bureau of Political Affairs at the Ministry of Foreign Affairs. He returned to Qing China as Japan's resident minister in 1901 and confronted the issue of Russia's also lacked details in their content, other than the secret agreement whereby Russia recognized Japan's interests in Manchuria and Mongolia, which had also been shared confidentially with the United Kingdom and France.

On the diplomatic front, meanwhile, Japan had to emphasize that its special interests did not constitute an exclusive sphere of influence. That line of argument may have been accepted in the era of imperialist diplomacy, but it clearly ran counter to the Washington System of guaranteeing mutual open-door policies, ensuring equal opportunity to all, and opposing the formation of exclusive spheres of influence. Some Ministry of Foreign Affairs officials began to harbor doubts about Japan's interpretation of the situation—that the international community had already recognized Japanese interests in Manchuria and Mongolia—and worried that Japan might end up violating the Nine-Power Treaty. The voices of concern were in the minority, however, as most officials maintained the prevailing argument. Foreign Minister Shidehara, for example, never wavered from his belief that, while China's sovereignty extended to Manchuria, Japan's interests in Manchuria and Mongolia had a firm foundation in treaty provisions and the approval of the international community.

The Japanese government would not budge from this line. Japan's Army General Staff refused to accept the new consortium negotiations of 1920, calling them a "failure." Japan never backed down from seeking recognition of the special nature of its interests in Manchuria and Mongolia, regardless of ongoing shifts in international relations and the international order. Even as China's move to reclaim sovereign rights began to encroach on Manchuria in the late 1920s and into the 1930s, Japan was relying heavily on its special rights in this region in terms of national defense and economic survival, leading to strident declarations rooted in the "Manchuria-Mongolia lifeline" theory.

refusal to withdraw its troops from Manchuria after the Boxer Rebellion. When Uchida got wind of secret Russo-Qing negotiations surrounding the Manchurian withdrawal in April 1903, he determined that Russia had no intention of pulling its military out—rather, he thought, it was using the time to prepare for war with Japan secretly. Uchida responded by urging Foreign Minister Komura Jutarō to launch hostilities against Russia as quickly as possible. He also requested that the Qing government refuse Russia's demands to delay the troop withdrawal. Uchida's tactics proved successful, dealing a significant blow to Russia's maneuvers. Later, he recalled that his "blood had never boiled as much" as it did when he learned of the behind-the-scenes dealings between Russia and Qing China. In 1904, Uchida met with Prince Qing and forced the Qing ruler to admit the existence of a secret pact and show him the clandestine Russo-Qing agreement, which he copied down in full.

After a stint in Vienna, Uchida went on to fill a variety of key posts, becoming Japan's ambassador to the United States in 1909 and later signing the US-Japan Treaty of Commerce and Navigation. He made his cabinet debut in October 1911, becoming Saionji Kinmochi's second foreign minister and immediately being faced with the 1911 Revolution in China. Uchida initially adopted a wait-and-see approach to the situation—until it became clear that Yuan Shikai was looking to quell the uprising by instituting a constitutional monarchy. Uchida called on the United Kingdom to help subdue the anti-Qing unrest via an international collaboration. The British side, however, had already made secret contact with Yuan Shikai and was working to mediate peace talks between the Qing dynasty and the revolutionary forces around a compromise that involved approving the creation of a Chinese republic. In late December 1911, Japan had to scrap its plans to help establish a constitutional monarchy in China. A year later, Uchida joined the rest of the Saionji cabinet in stepping down from his position.

4-6. Uchida Yasuya

The Russian Revolution unfolded in 1917 while Uchida was serving as ambassador to Russia. When Russia eventually signed a separate peace with Germany, Uchida returned to Japan. He later voiced his opposition to a Siberian Expedition, arguing that the likelihood of the "German peril" pushing eastward (i.e., a German advance into the Far East) through a Russo-German partnership was slim, and that the revolutionary forces would be able to sustain their strength. Uchida also began his second stint as foreign minister as part of the Hara cabinet in September 1918 and remained in that position after Hara's death, serving under subsequent prime ministers Takahashi Korekiyo and Katō Tomosaburō. During these years, Uchida filled his leadership teams in the Ministry of Foreign Affairs with "internationalists" like Shidehara Kijūrō, Hanihara Masanao, Debuchi Katsuji, Matsudaira Tsuneo, Matsuda Michikazu, and Yamakawa Tadao to arrive at a vision that guided Japan through the Paris Peace Conference and the Washington Naval Conference. He eventually stepped down as foreign minister in 1923, after which he became a privy councillor and later served as Japan's representative in signing the Kellogg-Briand Pact (the General Treaty for Renunciation of War as an Instrument of National Policy) in 1928. However, Uchida came under fire for giving Japan's consent to the agreement's provision stipulating that the governments would condemn war "in the name of the people"—a provision that the opposition parties criticized as encroaching on the supreme authority of the emperor, leading to his resignation from the Privy Council.

In June 1931, Foreign Minister Shidehara appointed Uchida the president of the South Manchuria Railway. In that capacity, Uchida worked to reform the struggling operation and tried to reinvigorate stagnant railway negotiations. He would soon find himself facing another difficult development when the Manchurian Incident unfolded in late 1931. Although Uchida initially favored a non-aggression policy, he gradually subscribed to the notion that the Kwantung Army's military actions were in "self-defense" and represented no breach of the anti-war pact that he himself had signed in 1928. He also backed the formation of a new Manchuria-Mongolia administration. Becoming foreign minister again in July 1932 as part of the Saitō Makoto cabinet, Uchida argued at an August session of the Imperial Diet that the recognition of the state of Manchukuo was the only solution to the Manchuria issue, even if it meant "reducing the country to scorched earth." Uchida soon fell ill, however, and resigned as foreign minister the following year.

In 1934, diplomacy expert Kiyosawa Kiyoshi suggested that Uchida's diplomacy had initially been as flexible and resilient as rubber—but the tragedy for Japan was that the rubber fossilized and hardened. In the 1930s, Uchida's diplomacy showed little of the flexibility he had once prided himself on.

Yokohama Specie Bank as its designated bank. The following year, the newly elected administration of Woodrow Wilson dropped support for US participation in the consortium out of concerns that the loan conditions would impair China's administrative independence. Accordingly, US banks withdrew, leaving in place a five-power consortium. This consortium and its reform loans for China helped to stabilize the Yuan Shikai regime.

Meanwhile, the conflict between Yuan Shikai and the Revolutionary Alliance had heated up. When Song Jiaoren, one of the leaders of the revolution, was assassinated, Sun Wen precipitated a second revolution in July 1913. Yuan Shikai immediately suppressed it, and when he was formally elected president that October, Japan and twelve other countries extended recognition to the new government. Sun Wen sought refuge in Japan, and China entered an era of conflict between its north and south.

On September 5, 1913, Abe Moritarō, head of the Political Affairs Bureau of the Ministry of Foreign Affairs, was assassinated in a move directed by Iwata Ainosuke, a political agitator active in mainland China. Iwata was motivated by his support for Yuan Shikai and the belief that Japan had turned its back on its interests in Manchuria and Mongolia. Japan's minister to China, Ijūin Hikokichi, was also an assassination target, but it was Abe who had led the opposition to intervention in China within the Ministry of Foreign Affairs. In an opinion paper submitted to Foreign Minister Uchida, he had argued that there was a pressing need to keep the army from intervening in internal Chinese affairs and for all diplomatic efforts to be handled by the Foreign Ministry. However, there were ongoing, relentless machinations by private citizens such as Kawashima Naniwa, who had schemed to push out Yuan Shikai, bring out Prince Shanqi in his stead, and achieve both a restoration of the Qing court and independence for Manchuria and Mongolia. The

4-7. Japanese troops enter Tsingtao (Qingdao)

actions of factions of the army in the field who sought to boost their own interests in response also proved serious. The nonintervention policy was turning into a mere formality. This was also due in part to the increasingly widespread view, both within and outside government circles, that coordination with the United Kingdom and the United States and the nonintervention policy were blocking a more proactive China policy. This lent greater prominence to voices saying that the Anglo-Japanese alliance was no longer necessary. The outbreak of World War I finally ended the stalemate.

2 The Start of World War I and Japan's Participation

Entering the War against Germany and the Occupation of Shandong

World War I began as a local conflict on the Balkan Peninsula, but it would generate losses and slaughter on a scale humanity had never experienced before, leaving Europe in ruins. It was described as "total war." When fighting broke out at the end of July 1914, there was still the possibility it would proceed as a traditional conflict between Austria-Hungary and Serbia. However, the network of alliances and ententes provided the spark that in no time at all caused it to develop into a great war that enveloped all five of the major European powers. Regardless of the fact that Japan had not been actively involved in starting this European war, and even though many other countries were quick to declare their neutrality, Japan promptly joined in.

On August 5, Katō Takaaki, in his capacity as foreign minister in the second Ōkuma Shigenobu cabinet, called on the British ambassador to Japan. He conveyed Japan's intention to support the United Kingdom, which clearly appeared determined to involve itself in the conflict. He also said that, in the event that the war spread to East Asia, Japan would act in accordance with the Anglo-Japanese alliance. When the United Kingdom declared war on Germany that same day (Japan time), it requested Japan's participation in the conflict, though this was limited to asking the Japanese navy to attack German warships stationed in the Far East. On August 7, in an emergency session, the cabinet decided to declare war on Germany. Its reasoning was that while the Anglo-Japanese alliance did not oblige Japan to join in, doing so was in keeping with the "fellowship" of the alliance and would also improve Japan's international standing.

The decision was passed on to the elder statesmen on August 8. For his part, Yamagata Aritomo was somewhat concerned that Japan would be left isolated once the Western powers returned to East Asia after the war. He wanted to act cautiously, but Katō overrode him immediately. Inoue Kaoru, another of the elder statesmen, was very much in favor of participating in the war. In a memorandum paper to the Ōkuma cabinet, he argued that Japan should unite in accepting this as "god-sent aid" and end, for once and for all, the Western powers' habit of isolating Japan. His view was that Japan should make the most of the Western powers' attention on

Katō Takaaki (1860–1926)

Katō Takaaki was from the Owari domain (Aichi Prefecture). He attended Tokyo Imperial University, and took a position in shipping operations at the Mitsubishi zaibatsu after graduation. The company quickly posted him to the United Kingdom, where he made the acquaintance of Mutsu Munemitsu. Katō married the eldest daughter of Mitsubishi president Iwasaki Yatarō in 1886, creating a bond that would have essentially put him on track for a promising career in the company—but a recommendation from Mutsu prompted Katō to go into government service and assume a post at the Ministry of Foreign Affairs in 1887. In 1890, Katō moved to the Ministry of Finance, but soon returned to the Ministry of Foreign Affairs under Mutsu, this time as the director-general of the Bureau of Political Affairs. Katō's tight association with Mutsu made him one of the "three crows of the Mutsu faction," as some called the coterie of Katō, Vice-Minister Hayashi Tadasu, and Bureau of Trade director-general Hara Takashi. After the Sino-Japanese War, Katō was named minister to the United Kingdom despite being only thirty-five years old. He took up his post in 1895 and spent the next four years in London, constantly working to convince the Japanese government of the need for a partnership with the United Kingdom. In a written report dated March 1898 and addressed to Foreign Minister Nishi Tokujirō, Katō blasted the "Man-Kan Kōkan" doctrine of exchanging freedom of action in Manchuria for the same in Korea as a form of "weak-kneed diplomacy toward Russia" and implored Nishi to "fight for Japan's existence" by "collaborating with the United Kingdom in anticipation of a confrontation with Russia."

Katō maintained that same perspective as foreign minister in the fourth Itō Hirobumi cabinet, which formed in January 1900. Always wary of the Russian threat, he grew increasingly apprehensive about a southward advance by Russia in the wake of the Boxer Rebellion, and adopted a harsh diplomatic stance against the country accordingly. Germany's proposal for a tripartite agreement between Japan, Germany, and the United Kingdom in the spring of 1901 led Katō to task Hayashi, Japan's envoy to the United Kingdom at the time, with initiating informal negotiations about a possible Anglo-Japanese alliance. However, Katō resigned as foreign minister—along with the rest of the Itō cabinet—that June with no alliance to show for his efforts. He would make a comeback as minister for foreign affairs in Saionji Kinmochi's first administration after Japan and Russia made peace, but he resigned from the post almost immediately over his opposition to nationalizing the railroads. The third Katsura Tarō cabinet made Katō foreign minister for a third time, following the death of Komura Jutarō. Katō took the position on one important condition: that the cabinet would address the negative impact of Japan's "dual diplomacy," which Katō saw as a result of the army's intimate involvement in shaping Japan's policy on China. The 1913 Taishō political crisis in which the entire Katsura cabinet stepped down, however, ended his efforts after little more than fifty days. At the end of 1908, Katō was once again appointed ambassador to the United Kingdom in London, and successfully steered the negotiations for the Third Anglo-Japanese Alliance. Concerned that the renewal of the Russo-Japanese Agreement might

4-8. Katō Takaaki

the war to solidify its foothold in East Asia.

On August 15, the Ōkuma cabinet sent an ultimatum to the German government, demanding that German warships withdraw from East Asian waters and that the Kiautschou (Jiaozhou) Bay leased territory be handed over to Japan so that it could be returned to China. Germany ignored these demands, and so, on August 23, Japan declared war on Germany. Japanese army units began landing on the Shandong Peninsula in early September. After they had seized the railroads in Shandong, they worked with British forces to capture Qingdao. In late November, they forced the German troops in the region to surrender.

In the meantime, on August 6, the Yuan Shikai regime had issued a declaration of its neutrality which forbade combatants from engaging with one another on Chinese territory. In response to Japanese demands, China accepted the establishment of certain neutral zones, as it had during the Russo-Japanese War. However, the Qingdao-Jinan railway (the "Shandong railway") was make Japan see Russia in too amicable a light, Katō promoted a strong Anglo-Japanese alliance as the "essential framework of imperial diplomacy."

In April 1914, Katō assumed leadership of Katsura's Rikken Dōshikai (Association of Allies of Constitutional Government) party. The Rikken Dōshikai was the ruling party of the second Ōkuma cabinet, which made Katō foreign minister and deputy to the prime minister. Katō eliminated the practice of sharing classified documents with the elder statesmen in order to keep them from interfering with diplomatic matters, a move that invited an excited backlash from the elders. He also rejected participation in the Advisory Council for Foreign Affairs created by the Terauchi Masatake cabinet, because he believed it violated the constitution's principle of centralizing diplomacy. On the international front, World War I broke out not long after the second Ōkuma administration was established. Katō led Japan toward declaring war on Germany, seeing the conflict as a god-sent opportunity for securing a better foothold for Japanese growth. The overall diplomatic strategy rested on leveraging the Anglo-Japanese alliance to expand Japan's interests in Manchuria and Mongolia. To establish and enlarge the then-pending Manchurian interests, Katō submitted the Twenty-One Demands to China—but his rash, hasty negotiations were high-handed and often inconsistent. Not only did the Chinese oppose them fiercely, but both the United Kingdom and the United States criticized Japan heavily for its overbearing, imperious tactics. The consequences of the Twenty-One Demands would leave a stain on Japanese diplomacy for years to come. With the Ōkuma cabinet lacking a strong base, Katō's inability to keep the sprawling array of demands from the army and hard-liner groups under control, along with his failure to foresee the opposition from China and the United States, would prove fatal.

Katō stepped down as foreign minister in August 1915 and spent the next decade or so leading the Kenseikai (Constitutional Politics Association), an opposition party. In 1924, he launched the Second Movement to Protect Constitutional Government and finally acceded to the premiership. Katō's successor as prime minister, Wakatsuki Reijirō, called Katō "a man incapable of pleasing his elders," in contrast to Hara, who was "a man who knew exactly how to make his elders happy." (The "elders" in Wakatsuki's statement were, of course, Japan's elder statesmen [*genrō*]). Katō was a proud man who loathed obeisance, and he was shunned by Yamagata. Only once both Yamagata and Hara had died was Katō's path to the premiership finally clear, and he formed his own cabinet.

As prime minister, Katō steered Japanese foreign policy in a new direction. He selected his brother-in-law Shidehara Kijūrō to serve as foreign minister and became a powerful advocate of so-called Shidehara diplomacy, which valued cooperation with the United Kingdom and the United States, a commitment to non-intervention in internal affairs, and the pursuit of economic interests—all policies that Katō embraced. Katō fell ill while in office in January 1926 and died shortly thereafter. Looking back, it would not be too much of a stretch to argue that, had Katō lived longer, Japan's policy toward China would have shifted, the Manchurian Incident would never have occurred, and party politics would have taken root much earlier.

to be outside of the combat zone recognized by the Chinese government. Hence, there were concerns about a breach of neutrality. Japan pushed for its possession of the Qingdao-Jinan railway on the grounds that the railway was equivalent to a German leased territory.

Given that Japan had no railway interests in China proper outside those in Manchuria, placing the Qingdao-Jinan railway under Japanese administration after the Russo-Japanese War was a necessary step as a means for compensating Japan in the event that the Kiautschou (Jiaozhou) Bay leased territory was restored to China after the war.

The Japanese army was to withdraw after the German forces' surrender. However, a 2,500-strong garrison had been put together to protect the Qingdao-Jinan railway and other holdings. These developments marked the start of the so-called Shandong problem, which would lead to eight years of conflict over the return of interests in Shandong to China.

Furthermore, the naval operations against the

islands that would become part of the South Seas Mandate—another German territory in the Far East—were successful. By the end of October 1914, Japan had occupied Yap Island, Saipan, and various other territories. Aside from Guam, which was US territory, all parts of Micronesia north of the equator came under Japanese jurisdiction.

Katō's haste to get Japan to declare war arose from his expectation that the European conflict would end quickly. Japan's leaders shared the sense that a critical moment was at hand. They feared that if Japan did not get involved promptly, Western powers would intervene and Japan would miss out on an opportune moment to expand its interests in China. In fact, even after Yuan Shikai had declared China's neutrality, he had approached the powers about obtaining the return of the Shandong Peninsula from Germany. Japan's quick entry into the war would limit such multinational efforts.

Domestic opinion strongly supported Japan's prompt entry and the expansion of its interests. The only major media organization to clearly state a case against entering the war was the *Tōyō Keizai Shinpō* (Eastern economic journal) helmed by Ishibashi Tanzan.

Foreign Minister Katō and the Effects of the Twenty-One Demands

When Japan entered the war against Germany, the Ministry of Foreign Affairs was bombarded with proposals from the army and civilians alike about pushing into China and expanding Japan's interests in Manchuria and Mongolia. Foreign Minister Katō Takaaki pulled together these various suggestions to form a set of demands for China. Following a cabinet decision in December 1914, after Qingdao had been occupied, he issued the "Twenty-One Demands" as an official instruction ("On the matter of China policy") to the minister to China, Hioki Eki. In January 1915, Minister Hioki in Beijing submitted the demands to Yuan Shikai and pressed him to accept them.

Broadly speaking, the Twenty-One Demands consisted of five groups, the first four of which were "required items"; the fifth consisted of "requested items." The first group (four demands) addressed Japan taking over German interests in Shandong Province, while the second group (seven demands) was concerned with Manchuria. Among the items were extensions to ninety-nine years on the leases for both the Shandong Leased Territory (Lushun and Dalian) and the South Manchuria Railway (including the right to operate the Chinese Eastern Railway's branches south of Changchun), along with a significant expansion of Japanese holdings in eastern Inner Mongolia. The second group contained the core demands for solidifying the foundations of Japan's Manchurian and Mongolian interests. Among the Russian interests that Japan had acquired through the Russo-Japanese War, the lease on Lushun and Dalian lasted only until 1923, while that on the South Manchuria Railway was to end in 1939. Thus, getting those leases extended had always been regarded as a crucial issue for Japanese diplomacy.

The third group (two demands) stipulated joint Sino-Japanese administration of the Han-Ye-Ping Company, which was China's leading iron-ore mining and steel-manufacturing enterprise. The fourth "group," a single demand, was that no further concessions be made along the Fujian coast.

Katō's primary objectives had been to get the leases extended on the Shandong Peninsula and on the Manchurian Railroad. He made the most of the opportunity presented by World War I and used the interests Japan had seized from Germany in Shandong as bargaining chips to try to stabilize and strengthen Japan's shaky Manchurian and Mongolian interests.

Japan revealed the "required items" in those four groups to the United Kingdom, France, Russia, and the United States, and those powers voiced no objections. While it anticipated fierce opposition

4-9. Leaflet calling for Chinese resolve in the face of Japan's demands

from China, had Japan limited itself to those fourteen demands, it probably would have been able to get the powers' consent. Political thinker Yoshino Sakuzō regarded the Twenty-One Demands to be "measures that are quite appropriate viewed from the perspective of the Empire's future standing in China," representing the perception that they were sensible for their time.

However, the list of demands also included a fifth group of "requested" items that were concealed from the Western powers. This comprised a miscellaneous set of demands—among others, that the Chinese government appoint Japanese advisors, that there be joint Sino-Japanese police forces in certain areas, that Japan be granted railroad construction rights, and that Japan have special privileges in supplying arms—that would inevitably anger China and the West. Because Katō set aside those "requested items" for last, and because no explicit directions were issued on how these demands would be handled, even today they yield varied interpretations.

In any case, Katō's plan was to keep the negotiations secret and conclude them quickly. However, Yuan immediately leaked their contents to the newspapers, which stirred up public sentiment against Japan. By late January 1915, the news that Japan had in fact made twenty-one demands had been reported over and over again in China, and in spite of the attempted distinction between "required" and "requested" items, the list was firmly in the public mindset as the "Twenty-One Demands."

Sino-Japanese Negotiations and the United States

Negotiations between Japan and China became deadlocked over whether or not the second group of demands applied to eastern Inner Mongolia as well as to Manchuria. Central to this debate was whether or not to recognize the spheres of activity and "preferred" status held by Japanese citizens living in South Manchuria—that is, residence rights, the commercial activities they could pursue, and the property rights available to them—as extending to eastern Inner Mongolia as well. With negotiations at a standstill, on March 13, 1915, the United States sent a memorandum (the Bryan Note) to both Japan and China, indicating that, while it thought that some of Japan's demands contradicted the spirit of equal opportunity and commerce, it nonetheless respected Japan's arguments regarding its interests in Shandong Province and increasing its interests in South Manchuria.

Some believe that Katō overestimated the favorable response expressed in the Bryan Note, and suggest that he was trying to keep the fifth group of "requested" demands under wraps for greater bargaining power. Furthermore, seeking to push negotiations forward, in early March Katō arranged for reinforcements for Japan's North China garrison to apply short-term military pressure. Concerned about a military engagement, the United Kingdom pushed Japan to reach a peaceful settlement while counseling China to compromise.

Meanwhile, US ambassador to China Paul Reinsch saw the fifth group of demands as an expression of Japan's ambitions, and the telegrams he sent to Washington on this point moved President Wilson to act. In mid-April, Wilson shifted the previously conciliatory position of the United States toward greater support of China. Aware of this change in the US position, China shifted to a hard-line stance, withdrawing its previous willingness to consider the second and fifth groups of demands, and negotiations again stalled.

On May 5, after removing the fifth group of demands, the cabinet decided to issue its ultimatum. Four days later, having also received communications on the issue from the Western powers, China told Japan that it would accept the remaining demands. On May 13, the United States notified Japan via the second Bryan Note that it would not recognize any treaties currently in force, or expected to be concluded, that infringed on Chinese territorial integrity or the open-door principle. This note was the first instance of the US policy of nonrecognition. It became the template for the Stimson

The Terauchi Masatake Administration and the Nishihara Loans

A darling of the Chōshū clique and the recipient of Yamagata Aritomo's personal patronage, Terauchi Masatake (1852–1919) was seen as the ideal successor to Katsura Tarō. While Terauchi had a serious, honest personality that helped him distinguish himself as a military bureaucrat with a knack for practical business, political clout was his weak suit. Terauchi served as the minister of the army for roughly a decade, starting in 1902, and played a central role in the government's military administration during the Katsura-Saionji era. He also became the first governor-general of Korea in 1911. In that capacity, he not only worked to push military-government policies but also poured his efforts into propelling economic development. After attaining the rank of field marshal in 1916, Terauchi became prime minister on the recommendation of Yamagata Aritomo and formed his cabinet in October 1916, bringing in a host of former bureaucrats rather than members of political parties. This nonpartisan cabinet even drew sarcastic barbs for being an "unconstitutional cabinet." Terauchi also created the Advisory Council for Foreign Affairs—the first all-party advisory body on diplomatic affairs in the history of constitutional politics—in order to unify public opinion and place foreign policy outside the arena of political strife. The group deliberated on a variety of key issues, including the Siberian Expedition and Japan's policy toward China (see sidebar on pages 174–75). In terms of China-related policy, the previous administration under Ōkuma Shigenobu had left Japan in an unenviable position; the controversy surrounding the Twenty-One Demands had subjected the government to pointed criticism both at home and abroad for what many saw as blatant interference in a foreign country's internal affairs. The Terauchi cabinet thus reached a decision to "maintain an attitude of unbiased impartiality" in relation to all the various parties and factions in China and to "refrain from interfering in any disputes that may arise in China's internal affairs." However, when the major powers of the world recognized the administration of Duan Qirui (a leader from northern China) as the ruling regime in China, the Terauchi cabinet moved away from its existing "impartiality" policy in July 1917 and instead gave the Duan cabinet "considerable friendly assistance."

4-10. Terauchi Masatake

The Nishihara loans were at the core of the government's support of Duan. The origins of the effort trace to a private entrepreneur named Nishihara Kamezō, who set up the trading company Kyōekisha, dealing in cotton goods, in Korea in 1906. Nishihara continued to develop the operation through 1916, making the acquaintance of Terauchi (then governor-general of Korea) along the way. When Shōda Kazue was appointed governor of the Bank of Korea at the end of 1915, Nishihara and Shōda became advisors on

Doctrine after the Manchurian Incident. The close cooperative relationship between China and the United States would continue until the Washington Naval Conference.

Finally, on May 25, the various problems presented by the Twenty-One Demands were resolved in Beijing through two treaties and thirteen exchanges of notes. The two treaties were the "Treaty on Shandong Province" and the "Treaty Respecting Southern Manchuria and Eastern Mongolia." The Treaty on Shandong Province stated that China would consent to whatever agreement Japan and Germany reached concerning the disposition of German interests in that province. The Treaty Respecting Southern Manchuria and Eastern Mongolia extended the terms on the lease to Lushun and Dalian and the terms for operating the South Manchuria Railway and the An-Feng Line to ninety-nine years. It also stipulated that Japanese were free to live where they chose in South Manchuria, allowed them to engage in business there, and allowed them to lease land through free contracts for the purposes of trade and manufacturing or agriculture.

Furthermore, attached to the Manchuria and Mongolia treaty were exchanges of notes granting Japan permission to exploit the principal coal and iron-ore mines in South Manchuria, giving it

---

continental operations. When Terauchi became prime minister of Japan in 1916, he named Shōda his finance minister, and Shōda once again teamed up with Nishihara to chart Japan's economic policies on the continent in an advisory role. Fortunately, Japan enjoyed an unprecedented wave of economic prosperity during World War I, and its international balance of payments recorded its first ever surplus. By the end of 1918, Japan held as much as 1.6 billion yen in foreign currency. A proponent of fiscal activism, Shōda was in agreement with Nishihara that Japan should take advantage of the accumulated foreign currency to invest large amounts of capital in China, in preparation for postwar economic battles, and provide support to the Duan regime at the same time. Shōda formulated the plan for the loan agreement and put Nishihara in charge of negotiations. In 1917 and 1918, the Duan administration signed eight loan agreements totaling 145 million yen. Foreign loans were Duan's only option for overcoming his administration's financial woes.

By that time, there was already an international consortium in place to help prevent excessive investment competition in China. The consortium's regulations initially applied to all loans, but changes in 1913 limited the scope of the restrictions to government loans and thus lifted regulatory control over business loans. The Nishihara loan program made itself out to be a business-loan program, exempt from the consortium's sphere of authority, but the funds from the Nishihara loans were basically government loans intended to assist the Duan administration; in fact, virtually all of the Nishihara loans went to cover Duan's administrative expenses and campaigns to quell revolutionary factions. The basic vision shaping the loan framework was Nishihara's belief in the neo-Confucian concept of the "kingly way" (*ōdō-shugi*), which he saw as vital to forming a Sino-Japanese "economic alliance" that could prepare Japan for heated trade and investment competition after the war. In Nishihara's conception of the "kingly way," the peoples of Japan and China would create an "economic fusion" grounded in good faith, "leading to truly friendly relations between Japan and China, going beyond the veneer of so-called diplomacy." The Nishihara loans thus made funding available without any fees or discounts, an approach that served to uphold Nishihara's harmonious vision but also edged out the private sector.

Coming at a time when the United States was spearheading an effort to form a new four-power loan consortium, however, Terauchi, Shōda, and Nishihara's initiative was viewed with suspicion, as it was seen as being in conflict with the international consortium. In addition, the Ministry of Foreign Affairs—which had been supporting the Yokohama Specie Bank's loan-consortium activities—ramped up its opposition to the scheme. After the Terauchi cabinet disbanded amid the Rice Riots (unrest over rising rice prices) in September 1918, the subsequent Hara Takashi administration not only reversed course on supporting Duan, but also terminated the Nishihara loans before they had yielded any results.

preferential lease terms in South Manchuria and eastern Inner Mongolia, and giving preference to Japanese in the hiring of foreign advisors in such fields as politics, public finance, military affairs, and the police. These formed the core of Japan's Manchurian and Mongolian interests. Through these two treaties, it appeared that Japan had achieved its primary goals with respect to resolving various issues that remained outstanding after the Russo-Japanese War: gaining semipermanent security for its Manchuria interests, and inheriting German interests that would give it a foothold for moving into China proper.

However, while negotiations over the Twenty-One Demands were continuing, in China there were numerous anti-Japan demonstrations and attempts to boycott Japanese goods. The day the final note was received (May 9) was regarded as "a day of national humiliation," and slogans urging Chinese to not forget this "national humiliation" became a feature of assemblies and demonstrations.

Japan had entered World War I in order to achieve a favorable resolution to its China problems. While it did acquire new interests there, they came at the expense of stirring up anti-imperialist Chinese nationalism that was in fact directed most of all at Japan.

When negotiations between Japan and China ended in May 1915, the environment in which Japanese diplomacy operated had deteriorated considerably. Japan's relationship with China worsened and the United States' trust in Japan eroded. The fallout from the Twenty-One Demands would prove to be a negative legacy that would plague future Japanese diplomacy.

Ishii Kikujirō (1866–1945)

Born in Mobara, Kazusa Province (present-day Chiba Prefecture), Ishii Kikujirō graduated from Tokyo Imperial University and entered the Ministry of Foreign Affairs in 1890 as part of a class that also included Ijūin Hikokichi. After serving in Europe for five years, Ishii was posted to Qing China in 1897 and later spent a full six months stranded in Beijing during the Boxer Rebellion. Recognized as a hard worker, Ishii was working as director-general of the ministry's Trade Bureau when he caught the attention of Foreign Minister Komura Jutarō, showing his mettle at the Portsmouth Peace Conference. In 1908, he leapfrogged over Yamaza Enjirō, who was his senior, and was made vice-minister. Ishii was recommended for the post of foreign minister in 1915, after the resignation of Katō Takaaki. The following year, Ishii negotiated the Fourth Russo-Japanese Agreement. He infused his approach to the talks with a historical perspective, reaching back to the eighteenth century to draw on the lessons of the Seven Years' War. In that conflict, Russia had agreed to a separate peace with Prussia—a precedent that led Ishii to worry that Russia might again forge a separate peace with a combatant, break off from its allies, and turn against Japan. In negotiating the agreement, therefore, Ishii attempted to position Europe as the main threat to Russia. History did indeed repeat itself, proving Ishii correct, when Russia forged a separate peace with Germany after the Russian Revolution.

4-11. Ishii Kikujirō

In September 1916, Ishii resigned as foreign minister and became a member of the House of Peers. Recent incidents on the international stage, especially the Twenty-One Demands, had deepened American suspicions about Japan's intentions. In that delicate diplomatic climate, Ishii headed off to Washington as a special envoy to secure the United States' approval of Japan's predominant rights in China. Secretary of State Lansing responded to the appeal by demanding that Japan, which then had a competitive edge in the Chinese market, eliminate its sphere of influence and agree with the United States to protect China's territorial integrity, uphold an open-door policy, and ensure equal opportunity. Ishii was ready to concur to the terms, but Prime Minister Terauchi Masatake, Foreign Minister Motono Ichirō, and the Advisory Council on Foreign Relations continued to push for

Anti-Yuan Policy, Pro-Duan Policy, and the Nishihara Loans

With the Twenty-One Demands affair concluded, Yuan Shikai—who had no fondness for republican institutions—became the president of the Republic of China. Having strengthened his political base through the Twenty-One Demands issue, he now aimed to claim the position of emperor himself. In late 1915, military units in Yunnan launched what might be termed a third revolution in opposition to Yuan's plan to assume the status of emperor (National Protection War). The Ōkuma cabinet in Japan invited the United Kingdom, France, and Russia to join it in urging Yuan to defer his imperial ambitions. In doing so, Japan hoped to mitigate further chaos and protect the interests of other countries. In March 1916, the Ōkuma cabinet decided it would support the anti-government forces in the south to prevent Yuan's efforts. Yuan died in June a broken man.

China then entered an era of conflict among military cliques, which were groups that had gained power through their own private armies. Yuan was succeeded by Li Yuanhong as president, with State Premier Duan Qirui forming a cabinet. Parliament was restored. While the Duan regime in Beijing now stood as the de jure government, it was opposed by Sun Wen's rebel forces in the south, and was in fact little more than one of the military cliques that were rampant in northern China. In the north, Duan's Anhui Clique competed with other powerful groups such as the Zhili Clique led by Feng Guozhang, and the Fengtian Clique led by Zhang Zuolin.

The Terauchi Masatake cabinet took office in Japan in October 1916, and its principal foreign-policy concern was overturning the previous

the United States to recognize Japan's "special position" in China. The negotiations reached an impasse over what "special position" was to signify. Eventually, however, the two sides came to a compromise by rephrasing "special position" as "special interests." The resulting Lansing-Ishii Agreement thus gave Japan the United States' official approval of its special interests in China. Ishii went on to become Japan's ambassador to the United States in 1918, and struggled with the diplomatic repercussions of Japan's reluctance to join the other major powers in withdrawing troops from the Siberian Expedition. In 1920, Ishii took over as the Japanese ambassador to France and served as the government's representative at meetings of the Supreme War Council to discuss the implementation of the Treaty of Versailles. Ishii also went on to play a prominent role in the League of Nations for seven years, garnering praise from other delegates for his fair, even-minded work. In 1927, Ishii joined Saitō Makoto as a plenipotentiary at the Geneva Naval Conference (also known as the "Disarmament Conference") and argued to make Japan's case. Not long after the conference, however, Ishii retired from office.

Ishii later served as Japan's representative at the 1933 London Economic Conference. On his way to London, he stopped in the United States and met with Franklin Roosevelt for preliminary negotiations on the recognition of Manchukuo as an independent state. He also proposed an arbitration treaty in hopes of easing the tensions between Japan and the United States, but the idea never made it to formal negotiations. Hopes were high that an agreement would take shape, with some calling the negotiations the "revival of the Lansing-Ishii Agreement." The expectations went unmet, however, as the talks failed to progress. With international public opinion of Japan souring through the mid-1930s, Ishii was chosen to be a "people's ambassador" in 1937 and traveled around Europe explaining Japan's position. In May 1945, during the firebombing of Tokyo, Ishii went missing on his way to Meiji Shrine and was never seen again.

In his memoirs, *Gaikō yoroku* (Diplomatic commentaries), Ishii wrote, "One's success in diplomatic pursuits hinges on preparing documents properly," underscoring the importance of keeping meticulous diplomatic records. He also envisioned the ideal diplomat as one "adept in both governing and negotiating" but at the same time attributed the successes of past Japanese diplomats "not to expertise in governing nor skills in negotiation, but rather to sincere honesty and moderation." He was a true diplomat who lived out those dual ideals.

cabinet's China policy. Japan's minister to China Hayashi Gonsuke stated that the Ōkuma cabinet's China policy had been an "inconstant" one. On the one hand, Japan provided indirect support such as selling arms through trading companies to the southern rebel factions opposing the Beijing government in the north. On the other hand, it also provided secret assistance to the Royalist Party in the north that was seeking to restore the Qing court. Japanese forces on the ground in Shandong had also tried repeatedly to take advantage of the chaos in order to expand Japanese interests there.

In January 1917, the Terauchi cabinet settled on a new policy toward China based on the views of Foreign Minister Motono Ichirō. It would adopt an "attitude of unbiased impartiality" toward both the northern and southern factions in China while working to expand Japan's interests with moderate measures. However, the Terauchi cabinet gradually became more involved with domestic Chinese politics. At a cabinet meeting held that July, the government settled on a pro-Duan policy that would provide the Duan Qirui regime with "a sizable amount of friendly assistance in anticipation of bringing tranquility to the current situation." In other words, Japan would extend the credit China needed for a financial rescue.

In August 1917, the Duan regime aligned with the Triple Entente (the United Kingdom, France, and Russia) and entered the war, which gave it the opportunity to speak out at the peace talks two years later. Entering the war on the side of the Entente nullified the treaties that had existed between China and Germany. China's position was that Germany's interests in Shandong Province had already been terminated, a stance that would prove incendiary in those postwar talks.

In an attempt to increase its political influence, Japan unilaterally provided loans—the so-called Nishihara loans (see sidebar on pages 156–57)—to the Duan regime, which had already decided to go to war. The nations of Europe had no financial leeway. Meanwhile, Japan had entered a period of unprecedented prosperity, and for the first time since the Meiji era, its international balance of payments had become favorable. Through Finance Minister Shōda Kazue's expansionary fiscal policy, Japan was attempting to make the most of the foreign currency it had accumulated through wartime special procurements by investing it in China. Nishihara Kamezō had run a cotton business in Korea. Friendly with Terauchi, he had suggested reshuffling China policy to change its focus to the economy.

However, the massive Nishihara loans were put exclusively toward the Duan regime's administrative expenses and toward the military expenses needed to suppress the southern rebels. They did not lead to any Sino-Japanese economic partnership. When the Hara Takashi (informally called Hara Kei) cabinet took office, the Nishihara loans were halted out of concern that they were benefiting only certain forces in the world of Chinese politics, and could encourage a drawn-out north-south conflict.

3 The Russo-Japanese Alliance and the US Entry into the War

The Completion of a "Russo-Japanese Alliance"

When the front lines of the war in Europe expanded to the Far East with Japan's entry into the war, the Triple Entente countries—the United Kingdom, France, and Russia—paid even closer attention to Japan's moves. France in particular was worried that the war's impact would spread to Indochina. It became interested in either joining the Anglo-Japanese alliance or in pushing Japan to form a four-power alliance that would also include

Russia. Worried about the possibility of rupturing the Anglo-Japanese alliance, Foreign Minister Katō Takaaki chose not to respond. Meanwhile, Russia, concerned about its extreme deficiencies in munitions and ordnance, sought a rapprochement with Japan in the hope that it could serve as an arsenal for the Far East.

At the same time, the discord in Anglo-Japanese relations with respect to China had become ever more prominent since the Chinese Revolution. Despite this, the United Kingdom indirectly gave its support to a rapprochement between Japan and Russia, hoping to keep Russia, as a member of the Triple Entente, from pulling its troops from the front lines. The expression of this was the inclusion of Japan as a signatory in the October 1915 "Declaration of London" in which the United Kingdom, France and Russia committed to not making unilateral peace. The Declaration of London was generated because the Triple Entente did not have a formal three-way alliance agreement, even though Germany was their common enemy with the outbreak of World War I. Foreign Minister Katō did not approve of Japan signing on to the declaration, and he resigned from his post in August 1915. His successor, Ishii Kikujirō, felt signing was necessary in order to preserve Japan's right to speak up in any postwar peace talks. In response to the United Kingdom's request, he added Japan as a signatory at a single stroke.

However, adding Japan to the list of signatories to the Declaration of London did not satisfy Russia, which was determined to achieve a Russo-Japanese alliance in order to prevent Japan and Germany from making peace on their own and turning on Russia. As foreign minister, Katō had been uninterested in a Russo-Japanese alliance, but once he resigned, elder statesmen such as Yamagata Aritomo and Inoue Kaoru were able to win support from such army leaders as Terauchi Masatake and Tanaka Giichi, and increased their pressure on Foreign Minister Ishii and others. Their goals were to conclude an offensive and defensive alliance with Russia, and also to obtain concessions reaching to Harbin on the Chinese Eastern Railway that had not been achieved in the Russo-Japanese War. In early 1916, Grand Duke George Mikhailovich visited Japan as Russia's envoy and conveyed the wishes of Foreign Minister Sergey Sazonov to see closer ties between Russia and Japan, leading to talks between Sazonov and Motono Ichirō in short order. However, Russia was reluctant to transfer rights to the Chinese Eastern Railway, so the issue was set aside to be settled at a later date. In July 1916, the Russo-Japanese Treaty of Alliance was signed in Petrograd.

This agreement differed from previous treaties in that it mentioned nothing about preserving Chinese territorial integrity or equal opportunity for other countries, but focused entirely on Japanese and Russian interests. In the secret parts of the treaty in particular, Japan prepared the essentials of a military alliance. It included talk of Japan and Russia supporting one another and providing military assistance in the event that one or the other went to war with "a third country harboring ill intentions" over China. For these reasons, it could be described as both an offensive and defensive alliance. The "third country harboring ill intentions" naturally was presumed to be Germany. However, in the December 19, 1917 edition of the daily *Izvestiya*, parts of the secret agreement were printed with an explanation appended suggesting that "third country harboring ill intentions" might refer to the United Kingdom or the United States, which shocked the countries concerned. Whatever the case, the Treaty of Alliance was a landmark in that its objective was to exclude any third force that had its eyes on China, rather than to coordinate spheres of influence in Manchuria and Mongolia as previous Russo-Japanese treaties had done. However, the agreement was nullified by the October Revolution.

If the Russian Revolution had not occurred, then the treaty would have remained in force, providing the grounds for Japan and Russia to divide up and rule the whole of China. Any conflict over China between the Anglo-American camp and the Russo-Japanese camp would have drawn in the other Western powers as well.

The Lansing-Ishii Agreement

In the wake of the Twenty-One Demands affair, relations between Japan and the United States grew cooler over the issues of China and immigration. However, the situation changed completely when the United States entered World War I in April 1917. Since the start of the year, President Woodrow Wilson had been furious about Germany's campaign of unlimited submarine warfare. He severed relations with Germany and called for war "to make the world safe for democracy" in a speech to Congress, which responded by approving a declaration of war. Having decided from the start that this was to be all-out war, Wilson committed the US navy to the anti-submarine campaign, as well as to sending massive numbers of troops to the Western Front as quickly as possible. To achieve these goals, in May 1917 he introduced a conscription bill, and also provided up to US$11.6 billion in wartime loans to its allies in the conflict.

The Japanese government expected that, with the United States' entry into the war, it would have a powerful voice about peace conditions and rebuilding the international postwar order. Accordingly, Japan sought to repair its chilled relations with Washington and worked to get its consent over Japan's special position in East Asia. Wilson, too, thought adjusting the US-Japan relationship would further his goal of prioritizing the war against Germany.

In late May 1917, the Terauchi Masatake government approved the dispatch of a special envoy to the United States to take up the problems of immigration and China. Former foreign minister Ishii Kikujirō was appointed as envoy, and he began negotiations that September. Ishii had prepared a "Japan-US Joint Declaration on China" stipulating that if the other nations concerned would renounce their spheres of influence in China, then Japan would do the same. It may be described as a proactive response to Wilson's diplomatic position, which opposed any one country having a monopoly position in China.

After reviewing the draft, however, the Advisory Council on Foreign Relations removed the section about eliminating spheres of influence out

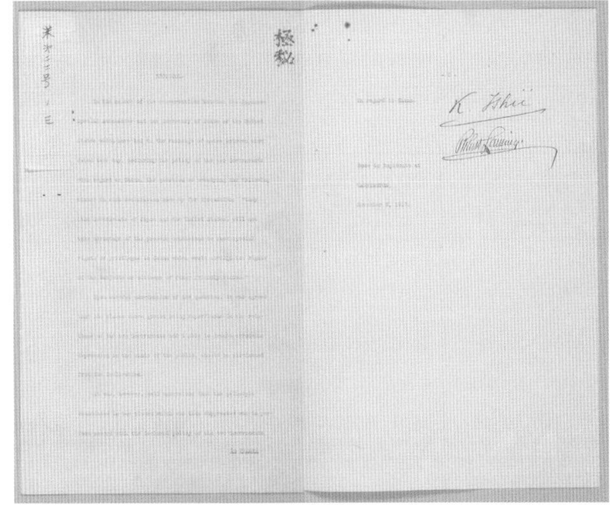
4-12. The Lansing-Ishii Agreement

4-13. Ishii Kikujirō and Robert Lansing

of consideration for the United Kingdom and Russia. In the end, Ishii refrained from touching on this point, and approached negotiations with the goal of getting the United States to acknowledge that Japan had a special status in China owing to its geographical proximity.

Once the United States recognized that "territorial propinquity creates special relations between countries" was within the framework of the negotiations, the United States then recognized that Japan had "special interests" in China. Japan had sought recognition that it had "preeminent interests" in China, but Ishii's counterpart Robert Lansing did not recognize this, and so the text settled on "special interests." The resulting Lansing-Ishii Agreement, which would replace the Root-Takahira Agreement, took the form of a joint declaration based on the diplomatic notes that Lansing and Ishii had exchanged. While the immigration problem still remained for Japan, this was a watershed agreement in that none other than the United States had recognized that Japan had special interests in China. Furthermore, the agreement elaborated on those interests, stating that "the territorial sovereignty of China, nevertheless, remains unimpaired" and promising that Japan would not discriminate against the trade of other nations. These stipulations could be seen as trying to guarantee the rights of the Western powers in China while also preventing Japan from seizing any superior interests.

In the context of the international environment surrounding Japan after the Russo-Japanese War—as well as the alliances and agreements Japan had with Russia, the United Kingdom, and France that formed the basis for trade and cooperation with each—the Lansing-Ishii Agreement was the crowning touch on the wartime web of alliances and agreements that hemmed in Germany. Immediately after this agreement was reached, however, the October Revolution occurred, ending Russia's participation.

4 Friction over Immigration between Japan and the United States

"Picture Brides" and the California Alien Land Law of 1913

One of the consequences of Japan's voluntary restraints on emigration arising from the Gentlemen's Agreement of 1908 was that it kept down any net increase in the numbers of Japanese immigrants coming into the United States. Eventually, the families of Japanese residing in the United States came to feature an abundance of "picture brides," owing to a loophole in the Gentlemen's Agreement that allowed for family members to immigrate. A marriage proposal would be arranged through exchanges of photographs and letters only, and after the marriage had been registered, the bride would be issued a passport and travel to the United States. This form of marriage struck Americans as odd. Furthermore, when these "picture brides" gave birth, the children automatically obtained US citizenship. The increase in the numbers of such children helped generate a sense of crisis about the growth of Japanese communities, and in due course it rekindled an anti-Japanese movement that had been quiescent.

At the same time, the numbers of Japanese seeking to get away from being simple laborers and hoping to reside permanently in the United States was increasing. This provoked a rising sense of alarm in agricultural sectors that led to the imposition of restrictions on land use. Specifically, they took the form of a bill on land use submitted to the California legislature in early 1913 that would prohibit aliens ineligible for citizenship from owning agricultural land. In practical terms, it was targeted

4-14. "As to Japanese Exclusion." Illustration by Frank A. Nankivell showing a group of "undesirables" dressed in kimono and pretending to be Japanese immigrants

at Japanese immigrants. Laws of this sort had been submitted numerous times since 1907, but each time they had been staved off owing to pressure from the Republican presidents Theodore Roosevelt and William H. Taft. However, the victory of Democratic Party candidate Woodrow Wilson in the 1912 presidential election presaged a change in position. Unlike his Republican predecessors, the new president had stressed states' rights even in the election campaign, and had voiced his support for restrictions on Japanese immigrants.

After going through numerous revisions, in May 1913 the bill was finally passed by both houses of the California legislature as the California Alien Land Law of 1913. Through Ambassador Chinda Sutemi, the Japanese government issued a strong protest to the US government on the grounds that the law unfairly discriminated against Japanese, and that it also contravened the US-Japan Treaty of Commerce and Navigation of 1911. President Wilson asked California governor Hiram Johnson to exercise his veto against the bill, and in late April he also hastily dispatched Secretary of State William Jennings Bryan to the state.

The US-Japan Treaty of Commerce and Navigation had made no mention of land ownership. The only terms it set down related to land were in regard to leasing property for residential purposes or the conduct of business, or with respect to home ownership. The 1913 bill was revised to stipulate the following so as to not contravene the Treaty of Commerce and Navigation: (1) All aliens eligible for citizenship would have all rights of land ownership; (2) aliens who were not eligible for citizenship would still have the right of land ownership as prescribed in the treaties the United States had signed with other countries, and (3) land for agricultural purposes could be leased for terms not exceeding three years. This marked the first time since the Russo-Japanese War that the anti-Japanese movement on the West Coast had succeeded in passing legislation.

However, there was a loophole in this land law. For example, land could be bought in the name of a child born in the United States (with US citizenship) and subsequently leased to the parent who was the child's ward. President Roosevelt was not indifferent to the existence of this loophole, but he ignored it in the interests of maintaining friendly relations with Japan. For the California governor, too, getting the land law itself passed was more important than its actual effects.

Ambassador Chinda's Struggle

The California Alien Land Law of 1913 was roundly criticized in Japan from the moment the California legislature began to debate it. People viewed it as an affront to the status Japan had achieved through its victory in the Russo-Japanese War, which was supposedly on a par with that of the Western powers. At a massive anti-US gathering convened in Tokyo at the Kokugikan national sumo stadium on April 17, 1913, it was argued that passage of the Alien

4-15. Chinda Sutemi

Land Law was a matter of great concern that had an effect on "the nation's prestige." Demonstrators advocated gunboat diplomacy, demanding that Japan's fleet be sent immediately to the US West Coast to prevent the law's passage. The scale of the protests in Japan was reported widely enough to attract the attention of the *New York Times*. The situation grew so extreme that the US military started to draw up a strategic plan in readiness for attacking Japan, should war be declared.

After the law was passed, the Japanese government presented the US government with a strong letter of protest. Having determined that war with Japan was unavoidable under the circumstances, Chief of Naval Operations Bradley Fiske asked Secretary of the Navy Josephus Daniels to move the fleet. As a result of this action, navy leaders held back on any hurried aggressive moves.

For Japan, the best solution to the immigrant problem would have been for the United States to grant Japanese residents of the country the right to naturalize, but this was extremely complicated. Since the law had been passed in August 1913, Ambassador Chinda Sutemi had been looking for

Imagined Tales of a "Future War" between Japan and the United States

For the United States in the early twentieth century, the influx of Japanese immigrants flocking to the West Coast created issues that went far beyond racial friction and labor-market competition. The growing Japanese presence also stoked fears about Japan as a nascent global power with imperialist designs, especially given Japan's victory in the Russo-Japanese War. For example, in *The United States as a World Power* (1909), author Archibald Coolidge sounded the alarm by stating that Japan, whose triumph over Russia had made her a "world power," had ambitions to seize "mastery of the Pacific" with Japanese immigrants forming "a vanguard" of Japanese power, and that it would be the "white man," rather than the Japanese immigrants, who would beat a retreat.

One of the more unusual books to emerge from that national mood was Homer Lea's *The Valor of Ignorance* (1909), which depicted a "future war" between Japan and America in the Pacific. In Lea's imagined account, should the Japanese army want to invade America, they would make quick work of conquering the West Coast and pushing into the Rocky Mountains. The United States would have no way of stopping the onslaught, leading Lea to conclude that American defenses were extremely vulnerable. Although *The Valor of Ignorance* portrayed Japan as a dangerous hypothetical enemy, the narrative cast the Japanese not as objects of hatred but rather as valorous adherents to the bushido code. That favorable presentation is likely why the book appeared in several different Japanese translations, making waves among Japanese readers.

4-16. The 1909 geopolitical analysis *The Valor of Ignorance* by Homer Lea

Such concerns about a looming Japanese threat were also seen in the US government and among military officials. In an October 1906 Department of State memorandum, Secretary of State Elihu Root wrote that Japan had "probably the most effective equipment and personnel now existing in the world." If Japan were to go to war with the United States, which was unprepared for such a conflict, Root predicted that the United States would suffer "the loss of the Philippines, Hawaii, and probably the Pacific coast, with the complete destruction of our commerce on the Pacific."

a way, in tough discussions with Secretary of State William Jennings Bryan, to guarantee the rights of Japanese immigrants in terms of land ownership via a new Japan-US treaty, seeing this as a realistic strategy for solving the problem. Chinda proposed a bilateral treaty that would provide treatment to Japanese on par with that granted to citizens of most-favored nations when it came to acquiring, disposing of, and inheriting the rights to agricultural land. Although an agreement had been reached by April 1914, Bryan hesitated to present it to the Senate's Foreign Relations Committee. Furthermore, because the Democratic Party, which at the time stressed states' rights, held a majority in the Senate, it was therefore decided that getting it passed through Congress would be too difficult. To make matters worse, Katō Takaaki, who became foreign minister in Ōkuma Shigenobu's cabinet in April 1914, dropped all of the draft treaties that had been proposed under his predecessor, Makino Nobuaki. Accordingly, all discussions were brought to halt, and Chinda's efforts were in vain.

Even so, in October Chinda asked Bryan to begin negotiations based on a new proposal that would prevent states from enacting these sorts of anti-Japanese land use laws. This second round of talks was cut short by Bryan's resignation, but Chinda's efforts would bear fruit seven years later in the Morris-Shidehara Talks.

Imagined Tales of a "Future War" between Japan and the United States

Japan's efforts to bolster its naval might after World War I put many American observers on alert. Around the time of the Washington Naval Conference (1921–22), books offering accounts of an imagined war between Japan and the United States were flying off the shelves on both sides of the Pacific. British journalist Hector Bywater's speculative tale of a Pacific war took the world by storm, while Japanese authors like Ishimaru Tōta and Mizuno Hironori penned similar bestselling works along similar thematic lines—subject matter that continued to capture the popular imagination well into the 1930s.

In Washington, US president Roosevelt ordered sixteen battleships from Hampton Roads Harbor on the Atlantic coast all the way to San Francisco Bay on the Pacific Coast in December 1907. Relocating battleships from the East Coast to the West Coast would entail a round-the-world voyage—and that was exactly what Roosevelt was planning. As the fleet sailed the Pacific, Roosevelt was aiming to demonstrate American sea power and dispel the talk of an all but inevitable showdown between the United States and Japan that had been gaining currency at ports in both countries, leading the Japanese government to request that the fleet also make a stop in Japan.

The American fleet eventually sailed into Yokohama in mid-October 1908, painted gray and white instead of its normal wartime colors. Japan welcomed the "Great White Fleet" with open arms. The friendly reception gave way to a general enthusiasm for warmer Japan-US relations and created a favorable context for the signing of the Root-Takahira Agreement (November 1908), which sought to maintain the existing status quo in the Pacific. For the United States, the fleet's globe-spanning voyage also provided an opportunity to showcase the transformation of an aging naval force into a brand-new, battle-ready outfit.

CHAPTER 5

The "New Diplomacy" and Japan

1. British prime minister David Lloyd George
2. US president Woodrow Wilson
3. French prime minister Georges Clemenceau
4. Italian prime minister Vittorio Emanuele Orlando
5. Marquis Saionji Kinmochi of Japan
6. Ulrich von Brockdorff-Rantzau of Germany

5-1. Plenipotentiaries present at the signing of the Treaty of Versailles

TIMELINE

1918 (Taishō 7)

January 8 US president Woodrow Wilson issues his Fourteen Points principles for peace

March 3 Germany and Russia sign Treaty of Brest-Litovsk

March 25 Japan and Beijing government sign Sino-Japanese Military Defense Agreement of 1918, aimed at Germany and Austria-Hungary

April 5 British and Japanese troops land at Vladivostok

May 14 Czechoslovak Legion precipitates incident at Chelyabinsk, sparking uprisings throughout Russia

July 8 US proposes to Japan to dispatch troops to aid the Czechoslovak Legion

July 22 Rice riots begin (end in September)

August 2 Declaration of troop dispatch to Siberia

August 7 De facto diplomatic relations between Japan and Soviet Union break off

September 29 Hara Takashi (Kei) cabinet formed

November 11 Allied Powers and Germany sign cease-fire agreement, ending World War I

November 18 Coup d'état by Omsk government; anti-revolutionary government forms under Admiral Alexander Kolchak

1919 (Taishō 8)

January 18–June 28 Paris Peace Conference

March 1 March First Movement erupts in Korea

March 2–6 Communist International (Comintern) organizes first congress in Moscow

May 4 May Fourth Movement emerges in China

May 16 Japan recognizes Kolchak government

June 28 Signing of Treaty of Versailles signed

July 25 Karakhan Manifesto (statement of Soviet policy toward China) issued (second version issued September 27, 1920)

1920 (Taishō 9)

January 10	League of Nations formed, with both Japan and China among its founding members
January 13	Japan decides to boost number of troops being sent to eastern Siberia
April 1	US army completes withdrawal from Siberia
April 4	Japanese army begins to demilitarize revolutionary forces in the Maritime Province of Siberia
April 6	Creation of Far Eastern Republic (Russia)
March 12–May 27	Nikolayevsk Incident occurs, in which 735 Japanese soldiers and civilians are killed
June 28	Japan decides to occupy northern Karafuto (Sakhalin)
July 15	Japanese army and Far Eastern Republic agree to cease-fire
July 21	Japanese army begins to withdraw its troops from Transbaikal regions (completed in August)
September 21	Morris-Shidehara Talks held to discuss the issue of Japanese immigration in California (through January 24, 1921)

1921 (Taishō 10)

March 3	Crown Prince Hirohito sets out on tour of Europe
May 13	Japan decides to start withdrawing troops from the Russian Far East once an agreement with the Far Eastern Republic has been reached
September 2	Crown Prince Hirohito returns from tour of Europe
November 4	Prime Minister Hara assassinated at Tokyo Station
November 12	Washington Conference opens (through February 6, 1922)
November 13	Takahashi Korekiyo cabinet formed

1 The Paris Peace Conference and Its Legacy

Wilson's "New Diplomacy"

In November 1917, the newly created Bolshevik regime issued its "Decree on Peace," directed at all parties involved in World War I. With "democratic peace" as its guiding principle, it called for peace without forcible annexations and indemnities, and lauded the principle of national self-determination. The new regime also made public the secret treaties that Imperial Russia had concluded during the war. Its goal was to impress upon the world that the war's aims had been imperialistic rather than a matter of self-defense, but global interest lay less in the Bolshevik regime than in what direction the United States would take, having demonstrated its overwhelming power following its entry into the war.

In January 1918, US president Woodrow Wilson gave a speech to the US Congress in which he laid out in fourteen points his ideas for restructuring the international order after the war. These included the principles that diplomacy should always proceed frankly and in the public view; navigation (i.e., trade) should be free; armaments should be reduced; a nation's people should be able to govern themselves or be independent; and some international organization should be formed to maintain the peace.

With defeat inevitable, Germany and Austria-Hungary proposed a cease-fire and peace based on Wilson's Fourteen Points in October 1918. One month later, a cease-fire agreement was signed, and after four years, World War I finally came to an end. It appeared that the Fourteen Point principles of peace might serve as the basic conditions for a new international postwar order.

Among Wilson's Fourteen Points, the ideas of open diplomacy and the founding of a general association of nations would leave their mark on international politics. The principle of open diplomacy arose because up until that point it had been conducted exclusively by nobles and the privileged classes, and secret negotiations had become the norm. Wilson believed that opening diplomatic activities to public view was the most important change of all; this "New Diplomacy" would reform the old-style diplomacy that deployed Machiavellian maneuvers and secret interchanges aimed at maintaining the balance of power and acquiring special interests. Resolving conflicts through open debate and conference diplomacy was now the ideal.

As to the principle of national self-determination, Wilson incorporated within it a criticism of colonialism, but he did not try to take up the issue at the peace talks. For Wilson, democracy was more important than national self-determination. In this sense, the New Diplomacy was also a way of ideologizing foreign relations, since he viewed democracy as evidence of the superiority of Western civilization.

Hara Takashi (Kei) (1856–1921)

Hara Takashi, born to the chief retainer of the Morioka domain, pursued studies in the Ministry of Justice law school but dropped out before completing his degree. He then held down a variety of jobs, working as a reporter for the *Yūbin Hōchi* and editor-in-chief for the *Daitō Nippō* (a government-affiliated paper), before he eventually caught the eye of Inoue Kaoru. Hara was offered a position at the Ministry of Foreign Affairs in 1882, when Inoue was foreign minister, at the age of twenty-six. His service in the ministry included stints at the Japanese consulate in Tianjin and Japan's legation in France, but he followed Inoue to the Ministry of Agriculture and Commerce in 1889 and was named councillor. It was at the Ministry of Agriculture and Commerce that Hara would make the acquaintance of lifelong friend Uchida Yasuya (Kōsai), then the minister's secretary. When, upon

Previously, peace negotiations had focused on adjusting interests with respect to territory and reparations. Now, however, issues to be debated would be presented in the form of ideologies and principles. In an article titled "From Imperialism to International Democracy," Yoshino Sakuzō wrote, "In the past, international relations were simply a matter of imperialism, of the strong being victorious, and of the weak being prey to the strong. . . . [Now, however] I believe that the world will gradually be refashioned into one where the principle of equality among all peoples applies on an international scale. It will be one in which international relations will have to be rebuilt, based on equality among nations, harmony, and trust."

However, Japan's diplomatic establishment had become quite accustomed to the previous way of doing things, and so Wilson's declaration left them puzzled. They were particularly wary of the idea of creating a league of nations. Discussing this, Vice-Foreign Minister Shidehara Kijūrō spoke of how "bothersome" it would be to have Japan's fate decided not by direct negotiations with the specific nation whose interests were involved, but rather through some roundtable conference. Meanwhile, some in the Ministry of Foreign Affairs—such as Komura Kin'ichi (eldest son of early twentieth-century foreign minister Komura Jutarō), who then headed the first division in the Political Affairs Bureau—argued that the diplomatic failures of the Ōkuma Shigenobu and Terauchi Masatake cabinets in relations with China showed the need for Japan to do away with spheres of influence and extraterritoriality, and actively take part in the New Diplomacy. However, it was not until after the peace talks that such opinions held sway within the ministry.

The Hara Cabinet and a Change in China Policy: Repairing Relations with the United States

The Hara Takashi (Kei) cabinet, which took office in September 1918, finally fully addressed the idea of the "New Diplomacy." In a parliamentary question at the House of Representatives, Hara pointed out that diplomacy was not a matter of "possibly achieving something just by banging your fist on

his return from the United States in 1890, Mutsu Munemitsu was appointed Minister of Agriculture and Commerce, he became aware of Hara's capabilities.

When Mutsu was appointed foreign minister in Itō Hirobumi's second cabinet in 1892, he decided to pull Hara away from the Ministry of Agriculture and Commerce and install him as the director-general of the Trade Bureau at the Ministry of Foreign Affairs. In 1895, Mutsu placed Hara even further up the ladder, making him vice-minister for foreign affairs. Hara poured his energies into assisting Mutsu in negotiating the Anglo-Japanese Treaty of Commerce and Navigation and implementing a system for testing and appointing aspiring diplomats and consuls. For Hara, who hated oligarchy, the existing approach of appointing people without requiring them to pass a fair test amounted to clan favoritism pure and simple. Hara became Japan's envoy to Korea in 1896, around the time that Mutsu bowed out of the cabinet due to illness; but he, too, left the Ministry of Foreign Affairs the following year. Hara then served as editor-in-chief of the *Osaka Mainichi Shimbun*, and later became the newspaper's president. In 1900, however, Hara joined the Rikken Seiyūkai party at the urging of Itō and Inoue, and was appointed minister of communications in the fourth Itō cabinet. Following Itō's exit from the Seiyūkai in 1903, Saionji Kinmochi became president, but Hara was the one doing most of the actual leading. In 1914, Hara was appointed president of the party.

5-2. Hara Takashi (Kei)

In the fall of 1908, during his time out of office, Hara spent six months traveling in Europe and the United States. The experience brought him face to face with the surging power of the United States, which he saw as the "nation that Japan should fear most in the coming years," and the reality of American political democratization (the "advance of national power"). As the official leader of the Seiyūkai, Hara sat on the Terauchi Masatake cabinet's Advisory Council for Foreign Affairs and used his membership as a platform for voicing his thoughts on Japan's relations with the United States. The pending Siberian Expedition issue was one topic that Hara considered to be key in that context. Arguing that "it would be reasonable to say that the fate of our country rests on the intimacy of our relationship with the United States," Hara recommended that Japan go along with the American proposal to send a limited dispatch of troops to Siberia—a strategy that went against the views of Prime Minister Terauchi and Army Minister Tanaka Giichi, who were aiming for a full-scale military expedition.

Hara also urged a closer relationship with China. "Japan must make a radical change in its attitude toward China," he said, "and take whatever measures possible to pave the way to friendship." He was critical of the domineering diplomacy of Ōkuma Shigenobu and Katō Takaaki, who had made a strong-armed push for the Twenty-One Demands. Hara was also against the Terauchi administration's policy of supporting Chinese premier Duan Qirui, which he saw as meddling in China's internal affairs.

The Rice Riots of 1918 ended the Terauchi administration, and Hara rose to the premiership in September 1918 with the backing of elder statesman Saionji Kinmochi. Hara proceeded to form Japan's first bona fide partisan cabinet: aside from the ministers of the army, navy, and foreign affairs, every cabinet minister was a Seiyūkai member. Hara appointed his close friend Uchida Yasuya as foreign minister. Domestically, Hara focused on railway construction and implanting the Seiyūkai around Japan; on the diplomatic front, he strove to repair the damage that the Ōkuma and Terauchi administrations had done to relations with the United States by shifting Japan's policy on China, including discontinuing the Nishihara loans. In 1920, Hara brought Japan into a new Four-Power Consortium formed to make loans to China. As a proponent of providing support to China via international cooperation, Hara laid a diplomatic foundation for Washington to build on, but was also careful in defending Japan's vested interests on the continent.

Hara's life ended abruptly in November 1921, just before the Washington Naval Conference, when he was stabbed to death by a young assailant. "I don't know what Hara did for others," Saionji recalled, "but he was not the kind of man to pursue his own self-interest." Had Hara's life not been cut short, he probably would have succeeded Yamagata Aritomo and Matsukata Masayoshi as one of Japan's preeminent elder statesmen.

the table." He argued that imposing this new style of diplomacy based on the idea of democracy would "completely change the thinking about international relations among civilized peoples." However, the prospects for the Hara cabinet were not bright. Japan's treaty with Russia was invalid due to the collapse of that country's imperial government, and the "voluntary dispatch" of troops to Siberia (discussed below) had invited Wilson's distrust. In forming his own cabinet, Hara was burdened with the legacy of the China policies of the Ōkuma and Terauchi cabinets, which had roused the suspicions of the United States and inflamed anti-Japanese sentiment in China.

Hara had spent a half year traveling around the United States and Europe before he became prime minister, and he foresaw that the coming of peace due to America's entry into the war would be conducive to "American influence" and a sudden rise in democracy in the world. For Hara, adjusting relations with the United States was a crucial issue that would determine Japan's fate. Thus, he made it a top priority, and worked to transform the China policy that Japan had pursued during the war, which had led to conflict and frictions with the United States. One month after the cabinet was formed, Hara's government decided to halt independent loans to China and liquidate the Nishihara loans. It also stopped providing loans and weapons to the Beijing government on the grounds that it drew suspicion from the Western powers and contributed to China's internal chaos.

Some within the Ministry of Foreign Affairs, such as minister to China Obata Yūkichi, had been arguing since the days of the Terauchi cabinet for consolidating the diplomatic channels dealing with

China. They advocated abandoning backchannel diplomacy involving the military and private actors in favor of centralizing matters through the diplomatic establishment. Hara responded by consolidating diplomatic efforts, seeing this as a way to restore to the cabinet the rights to make foreign policy decisions that had been partially stolen by the Advisory Council on Foreign Relations (see sidebar on pages 174–75). But even as Hara skillfully manipulated the council, his ultimate goal was actually to eliminate it. The transformation in Japan's diplomacy by Hara was not so much a direct response to Wilson's New Diplomacy as an effort to "correct" Japan's existing China policies.

The Struggles of Makino Nobuaki

The Advisory Council on Foreign Relations, which for all practical purposes was responsible for deciding Japan policies at the peace talks, began its deliberations in November 1918. The comments of Vice-Plenipotentiary (and privy councillor) Makino Nobuaki in the Advisory Council debates were particularly striking in their agreement with the "New Diplomacy." Makino correctly understood the objectives of the Paris Peace Conference as being to eradicate the old diplomacy. Speaking of China at the Advisory Council on Foreign Relations meeting of December 1918, he pointed out that "dual diplomacy"—such as talking of "righteousness and justice," Sino-Japanese amity, and nonintervention in the internal affairs of other countries on the one hand while actually promoting coercive and imperialistic diplomacy such as that expressed through the Twenty-One Demands on the other—itself damaged any trust any nation would have in Japan. He argued instead for the abolition of extraterritoriality and the withdrawal of Japanese troops. While it became an issue for debate between former prime minister Terauchi Masatake and Army Minister Tanaka Giichi, most Advisory Council members approved of doing away with extraterritoriality rights and withdrawing the armed forces.

Makino also argued in favor of approving the proposal for what would become the League of Nations, but many were critical of the idea. For example, Itō Miyoji regarded it as "a sort of political alliance whose objective was the maintenance of the status quo for the Anglo-Saxon peoples." He was concerned that it would threaten the Anglo-Japanese Alliance.

Other than certain economic interests, all members of the Advisory Council approved of restoring the former German interests—including the leased territories—to China. The decision was made keeping Japan's relations with the United States in mind. However, rather than restoring these interests directly, they settled on doing so indirectly, through bilateral negotiations between Japan and China based on the 1915 "Treaty on Shandong Province," after the unconditional transfer of German interests in Shandong to Japan had been completed.

After various deliberations, Japan's position on the peace talks was finally decided late that December. In sum, Japan was making a "demand for the voluntary conveyance" of Germany's previous rights in Shandong and the South Sea Islands. Any other issues were to be handled with a "follow-the-crowd" approach (*taisei junnō shugi*). The Japanese government's view regarding Wilson's Fourteen Points was that it agreed with them in principle, but—considering the impact they would have on Japan—it would either align itself with the United Kingdom or simply follow along with what other countries were doing. In particular, on the matter of creating an international league, it decided to postpone any agreement on a concrete proposal. The policy on the peace talks the government adopted did not reflect Makino's advocacy of the New Diplomacy, but rather sought to formalize the holdings Japan had acquired during the war.

What surfaced in connection with the proposed

Makino Nobuaki (1861–1949)

Makino Nobuaki was born in the Satsuma domain (Kagoshima Prefecture), the second son of Ōkubo Toshimichi. In 1871, he was sent abroad with the Iwakura Mission and remained in the United States to study, returning to Japan in the fall of 1874. He immediately enrolled at the Kaisei Gakkō (a forerunner of the University of Tokyo). In 1878, however, his father was assassinated, and his mother died of an illness in December. Makino then changed his given name from Nobukuma to "Nobuaki." In 1879, he joined the Ministry of Foreign Affairs. While working at the Japanese legation in the United Kingdom in 1882, he met Itō Hirobumi, who was in the United Kingdom researching constitutional systems. Impressed with the young man's resourcefulness and abilities, Itō decided to take Makino under his wing, overseeing his training, including taking him along on a trip to China. After a stint in Japan, Makino then spent the next ten years in Europe, serving in a variety of posts, including as minister to Italy and Austria, between 1897 and 1906.

After the Russo-Japanese War, Makino developed close ties with Saionji Kinmochi, serving as the minister of education and minister of agriculture and commerce, respectively, in Saionji's first and second cabinets. In 1913, Makino was appointed foreign minister under the Yamamoto Gonnohyōe administration—a cabinet that the Satsuma faction had long been hoping to see take shape. Public opinion was incensed during his two-year tenure due to the murders and assaults of several Japanese citizens in China, but Makino remained firm in his determination to resolve problems through diplomatic negotiations. Across the Pacific, the first California Land Law of 1913 created another issue for Makino to contend with. He looked for ways to guarantee the rights of Japanese immigrants via a new Japan-US treaty, enlisting Japanese ambassador to the United States Chinda Sutemi to negotiate a solution, but the effort proved fruitless. With public opinion heavily in favor of a hard-line anti-foreign stance, many lambasted Makino for his "weak foreign policy" in hesitating to take an uncompromising stand against the oppression of their fellow citizens.

5-3. Makino Nobuaki

As a member of the Advisory Council for Foreign Affairs, a new body under the Terauchi Masatake administration,

The Ad Hoc Advisory Council on Foreign Relations

The Terauchi Masatake administration formed an ad hoc Advisory Council for Foreign Affairs in June 1917 as an investigative and advisory body that would report directly to the emperor. Providing counsel on diplomatic issues, the organization would remain in place under the administrations of Hara Takashi, Takahashi Korekiyo, and Katō Tomosaburō and act as a "watchdog" with an enormous amount of influence over Japan's foreign affairs. On the first Advisory Council roster were ten members: several leading cabinet ministers representing the government side, along with Makino Nobuaki, Privy Councillor Hirata Tōsuke, Privy Councillor Itō Miyoji, Seiyūkai leader Hara, and Rikken Kokumintō (Constitutional Nationalist Party) leader Inukai Tsuyoshi. With diplomacy-related issues piling up in the late 1910s, the pretext was to help foster a unified national consensus and keep diplomatic matters out of political squabbles, but the Terauchi cabinet also wanted to pave the way for the Seiyūkai and Rikken Kokumintō to become the ruling parties. The actual operations of the advisory body involved Itō formulating ideas and also drafting the corresponding legislation. Initially, the hope was that the Advisory Council would be a non-partisan body, but Katō Takaaki—then the president of the Kenseikai (Constitutional Politics Association), a party whose influence rivaled that of the Seiyūkai—declined his invitation to join the board. It was natural for Katō to refuse the offer, given that his philosophy had always been to unify diplomacy under the Ministry of Foreign Affairs. Opposition was also widespread in academic circles and the national news media, who claimed that creating an imperial advisory council separate from the cabinet ministers was unconstitutional. Katō remained unwavering in his refusal to join the council, and it saw its significance considerably reduced, but it nonetheless served as a deliberative body on several important diplomatic issues, including the Siberian Expedition and the Paris Peace Conference.

Hara in particular took an interesting approach to the Advisory Council for Foreign Affairs after becoming prime

Makino joined Hara Takashi in calling for a "limited" Siberian Expedition dispatch in a cooperative arrangement with the United States—contradicting the all-out dispatch that Prime Minister Terauchi favored. Makino was appointed as assistant ambassador and plenipotentiary to the Paris Peace Conference in late 1918. He advocated abandoning the "old diplomacy" of the Ōkuma Shigenobu and Terauchi administrations in favor of Woodrow Wilson's "New Diplomacy." He was in favor of ending the "dual diplomacy" of Japan's China policy, revising unequal treaties, withdrawing the Japanese army, and collaborating more actively with the League of Nations, but his proposals made no impact on Japan's conformist approach at the peace talks.

Makino went on to occupy several other high-ranking offices. He became the imperial household minister in 1921 and assumed the post of Lord Keeper of the Privy Seal in 1925. For the next ten years, he and Saionji Kinmochi were among the young Emperor Shōwa's trusted advisors. In 1929, he picked Admiral Suzuki Kantarō (the former chief of the Navy General Staff) to serve as grand chamberlain of the Imperial Household Agency, filling out a cadre of close aides to the emperor. The trust Makino gained from the emperor established him as an influential "court politician." His influence played into Japan's stance on several issues, including the assassination of Zhang Zuolin in the Huanggutun Incident (see page 228). Prime Minister Tanaka Giichi was eager to bring the controversy to an end, even though the party responsible for the killing was unknown, but Makino, who felt Tanaka "lacked any of the qualities required of a politician," encouraged the emperor to take the unorthodox step of directly rebuking the prime minister for his culpability. Tanaka resigned, and passed away suddenly not long afterward. In terms of diplomacy, Makino embraced a policy of non-intervention in China's domestic affairs and favored a "Shidehara diplomacy" approach that rested on cooperation with the Western powers. As the issues surrounding the 1930 London Naval Treaty swirled, meanwhile, Makino maintained steadfast support of the Hamaguchi Osachi cabinet.

According to Chamberlain Irie Sukemasa, the emperor "cried out in sorrow" when he learned that Makino had resigned as Lord Keeper of the Privy Seal in 1935. In the Shōwa era, Makino become a prime target for segments of the military and radical nationalist groups that saw him as the center of a pro-British, pro-American faction. The antagonism culminated with an attempt on Makino's life during the February 26 Incident, but he narrowly escaped the attack. He died in 1949 at the age of eighty-seven.

minister in 1918. In full awareness of the council's inherent faults, he decided to use the organization as a valuable tool in winning elder statesmen and members of the Privy Council over to his ideas. However, he eventually clashed with council members Itō, Gotō Shinpei, and Inukai over decisions concerning Japan's delegation to the Paris Peace Conference. Hara was especially critical of Itō's opposition, seeing the elder statesman's "nonsensical nitpicking" as criticism for its own sake. To keep Itō from interfering in the decision-making process, Hara effectively reduced the scope of the Advisory Council's activities to little more than making reports; meetings grew fewer and farther between. Itō had hoped to keep the Advisory Council alive after the conclusion of the Paris Peace Conference, but Hara soon began to see little purpose for the organization. The council was abolished in September 1922, during the Katō Tomosaburō administration.

League of Nations was a demand for doing away with racial discrimination. Some at the Ministry of Foreign Affairs' Peace Preparations Committee voiced the opinion that a clause on racial discrimination should be included to keep the proposed league from becoming a venue for Caucasians to do business while excluding other races. This reflected the force displayed by the anti-Japanese movement in the United States, as symbolized by the California Alien Land Law of 1913. The issue became a matter of debate in the Advisory Council on Foreign Relations, which came up with a proposal for eliminating the "disadvantages to our empire" resulting from racial prejudice. Many among the press and public also supported the proposal on the grounds that it would be useful for resolving immigration issues, and would also safeguard against future racial conflicts.

It was decided that Japan would play for time

during discussions regarding Wilson's League of Nations at the Peace Conference. If its establishment appeared to be inevitable, Japan would then demand that the association's charter include a clause for the elimination of racial discrimination. That said, Japan's reasons for making this proposal had less to do with touting the ideal of racial equality than with the restrictions imposed on Japanese immigrants to the United States with respect to owning businesses and land and acquiring citizenship.

In Paris: The Demands and Their Outcome

Japan selected Saionji Kinmochi to be the head of its delegation of plenipotentiaries to the Paris Peace Conference. (Makino Nobuaki was in charge of negotiations; Saionji's participation was symbolic.) Makino was elected to be the de facto head; the chief aides included Chinda Sutemi (ambassador to the United Kingdom), Matsui Keishirō (ambassador to France), and Ijūin Hikokichi (ambassador to Italy). The delegation from the Ministry of Foreign Affairs included Nagai Matsuzō, Nagaoka Harukazu, Saburi Sadao, Matsuoka Yōsuke, Yoshida Shigeru, Kimura Eiichi, Arita Hachirō, Shigemitsu Mamoru, and Ashida Hitoshi. The entourage also included Nara Takeji, Ninomiya Harushige, Tanaka Kunishige, and Hata Shunroku from the army; Takeshita Isamu and Nomura Kichisaburō from the navy; and Yamakawa Tadao, Tachi Sakutarō, and Fukai Eigo.

Other than the official members, such figures as Konoe Fumimaro, Saionji Hachirō, and Akizuki Satsuo attended, bringing the total number of participants to sixty. Journalists and political figures such as Nakano Seigō, Baba Tsunego, Nagai Ryūtarō, Uehara Etsujirō, and Kojima Kazuo also made the trip to Paris. It is clear from the list of participants that the group included many of the diplomats and thinkers who shaped Shōwa-era diplomacy. As vice-minister of the Ministry of Foreign Affairs, Shidehara Kijūrō also oversaw the ministry end of the negotiations.

The Paris Peace Conference was held from January to June 1919. Invitations were sent to twenty-nine members of the Allied powers, though the initiative was largely in the hands of the leaders of the "Big Four": British prime minister David Lloyd George, French prime minister Georges Clemenceau, US president Woodrow Wilson, and

5-4. Japanese delegates to the Paris Peace Conference

Italian prime minister Vittorio Orlando. Japan initially was also part of the leading nations, rounding out a "Big Five," but it gradually found itself sidelined. It eventually came to be ridiculed as a "silent partner," but the delegation did its best under the circumstances.

Although Konoe had thought he saw signs that secret diplomacy was becoming a thing of the past, and that the age of people's diplomacy and diplomatic transparency was at hand, he was also shocked by the undeniable fact of the "rule of power." This view of the new diplomacy combining "acceptance and backlash" was proof that Japanese diplomacy was still seen as shaky.

5-5. The Paris Peace Conference

(1) The South Seas Mandate

Debate at the Peace Conference was based on the assumption that any treaty signed with Germany would include a covenant for the proposed League of Nations, and the first item on the agenda was deliberation on setting up the international league proposed by Woodrow Wilson. In parallel with this, discussions focused on how to dispose of former German territories in Africa and the Pacific, including its South Sea Islands.

Wilson believed that immediate annexation of these former colonies by the winners of the war would go against the principle of national self-determination expressed in his Fourteen Points, and feared that doing so would give the world the impression of a return to the old international order. In the end, the conference adopted a mandate system for administering the former colonies, dividing the territories up into three categories—Class A, B, and C—based on such factors as their levels of cultural development and their location. Their administration was then entrusted to various Allied nations. The South Sea Islands were determined to be a Class C mandate, and were placed under Japan's administration because of its geographical proximity. In 1922, military administration was lifted in the islands and the defense garrison withdrawn, and Japan created the South Seas (Nan'yō) government to administer the islands. While the mandate system imposed various restrictions, such as a ban on militarization, in substance the islands were governed as a Japanese territory until the end of World War II.

(2) Setbacks for the Article on Racial Discrimination

Japan's request to insert a clause on eliminating racial discrimination into the covenant of the League of Nations made slow progress. Speaking to the League of Nations Commission in mid-February, Makino made a proposal "that the covenant of the League of Nations should state clearly that foreigners in signatory countries, regardless of race or nationality, should face no discrimination whatsoever, be it legal or factual, and be treated equally in all ways." He stressed that discrimination based on race and religion had frequently been a source of trouble and war, and that the regrettable devastation caused by this was on a scale too large to recount. This proposal, coming from the one non-Caucasian nation among the Big Five, did not go unnoticed. In Japan, support for the proposal was broad. A group of some 300 interested parties, including members of the House of Peers and politicians from the Seiyūkai, formed the Alliance to Achieve Early Adoption of the Racial Equality Article, and took action, including sending a telegram to French Prime Minister Clemenceau, urging him to end racial discrimination.

While Wilson supported the proposal, France opposed it, as did the United Kingdom, which feared an influx of Japanese immigrants to its commonwealth of Australia. Makino and Chinda worked nonstop until the end of March trying to get their counterparts at the conference to agree to the proposal. Meanwhile, Makino tried to break through the impasse by suggesting that principles of equality among nations and just treatment for alien nationals be included instead in the preamble to the League covenant. In a vote taken at the final meeting of the League of Nations Commission held in mid-April, eleven of the sixteen commission members voted in favor of the proposal. However, Wilson said that a unanimous vote was necessary to adopt such an important item, and so the Japanese proposal was rejected. One of the reasons that Wilson hesitated was his fear that adoption of the proposal would be used in debates over the immigration issue in Congress.

(3) The Complicated Shandong Problem

For Japan, the most important issue was the matter of transferring Germany's interests on the Shandong Peninsula, which Japan had acquired through its entry into the war against Germany. Foreign Minister Motono Ichirō (from the cabinet of Terauchi Masatake) had negotiated secretly with the Allied powers to guarantee the unconditional transfer of German interests there as a reward for Japan's participation in the war as an Allied power. In January 1917, Japan had complied with a British request to dispatch a destroyer flotilla to the Mediterranean. In exchange, Japan had secured a secret memorandum from the British agreeing that the United Kingdom would support Japan's demands for the unconditional transfer of German interests at any postwar peace conference. Japan had also secured similar secret memoranda from France, Italy, and Russia. Accordingly, Japan was mainly seeking the agreement of the United States. However, since the United States had already indicated that it did not accept the Treaty on Shandong Province of 1915 (see page 157), the Japanese negotiators anticipated difficulties.

Meanwhile, in China, the Beijing government's fierce conflict with the southern regime continued even after the Beijing regime entered the war against Germany. However, as the war was coming to a close, the northern and southern factions reached a peace of sorts, and together sent a delegation of some fifty people to the Paris talks. For China, the most important objective was to achieve the unconditional return of its interests in Shandong. Substantive deliberations about the Shandong problem began in April 1919, and the United States initially gave strong support to the Chinese position. As they had been directed, the members of the Japanese delegation insisted that, having acquired the Shandong concessions from Germany freely and unconditionally, they expected to discuss returning those concessions to China through direct bilateral negotiations in accordance with the Treaty on Shandong Province. Their attitude suggested that they were willing to walk out of the conference over the issue. Getting the League of Nations established was Wilson's top priority, so he was receptive to Japan's demands, and they were included in an article about Shandong in the Treaty of Versailles.

Wilson's decision to accept Japan's demands was not solely due to the hard-line stance taken by the Japanese delegation, backed up by the secret agreements its government had made with various European countries. Following an agreement reached in talks with Wilson, in May 1919 Makino again declared Japan's intention to restore all sovereignty over the Shandong Peninsula to China, and said that Japan would preserve only its right to secure Germany's former economic interests and to establish a foreign settlement in Qingdao. This left Wilson hopeful that the Shandong problem would finally be resolved through the League, and progress would be made in international cooperation with respect to China.

Wilson attached great importance to cooperation among the great powers as a way to make a new international order a reality, and feared that the Shandong problem could trigger a return to the former rivalry among powers. Sustaining cooperation among the great powers was the premise for the collective security that Wilson sought. Wilson's concept was repudiated within the United States, however, reigniting the crisis in relations with Japan. They did not become stable again until the Washington Naval Conference, when the Harding administration asserted its leadership on East Asia policy.

The May Fourth Movement and Propaganda

The approval of the transfer of the concessions in Shandong to Japan despite China's objections sparked massive demonstrations by students in Beijing. This developed into a nationwide mass anti-imperialism movement later known as the May Fourth Movement, leading to sweeping boycotts of Japanese goods and acts of protest across the country. The Beijing government managed to suppress these demonstrations, and then ordered its delegation to sign the Treaty of Versailles. The Chinese delegation had considered signing the treaty with the stipulation that the parts referring to Shandong concessions be deferred, but since this deferment was not accepted, it refused to sign.

Once the Treaty of Versailles had come into force, Japan offered to negotiate the return of Shandong with China. The conditions for this included the withdrawal of Japanese troops and joint Sino-Japanese administration of the Shandong railway (Qingdao-Jinan railway). While maintaining a firm stance regarding an unconditional return, China was also pressured by public opinion calling for the decision to be left up to Anglo-American intervention or to the League of Nations. It rejected Japan's various proposals, and the matter remained unresolved until the Washington Naval Conference. In the latter half of the 1910s, Japan was a prominent target of anti-imperialist and anti-Japanese movements in China. During this period, Japan sought to "correct" the "anti-Japan sentiment" in China's history textbooks.

Japan optimistically believed that the Shandong problem would be resolved through bilateral cooperation in peace talks. In December 1918, Foreign Minister Uchida Yasuya (Kōsai) had met with Lu Zhengyiang of the Beijing government, who stopped in Japan en route to the Paris Peace Conference. Uchida conveyed Japan's support for revising the unequal treaties with China, and reaffirmed that Japan and China would work together. However, China had been making its own efforts behind the scenes. China's envoy to the United States, Wellington Koo, had started to explain his country's position to the US delegation before it arrived in Paris, and had declared its support for Wilson's New Diplomacy. The Chinese delegation in Paris also repeatedly engaged in its own maneuvering and propaganda directed toward the United States in the run-up to the Shandong negotiations.

The head of Japan's delegation, Saionji Kinmochi, wrote in his mission report of how difficult the talks on the Shandong problem were. He noted how China's propaganda efforts had managed to influence the great powers, observing that the opposition of the entire Chinese delegation and a certain degree of sympathy for China on the part of the United States created enormous barriers to resolving the issue. Likewise, delegation member Konoe Fumimaro, in recounting his personal experiences of the peace conference, wrote that diplomacy had become driven by public sentiment. He noted, "In an age in which nothing can be accomplished

The Yap Island Controversy

In the wake of World War I, the South Seas Mandate gave Japan control over the Mariana Islands, the Caroline Islands, and the Marshall Islands. One of the territories—Yap, a tiny piece of land in the Western Carolines—ended up being the center of an international controversy. The United States was opposed to giving Japan control over the island due to what lay under it. Yap sat on three submarine power cables, including the line connecting Guam (a US territory) and Celebes (a Dutch territory), fueling concerns that the submarine cables might come under the control of a single country.

At the International Radiotelegraph Conference, held in Washington in October 1920, the American delegation proposed removing Yap from the scope of Japanese mandatory rule and placing the territory under international control. Japanese ambassador to the United States Shidehara Kijūrō countered, saying that it was impossible to overturn a mandate that had already become official. The United States then proceeded to submit a protest note to the League of Nations in February 1921. That April, the US government informed Japan, the United Kingdom, France, and Italy that it was not bound by the terms of the Treaty of Versailles (which stipulated the South Seas Mandate) because it had never ratified the agreement. In an effort to break the deadlock, Shidehara—dealing directly with US secretary of state Charles Evans Hughes—offered to grant the United States the same special rights and interests that Japan held over the laying of, operation of, and telegraphy via the submarine power cables if the United States would relinquish its objections to Japan's mandate over Yap. The United States accepted the compromise, and the two sides signed the Treaty as to Yap and the Mandated North Pacific Islands in February 1922.

without winning public consensus and sympathy... propaganda is simply a new weapon for diplomacy that has been created in keeping with the needs of these times," suggesting there was a need for a "propaganda organization."

Reforming the Ministry of Foreign Affairs and a Shift toward Greater Autonomy

The Paris Peace Conference was the first time that members of a Japanese delegation had attended a full-blown international conclave. Japan had been invited as one of the Five Powers, but the delegation became painfully aware of how unprepared it was, of its poor performance in terms of public relations, and of its inadequate linguistic abilities. Konoe Fumimaro mentioned that one of the impressions he came away from the conference with was the need to overhaul the systems in place for diplomatic officials. He was not alone in his thinking.

Younger diplomats in the delegation, such as Arita Hachirō, Shigemitsu Mamoru, Saitō Hiroshi, and Horinouchi Kensuke, also had a sense of impending crisis regarding the future of the Ministry of Foreign Affairs, and they decided while in Paris to start a movement to reform the ministry. The movement focused on three objectives: opening the door to a wider range of potential staff, educating ministry personnel, and expanding and strengthening the ministry's organizational apparatus. After they returned to Japan, they sent out a manifesto to others, including diplomatic missions overseas. They put together a group of nearly fifty like-minded colleagues, and in September 1919 organized a ministry reform society with Arita in the lead. With the founding of the society, the ministry picked up on the movement and initially set up an internal interim committee that eventually became the Systems Investigation Committee. The committee was headed by Tanaka Tokichi (chief of the ministry's Trade Bureau). After numerous lively meetings, it submitted its report to Foreign Minister Uchida Yasuya in May 1920.

The report's suggestions encompassed a broad range of issues related to organization, personnel, budget, compensation, and education. Most of them would be incorporated into the ministry's reforms. To expand and strengthen the organizational apparatus, the ministry added a Treaties Bureau to its two existing bureaus in July 1919. In October 1920, the overly busy Government Affairs Bureau was split into an Asia bureau and a Europe-America bureau, bringing the number of bureaus to four. The Trade Bureau remained in place, but now the ministry put in place a regional bureau system that continues to this day.

As to the training of personnel, in January 1921 the ministry decided to implement a system to provide opportunities for new appointees to study the language and political conditions of their new posts. Aside from personnel who had already studied overseas, the ministry would finally be producing diplomatic officials who could handle foreign languages. On the matter of an open-door policy in hiring practices, there was a vast increase in the number of staff both at the ministry itself and at its overseas diplomatic missions after World War I. In addition to those who had passed the foreign-service examination, personnel were now also being hired from outside the ministry by means of a special appointment system. Among those who would go on to leave a notable track record at the ministry on par with peers who had passed the foreign-service exam were Matsumoto Shun'ichi (who came from the Ministry of Finance), Mitani Takanobu (Ministry of Home Affairs), Yamamoto Kumaichi (successful civil-service examinee), Usami Uzuhiko (Ministry of Agriculture and Commerce), Harada Ken (Ministry of Home Affairs), and Tsukamoto Takeshi (successful civil-service examinee). The ministry rapidly grew from 586 people on staff in 1918, almost doubling to nearly 1,108 in 1921.

As to public communication efforts, Prime Minister Hara himself was enthusiastic about creating a large information bureau, and his aide Ijūin Hikokichi was at the center of an effort to study the matter. A proposal emerged to create a powerful information agency attached to the cabinet in accordance with Hara's wishes. However, this was set aside as unrealistic in the short term, and in its stead the government created an Information Department within the Ministry of Foreign Affairs in August 1921. Ijūin became its first chief.

As the mechanism for dealing with foreign affairs was expanded through organizational reforms and a dramatic increase in staff, there was also a growing trend over the course of World War I toward greater autonomy from both the elder statesmen and the Imperial Diet—both of which had previously constrained the ministry's efforts to conduct diplomacy. First, with the 1893 introduction of the examination system for foreign-service officers and consular personnel, in principle it was no longer possible to work at the ministry without having passed the qualifying examination. It was also, as a rule, no longer possible to move from one ministry to another. With this personnel system firmly established, the war period and postwar years saw the emergence of men like Shidehara Kijūrō who passed the foreign-service exam and subsequently became ambassadors and vice-ministers. This marked the apex of the 1893 reforms.

At the same time, this shaping of "Kasumigaseki diplomacy" was also part of the effort to centralize diplomacy under the Ministry of Foreign Affairs. Determined efforts were being made to eliminate the harmful effects of dual diplomacy carried out by the military authorities, as well as interventions by the elder statesmen or the Privy Council. With such moves, the ministry was gradually acquiring an autonomy in diplomacy better suited to the age of New Diplomacy. However, it lacked a framework for unifying the sense of purpose within the ministry. Additionally, when it came to consolidating diplomatic policy at the national level, the ministry's clashes with the military authorities and the Privy Council continued unabated. Thus, the most important of the necessary conditions for implementing New Diplomacy—that of civilian control over diplomacy—remained unmet as the 1920s began.

2 The League of Nations and Japan

Collective Security and International Cooperation

In March 1919, the Covenant of the League of Nations that had been incorporated in the first version of the Treaty of Versailles was adopted by thirty-two countries. The League of Nations was formally launched the following year, with forty-two founding members. The League did not turn out to be the "world government" that Wilson had heralded. Rather, it ended up being a system of partnership among sovereign states. As had been the case with the various collaborative relationships among the European powers in the past, the five major powers—the United Kingdom, France, Italy, the United States, and now Japan—were to be standing members of this new organization, and would have special responsibilities when it came to world peace and security. (As the United States did not join, the remaining four Great Powers would be the permanent members at the time of the League's founding.)

In the process of establishing the League, the signatory countries would affirm their thinking about restrictions on armaments and on collective security. Until World War I, maintaining national security had been considered a domestic issue that was secured either singlehandedly or by forming alliances with other countries that shared the same interests. Being free to militarize or to ally with others, and having the recourse to go to war, countries sought to achieve their own safety on the premise of a global balance of powers. However, these means for guaranteeing national security were unstable, giving rise to arms races, intensifying conflicts between sets of allies, and making it difficult to prevent frequent international conflicts, which had ultimately caused an unprecedented world war. Reflections on this situation led to new ways of thinking, including ideas about arms control and preserving collective security. Of these, collective security was a new concept. It called for creating a standing international organization in which certain groupings of nations would work to keep the peace and resolve conflicts; through this, its member states would guarantee security for one another. The League of Nations was supposed to realize this vision.

5-6. League of Nations headquarters

However, as it was actually formed, the League went no further than endorsing the foundations for an international organization in which the resolution of conflicts and the maintenance of peace would rest on agreement between member nations. For this reason, the League had many deficiencies on such matters as arbitrations connected to its obligation to find peaceful solutions to international conflict and its approach to joint sanctions in response to aggression.

Its greatest deficiency lay in the fact that it only had moderate tools for applying sanctions in response to aggression. In terms of sanctions to combat aggression, Wilson put greater weight on the "moral authority" of international public opinion and economic sanctions than on creating some world government or multinational army. As for measures for preventing war, the League Covenant did clearly call for the reduction of national armaments by member states. However, encouraging international arms reduction eventually resulted in a power vacuum that tempted nations to expand their spheres of influence; this would wind up exposing the powerlessness of moderate sanctions.

Aside from security issues, the League of Nations also undertook international partnership projects aimed at encouraging the socioeconomic development of member states. For example, as stated in the preamble to its constitution, the International Labour Organization (ILO) created concurrently with the League was intended to achieve "social justice" by improving working conditions. Its specific function was to adopt agreements and recommendations for the establishment of international labor standards, and then to monitor how they were being implemented. Japan was a standing member of the ILO from its inception. However, it withdrew from the organization in 1938 after the Manchurian Incident and the Second Sino-Japanese War. (It rejoined the body in 1951.)

Japan's Contributions to the Work of the League

Japan joined the League of Nations not so much out of support for the ideology and ideals the League espoused, but rather because it opened the way for it to conform with others and be seen as a great power. Still, Japan attained the enviable status of being one of the permanent members of this body. It may not have been able to flex its muscles in the workings of the Paris Peace Conference, but as a permanent member, Japan played a major role in the League's activities. Its official involvement with the League lasted for thirteen years. The Ministry of Foreign Affairs would dispatch two officers with international experience—Nitobe Inazō and Sugimura Yōtarō—to serve as under-secretary-general, a core operational position. As the author of *Bushido: The Soul of Japan*, Nitobe was one of the best-known Japanese figures of the time, and he put in a great deal of effort to make the work of the League widely known. Nitobe played a major role in launching and then overseeing the League's International Committee on Intellectual Cooperation (ICIC), which handled matters related to education, cultural affairs, and scholarship. His successor, Sugimura Yōtarō, concentrated specifically on helping to resolve various European conflicts.

Japan also dispatched Ishii Kikujirō, Matsui Keishirō, Adachi Mineichirō, Yoshizawa Kenkichi,

The International Committee on Intellectual Cooperation and the "Textbook Controversy"

At the League of Nations Assembly meeting in 1921, the members voted to establish the International Committee on Intellectual Cooperation (the forerunner of UNESCO) as an advisory body to the League in 1922. At the heart of the effort to create the organization was League of Nations under-secretary-general Nitobe Inazō. The committee was a unique consortium of some of the day's brightest minds and most eminent thinkers—Albert Einstein and Marie Curie, to name two—who all joined the initiative in a private capacity. Together, the participants worked to coordinate with educators worldwide to put in place a textbook movement. The organization knew that if a country's government chose to teach "convenient" history, students could very well end up harboring unfounded prejudices or enmity toward other countries—circumstances that could also prepare citizens for war on a psychological level. The movement aimed to eliminate content that might lead to major misunderstandings concerning other nations by having various countries check one another's history books.

In Japan, too, the newly formed "Keimeikai" teachers' union was working to promote internationally minded history textbooks that did not in any way encourage hostile feelings, in anticipation of the League of Nations Assembly. The Keimeikai movement would eventually peter out in the mid-1930s before the sway of imperialism infringed on textbook rights and interfered in domestic affairs. But it is worth noting that the 1929 report by the International Committee on Intellectual Cooperation was based on the guiding principle that approaching the teaching of European history as a single entity, rather than that of individual nations, would help to achieve unity.

Satō Naotake, and Nagaoka Harukazu as envoys to the League's council. The impartiality and honesty they showed in their work earned them high praise as a "good example for others." Ishii in particular came to be well regarded within the League for his work as head of the special commission on the Upper Silesia problem and the commission dealing with Åland Islands issue.

Furthermore, in the latter half of the 1920s, Ishii was also entrusted with handling the issue of minority peoples, as Japan could be expected to take an impartial position. The Japanese delegation

Yoshizawa Kenkichi (1874–1965)

A native of Niigata Prefecture, Yoshizawa Kenkichi was drawn to Chinese classics early on. After graduating from Tokyo Imperial University with a degree in English literature in 1899, he passed the foreign-service examination and launched his career as a diplomat. He was posted to Qing China in 1900 and remained there until 1918, except for a two-year stint in London. After returning home to Japan, Yoshizawa took part in the diplomatic negotiations on the Siberian Expedition in 1919 as director-general of the Bureau of Political Affairs in the Ministry of Foreign Affairs. He then returned to China to serve as Japan's minister from 1923 to 1929, working to mitigate anti-Japanese sentiment, de-escalate mounting boycotts of Japanese products, and protect Japanese citizens in China. In the events surrounding the Tanaka Giichi administration's Shandong Expedition, Yoshizawa advised Zhang Zuolin to withdraw to Manchuria, but remained critical of the Japanese army's belligerent stance on the matter. Yoshizawa, along with Hioki Eki, also represented Japan at the Special Conference on the Chinese Customs Tariff, pursuing negotiations across a protracted nine-month process, and also engaged in the talks to normalize relations between Japan and the Soviet Union—an effort that resulted in the signing of the Soviet-Japanese Basic Convention in Beijing in 1925.

5-7. Yoshizawa Kenkichi

Yoshizawa went to Paris as Japan's ambassador to France in 1930. He also served as Japan's official representative to the League of Nations, bearing the brunt of the criticism when the Council of the League of Nations began addressing the implications of the Manchurian Incident. In January 1932, Prime Minister Inukai Tsuyoshi appointed Yoshizawa as his foreign minister. During his term, Yoshizawa made efforts to restrain the Japanese military, which was

Nitobe Inazō (1862–1933) and Sugimura Yōtarō (1884–1939)

Nitobe Inazō graduated from Sapporo Agricultural College in 1881, along with fellow classmate Uchimura Kanzō. He traveled to the United States and enrolled at the newly established Johns Hopkins University. He married an American woman and joined the Religious Society of Friends (Quakers). He became a professor at his alma mater, Sapporo Agricultural College, and wrote *Bushido: The Soul of Japan*—in English—in 1899. The book, which was translated into more than ten languages, gave international audiences an introduction to the Japanese spirit. After a stint as professor at Kyoto Imperial University, Nitobe was appointed headmaster of the First Higher School. While Nitobe's academic specialties lay in colonial studies and agricultural policy, he is most admired as a social educator representative of Taishō-era liberalism.

5-8. Nitobe Inazō

5-9. Sugimura Yōtarō

Nitobe later served as an under-secretary-general of the League of Nations, securing the position on the recommendation of Makino Nobuaki in 1920. Over his seven years in this role, Nitobe worked under Secretary-General James Eric Drummond as the director of the International Bureaux Section and played an instrumental part in forming and overseeing the International Committee on Intellectual Cooperation (the forerunner of UNESCO). In all, Nitobe left collaborated with the League Council as it poured its energies into resolving the issues between Germany and Poland with regard to minorities. It served as mediator in direct negotiations between the two countries and laid a path toward a diplomatic solution. These contributions were the embodiment of the "Geneva spirit" of reconciliation and compromise. Aside from this, Japan also actively participated in the work of the ILO, the ICIC, and the Permanent Court of International Justice. Miyajima Mikinosuke was particularly active in the area of health and hygiene. He carried

pressing for the creation of an independent Manchurian state. When the May 15 Incident resulted in the dissolution of the Inukai cabinet, however, Yoshizawa withdrew from diplomatic service. Subsequently, he led the Japanese delegation in economic talks with the Netherlands to help Japan secure supplies of oil, and served as Japan's ambassador extraordinary to French Indochina from October 1941 to the end of 1944, returning to Japan as the Pacific War entered its final stages. In the postwar years, he became Japan's first ambassador to the Republic of China (Taiwan) upon the conclusion of the Treaty of Peace between the Republic of China and Japan in 1952.

Over his six-decade career in diplomacy, Yoshizawa spent much of his time in China. After the onset of China's "Warlord Era," a frequent partner at the negotiating table was Wellington Koo, a Chinese representative with pro-Western leanings.

Koo, who held a doctorate from Columbia University, leveraged his exceptional command of English to represent China at the Paris Peace Conference, the Washington Naval Conference, and other international gatherings. He also presided over diplomatic affairs for the First Republic of China (the Beiyang government) and the Nationalist government in Nanjing, engaging in international negotiations on a personal mission to eliminate unequal treaties. Koo was the Chinese member of the Lytton Commission in the aftermath of the Manchurian Incident, and also served as China's representative to the League of Nations, where he clashed with the Japanese delegation over the invasion of Manchuria in 1933. Koo served as China's ambassador to France, the United Kingdom, and—after World War II—the United States, striving in all those roles to improve the international standing of the Republic of China. His friendship with Yoshizawa deepened when they were both in Paris as ambassadors to France. Yoshizawa and Koo apparently sparred at the negotiating table but were also very close. The two would remain friends through the postwar years.

an indelible mark on the League's global educational initiatives—part of his lifelong vision of embodying a "bridge across the Pacific." Upon returning to Japan, Nitobe became a member of the House of Peers. The aftermath of the Manchurian Incident would largely shape the rest of his life: he traveled throughout North America giving lectures and doing everything he could to repudiate any "misunderstanding" of Japan's actions in Manchuria until he died unexpectedly in Canada in 1933.

Sugimura Yōtarō entered the Ministry of Foreign Affairs before going to study at the University of Lyon, ultimately receiving a doctorate in law from the institution. In 1923, he became deputy director of the Imperial Japan Office of the League of Nations, where he distinguished himself, working side by side with Director-General Matsuda Michikazu on a variety of international issues. In 1926, he assumed the directorship of the same office; just one year later, he relocated to Geneva to take over for Nitobe as under-secretary-general and director of the Political Section. While Sugimura managed to prevent China from submitting an official complaint over the Jinan (Tsinan) Incident, the Manchurian Incident put him in the difficult position of having to negotiate from the conflicting standpoints of the League and Japan. After Japan withdrew from the League of Nations, Sugimura spent time in the Swiss mountains to recuperate from stress and ill health. In *Kokusai gaikōroku* (A record of international diplomacy), which he wrote shortly after Japan's exit from the League of Nations, he stressed the need for Japan to adopt a new policy in the international context. "Should Japan wish to establish itself as a preeminent force in the Far East, assume leadership in the Orient, and forge cooperative bonds with its neighboring nations," Sugimura wrote, "it must embark on a policy shift with all the purpose, resolve, and forethought it can muster." In 1937, he was appointed Japan's ambassador to France, but he succumbed to an intestinal occlusion in March 1939. He received an official Ministry of Foreign Affairs funeral, a testament to his diplomatic achievements.

out local surveys of epidemics in the Far East, and his work helped lead to the creation of the League's Eastern Bureau of Epidemiological Intelligence.

According to Satō Naotake, the purpose of Japan's active involvement in the League was to win the trust of member nations and put itself into an advantageous position in the event that the standoff between Japan and China over the Manchuria question became a topic of debate at the League. However, the increasing severity of the Manchuria problem rendered that hard-earned trust immaterial.

The Japanese delegation had acted impartially with respect to various European issues. However, the situation was different when it came to issues in the Far East. When the Jinan Incident occurred in 1928, China's case was blocked before it could be brought. However, with the Manchurian Incident of 1931, for the first time Japan became the subject of League deliberations as one of the combatant nations, and it had a tough time of it. Japan gave notice in 1933 that it would pull back from the political aspects of the League, although it also declared that it would continue to cooperate in peaceful specialized areas. Its cooperative relationship with the League would last until November 1938.

In the meantime, Germany joined the League as a permanent member of the Council in 1926. China provided the bulk of the support to secure Germany that status. While China had refused to sign the Treaty of Versailles, it did sign the Treaty of Saint-Germain reached with Austria in 1919, and became a founding member of the League as per Article 1 of that treaty. China took on a considerable financial burden for the League, worked hard to improve its status within the body, and managed to get itself elected to the Executive Council several times, making use of the allotment set aside for nonpermanent Asian members.

3 International Consortia and Japan

The Origins of International Consortia

The idea of providing China with financial assistance and developing the country's market through foreign loans (investment) went back to Qing times. In particular, the Beijing government established after the 1911 Revolution (first under Yuan Shikai, and then Duan Qirui) got into financial straits due to internal conflicts, and repeatedly had to rely on foreign loans to get back on their feet. Because the Western powers were not unified in their response to such requests, however, the loans proved ineffective. The decision was therefore made to try joint enterprises financed through international consortia. In 1909, a group of banks from the United Kingdom, France, and Germany concluded a loan contract with the Qing court to fund the Hukuang Railway (with lines between Guangdong and Hankou, and between Sichuan and Hankou). When US banks joined in 1911, the Four-Power Consortium took shape just ahead of the revolution. US secretary of state Philander C. Knox's plan to internationalize (neutralize) the South Manchurian Railway may have been shelved (see chapter 3), but the underlying concept was realized in a different form with the establishment of international consortia that jointly administered China's railways. The Four-Power Consortium's project contracts went beyond railways, also calling for reforms to China's monetary (currency) system and for the development of Manchuria.

Upon hearing of the newly created Four-Power Consortium, both Japan and Russia grew even more wary about protecting their respective Manchuria interests. However, at the request of the post-revolution Beijing government (under Yuan), the consortium agreed to embark on large-scale reform financing, and added both Japan and Russia to the group (June 1912, the Six-Power Consortium). The Japanese government had envisioned a situation in which China's administrative and financial functions would be placed under some sort of joint international management structure led by the Western powers, and so it decided that becoming a part of structure was the sensible thing to do. Accordingly, while keeping a close eye on the powers' reservations about and tolerance of its Manchurian interests, Japan ended up joining the financial consortium.

However, the Six-Power Consortium soon had to deal with the United States withdrawing from the group in March 1913. President Woodrow Wilson's administration, which succeeded Taft's, had decided that the consortium's projects infringed on Chinese sovereignty and administrative independence. Upon the withdrawal of the United States, the consortium decided that it would restrict its projects to loans for governmental purposes. Private loans for business purposes would be left up to the individual countries involved. Then, in 1914, World War I began. As Germany was now a combatant against the United Kingdom, France, and Russia, it withdrew from the consortium, and the group's projects stagnated. However, the Japanese economy benefited from the wartime conditions. Its balance of trade moved from deficit conditions to a surplus at a single stroke, and it shifted from being a debtor country to a creditor. In light of this financial growth, Japan embarked on a policy of actively providing loans to China. However, its projects—typified by the Nishihara loans undertaken by the Terauchi Masatake cabinet—deviated from the framework of international consortia. These loans, which were arranged in secret with the intention of assisting the northern Duan regime, generated mistrust of Japan among the Western powers, and also drew domestic criticism. They were put to a halt by the Hara cabinet formed in September 1918, and the pro-Duan policy was cancelled. Hara was moving forward on efforts to repair relations with the United States that had been damaged during the war years by Japan's aggressive China policy, and Japan's participation in a new Four-Power Consortium would become part of that effort.

The New Four-Power Consortium; Manchurian and Mongolian Interests

In May 1919, just as the Peace Conference was reaching its final stages, Thomas W. Lamont of J. P. Morgan and Company chaired a meeting in Paris of representatives from the banks of four countries. The meeting came about as the result of a proposal the US government had made in July 1918 to the United Kingdom, France, and Japan to form a new international financial consortium. The United States proposed that the consortium be put together to avoid overheated competition among banks for investments in China. The governments would provide assistance only to this consortium. The US government asked the three other governments to form groups of banks, with the idea that these groups from the four countries would jointly invest in China. One of the underlying political motives for this plan was to restrain monopolistic investment efforts such as those represented by the Nishihara loans. Specifically, the new consortium would handle business loans as well as government loans; additionally, each country would assign its existing loan priority rights in China to the new consortium. The first condition developed because the Nishihara loans were seen as an abuse of the freedom to provide business loans under the old Four-Power Consortium and an attempt to establish Japanese influence over China.

The Terauchi cabinet did not settle on a formal opinion on either of the conditions and delayed in offering a response. However, following the decision by the successor Hara cabinet that the Yokohama Specie Bank would serve as Japan's representative financial institution, the banking

Itō Miyoji (1857–1934)

Nagasaki native Itō Miyoji studied English in his home province before taking a job at a foreign-language newspaper in Kobe. His work there eventually attracted the attention of Hyōgo Prefecture governor Kanda Takahira, who made Itō an official interpreter for the prefecture. When Kanda became a member of the Chamber of Elders, Itō moved to Tokyo and became a protégé of Itō Hirobumi. He remained a faithful follower of Itō; his posts included secretary to the prime minister in Itō Hirobumi's first cabinet, chief secretary in the second cabinet, and minister of agriculture and commerce in the third administration. He became a member of the Privy Council in 1899 and spent the next thirty-five years—until his death in 1934—maintaining a commanding presence in the organization. After the death of Itō Hirobumi, Itō Miyoji established a closer relationship with Yamagata Aritomo. Then, as the aging Yamagata gradually faded out of the political picture, Itō regularly involved himself in diplomatic issues as a self-proclaimed elder statesman. Itō was a key figure behind the creation of the Advisory Council for Foreign Affairs and criticized Foreign Minister Motono Ichirō's argument for an independent Siberian Expedition so fiercely that Motono ended up stepping down from his position. He also effectively silenced the voices of Makino Nobuaki, Hara Takashi, and others advocating a joint Japan-US expedition. Itō's presence would take on even more weight after Yamagata's passing, as he became a "backroom fixer" in diplomatic circles—and often created problems for the administration in power. In 1927, he took the Wakatsuki Reijirō cabinet to task for the emergency imperial decree ordering a bailout for the Bank of Taiwan, which he said was unconstitutional, and the Privy Council thwarted the bailout. He followed a similar line of attack against the Tanaka Giichi administration's agreement to the Kellogg-Briand Pact the following year, charging that the phrasing of the declaration in Article 1—which stipulated that governments would condemn war "in the names of their . . . peoples"—was unconstitutional. In 1930, as chair of the Privy Council Review Committee, Itō also railed against the Hamaguchi Osachi cabinet for signing the bill to ratify the London Naval Treaty, which he saw as an infringement on the prerogatives of the emperor.

5-10. Itō Miyoji

groups from the four countries held their meeting in Paris in May 1919.

The most difficult aspect of negotiating the formation of this new consortium was determining how Japan's vested interests in Manchuria and Mongolia would be handled. Based on a cabinet decision reached in May 1919, the Hara government instructed its Paris delegation to get Manchuria and Mongolia excluded completely from the scope of the consortium's joint projects. It also notified the United Kingdom and the United States of its decision via memorandum. This demand was an example of *gaikatsu shugi* ("generalism"), a method for excluding certain groups of regions. It was rejected by the United States at the end of July.

Early the following month, a meeting of the Advisory Council on Foreign Relations was held. Recognizing that it would be difficult to get the consortium to consider excluding Manchuria and Mongolia, Foreign Minister Uchida Yasuya proposed an approach described as *rekki shugi* ("enumerationism"), enumerating each of Japan's interests and requesting that they be excluded individually. Meanwhile, with the army pressing the government to maintain and defend Japan's Manchurian and Mongolian interests, Army Minister Tanaka exhorted the council to endorse the all-encompassing *gaikatsu shugi* approach. Itō Miyoji then pointed out that a *rekki shugi* approach would also assert Japanese interests in Manchuria and Mongolia, and that any negotiations with the United Kingdom and the United States would not yield satisfactory results. Therefore, he said, Japan should either pursue the *gaikatsu shugi* approach or

The Foreign Travels of Crown Prince Hirohito

In March 1921, twenty-year-old Crown Prince Hirohito (later Emperor Shōwa) and a retinue of fifteen attendants boarded the battleship *Katori* at the Port of Yokohama and set off for Europe. The primary destination for the voyage was the United Kingdom. With Emperor Taishō in failing health, Prime Minister Hara Takashi, elder statesman Saionji Kinmochi, and fellow elder statesman Yamagata Aritomo recommended that the crown prince see the world for himself so that he could gain some of the insights that he would need as a future monarch. Above all, however, the trip was one that the crown prince personally wanted to take. Upon arriving in the United Kingdom in May, the prince and the rest of the traveling party commenced a busy schedule of tours and functions as official guests of the British royal family and government. Following their British stay, they made stops in France, Italy, and other locations on the continent. The group arrived back in Yokohama that September, just two months before Crown Prince Hirohito became the regent of Japan (*sesshō*) for his ailing father.

The day after the group's welcome banquet in the United Kingdom, King George V paid an unexpected visit to the prince's room at Buckingham Palace and spoke with Hirohito about the country's current conditions and its travails during the World War I. Asked later about his European visit, Emperor Shōwa commented, "The things I learned from King George V about the ideals and workings of a constitutional monarchy have formed the basis of my views ever since." In London, the crown prince went shopping by himself, rode the subway, and bought paintings and antiques. In Gibraltar, he bet on horse races. In Paris, he bought himself a tie. His jaunt on the Parisian subway even took an unexpected turn when he got off the train and went through the gate with his ticket still in his hand. That ticket would stay with the emperor, who kept it as a treasured memento of his European trip for the rest of his life. During a visit to World War I–ravaged Verdun in June, he witnessed the scars of war firsthand. Seeing shell fragments and gas masks strewn across the ground and ravines filled with freshly dug graves, the prince conveyed his shock, reportedly calling war "a truly atrocious thing."

Crown Prince Hirohito's tour of Europe may not have had any explicit political intentions, but it did have symbolic ramifications. By the advent of the 1920s, political circles had begun to buzz with questions surrounding the renewal of the Anglo-Japanese Alliance (first signed in 1902)—a pact that had been central to Japanese diplomacy for almost twenty years. In that context, the crown prince's visit to the United Kingdom in 1921 and the reciprocal visit by Prince Edward in 1922 symbolized hope for an enduring friendship between the two nations. On looking back at his travels in September 1970, Emperor Shōwa said, "Until my trip to Europe, I had lived a life like that of a bird in a cage, but the experience of freedom on that trip serves me to this day."

5-11. Crown Prince Hirohito visits Europe

simply withdraw from the proposed consortium.

Ambassador to the US Debuchi Katsuji opined that *gaikatsu shugi* should be eschewed on the grounds that it would lower Japan's international standing, and stated that there would be little to lose even if the five Manchuria and Mongolia railways in which Japan held preferential investment rights were offered to the consortium. Debuchi argued that, with that retraction as a condition, Japan should be able to get the United Kingdom and France to promise to do away with spheres of influence, appease anti-Japan sentiment in the United States, and secure a leadership role in administering the consortium. The Japanese banking group in Paris argued that the idea of *kakkyo shugi* (sectionalism) that called for fencing off specific regions was out of date. It asked that the *gaikatsu shugi* approach be retracted, given that Japan was better positioned than other countries for free competition in the Chinese market, and any joint investment in the Manchuria and Mongolia railways posed no threat. Despite much criticism of the *gaikatsu shugi* approach, Prime Minister Hara decided to maintain that stance while seeking a resolution to the issues through compromise (*rekki shugi*), and gingerly watched to see the response of the United Kingdom and the United States.

With negotiations at an impasse, in March 1920, J. P. Morgan's Lamont visited Japan at the US State Department's request. In talks with Inoue Junnosuke, an agreement was reached in principle along *rekki shugi* lines; i.e., one in which the parties would enumerate only those interests to be excluded. This compromise was reached because the United States prioritized the creation of a new consortium. Toward the end of March, the Hara cabinet decided on its response to the United Kingdom and the United States. It sought their understanding of Japan's position on establishing special and fair retention, for reasons of both national defense and state survival due to Japan's "vital interest" relationship with Manchuria and Mongolia. For that reason, the response said, Japan wished to exclude those individual interests from the consortium's scope of investment. In short, the decision moved away from *gaikatsu shugi* in favor of trying to achieve a resolution through *rekki shugi*.

The British and US governments responded in early May, reaffirming they had no intention to take any sort of action that would infringe on Japan's "pressing interests" in Manchuria and Mongolia. This proved the decisive step for negotiations to come to a satisfactory conclusion. The United Kingdom and the United States no longer expected unconditional participation from the Japanese banking group, and instead assented to the *rekki shugi* principle. Also, based on the general principle that geographical accessibility creates special relationships among nations, they affirmed that pressing interests existed for Japan in Manchuria and Mongolia, and they promised to not infringe on them. Meanwhile, the Japanese government declared that "pressing interests" did not mean it had exclusive special rights or a set sphere of influence. Japan narrowly managed to secure the grounds for asserting the validity of its Manchurian and Mongolian interests.

In May 1920, one year after the negotiations began, the Japanese banking group declared that, in accordance with a government directive, it was retracting the correspondence of June 1919 seeking for Manchuria and Mongolia to be excluded in their entirety. In its place, the group would now join a new consortium under the same conditions as its counterparts from the United Kingdom, France, and the United States. The new Four-Power Consortium was formally launched in October 1920. All loans to China, including those made for economic purposes, would henceforth be handled as joint projects by the consortium. However, the consortium would eventually conclude its activities without having actually done anything.

Resolving the consortium issue kept the Manchuria and Mongolia issue from once again becoming a point of contention between Japan and the United States. It also demonstrated that any policy seeking to obtain an exclusive and dominant position for Japan in China was simply not a realistic option. International relations in East Asia had developed around a basic structure of opposing Japan's expansionist policies. Now, however, they would start moving toward creating an international order in which Japan was a partner, hinging on stability in the Japan-US relationship. The Washington Naval Conference was the culmination of this process.

4 The Siberian Expedition: Interventionist War and Japan

Send Troops or Prudently Watch? The Joint Japan-US Troop Dispatch

The Bolshevik regime headed by Vladimir Lenin that seized power through the October Revolution was the world's first communist government. Lenin had called on all warring countries to make a peace with no indemnities or annexation of territory to achieve the result that all people wanted, but not a single country responded to his plea. Meanwhile, Germany, which was at war with the Allied powers, now took advantage of the chaos caused by the revolution and launched a military offensive against Russia. The Russian army lacked the ability to fight back, and in December 1917 Lenin sued for peace with Germany. With Russia's withdrawal, Germany's Eastern Front was no longer an issue. This meant that Germany could now focus its offensive efforts on the Western Front. In response, the United Kingdom and France began maneuvering to topple the Bolshevik regime, unite elements in Russia that would support continuing the war effort, put together a new government, and resurrect the Eastern Front. Based on these plans, the two governments approached their Japanese and US counterparts at the end of 1917 in an attempt to persuade them to jointly dispatch troops to Siberia.

At first, both Japan and the United States were unenthusiastic about the plan. President Wilson had called for the evacuation of all Russian territory in his Fourteen Points memo, and so he rejected the British and French efforts at persuasion. In March 1918, the Japanese government received a memorandum saying the US was wary

5-12. Troops sent to Siberia

about a troop dispatch at that moment. Around the same time, Germany and Russia signed a peace treaty, the Treaty of Brest-Litovsk. Having the upper hand, Germany did not accept Lenin's call for peace with no annexations or indemnities, and demanded Russia cede territory to it. Accordingly, Russia lost a large amount of land, although it was able to extract itself from the ongoing war and restore peace for itself. For its part, Japan saw the peace that had been reached between Germany and the new Russian government as posing the threat of a German advance into Siberia.

Within the Japanese government, Foreign Minister Motono Ichirō now argued for accepting the request for a dispatch of troops on the grounds of "self-defense" to prevent any eastward move by German forces. Motono had been stationed in Russia for many years, and had built close relations with many in the Imperial regime. Accordingly, he harbored a deep hatred for the Bolshevik revolution. He also argued for the dispatch on the grounds that it would increase Japan's international influence once the war was over.

Motono made his arguments for the dispatch at the Advisory Council on Foreign Relations in December 1917. However, Hara Takashi (then president of the Seiyūkai) argued strongly against it, saying that a troop dispatch was a warmongering act that would invite an immediate outbreak

5-13. Rice Riots, August 1918

of conflict with Russia. Other Council members endorsed this view, and the matter was shelved. Prime Minister Terauchi and leading elder statesman Yamagata Aritomo were also voices of caution. Yamagata argued that, so long as no predictions could be made about either how to raise the funds for such a dispatch or how to handle troop withdrawal, he was opposed to Japan sending troops unilaterally. They thought that, at the very least, Japan needed the United States to agree or to also send troops. Hence, in April 1918, although the Terauchi cabinet affirmed the need for a troop dispatch to eastern Siberia to maintain public order and protect the Japanese empire, it also decided that, as long as approval had not been obtained from the United States, it would remain cautious. Motono resigned his post as foreign minister at this juncture, but his successor, Gotō Shinpei, was equally in favor of the dispatch.

Meanwhile, the Army General Staff Office retained its aggressive attitude, quite unconcerned with the circumspect arguments about the troop dispatch taking place at the Advisory Council on Foreign Relations and within the government. Deputy Chief of Staff Tanaka Giichi had devised a plan for creating an autonomous regime east of Lake Baikal (the Transbaikal region) to oppose German forces, thereby securing Japan a foothold on Siberian development. Army General Staff Office had constructed a plan to dispatch Japanese forces to an area stretching from Russia's Maritime Province to northern Manchuria, under the guise of "Protecting Japanese Residents." At the end of February 1918, the heads of the relevant division within the Army Ministry and Army General Staff were brought together to create the Joint Committee on Military Matters in order to formulate a mobilization plan, with Tanaka as chairman. The final proposal, put together in March, reflected the views of the army. It called for seizing eastern Siberia, which was seen as the extent to which an advance through the Transbaikal would reach; taking control of important points along the Chinese Eastern Railway; and establishing a pro-Japanese government in the occupied region.

The Revolt of the Czechoslovak Legion and Joint Troop Dispatch

In order to concentrate the US army's forces along the Western Front, and because a joint troop dispatch might lead to Japan expanding its sphere of influence in Northeast Asia, President Wilson remained halfhearted about sending forces. But the revolt of the Czechoslovak Legion pushed Wilson toward taking that step.

In May 1918, Czechoslovak Legion forces (see sidebar on page 193) traveling on an eastbound train on the Trans-Siberian Railway skirmished at Chelyabinsk Station with a group of Hungarians who were headed west as prisoners of war. The fighting was brought under control, but the Bolshevik government demanded the Legion troops be disarmed before being allowed to continue their eastward journey. The Legion forces rejected this demand and signaled that they would rise up against the Bolsheviks. They quickly wound up occupying several cities along the Trans-Siberian Railway.

The uprising of the Czechoslovak Legion was an unexpected development, but the British and the French tried to take advantage of it to redraw the battle lines against Germany. The Legion, too, for

The Tragedy of the Czechoslovak Legion

The Czechoslovak Legion was a unit of Czechs and Slovaks who had been captives of the Russian army in World War I, along with Czechs who had fled Habsburg dominance and moved to Russia generations prior. The group's aim was to win the support of the Russian Empire, which would help them in their cause of gaining independence from the Austrian Empire. Having fought for the Russian side in World War I, the Czechoslovak troops secured the backing of the post–February Revolution provisional government and had already grown to nearly 40,000 by the end of 1917. However, when the Bolsheviks made peace with Germany and Austria—the powers that the Czechoslovak Legion had been fighting—via the Treaty of Brest-Litovsk, the Legion was left with nowhere to go in Russia. When the Soviet government agreed to permit the forces to keep fighting on the Western Front, the Czechoslovak Legion headed east on the Trans-Siberian Railway. The plan was to embark on a great expedition that would take them to Vladivostok, then across the Pacific, over the United States by land, and finally to the battleground in France.

The Czechoslovak Legion's ultimate objective was ethnic independence. That goal did come to fruition with Czechoslovakia's declaration of independence in October 1918, which was recognized the following year by the delegations to the Paris Peace Conference. The nascent republic's first president was Tomáš Masaryk, a renowned thinker and titular commander in the Czechoslovak Legion. However, the withdrawal of the Czechoslovak Legion was delayed, and they found themselves under the orders of the anti-revolutionary British and French forces, and even took up arms against the Japanese army. They signed a cease-fire with the Soviet government in February 1920, but by the time they withdrew from Siberia, only 72,000 soldiers remained to return home. In all, 3,600 of the Legion's troops died—more fatalities than those suffered by the Japanese army.

the moment at least gave signs that it was receptive to this idea. Around this time, the Legion was cut off to the west of Lake Baikal. There were rumors that they had been attacked by German and Austro-Hungarian prisoners-of-war and were now isolated. The Allied Supreme War Council, led by the United Kingdom and France, strongly urged Japan and the United States to come to the rescue of the Legion forces. The Legion also asked President Wilson for assistance and support for their independence. Wilson had a change of heart, and in July 1918, proposed that Japan and the United States each dispatch 7,000 soldiers to Vladivostok to both rescue the Legion troops and help democratic forces in Siberia to establish themselves.

At a meeting of the Advisory Council on Foreign Relations held in mid-July, Hara Takashi signaled that he approved on the grounds that a limited dispatch to Vladivostok would be the first phase of future Japan-US collaborations, but that he also remained opposed to any large-scale troop dispatch to Siberia. Makino Nobuaki also argued that Japan should limit itself to landing a small force in Vladivostok out of consideration for the United States, contradicting Prime Minister Terauchi Masatake and Foreign Minister Gotō Shinpei's calls for an all-out troop dispatch. In the end, the Advisory Council decided on August 1 to send troops to Vladivostok with the limit set at 12,000 men, though this number could be increased if need be. At a cabinet meeting the following day, with Prime Minister Terauchi having pledged that no more than two army divisions would be sent to Vladivostok and Siberia, the body decided to participate in a joint troop dispatch on the proviso that Japan consult with the United States. That same day, the government announced the dispatch at home and abroad, strongly emphasizing that it was being done "in response to a US proposal, as a way to pay back its friendship." This was not a declaration of war, but rather a declaration that troops were being dispatched to Vladivostok. The United States, along with the United Kingdom and France, now also announced that they would send troops.

The Far Eastern Republic

In April 1920, while Japan was on its Siberian Expedition, revolutionary leader Alexander Krasnoshchyokov founded a new state: the Far Eastern Republic. A native of the Russian Far East, Krasnoshchyokov conceived of the Far Eastern Republic as a type of Red Army "buffer" in the Far East; he convinced Lenin and Trotsky to create the state in part to ward off potential conflict with the Japanese army. The government operated out of Chita and gradually expanded its sphere of control from western Transbaikal into locations throughout Siberia, absorbing local regimes along the way. Although the Far Eastern Republic was under the direct influence of the Soviet government, the state avoided claiming that revolutionary identity outright; by making itself out to be a democratic nation, the Far Eastern Republic sought to deprive Japan of political justification for intervention and hoped to drum up support in the international community. The nation did act as a buffer to reduce the likelihood of a situation that might spark a military confrontation with the Japanese army prompting a large-scale, armed intervention.

Having extended its power across the entirety of Eastern Siberia, the Far Eastern Republic absorbed the last Siberian outposts of the counter-revolution and established its authority across the entire region. The government even sent a representative to the Washington Naval Conference, working to make other attendees sympathetic to the idea of having the Japanese army withdraw from Siberia as quickly as possible. But once the Japanese army had withdrawn, the Far Eastern Republic no longer served its original purpose as a buffer state, and was absorbed into the USSR in November 1922.

The Rise and Fall of the Kolchak Regime

The Japanese and US forces landed in Vladivostok in mid-August 1918. In a considerable departure from what the two countries had agreed upon, by mid-October Japan had dispatched some 73,000 troops to the three provinces of the Russian Far East—Zabaikal, Amur, and the Maritime Province—stretching from northern Manchuria to the Transbaikal. Furthermore, it appeared that Japan would keep control of the Chinese Eastern Railway for itself. Following strong objections by President Wilson to the Japanese army's actions, the Hara cabinet (formed September 1918), which prized the relationship with the United States, reduced the expeditionary force to 26,000, and also reached an agreement with the United States on an approach for multinational administration of the Chinese Eastern Railway.

That November, around the time when the cease-fire brought World War I to an end, the anti-revolutionary White Russian movement under Alexander Kolchak formed a government in Omsk. With equipment and numbers superior to the Red Army's, the Kolchak forces gained the allegiance of other anti-revolutionary forces. They forced the Red Army back to the Ural Mountains by spring 1919, and had the momentum to press on to Moscow. The United Kingdom and France gave indications they would support a Kolchak regime. Hoping for an independent regime that it could have a friendly relationship with, Japan became the first country to provisionally recognize the Kolchak government in May 1919. This might cede a favorable resolution to questions that had been pending since the Imperial Russia era: Siberian development, the transfer of the Chinese Eastern Railway, fishing rights, and other such matters. Katō Tsunetada, a member of the House of Peers and one of Prime Minister Hara's closest friends, was appointed ambassador to the Kolchak regime, and took up his post in October. Once formal diplomatic relations had been established, Japan would then open consulates in Khabarovsk, Irkutsk, and other locations in Kolchak-controlled territory.

Very shortly, however, the Red Army counterattacked, and the Kolchak government retreated eastward. In July 1919, the Kolchak regime asked for an increase in the size of the Japanese forces, but the Hara cabinet refused. Both the Army General Staff Office and Army Minister Tanaka Giichi also wanted to dispatch more troops to Siberia. The former wanted a larger force to halt the Red Army's advance at Lake Baikal, while the latter feared the front lines defending Japan's Manchurian and Mongolian interests would be trampled by the Bolshevik forces. However, again in deference to the relationship with the United States, Prime Minister Hara denied the troop requests and avoided getting too deeply involved with the Russian internal conflict.

The Red Army became further emboldened, and by mid-November they had occupied Omsk. The Kolchak regime then moved its capital to Irkutsk. Army Minister Tanaka again submitted a troop increase request in a cabinet meeting, but it was turned down. The Red Army was working with local partisans as it fought its way east, and the Hara government's policy was to avoid direct engagement. In March 1920, the Red Army entered Irkutsk, and the Kolchak regime collapsed, leaving all of the Transbaikal under Bolshevik control. Given the situation, the United Kingdom and France ended their military intervention in Siberia. Even before that point, in January, the United States had informed Japan that it was putting an end to its part of the joint dispatch. Japan was now the only country with forces stationed in Siberia.

After the collapse of the Kolchak regime, Bolshevik forces had now reached as far as the Maritime Province that had been the Japanese army's greatest concern. Partisan forces took control of Vladivostok in January, and they formed a temporary government that was heavily influenced by the Bolsheviks. A similar government was formed the next month in Khabarovsk, another of the major cities in the Maritime Province. Thus, the danger of a clash between the revolutionary forces and the Japanese army was on the rise. However, the Bolshevik government, seeking to avoid such a conflict, forbade the Red Army from advancing into the Transbaikal. That February, seeking to encourage a withdrawal of Japanese forces through negotiations rather than military means, the Bolshevik government sent a proposal for talks to its Japanese counterparts through Japan's ambassador to France, Matsui Keishirō.

The following month, the Hara cabinet settled on a new policy. Japan was to pull out of Amur and Zabaikal and reduce the size of its forces. Its troops would now be concentrated in the southern part of the Maritime Province and along the Chinese Eastern Railway in order stop the influence of the revolution from reaching Manchuria and Korea. The pretext for the troop dispatch had changed from rescuing the Czechoslovak Legion to "self-defense" against the Bolsheviks. Just as the Japanese government was laying plans to reduce the force size and restructure its deployment, however, the Nikolayevsk Incident occurred.

The Impact of the Nikolayevsk Incident

The Japanese naval landing force had taken control of the city of Nikolayevsk (Nikō) at the mouth of the Amur River without resistance in September 1918. In early 1920, partisan forces assisting the Red Army surrounded the city. With the collapse of the Kolchak regime, the Japanese army had replaced the White Russian forces as the target for attack. After some clashes, however, in late February the Japanese and partisan forces agreed to a cease-fire. After executing White Russian soldiers and collaborators, the partisans then demanded that the Japanese hand over their weapons. Repeated requests for assistance had already been made to the government in Tokyo, but no measures had been taken. Left isolated and under pressure to make a decision, the Japanese forces and civilians in the city tried to find a solution by launching a surprise attack on the partisans rather than handing over their weapons.

The Japanese army took the partisan forces by surprise before dawn on March 12. The partisans were not their only foe: Chinese gunships also bombarded the Japanese forces, and a group of Korean volunteers also fought the Japanese army. The action ended in the defeat of the Japanese side, and on the 18th they surrendered to the partisans. Most of the Japanese soldiers and the Japanese civilians who had been resisting from inside the consulate had either died in the fighting or been taken prisoner. Vice-Consul Ishida Toramatsu and his family committed suicide. By the time a Japanese relief battalion finally arrived in early June, the partisan forces had already withdrawn. City streets had been reduced to ashes, and all of the Japanese who had been taken prisoner had been executed. A total of 735 victims (384 civilians, 351 soldiers) were killed in the Nikolayevsk Incident, including 183 women.

The horrific tragedy at Nikolayevsk infuriated the Japanese public. Anger was also directed at the authorities for having left those victims isolated and helpless. Back in Japan, twelve-year-old Ishida Yoshiko, the eldest daughter of the vice-consul and the only member of the family to escape, put her grief over losing her parents and siblings into a poem titled "Kataki o utte kudasai" (Please avenge them), which was published in the *Kokumin Shimbun*, and drew tears. Ishibashi Tanzan warned that the public's desire for revenge would serve only the military and financial cliques, and would cause the nation more harm than good. However, with the plan to reduce and reconfigure Japanese forces shelved for the time being, following the Nikolayevsk Incident, the door was now open for a fresh dispatch of forces to occupy Karafuto (Sakhalin).

The Occupation of Northern Sakhalin

The Treaty for the Exchange of Sakhalin for the Kurile Islands of 1875 had resulted in all of Sakhalin becoming the territory of Imperial Russia. Then, as a consequence of the Russo-Japanese War, Japanese troops occupied the entire island. With the Treaty of Portsmouth, Japan got those parts of the island below latitude 50 degrees north. Since that time, Sakhalin had been divided between Japan to the south and Russia to the north. The Japanese navy had been seeking since before the Russian Revolution to secure drilling rights in the Russian half of the island, as it was a promising source of crude oil, which the navy required to fuel its ships (it had stopped using coal as fuel in 1906). In May 1919, the cabinet had decided that it would seek to acquire oil exploitation rights in Sakhalin in exchange for recognizing the Kolchak regime.

In July 1920, the Hara cabinet issued a declaration that Japan would undertake a "protective occupation" of the island until a legitimate Russian government had been established in northern Karafuto and the Nikolayevsk Incident had been resolved, making the Nikolayevsk Incident a pretext for occupying northern Sakhalin. The Japanese army occupied the north in a flash and placed it under military rule. Because the "protective occupation" was meant to be a temporary measure, the government refrained from encouraging either full-scale investment or immigration to the region. Nevertheless, with private capital investing aggressively in the development of the area's coal mines and oil fields, immigration also increased. Hokushinkai, a consortium of Japanese companies, was granted preferential development rights by the expeditionary force, while the extraction of mineral resources was supervised by the navy. The Sinclair Oil and Refining Corporation (a US company), along with British companies, also sought to get involved with oil-field development, but the expeditionary force blocked their efforts. This closing of the "open door" contributed to the deterioration of Japan-US relations.

While Japanese forces were occupying northern Sakhalin, the Hara cabinet decided to pull troops out of the Zabaikal area in accordance with its new policy of March 1920. This decision was taken in the face of strong opposition by the forces on the ground in Vladivostok and the Army General Staff Office, who felt it was abandoning the anti-Bolshevik regime of Ataman Grigory Semyonov that had been established in Chita. Meanwhile, local Bolshevik forces approached Moscow about creating a buffer state in Siberia. Seeking to avoid a clash with the Japanese army, Lenin supported this idea, and so, in April 1920, the founding of the Far Eastern Republic was declared. The Far Eastern Republic's revolutionary army then asked for permission to advance on Semenov's home base of Chita, but Lenin refused, as expected. With the support of Army Minister Tanaka Giichi, Prime Minister Hara now hastened the pullout from Zabaikal. After reaching an agreement with the Far Eastern Republic in July, Japan completed the withdrawal in August. The troops occupying northern Sakhalin remained in place.

The Emergence of Gotō Shinpei

The Japanese government continued to occupy northern Sakhalin, arguing that this was a response to the Nikolayevsk Incident and unrelated to the Siberian Intervention. Until these two pending questions could be resolved together, it did not wish to establish diplomatic relations with the Bolshevik regime. It was previous foreign minister Gotō Shinpei who offered to handle the difficult task of mediating between Japan and Bolshevik Russia over these issues. Gotō—who had become mayor of Tokyo and also head of the Japan-Russia Society—had fervently pressed for the Siberian dispatch when he was foreign minister. He sought to normalize relations with the Bolshevik regime because he thought that such a partnership would replace the Anglo-Japanese Alliance, which had

Gotō Shinpei (1857–1929)

Born in the Mizusawa domain (Iwate Prefecture), Gotō Shinpei attended Sukagawa Medical School and initially worked as a hospital doctor, but he broadened his interests to encompass health administration, and joined the Home Ministry's Health and Medical Bureau in 1883. Gotō began serving in the Ad Hoc Army Quarantine Office in 1895. His performance impressed vice-minister of the Army and Ad Hoc Army Quarantine Office director Kodama Gentarō, who, upon becoming governor-general of Taiwan, named Gotō the director-general (later the civil governor) of his Civil Affairs Bureau. In 1906, Gotō became the first president of the South Manchuria Railway and worked to lay the groundwork for the railway's operations. Always aware that stable relations with Russia were tied to stable management of Manchuria, he even made a visit to Russia in 1908. The stated purpose of this trip was apparently to begin forging a transportation network joining Europe and Asia via connections between the South Manchuria Railway, the Chinese Eastern Railway, and the Trans-Siberian Railway, but that specific venture was part of Gotō's larger, singular philosophy: he wanted to expand an alliance between Japan, China, and Russia across the Eurasian continent (the Old World) to contend with the United States (the New World) in an "Old World–New World continental divide." It was Gotō who recommended that Itō Hirobumi visit Harbin in October 1909 to explore the possibilities of a Russo-Japanese partnership, but Itō's assassination shortly after his arrival brought an abrupt end to that diplomatic foray.

After Itō was assassinated, Gotō began working to enlist Prime Minister Katsura Tarō's help in forging closer ties with Russia. He ended up accompanying Katsura on a visit to Russia in 1912 and later became the minister of communications in Katsura's third cabinet. Other ministerial appointments would follow; when Motono Ichirō resigned as foreign minister in the Terauchi Masatake cabinet in April 1918, Gotō was his replacement, jumping from the Ministry of Home Affairs to the Ministry of Foreign Affairs. Gotō was also a party politician, dueling with Katō Takaaki for leadership of the Rikken Dōshikai. His term as foreign minister, albeit just five months in duration, marked the first time a party politician had filled the position. In the debate over the Siberian Expedition, Gotō favored a joint Japan-US intervention in order to prepare for an eastward push by Germany, which had made peace with Russia in World War I, and to cement a "Japanese, British, and American confederation" for greater stability in the wake of the war. That stance gradually shifted, however, as Gotō began to side with Prime Minister Terauchi and army leaders in calling for an aggressive independent expedition that would give Japan a stronger foothold in Siberia. In August 1918, Gotō led the call for Japan's expedition declaration.

After resigning as foreign minister, Gotō worked to foster goodwill between Japan and Soviet Russia as president of the Japan-Russia Society. He built a wide network of connections in the private sector, including the chairman of Nichi-Ro Gyogyō (a fishing company), Tsutsumi Seiroku. In early 1923 he resigned as mayor of Tokyo, and with the agreement of Prime Minister Katō Tomosaburō, invited Adolph Joffe, the Soviet Union's diplomatic representative to the Far East, for unofficial talks on establishing diplomatic relations. These talks did not yield any tangible results, but they were an important first step in facilitating the process when official talks took place the following year, leading to the normalization of Soviet-Japanese relations in 1925.

Late in 1927, Prime Minister Tanaka Giichi sent Gotō to Soviet Russia to meet with Joseph Stalin, People's Commissar for Foreign Affairs Georgy Chicherin, and other Soviet leaders. The visit had a dual purpose. First, Japan wanted to show the Soviets that it was willing to depart from its traditional Anglo-American diplomacy in favor of stronger ties with both Soviet Russia and China. Second, Japan also wanted to reach an understanding with the Soviets on the China issue. At the core of that diplomatic outlook was the idea of forming a tripartite alliance among Japan, China, and Soviet Russia to stand in opposition to the United States, a stance that had clear roots in Gotō's concept of an "Old World–New World continental divide." Gotō constantly saw international affairs through that scope of geopolitical confrontation, from the days of Czarist Russia through to the post–World War I era of "new diplomacy" and ideological diplomacy. His diplomatic vision stood in stark contrast to the "Kasumigaseki diplomacy" under the Washington System, which favored cooperation with the United Kingdom and the United States.

been abrogated in 1922 in order to stand up to China and the US in East Asia. Furthermore, Gotō wanted to prevent any direct collaboration between China and Russia, seeing a three-way partnership between Japan, China, and Russia as the way to stand up to the United Kingdom and the United States. This approach had its roots in the grand conception of the world that saw the Old (the Eurasian continent) and the New (the Americas) facing off against one another, but it was becoming clear that geopolitical considerations had taken precedence over ideology.

5-14. Gotō and Joffe

Gotō began talks with his Soviet counterpart Adolph Joffe in January 1923, but as they were unable to agree on the timing of a troop withdrawal from northern Sakhalin, on a resolution to the Nikolayevsk Incident, or on the amount to be paid for the acquisition of northern Sakhalin, Gotō then handed over his role in the talks to Japan's minister to Poland, Kawakami Toshitsune. No progress was made, however, and the talks broke down in July. Prime Minister Katō Tomosaburō died the following month, and then on September 1, the Tokyo area was rocked by the Great Kanto Earthquake. As a result of these domestic developments, negotiations were put on hold. But—feeling pressure from the Soviet Union's growing international standing through its recognition by the United Kingdom and Italy, and the establishment of diplomatic relations with China—Matsui Keishirō, the foreign minister in the cabinet of Kiyoura Keigo, restarted talks with Soviet representative Lev Karakhan in May 1924. These, too, came to an end when the Kiyoura cabinet fell. They resumed under the auspices of "Shidehara diplomacy" the following month.

The Siberian Intervention that had begun in the summer of 1918 was in essence an interventionist war on the part of the Allied powers worried about the influence of the Russian Revolution. It had been a joint effort at first, centered on Japan and the United States, but after 1920, only Japanese forces remained in eastern Siberia. Japanese troops would not withdraw from northern Sakhalin until 1925. During those seven-odd years, some 240,000 troops were dispatched, and more than 3,300 died. If the people killed in the Nikolayevsk Incident along with other civilian and volunteer soldier deaths were added, the number of casualties exceeded 10,000. Why did the troops remain there for seven years? According to historian Asada Masafumi, one of the main reasons lay in the army's—and above all, the Army General Staff's—refusal to withdraw. All of the military commanders shared the idea that the more casualties Japan suffered, the greater the reluctance to pull the troops out would be, and that the spoils of war should be on a par with the sacrifices.

The Jiandao Expedition

The Jiandao region (now Yanbian Korean Autonomous Prefecture, Jilin Province) is a rugged, mountainous area in the southeast of China's Jilin Province in Manchuria, across the Tumen River from the Korean Peninsula. Although it lay in Chinese territory, Jiandao bordered both Korea and Russia and was home to large numbers of Koreans and Japanese. In 1919 and 1920, Jiandao also became the center for the Korean independence movement, as it turned into a haven for Korean activists who had escaped Japan's military suppression of the March First Movement or had relocated to avoid the path of the Japanese army's Siberian Expedition. As the movement gained local momentum, clashes between Japanese residents of Jiandao and anti-Japanese, pro-independence groups became frequent. Anti-Japanese groups even formed their own independent army and made forays into Korea.

October 1920, a *bazoku* ("bandit") group attacked the Japanese consulate in Hunchun (a central city in Jiandao) and burned the facility to the ground. The incident left numerous casualties in its wake, claiming the lives of more than ten Japanese residents as well as injuring or killing many people of Chinese and Korean descent. Asserting that the *bazoku*'s ranks were made up of "insubordinate Koreans" and extremists, including Russians, the Japanese government decided to respond with an aggressive display of force. The cabinet activated troops garrisoned in Korea and diverted a portion of the Siberian Expedition forces (army personnel scheduled to ship out of Vladivostok), dispatching both groups to Jiandao. Leaders also reached out to Zhang Zuolin, who had just become inspector-general of the Three Northeast Provinces, about suppressing the unrest in a joint mission. Although hesitant at first, Zhang eventually agreed to take part in the initiative. The combined forces—approximately 10,000 troops from the Kwantung Army, the Japanese Army in Korea, and the Siberian Expedition troops—undertook a punitive expedition into November. The Japanese army gunned down just under 400 "insubordinate Koreans," including civilians; the forces even attacked schools and churches. When the details of the offensive came to light by way of Canadian missionaries in the area and the US Consulate General in Mukden, Japan came under heavy international criticism.

Yamagata Aritomo suggested withdrawing Japanese troops from Vladivostok, but Prime Minister Hara Takashi opposed the proposal. To make the Jiandao Expedition a success, Japan needed to intimidate the opposition by stationing forces in the southern reaches of the Southern Maritime Province (Primorsky Krai). The Jiandao Expedition was thus one of the reasons behind the delay in Japan's Siberian pullout. At the same time, the presence of the Czechoslovak Legion—itself fighting for its own ethnic independence—was also stoking the flames of the Korean independence movement; the creation of the National Congress of Great Korea, which took shape in Vladivostok in March 1919, drew some of its inspiration from the birth of the Czechoslovakian National Assembly. In that sense, the issues of the Jiandao Expedition and the Siberian Expedition were deeply intertwined.

CHAPTER 6

The Ups and Downs of International Cooperation:
The Era of "Shidehara Diplomacy"

6-1. National representatives at the Washington Naval Conference

TIMELINE

1922 (Taishō 11)

February 1	Yamagata Aritomo dies
February 4	"Treaty for the Settlement of Outstanding Questions Relative to Shantung" signed
February 6	Treaties related to Pacific Ocean affairs, China, and naval disarmament are signed at the Washington Conference
June 12	Katō Tomosaburō cabinet formed
June 23	Katō cabinet decides to withdraw troops from Siberia by end of October
August 15	Army force reduction plan carried out (Yamanashi force reduction)
October 25	Final Japanese troops withdrawn from Vladivostok
December 30	Union of Soviet Socialist Republics (Soviet Union) formed

1923 (Taishō 12)

January 26	Sun-Joffe Manifesto issued, formalizing Republic of China's support for the Soviet Union
January 29	Adolph Joffe visits Japan, holds talks with Gotō Shinpei
June 28	Kawakami Toshitsune begins talks with Joffe
September 1	Great Kanto Earthquake and Fire occurs
September 2	Second Yamamoto cabinet formed
December 27	Toranomon Incident (Yamamoto cabinet resigns en masse)

1924 (Taishō 13)

January 7	Kiyoura Keigo cabinet formed
January 11	Seiyūkai, Kenseikai, and Kakushin Club drive to take down the Kiyoura cabinet (second movement to defend constitutional government)
January 31	Formation of First United Front in China proclaimed
February 1	United Kingdom recognizes the Soviet Union
May 15	Yoshizawa Kenkichi and Lev Karakhan begin talks in Beijing on establishing diplomatic relations between Japan and the Soviet Union (talks end January 20, 1925)
May 26	Immigration Act of 1924 signed into law by President Coolidge (in effect until June 1952)
June 11	First Katō Takaaki cabinet formed (three-party constitutional defense cabinet)
September 18	Second Zhili-Fengtian War breaks out; Zhang Zuolin seizes control of Beijing-based government

1925 (Taishō 14)

January 20	Soviet-Japanese Basic Convention signed
April 22	Public Peace Maintenance Law promulgated
May 5	General Election Law promulgated
May 15	Japanese army withdraws troops from northern Karafuto (Sakhalin)
August 2	Second Katō cabinet formed
October 26	Special Conference on Chinese Customs Tariff in Beijing (ends July 3, 1926)

1926 (Taishō 15/Shōwa 1)

January 30	First Wakatsuki Reijirō cabinet formed
April 26–May 5	Near East Trade Conference of 1926 held in Constantinople to discuss promoting trade in the Middle East and the Balkans

July 6 Chinese Nationalist Party announces its Northern Expedition

July 9 National Revolutionary Army led by Chiang Kai-shek (Jiang Jieshi) launches its Northern Expedition

September 13 South Seas Trade Conference held at House of Representatives in Hibiya

December 25 Emperor Taishō passes away; Prince Hirohito ascends to the throne; era name changed to Shōwa

1927 (Shōwa 2)

March 14 Shōwa Financial Crisis (until May 13)

March 24 National Revolutionary Army forces attack Japanese and British consulates and other interests (Nanjing Incident of 1927)

April 12 Chiang Kai-shek launches anti-Communist coup d'état in Shanghai

April 20 Tanaka Giichi cabinet formed

May 28 Japan decides on first Shandong troop dispatch

June 27–July 7 Eastern Conference (Tōhō Kaigi) held

1928 (Shōwa 3)

February 20 First election based on universal male suffrage held

April 19 Japan decides on second Shandong troop dispatch

May 3 National Revolutionary Army forces and Japanese troops engage in direct combat (Jinan Incident)

May 8 Japan decides on third Shandong troop dispatch

June 4 Zhang Zuolin assassinated in bombing (Huanggutun Incident)

June 9 National Revolutionary Army enters Beijing (Northern Expedition completed)

August 27 General Treaty for Renunciation of War as an Instrument of National Policy (Kellogg-Briand Pact) signed

October 1 Soviet Union declares start of first Five-Year Plan

December 29 The "Three Eastern Provinces" regime (under Zhang Xueliang) joins with Nationalist government (Northeast Flag Replacement), uniting China under one government

1929 (Shōwa 4)

June 3 Japan recognizes China's Nationalist government

July 2 Hamaguchi Osachi cabinet formed

July 19 Soviet Union and Zhang Xueliang regime engage in border conflict related to administration of Chinese Eastern Railway

October 24 Wall Street Crash in New York (start of the global financial crisis)

1930 (Shōwa 5)

January 11 Embargo on gold exports lifted (return to the gold standard)

April 22 Signing of London Naval Treaty

April 25 Seiyūkai questions London Naval Treaty as encroachment on supreme authority of the emperor

May 6 Japan-China Tariff Agreement signed, restoring China's tariff autonomy

November 14 Prime Minister Hamaguchi shot and fatally injured at Tokyo Station; dies on August 26, 1931

1 The Washington Naval Conference

The Anglo-Japanese Alliance in Flux

In March 1921, Crown Prince Hirohito (later Emperor Shōwa) visited the United Kingdom as an official guest of the British Royal Family. He would also stop in France and Italy before returning to Yokohama Harbor that September (see sidebar on page 189). There was no political intent to the crown prince's European visit, but the reciprocal visit made by the British crown prince the following year was seen as a symbol of the enduring friendship between the two countries. However, the Anglo-Japanese Alliance, which had been the backdrop for Hirohito's visit, was about to expire, having been in place for twenty years.

Since the Anglo-Japanese Alliance had been renewed for a third time in 1911, Russia—which was the object of the original pact—had lost its great-power status through revolution, and Germany, which had been seen as a threat in Russia's stead, had been defeated in World War I. As a military alliance, the formal Anglo-Japanese partnership had become a ceremonial affair. However, the Japanese government sought to maintain the alliance to avoid becoming isolated and to preserve Japan's international standing. For its part, the United Kingdom may have been increasingly concerned about conflicts of interest caused by Japan's further advances into China, but for that very reason it also did not wish to see the collapse of what was an effective channel for keeping those advances under control. The United Kingdom was also concerned about the potential threat to its colonies and its dominions in the event that the Anglo-Japanese Alliance was dissolved.

Meanwhile, one of those dominions, Canada, had started to seek greater independence in diplomacy and military affairs at the Imperial Conference held in London in June 1921, and argued vigorously against continuing the alliance. Views within the British Empire were not unified, but the greater problem lay in US opposition. For the United States, the Anglo-Japanese Alliance was simply a product of the age of the "old diplomacy." It incorporated exclusive arrangements to recognize the two countries' mutual special interests, and would put the United Kingdom in a position where it could not help but be complicit with Japan's advances into China. Toward the end of June, US

6-2. First day of the Washington Naval Conference

6-3. Japanese delegation to the Washington Naval Conference

secretary of state Charles Hughes showed a very negative attitude to the United Kingdom concerning the alliance being renewed.

The United Kingdom was driven by the need to dispel the United States' distrust. In an attempt to resolve the alliance issue, Foreign Secretary Lord Curzon proposed holding a conference between Japan, the United States, and the United Kingdom—with China also included if desired—in London as part of a conference among the Pacific nations. Support for this proposal was also voiced at the Imperial Conference, and it was conveyed to Japan and the United States in early July. Japanese ambassador to the United Kingdom Hayashi Gonsuke—mindful that the Russo-Japanese Agreement had already been lost and that Tokyo's only pillar of support in the Anglo-Japanese Alliance was under threat—encouraged his government to take part to prevent Japan from becoming isolated internationally.

US president Warren G. Harding was wary of the leadership role in such a conference shifting to the United Kingdom, so in mid-July he privately suggested to the United Kingdom, France, Italy, and Japan that an arms reduction conference already under consideration be combined with the proposed Far East and Pacific conference, with the resulting event to be held in Washington.

Reduction of Naval Forces

In 1916, with World War I raging, the United States embarked on a shipbuilding program aimed at creating the most powerful navy in the world. However, the recession that followed the conflict increased the momentum toward arms control among the great powers. The efforts to bring about arms reduction around the world, as inscribed in President Wilson's Fourteen Points, would be pursued in earnest in the 1920s. Even US senator William Borah—who had staunchly opposed his country's joining the League of Nations—advocated that the world's major naval powers hold an arms-reduction conference. The Republican Party and big business also actively supported such a move, believing that arms reduction accomplished through cooperation among the major powers, unfettered by any global institution, would be an effective method for keeping government expenditures under control.

Thus, in July 1921, the United States issued its proposal for a five-nation conference to discuss the issue of arms reduction. At the time, Japan had been pursuing a plan to build up its navy so that it could hold its own against the United Kingdom and the United States (the Eight-Eight Fleet Program).

Even as government expenditures ballooned dramatically after the war, military spending—most of which was going toward the shipbuilding program—accounted for close to half of the total budget. With growing strain on the government's finances, sustaining that effort was becoming difficult. This is why the Japanese navy was in favor of establishing a balance of military power that would make it possible to maintain peace in the Pacific among the three major naval powers of Japan, the United States, and the United Kingdom. For its part, the United Kingdom had become aware that its traditional strategy of maintaining the world's most powerful fleet belonged to a bygone era. It had no objection to arms reductions that would put UK and US naval strength on a par with one another.

The US proposal for the international conference also included discussion of issues in the Far East, including the China question. Japan's foreign policy had steadily worsened relations with both China and the United States over the course of World War I. Regardless of whether or not the Anglo-Japanese Alliance was renewed, Japan needed to come to some sort of understanding with the United States through international discussions of Far East problems. The US Department of State had grasped this trend in Japan's thinking and had decided that the time had come to use its traditional open-door policy to reach a final settlement over the various faits accomplis that Japan's forays into the Asian continent during World War I had produced, as well as over such conflicts as the Shandong problem, and redress the balance of power in the Far East.

The Positive Response of the Ministry of Foreign Affairs

In the summer of 1921, the Hara Takashi cabinet received successive proposals for an international conference from the United Kingdom and the United States. The majority was of the opinion that it should respond positively, seeing this as a good opportunity to improve relations with the United States and put relations with China on a different track. However, there were some who predicted that, when it came to Far East and Pacific problems, the United States—which was likely to play the leading role in such a conference—would not treat Japan as a "winner" (as had been the case at the Paris Peace Conference), but would rather focus on criticizing Japan's China policy during World War I.

Some within the government were worried that bilateral issues between Japan and China, such as the Shandong problem and the Twenty-One Demands, would become topics for discussion in multinational talks. They feared that Japan would find itself on the defensive, and so there was a strong inclination to avoid debate on these problems. However, the Hara cabinet welcomed establishing a new international consensus on naval arms limitation and Far East issues that would include the United States. Although it was aware that the Anglo-Japanese Alliance had become difficult to extend in its existing form, it was keen to preserve it within a three-power framework that also involved the United States.

As of the summer of 1921, the Ministry of Foreign Affairs was hoping to use the international conference as an opportunity to urge reform of "dual diplomacy" and "military diplomacy" with regard to the China strategy, while leaving those reforms to someone else. In particular, the Political Affairs Bureau's First Division—led by Komura Kin'ichi, eldest son of Jutarō—was a driving force pushing for a change in diplomatic strategy. In light of the Paris Peace Conference and the formation of the new Four-Power Consortium in 1920, the First Division aimed to move away from the past strategy, which had been based on mutual regard for each great power's sphere of influence in China, toward one that was more in tune with the New Diplomacy.

The instructions given to Japan's delegation

included pushing for the "lifting of consular jurisdiction" by encouraging the creation of judicial systems, the "removal of foreign troops stationed in China," and the "elimination of spheres of influence." The second item would call for all the powers to pull out their troops stationed in northern China, including a withdrawal of Japanese forces from Shandong. Meanwhile, the third item specifically focused on a uniform erasure of any claims to exclusivity by the powers along the Yangtze River and in Guangdong, Guangxi, and Yunnan.

These proposals were not put forth at the Washington Naval Conference, but they illustrate how the Ministry of Foreign Affairs was trying to shake up Japan's China policy. With regard to the "elimination of spheres of influence," however, the guarantees over Japan's national defense concerns and economic presence in Manchuria and Mongolia had already been covered when the new Four-Power Consortium was formed, with the assertion that they had already been retained and would not be affected by the elimination of spheres of influence. Hence, it is evident that the talk about excluding Manchurian and Mongolian interests was in keeping with Japan's already-declared stance. Plenipotentiary Shidehara Kijūrō already understood this as well.

Whatever the case, the Ministry of Foreign Affairs anticipated that the conference would have a broad and varied agenda. It made careful preparations, and put together a delegation that was equal, if not superior, to that which had attended the Paris Peace Conference. The chief plenipotentiary was Katō Tomosaburō (navy minister). The delegation also included three full plenipotentiaries: Shidehara Kijūrō (ambassador to the United States), Hanihara Masanao (vice-foreign minister), and Tokugawa Iesato (lord speaker of the House of Peers). The rest of the entourage included numerous individuals from the Ministry of Foreign Affairs who would become core figures in the ministry's work over the following decades, such as Saburi Sadao, Ishii Itarō, Saitō Hiroshi, Sawada Renzō, Matsudaira Tsuneo, Kimura Eiichi, and Shiratori Toshio. The official delegation numbered eighty-five people, and more than forty members of the press traveled with them.

Holding the Washington Conference and the Naval Treaty

Shortly after the members of the Japanese delegation arrived in Washington in early November 1921, they received the shocking news from Tokyo that Prime Minister Hara had been assassinated. Yasuya (Kōsai)—then serving as acting prime minister as well as foreign minister—asked the delegates to continue to serve as Japan's plenipotentiaries regardless of the makeup of the next cabinet. In the event, the incoming Takahashi Korekiyo cabinet kept all of the previous administration's ministers in place.

The Washington Conference began on November 12 with a speech from US president Warren Harding. Secretary of State Hughes followed with an unexpected proposal for arms reductions that surprised the assembled delegations. This proposal stated that (1) any capital ship (battleships and cruisers) under construction and some of the existing warships should be scrapped; (2) a 5:5:3 ratio should be used for tonnage of existing capital ships held by the United States, British, and Japanese navies as the measurement of relative power; (3) these ratios would be used to determine the size of each navy; and (4) there would be a ten-year moratorium on shipbuilding after any agreement went into force. Japan was being asked to scrap three capital ships (the already-launched *Mutsu*, as well as the *Tosa* and *Kaga*, which were under construction) and four battle cruisers (the under-construction *Amagi* and *Akagi*, as well as two ships for which building materials were still being sourced, the *Atago* and the *Takao*). Japan would also have to abandon any plans for building battleships and battle cruisers, as well as scrap all super dreadnoughts. However, given that it was the United States that had the largest number of battleships under construction at the time, Hughes's proposal for their total elimination was praised as being both bold and fair. The United Kingdom agreed to it forthwith.

France and Italy were to be permitted tonnages that were 30 percent of those of the United Kingdom and the United States. With its tradition as a major naval power, France was affronted by having been kept in the dark, and then being limited to the same tonnage as Italy. However, mindful of the negative effects that being isolated at this arms reduction conference would have on its standing in Europe, it reluctantly went along with the proposal.

Japan's chief plenipotentiary Katō Tomosaburō was determined to accept the Hughes proposal in principle. However, a panel of experts from the Japanese side that included naval officials argued that Japan should be allowed 70 percent of the British and US tonnages, and this brought negotiations in Washington to a deadlock. Conventional wisdom in Japan since the adoption of the Imperial Defense Policy in 1907 had been that Japan's navy needed to have at least 70 percent of the tonnage of its US counterpart in order to engage the US fleet in the Western Pacific. Individuals such as Vice Admiral Katō Hiroharu, the chief delegate from the navy, would not easily compromise. However, plenipotentiary Katō rejected the narrow technical arguments and decided to take a broader perspective and accept the proposal. In turn, plenipotentiary Katō proposed that, in return for accepting 60 percent, Japan, the United Kingdom, and the US pledge to maintain their defenses and military installations at their current levels on islands in the Pacific. This proposal was accepted. As a result, the parties concluded the Five-Power Treaty on the Limitation of Naval Armament in February 1922. Based on Article 19 of this treaty, the United States would be forbidden from fortifying its advanced bases in the Pacific at the Philippines and Guam, and so Japan would hold on to its relative dominance as a naval power in the Western Pacific.

While the figures for the total tonnage of aircraft carriers had been settled, auxiliary vessels were only limited in the tonnage of individual crafts and their armaments. Submarines were not addressed at all. In particular, the inadequacy of restrictions on auxiliary vessels wound up inviting a new shipbuilding competition in order to make up for the numerical inferiority of capital ships with auxiliary vessels.

The Abrogation of the Anglo-Japanese Alliance and the Four-Power Treaty

Japan and the United Kingdom had been considering proposals for a multinational treaty to replace the Anglo-Japanese Alliance since before the Washington Conference. On the eve of the conference, British plenipotentiary Arthur Balfour suggested a "three-power agreement" that essentially would bring the United States into the framework of the existing alliance with Japan. However, plenipotentiary Shidehara Kijūrō did not think it would be possible to get the United States to agree to the Balfour proposal, which amounted in practical terms to the continuation of a military alliance. In late November 1921, Shidehara offered his own draft proposal, which did away with any military obligations or alliance-type characteristics. Rather, in the event of an imminent threat, it called for signatories to first exchange views on what measures should be taken. It would be strictly a "consultative" treaty, and, after some revisions, the United Kingdom and the United States accepted it as a basis for negotiations. After Hughes had made further rewrites that turned it into a "harmless" general arrangement, the Four-Power Treaty on Insular Possessions and Dominions in the Pacific—now including France—was signed in February 1922.

The reason that, despite wishing to continue

with the Anglo-Japanese Alliance, both the United Kingdom and Japan decided to go instead with the harmless Four-Power Treaty, which was devoid of any military implication, lay in the disappearance of the threat that had given rise to the alliance and the United States' opposition to it. The United Kingdom finally decided to abrogate the alliance once the United States had joined the Washington Naval Treaty and ensured its commitment to the Far East.

The Four-Power Treaty ensured that the signatory powers would mutually respect one another's territorial rights over island groups in the Pacific. It committed the signatories to holding joint discussions in the event of a conflict among signatory powers, and to conferring about how to respond to aggression from third parties, and stipulated that the Anglo-Japanese Alliance would be scrapped once the agreement went into effect. For Japan, the Four-Power Treaty had value, because it kept the country from being isolated diplomatically and eased tensions with the United States. However, it was no substitute for the military alliance that had once existed between the United Kingdom and Japan. Furthermore, in actual fact, the Four-Power Treaty was never invoked.

The Nine-Power Treaty on China

Of the three major treaties signed at the Washington Conference, the only one to which China's Beijing government was a signatory was the Nine-Power Treaty. The Japanese delegation had been concerned about bringing up the US government's objections regarding Japan's interests and standing in China at the conference. At the opening of negotiations on this treaty in mid-November, Chinese plenipotentiary Alfred Sao-ke Sze (Shi Zhaoji) led by presenting the ten principles upon which his government was operating. These included getting the powers to preserve China's territorial integrity, respect its political independence, and abolish the unequal treaties. However, US plenipotentiary Elihu Root rejected China's sweeping demands, and instead presented the "four Root principles." These were, first, to respect the sovereignty, the independence, and the territorial and administrative integrity of China; second, to provide China the opportunity to establish an effective and stable government; third, to establish and maintain the principle of equal opportunity for the commerce and industry of all nations throughout China; and fourth, to refrain from taking advantage of conditions in China in order to seek "rights or privileges which would abridge the rights of subjects or citizens of friendly States," and from countenancing action inimical to the security of such states. Japan's understanding of the fourth principle was that it tacitly accepted Japan's prior calls to disallow any interference with or challenges to the Manchurian and Mongolian interests that Japan saw as indispensable to its national defense and economic survival. In fact, Japan received support for this interpretation through private channels from Root himself.

The four Root principles were approved at a general meeting in December. These provided the basic framework for an agreement, to which were added other stipulations such as bans on special rights and on the establishment of new spheres of influence. The resulting Nine-Power Treaty on China was signed in February 1922. As a document that in a sense legitimized the United States' traditional open-door policy, it also halted to a certain degree Japan's penetration of China. However, even though the treaty forbade the acquisition of new exclusive rights and interests, it posed no threat to the rights and interests that the powers had already acquired, or to Japan's own Manchurian and Mongolian interests. Signing the Nine-Power Treaty led Japan and the United States to terminate the Lansing-Ishii Agreement. Japan interpreted the new treaty as endorsing its hold on its Manchurian and Mongolian interests, so the prior agreement was no longer necessary.

Also, while the second of Root's principles called on signatories to agree to provide an opportunity for China to consolidate itself and develop, the powers did not pledge to work actively toward that aim. It was assumed that the consolidation and development of China was up to China, and the role of the powers was to support its efforts to that end.

The Restoration of Shandong Interests and the Retention of the Treaty Respecting Southern Manchuria and Eastern Mongolia

The Shandong problem had been an important unresolved issue ever since the Paris Peace Conference. Japan wanted its resolution to be a bilateral issue between it and China, rather than a topic for discussion at the Washington Conference. The United States believed that solving this problem was indispensable for stabilizing the East Asian order and entrusted this process to direct Sino-Japanese talks held in parallel with the Washington Conference. The United Kingdom and the United States attempted to mediate by sending representatives as observers.

A Japanese delegation led by plenipotentiary Hanihara Masanao participated in the talks, but progress was slow, as China expected US backing for its demand for unconditional restoration of all Shandong interests. An apprehensive Shidehara Kijūrō had been taken quite ill, but he took part in the negotiations after they were underway. Fearing that a breakdown in talks would cause American public opinion to worsen again after it had improved, he pleaded with Tokyo for concessions. The United States was also worried that any such breakdown would have a negative impact on dealing with other problems. Since the Japanese side had already

Shidehara Kijūrō (1872–1951)

Born to a wealthy farming family in Kadoma, Osaka Prefecture, Shidehara studied at Osaka Middle School, one of the leading bastions of English education in Japan, from 1883, and then attended the Third Higher School in Kyoto and the School of Law at Tokyo Imperial University. After graduating, he joined the Ministry of Foreign Affairs in 1896 as part of the fourth group of successful recruits under the examination system for diplomats and consuls. He spent six years in various posts abroad before returning to Japan and marrying Iwasaki Masako, the sister of Katō Takaaki's wife, in 1903. From 1904 to 1911, Shidehara worked at the ministry's home office, spending most of his time in the Telegraph Communications Division. During this time, he was tutored by Henry Denison, a ministry advisor, in English composition as well as diplomatic practices and negotiating tactics. In 1915, Shidehara became vice-minister under Foreign Minister Ishii Kikujirō and served under five successive foreign ministers, also holding concurrent positions along the way. After becoming ambassador to the United States in 1919, Shidehara worked on the Japan-US immigration issues in the Shidehara-Morris and other negotiations. At the same time, under the Hara Takashi administration's collaboration-oriented policy toward the United States, he pushed for a new mode of Japanese diplomacy on the global stage through his work at the Paris Peace Conference and the Washington Conference, seeking to move away from the old style of Japanese foreign relations centered on jostling with other powers to stake out spheres of influence, and embracing international cooperation as a guiding principle.

6-4. Shidehara Kijūrō

Almost immediately upon becoming foreign minister in the Katō Takaaki cabinet in June 1924, Shidehara declared in his first official address that "the age of scheming strategies and aggressive policies [had] passed." His intentions to overhaul Japan's China policy were clear. At the foundation of his stance on China were three key elements: coordinated action with the United Kingdom and the United States, a complete noninterference policy toward armed conflict in civil wars, and a focus on the economy. Shidehara decided to avoid meddling in China's affairs in hopes of facilitating the unification and stabilization of that country, a noninterference policy that was also in tune with pledged to withdraw its troops from Shandong, the focus of the talks was on how to deal with the Shangdong railway. However, China rejected both a proposal for joint Sino-Japanese management and a railway lease proposal. In the end, a compromise was agreed on in which the railway would be restored to China in exchange for a payment of 40 million yen in Chinese government bonds.

And so, after thirty-six rounds of talks, Japan and China signed a treaty that settled the outstanding questions relative to Shandong in February 1922. Shidehara would speak later of the unprecedented expressions of gratitude he received from all over the United States for having signed this treaty, and also of how he had subsequently struck up a deep friendship with China's Wang Ch'unghui, who had been involved with drafting the treaty. At the end of 1922, Japan withdrew all its forces from Shandong. The Shangdong railway was turned over to China in January 1923, bringing Japan's nine-year rule over Shandong to an end. Some Japanese industries such as cotton mills remained, mainly in Qingdao and Jinan. Shandong became one of the locations in China where Japanese economic interests were concentrated.

Though China had demanded the expungement of the Twenty-One Demands, the United States did not entirely support China's arguments. Still, while asserting that Japan would maintain the Twenty-One Demands, based on the decisions made during preparations for the Washington Naval Conference, Shidehara had voluntarily withdrawn the fifth group of demands and renounced preferential investment rights in Manchuria and Mongolia.

Thus, while China's objectives regarding the recovery of Shandong interests were largely accomplished, Japan succeeded in retaining the 1915 treaty

---

the view that national interest lay in economic gains. For Shidehara, there was little issue with China unifying under a communist regime—as long as the country maintained a degree of order, the need for trade and economic development would remain intact. Japan thus joined the United States and the United Kingdom in providing support to Chiang Kai-shek, who they thought was capable of stabilizing and unifying China, and also started pursuing diplomatic relations with the Soviet Union.

Shidehara's defining characteristic was his devotion to treaties. Looking back at the Shandong problem at the Washington Naval Conference, Shidehara mused, "If we make it possible for a treaty that a country has already signed and ratified to be nullified solely on the grounds of a country declaring it had not intended to sign it, how can we ever guarantee world peace and stability?" This devotion to treaties served to maintain the status quo, but it could also be incompatible with changing circumstances in the real world.

Shidehara would retain his position as foreign minister in the first Wakatsuki Reijirō cabinet, which formed after Prime Minister Katō died in office. He lost his cabinet position for a time when Tanaka Giichi took over as premier in April 1927, but he was back as foreign minister when Hamaguchi Osachi formed his cabinet in July 1929. The two pillars of the Hamaguchi cabinet were Finance Minister Inoue Junnosuke's focus on budgetary austerity and Shidehara's commitment to international cooperation. He started by giving top priority to working together with the United States and the United Kingdom at the London Naval Conference in early 1930, making the gathering a success for Japan. On the China front, meanwhile, Shidehara made Shigemitsu Mamoru Japan's resident envoy and negotiator, catching up with the United States and the United Kingdom in securing recognition of China's tariff autonomy. Just as Shidehara's team was about to start negotiating a revocation of extraterritoriality, however, the Ryūjōko Incident (Liutiaohu Incident)—the explosion that triggered the Manchurian Incident—occurred.

Shidehara tried to handle the Manchurian Incident response in a way that would maintain a non-expansionist policy and search for a solution through face-to-face talks with China, but he resigned with the rest of the cabinet when diverging opinions among Japan's top ministers prompted the folding of the Wakatsuki administration in December 1931.

respecting its interests in southern Manchuria and eastern Mongolia that was based on the Twenty-One Demands. For Japan, the 1915 treaty provided the basis for extending the freedoms of Japanese (and colonial Korean subjects) to do business and move about that had heretofore been limited to lands attached to the South Manchuria Railway and the Kwantung Leased Territory to encompass all of South Manchuria. This would not have been possible had the 1915 treaty been expunged.

2 The Washington System and Shidehara Diplomacy

The Vagaries of the "Washington System"

In Japan, scholars describe the international order created in the Asia-Pacific region by the various treaties concluded under the auspices of the Washington Naval Conference as the "Washington System." Essentially, that system was created through the joint actions of Japan, the United Kingdom, and the United States. The economic strength of the United States had enabled it to raise its profile in the Asia-Pacific through World War I, and it took the initiative in this new context. In particular, the Washington Naval Treaty was historic for being an international agreement to reduce armaments. It was the product of an effort at international cooperation that generated mutual concessions and compromises between Japan, the United Kingdom, and the United States.

On the other hand, there is a compelling argument that the United Kingdom, which viewed the Washington treaties as the products of traditional diplomatic dealings, had no sense at all of being constrained by a system of international cooperation. Even so, there is no denying that a collaborative approach that might be termed the "Washington System" existed. Secretary of State Hughes had greater regard for the cooperative spirit and mutual trust created among the signatory nations than he did for the actual treaties that were signed at the Washington Conference. He would go on to emphasize the "spirit" of the Washington Naval Conference, a view that was shared by the leaders of the countries involved.

The question was whether any joint efforts by the United Kingdom, the United States, and Japan could be maintained in a China that remained politically unstable. The Nine-Power Treaty certainly made no promises of any joint action to stabilize and unify China. The assumption was that China would be making its own efforts, and the powers would then determine how to support it. For Japan, whose objective was to retain its interests in Manchuria and Mongolia, the most important diplomatic issue was how to cooperate with the United Kingdom and the United States while addressing the issue of China as a whole.

However, as the mid-1920s drew near, two issues threatened Japan's focus on working with the United Kingdom and the United States. One was the emergence of "revolution diplomacy" in China, impelled by a fierce movement seeking to recover national sovereignty. The other was the threat posed by the Soviet Union, which was trying to surmount the chaos of the Russian Revolution to rebuild the country's economy while also pushing forward into the Far East. Japanese diplomacy had not anticipated these new developments, and it was rocked by them, as was the Washington System itself, which centered on Japan, the United Kingdom, and the United States. The Washington System had excluded China and the Soviet Union from the very start.

Chaos in China: The Beijing Government and the Growth of the Kuomintang

The Republic of China arose out of the Chinese Revolution (Xinhai Revolution) of 1911. The leader of the Beiyang Group, Yuan Shikai, became president and ruled from Beijing, having crushed the parliamentary government and built up his authoritarian rule. In opposition was Sun Wen (Sun Yat-sen) at the head of the Chinese Revolutionary Party (later the Kuomintang Nationalist Party of China), who established a separate government based in Guangdong. For all intents and purposes, China was fractured into northern and southern halves.

Following Yuan's sudden death in 1916, leadership of the northern government in Beijing was assumed by Duan Qirui of the Anhui Clique, who was favored by Japan in the framework of its "pro-Duan policy." However, the unifying power that Duan had acquired by seizing the reins of government was diminished as a consequence of the May Fourth Movement of 1919, leading to the rise of Wu Peifu (of the Zhili Clique) in Beijing, and the ruler of Manchuria, Zhang Zuolin (of the Fengtian Clique). The two rival cliques joined forces in 1920 to drive Duan from Beijing in what became known as the Zhili-Anhui War, and established a joint Zhili-Fengtian government. However, the rivalry between Wu and Zhang for political control in Beijing grew fierce, and the two cliques twice engaged in a bruising struggle for power.

In the first Zhili-Fengtian War of 1922, Zhang was forced to retreat back to Manchuria. However, Zhang still sought to make inroads in Beijing, and in September 1924 launched the Second Zhili-Fengtian War. Zhang met with serious difficulties, but he was saved the following month by a coup d'état carried out by Feng Yuxiang, a general within the Zhili Clique, and Wu retreated. The Kwantung Army was generally understood to have been pulling the strings behind Feng's coup by helping to finance its operations.

Meanwhile, in southern China, new political forces were rising. The Kuomintang Nationalist Party led by Sun, which was seeking to unify China, had the support of both the Chinese Communist Party (CCP) and the Soviet Union, and it was building up strength. In January 1924, the First National Congress of the Nationalist Party was held in Guangzhou. There, they hammered out the "three great policies" of alliance with the Soviet Union, alliance with the First United Front (of the Nationalist Party with the CCP), and—generally—support for peasants and workers. Thus, based on the alliance it formed with the CCP, the Nationalist Party won the support of laborers and peasants, which enabled it to launch its Northern Expedition (later termed the National Revolution). The primary objectives of the expedition were to overthrow the clique-based regime in the north while also doing away with the unequal treaties that dated back to the Qing era. In short, it sought to recover the sovereignty that China had lost.

Even with a civil war underway, the southern government and its Beijing counterpart shared the foreign-policy goal of recovering national sovereignty. In 1923, that desire took the form of a request from the Beijing government for the restoration of Lushun and Dalian by Japan. The twenty-five-year leases that (now-defunct) Imperial Russia had for Lushun and Dalian had expired, and the territories were to be returned to China. The Beijing government notified its Japanese counterpart that it would not accept Japan taking over those leases, nor the ninety-nine-year extension requested in the Twenty-One Demands, and that all territories should be returned at once. Beijing's demand came as a tremendous shock to the Japanese government, and the request was rejected.

The Soviet Union's Inroads into East Asia

In two manifestos issued in 1919 and 1920 by its deputy commissioner for foreign affairs, Lev

Karakhan, the Soviet Union declared that it would abrogate Russia's unequal treaties with China and rescind its special privileges there. The Soviets also called for the establishment of diplomatic relations. Soviet representative Adolph Joffe followed up by meeting with Sun Wen in Shanghai, and in January 1923 the pair signed the Sun-Joffe Manifesto. Observing that the most urgent problems facing China at the moment were the "unification of the republic and the completion of national independence," the Soviet Union expressed its "empathy" and offered assistance, making its support for China—specifically the Nationalist Party—clear. The following month, Joffe went to Japan where he held unofficial talks with Gotō Shinpei on the matter of establishing diplomatic relations between Japan and the Soviet Union. The invitation for those talks had been extended by Gotō, who was concerned about the rapprochement between China and the Soviet Union (see sidebar on page 197).

In May 1924, the Soviet Union and the Beijing government signed an agreement that established diplomatic relations. However, the Fengtian regime of Zhang Zuolin would not accept this, and signed its own treaty with the Soviet Union in October, despite the objections of the Beijing government. The Fengtian-Soviet treaty called for joint administration of the Chinese Eastern Railway, which was controlled by Zhang's regime. It also stated that Chinese (Fengtian) authorities would be responsible for the legal affairs and administration of lands attached to the railway. The Duan regime in Beijing went on to ratify the agreement in 1925, making it official. However, in practical terms the Soviet Union had seized control of the Chinese Eastern Railway, and the Zhang regime and the Soviets remained at loggerheads over the matter.

In response to Moscow's efforts to make inroads into East Asia, Shidehara reached out to the Soviet Union to establish diplomatic relations. On the other hand, the Japanese army sensed a potential threat, and leaned toward strengthening ties with Zhang while also looking for an opportunity to move into North Manchuria.

Cultural Programs for China

In an effort to bridge a widening divide on culture and education between Japan and China, the Japanese government launched a series of "cultural programs for China" in the 1920s. One of the originators of the initiative was Hayashi Gonsuke, then Japan's minister in China. In March 1918, Hayashi issued a proposal that recommended using the reparations from the Boxer Rebellion to help repair the damage that the Twenty-One Demands had done to Sino-Japanese relations. The idea was to use "vocational and general education, as well as health-related projects" instead of funding loans and economic development with an eye to securing Japanese rights in China. The suggestion coincided with numerous Diet proposals on education for Chinese students in Japan, which eventually led to the passing of the China Cultural Project Special Account Act of 1923. The following February, Wang Jung-pao, China's minister in Japan, and Debuchi Katsuji, director-general of the Asia Bureau, signed an agreement (the Wang-Debuchi Agreement) to forge a bilateral basis for the initiatives. Within the new framework, a general committee comprising members from both China and Japan took the lead in overseeing operations, while the Asia Bureau's Cultural Programs Department (which broke off from the Asia Bureau to operate independently in 1927) was in charge of actually implementing the projects. The overall initiative also got a new name: "Oriental Cultural Programs."

6-5. Tung Wen College, Shanghai

Conceived as joint non-political enterprises that would remain impervious to shifts in the Chinese and Japanese political landscapes, the Oriental Cultural Programs covered a wide range of efforts that included providing exchange

The Beginning of Shidehara Diplomacy

In June 1924, Shidehara Kijūrō became foreign minister in the first cabinet of Katō Takaaki—the first foreign minister in Japan to have been a diplomat who had passed the examination for foreign service and consular officers. The Katō cabinet was a coalition government centered around the two main political parties of the day, the Kenseikai and the Seiyūkai (known as the "three-party constitutional defense cabinet"). Hence, "Shidehara Diplomacy" was launched based on a foundation of true party politics. Prime Minister Katō also vigorously supported Shidehara's approach to diplomacy. Helping Shidehara's efforts in such capacities as vice foreign minister, bureau chief, and assistant bureau chief were individuals like Debuchi Katsuji, Saburi Sadao, Kimura Eiichi, and Komura Kin'ichi. They had all worked with Shidehara during his participation in the Washington Naval Conference as Japan's ambassador to the United States.

Shidehara laid out his diplomatic stance in a foreign-policy address delivered to the forty-ninth extraordinary session of the Imperial Diet in July 1924. Written by Shidehara himself, the speech argued that the provisions outlined in the various Washington treaties were congruent with the Japanese government's stance. "The government's position is consistently based on the spirit of these treaties," he declared. Shidehara's predecessor in the post, Matsui Keishirō, had also spoken of how Japan "fully respected the spirit" of the Washington Naval Conference. However, Shidehara had worked hard to bring the Washington treaties into force, and was uncommonly determined to see them defended. That said, the focus of attention when it came to this speech was his comments on problems with the United States. This was a matter of timing, for the US Congress had passed the Immigration Act of 1924 (which was known by some in Japan as the Japanese Exclusion Act) and Shidehara's speech was delivered that May, on the day it came into effect.

Shidehara's speech included remarks that were critical of the United States with reference to the

students with financial aid, offering grants to related organizations, establishing the Peking Humanities Research Institute and the Shanghai Natural Sciences Research Institute, and opening Academies of Oriental Culture in Tokyo and Kyoto. However, as Japan-China relations soured in the late 1920s, some began accusing the programs of being a form of "cultural invasion." The Chinese movement to reclaim the country's educational rights also zeroed in on the programs as examples of Japanese control. China quickly distanced itself from the operations; the Chinese contingent on the Oriental Cultural Program Committee withdrew from the organization after the Jinan Incident, and the Chinese government officially abrogated the Wang-Debuchi Agreement in 1929.

Foreign Minister Shidehara Kijūrō aimed to restart the programs as efforts "completely independent of politics" in 1930, but was unable to obtain the cooperation of the Chinese side. Going ahead unilaterally would taint the initiative. The original idea of contributing to forging a closer Japan-China friendship through joint cultural programs had become distorted, but the Academies of Oriental Culture were conceived unilaterally by Japan as research institutions that would "inspire research into Oriental cultures." In the late 1930s, after the outbreak of the Second Sino-Japanese War, the Japanese government established the Asia Development Board, which assumed control of the cultural programs from the Ministry of Foreign Affairs. From that period onward, the cultural programs transformed into an outfit for cultural maneuvering under Japan's occupying regimes in north and central China.

The cultural programs for China started out as a trailblazing effort to leverage Japan's soft power in the "new diplomacy" environment of the 1920s, but they ultimately failed to meet their original purpose.

legislation, but he also spoke of his determination to work toward preserving lasting friendly relations between Japan and the United States. However, domestic public opinion was strongly opposed to the Act; on the day of the speech someone even stole the flag from the US Embassy in Tokyo. Shidehara promptly issued an apology to the US government. The perpetrator was arrested the next day and the flag was returned undamaged. The quick Japanese response showed the US government it could rule out any involvement by its Japanese counterpart. Thereafter, even as he doggedly argued against the anti-Japanese sentiment in the United States, Shidehara still sought to downplay the issue, treating it as something that would only "stir up nationalistic feelings in both countries to no purpose."

The Ravages of War in North China and the Nonintervention Policy

China was the biggest outstanding issue throughout the years of Shidehara's service as foreign minister. Shidehara's goal was to establish a harmonious relationship with a stable and unified China. He held firm to a position of "nonintervention in the internal affairs of other countries" with respect to China that was grounded in preserving the Washington System.

The cabinet made the decision to adopt a

The Japan-US Immigration Crisis

The Shidehara-Morris Talks

World War I brought a lull in the anti-Japanese fervor in California, but the sentiment reignited after the war as Japanese-American relations grew increasingly chilly. A Japanese-exclusion league took shape in September 1919 and worked with local anti-Japanese groups around the state to rally bipartisan support for prohibiting Japanese immigrants from leasing land and ban the practice of "picture brides" (a matchmaking process by which women would come to the United States to wed locally based Japanese individuals after a mere exchange of photographs), calling to nullify the gentlemen's agreement between Japan and the United States. Even as the Japanese government took measures to stop picture brides from traveling to the United States in 1920, the anti-Japanese groups had begun narrowing their focus to reshaping the existing land laws. In the fall of 1919, groups launched a campaign to propose an initiative measure (subject to a direct vote by state residents) on the land issue. By August 1920, over 84,000 people had signed the petition—far exceeding the minimum requirement—and the matter was up for popular vote.

State residents cast their ballots on the initiative in November 1920, approving the Second California Alien Land Law of 1920 by an overwhelming margin: roughly 670,000 to 220,000, or more than three to one. While the US government issued a statement on the eve of the vote opposing the process of enacting a law via an initiative, the movement had gained unstoppable momentum—there was little the federal government could do. The law left Japanese immigrants with no rights to own land (which the 1913 Alien Land Law had already revoked) or lease land (as a result of the 1920 law)—and it also banned guardians of American-born children of Japanese immigrants (who were US citizens, by definition) from owning land.

During this time, the Morris-Shidehara negotiations took place in a bid to find a solution to the immigration problem. Both the Japanese and American governments recognized that it would be difficult to stop the enactment of the Second California Alien Land Law as they continued negotiations, meeting on twenty-three separate occasions before finally coming to an agreement at the end of January 1921. Under the agreement, the Japanese government was to keep its voluntary emigration-restraint policy in place and extend the scope of its travel ban through revisions to the gentlemen's agreement. In exchange, the US government promised to guarantee equal treatment for Japanese citizens in the United States via a separate treaty between the two countries. For the Japanese government, it was a rational, practical solution to the issue. Foreign Minister Uchida Yasuya (Kōsai) praised Shidehara for his efforts, saying that "resolving the issue and eradicating the roots of similar future evils would be a favorable outcome for both nations."

However, the administration of US president Warren G. Harding never acted on the new treaty proposal. Secretary of State Charles Evan Hughes, who was devoting most of his time to preparations for the Washington Naval Conference, nonintervention policy in the Second Zhili-Fengtian War, which broke out in September 1924, and left the policy to Debuchi Katsuji, the head of the Asia Bureau at the Ministry of Foreign Affairs, to communicate the policy at home and abroad. Both the Fengtian and Zhili cliques had been making vigorous approaches to Japan in order to create advantageous positions for themselves, but Japan remained impartial. When the Zhang Zuolin–led Fengtian Clique was losing ground to the Zhili Clique, the Japanese government considered dispatching forces, but then Feng Yuxiang launched a coup d'état that reversed the situation, and the Japanese government narrowly escaped getting involved in a civil war. Shidehara would later recollect that, at that moment, he had been prepared to resign his post in order to maintain Japan's policy of nonintervention.

After the Feng Yuxiang coup d'état, Duan withdrew to Tianjin. Zhang, with support from Feng, tried three times to restore his regime in Beijing, but the political situation remained unstable.

Zhang expanded his influence from Northern China into Central China, but this created frictions with the other military cliques, so he pulled back. Furthermore, in November 1925, Guo Songling—a general under Zhang's command who had been a force within the Fengtian Clique, and had even

was expecting that the issue would be resolved within the cooperative framework of the Washington System. The Second California Alien Land Law of 1920 started to spread, with states like Washington, Arizona, and Texas all enacting similar land laws. Although Japanese residents waged court battles in hopes of turning the tide, the US Supreme Court ruled against a Japanese naturalization lawsuit, and most of the legal action in relation to land laws was unsuccessful.

The Hanihara Note

Prior to the passage of the Second California Alien Land Law of 1920, a gentlemen's agreement between Japan and the United States had been in place to keep the numbers of Japanese migrants down through voluntary limitations by the Japanese government. The annual net increase in immigrant counts from 1909 to 1923 came to an average of just under 600, a relatively low rate of growth. From 1921, the year after the California Alien Land Law came into effect, the numbers went into a net decrease. Discourse on the topic went quiet in both nations.

However, an immigration bill that came up for deliberation in the House of Representatives in December 1923 changed the issue. The proposed legislation essentially sought to make the existing temporary immigration quotas—originally enacted on a temporary basis to stem the tides of immigrants coming from Europe—permanent. Under the provisions of the legislation, the government would set the total annual quota to 150,000 immigrants and cap the immigration total for any one nationality to 2 percent of the number of individuals from that country currently residing in the United States. Had that been applied to Japan, the maximum number of Japanese immigrants would have been around 185 per year. However, the new immigration bill would also ban the entry of aliens ineligible for US citizenship—which meant that the quota system would not apply to Japanese citizens. A US Supreme Court ruling in 1922 had found that Japanese citizens could not be naturalized, so they were ineligible for US citizenship.

The new immigration bill passed the House of Representatives by a sizable margin and made its way to the Senate. In a Senate environment that devoted considerable attention to diplomatic matters, the legislation encountered opposition from lawmakers who saw the bill as potentially detrimental to foreign relations. Recognizing that legislative roadblock, diplomatic leaders on both the Japanese and the American sides were optimistic that the Senate would vote the proposal down. The Senate deliberations did not go as expected, however. One of the vocal proponents of the bill was Senator Hiram Johnson, who led a chorus of voices arguing that the gentlemen's agreement gave the Japanese government authority over Japanese emigration to the United States, which he felt violated the Senate's "moral authority" and therefore constituted an attack on American sovereignty. The relationship between the gentlemen's agreement and congressional authority had been an issue for some time, but this ambiguity had been left unchallenged in consideration of relations with Japan. Now it had resurfaced.

The Japan-US Immigration Crisis

Another issue was a note that Japanese ambassador to the United States Hanihara Masanao had given to US secretary of state Charles Evan Hughes in April 1924. At the end of the note was a passage mentioning "the grave consequences which the enactment of the measure [the immigration bill] . . . would inevitably bring upon the otherwise happy and mutually advantageous relations between our two countries." Upon learning of the note's content, Senate Committee on Foreign Relations chairman Henry Cabot Lodge denounced the "grave consequences" as a veiled threat by the Japanese government. That triggered an avalanche of support for the new immigration legislation, with numerous once-ambivalent senators throwing their weight behind the measure. The bill thus passed the Senate in mid-April 1924 with an enormous majority. After a handful of minor revisions, President Calvin Coolidge signed the bill into law in late May. Despite expressing reservations about the legislation, Coolidge did not exercise his veto power.

The text of the Hanihara Note actually came about after several consultations between Japanese and American officials, who worked together to formulate a statement to clarify the purport and application of the gentlemen's agreement due to rampant misinformation on its contents circulating in Congress. The note included the following passage:

> . . . It is not the intention of the Japanese government to question the sovereign right of any country to regulate immigration to its own territories. . . . The Japanese government showed from the very beginning of this problem their perfect willingness to co-operate with the United States government to effectively prevent . . . the entrance into the United States of such Japanese nationals as are not desired by the United States. . . . To Japan, the question is not one of expediency, but of principle. . . . The important question is whether Japan as a nation is or is not entitled to the proper respect and consideration of other nations [and] . . . the self-respect of another, which, after all, forms the basis of amicable international intercourse throughout the civilized world.

The message that the Japanese and American officials had crafted, however sincere, failed to resonate with lawmakers. What led to Lodge's about-face? At the time, the Republican Party was embroiled in an oil-field scandal (the Teapot Dome scandal), and with a presidential election coming up in November, the Republican leadership used the new immigration bill as a way to rally the ranks. That focus on party unity, however, clouded Republicans' long-range perspective on foreign relations.

Japan and Canada also had a gentlemen's agreement (the Lemieux Agreement) that stipulated voluntary limits on emigration from Japan. Unlike the United States, Canada chose to temporize its immigration problems, and avoided enacting anti-Japanese legislation by revising the existing gentlemen's agreement.

been a teacher of Zhang's son Xueliang—rebelled, leaving Zhang in a perilous position. Out of concern that Guo's influence would reach into Manchuria, all of Japan's local outposts—the consulates, the offices of the South Manchuria Railway, and the Kwantung Army—were united in their view that Japan should attempt to maintain the status quo in Manchuria by providing aid to Zhang Zuolin. The Ministry of Foreign Affairs and the army leadership were doing their best to address matters through the nonintervention policy. However, as Guo's forces gained the upper hand, the cabinet decided in mid-November to dispatch troops. With that, a force of some 3,500 men combining units in Japan and already in place on the Korean Peninsula was sent to Fengtian (Mukden). Shidehara informed Fengtian Consul General Yoshida Shigeru that the purpose of the dispatch was to be a determinedly "supplementary force" only, and that there was no change whatsoever in "Japan's absolute stance of nonintervention and strict neutrality."

In the end, Zhang Zuolin's forces were able to suppress Guo's insurrection with the intervention and assistance of the Japanese army. Japan thus escaped any incursion by Guo into Manchuria.

The Shockwaves of the Immigration Act of 1924

The Immigration Act of 1924 would lodge itself in the Japanese memory not as a diplomatic matter but rather as an undeniable racial discrimination issue, a virtually unbridgeable chasm between the United States and Japan. Emperor Shōwa noted in his *Dokuhakuroku* (Emperor's monologue) after the Pacific War that racial discrimination was one of the underlying factors behind the outbreak of war between Japan and the United States in 1941; there was a link between the Immigration Act and Japan's involvement in World War II. "Discrimination between yellow and white continued as before, as in California's prohibition against immigration, and this was more than enough to cause resentment among the Japanese people," the emperor said. "With such popular resentment in the background, it was no easy task to bring the military to heel once it came to the fore."

Fourteen Tokyo-based newspapers published a joint article shortly after the passage of the Immigration Act, saying that the enactment of the legislation was an outrage that "not only runs contrary to the spirit of humanity and represents a serious injustice but also . . . constitutes a reckless act that completely ignores the long-standing friendship between Japan and the United States." Anti-American protests and boycotts of American products sprang up nationwide. In the eyes of the Japanese people, the Immigration Act was an unjust, inhumane affront.

On the day that the Immigration Act of 1924 went into effect (July 1, 1924), the *Kokumin Shimbun* (People's newspaper) president Tokutomi Sohō wrote, "Today is the day that we sever relations with the United States and join hands with our Asian brethren." Faced with this rejection of Japanese immigration, the Japanese confronted an identity crisis, and there followed a shift in national consciousness away from "the West" toward looking to "Japan as part of Asia."

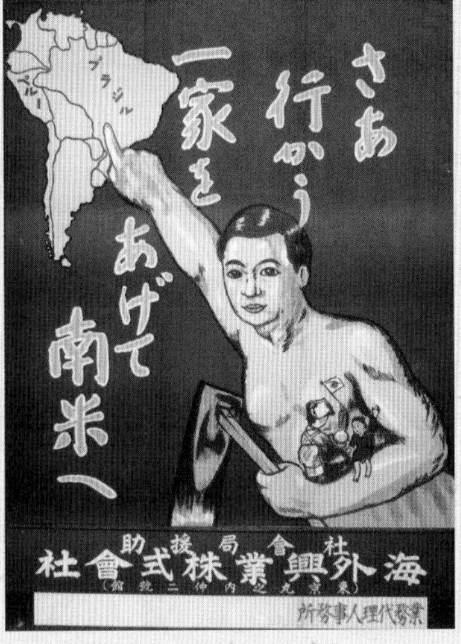

6-6. Poster promoting emigration from Japan to South America

Japanese-Owned Cotton Mills in China and the May Thirtieth Movement

In China proper, following the formation of the First United Front in January 1924, mass movements opposing the military clique governments and seeking the abolition of the unequal treaties were gathering force. The labor movement was also intensifying. At the start of 1925, massive strikes broke out at Japanese-owned cotton mills in Shanghai and Qingdao. Japanese cotton-spinning companies had made enormous profits during World War I. With the lifting of import duties on Chinese cotton fabrics in 1919, companies such as Tōyō Bōseki, Kanebuchi Bōseki, and Dai-Nippon Bōseki entered the market through direct investments in Shanghai and Qingdao. The scale of the investments in these Japanese cotton mills amounted to nearly 30 percent of all direct business investments in China proper, excluding Manchuria, surpassing all other domestic private investment in China by a significant margin. In terms of Japanese investments in China, only the South Manchuria Railway accounted for a larger share.

The Japanese companies applied Japanese techniques and management practices to their Chinese cotton mills, but the Chinese laborers earned lower wages than their counterparts in Japan. Furthermore, the fact that these companies partnered with Japan's great trading houses—which had plentiful capital resources and powerful sales networks—also put them in a superior position over Chinese private investors. Chinese-run mills were placed in a difficult business position. One after another they went bankrupt or halted operations, which resulted in worker unemployment and wage reductions. Amid these circumstances, mill strikes began at the Naigaimen (Naigai Textile) facility in Shanghai in February 1925. When a Japanese foreman shot and killed a worker at the mill, Chinese workers at all of the Japanese cotton mills united and initiated a massive strike.

At about the same time, a municipal council operated by the British in the International Settlement arrested a large number of students in connection with demonstrations over a proposed law that discriminated against Chinese merchants and workers. This led to riots calling for the students' release, and British Shanghai Municipal Police fired on the demonstrators, leaving several dead and injured. This was the "May Thirtieth Massacre" (Nanjing Road Incident) that sparked the May Thirtieth Movement and led to unparalleled anti-British and anti-Japanese demonstrations and actions across China. The Communist Party lost no time in calling for a national struggle against imperialism. It brought representatives from unions together to form a Shanghai General Labor Union that would be at the center of the strikes there. The party also brought together various merchants' associations and student federations to form a federation of workers', merchants', and students' organizations to pursue the anti-imperialist struggle in an organized fashion.

Responding to the situation, the Beijing government, which saw the unequal treaties as the fundamental cause of these incidents, lodged a protest with the Japanese, American, British, Italian, and Dutch envoys that made up the diplomatic corps in China, seeking revision of the treaties. In response, Shidehara pursued a policy that prioritized "trilateral cooperation between Japan, the United Kingdom, and the United States" to resolve the incident by punishing the police involved in the shooting and providing aid to victims. As to the revision of the unequal treaties, his position was that they were not directly related to the immediate incident, and the matter did not require review. Negotiations pursued by the diplomatic corps made little headway at first, but eventually, in August 1925, Shanghai Consul General Yada Shichitarō worked out a compromise with the Beijing government that was welcomed by all the countries involved except the United Kingdom, and the situation was brought under control. The issue of unequal treaty revision would be brought up again by the Beijing government at the Special Conference on Chinese Customs Tariff in Beijing.

The Special Conference in Beijing

In October 1925, the representatives of thirteen countries (including Japan, China, the United Kingdom, the United States, and France) gathered in Beijing to hold what became known as the Special Conference on the Chinese Customs Tariff. This was based on the treaty on customs tariffs that had already been agreed to at the Washington Naval Conference, but had been delayed because France had been late in ratifying it. Japan's plenipotentiaries officially were Ambassador Hioki Eki and Minister to China Yoshizawa Kenkichi, but it was Saburi Sadao (then chief of the Trade Bureau at the Ministry of Foreign Affairs), dispatched to Beijing by Shidehara himself, who actually oversaw Japan's delegation.

The conference had two main objectives. The first was to raise China's import tariffs, which heretofore had been held at the relatively low rate of 5 percent. This was to increase fiscal revenues for the Beijing government (which was still under Duan Qirui at the time). Given that most of the tariff revenues went toward repaying foreign loans, an increase for all practical purposes was implemented after the Washington Conference based on a revision to the tariff schedules. The understanding at the tariff conference was that the rates would go up by another 2.5 percent (5 percent for luxury items).

The second goal was to get the Beijing government to promise to abolish the so-called *likin*. The *likin*, a form of domestic transit tax that each of the local military cliques imposed, was an obstacle to the distribution of goods. It may have been profitable to the various military cliques, but it was simply a hindrance to the central government's efforts to secure revenues. It was expected that the Tariff Conference would strengthen the financial base for the Beijing government while weakening the regional rule of the military cliques. In short, it was expected to help to unify China.

Meanwhile, in light of a growing nationalist movement aimed at recovering sovereign rights, the Beijing government embarked on a diplomatic drive to revise China's unequal treaties with the Western powers. China had already met with some success, such as revising its treaty with Germany through separate negotiations, but it was the tariff conference to be held in Beijing that would provide a platform for accomplishing the same through diplomatic efforts with other nations. For that reason, the Beijing government made restoration of China's tariff autonomy a priority at the event.

In their opening remarks to the conference, the Japanese delegation surprised the other participants by taking the initiative in declaring their readiness to support China's desire to regain tariff autonomy. The proposal for this pro-China declaration originated with Saburi Sadao. The Japanese government had feared the potential ill effects on trade with China should the latter increase its tariffs, but it also hoped to reach a separate deal with China on a favorable tariff. Accordingly, it supported its delegation's stance. Having seized the initiative, the delegation then pressed the other participants to follow suit, with the result that in November 1925, an agreement was reached on the principle of restoring tariff autonomy to China. In exchange, China declared that it would end the *likin* as of January 1929.

However, the negotiations that followed were difficult. Japan's desire for a 2.5 percent provisional tax rate to last until tariff autonomy was formally restored conflicted with the Chinese desire for a higher rate. The participating governments also did not agree on matters such as how the extra revenue from surtaxes would be spent. In the end, the parties involved arrived at a general agreement to set a graded tax rate thanks to ardent American efforts at mediation. However, owing to the coup d'état of April 1926 that brought down the Duan regime, the conference was postponed indefinitely and the agreement was not formalized.

There is also a point of view that the adjournment marked the beginning of the end of efforts to deal with the various issues associated with China under both the Washington System and the trilateral cooperative framework between Japan, the United Kingdom, and the United States. The argument is that, unlike the United Kingdom and the United States, Japan saw preserving its interests in the Chinese market as vital to its national well-being, and sacrificed the trilateral relationship to that end. However, it should also be remembered that Shidehara and Saburi managed to get the other participating nations to agree in principle on the restoration of tariff autonomy to China, and they put forth strenuous efforts toward making the conference a success; for example, they convinced the United Kingdom to remain involved despite its wishes to end the proceedings early.

The Northern Expedition and the Nanjing Incident of 1927

In the mid-1920s, Zhang Zuolin was in ascendancy in Manchuria; Duan Qirui and Feng Yuxiang were holding sway in northern China; and Sun Wen's revolutionary government was ruling the south.

6-7. The signing of the Soviet-Japanese Basic Convention

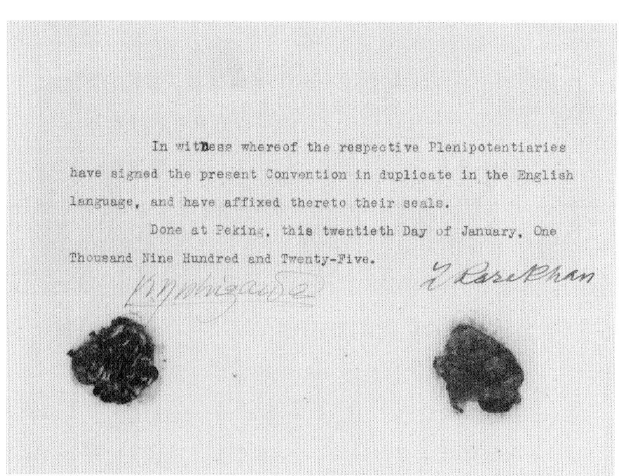

In witness whereof the respective Plenipotentiaries have signed the present Convention in duplicate in the English language, and have affixed thereto their seals.

Done at Peking, this twentieth Day of January, One Thousand Nine Hundred and Twenty-Five.

6-8. Document signed by Yoshizawa and Karakhan

Furthermore, though it was still in its infancy, the Chinese Communist Party (CCP) was also on the scene. Such was the power structure when Sun Wen died in 1925. He was succeeded by Chiang Kai-shek (Jiang Jieshi). Seeking to unify China under the Nationalist government, in July 1926 Chiang set out from Guangdong at the head of the National Revolutionary Army to embark on the so-called Northern Expedition.

The National Revolutionary Army swiftly swept across South and Middle China, and before long was pressing on toward Shanghai and Nanjing. The Northern Expedition was also a national revolutionary movement that assumed an anti-imperialist and anti-military stance. The increase in tensions between Japan and China after World War I originated in the Northern Expedition. The Nationalist government's policies were inclined toward a hard-line effort to recover China's sovereign rights; it termed them "revolutionary diplomacy." In January 1927, it reclaimed the British concessions at Hankou and Jiujiang by force. The United Kingdom sent a request to the Japanese government for a troop dispatch, but Shidehara Kijūrō turned it down, citing Japan's policy of nonintervention in the internal affairs of other countries.

That March, with the National Revolutionary Army having occupied Nanjing, both the British and Japanese consulates, as well as foreigners in the city, were attacked in what is known as the Nanjing Incident. This 1927 incident was the first time that Japan, rather than the United Kingdom, was targeted. British and US warships bombarded the city in response. However, Foreign Minister Shidehara argued that Japan should abide by the nonintervention policy and leave the reprisals and sanctions to the other two countries. Domestically, Shidehara's response was labeled "weak-kneed diplomacy," and he was criticized fiercely by both Japanese residing in China and opposition parties at home.

For local Japanese residents sympathetic to the National Revolutionary Army, the Nanjing Incident was a betrayal of the perception that this army was fair and adhered to strict military discipline. Mass acts of violence against resident foreigners continued after the incident. Many Japanese living in Suzhou, Hangzhou, Jiujiang, Yichang, Chongqing, Chengdu, and elsewhere abandoned their homes in China and returned to Japan.

Foreign Minister Shidehara regarded Chiang Kai-shek as the "moderating force" within the Northern Expedition, and tried to defend Japan's interests by working together with him. Shidehara believed the Nanjing Incident was a plot undertaken by extremist anti-Chiang elements, and clamped down on the attempts at finger-pointing. Then, the financial panic of April 1927 caused the Wakatsuki Reijirō cabinet to collapse, and Shidehara stepped down with the rest of the administration.

Immediately after this, Chiang staged an anti-Communist coup d'état in Shanghai and founded a Nationalist government of his own in Nanjing, in opposition to the pro-communist Wuhan Nationalist government. In September 1927, the Wuhan Nationalist government led by Wang Jingwei reconciled with the Nanjing government and joined forces. Thus, the First United Front that had been created in 1924 was dissolved in 1927, and the rivalry between the Nationalists and the Communists would go on for another decade.

Concluding the Soviet-Japanese Basic Convention: The Persistence of Envoy Yoshizawa

Ever since the dawn of Shidehara diplomacy, the Japanese government had pursued negotiations with the Soviet Union out of a desire to normalize relations. As discussed earlier, negotiations had stalled over numerous thorny issues, including the withdrawal of Japanese troops from northern Karafuto (Sakhalin), the rights to exploit oil resources and fisheries in the northern Pacific, and resolution of the Nikolayevsk Incident (see pages 195–96). When he became foreign minister, Shidehara Kijūrō designated Yoshizawa Kenkichi, Japan's minister to China who had also been working on negotiations with Russia, to continue discussions with the Soviet representative Lev Karakhan. Finally, after sixty-one rounds of official talks, in January 1925, the two signed the Soviet-Japanese Basic Convention.

One of the most important items on the negotiating table was recognizing that the Treaty of Portsmouth remained in force. Having managed to integrate the Far Eastern Republic, the Soviets declared that they would abrogate pacts that had been signed by Imperial Russia, and Japan was concerned that the Treaty of Portsmouth was one such agreement. Above all, the Russian-Japanese Fisheries Convention of 1907 that laid the foundation for exploiting the northern Pacific fisheries was itself based on the Treaty of Portsmouth, and Japan attached a great deal of importance to its continuation. Happily, in Article II of the Basic Convention, the Soviet Union agreed that this treaty would remain in force. The two parties also agreed that Japan would withdraw its troops from northern Sakhalin within a specific timeframe.

The Japanese navy had been anxious about acquiring the right to develop oil fields in northern Sakhalin so as to secure a fuel supply for its ships; this, too, was covered in the Basic Convention, with the Soviet Union granting discovery and exploitation rights in exchange for the Japanese troop withdrawal.

What remained a problem to the end was the question of whether or not Article V (on banning propaganda activities in one another's countries) applied to the activities of the Communist International (Comintern) organization. Yoshizawa regarded the activities of the Comintern as behavior that threatened the order and public peace of the partner country (i.e., Japan), but Karakhan strenuously objected to this. Finally, Karakhan's argument that the Comintern had a separate existence from that of the Soviet government was accepted. However, the Japanese government, in its application of the Basic Convention, stuck to its interpretation that the Comintern's activities came under Article V. This issue was one of the reasons why the Japanese government enacted the Public Peace Maintenance Law at the same time as it entered into the Basic Convention.

One of the reasons Shidehara believed normalizing relations with the Soviet Union was necessary was that the latter's international standing was gaining a more solid footing, and Japan had economic interests at stake. Establishing diplomatic relations with the Soviet Union was significant as an attempt to usher the Soviets—who had finally begun stable administration of their nation—into the Washington System not as a "critic" but as an "accepter," and to broaden the foundation for international policy cooperation.

The expansion of trade between the two countries and resource development in northern Sakhalin signaled that Shidehara's economy-focused view of the national interest was now being applied to the post-revolutionary Soviet Union as well. He appointed Tanaka Tokichi, who had served in the Bureau of Trade at the Ministry of Foreign Affairs, to be Japan's first ambassador to the Soviet Union, and continued to pursue these views.

The Globalization of Trading Blocs

At the core of the economic diplomacy pursued by Shidehara was the effort to expand trading outlets. The years of the first period of Shidehara diplomacy were marked by the global post–World War I slump and the Japanese economy hitting bottom with the Great Kanto Earthquake of 1923. Japan had slipped into a massive foreign trade deficit, and needed to boost trade by developing new markets.

Accordingly, Shidehara enlisted the help of previous chiefs of the Trade Bureau at the Ministry of Foreign Affairs, starting with his trusted friend Saburi Sadao, as well as Saitō Ryōe and Taketomi Toshihiko, to implement organizational improvements such as expanding the Trade Bureau and establishing a new system for commerce secretaries. At the same time, aiming to diversify, he also made efforts to expand trade with regions that previously had not received much attention. Having pinpointed eastern Africa and various parts of the Middle East such as Egypt, Turkey, and Asia Minor, Shidehara arranged for a Near East Trade Conference to be held from April to early May 1926 in the Turkish capital Constantinople (now Istanbul). Among the matters settled at the conference were the opening of direct shipping routes to boost trade, the expansion of diplomatic missions, the dispatch of commerce attachés, and the holding of trade fairs. One concrete result was that the shipping company Nippon Yūsen opened a shipping route to the Near East. In parallel with these moves, the Ministry of Foreign Affairs also held its first trade conference (the South Seas Trade Conference) to promote trade around the South Seas Pacific and India, in September 1926.

During this first period of Shidehara diplomacy, Japan signed new commercial treaties or revised existing ones with more than a dozen countries, including Belgium, Peru, Spain, Czechoslovakia, Egypt, Lithuania, Romania, Ethiopia, and French Indochina. These efforts to increase Japan's economic strength within a diversified commerce and trade network, thereby expanding national power, represented a new undertaking for Japanese diplomacy.

3 The Tanaka Cabinet and the Separation of Manchuria and Mongolia

The Eastern Conference (Tōhō Kaigi) and the Jinan Incident

In April 1927, Seiyūkai party president Tanaka Giichi formed a new cabinet. Serving also as foreign minister, Tanaka, along with the United Kingdom and the United States, acknowledged the positions of both the Nationalist government and the Three Eastern Provinces regime (now under

Zhang Zuolin) in China, while at the same time attempting to resolve the Manchuria problem and push for development there. However, while the Seiyūkai gave Tanaka the backing he needed for his diplomatic efforts, the party's foundations were unstable. This forced him to adopt an excessively hard-line stance to satisfy public opinion. In a complete reversal of the policy of nonintervention in the internal affairs of other countries pursued by Shidehara, Tanaka embarked on a policy of protecting Japanese living overseas, and dispatched troops to the Shandong Peninsula that June.

However, the Tanaka cabinet had been wary of a dispatch of troops from the start. Accordingly, rather than sending any forces directly from Japan, they instead handled the matter by using troops stationed in Manchuria. The forces in question were stationed in Qingdao for a month, but this led to more domestic criticism of Tanaka's diplomacy, and they were eventually sent on to Jinan. At this point, with their flank under threat from the Wuhan forces, the National Revolutionary Army retreated, leading the Japanese forces to pull back also, avoiding a direct encounter between the two

The "Tanaka Memorial" and International Propaganda

The "Tanaka Memorial" was an anonymous document allegedly presented to Emperor Shōwa by Prime Minister Tanaka Giichi shortly after the Eastern Conference in July 1927. Of all the passages in the lengthy document, one has drawn significant attention over the years.

> ... In order to conquer China, we must first conquer Manchuria and Mongolia. In order to conquer the world, we must first conquer China. . . . This is the plan left to us by Emperor Meiji, the success of which is essential to our national existence.

From early on, this memorandum to the throne was believed to be a fake in Japan, and no scholar today considers it authentic. In China, however, the theory that the document is a fake has not been totally rejected. The logic that in order to conquer Asia, Japan would need to conquer China, which would require conquering Manchuria, is consistent with the prevailing historical view in China emphasizing that Japan's invasion of China was a planned, consistent maneuver. For that reason, the Tanaka Memorial came to be used as a tool of international propaganda and intelligence activity, and it had considerable influence.

It is highly likely that the document was forged around 1929 (during the time of the Zhang Xueliang administration) in the northeast part of China, where it made frequent appearances in local anti-Japanese newspapers and magazines. The local Japanese legation was aware of the information going around, too, and submitted a protest note to the Nationalist government's diplomatic branch. Officials at the branch also recognized the document was a fake. The Manchurian Incident, however, led to the document circulating throughout China and the United States, where it became a vehicle for anti-Japanese propaganda. At a meeting of the League of Nations, for example, Chinese representative Wellington Koo quoted a passage from the memorial—without addressing its authenticity—arguing that the document laid out Japan's pursuit of hegemony over North China and East Asia, and showed how its control over northeast China was "merely the first step to world conquest." It was the Manchurian Incident that prevented the Tanaka Memorial from sinking into obscurity as one of the countless anti-Japanese tracts making the rounds at the time.

The Tanaka Memorial even came up at the Tokyo Trials following World War II, where the prosecution intended to use the document in arguing its case, but as its authenticity could not be established, the document was not submitted as evidence of a conspiracy. Still, the Tanaka Memorial circulated in America and the Soviet Union during the Cold War, and made numerous appearances in the *People's Daily*, the official newspaper of the Chinese Communist Party.

The world of international politics does not operate solely on the basis of accurate information and actual facts. The worldwide diffusion of the Tanaka Memorial is a perfect illustration of how often international politics is swayed by misunderstanding and prejudice fueled by propaganda campaigns and information warfare, even when these are rooted in a forgery.

armies (First Shandong Expedition).

Around the same time as the Shandong Expedition in late June, the Japanese government under Tanaka held a Eastern Conference (Tōhō Kaigi) that brought together senior officials from the Ministry of Foreign Affairs and the army posted in China, along with other senior government officials. The "China policy platform" briefing issued by Tanaka at the end of the conference called for a separation of the main part of China from Manchuria and Mongolia, with a neutral stance toward China but a separate policy toward Manchuria and Mongolia based on special interests that were considered vital to national security and the people's survival. This separation policy was not intended to turn the two regions into separate territories or grant them independence. Rather, while recognizing that Manchuria and Mongolia were under Chinese authority, Japan would insist that China's leaders honor what Japan considered its vital interests. The fact was that it was inconceivable for the Nationalist government, which set store by "revolutionary diplomacy," to honor Japan's vital interests in Manchuria.

In August 1927, having stepped down from public office to encourage the Wuhan and Nanjing

Tanaka Giichi (1864–1929)

A native of Hagi, a community in the Chōshū domain, Tanaka Giichi worked his way to Tokyo in 1882 and entered the Rikugun Kyōdōdan (an academy for training noncommissioned officers), going on to the Army Academy and Army War College, and later fighting in various battles around Manchuria during the First Sino-Japanese War. In 1896, after the conclusion of the war, Tanaka became a member of the Intelligence Department in the Army General Staff Office and spent time on an official assignment in Russia. On returning to Japan, he was appointed to serve as the Russia Section chief in the Military Operations Department of the Army General Staff Office, where he led planning for Japan's Russia strategy. During the Russo-Japanese War, Tanaka departed for the front in Manchuria to serve on the staff for the new Manchuria Army Headquarters. Known as the "darling boy of the Chōshū group," he went on to amass a solid military record in the postwar years. He developed the plan to create two additional army divisions in 1911, climbed the hierarchical ladder to become vice-chief of staff in 1915, and coordinated plans for the type of aggressive actions like the Siberian Expedition that the army was hoping for. In 1918, after being appointed army minister in the Hara Takashi cabinet on the recommendation of fellow Chōshū native and elder statesman Yamagata Aritomo, he adopted an entirely new tack. He backed Hara's policy of cooperating with the United States and led initiatives to withdraw troops from the Shandong Peninsula and Siberia. Health issues prompted Tanaka to resign as army minister in 1921, but he would maintain a powerful voice within military circles by stepping into the leadership void created by Yamagata's death in 1922. After retiring from the army in 1925, Tanaka joined the opposition Seiyūkai party as president.

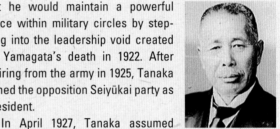

6-9. Tanaka Giichi

In April 1927, Tanaka assumed the office of prime minister—and concurrently the office of foreign minister—as the leader of the ruling Seiyūkai. In contrast to the approach of Shidehara diplomacy, which had been called "weak-kneed" for its focus on international cooperation and noninterference in internal affairs, Tanaka embraced a more aggressive form of diplomacy, such as pressing ahead with the Shandong Expedition to help protect Japanese residents in China. At the core of Tanaka's China policy, however, was a clear distinction between the Manchuria-Mongolia area (the Three Northeast Provinces) and the main part of China. In political terms, that meant supporting different leaders in the two areas: leaving control of Manchuria in the hands of Zhang Zuolin while permitting Chiang Kai-shek to govern the main part of China from a moderate position. The stance was not necessarily a move away from a commitment to cooperating with the United Kingdom and the United States, however. In Manchuria, Tanaka was aiming to use Zhang Zuolin to maintain order so that foreign capital could come flowing in—and thereby keep Japan's economic interests growing through bigger investments in railroad construction and other forms of economic development. In fact, Tanaka was nationalist governments to merge, Chiang Kai-shek went to Japan, where he met with Tanaka. The prime minister warned Chiang against impetuously renewing the Northern Expedition, and encouraged him to strengthen his position south of the Yangtze River for the time being. Tanaka was seeking to stabilize Sino-Japanese relations, just as Shidehara had, by working and partnering with Chiang. While signaling Japan's approval of a China unified under Chiang, Tanaka was also seeking to restore the "Three Eastern Provinces" (Manchuria) to Zhang Zuolin to achieve stability there as a local regime.

However, heedless of Tanaka's warning, in April 1928 Chiang—who was now once again at the head of the Revolutionary Army under the now-unified Nationalist government (the Wuhan and Nanjing factions having united in September 1927)—resumed the Northern Expedition. This time, Tanaka abruptly dispatched Japanese forces stationed in Japan to Shandong under the pretext of protecting local Japanese residents. The move was a demonstration of strength by the Seiyūkai, which had effectively been defeated in the general election that February. The 5,000-strong Sixth Division that was sent as the second Shandong troop dispatch

so focused on implementing a sound railroad policy that he asked Yamamoto Jōtarō (a Seiyūkai leader who had been appointed president of the South Manchuria Railway) in May 1928 to secure an agreement with Zhang Zuolin for the construction of five rail lines in the Manchuria-Mongolia region. As shown in his hesitancy about the First Shandong Expedition, Tanaka was by no means a vocal proponent of military action in the area.

However, Tanaka's lack of a sturdy support base in the Seiyūkai made it hard for him to push policies through. As the "adopted leader"—a moniker that tied into his straight-to-the-top installation as party president when no Seiyūkai member agreed to take leadership of the group—Tanaka found himself not only having to bend to the hard-line currents running through the party and Japan's public discourse, but also forced to give consideration to policy-related differences with the opposing Minseitō (Constitutional Democratic Party). This climate of divergent interests and political compromise frustrated the pursuit of his vision for a moderate China policy. For example, Tanaka's decision to approve the second Shandong Expedition in 1928 was entirely rooted in putting political considerations first. This opened the way for the Jinan Incident, which took a heavy human toll on both the Chinese and Japanese armies, further inflaming anti-China sentiments among the hard-line elements of the Japanese general public and army leadership. After the Jinan Incident, Chiang Kai-shek's National Revolutionary Army bypassed Jinan, advanced on Beijing, and, by mid-May, was on the verge of routing Zhang Zuolin's forces and invading Manchuria. Tanaka wanted to send the Kwantung Army to the Shanhai Pass in hopes of disarming Chiang's and Zhang's forces and staving off a Manchurian invasion, but he was hesitant, as that move would have required an official imperial order. The Kwantung Army grew impatient and bombed Zhang Zuolin's train en route from Beijing to Mukden, killing him. The Kwantung Army had planned to put a pro-Japanese government in place in southern Manchuria, but there was not even a consensus about this. Zhang Zuolin's son, Zhang Xueliang, eventually emerged as his father's successor, but took no action. Zhang Xueliang eventually began leaning toward merging with Chiang's Nationalist government, and, by the end of 1928, Chiang's regime had unified China. Zhang Xueliang took a tough stance on Japan, effectively stalling Tanaka's Manchuria policy initiatives.

When Tanaka learned of how Zhang Zuolin's assassination had unfolded in late June 1928, he gave the emperor his word that the perpetrators would be punished. However, the ministry declined to identify those responsible for the attack and remained reluctant to impose severe punitive measures, instead choosing simply to suspend alleged mastermind Colonel Kōmoto Daisaku and hand out some relatively light administrative punishments. Tanaka presented a report on the measures to the emperor, who immediately recognized that Tanaka had failed to deliver on his promised punishments. When Tanaka tried to explain the situation, the emperor cut him off. Tanaka eventually dissolved his cabinet in July 1929, saying that he had lost the trust of the emperor, and died of chronic heart disease two months later.

would end up clashing with the National Revolutionary Army in Jinan. In retribution for losses inflicted on resident Japanese and putting its own prestige on the line, the Japanese army attacked Jinan, inflicting more than 3,500 casualties on the Chinese side (Jinan Incident). In Japan, the incident was seen as a consequence of Chinese scorn for Japan; people characterized it as a "punishment" for impudence. In short, the original objective of protecting Japanese residing in China had turned into one of punishing the Chinese army.

The Jinan Incident did not just have the effect of strengthening Chiang's distrust of Japan, but was also the first time that anti-imperialist and anti-foreign movements in China, which heretofore had seen the United Kingdom as their main enemy, had directed their hostility toward Japan instead. The negotiations aimed at settling the incident and its aftermath were difficult, but finally, in March 1929, after compromises on both sides, Japan and China signed an agreement resolving the dispute.

The Huanggutun Incident and the End of the Northern Expedition

After Duan Qirui's downfall in 1926, Zhang Zuolin and his Fengtian army in Manchuria once again advanced on Beijing. The following year, Zhang put together a military government and attempted to stave off the National Revolutionary Army then advancing to the north. Having cleared out of Jinan to continue his drive north, Chiang Kai-shek would now be confronting Zhang Zuolin.

The Tanaka government sought to maintain a stance of strict neutrality between Zhang and Chiang. However, in mid-May 1928, Japan notified both parties that, should the civil war spill over into Manchuria, it would take appropriate and effective measures to maintain public security there. This notice signaled that, in the event that either of the Chinese armies should enter Manchuria in a state of disarray, they would be disarmed. Overpowered by the National Revoluionary Army and on the brink of defeat, Zhang Zuolin paid heed to the Japanese warning, and decided to withdraw from Beijing and return to Manchuria.

The Kwantung Army then relocated its headquarters from Lushun to Fengtian, and made preparations to advance into Jinzhou in order to disarm the Chinese forces. The Kwantung Army would of course have attempted to disarm the National Revolutionary Army should it enter Manchuria. Likewise, it would have sought to do the same to Zhang Zuolin's forces, and also to remove Zhang by force. However, the primary mission of the Kwantung Army was to protect the South Manchuria Railway. Jinzhou lay a considerable distance away from the railway's lines, and so the army required imperial approval in the form of an official decree for such a move.

After receiving the Kwantung Army's report, the Army General Staff Office sought Prime Minister Tanaka's approval for the advance before going to the emperor with the request. However, Tanaka still wanted to maintain Japan's relationship with Zhang Zuolin, and in late May he made it clear that he did not approve of the advance to Jinzhou. The plan had met with Tanaka's opposition before the emperor could be asked. At the Kwantung Army's headquarters, where they had been awaiting the emperor's approval, the unit's commander Muraoka Chōtarō and his staff lost patience and decided to remedy the situation by assassinating Zhang Zuolin. At the heart of this plot was senior staff member Colonel Kōmoto Daisaku.

Colonel Kōmoto devised a scheme to bomb the special train that Zhang was riding in as he returned to Fengtian from Beijing, and he assigned Captain Tōmiya Kaneo of the Independent Garrison in Manchuria to carry out the assassination. Early on the morning of June 4, the train carrying Zhang was bombed; Zhang died shortly thereafter. Kōmoto and his collaborators had wanted to take advantage of the chaos in Manchuria that would result from

Zhang's death to prop up a regime in South Manchuria that would be more favorable to Japan. However, a unity of views within the Kwantung Army alone was not enough for the task. Zhang Zuolin's son Xueliang succeeded him, and he did not comply.

6-10. The bombing of the train carrying Zhang Zuolin

Hence, with Zuolin's assassination, Zhang Xueliang had now seized power in Manchuria. At the end of 1928, the Zhang Xueliang regime merged with the Nationalist government in Nanjing, and the Northern Expedition was brought to an end. With Zhang's announcement, known as the "Northeast Flag Replacement," China was now unified.

The Zhang Xueliang regime was a coalition of commanders from the old military cliques from his father's era as well as influential figures from each of the three provinces. To create a centralized regime, he pursued administrative and financial reforms. Unlike his father Zuolin, Zhang Xueliang refrained from making any moves into China proper. Instead, he tried to stand up to Japan by building a collaborative relationship with the Nationalist government and modernizing governance in Manchuria.

One of the steps he took was to encourage railway construction through private capital. If this plan could be achieved, it would halt the agreements made during his father's regime on the construction of five railways in Manchuria and Mongolia (these included such contracts as the one of May 1928 signed between Zhang Zuolin and South Manchuria Railway President Yamamoto Jōtarō). Under the administration of a Northeast China Transportation Committee, Zhang Xueliang sought to hasten railway construction that would circumvent the lines of the South Manchuria Railway. Japan feared that its South Manchuria Railway profits would be threatened by competition for freight. Above all, it believed the construction of a Datong line (between Dahushan and Tongliao) and a Jihai line (between Jilin and Hailong) would wipe out the South Manchuria Railway. Hence, Japan would repeatedly argue that this would infringe on the clause within the 1905 Treaty and Additional Agreement between Japan and China Relating to Manchuria forbidding the creation of railways parallel to the South Manchuria Railway.

The Radicalization of Chinese Nationalism over the Recovery of Sovereignty

Meanwhile, in the main part of China, the Nationalist government once again pursued its policy of "revolutionary diplomacy" as part of its efforts to complete the unification of the country, taking an anti-imperialist stance and declaring its intention to abrogate the country's unequal treaties. However, the influence of the Soviet Union and the Chinese Communist Party, which had been the guiding forces behind revolutionary diplomacy, had waned. The main goal now was to achieve, through bilateral negotiations, the tariff autonomy that was essential to building a self-sustaining economy. The Western powers likewise preferred to respond to China's demands for restoration of its national sovereignty through bilateral negotiations with the Nationalist government rather than through collaborative efforts as they attempted to preserve their own interests. The United Kingdom had suffered due to a boycott of British goods ever since the days of the May Thirtieth Movement. Accordingly, it opted to deal with Chinese nationalism in a more realistic fashion. In a "Christmas message" delivered in 1926, the British government made it clear that it was ready to enter negotiations on returning sovereign rights if China could create a new government on its own. In July 1928, the United States took the initiative to recognize China's tariff autonomy, and the United Kingdom followed suit that December.

4 The Second Period of Shidehara Diplomacy

Finalizing the Japan-China Tariff Agreement

In July 1929, Tanaka Giichi and his cabinet took responsibility for the assassination of Zhang Zuolin by resigning. They were replaced by a Minseitō (Constitutional Democratic Party) cabinet led by Hamaguchi Osachi, and Shidehara Kijūrō once again became foreign minister. The most pressing diplomatic issues for Shidehara to deal with were the various problems related to approving China's tariff autonomy left behind by the Tanaka cabinet. For the Hamaguchi cabinet, which had lifted its gold embargo in January 1930, but had delayed the introduction of Chinese statutory tariffs planned for the following month, it had become urgent to iron out any trade issues with China.

Shidehara prioritized the profits from exports to China by the cotton-spinning industry—Japan's largest—through international cooperation. He was unenthusiastic about any unconditional increase in tariff rates or any hasty restoration of tariff autonomy. However, the boycotts of Japanese goods throughout China by merchants and industrialists following the Jinan Incident had had a severe impact on exports to China, and those exports needed to be restored. After difficult negotiations, a settlement of the Jinan Incident had been achieved in March 1929. Aided by this, Shidehara ordered his trusted friend Saburi Sadao to serve as minister to China, where he was to pursue negotiations on the economic issues. However, Saburi met with an untimely death (possibly a suicide) in November, and China refused the appointment of Obata Yūkichi as his successor, rejecting his *agrément* (see sidebar on page 231).

Accordingly, Shidehara appointed Shanghai consul general Shigemitsu Mamoru to also serve temporarily as Japan's representative. Shigemitsu then took over negotiations with China, and from the start of 1930 began meetings with Finance Minister T. V. Soong (Soong Tse-ven). That May, Shigemitsu and Foreign Minister Wang Zhengting signed the Japan-China Tariff Agreement. This agreement made Japan the fourth country to recognize Chinese tariff autonomy, following the United States, the United Kingdom, and Germany, while leaving tax rates on Japan's primary exports to China (cotton goods, marine products, and so forth) unchanged for three years. For China, restoring its tariff autonomy through such agreements with the powers was a necessary condition for rebuilding its finances and achieving independent economic development.

Shidehara had made every effort to remain in step with United Kingdom and the United States, from the point of view of cooperating with those countries. Meanwhile, Shigemitsu's focus was on avoiding radicalizing the forces

Obata Yūkichi (1873–1947) and the Refusal of *Agrément*

The term *agrément* refers to a diplomatic practice in which a state formally agrees to receive the representative of a diplomatic mission from a foreign country. It was an *agrément* that would spark another conflict between Japan and China. In July 1929, Foreign Minister Shidehara Kijūrō appointed Obata Yūkichi to replace Saburi Sadao, who had died the previous November, as Japan's minister to China. When Shidehara notified China of the transfer of authority, the Chinese government refused the corresponding *agrément*—and the news made its way back to Japan via newspaper reports. The articles, operating on information from the Nationalist government in Nanjing, indicated that China had refused the *agrément* because Obata had been the "ringleader of Japan's invasive diplomacy toward China" in the events surrounding the Twenty-One Demands. There was no denying that Obata had been involved in the process; he had been the first secretary at the Beijing legation, and he had assisted Hioki Eki in presenting the Twenty-One Demands to Yuan Shikai (and the Beiyang government) in January 1915.

To the Japanese government, however, the situation seemed suspect, given that, following the Twenty-One Demands controversy, Obata had subsequently served as Japan's minister to China for more than five years, and had even been decorated by the Chinese government for his work. Furthermore, the fact of announcing the refusal of *agrément* via the press was an unpardonable insult. Hoping to defuse the situation, Shigemitsu Mamoru and others at Japan's Consulate General in Shanghai enlisted notable figures like renowned Japanophile Hu Hanmin to dispel the miscasting of Obata as the "ringleader" of Japan's diplomacy with China. The Nationalist government would not hear the arguments, however. Foreign Minister Wang Zhengting ultimately disavowed the information that the media had cited as grounds for the refusal, but he declined to revoke the refusal itself.

6-11. Obata Yūkichi

Unable to serve in China, Obata instead became Japan's ambassador to Germany in 1930 and retired from the diplomatic corps in 1933. Hayashi Senjūrō offered him a cabinet position as foreign minister in February 1937, but Obata turned him down, recommending ambassador to France Satō Naotake instead.

within China, providing broad concessions to the moderate "realists" there, and helping them to cement their leadership.

The Sino-Soviet Conflict (1929) and the Kellogg-Briand Pact

Regardless of the fact that the Fengtian regime under Zhang Zuolin and the Soviet Union had signed a treaty in 1924, a conflict persisted over who would administer the Chinese Eastern Railway. In July 1929, after the conclusion of the Northern Expedition, the Nationalist government set out to recover authority over the railway. This developed into an armed clash with the Soviets. The Red Army overwhelmed Zhang's forces with its military strength, and at the end of the year the Nationalist government signed a cease-fire agreement that restored the status quo ante.

Prompted by the threat of an all-out clash, Zhang complained of infractions to the signatories of the newly enacted Kellogg-Briand Pact (General Treaty for Renunciation of War as an Instrument of National Policy), and he attempted to get other powers to mediate. However, even though the powers reproached the Soviet Union, they also saw Zhang's unilateral takeover of the Chinese Eastern Railway as inappropriate, and sidestepped any proactive intervention. Foreign Minister Shidehara held separate talks with representatives of both countries in Japan. He attempted to arrange direct talks between China and the Soviet Union, but the Soviet Union rejected the overture.

Meanwhile, US secretary of state Henry Stimson

The Implications of the Treaty for Renunciation of War (Kellogg-Briand Pact)

After the First World War, France was looking to sign a security treaty with the United States for protection against the threat of Germany—a longstanding source of French anxiety. Although the United States was providing economic support to Europe in the discussions surrounding German reparations, it was moving toward a more isolationist stance at home. Against that backdrop, US secretary of state Frank Kellogg extended a different proposal to French foreign minister Aristide Briand: instead of a French-American security treaty, the idea was for a treaty that would make war of any kind an illegal act. France was not satisfied with this, but the French government was apprehensive about having to withdraw its army from the Rhineland German border in two years' time, and felt the need to keep the United States involved, one way or another. The General Treaty for Renunciation of War as an Instrument of National Policy (Kellogg-Briand Pact) was signed in Paris in August 1928 by fifteen nations. It met the needs of France, which sought to ensure its national security, and the United States, which wanted to keep itself out of European power politics. Ultimately, the impetus was more a desire to secure the interests of the United States and France than a shared belief in a righteous anti-war ideal.

Article 1 stipulated that the signatories were to "solemnly declare in the names of their respective peoples that they . . . renounce [war] as an instrument of national policy." The treaty was an extension of the League of Nations' 1924 Geneva Protocol, and marked the first time in history that war had been declared illegal in the interest of total renunciation. Until that point, waging war had been a legitimate state right, and even the Covenant of the League of Nations had placed only partial prohibitions on warfare. However, the Treaty for Renunciation of War only applied to renouncing war "as an instrument of national policy"—it did not apply to self-defensive war. Article 9 of the Japanese Constitution is said to have its origins in the Treaty for Renunciation of War.

The Tanaka Giichi cabinet made Japan one of the original signatories to the treaty, with Privy Councillor (and former foreign minister) Uchida Yasuya signing the document on Japan's behalf. Japan had initially sought to retain its right to act at its own discretion in China, but Uchida's consultations with other powers showed them to be unfavorable to the idea so that, in the end, he only went as far as confirming that defensive war was not forbidden when accepting the conditions.

Back in Japan, criticism surfaced that Article 1 condemning war "in the name of the people" contradicted the constitutional principle of imperial sovereignty. The objections emanated from what constituted the national identity. With the opposition Minseitō seizing the debate as an opportunity to attack the majority, the Treaty for Renunciation of War became a point of intense political contention in the fall of 1928. The Tanaka administration eventually laid the furor to rest in late June 1929 by issuing an official government declaration that the phrasing of the treaty, "viewed in the light of the provisions of the Imperial Constitution," was "understood to be inapplicable in so far as Japan is concerned." Uchida promptly resigned his position as a privy councillor, angered that the government would attach an official declaration to a treaty that he himself had already signed. The effectiveness of the Treaty for Renunciation of War would be rapidly put into question when the Sino-Soviet conflict between the Zhang Xueliang administration and the USSR erupted in the fall of 1929.

called on Japan, the United Kingdom, and France to find a solution through a joint commission. In December 1929, the United States, along with the United Kingdom and France, issued a joint statement on the matter. The statement criticized the Soviet Union's use of force as an infraction of the Kellogg-Briand Pact, while calling for the suspension of hostilities in light of their readiness to mediate. The Soviet Union responded that its use of military force was justified in the name of self-defense. It rejected any intervention by third countries, but it was also amenable to a directly negotiated cease-fire. Shidehara did not respond to Stimson's call, judging it necessary to accept the Soviet position in order to create some sort of balance of power in Manchuria that would preserve Japan's interests in Manchuria and Mongolia.

The London Naval Conference of 1930

At the Washington Naval Conference, Japan, the United Kingdom, and the United States had agreed on tonnage-based restrictions on the numbers of capital ships each could have, as well as a ten-year moratorium on the construction of such vessels. Afterward, however, each country began pouring its energies into building auxiliary vessels. Accordingly, in 1927, in response to a proposal from US president Calvin Coolidge, the powers held a conference in Geneva to discuss tonnage limits for auxiliary vessels as well. Neither France nor Italy participated in the Geneva Naval Conference; Japan's plenipotentiaries were Ishii Kikujirō and former navy minister Saitō Makoto. Japan argued that its auxiliary vessels should be limited to 70 percent of the US tonnage allowance, but as the United States and the United Kingdom could not reach an agreement despite mediation, the conference ended in failure.

In 1929, Coolidge's successor, Herbert Hoover, called for arms reductions based on the Kellogg-Briand Pact that had been signed the previous year. In the United Kingdom, too, the Labour Party cabinet of Ramsay MacDonald was pushing for arms reduction. Following three months of preliminary talks between the United Kingdom and the United States, the London Naval Conference was called into session in January 1930. The Japanese delegation was led by former prime minister Wakatsuki Reijirō; his plenipotentiaries included Navy Minister Takarabe Takeshi and ambassador to the United Kingdom Matsudaira Tsuneo.

The Hamaguchi cabinet decided in November 1929 that Japan's demands in principle would be for total tonnage of auxiliary vessels and number of battle cruisers to be 70 percent of those of the United States. They reasoned that, while this would not be sufficient to carry out an offense, it would be enough to defend Japan. However, they stepped aside from making a public statement about these ratios. After talks with the US delegation in London, the two sides came up with a compromise draft agreement. Under it, Japan would be allowed to have 62 percent of the number of battle cruisers that the United States had, while the tonnage of cruisers, destroyers, and submarines could be 69.7 percent of the US

6-12. The London Naval Conference

Abandoning the "Shina" Name for China

In June 1913, the Japanese cabinet had arrived at a decision to refer to China as "Shina" in all uses except for treaties and sovereign letters. The nomenclature did not sit well with China, which claimed that "Shina" had derogatory overtones, and thus frequently demanded that Japan refer to the country as the "Republic of China" (Chūka Minkoku). When Japan used "Shina" in the text of a tariff agreement with China in May 1930, for example, Nationalist government Document Bureau director-general Yang Xiji objected, saying, "Should Japan continue to use this rude phrasing, we shall return the disgrace in kind by rejecting any document containing said nomenclature and issuing a strong reprimand accordingly." In light of the fiery sentiments running through both the private and public sectors in China, the Hamaguchi Osachi cabinet resolved that October to make "Republic of China" (Chūka Minkoku) its standard designation for the country.

limit. Wakatsuki then asked the government for its approval to accept the agreement. The Navy General Staff opposed the draft from a military perspective, on the grounds that it would threaten national security, but Prime Minister Hamaguchi took a broader view and decided to accept it. On April 1, the cabinet sent a telegraph to the delegation that agreed to this draft as the basis for a treaty. As a result, the London Naval Treaty came into force in late April.

However, in the subsequent process of ratifying the treaty, the issue of encroachment on the supreme command of the emperor arose. At a special session of the Imperial Diet in April, representatives of the Seiyūkai opposition party launched a criticism of the government. They argued that, on the basis of Article 12 of the Meiji Constitution, for the government to have decided on the force size while disregarding the objections of the Navy General Staff—a supreme command institution—was an infringement on the emperor's own rights of supreme command. The Navy General Staff now also stopped arguing about force-size insufficiency and began talking about imperial authority. Retired navy admiral Tōgō Heihachirō also sounded off, and nationalist groups responded as well. This created an uproar. Above all, in the course of vetting at the Privy Council prior to ratification, Councillor Itō Miyoji directed harsh questioning toward the government's leadership. However, neither Prime Minister Hamaguchi nor

Takahashi Korekiyo (1854–1936) and Inoue Junnosuke (1869–1932)

Ups and Downs

Born in Edo, Takahashi Korekiyo was adopted by Sendai domain foot soldier Takahashi Koretada. After studying English, he traveled to the United States in 1867, when he was just fourteen, and having unwittingly signed a document he could not read, was sold as a slave. He eventually made his way home to Japan and started learning under Mori Arinori. He went on to hold a variety of jobs, including working at the Ministry of Education and Finance, serving as an interpreter and translator, teaching at English schools, and even working as a stockbroker. Even as he led a dissipated life, there were indications of his talent for financial administration. At the age of twenty-four, he gave a speech rebutting Baba Tatsui's wildly popular free-trade argument, saying that protective trade was the only means by which a yet-underdeveloped nation could develop its industry and promote exports. That was the genesis of Takahashi's basic approach to finance: prioritizing the protection and cultivation of domestic industry, rather than pursuing the free trade that suited the United States, the United Kingdom, and other first-world countries.

At the age of twenty-eight, Takahashi took a position handling trademark registration and patent issues at the Ministry of Agriculture and Commerce. During his time there, he was approached about investing in the development of a Peruvian silver mine. He resigned from his post in 1889 and headed to Lima only to find the mines abandoned and himself bankrupt. Having lost everything, Takahashi decided to start afresh as an "apprentice boy,"

Foreign Minister Shidehara made any concession, and they refuted the arguments directly. As a result, the Privy Council eased its stance, and the treaty was ratified in October 1930.

Hamaguchi had made the following argument: "On the matter of the force size of the Imperial Navy, the government has given careful consideration to the professional opinion of the General Staff. That having been done, the government reached this decision. Based on the decisions that the government has already made, the responsibility for this is one to be taken by the government. With respect to this decision, scholarly arguments about the Constitution such as issues about a matter being in accordance with this or that article should each be subject to study. We do not have the free time for such research." It was statement befitting the prime minister of a party cabinet that had the backing of an absolute majority in the House of Representatives.

On November 14, Hamaguchi was shot and seriously wounded by a youth who was dissatisfied

---

taking a position at the Bank of Japan where he quickly made his mark. In 1895, he was made manager of the main branch of the Yokohama Specie Bank. Two years later, the second Matsukata Masayoshi cabinet adopted the gold standard. Takahashi supported Matsukata (who was both prime minister and finance minister at the time) and recommended devaluation on the implementation of the gold standard system.

The Russo-Japanese War created a pressing need for war funding, and the government decided to entrust Takahashi—then deputy governor at the Bank of Japan—with floating foreign bonds. Japan had not yet cultivated much in the way of international trust at that point, and had misgivings about floating bonds in the United States and Europe. Help arrived in the form of Jacob Schiff, head of Kuhn, Loeb & Co., an American investment bank, who successfully acted as agent in the British and American markets. Working together with American rail baron E. H. Harriman, the German-born Schiff—who had made a name for himself on a predilection for bold investments—laid his bets on Japan's future. In later years, Takahashi called Kuhn, Loeb & Co. "Japan's benefactor," and remained friends with Schiff and his family. Takahashi also worked to nurture international financiers, sending promising young staffers from the Bank of Japan and the Ministry of Finance to London and New York. The list of Takahashi's protégés includes such illustrious names as Inoue Junnosuke, Tatsumi Kōnojō, Mizumachi Kesaroku, Fukai Eigo, Mori Kengo, and Tsushima Juichi.

Stabilizing China

Takahashi became finance minister in 1913, at the age of sixty, in the first Yamamoto Gonnohyōe administration on the recommendation of Matsukata, but the cabinet resigned in just over forty days, preventing Takahashi from demonstrating his fiscal prowess. He would return to the position in September 1918 under Prime Minister Hara Takashi, whom he worked with to discontinue the Nishihara loans and bring Japan's interventionist policy to an end. From that point forward, Takahashi focused on stabilizing China and enabling peaceful, orderly economic expansion into the country. In a May 1921 position paper that marked the start of his vision, Takahashi posited that if an "East Asian Economic Power" could be created, combining Japan's capital and industrial might with China's resources and labor, there would be no reason to fear the advance of American and British capital into East Asia. To pave the way for this, Takahashi argued that Japan would have to abandon its "meddlesome" stance and withdraw its military presence from China—a position on China that echoed Hara's.

6-13. Takahashi Korekiyo

6-14. Inoue Junnosuke

After Hara's assassination in November 1921, Takahashi was appointed prime minister while retaining his position as finance minister. His "expansionist fiscal policy" met criticism from Hamaguchi Osachi and other members of the Kenseikai who pursued deflationary theory rooted in a high-interest strategy, but Takahashi was not swayed. Takahashi was also president of the Seiyūkai, but he had not been a party member long, and was felled by his lack of authority in quelling the criticisms within the party, resigning his post after just seven months.

Takahashi later found himself back at the helm of the Ministry of Finance as part of Tanaka Giichi's all-Seiyūkai cabinet, which formed after the Shōwa financial crisis ended the Wakatsuki Reijirō administration. The Japanese public was ill at ease amid the financial tumult, but even though Takahashi was already seventy-four at the time of his appointment, his warm, positive personality reassured the public. He efficiently steered the country through the financial crisis and then resigned as minister of finance after a mere forty days in office.

Inoue and Lamont: Forging Japan-US Economic Ties

World War I allowed the United States to increase its presence in the world of international finance considerably, with J. P. Morgan & Co. displacing Kuhn, Loeb & Co. as the leading company. During the war years, J. P. Morgan had helped the allies procure substantial funding and war equipment, and it was Inoue Junnosuke who was instrumental in building a relationship of trust with Morgan executive Thomas Lamont and leading the development of Japan's foreign financing.

Hailing from Hita, Ōita Prefecture, Inoue moved to Tokyo at age seventeen and studied English and mathematics. After graduating from the Second Higher School in Sendai and obtaining a degree from Tokyo Imperial University, he got a job with the Bank of Japan in 1896. He was sent to the United Kingdom for training in the business of banking. Inoue returned to Japan in 1899 and worked at the Bank of Japan's Osaka branch, where he served as manager. He was then sent to New York for training, at the initiative of bank deputy governor Takahashi, for a second stint abroad that lasted three years. Returning to Japan in 1912, he was appointed head of the Specie Bank in 1913 and became governor of the Bank of Japan in 1919. His path to the top had followed an elite track, going from Tokyo Imperial University to the Specie Bank and on to the Bank of Japan. This was in stark contrast to the tribulations that had characterized Takahashi's rise.

As governor of the Bank of Japan, Inoue worked with Lamont to bring Japan into the new Four-Power Consortium in China. The loan negotiations made a powerful impression on Lamont, who later called Inoue "the epitome of a liberalist in modern Japan." Yamamoto Gonnohyōe made Inoue his second minister of finance in 1923, and Inoue quickly got to work on his plan to lift the gold embargo and institute the gold standard. Not long after he took over at the Ministry of Finance, however, the Great Kantō Earthquake reordered Inoue's priorities. With Lamont's help, he worked on the issue of foreign bonds for post-earthquake recovery and putting in place credit conditions in preparation for the repeal of the gold embargo. Inoue continued to forge closer ties with British and American banking syndicates over the course of the 1920s, bolstering the Washington System on the economic front along the way.

Inoue believed that restoring the gold standard would stabilize currency values, steady exchange rates, and effect a self-correcting mechanism to bring Japan's international balance of payments into equilibrium. He also subscribed

by the naval treaty. The following April, in 1931, he turned the office of prime minister over to Wakatsuki, and died that August.

The London Naval Treaty marked the apex of Japan's cooperation with the United Kingdom and the United States. The combined leadership of Shidehara and Wakatsuki enhanced Japan's international standing. Shidehara retained his post in the second Wakatsuki cabinet, and the partnership seemed poised to become even stronger.

The Great Depression and the Manchuria "Crisis"

At the initiative of Chargé d'Affaires Shigemitsu Mamoru, Japan and the Nationalist government finalized the Japan-China Tariff Agreement, giving China the recognition of its tariff autonomy that it had wanted. Furthermore, Shigemitsu pursued bilateral negotiations with China's T. V. Soong over such issues as the introduction of a surtax on exports to China, and China's debts to Japan that had originated with the Nishihara loans. They also addressed the elimination of extraterritoriality. Shigemitsu's idea was to avoid negotiating with fully to the idea of implementing austerity measures to stockpile specie reserves, which he saw as essential to an effective gold-standard system—and he also knew that constraints on spending, along with military reductions, would be crucial to securing the support of British and American financiers if Japan were to repeal its gold embargo. In fact, Inoue's commitment to austerity was an important factor in securing the trust of Lamont and other financial heavyweights.

The Turbulent Years of the Great Depression

Upon becoming finance minister under Prime Minister Hamaguchi Osachi in 1929, Inoue implemented a string of austerity measures and finally lifted the gold embargo—thereby reinstating the gold standard—in January 1930. The Japanese economy burst into the open system under the gold standard, throwing its doors wide open to the world economy. Almost as soon as it had embarked on that new chapter, however, the global financial crisis devastated global markets and thrust Japan straight into the "Shōwa Depression." Shortly after the Manchurian Incident, the United Kingdom declared that it would be abandoning the gold standard—just the beginning of a worldwide shift away from gold. As the global financial crisis continued to shake the very foundations of the gold-standard system, Japan soon found itself on the brink of having to reimpose the gold embargo. In December 1931, Inoue stepped down as minister of finance along with the rest of the second Wakatsuki cabinet. He became a leading voice in the Minseitō, and criticized Takahashi's aggressive fiscal policies. He was waiting for an opportunity to bring the gold standard back, but was assassinated in February 1932.

The global financial crisis wiped out the gold standard system, giving Takahashi another opportunity to shine. As minister of finance in the new Inukai Tsuyoshi cabinet, Takahashi promptly abandoned the gold standard. As the yen plummeted against the dollar, there followed an improvement in the performance of Japan's export industries and a sharp rise in the export of light-industry goods. From that point on, until his assassination in the February 26 Incident of 1936, Takahashi's main focus was rescuing Japan from the effects of the depression. Aiming to get the economy back on track and still avoid raising taxes, he initiated the issue of deficit-covering bonds underwritten by the Bank of Japan and expanding government expenditures to cover growing demands for military funding. In the end, the jump in Japanese exports and the increase in government spending—both under Takahashi's watch—were what allowed the Japanese economy to recover from the depression as quickly as it did. Some of Takahashi's policy moves ended up having complicated implications, however. As he worked to rein in the unbridled expansion of military demand in the aftermath of the Manchurian Incident, Takahashi set out to reduce deficit-covering bonds to maintain a healthier budget. That shift naturally drew the ire of the military, which was a factor in Takahashi's demise.

the forces seeking to radicalize China, and to offer concessions to the moderating elements, thereby helping them to impose their leadership. He also pinned his personal hopes on "the opportunities presented by Shidehara diplomacy at its height." Shigemitsu's collaborative line between Japan and China would continue even after the Manchurian Incident of 1931. In 1930, China had completed its effort to win back tariff autonomy from Japan, the United Kingdom, and the United States, and it appeared as though a path had opened to including China in a rebuilt Washington System.

But Manchuria was a separate matter. At the start of 1931, having ascertained that the Nationalist government's revolutionary diplomacy program included the restoration of its interests in Manchuria, Shigemitsu grew pessimistic about future negotiations. There had been a tacit understanding in bilateral negotiations up to then that the two parties would not touch on the delicate problem of Manchuria. The priority was to be revision of unequal treaties for China. But now, in Shigemitsu's view, Japan's negotiating stance appeared to be collapsing.

There was a sense of crisis about revolutionary diplomacy extending to encompass China's recovery of its interests in Manchuria. Japanese residing in Manchuria under Zhang Zuolin's "Three

Eastern Provinces" regime, as well as those in China proper, were feeling a similar sense of crisis. Since the start of the 1920s, Japan's basic policy had been to protect its Manchurian and Mongolian interests by steering Zhang Zuolin's regime. However, after his assassination, the regime under Zhang's heir, Zhang Xueliang, drew closer to the Nationalist government. Xueliang transferred much of the authority to rule Manchuria over to the central government, and he grew increasingly anti-Japanese. Anti-Japanese propaganda from Nationalist government bureaus in Manchuria and leftist elements grew ever more strident, boycotts on Japanese goods stiffened, and growing encroachment on many of the vested interests that Japan had regarded as grounded in treaties was evident.

Furthermore, the global financial crisis was making its effects felt in Manchuria as well, with the collapse in the price of silver and the slump in exports of soybeans, which were a major product. Starting in 1930, the South Manchuria Railway experienced a sharp downturn in business. The repercussions on affiliated companies and businesses were even more severe. The 200,000 Japanese expatriates living in Manchuria recognized the idea that Manchuria and Mongolia were lifelines for Japan as a fact of life. In July 1931, the Manchurian Youth League, which brought together Japanese youths throughout Manchuria, even went so far as to send a group to campaign around Japan for Manchuria and Mongolia to separate the regions from Chinese control and declare independence.

Japan, too, was affected by the global financial crisis. Agricultural product prices had fallen dramatically, which had a direct impact on the livelihoods of farming families. As 1931 began, through local veteran's associations and in speeches at meetings, the army began complaining of a "crisis in Manchuria and Mongolia" to a Japanese public that previously had not displayed much interest in either place. In doing this, they stirred up anger within Japanese society in East Asia against Chiang Kai-shek and the Three Eastern Provinces regime, who had been using boycotts as a strategic tool. This anger would give the Kwantung Army the impetus to act on its plan to occupy Manchuria.

The Kwantung Army was provoked still further by the Nakamura Incident on June 27. Captain Nakamura Shintarō from Army General Staff Office and an aide, who had been traveling on a reconnaissance mission through China's Taonan region since the start of the month, were killed by the Chinese Reclamation Army. News of the deaths reached the Kwantung Army in mid-July, and the soldiers advocated using the incident as an opportunity to resolve the problems of Manchuria and Mongolia through military force. The Ministry of Foreign Affairs Asia Bureau chief Tani Masayuki and Fengtian consul general Hayashi Kyūjirō worked frantically to negotiate with the Three Eastern Provinces regime to settle the matter diplomatically. Hayashi began talks with Fengtian governor Zang Shiyi on August 17. The fact that the Chinese initially would not acknowledge that the killing had occurred made the situation worse, and was one of the factors that encouraged the Kwantung Army to make the decision to use military force.

CHAPTER 7

The Impact of the Manchurian Incident

7-1. Official photo following the coronation of the emperor of Manchukuo

TIMELINE

1931 (Shōwa 6)

January 23	Matsuoka Yōsuke gives an address on Manchuria and Mongolia in the House of Representatives
April 14	Second Wakatsuki cabinet formed
June 27	Nakamura Incident (killing of Japanese army officer in Manchuria)
September 18	Liutiaohu Incident occurs (start of the Manchurian [Mukden] Incident)
September 19	Wakatsuki cabinet decides on policy to keep the Manchurian Incident contained
September 21	China initiates proceedings over the Manchurian Incident with the League of Nations (deliberations begin the following day at the Council of the League of Nations)
September 30	Council of the League of Nations ends meeting with a decision to pull back Japanese forces to lands attached to the South Manchuria Railway (with Japan's approval)
October 8	Kwantung Army bombards Zhang Xueliang regime's final stronghold of Jinzhou
October 15	Council of the League of Nations decides to invite the US to its deliberations as an observer (Japan opposes)
October 17	Plans by a group of army officers to carry out a coup d'état discovered (October Incident)
November 16	Council of the League of Nations reconvenes
November 18	Kwantung Army occupies Qiqihar in North Manchuria
December 10	Council of the League of Nations opts to dispatch a fact-finding commission to report on the Manchuria situation; closes its session
December 13	Inukai Tsuyoshi cabinet formed (a Seiyūkai cabinet)
December 17	Gold exports banned again (halt to the gold standard)

1932 (Shōwa 7)

January 3	Kwantung Army occupies Jinzhou
January 8	US secretary of state Stimson issues the Stimson Doctrine (non-recognition policy)
January 28	Shanghai Incident (January 28 Incident)
February 2	Japan decides to reinforce troop deployment in Shanghai
February 29	Lytton Commission begins its investigations
March 1	Announcement of the founding of Manchukuo

March 11 Assembly of the League of Nations creates 19-member committee to compile report on the Sino-Japanese dispute; adopts policy of non-recognition of Manchukuo

May 5 Shanghai Cease-Fire Agreement of 1932 signed

May 15 May 15 Incident (Prime Minister Inukai assassinated)

May 26 Saitō Makoto cabinet formed

June 14 House of Representatives decides unanimously to recognize Manchukuo

August 25 Foreign Minister Uchida Yasuya (Kōsai) gives "scorched-earth" address in response to a question by Mori Kaku of the House of Representatives, stressing his determination to obtain recognition for Manchukuo

September 15 Japan-Manchukuo Protocol signed, recognizing "Manchukuo" as a country

October 2 Lytton Report issued

November 4 Soviet Union proposes Soviet-Japanese Non-Aggression Pact

November 8 Franklin Roosevelt elected president of the United States

November 21 Council of the League of Nations holds session to discuss the Lytton Report

1933 (Shōwa 8)

January 1 Kwantung Army attacks Shanhaiguan district in Qinhuangdao (Hebei Province); district captured on January 3

February 23 Kwantung Army launches Operation Nekka in Jehol (Rehe) Province in Inner Mongolia

February 24 Assembly of the League of Nations adopts the Lytton Report; Japanese delegation walks out

March 4 Kwantung Army occupies capital of Jehol Province, Chengde

March 11 Operation Nekka brought to an end

March 27 Japan notifies League of Nations of its withdrawal; imperial rescript on same issued

May 31 Tanggu Truce signed (conclusion of the Manchurian Incident)

June 12–July 27 London Economic Conference

1 The Occupation of Manchuria

The Liutiaohu Incident (Start of the Manchurian Incident)

On September 18, 1931, just before dawn, the first reports from the Kwantung Army arrived at the Army Ministry in Tokyo with the news that tracks on the South Manchuria Railway had been destroyed by Chinese forces at Liutiaohu on the outskirts of Fengtian, and a battle had ensued. It was the Kwantung Army itself, however, that had bombed the railway line. This was a plot that had been devised by Lt. Colonel Ishiwara Kanji and Colonel Itagaki Seishirō from the Kwantung Army's General Staff, and carried out by a garrison stationed in the region.

The actual explosion along the rail line was small, but in accordance with the plans for the Kwantung Army, around 10,000 troops were assembled in Fengtian, the home base of the Three Eastern Provinces regime. By the following morning, Mukden had been occupied. Furthermore, nearly all of the major cities that lay along the South Manchuria Railway were brought under the control of the Kwantung Army on the 19th.

Meanwhile, Fengtian consul general Hayashi Kyūjirō dispatched numerous telegrams surmising that this was a plot by the Kwantung Army and an all-out display of military force. On the morning of September 19, in an extraordinary meeting, the Wakatsuki Reijirō cabinet decided to contain the damage in light of the uncertainties about the facts. The situation became even more unsettled. That same day, responding to strong entreaties from Itagaki and Ishiwara, Kwantung Army commander-in-chief General Honjō Shigeru ordered a troop dispatch to Chi-lin, which lay a considerable distance away from the lines of the South Manchuria Railway, on the pretense of protecting Japanese in the area. On the 21st, in response to this, commander-in-chief of the Japanese army in Korea Hayashi Senjūrō ordered forces stationed in Sinuiju to cross the border from the Republic of China into Manchuria. That evening, chief of the

7-2. September 18 History Museum, Shenyang, Liaoning Province

Army General Staff Kanaya Hanzō reported the details to Emperor Shōwa. Faced with the fact that troops had already crossed the border, the emperor accepted the situation post facto, though only after he admonished Kanaya, saying, "There's no helping what has already happened, but be much more cautious in the future."

Chief aide-de-camp Nara Takeji, who had followed the incident at the emperor's side, later wrote in his diary that it would be necessary to investigate the "arbitrary action" undertaken by the commander-in-chief of the Japanese army in Korea once the situation had quieted down. In the end, however, there was no punishment. Crossing the border with troops required government approval. On the 22nd, the cabinet decided that, while it would not approve increasing Japan's forces in Manchuria, it would cover the additional costs associated with that crossing of the border.

Japan's minister to China, Shigemitsu Mamoru, and the Nationalist government's then minister of finance, T. V. Soong (the younger brother-in-law of Chiang Kai-shek [Jiang Jieshi]), had begun working from the morning of the 19th to resolve the incident at a regional level. Soong proposed creating a joint Sino-Japanese commission. Shigemitsu accepted this, and then passed the suggestion on to the Ministry of Foreign Affairs in Japan. Foreign Minister Shidehara hoped to achieve a breakthrough over the situation through direct bilateral negotiations, and immediately sent a telegram to Shigemitsu agreeing to the proposal. However, the Chinese government held that a state of war now existed with Japan. They questioned whether they could get the Japanese army to withdraw to its original positions even if a joint commission were organized, and so they rejected the notion of holding direct bilateral negotiations. On September 21, the Chinese government appealed to the League of Nations regarding the incident.

At the time, although the Chiang-led Nationalist government had managed to unify the country, it was also midway through an effort to mop up Communist forces based in Jiangxi Province, and was also in conflict with an independent regime based in Guangdong that had been formed in May 1931. For these reasons, the Nationalist government had few resources to resist the Japanese army. Even before the incident, Chiang had ordered Zhang Xueliang not to do anything to incite the Japanese. Despite having in place an overwhelming force of 200,000 troops to confront the Japanese army, Zhang had chosen a policy of nonresistance. Zhang feared that, in the event of an all-out war with Japan, his own forces—which were inferior in both men and equipment—would be dealt a blow and he would lose his base in Manchuria. He had to avoid an all-out confrontation for the sake of self-preservation. Taking advantage of the openings created by these Chinese policies of non-resistance, the Japanese army stepped up its military actions.

The Dispute at the League of Nations

On September 22, 1931, in response to China's appeal, the Council of the League of Nations met in Geneva. Japan's representative, Yoshizawa Kenkichi, argued that the military action had been undertaken in self-defense to guarantee the safety of the South Manchuria Railway and to protect Japanese residing in the area. He also argued that the incident had occurred in response to infringements on Japan's rights and interests, and was justified by treaty. Furthermore, in keeping with the policies set down by Foreign Minister Shidehara, Yoshizawa rejected any intervention by third countries and argued that a solution should be arrived at through direct negotiations between Japan and China. In contrast, China's representative, Alfred Sao-ke Sze, pointed out how the Japanese army was expanding its operations and protested that direct negotiations were inconceivable while parts of China were under military occupation. Hence, the two sides were at an impasse from the start.

In the end, all fourteen members of the Council adopted a resolution unanimously stating that, once the safety of Japanese citizens and their assets had been secured, Japanese forces would be asked to withdraw as quickly as possible to lands attached to the South Manchuria Railway. The Council then recessed at the end of September. Japan also agreed with this resolution. The decision indicated that, so long as Japan's actions were to be treated as self-defense measures aimed at protecting Japan's local assets, the League would give consideration to Japan's stance while also encouraging self-restraint.

On October 8, however, the Kwantung Army began bombing Jinzhou, where Zhang Xueliang had moved his base of operations. The attack on Jinzhou occurred before the Council had reconvened, and it caused a rapid negative shift in the attitudes toward Japan in Geneva. When the Council did reconvene in mid-October, Yoshizawa presented a five-point draft for an agreement that laid out the conditions for a Japanese troop withdrawal. These included the preservation of China's territorial integrity—including Manchuria and Mongolia—by Japan, while China was expected to guarantee the freedom of movement and activity of Japanese residing in Manchuria. If such an agreement could be achieved through direct negotiations between Japan and China, Japan would withdraw its troops. However, the Council rejected the proposal. Instead, overriding Japanese objections, it opted for a plan to invite US observers to its deliberations as a due process provision. In late October, the Council voted on a troop withdrawal recommendation stipulating that if Japanese forces withdrew from the occupied territories by the time of the next Council meeting (November 16), then bilateral negotiations would commence. This timetable was the reverse of the Japanese proposal, and the recommendation did not pass owing to Japan's "nay" vote (13–1). On the other hand, Japan's broad-based proposal was also rejected, and the Council again recessed.

The Impact of Occupying Qiqihar

In late October, while the League Council was in recess, the Kwantung Army made plans to occupy the capital of Heilongjiang Province, Qiqihar. Occupying Qiqihar was the crucial next step for the army's move into North Manchuria. In November, using the destruction of a railway bridge on the Taoang line (a Japanese concession) by Chinese forces loyal to Ma Zhanshan as a pretext, the Kwantung Army began its attack on Qiqihar. Imperial Army leaders in Tokyo had expressly forbidden any military maneuvers that would go beyond the Chinese Eastern Railway. They feared that any such move would incite the Soviet Union and induce a military intervention. The Red Army's proficiency had been demonstrated by the Sino-Soviet conflict of 1929 over the Chinese Eastern Railway, in which it had dealt a crushing blow to the Chinese forces under Zhang Xueliang in a matter of days. However, the Kwantung Army's leadership argued that, to the contrary, the very fact of leaving North Manchuria "vacant" was an invitation for the Soviets to invade.

In mid-November, ambassador to Italy Yoshida Shigeru sent a telegram to Foreign Minister Shidehara arguing that the invasion of North Manchuria would have grave consequences for Japan's very existence, and he urged that the assault on Qiqihar be promptly halted and that Japan should return to its policy of maintaining its interests in South Manchuria. Minister to Austria Arita Hachirō likewise sent a dispatch deploring the Qiqihar attack as imprudent. Heedless of such concerns, the Kwantung Army routed Ma's forces and occupied Qiqihar on November 19.

The fact that the Kwantung Army had crossed the lines of the Chinese Eastern Railway (the Manzhouli-Suifenhe and Harbin-Changchun lines) to advance into North Manchuria shook up the status quo that had been in place in Manchuria and Mongolia since the time of the Russo-Japanese War, and looked set to have a grave impact on

Soviet-Japanese relations. However, the Soviet Union viewed Japan's moves cautiously and took a neutral position over the Manchurian Incident. It avoided doing anything to provoke the Kwantung Army or upset relations with Japan.

7-3. The Japanese army enters Qiqihar

The occupation of Qiqihar took the Manchurian Incident to a new level. At that stage, the Wakatsuki Cabinet had become resigned to the notion that, in order to obtain a fundamental resolution to the Manchurian problem, dealing with a new Manchurian administration that the Kwantung Army had been working to put in place, rather than the Nanjing government, was the only option. It therefore fell into line with the army's approach. This was a major about-face for Shidehara diplomacy, which had very much focused on finding a solution with the Nanjing government.

Furthermore, the occupation of Qiqihar completely changed the atmosphere at the Council of the League of Nations, which had been searching for a solution that would be acceptable to both Japan and China. China's representative, Alfred Sao-ke Sze, demanded that Article 16 of the League's Covenant (on sanctions against a member committing an act of war on another member) be applied to Japan. On November 21, 1931, the Japanese delegation proposed to the Council that a fact-finding commission be dispatched to Manchuria. With things getting bogged down, the dispatch of such a commission was one of the few options available for breaking the deadlock. Lacking an effective plan of its own, the Council welcomed the proposal. However, the Japanese delegation attached several conditions to the dispatch. First, participation in the commission would be limited to delegates from the great powers. The delegation sought this restriction out of the belief that it was necessary to exclude representatives from the numerous minor countries who might ignore conditions on the ground in favor of arguing for the strict application of the League's Covenant.

Second, it wanted the commission to examine conditions not only in Manchuria but across China as a whole. The hope was that, if it observed the fierce anti-foreign movement across China and the reality of infringements on treaty-based rights, the commission would be forced to acknowledge that Japan's actions had been justified. The Council of the League of Nations approved the proposal to dispatch a fact-finding commission on December 10, and recessed. Even though the decision to dispatch a commission had been made, the League had effectively postponed moving toward a resolution.

The October Incident and the "Coalition Cabinet" Effort

There was another facet to the Manchurian Incident in that it had been a coup d'état conducted by middle-ranked officers working together both overseas (in Manchuria) and in Japan. Staff in the Kwantung Army saw the Manchurian Incident as one part of a "national reconstruction" aimed at fighting a total war in the future. They were plotting to put in place a government under military command. In fact, Lieutenant Colonel Hashimoto Kingorō of the ultranationalist Sakura-kai (a group consisting of junior army officers) plotted to overthrow the Wakatsuki cabinet through a coup d'état (October Incident) in concert with the Kwantung Army. News of the plot leaked out and it failed, but the incident had a broad impact on the political realm. The incident added momentum to the effort to create a "coalition cabinet" that would shift the government from one dominated by the Minseitō to a grand coalition involving both the Minseitō and the Seiyūkai.

While the then president of the opposition Seiyūkai party, Inukai Tsuyoshi, had been aware of the coup d'état plan, he grew enthusiastic about the idea of an coalition. Even though he was a member of the ruling Minseitō, Home Minister Adachi Kenzō was also enthusiastic about creating a "coalition cabinet" as a way to "maintain trust in political parties while also achieving breakthroughs in a time of external crisis." Even Prime Minister Wakatsuki, who was dubious about a "Coalition Cabinet," nonetheless leaned toward approving it when it became clear that Japan would be isolated in the Council of the League of Nations. Elder statesman Saionji Kinmochi was also inclined to support this development. However, in November, both Shidehara and Finance Minister Inoue Junnosuke began voicing their objections within the Minseitō over creating such a cabinet, arguing that an alliance with the opposition parties would bring with it a reversal of the government's foreign and financial policies. Mindful of the dissenting forces within his own party, Inukai also turned negative.

By late November, the movement was rekindled from within the Seiyūkai. Although he had been opposed to the idea, Seiyūkai secretary-general Kuhara Fusanosuke drafted a memorandum in early December with Minseitō advisor Tomita Kōjirō regarding a "coalition cabinet." Tomita then presented this to Wakatsuki, who summoned his cabinet ministers and reconfirmed his opposition to such a coalition. Home Minister Adachi Kenzō was isolated in his support of the coalition, but he refused advice to step down, leading to the resignation of the entire Wakatsuki cabinet on December 13, 1931, over the lack of internal agreement. With the leaders of both parties refusing to enter into a coalition, Prince Saionji had no choice but to appoint a single-party Seiyūkai cabinet with Inukai as prime minister.

The Demise of Shidehara Diplomacy

The international cooperation that was a hallmark of Shidehara diplomacy did not extend to working cooperatively with the League of Nations on matters related to China. In an October 6 dispatch to Shidehara, ambassador to Belgium Satō Naotake—who had been making strenuous efforts at the League—criticized Japan's position ruling out League mediation. He wrote, "Japan has been a staunch supporter of the League on European issues, but we risk becoming ostracized when it comes to issues that have a direct bearing on ourselves. This is not something that will turn global public opinion to our advantage." Nevertheless, there was no change to Shidehara's policy.

The second period of Shidehara diplomacy, which had begun in 1929 just prior to the Manchurian Incident, was conducted in close partnership with Finance Minister Inoue Junnosuke. Determined to keep the gold standard, Inoue set great store in international cooperation from an economic and financial perspective, and therefore supported Shidehara diplomacy. However, the Manchurian Incident and the global financial crisis made it difficult to sustain international cooperation on both diplomatic and economic fronts. The global financial crisis not only contributed to the Manchurian Incident, but also made it hard for the major powers to maintain the gold standard. In particular, the United Kingdom's withdrawal from the gold standard shortly after the Manchurian Incident placed the future of international economic cooperation in doubt. Japan, too, would withdraw from the gold standard under the Inukai cabinet that followed.

2 The Inukai Cabinet

The Occupation of Jinzhou and the Stimson Doctrine

Taking office in December 1931, the first task of the Seiyūkai cabinet of Inukai Tsuyoshi was to rebuild Japan's economy and finances, which had fallen into disarray, as the United Kingdom's abandonment of the gold standard had resulted in dollar-buying. To address this, Inukai appointed the accomplished Takahashi Korekiyo to the post of finance minister. Takahashi immediately broke away from the gold standard, reimposing an embargo on gold exports and prohibiting gold-to-dollar conversion, thus adopting an expansionary fiscal policy.

Because of his close relations with China, Inukai had envisioned turning Manchuria into a self-governing region under China's suzerainty and driving economic development through an equal Japan/China union. His aim was not to found the new country of Manchuria, but rather to find a solution that was in keeping with the existing international order. To that end, he appointed his son-in-law, Yoshizawa Kenkichi, then serving as Japan's ambassador to France, but with years of experience in China and a solid reputation at the League of Nations, to be his foreign minister. In late December 1931, while he was en route to Tokyo to take up his new post, Yoshizawa stopped in Moscow, where the Soviets unofficially proposed signing a non-aggression pact with Japan. However, Inukai did not make it clear whether he accepted or rejected the proposal.

In China, just as the Inukai cabinet was coming together, the new regime of Sun Ke (Sun Fo) came into being as the result of a merger between the independent Guangdong regime (Guangzhou Nationalist government) and the Nationalist government in Nanjing. The foundations for Sun's government came more from the Guangdong regime. Unlike Chiang Kai-shek, who was then out of office, Sun's government was motivated to settle the Manchurian Incident through direct negotiations with Japan. Prime Minister Inukai sent a secret emissary to China in an attempt to resolve the incident through such negotiations. That emissary, Kayano Nagatomo, made contact with Sun and other important figures, and the negotiations made good progress. However, lacking the support of both the Seiyūkai's leadership and the Imperial Army, who were concerned about the Nationalist government's sovereignty extending to Manchuria, the negotiations came to a standstill.

In the meantime, the Kwantung Army advanced toward Zhang Xueliang's final stronghold of Jinzhou in late December, and had occupied it by early January. By that stage, neither Chiang nor Zhang were particularly inclined to fight to the death for Jinzhou. The fall of Jinzhou signaled that the local government institutions that the Nationalists had used to govern the Manchuria region had ceased to function, leaving the way wide open for the founding of Manchukuo.

At the time the Manchurian Incident occurred, the Western powers were all struggling with the global financial crisis. They were under pressure to respond to the crisis, but they had no leeway to get seriously involved in a conflict in the Far East. Under those circumstances, it was the actions of the United States—not a League member—that made an impact. Secretary of State Henry Stimson had expected that the Wakatsuki-Shidehara pair, who had made their presence known at the London Naval Conference while working in concert with the League of Nations, would rein in the Japanese forces on the ground and get the situation under control.

But Stimson's attitude changed with the fall of Jinzhou. On January 7, 1932, he sent memoranda to both Japan and China stating that the United States would not recognize any situation created through methods that ran contrary to the obligations under the Kellogg-Briand Pact. He also demanded that Japan respect the terms of the Nine-Power Treaty, under which signatories promised to respect one another's territorial integrity and the open-door policy (Stimson Doctrine).

7-4. The Shanghai Incident (January 28 Incident)

The Shanghai Incident (January 28 Incident)

At the end of January 1932, Sun Ke resigned his position as head of the Nationalist government. Wang Jingwei took over as premier, while Chiang Kai-shek became chairman of the National Military Affairs Commission, creating the Wang-Chiang regime. But just before this, the Shanghai Incident occurred on January 28.

In Shanghai, the boycott of Japanese goods had grown more intense as a consequence of the Manchurian Incident, and the situation had grown so severe that the lives of Japanese residents were under threat. In mid-January, a group of Japanese Buddhist priests belonging to the Nichiren sect were attacked by Chinese as they were evangelizing at the Shanghai International Settlement. At the time, the powerful and fiercely anti-Japanese Nineteenth Route Army under the Nationalist government was stationed in the vicinity of Shanghai. The situation suddenly grew strained, and progressed to fighting between Japanese and Chinese forces at the end of the month. Japanese naval land forces repeatedly engaged in fierce exchanges with the Chinese forces, but they were pushed back. On February 2, the Inukai cabinet decided to reinforce the Japanese army forces in the area. Thus, early that month, the Japanese army landed forces in Shanghai for the first time ever. The troop reinforcements found themselves pressed into a difficult battle.

The Western powers were shocked that the conflict in China had spread to Shanghai, where their concessions were concentrated. Fearing that expansion of the Shanghai Incident now posed a threat to its interests in the Chinese market and the Yangzi River Delta region, the United Kingdom made feverish attempts to mediate between the League of Nations and Japan.

Under UK leadership, the United Kingdom, France, and the United States sent a cease-fire mediation proposal to both Japan and China in early February. It called for the implementation of a cease-fire and a neutral zone, and the start of negotiations to settle all the pending issues, including the Manchuria problem. The Japanese side saw the Manchurian Incident and the Shanghai Incident as two separate issues and turned down the request. The fact is that the Japanese government treated the two incidents as distinct from one another, its main objective being to keep the situation as contained as possible.

The Council of the League of Nations, having received China's request, decided that it would move deliberations over the conflict to the Assembly, applying Article 15 of the League Covenant, which stated that a resolution could be passed by a majority vote in that body. Ambassador to Belgium Satō Naotake, who had been working tirelessly to make Japan's case in the Council, reported back to Tokyo that Japan had been driven into "completely friendless isolation in the face of global public opinion." Meeting in early March, the League Assembly unanimously (with Japan abstaining) adopted a resolution giving full support to the Stimson Doctrine. The resolution called for organizing a nineteen-member committee, meaning that the League would play a major role in settling the Sino-Japanese conflict.

By early March, the fighting in the Shanghai Incident had turned to Japan's advantage. Shanghai Expeditionary Army commander-in-chief Shirakawa Yoshinori unilaterally declared that he would halt combat activities so long as the Chinese forces did not counterattack. Chiang Kai-shek had been looking for a way to reach an understanding with Japan, and had no desire to find himself in an all-out confrontation with the Japanese forces. A de facto cease-fire came into effect by mid-March, and a formal cease-fire agreement was signed in early May. In late April, just before the agreement was signed, Shirakawa Yoshinori and Shigemitsu Mamoru were gravely wounded by a bomb thrown by a Korean activist at a ceremony being held to celebrate the emperor's birthday in Shanghai. Shigemitsu signed the agreement from his hospital bed. The January 28 incident did not last long, but Japan suffered more than 3,000 casualties, while China lost upward of 14,000.

As this was going on, the Kwantung Army made steady progress toward establishing an autonomous state in Manchuria. The incident helped shift international attention away from Manchuria.

The Founding of Manchukuo

When they set the Manchurian Incident in motion, what Ishiwara Kanji and his fellow officers of the Kwantung Army first had in mind was to occupy Manchuria. However, since the Imperial Army's central command did not approve, from around late September 1931 the Kwantung Army officers turned their attention toward founding an autonomous nation that would lay claim to all of the four northeastern provinces. In the face of the concerns voiced by central command regarding rushed state-building, the Kwantung Army redoubled its efforts to set up the new country. In January 1932, Itagaki Seishirō of the Kwantung Army's General Staff returned to Tokyo with a concrete plan for the new nation. The thinking within the Japanese government in Tokyo, however, was that Manchuria and Mongolia for the time being should be treated as a single political entity separate from the Chinese central government, and that they should be gradually "encouraged" to turn themselves into an autonomous nation. Prime Minister Inukai was concerned about actions that would be incompatible with the Nine-Power Treaty, and so leaned toward establishing a single regional regime that would be under Japanese influence.

However, with the attention of the Western powers focused on the Shanghai Incident, the Kwantung Army steadily pushed ahead with the creation of the "new independent nation of Manchuria and Mongolia." Whether it was to be the creation of a new administration or a new nation, it would be necessary to destroy the base of the Zhang Xueliang regime that ruled Manchuria. Accordingly, immediately after the Manchurian Incident broke out, the Kwantung Army embarked on a plan to win over influential Chinese in the Three Eastern Provinces regime through persuasion, inducements, bribery, and coercion. Among these influential people were members of the "restoration faction" who sought to reestablish the Qing court. They hoped to bring Puyi back to Manchuria, the birthplace of the Qing regime, and use that as leverage to restore the court.

By mid-February 1932, through leadership and persuasive tactics, the Kwantung Army's commanders had managed to gather together a group of influential Chinese who represented the three Manchurian provinces and who had all issued declarations of independence and agreed on the founding of Manchukuo. On March 1, 1932, a declaration was issued in the name of the "Northeast Administrative Committee" claiming that, based on the will of 30 million people, the provinces of Fengtian (Hōten), Chi-lin (Kitsurin), Heilongjiang (Kokuryūkō), Jehol (Nekka), and Mongolia were severing ties with the Republic of China to found the new state of Manchukuo. This created a fait accompli in the form of a new nation before the League of Nations' fact-finding team (the Lytton Commission) could arrive on the scene.

The "Puyi Letter" and the Reality of Control

Since his abdication, Puyi, who had been earmarked as chief executive (governor) of Manchukuo, had been living in seclusion in Tianjin with his entourage, but immediately after the Manchurian Incident, he was placed under the protection of the Japanese army's Tianjin garrison. In November 1931, a plot was hatched to move him to Lushun. He was then moved from Lushun to Changchun in early March 1932. Then, following the ceremony appointing him chief executive, Puyi sent a secret letter dated March 10 to Kwantung Army commander-in-chief Honjō Shigeru. The letter had been drafted by Colonel Itagaki, who had made Puyi sign it in advance. It said that Manchukuo would entrust to Japan the authority to handle its national defense and the maintenance of public security at home. It also said that Manchukuo would grant the Kwantung Army the rights to administer and build railroads, harbors, and runways as deemed necessary for national defense. This was intended to serve as the foundation for formally signing a treaty between the two nations in the future. Thus, the Puyi Letter provided the basis for the Japan-Manchukuo Protocol that would follow.

7-5. The installation of the Puyi administration

Manchukuo was to be an independent country arising from an autonomous and spontaneous nation-building movement on the part of local people. The guiding ideas in the declaration on founding the new nation included total independence from the Republic of China, the principle of equality among ethnic groups, continuing to respect previously agreed treaty responsibilities, and maintaining the open-door policy. However, real power over each section of the administrative apparatus was in the hands of Japanese bureaucrats. The secretary-general, who was the highest-ranked Japanese official in the new state, had absolute control over the central administration of Manchukuo. Furthermore, authority over national defense, public finance, diplomacy, and transportation—the key functions of a nation—was in the hands of the Kwantung Army.

In mid-March, after having created basic laws on government administration, human-rights protections, and so forth to go with establishing the organizations for central and local governments, the new Manchukuo regime dispatched the "Announcement of the Establishment of Manchukuo" to seventeen nations, including the United Kingdom, Japan, and the United States. The dispatch notified the recipient countries that the new state would respect the goodwill that had been established with them, along with international laws and customs. In particular, it also stated that the new state would discharge the treaty obligations it had inherited from the Republic of China, and also respect the principle of maintaining an open-door policy. It was delivered with the goal of obtaining international recognition for the new Manchu state. Despite such measures, it was clear to foreign observers that the creation of Manchukuo was the product of a military operation by the Kwantung Army. The United States had already made it clear that it would not recognize such a state, and Japan had no expectation of winning recognition from any of the major powers involved, including the United Kingdom and France, as well as China itself.

7-6. Fengtian (Mukden) Station in former Manchuria

3 The Pluses and Minuses of Withdrawing from the League of Nations

Foreign Minister Uchida and "Scorched-Earth Diplomacy"

Prime Minister Inukai Tsuyoshi, who had opposed the recognition of Manchukuo as a state, was assassinated in May 1932 in an act of terrorism carried out by a group of junior navy officers. This event, known as the May 15 Incident, delivered a major blow to party politics in Japan. The Seiyūkai had scored a crushing victory in the general election held that February. However, only a minority within the Seiyūkai wanted a cabinet comprised solely of the members of their party. Elder statesman Saionji Kinmochi then sought to hand the reins of government over to the Minseitō and to Ugaki Kazushige, governor-general of Korea, who represented moderates in the government and in the army. However, support for Ugaki in the House of Representatives collapsed with the Minseitō's decisive defeat in the February election, and even the moderates in the army retreated in the face of the rise of the so-called "Imperial Way" faction.

Saionji, who had the authority to endorse candidates for prime minister to the emperor, had only two options: endorse another Seiyūkai cabinet, or select a non-party cabinet with a prime minister not from the world of party politics. In the end, Saionji named as the next prime minister the seventy-four-year-old former navy minister Saitō Makoto. This marked the end of the eight-year-long stretch of party cabinets. With someone who was not the leader of a political party serving as prime minister, there was now a national unity cabinet comprising members from both political parties, as well as from the military and the bureaucracy.

Saitō appointed South Manchuria Railway

president Uchida Yasuya (Kōsai) as foreign minister. Uchida's position on the Manchuria question was clear in light of his having cooperated with the Kwantung Army's maneuvering to create Manchukuo while presiding over that company. He laid this out in a note from May 1932, writing, "Viewed from Japan's position, the Manchuria problem no longer exists. All that remains is the issue of extending recognition to Manchukuo."

In a foreign-policy address delivered to the sixty-third session of the Imperial Diet that August, Uchida argued that recognition for Manchukuo was the only means of bringing peace to Manchuria, Mongolia, and the Far East. Responding to criticism that Japan's actions violated its responsibilities as a signatory of the Kellogg-Briand Pact, Uchida responded: "The Kellogg-Briand Pact does not restrict the exercise of self-defense to protect against acts that infringe on crucial interests related to Japan's very existence. That exercise can be extended to Manchuria as well, outside of territorial Japan."

He also went on to argue that the founding of Manchukuo was the "result of an independence movement" undertaken by Manchurians and Mongolians themselves. He said that extending recognition to a nation created on the initiative of its own people did not contravene the Nine-Power Treaty. As to the fact that so many Japanese were being employed by the Manchukuo government, he argued there were numerous precedents for a new nation to make use of the talents of foreigners at its founding, such as the many who had been hired by the Meiji-era Japanese government.

In response to this address, Mori Kaku of the Seiyūkai asked Uchida what preparations were being made by the government, as the issue of recognizing Manchukuo would worsen relations with the other powers. Uchida responded that Japan "would remain determined to not budge even an inch in pressing its case, even if the country should be burned to the ground." This moment became famous as the "scorched-earth" address. According to Arita Hachirō (who was vice-foreign minister at the time), Uchida worded his answer as a rebuke to Mori's "malicious question."

One-Sided Recognition of Manchukuo: The Japan-Manchukuo Protocol

Domestic public opinion was in favor of recognizing Manchukuo as soon as possible. In mid-June, a House of Representatives plenary session unanimously approved of doing so, and with that, the domestic debate over the issue of recognition ended.

And so, on September 15, 1932, based on the aforementioned letter signed by Puyi, the Japan-Manchukuo Protocol was signed by Kwantung Army commander-in-chief Mutō Nobuyoshi and prime minister of Manchukuo Zheng Xiaoxu. Their act formalized Japan's recognition of Manchukuo. The Japan-Manchukuo Protocol established that Japan retained its rights to station troops in Manchuria. Moreover, it also guaranteed that those rights and interests already obtained in Manchuria through existing Sino-Japanese agreements and treaties remained in force.

The reason the Kwantung Army commander-in-chief was Japan's representative at the signing was that Honjō Shigeru's replacement, Mutō Nobuyoshi, had become Japan's special plenipotentiary to Manchuria in addition to his duties as commander of the Kwantung Army.

The Work of the Lytton Commission

The Lytton Commission had been created by a Council of the League of Nations decision reached in December 1931. Headed by Victor Bulwer-Lytton, it began its investigations in late February 1932. The commission conducted interviews with numerous leaders and important officials from the Japanese government, the Nationalist government, the Kwantung Army, and the Manchukuo

The Lytton Commission

In December 1931, the League of Nations decided to send an official commission to Manchuria and China. Comprising five members—one each from the United Kingdom, France, Italy, Germany, and the United States—the group gathered in Geneva in late January 1932 and chose Victor Bulwer-Lytton as head of the commission. The son of a former viceroy of India, Lytton had studied at the University of Cambridge and served in a number of important positions, including that of governor of Bengal and acting viceroy of India. German representative Heinrich Schnee, who had spent significant time in the German Foreign Office's Colonial Department and written extensively on colonial relations, contributed greatly to the investigation. As the majority of the five members had considerable experience in colonial administration, they were expected to conduct a fair and objective investigation. Lytton in particular was an ideal choice to lead the commission given his long-standing commitment and affinity with the League of Nations' role in maintaining international order.

From late February to July 1932, the commission conducted thorough research and met with key figures in Tokyo, Beijing, Shanghai, and Manchuria. Important stops on the group's tour included central Shanghai, which lay in ruins, and the site of the Ryūjōko (Liutiaohu) Incident. As detailed in the main text, holding talks with the upper echelons of the Nationalist government was useful in helping the commission achieve its objective of suggesting resolutions to the incident. However, the meetings with Japanese officials proved completely fruitless in that regard.

In late March 1932, Matsuoka Yōsuke (the former vice-president of the South Manchuria Railway), who had been appointed Japan's special envoy to the commission by foreign minister Yoshizawa Kenkichi, stated that the Japanese military action had been an inevitable consequence of repressive anti-Japanese sentiment in Manchuria and Mongolia. The Lytton Commission members also met with Kwantung Army leaders in Mukden on six separate occasions. Staff Officer Ishiwara Kanji took most of the responsibility for detailing the Kwantung Army's actions on the night of the Ryūjōko Incident. Ishihara was adamant that the troops, which had been training constantly for emergency situations, had taken necessary action out of self-defense at the initiative of the commanding officers present. Kwantung Army commander Honjō Shigeru argued that defending Manchuria was not for the exclusive benefit of Japan, but rather to prevent the civilized world from the threat of Comintern turning nations "red" (communist)—and given that context, the only effective resolution would be to recognize Manchukuo.

The commission also held two meetings with Uchida Yasuya (Kōsai), who had left the presidency of the South Manchuria Railway to become Japan's foreign minister, and repeatedly pressed for resolutions other than recognition of the state of Manchukuo. In reply, Uchida only kept repeating that there was no other resolution. And when the commission members suggested as a resolution the Chinese proposal of granting broad autonomy instead of reverting to the old system and discussing the recognition issue with the signatories to the Nine-Power Treaty, Uchida bluntly refused. He told the commission that he had no interest in talks with the other countries because Manchukuo was the product of the residents' free will, which put it outside the scope of the Nine-Power Treaty to begin with.

7-7. The Lytton Commission

government. It visited the concession sites that had been left in ruins by fiercely contested battles, as well as the site of the Liutiaohu Incident.

The goal of the Lytton Commission was not to simply look into how the Manchurian Incident had occurred, but rather to come up with a proposal that would resolve all aspects of the Sino-Japanese conflict. For example, when Zhang Xueliang met with the commission in April, he argued that the roots of the bilateral crisis lay in the aggressive strategy toward China that Japan had taken ever since the Meiji era, and attributed this entirely to Japanese territorial ambitions. Lytton responded that the work of the commission was not to pass judgement on past actions, but rather to look to the future and somehow resolve the conflict in accordance with the League's Covenant. He pointed out that focusing on Japan's aggressive strategies or territorial ambitions would not help resolve the current situation.

Among the most crucial of the commission's interviews with key officials were the two rounds of talks conducted with leaders of the Nationalist government. In the second talks held in June, Lytton said that, based on the results of their surveys in Manchuria, the Chinese living in that area did not wish to see a return to the status quo that had existed prior to the Manchurian Incident, and wished to have an autonomous government with a civilian-led administration and a special police force. Lytton's comments amounted to a rejection of the Zhang regime's rule over the Three Eastern Provinces (i.e., Manchuria). In responding, Wang Jingwei gave signs that he would accept an "independent government" for Manchuria, and that he would not insist on retaining Zhang's regime there. The comment was an important contributing factor to the report that the investigative commission would draft. Following a final visit to Tokyo in mid-July, the commission set about compiling its report.

The Lytton Report

The Lytton Commission released its report in early October 1932. The report recognized Japan's special status in Manchuria, and also took into consideration Japan's position in the face of intense anti-Japan boycotts among the Chinese. That said, it also rejected Japan's assertions that its military actions had been undertaken in self-defense, and that Manchukuo was the product of a spontaneous independence movement. Rather than returning to the status quo ante, it urged Japan and China to instead take a number of steps to settle the Manchurian Incident. These may be summed up as follows:

First, establish an "autonomous government" with wide-ranging authority under the sovereignty of China; second, appoint foreign advisors under League guidance to this autonomous government; and third, set up a "special police force" to maintain public order in the region, which would gradually be disbanded following the withdrawal of Japanese and Chinese forces from the region. Special considerations for Japan included the recommendation that Japanese be given priority in the designation of advisors to the autonomous government, and also called for forbidding organized boycotts of Japanese businesses and trade activities.

However, the Japanese government, which had already extended official recognition to Manchukuo, gave not even the slightest consideration to the report's recommendations. In particular, Foreign Minister Uchida remained adamant that the only option for resolving the Manchuria question was to officially recognize Manchukuo.

In mid-August 1932, three Japanese ambassadors, including Nagaoka Harukazu in Paris, Satō Naotake, and Yoshida Shigeru, sent a joint dispatch to Tokyo suggesting that Japan should avoid being the only country to recognize Manchukuo. In short, they recommended that Manchukuo join the League of Nations, and that China should maintain sovereignty over the territory until then. They also said that Japan should support Manchukuo's entry to the League by acting as intermediary. Presenting such a proposal to the League would also help the League to save face, they added.

While Uchida did not accept the proposals to avoid the one-sided recognition issue, he also had no intention of pulling Japan out of the League of Nations. The fact is, the recognition of Manchukuo and the rejection of the Lytton Report were not immediately responsible for Japan's withdrawal.

Efforts to Keep Japan in the League of Nations

Matsuoka Yōsuke was appointed to head Japan's delegation to the Council and Assembly of the League of Nations as it deliberated over the Lytton Report. He arrived in Geneva in mid-November 1932. Colonel Ishiwara Kanji had also been dispatched to Geneva as an additional member of the Japanese delegation. Working on the premise that Japan would remain in the League, Foreign Minister Uchida sought to resolve the Manchuria problem through direct talks with China.

Deliberations over the Lytton Report in the League Council began in late November. At the meeting, Matsuoka and his Chinese counterpart Wellington Koo reiterated their countries' respective positions. The Council president made a proposal that the topic be transferred to the Assembly for discussion there, which was approved (Japan abstained).

At the General Assembly early the following month, one representative after another spoke on the matter, with the majority being critical of Japan. However, UK foreign secretary John Simon stressed that, rather than just voicing criticism, an effort needed to be made to reach a compromise. Matsuoka and the Japanese delegation pinned their hopes on the UK effort at appeasement, counting on its mediation to avoid leaving the League.

The extraordinary Assembly session then entrusted the nineteen-member committee with the drafting of a report on settling the Manchurian Incident that would take into consideration the deliberations of the Assembly. In parallel with the committee's work, Foreign Secretary Simon also proposed, based on the League's Covenant (Article 15, paragraph 3) that a "peace committee," which would include non-League members the United States and the Soviet Union, work to mediate the Sino-Japanese conflict. He presented the proposal to Matsudaira Tsuneo and Japan's standing League delegates in mid-December, and they offered their endorsement. However, the government back in Tokyo was concerned about how the United States' uncompromising attitude over such factors as the Nine-Power Treaty would influence such a committee, and so rejected the proposal.

Undeterred, Simon continued his efforts at mediation. In January 1933, he proposed creating a committee that did not include either the United States or the Soviet Union, and then holding direct talks between Japan and China under its oversight.

Senior officials at the Ministry of Foreign Affairs back in Tokyo were still hesitant about accepting the proposal. When the League's nineteen-member committee reconvened in mid-January, China and the minor countries reiterated their criticisms of Japan. The idea of holding direct negotiations between Japan and China guided by a peace committee became impossible. The League's committee likewise gave up on a settlement of the dispute under Article 15, paragraph 3, and leaned instead toward reporting to the Assembly that paragraph 4 ("If the dispute is not thus settled, the Council either unanimously or by a majority vote shall make and publish a report containing a statement of the facts of the dispute and the recommendations which are deemed just and proper in regard thereto") should apply instead.

It seems that Foreign Minister Uchida believed that if Japan showed the League an uncompromising attitude, the League would take steps to remedy the situation, and Japan could expect a favorable outcome through direct negotiations. However, the increasing severity of the Rehe (Jehol) problem delivered a major blow to these prospects.

The Rehe Problem and Withdrawal from the League

Rehe Province was supposed to be part of Manchukuo's territory. However, it was still under the influence of Zhang Xueliang, who sought to destabilize Manchukuo, and was very unstable. Hence, the Kwantung Army decided it would try to gain control over Rehe by force. From China's perspective, Rehe was not one of the three eastern provinces that made up Manchuria; rather, it was Chinese territory. Accordingly, the Nationalist government paid close attention to the Kwantung Army's moves to advance into Rehe.

Mindful of the international repercussions, both the Saitō cabinet and the Japanese army expressed disapproval concerning an attack on Rehe. However, faced with the persistence of the Kwantung Army's push to attack Rehe, the cabinet finally gave its approval in mid-January, on the condition that no troops be sent south of the Great Wall.

7-8. Matsuoka Yōsuke addresses the Assembly of the League of Nations

The problem was the connection between the timing of the Rehe campaign and the deliberations then going on in the League of Nations. It was easy to imagine that if the attack reached as far as Tianjin or Beijing, Japan would be subjected to international criticism, and attitudes toward Japan within the League would be strongly affected. According to Article 16 of the League's Covenant, any member state engaging in conflict with another member state was expected to accept the unanimously approved recommendations from all other members on resolving the conflict. Under Article 16, if the offending state did not accept that recommendation and resorted to acts of war, the League could impose sanctions on the state in question. Accordingly, one could foresee that if Japan resorted to military force in Rehe after the Assembly of the League of Nations had already approved of a proposal for recommendations under Article 16, and if that use of force spilled over into North China, then the League would regard it as a situation that called for sanctions, and would put them into effect.

With the situation becoming tense, the League's nineteen-member committee searched for a way to compromise with Japan, and the Japanese delegation came up with a number of modified drafts aimed at getting around the non-recognition of Manchukuo. However, these efforts, too, reached their limits. In early February, the committee asked for the final approval on whether the report with its core recommendation of Manchurian autonomy under Chinese sovereignty would be accepted. Matsuoka rejected the recommendation in mid-February, with the renewed rebuttal that recognition of Manchukuo was the only solution. With this, the committee then presented its draft recommendations to both Japan and China. The United Kingdom's assiduous efforts at achieving a compromise also finally collapsed. On February 20, the Saitō cabinet decided that if the Assembly of the League of Nations accepted the draft recommendation, then Japan would withdraw from the League. If Japan withdrew, then the legal grounds for accepting sanctions should disappear.

Even with Japanese domestic public opinion leaning heavily toward withdrawal, there were some in the mass media who proposed the option of ignoring the recommendations and remaining in the League. For example, the *Jiji Shinpō*, over a series of articles in the latter part of February, noted that "recommendations were just recommendations." Even in light of the League's Covenant, sanctions were inconceivable, and from a broader perspective there were advantages to remaining in the League. The *Asahi Shimbun* also ran an editorial in its February 18, 1933, edition titled, "The recommendations are not a court verdict." The article went on, "The decision of whether to accept or reject the recommendations is at the discretion of the member state concerned." Even if they were rejected, it argued, that would not necessarily mean the League really would resort to sanctions. Withdrawing from the League because the recommendations were in conflict with Japan's position, it concluded, demonstrated a lack of proper understanding of the nature of the League.

While the acceptance of the draft recommendations by the Assembly of the League of Nations and Japan's withdrawal were not directly linked, the problem was what might happen afterward. Even if Japan had remained a member, once it had carried out its Rehe campaign as already planned, it would have been regarded as resorting to war, and subjected to sanctions by the League for starting a new war. If it withdrew before launching the Rehe campaign, it would also escape sanctions.

On February 24, the League of Nations Assembly Report on the Sino-Japanese Dispute was approved by a 42–1 vote (Japan cast the lone dissenting vote). Matsuoka and the Japanese delegation then walked out of the Assembly, and Japan's withdrawal from the organization became inevitable. And since there was no longer any reason to hold off on the Rehe campaign out of fear of League sanctions, the Kwantung Army began its assault on Rehe in earnest the following day.

The Conquest of Rehe and the Tanggu Truce

The Chinese forces in Rehe were defeated in less than two weeks once the Kwantung Army began its all-out attack. Chiang Kai-shek, who had been leading a campaign to suppress the Communist Party's forces, now deployed a vast force for a defensive battle at the Great Wall. Nonetheless, the Kwantung Army breached the Great Wall and entered into China proper in April 1933. After Imperial Army Headquarters expressed disapproval, the Kwantung Army then temporarily pulled back from the Great Wall, only to break through again in May.

For China, the rout of Zhang Xueliang's army at Rehe was a tremendous shock. However, the outcome of the struggle with the communist forces remained uncertain. Chiang looked to reach an understanding with Japan. Rather than put up a stiff resistance against the Japanese forces pressing on Tianjin and Beijing and see more territory lost, he would yield for now, reach a settlement, and try to recover lost ground in the future.

Thus, at the end of May 1933, Japanese and Chinese military authorities met in Tanggu on the outskirts of Tianjin to sign a cease-fire agreement (the Tanggu Truce). Under the terms of the truce, in exchange for the Kwantung Army pulling back north of the Great Wall, a vast demilitarized zone extending 100 kilometers south of the wall would be created. The two armies pulled out of the demilitarized zone at the start of August. The Great Wall now became the de facto border of Manchukuo, and the area to the south now became a sort of buffer zone. China could not station troops in that area, and a Chinese "Peace Preservation Corps" (security force) was given responsibility for maintaining peace and order there.

After World War II, Okamura Yasuji, who handled negotiations for the Japanese side, spoke about this truce in the context of the foreign conflicts Japan fought from 1931 through 1945. He said, "This was the most crucial border line. It would have been best if we had stopped our aggressive policy toward the outside world around that time." However, Japan was not able to make the choice of strictly observing the truce and dedicating itself to building Manchukuo.

The Strengths and Weaknesses of Diplomacy under Uchida

Foreign Minister Uchida Yasuya resigned his post in September 1933 due to ill health. In later years, many criticized Uchida's diplomatic handling of the Manchurian Incident. Some, for example, held that he moved Japan's recognition of Manchukuo forward too quickly. Ugaki Kazushige criticized him on the basis that Japan recognizing Manchukuo on its own without the other powers worsened international relations. That said, the problem is that Uchida made the move before the Lytton Report was released, and then showed no interest in discussing the settlement recommended in the report. Additionally, in the final stages of diplomatic maneuverings with the League of Nations, he rejected the League's proposal for direct talks between Japan and China under a peace committee, and ignored the solicitous British efforts to keep Japan in the League.

It would appear that Uchida's approach to diplomacy led to Japan's withdrawal from that body, and that Japan had stepped away from its previous focus on international cooperation. But in fact, he was trying to use Japan's potential withdrawal as leverage to restore Japan's foreign relations on the foundation of international cooperation. For example, in February 1933, just prior to Japan's withdrawal, he accepted a US invitation to participate in the London Economic Conference that was to discuss measures to fight the global financial crisis. Furthermore, even after pulling out of the League of Nations, he made no move to withdraw from the World Disarmament Conference, as he recognized the importance of international arms reduction.

In the area of China policy, too, aware of the Chiang regime's desire to placate Japan, Uchida kept trying to come up with proposals to resolve longstanding problems through direct bilateral negotiations. In August 1932, the Saitō cabinet had settled on an approach for handling developing problems that prioritized international relations. Under this approach, the policy on Manchuria and Mongolia affairs was to be handled separately from

Anglo-Japanese Trade Friction

In the aftermath of the Great Depression, Japan recovered from its economic slump before many other major industrial powers, thanks to Takahashi Korekiyo's fiscal policy and a drive to boost exports of cotton and other textile products on the back of a weak yen and low wages. However, Japan's aggressive export strategy also posed a threat to British manufacturers looking to break into foreign markets. The situation led to noticeable Anglo-Japanese trade friction, starting with the problem of restricting exports of cotton products to British India. Japan's push to expand its exports, however, went beyond India, and looked to new markets like South America, the Middle East, and Africa. In the face of these developments, the British cotton industry began calling for restrictions on Japanese exports. In April 1933, the UK government proposed holding private-sector negotiations between leaders of the Japanese and British cotton industries in order to come up with a solution to the trade friction. At the negotiations which began in February 1934, the UK side demanded restrictions on Japanese textile exports across the entire global market, whereas Japan suggested restricting exports solely to the United Kingdom proper and its colonies. With both parties unwilling to compromise, the negotiations broke down.

The UK government responded to the collapse of the private-sector negotiations by making a retaliatory move. In May 1934, the United Kingdom announced that it would be instituting an import quota system. Japan began to formulate a rebuttal based on its right to most-favored-nation treatment, as per the Anglo-Japanese Treaty of Commerce and Navigation, but seeking retribution on legal grounds was not in Japan's best interest. Japan's ambassador to the United Kingdom, Matsudaira Tsuneo, warned that launching into legal arguments would only aggravate the situation. The Ministry of Foreign Affairs thus refrained from opposing the import quota system itself, choosing rather to focus on provisions concerning "equal treatment" as a structural problem.

Perceptions of Japan's export successes began to shift in the mid-1930s. Observers began to recognize that, rather than dumping, the contributing factors were the depreciation of the yen, efficient markets, and the rationalization of production. With that reassessment, the hostility toward Japanese products dissipated.

policy on the main part of China. When it came to China proper, in line with its objective of nurturing the formation of a unified government there, Japan would adhere to the open-door policy and seek to stimulate trade and the market for business based on international cooperation. Maintaining this stance was fundamental to Uchida's own policy. However, the insistence on resolving longstanding problems through direct bilateral negotiations leaned toward obstinacy, as can be seen during Hirota Kōki's years as foreign minister (1933–36), when he refused to allow any third-country mediation on disputes between Japan and China.

This does not mean that Japan was no longer interested in international cooperation in its diplomacy after having withdrawn from the League of Nations; it continued to direct effort toward improving relations with the other powers and above all toward restoring ties with China, and even achieved a certain degree of success in these areas. However, a movement that ran counter to such efforts by Japan's diplomats began to take shape in North China from the middle of 1935. This was the maneuvering undertaken by the local Japanese forces to separate North China from the rest of the country. The machinations by those army units were the underlying cause of developments that in the end would bring about the Marco Polo Bridge Incident (Lugou Bridge Incident).

The London Economic Conference

In June 1933, the League of Nations called a gathering of sixty-four countries to search for ways out of the global depression. The United States and the Soviet Union, both nonmember nations, were also in attendance. Japan's plenipotentiaries were Privy Councillor Ishii Kikujirō, Bank of Japan deputy governor Fukai Eigo, and ambassador to the United Kingdom Matsudaira Tsuneo. The United Kingdom was hoping to settle war-debt issues, outline conditions for restoring the gold standard, and reach a resolution on disarmament. The main focus of the talks, however, was newly elected US president Franklin Roosevelt's stance on the Allies' war debts. The previous US administration had made cooperation with the United Kingdom possible because of the willingness it had shown to write off European nations' debts to the United States. The Roosevelt administration, however, was reluctant to cancel the debt, given the domestic situation, and made war debts, disarmament, and measures to stabilize foreign exchange rates nonnegotiable.

As expected, UK prime minister Ramsay MacDonald (representing the host country) announced in his opening address that the discussions would focus on war debts—and, as expected, Roosevelt did not take up the matter. He went on to strongly criticize the joint declaration that France, Italy, and other gold-standard nations had given on currency stabilization from Washington, DC (June 30). He counterattacked by arguing that the world should be working to expand trade by removing trade barriers rather than focusing on stabilizing exchange rates. In the end, the conference adjourned without a consensus plan for overcoming the depression.

With the United States and the United Kingdom in opposition, Japan gave its full backing to US secretary of state Cordell Hull's proposal for helping global trade recover (starting bilateral talks on eliminating trade barriers and bringing down tariff rates)—a plan that would eventually come into being as the Reciprocal Tariff Act. In trying to overcome the recession, Japan adhered to the concept of increasing the export of low-cost goods by rationalizing production, all based on free trade, and this fit in well with the American position of expanding trade by eliminating trade barriers. Free-trade champion Japan was also keen on the removal of trade barriers to push back against the United Kingdom's protectionist trade policies.

The Reciprocal Tariff Act, which was enacted in June 1934, gave the US president the power to increase or decrease existing trade tariffs by up to 50 percent through bilateral agreements valid for three years. Japan's ambassador to the United States, Saitō Hiroshi, paid a visit to Hull to confirm that the new legislation would do away with protectionist industrial-recovery laws and import restrictions. The meeting, in a broader sense, was also a way to ensure that the free-trade–based partnership between the United States and Japan would endure, although it was diminished after the Second Sino-Japanese War.

Japan Leaves the League of Nations

In March 1933, Japan announced its withdrawal from the League of Nations, and stopped being a member two years later, in March 1935. Subsequently, in accordance with the pre-withdrawal cabinet decision and the associated imperial rescript, it had no involvement with any League initiatives that had political implications. However, it continued to cooperate on peace-oriented, humanitarian, and technical projects.

The vested interest that Japan wanted to maintain via its relationship with the League of Nations was the South Seas Mandate. In the eyes of League member nations, the Japanese mandate over the islands in the South Seas had been a resounding success. With the mandate territory under the supervisory authority of the League of Nations, Japan was concerned that its withdrawal might lead to the loss of the mandate. It therefore sought to remain involved as a "friendly non-member," rather like the United States. Article 22 of the Covenant of the League of Nations did not, in fact, specify requirements for holding a mandate. The South Seas Mandate had actually been granted to Japan not by the League of Nations itself, but rather by the "Principal Allied and Associated Powers." The understanding was that, once in place, the mandate came with a collateral condition under the supervision of the League of Nations. The League of Nations accepted that interpretation of the mandate on Japan's official withdrawal in 1935. Japan thus continued to take part in the Permanent Mandates Commission, submitting annual reports on the administration of the South Sea Islands under Japanese mandate to the Executive Council and sending a government representative to attend the yearly reviews in Geneva.

Japan also attempted to maintain equality among trading partners in the mandate territory. The League of Nations' official regulations stipulated parity of treatment in mandate territories—another provision that Japan's withdrawal theoretically jeopardized. At the time, Japan was committed to free trade and pinning its hopes on the United States' reciprocal trade program as a means of pushing back against the United Kingdom's protectionist policies. The issue was that maintaining equality among trade partners could well turn out to be a problem through its impact on the legal basis of free trade. Even though it had withdrawn from the League of Nations, Japan was mindful of the usefulness of the pro-free trade League, and saw the maintenance of equality among trade partners as an extension of its interpretation of the League Covenant.

In September 1937, shortly after the start of the Second Sino-Japanese War, China made a second formal appeal to the League of Nations to take action against Japan. The League invited Japan to send a representative, but Japan declined. The League went on to sanction Japan under Article 16 of the Covenant, but left the actual implementation of the sanctions up to the individual member nations. Japan did not actually face any sanctions, due to the fact that the members lacked the ability to actually enforce the measures. However, it reached the conclusion that, as long as relations with the League remained antagonistic, maintaining cooperative relations would be "impossible from the perspective of national honor," and cooperating with a League that had become little more than a mouthpiece for China and the Soviet Union would "invite the scorn of the powers." In November 1938, Japan announced that it was severing all ties with the League's organizations.

When Japan discontinued its involvement in the League of Nations, it had government representatives on the organization's Permanent Mandates Commission, the Advisory Committee on Social Questions, and the Advisory Committee on Traffic in Opium and Other Dangerous Drugs. Private (non-government) Japanese members also sat on the Permanent Mandates Commission (Sakenobe Nobumichi) and the International Committee on Intellectual Cooperation (Anesaki Masaharu). There were also private Japanese members taking part in the Far Eastern Epidemiological Intelligence Bureau in Singapore (Ōuchi Tsune, who served as vice-chair), the International Labour Organization, and the Permanent Court of International Justice. Furthermore, Japan had sent representatives to the League-sponsored World Disarmament Conference and London Economic Conference.

CHAPTER 8

The Disruption of International Cooperation and Japan-China Cooperation

8-1. The signing of the Japan-Germany Anti-Comintern Pact

TIMELINE

1933 (Shōwa 8)

January 30 Hitler becomes chancellor of Germany

May 2 Soviet Union proposes sale of North Manchuria Railway (Chinese Eastern Railway) to Japan

June 12 London Economic Conference (through July 27)

September 23 Japan-India Simla trade talks start (end in July 1934, with signing of Japan-India New Trade Agreement)

October 3–20 Five-Minister Conference to coordinate national defense, diplomacy, government finances

October 14 Germany withdraws from League of Nations, Disarmament Conference

1934 (Shōwa 9)

March 22 Japan proclaims exchange of friendly messages between Foreign Minister Hirota Kōki and US secretary of state Cordell Hull

April 17 Foreign Ministry Spokesman Amō Eiji policy proclamation (Amō [Amau] Doctrine)

June 8 Japan, the Netherlands hold negotiations for market liberalization in Dutch East Indies (through December 21)

July 8 Okada Keisuke cabinet formed

September 18 USSR joins League of Nations

October 23 Under the Washington Naval Treaty, US, UK, Japan begin negotiations leading to London Naval Conference

December 29 Japan notifies US of its intention to leave the Washington Naval Treaty

1935 (Shōwa 10)

January 21 Manchukuo reaches agreement with USSR to take ownership of North Manchuria Railway (Chinese Eastern Railway)

February 18 Kikuchi Takeo criticizes Minobe Tatsukichi in the House of Peers

March 23 Manchukuo, USSR sign agreement for transfer of ownership of North Manchuria Railway

May 2 The president and another head of a pro-Japanese news service murdered in Tianjin (Tianjin Incident)

May 4 Shanghai's weekly magazine *Xinsheng* publishes provocative article about Japan's emperor. Japan takes offense and lodges a strong protest; the Chinese government formally apologizes on July 8 and punishes those responsible

May 17 Japan, China promote envoys to ambassadors

June 10 To quell anti-Japanese sentiment, Chinese government orders restrictions on anti-Japan activities

June 18 Tianjin Army demands that Nationalist Party officials withdraw from Hebei Province and that the provincial leader Yu Xuezhong (Yu Hsueh-chung) be dismissed. Chinese side gives oral assent (He-Umezu Agreement)

June 27 Doihara Kenji, head of military intelligence in Mukden, compels China to promise that anti-Japanese forces and Song Zheyuan's army will leave Chahar Province (Chin-Doihara Agreement)

August 1 Chinese Communist Party issues a "Message to All Compatriots on Resistance against Japanese and National Salvation" (August 1 Declaration), calling for the organization of a National United Front to resist Japan

August 12 Nagata Tetsuzan, director-general of the Military Affairs Bureau of Army, assassinated by Kōdōha faction officer (Aizawa Incident)

September 6 Group led by Sir Frederick Leith-Ross, chief economic advisor to UK government, visits Japan

October 4 Hirota puts forward his "Three Principles" decision on China policies (submitted to Chinese side on October 7)

October 15 Chinese economic mission arrives in Japan

November 3 China's treasury announces currency reforms

November 25 Demilitarized zone established south of the Great Wall in the name of the East Hebei Anti-Communist Committee, led by Yin Ju-keng

December 9 Chinese protest the partitioning of northern China (December 9 Movement)

December 9 Second London Naval Conference (through March 25, 1936)

December 18 Start of Hebei-Chahar Political Council, which is to govern Hebei and Chahar from Beijing under chairman Song Zheyuan

December 25 Name of East Hebei Anti-Communist Committee changed to East Hebei Autonomous Government

1936 (Shōwa 11)

January 15 Japan gives notice of withdrawal from London Naval Conference

February 26 February 26 Incident (assassination of Lord Keeper of the Privy Seal Saitō Makoto, Finance Minister Takahashi Korekiyo)

March 9 Hirota Kōki cabinet formed

May 18 *Gunbu daijin geneki bukan-sei* (system allowing only active-duty officers to serve as army and navy ministers in the cabinet) reenacted

June 8 Third round of reforms of "Imperial Defense Policy" and "General Operation Plans"

June 8 UK group led by Leith-Ross visits Japan again

July 17 Outbreak of Spanish Civil War

August 1 Berlin Olympics begin

August 7 Five-Minister Conference decides Fundamentals of National Policies

August 24 Japanese reporters killed in Szechuan (resolved December 30 by official Chinese government apology)

September 3 Pakhoi Incident in Guangdong Province (resolved December 30 by official Chinese government apology)

September 15 Kawagoe-Chiang Qun talks begin (broken off December 3)

November 14 Inner Mongolian Army, with support from Kwantung Army, engages Chinese Army in battle in Suiyuan (Suiyuan Campaign)

November 25 Japan-Germany Anti-Comintern Pact signed in Berlin

December 12 Zhang Xueliang and associates detain Chiang Kai-shek (Xi'an Incident)

December 26 Trade friction between Japan and Australia leads to signing of interim agreement (followed by second interim agreement in July 1938, which remains in place until war between the United Kingdom and Japan breaks out in December 1941)

December 31 Washington, London naval treaties fail, starting era of absence of naval treaties

1937 (Shōwa 12)

February 2 Hayashi Senjūrō cabinet formed

March 15 Economic group led by Kodama Kenji (head of Yokohama Specie Bank, Ltd.) visits China

April 9 Japan, the Netherlands sign Hart-Ishizawa Agreement

June 4 First Konoe Fumimaro cabinet formed

1 The Era of Hirota Diplomacy

Hirota Diplomacy and the Army

In September 1933 (Shōwa 8), Hirota Kōki became foreign minister in the cabinet of Prime Minister Saitō Makoto, succeeding Uchida Yasuya (Kōsai) in that post. Hirota was to remain foreign minister in the cabinet of Okada Keisuke until March 1936, following the February 26 Incident, when he became prime minister. Important support for Hirota's style of diplomacy came from his vice-minister, Shigemitsu Mamoru. Particularly when it came to China policy, Shigemitsu played the lead role; some, in fact, went so far as to equate Hirota with Shigemitsu. One major issue faced by Hirota was how to rein in the power and influence of the army, which had increased in the wake of the 1931 Manchurian Incident.

At that time, the army was controlled by the Kōdōha (Imperial Way Faction). Araki Sadao, who was army minister under Prime Minister Inukai Tsuyoshi, used various personnel changes to install officers loyal to the Kōdōha and solidify his sway over the General Staff Office and the Army Ministry. The Kōdōha espoused radical reforms that were mainly anti-Soviet and anti-Communist in nature. One might think that this would result in a hard-line foreign policy, but that was not the case. Apart from their harsh opposition to the USSR, they seemed to avoid grappling deeply with any problems in Japan-China relations for fear of disrupting the governance of Manchukuo, and they strove to stay on an even keel with the United Kingdom and the United States. In terms of external policy, the Kōdōha formed the foundation of Hirota diplomacy.

In October 1933, the Saitō cabinet convened five meetings of the Five Ministers' Conference (the five ministers included the prime minister and the ministers of the army, the navy, foreign affairs, and finance). These sessions were intended to decide basic guidelines and achieve mutual coordination on matters of national defense, diplomacy, and domestic affairs. By tradition, the army had been oriented toward expansion to the north on the Asian mainland, and so it lobbied to focus on the threat posed by the Soviet Union and the need to strengthen Japan's defenses against that threat. The navy, in contrast, was oriented toward the south, toward the sea. It pushed back against the army, and stressed the need to maintain a hard line against the United States. On the importance of restoring amicable relations with the United Kingdom and the United States, however, the navy agreed with the rest of the government. In the end, the Five Ministers' Conference agreed to pursue moderate policies, focusing on restoring external relations based on collaboration among nations and on building up the nation's defenses while paying heed to government finances.

Then, in 1934, Araki and Vice-Minister of the Army Yanagawa Heisuke resigned their posts, weakening the power of the Kōdōha. This allowed Reserve General Ugaki Kazushige and a group of moderates to take control of the army. At the center of this was Major General Nagata Tetsuzan, who in March 1934 had been promoted to director-general of military affairs within the Army Ministry. In July 1934, the Saitō cabinet was dissolved as a result of the Teijin Incident, a corruption scandal. Admiral Okada Keisuke, who had been Saitō's minister of the navy, formed a new cabinet and took office as prime minister. Hirota stayed on as minister for foreign affairs. Control of the army was a significant issue facing the Okada cabinet, but Okada placed his hopes in Major General Nagata, who was the Military Affairs Bureau director-general, Army Minister Hayashi Senjūrō, and other middle-ranking officers.

The Purchase of the North Manchuria Railway

The Five Ministers' Conference set about getting everyone on board for creating a "good neighbor policy" with the Soviet Union. After the establishment of Manchukuo, one significant issue that remained between Japan and the Soviet Union was the purchase of the North Manchuria Railway (Chinese Eastern Railway). Shortly after Manchukuo was established, the Soviet Union had agreed that the Manchukuo government should take over the rights to the North Manchuria Railway, and that the two countries would handle management of the railway jointly. However, because the Manchukuo government had cut off transport at both ends of the railway, the economic and strategic value to the Soviet Union was greatly diminished, and in May 1933 it decided to sell its interests.

Negotiations began in late June 1933, with Japan acting as mediator. The main difficulty lay in deciding the purchase price, but after a long, arduous process, Manchukuo and the Soviet Union arrived at an agreement in March 1935. The Soviet Union recognized Japan's effective control over Manchuria, and it made efforts to stabilize relations with Japan, but tensions between the two continued because of a series of imbroglios along the border between the Soviet Union and Manchukuo.

Around the same time in 1933, the Soviet Union reestablished diplomatic relations with the United States, enhancing its status within the community of nations. It also built up its military presence in the Far East, greatly enhancing its ability to limit Japan's diplomatic actions.

Stabilization of Japan-China Relations: The Amō (Amau) Doctrine

At the outset of Hirota diplomacy, the state of affairs in North China was fluid. After signing the Tanggu Truce, the Nationalist government and Manchukuo opened the way toward restoration of stable relations, starting with the areas of postal delivery, transport, and customs. Leaving these negotiations up to the Kwantung Army, Hirota diplomacy strove to achieve stable relations with China through cooperation with the administration of Chiang Kai-shek, which was intent on appeasing Japan. To further stabilize relations, what was needed was the restoration of trade, which had fallen off sharply since the Manchurian Incident.

In mid-April 1934, Minister Ariyoshi Akira and Wang Zhaoming reached an agreement on Japan-China "co-prosperity," and pledged to work to put the Manchuria problem behind them in the interest of improving bilateral relations. Wang expressed confidence in the outcome, and Ariyoshi promised to report to the foreign minister and seek his consideration. Just as it seemed that bilateral relations were set to improve for the first time since the cessation of hostilities agreement the year before, the problem of the Amō Doctrine arose.

In late-April, Amō Eiji, who was spokesman for the Ministry of Foreign Affairs, made the following statement at a regular press conference: "It is Japan's duty to maintain peace and order in East Asia, and Japan must bear responsibility for doing so. Any act of joint aid to China by any country—whether of a financial or technical nature—would necessarily carry a political meaning, and we would have to oppose it."

These statements by Amō, which were widely publicized both within and outside Japan, came to be known as the "Amō Doctrine," but in fact, they were based on a diplomatic address given by Hirota in January of that year. The idea that Japan-China issues should be resolved directly between the two nations, without the intervention of third countries, had been expressed repeatedly at the League of Nations during Foreign Minister Uchida's time. Joseph Grew, the US ambassador to Japan, said the Amō Doctrine "expresses policies that Japan clearly wants to carry out." The prevalent view was that the

Amō Doctrine was intended to support the "pro-Japan" elements of the Chinese Nationalist government while keeping the "pro-Western" elements, which depended on assistance from the United States, the United Kingdom, and the League of Nations, in check.

Outside Japan, the Amō Doctrine was regarded—and feared—as a "Monroe Doctrine for East Asia." The Amō Doctrine was intended to warn against the League of Nations' plans to assist China, and it was met with opposition from League headquarters in Geneva. However, the League of Nations remained consistent in its policy of cool non-intervention in Japan-China problems. Major countries accepted Foreign Minister Hirota's view that the policy put priority on the principles of open markets and equality of opportunity.

The Problem of Withdrawal from Disarmament Agreements

Another issue for Hirota diplomacy, on a par with the China problem, was that of Japan's withdrawal from naval disarmament treaties. Both the Washington Naval Treaty and the London Naval Treaty were set to end in 1936, and so around 1933 the major nations of the world began to reassess the state of their naval strength. Following Japan's withdrawal from the League of Nations in March 1933, Nazi Germany also withdrew from the Geneva Disarmament Conference and the League of Nations in October, asserting its equal rights to militarization. This greatly upset the tide of international cooperation.

After the London Naval Treaty ended, changes were made to Japan's Navy General Staff regulations

Hirota Kōki (1878–1948)

The shock of the Tripartite Intervention led young Hirota Kōki, a native of Fukuoka Prefecture, to abandon his military ambitions and instead pursue a diplomatic career. He completed his studies at Shūyūkan (a leading prefectural school), the First Higher School, and then Tokyo Imperial University. While in school, Hirota enjoyed the favor of fellow Fukuoka native Yamaza Enjirō (then the director-general of the Political Affairs Bureau at the Ministry of Foreign Affairs) and married the second-eldest daughter of a prominent figure in the Gen'yōsha, which had provided Hirota with support. In 1906, Hirota passed the foreign-service examination and entered service in a recruiting class that included the likes of Yoshida Shigeru and Hayashi Kyūjirō. Upon joining the Ministry of Foreign Affairs, he served posts in Qing China, the United Kingdom, and the United States; accompanied Japan's delegation to the Paris Peace Conference; and, during his time in Paris, was active in a movement to spur reforms at the Ministry of Foreign Affairs. Hirota eventually became the director-general of the ministry's Europe and America Bureau in 1923; in that role, he teamed with Tōgō Shigenori (then the director of the bureau's First Division) on the marathon negotiations surrounding the restoration of diplomatic relations between Japan and the Soviet Union. After a stint as Japan's minister to the Netherlands came Hirota's 1930 appointment as ambassador to the USSR, where he oversaw Japan's diplomatic approach to the Soviet Union in the events surrounding the Manchurian Incident. Hirota's time in the Soviet Union brought frustrations with Foreign Minister Shidehara Kijūrō, who tended to stick to principle-based directives without fully accounting for developments within the Kwantung Army ranks on the ground.

8-2. Hirota Kōki

Hirota returned to Japan in October 1932, after Manchukuo had officially secured recognition as an independent state, and replaced Uchida Yasuya (Kōsai) as foreign minister in the Saitō Makoto administration the following year. Hirota took the position on one condition: that Japan's diplomacy would conform to the imperial rescript concerning the country's withdrawal from the League of Nations. That meant first ensuring the recognition of Manchukuo as its own state and then pursuing a "harmony among all nations" in which Japan would promote "mutual confidence" without standing "aloof in the Extreme Orient" or "isolating itself . . . from the fraternity of nations." Hirota's chief concern was dealing with the adverse diplomatic and other rules, and the military command structure (Navy General Staff Office) came to supersede the military administration (Navy Ministry). The military hard-liners in power were known as the "Fleet Faction." Their aim was to establish military autonomy for Japan, unrestrained by treaties, and this objective was reflected in their policies regarding disarmament conferences.

The navy's disarmament policy focused mainly on the idea of establishing equality of military power by abandoning the relative ratios (i.e., allowing Japan 70 percent of the power of the United States or the United Kingdom) in favor of limitations on total tonnage, as well as ending limitations on specific ship categories. Abandonment of the relative ratios and establishment of military equality had been a core desire for the navy since the 1907 establishment of the Imperial Defense Policy. This abrupt call for parity was a major change, showing that withdrawal from existing disarmament treaties had been Japan's plan all along.

To justify its position, the navy published frequent pamphlets, starting in about 1933, insisting that under the existing treaties, the gap in the number of naval vessels between Japan, the United States and the United Kingdom would reach its highest number from 1935 to 1936. This would imperil national security, so it was imperative to build up naval strength. The navy dubbed this impending situation "The Crisis of 1935–36." The army took a competing view, highlighting instead the threat posed by the Soviet Union. In 1933–34, senior military officials from the Kōdōha and the Fleet Faction published articles that can now be found in *Hijōji kokumin zenshū* (Complete works of the people from the time of emergency), published

fallout of the Manchurian Incident—and mending fences with China was the most urgent task at hand. A vital force on that front of Hirota's foreign-affairs efforts was his vice-minister, Shigemitsu Mamoru.

Hirota's efforts to improve Japan's relations were successful in some respects. Adopting a conciliatory diplomatic approach that focused on supporting the pro-Japanese faction within China's Nationalist government, Hirota worked to build a foundation for amity with China by easing tensions and forging a strong economic partnership between the two countries. However, Hirota's failure to take decisive action in stamping out local military forces' maneuvers to create a North China "buffer state" from mid-1935 onward ended up making Japan's exclusionary influence in North China even stronger and fueling distrust on the Chinese side.

After stepping down from the foreign-minister position as a result of the February 26 Incident, Hirota received an imperial command to be Japan's prime minister in early March 1936 and offered the foreign-minister position to Yoshida Shigeru. He encountered some challenges in forming his cabinet, however; Terauchi Hisaichi, Hirota's pick for army minister, turned down the post on the grounds that the would-be foreign minister had overly "liberal overtones." Hirota found himself facing a tough decision: either abort his administration altogether or compromise with the army. Hirota ultimately chose the latter option, pandering to army demands by naming Arita Hachirō foreign minister and setting out a policy line of "complete political overhaul." The "overhaul" was an objective that not only meant expanding the army's political influence but also signified a willingness to welcome compromise instead of conflict with the military. In that sense, Hirota aligned more with Arita and Shigemitsu than with "liberalists" like Yoshida and Shidehara.

Although internal strife prompted the Hirota cabinet to resign en masse in February 1937, Hirota was back in the foreign minister's seat that June as part of Konoe Fumimaro's first administration. With Japan in a celebratory mood due to the patriotic momentum stemming from the onset of the Second Sino-Japanese War and then the fall of Nanjing late in the year, Hirota's insistence on stringent conditions on peace during the ongoing Trautmann mediation brought the peace process to a stalemate.

After the Second World War, the US Occupation authorities brought war-crime charges against Hirota. In the end, he was the only civilian to receive a death sentence at the Tokyo Trials. One of the charges that proved to be most damning was that Hirota knew full well of the Nanjing Massacre but failed to take any official measures in response. Not once during the entire trial did Hirota even attempt to offer a defense or explain his actions; instead, he accepted the fate of his execution.

by Chūō Kōron. The army generals wrote passionately about the threat of the Soviet Union, while the navy admirals were equally fervent about the need to address the "crisis of 1935–36."

Prior talks in London between the United States and the United Kingdom began in June 1934, followed by preliminary negotiations with Japan in October. Japan was represented by ambassador to the United Kingdom Matsudaira Tsuneo and Rear Admiral Yamamoto Isoroku. Japan made two main arguments based on abandonment of the relative ratios: Firstly, that it would be preferable to set the same ceiling for all nations' military power; and secondly, that Japan wished to renounce the Washington Naval Treaty because it was clearly not advantageous to Japan. Some officials of the Ministry of Foreign Affairs and the army spoke up in favor of continuing the disarmament treaties because they had helped to maintain the balance of security systems in the Pacific Ocean. They expressed the hope that some mechanism would be devised to replace the Washington Naval Treaty (such as the trilateral non-aggression pact, discussed below).

The United States, as the main backer of the Washington System, hoped for the continuation of the Washington Naval Treaty, which was a key constituent element of that system. It called for continuation of the treaty and uniform 20 percent reductions. The United Kingdom, for its part, expressed resistance to the idea of scrapping the Washington Naval Treaty before some alternative mechanism could be decided, and opposed setting uniform ceilings for all participants.

Faced with halting progress, Foreign Secretary John Simon of the United Kingdom, as the chair, recognized the principle of equal rights for each nation and proposed that each country provide a self-assessment of its current military strength. Japan opposed this idea because it was based on the existing treaty's standards of military power. At the end of December 1934, Japan unilaterally notified the United States that the preliminary negotiations had failed, and announced that it would leave the Washington Treaty. When the United States and Japan met in late October, Matsudaira said the disarmament issue was "not necessarily a problem of fact, but a problem of Japanese people's emotions. If that passion can be satisfied, people will settle down." This statement demonstrates how much influence the feelings of the Japanese people had on the disarmament problem.

In December 1935, based on the terms of the Washington and London Naval Treaties, the United Kingdom convened negotiations that included Japan, the United States, France, and Italy. Japan sent Admiral Nagano Osami and Ambassador Nagai Matsuzō, but the meeting was nothing more than a repeat of the previous year's preliminary negotiations, and the three participant nations were unable to break their deadlock. In January 1936, Japan withdrew from the arms reduction conference. As a result, both the Washington Naval Treaty and the London Naval Treaty ended at the end of 1936, and Japan entered a period where it was unfettered by disarmament treaties.

Limits of Policy Coordination with the United States and the United Kingdom

In parallel with the disarmament talks, the idea arose of a tripartite non-aggression pact between Japan, the United Kingdom, and the United States. Foreign Minister Hirota and British ambassador to Japan Robert Clive held a meeting in July 1934 in which Hirota proposed a trilateral non-aggression pact that would include the United States. One aim of Hirota's proposal was to convey to the United States and the United Kingdom that Japan had no aggressive intentions. Another was to offer an alternative instrument for coordination with the United States and the United Kingdom in the wake of the collapse of the Washington Naval Treaty.

The United Kingdom took a positive view of the idea of a non-aggression pact, but the United States opposed the idea of an agreement that would include only a specified group of countries. For the United States, as the prime advocate of the Washington System, no non-aggression pact could substitute for the Washington Naval Treaty. Ever since the Manchurian Incident, the United States had been disinclined to meddle in East Asian political affairs. With the exception of the unofficial Hirota-Hull exchange of messages in March 1934, the United States exhibited little interest in Japan's activities.

For Japan and the United Kingdom, the Hirota-Clive dialogue was the starting point for a series of informal talks, but the United States did not participate. The talks did not focus on mutual non-aggression, but merely on the extension of the Four-Power Treaty established by the Washington Conference. In the end, no agreement was reached.

Japan and China: Friendly Relations, Economic Cooperation

For the Chinese Nationalist government, 1935 was the year when the threat from the Chinese Red Army was the weakest. The year before, the Nationalists had succeeded in a campaign to surround the Communists. The Red Army lost control of the city of Ruijin, the birthplace of the revolution, and was forced to take the Long March. Given these circumstances in China, the first half of 1935 was a time of exceptional friendliness between China and Japan. In December the previous year, Chiang Kai-shek had published an article entitled "Friend or Foe?" in the Nationalist-government-aligned journal *Waijiao pinlun* (Diplomatic review), in which he wrote that the Japanese people were ultimately not enemies of China. He suggested that direct, bilateral negotiations to resolve outstanding issues should be possible, and that Japan and China needed to work together. Foreign Minister Hirota, in an address at the end of January, floated a policy of "non-menace and non-aggression" with respect to China. Hirota went on to say, "I am confident

Fundamentals of National Policy

Changes in the military environment after the Manchurian Incident forced Japan to revise the Imperial Defense Policy that had been in place since 1907. One of the main factors prompting the amendment was the Soviet Union, whose moves had started to worry Japan. The military environment had changed for both the Japanese army and navy. The army was at a major disadvantage in terms of military balance vis-à-vis the Soviet Union in the Far East. The navy, on the other hand, was no longer part of the Washington Naval Treaty; it thus entered a "treaty-less" situation (where there would be no treaties binding naval action involving Japan) in 1936, making a strategic review necessary. The government overhauled its Imperial Defense Policy in June 1936, putting the Soviet Union alongside the United States as Japan's most likely war adversary ahead of the United Kingdom and China.

Meanwhile, since late 1935, army and navy leaders had been clashing over how to integrate Japan's national policy. Ishiwara Kanji, the director of the Army General Staff's Military Operations Division, advocated focusing on defenses against the Soviet Union. "We do not believe that Japan should divert any of its national strength away from Manchuria over the next decade," he argued, "so any plans to advance to the south should wait." On the other hand, the navy championed a national policy proposal that would involve "defending the north and advancing to the south" in order to sustain an "expansion in naval armaments" with a treaty-less future looming. The army and navy eventually came to a compromise: a core national policy under which Japan would "both secure a foothold for the empire on the East Asian continent and advance into the southern seas." That was the crux of the "Principles of National Policy," which the Five-Minister Conference made official as the "Fundamantals of National Policy" in August 1936. While the Fundamantals of National Policy became a focal point of the International Military Tribunal for the Far East, where the prosecution cited the policy to show that Japan had clearly been aiming to conquer East Asia, the document was less a grand scheme than it was a budgeting compromise between the army's continental approach and the navy's sea strategy.

there will definitely be no war during my tenure in office."

In February 1935, the Nationalist government issued an order barring newspapers throughout the country from printing anti-Japanese discourse. Then, in March, it forbade educational authorities in all cities and provinces to use anti-Japanese textbooks. In June, the Nationalist government promulgated an order for cordial relations with Japan and banned anti-Japanese groups. In May, the two nations elevated their legations to embassies, underscoring the steady change in the Nationalist government's attitude toward Japan. The mutual decision to exchange ambassadors had been made in 1924, but it had never been carried out. Japan's first ambassador to Nationalist China was Ariyoshi Akira; Nationalist China's first ambassador to Japan was Chiang Tso-pin (Jiang Zuobin).

In October 1935, a group of fifteen Chinese businesspeople visited Japan. An agreement was reached with economic organizations in Japan to establish standing business representative offices in each country, the objective being to realize equal economic cooperation between the two countries. Based on this agreement, in January 1936 the Japan-China Trade Association was set up in Tokyo, and the China-Japan Trade Association was established in Shanghai. Kodama Kenji was chairman of the former and vice-chairman of the latter, and Chow Tso-ming (Zhou Zuomin) was chairman of the latter and vice-chairman of the former.

2 Crisis in North China: 1935

The He-Umezu Agreement

In northern China, the Tanggu Truce established a demilitarized zone, but still there were repeated skirmishes along the Great Wall area between the Kwantung Army and an anti-Japanese militia led by General Sun Yong-qin calling itself the Northeast Volunteers. In mid-May 1935, the Kwantung Army, believing Sun had the support of Hebei Province chairman Yu Hsueh-chung (Yu Xuezhong), crossed the Great Wall and entered Hebei to attack Sun. This incident followed another earlier in May, in which two heads of the pro-Japanese news service had been killed in the Japanese settlement in Tianjin. In response to these incidents, the Tianjin Army, led by Chief of Staff Sakai Takashi, made a complaint to the Chinese authorities (acting chairman of the Peiping National Military Council He Yingqin) alleging that the cease-fire agreement had been violated. The Tianjin Army (officially the China Garrison) was the Japanese military force stationed in Beijing and Tianjin based on rights acquired following the 1901 Boxer Rebellion. Sakai demanded that anti-Japanese actors be dealt with sternly, that Yu Hsueh-chung be dismissed, and that Kuomintang (Nationalist Party) officials, military police, and the Blue Shirts Society and other anti-Japanese elements be driven out of Hebei Province.

At the end of May the Nationalist government, through Ambassador Chiang Tso-pin (Jiang Zuobin), appealed to Foreign Minister Hirota Kōki to intercede. Hirota turned down this request, however, saying military withdrawal was outside the purview of diplomatic negotiations, being a matter for the high command. In early June, the Tianjin Army gave the Nationalist government an ultimatum. On June 18, He Yingqin responded orally to the Japan embassy military attaché, Takahashi Tan. This what is known as the He-Umezu Agreement. There is no written statement of the Chinese response, only an acknowledgement of receipt (dated July 6) addressed to Umezu Yoshijirō, commander of the Tianjin Army. While China carried out the stipulations of the agreement, it maintained that it did so not because of Japan's demands, but for its own reasons.

As these negotiations were taking place, Army Minister Hayashi Senjūrō and Major General Nagata Tetsuzan of the Army Ministry visited Manchuria. Through the Kwantung Army, Hayashi knew of the Tianjin Army's demands. He recognized that the details and the methods of the negotiations were problematic, but he telegraphed Tokyo to insist that the Kwantung Army support the Tianjin Army to achieve its demands. His June 3 message states, "If the arrow has already been loosed from the bow, the central government (of Japan) should support the decision." Hayashi and Nagata, who were central figures in the army, were quick to support the actions of the Tianjin Army, and established a mutual understanding between the central command and the Kwantung Army to remove the power and influence of the Nationalist government from northern China.

The Chin-Doihara Agreement

As a matter of practical fact, the He-Umezu Agreement extended the Tanggu Truce to all of Hebei Province and forced Yu Hsueh-chung (Yu Xuezhong) and the Nationalist army to leave. This sequence of events was followed by the North Chahar Incident, in which soldiers under the command of Song Zheyuan, governor of Chahar Province, briefly detained undercover military agents of the Kwantung Army. The Kwantung Army had been striving to drive Song's forces out of Chahar Province in an effort to solidify its control of the borders of Manchukuo, as part of its plans for the Inner Mongolia Autonomous Region. In response to the North Chahar Incident, Major General Doihara Kenji, head of the military intelligence organ in Mukden, began negotiations on behalf of the Kwantung Army with Song's representative Qin Dechun (Chin Techun); the result was the Chin-Doihara Agreement, reached on June 27, 1935. The agreement included punishment for those responsible for the North Chahar

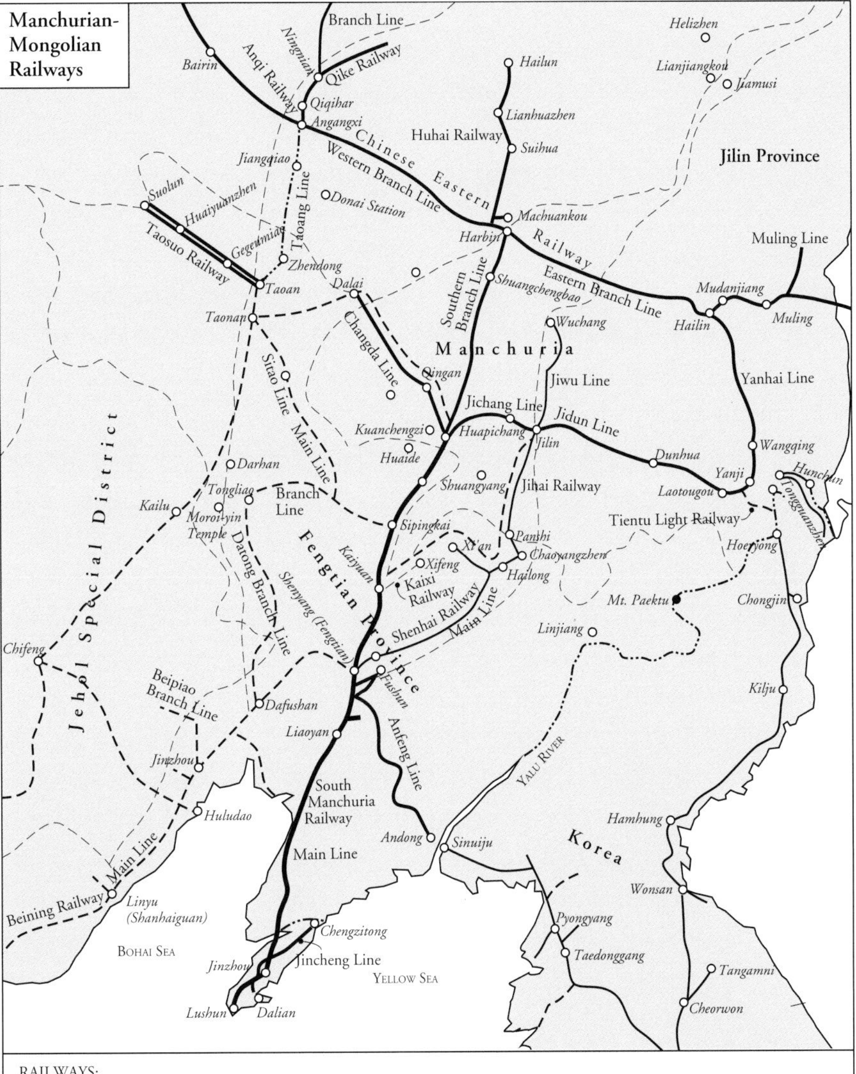

8-3. The railway system in Northern Manchuria and Mongolia

Incident, as well as a promise to expel Song's troops and anti-Japanese groups from Chahar Province. Song and his troops moved to Hebei Province. The Kwantung Army had hoped to persuade Song to take a friendly stance toward Japan, but such hopes were in vain. In fact, the Marco Polo Bridge Incident of 1937 was rooted in a clash between Song's troops and the Japanese army.

After these two agreements were reached, local troops, calling themselves the "North China Autonomous Movement," began a political and economic separation of North China—which bordered on Manchukuo—from the main Chinese territory, and they set about eliminating the power and influence of the Nationalist government. This came to be known as the "North China Buffer State Policy" (at the time, it was also known as the "North China Autonomous Movement"). As in Manchukuo, persuasion and threats were used to lead prominent Chinese citizens to disavow the Nationalist government and promote the declaration of autonomy. The aim of this policy was to turn the five northernmost provinces of China—with a combined area greater than the Japanese archipelago—into states like Manchukuo. The Ministry of Foreign Affairs wanted to build stable relations with the Nationalist government, which sought a unified China, but local Japanese army units believed the true intentions of the Nationalist government were "anti-Japanese." For the defense of Manchukuo, and to carry out their Soviet strategy, they sought to minimize the Nationalists' power and influence in North China. Unlike the process of building Manchukuo, however, the North China Policy did not proceed so smoothly. Instead, it was met with increasingly vehement resistance from Chinese nationalism.

Hirota's Three Principles

In October 1935, Hirota grew alarmed at how the North China Buffer State Policy was unfolding, and he devised, as a consensus among his colleagues in the cabinet, a new set of policies regarding China that came to be known as Hirota's Three Principles. In essence, they were three demands on China: First, zero tolerance for anti-Japanese words or actions in China; second, recognition of Manchukuo's independence (if possible, formal recognition); and third, cooperation in eliminating the threat posed by Communist forces (joint anti-Communism). In attached documents, Hirota said Japan would not strive to either assist or deter the unification or break-up of China; these stipulations were appended to keep the army in North China in check.

Hirota, having noticed Chiang Kai-shek's anti-Communism, basically reformulated long-standing Japanese demands in his Three Principles, adding a demand that China work with Japan against the Communists. Within the Three Principles was a demand for tacit recognition of Manchukuo by China, and a prioritization of "anti-Communism" as a shared goal as part of the North China policy. The Japanese troops in China, for their part, would make greater efforts to police their own behavior.

In early October, Hirota conveyed these goals to Ambassador Chiang Tso-pin (Jiang Zuobin) and asked for dialogue. The Chinese side had already, in September, communicated its own ideas for Three Principles (mutual respect for complete autonomy, maintenance of true amicable relations, and peaceful resolution of disputes) through Ambassador Chiang. Consequently, while Hirota's Three Principles were perhaps meant to be a response to the Chinese side's proposals, they ended up as a one-sided expression of Japan's aims, failing to touch upon the ideas of respect for mutual autonomy or peaceful resolution of disputes. The negotiations did not make much headway, as each side stuck to its own position and refused to yield.

While Japan stressed the common goal of anti-Communism, in fact China had already begun to seek rapprochement with the Soviet Union, and did not respond to Japan's overtures. Given the expanding threat posed in East Asia by the Soviet Union at that time, the Japanese side frequently brought up the ideology of anti-Communism in discussions of Japan-China cooperation.

General Nagata's assassination in mid-August by a member of the Kōdōha was a serious setback for Hirota's diplomatic policies. Nagata had been an advocate for greater restraint by Japan's military forces in China, and his death meant greater license for the military.

Leith-Ross Visit to East Asia: Seeking Avenues for Japan-UK Cooperation

The Nationalist government of the Republic of China faced an imminent economic crisis that threatened its political foundations. In 1934, the United States bought up a great deal of silver, causing a vast quantity of the precious metal to flow out of China. This was an unprecedented predicament for the Republic of China, as its monetary system and government finances were based on silver. The United Kingdom offered to help China out of this predicament, seeing the value in securing the stability of the Chinese market in the interests of its own industry.

Central to the UK's assistance to China were currency reform and loans to support it. The UK's aim, above all, was to stabilize the currency through modern management, by forcing China to end its silver standard and reestablish its currency on the basis of paper notes issued by the reorganized central bank. Additionally, from the perspective of Japan-UK cooperation, the financing was connected to the Manchukuo problem. Manchukuo benefited from a 10-million-pound loan backed jointly by Japan and the United Kingdom. That sum was, in fact, paid to China as compensation for its "Manchuria losses." Japan-UK cooperation was based on two main tenets: de facto recognition of Manchukuo and effective support for the Republic of China. This being the case, the United Kingdom dispatched the government's chief economic advisor, Frederick Leith-Ross, to visit China and Japan in June 1935.

When Leith-Ross arrived in Yokohama early in September 1935, he held lively discussions with his Japanese counterparts, conveying the message that currency reform, jointly backed by Japan and the United Kingdom, would be vital for China's financial reconstruction. He stressed that the United Kingdom was prepared to extend de facto recognition to Manchukuo. However, Japan's response was tepid. Hirota and Shigemitsu Mamoru responded to Leith-Ross's proposal by pointing out that if Japan and the United Kingdom were to provide financing, they would effectively control China. They argued it would be better for China to stand on its own, without help from other nations. The Manchukuo problem, they said, was a matter for resolution through bilateral negotiations between Japan and China.

It was difficult for Japan to consider Leith-Ross's proposals because the country was reaching the structural limits of its economy. Japan was faced with both a worsening current-account balance and a growing burden of investment in Manchukuo. It had little in reserve for additional financing for China.

At the end of his visit, Leith-Ross made a request the Japan side had not anticipated: he wished to deliver personally, to the emperor, a letter from the king of England communicating the importance of his role and asking for the emperor's understanding and cooperation.

When Leith-Ross went on to China, he worked with the Nationalist government on currency reform, largely in line with the details envisioned by the Nationalist government. With the United Kingdom pushing matters, on November 4 the Nationalist government acted decisively on the reform process. The main points of the currency reform were the abandonment of the silver standard and a transition to a managed currency. Silver could be held only by the national government, and only three banks would be allowed to issue currency. The United Kingdom did not actually provide its own financial backing, but in an effort to make the reform succeed, it did provide for a transfer of silver to China by British banks. The United States reached an agreement with China on the purchase of silver and assisted China in abandoning the silver standard.

The overwhelming majority of observers within financial and business circles in Japan expected the new currency regime to collapse quickly. Very few people expected it to succeed. But China's currency reform proved to be a success, providing undergirding economic support for national unification.

Radical Changes in North China Policy

For Japanese forces on the China mainland, the success of currency reform was a development that could not be overlooked. There was apprehension that the United Kingdom, which had supported the reform, would expand its power and influence, and that the foundations of the Nationalist government would be solidified. The Kwantung Army and the Tianjin Army pushed hard for their North China Policy, pressuring Song Zheyuan and other North China leaders to obstruct the currency reform and work to separate the economy of North China from the Nationalist government.

The North China Policy of the Kwantung Army, and particularly the Mukden secret military intelligence, made rapid progress, and in late November 1935 Yin Ju-keng (Yin Rukeng) formed the East Hebei Anti-Communist Committee. (This entity, whose territory included the demilitarized zone, was later reorganized as the East Hebei Autonomous Government). However, this did not serve to aid the cause of the North China Policy. On the contrary, it provoked a response from the China side.

Early in December, in Beijing, thousands of students opposed to the separation of North China demonstrated under slogans like "Oppose Japan, Save the Nation!" They clashed with police, and a wave of demonstrations spread throughout the land (December 9 Movement). Later in December, the Nationalist government preempted a move by Japan by setting up the Hebei-Chahar Political Council (Hebei-Chahar government), chaired by Song Zheyuan. Song had no direct connection to the Kuomintang, but he was an influential person who was being pressured by the Japanese army to establish an autonomous government. The Nationalist government decided to back him in hopes of constraining Japan's North China policy. The Japanese army wanted to combine the East Hebei and Hebei-Chahar governments into a more powerful political entity, but this effort failed in the face of Nationalist resistance.

The Nationalist government demanded repeatedly that Japan rein in its separation policy. Foreign Minister Hirota, while urging Japanese troops to curb their reckless behavior, regarded this as a matter of internal affairs and condoned North China's autonomy.

In the fall of 1935, the rapid progress of Japan's North China Policy diminished the power and influence of the pro-Japanese faction of the Chinese Nationalist government. Huang Fu, the effective leader of North China and a central figure in negotiations with the Japan side, resigned his post. In early November, Wang Zhaoming was gravely wounded in an attack by unknown persons, and had to resign his positions as president of the Executive Yuan and foreign minister. In December, Tang Youren, deputy foreign minister in charge of relations with Japan, was assassinated. Hirota sought to stabilize relations with China by working with the pro-Japan faction, but he lost the cooperation of some powerful people in China. By the end of the year, efforts to renegotiate the relationship based on his Three Principles came to a halt.

Chiang Kai-shek, who took over from Wang Zhaoming as president of the Executive Yuan, was still a proponent of placating Japan. Inside China,

Japanese diplomats like Ambassador Ariyoshi Akira, Nanjing consul general Suma Yakichirō, and Shanghai consul general Ishii Itarō were grasping for ways to build good relations and achieve compromise with the successors of Tang and Huang.

3 Japan's Final Negotiations with China: 1936

The Hirota Cabinet and the February 26 Incident

In the February 26 Incident of 1936, a group of young officers attempted a coup d'état, momentarily paralyzing the government and bringing diplomatic activity to a halt. General elections had been held shortly before this incident. The Minseitō and the Shakai Taishūtō (Social Mass Party), which were both critical of the extremist Kōdōha faction of the army, advanced in the polls, adding to the pressure on the Kōdōha and leading to predictions that a party cabinet would be restored. One aim of the February coup may have been to solidify the Kōdōha's grip on power and prevent a revival of party politics.

While Prime Minister Okada Keisuke miraculously escaped death in the coup, the entire cabinet resigned, and in early March Hirota Kōki took over as prime minister. Hirota's successor as foreign minister was Arita Hachirō, who had been ambassador to China. Horinouchi Kensuke, who had been the director-general of the America Bureau, replaced Shigemitsu Mamoru as vice-minister, but for the most part the entire senior management of the ministry remained the same, including Horinouchi, Kuwashima Kazue, Tōgō Shigenori, Kuriyama Shigeru, Amō Eiji, and Kurihara Shō.

8-4. The February 26 Incident

However, the February 26 Incident weakened support in Japan for Arita's diplomacy. After that incident, the army purged its ranks not just of Kōdōha generals and their sympathizers, but of many other senior leaders. Ugaki Kazushige and other moderates remained at the core of leadership, but for some time their support lacked full power. Because the Kōdōha had been weakened, it was difficult for the army to control the expansionist ambitions of the separatist policies pursued by Japanese troops in China.

Prime Minister Hirota and Foreign Minister Arita remained in their respective offices for less than a year—until January 1937—but the issues they had to deal with were important. One of these was the problem of North China; another was Japan's defense against the Soviet Union.

As foreign minister, Arita explored the possibilities for cooperation with the United Kingdom on China, and he decided to invite Leith-Ross for a return visit to Japan. The success of China's currency reform had bolstered Leith-Ross's reputation. Market stabilization in China through currency reform would be a desirable outcome in terms of Japan's trade with China. To achieve radical solutions in China, Ambassador Kawagoe Shigeru recognized the need for bilateral economic cooperation on infrastructure such as railways and harbors.

When Leith-Ross returned to Japan in June 1936, he met with Arita, Vice-Minister Horinouchi, and

Finance Minister Baba Eiichi. In the meeting with Finance Minister Baba, Leith-Ross spoke of bilateral cooperation to rebuild China's economy, and he made a proposal on joint investments. However, Baba rejected the idea, saying Japan was not in a position to make such investments. What Japan wanted was some kind of joint aid that did not require significant investment. Leith-Ross sought a pledge from Japan to rein in the North China Buffer State Policy, but Arita and other Japanese leaders would only reiterate that this was an "internal matter" for the Nationalist government, as it was difficult for them to restrain the actions of the Japanese troops in China.

In early August, the group of concerned ministers formulated the "Imperial Diplomatic Guidelines," as well as China policies that were the practical expression of those guidelines. The China policy that they emphasized showed little restraint with regard to North China—quite the opposite, in fact. More specifically, it aimed for the swift realization of two objectives, both intended to counter the urgent threat posed by the Soviet Union: making North China into a specially designated region, and making all of China opposed to the USSR and dependent on Japan. To those ends, anti-Communism was a particular priority, and the policy called for a concrete bilateral agreement to oppose Communism. The conclusion of such an agreement was an important goal of the talks between Kawagoe and Chiang Qun scheduled to begin in September.

The Kawagoe–Chiang Qun Talks: The Last Japan-China Negotiations

In late August and early September 1936, there were several terrorist attacks on Japanese residents of China, including the Chengdu Incident and the Pakhoi Incident. Most notably, the Pakhoi Incident took place in the vicinity of Hainan Island, which the Japanese navy regarded as a target of its southward-advance strategy, so it could not take passive measures to compete with the army. The

Smuggling in East Hebei

Of all the problems and incidents that continued to thwart progress in mending Japan-China relations from late 1935 onward, one of the most serious was the issue of "special commerce" (smuggling) in East Hebei. Prior to the Manchurian Incident, there were already rampant smuggling operations moving goods from the Kwantung Leased Territory to the coast of Hebei Province and other destinations via Bohai Bay. The incident spurred even more activity, as high tariffs on Japanese products and a Japanese ban on anti-smuggling ships off the coast of the demilitarized zone drove trafficking in rayon silk, sugar, and other products via the demilitarized zone. The smuggling also helped the fledgling East Hebei administration (East Hebei Autonomous Government) secure administrative funding. Almost as soon as it took shape, the government (with the assistance of the Kwantung Army) decided to permit ships to unload contraband as long as they paid a minimal examination fee (special tax) equivalent to around just one-quarter of the Nationalist government's official tariffs.

The contraband unloaded in the East Hebei area circulated throughout North China and even into regions south of Chang Jiang (the lower portion of the Yangtze River), establishing a market presence big enough to deal a major blow to the Nationalist government's tariff income and throw the domestic economy into disarray. In Japan's eyes, the activity was all within the scope of "East Hebei special trade"—fully sanctioned by the local government. To China, however, it was nothing more than illegal smuggling. The Chinese government lodged repeated protests against the arrangement, and Frederick Leith-Ross, the UK's economic advisor, who was on an official mission to China, also saw the smuggling as a potential problem. Japan decided not to get involved in the issue, however, as the government believed doing so would be meddling in China's internal affairs.

navy in particular regarded this incident as a serious matter, and it took a tough stance: If the Nationalist government were to seek to evade responsibility, the navy was prepared to respond militarily. The navy was beefing up its "Punish China" policy. The army was reluctant to take any military action outside North China, and it had managed to get by without incident, but any misstep threatened to provoke war.

In the end, the resolution of these incidents was left for the negotiations between Ambassador Kawagoe Shigeru and Foreign Minister Chiang Qun (Chang Ch'ün), which were scheduled to begin in September. Japan's Ministry of Foreign Affairs wanted to resolve the Chengdu Incident and the North China problem, among many others, as a way of improving relations.

Japan's main interests in these talks included creating a "special system" in North China; concluding a mutual pledge to oppose Communism; economic cooperation in North China; and lower customs and tariffs to combat smuggling in East Hebei. Of these goals, the first two were top priorities for Japan. The "special system" refers to the "Five Provinces of North China Special Political Association" that was enthusiastically backed by Consul General Suma Yakichirō as a counterproposal against the North China Buffer State Policy. Under this idea, the five provinces of North China would establish autonomous governments under the aegis of the Nationalist government, and would have special responsibility for their own affairs. This was aimed at restraining the expansion of the Japanese military's power in North China, dissolving the government of East Hebei, and restoring normalcy in Japan-China relations. In addition, for military reasons with regard to the Soviet Union, it was important for Japan to form a "hinterland"; this idea won the support of both the army and the navy.

In late September, the Chinese side lodged its own five demands, among which were the abandonment of the Tanggu Truce and the Shanghai Cease-Fire Agreement; the dissolution of the East Hebei government; cessation of smuggling in East Hebei; and the breakup of the Suiyuan Militia (a puppet army in inner Mongolia under the influence of the Kwantung Army). These were the first concrete demands that China had directed at Japan since the Manchurian Incident.

In subsequent negotiations, for the first time since the submission of Hirota's Three Principles, China indicated its willingness to consider "joint anti-Communism" in North China, which it had refused to accept up to that point, in exchange for the dissolution of the East Hebei government and the Suiyuan militia. The dissolution of the East Hebei government was important to the Chinese for reasons relating to sovereignty and administrative unification. However, the negotiations made little progress, because the Japan side was insistent on the establishment of an autonomous government, rather than the dissolution of the East Hebei government. In November, the Suiyuan militia, with the support of the Kwantung Army, entered the northern part of Suiyuan Province and skirmished with the Chinese Army (Suiyuan Campaign). In early December, negotiations were terminated. The Kawagoe-Chiang Qun talks were the last negotiations aimed at improving bilateral relations between Japan and China.

At the same time, the Ministry of Foreign Affairs, seeking to forge a connection with the negotiations for a Japan-Germany anti-Communist agreement it was conducting in parallel, continued to seek a Japan-China anti-Communism agreement that would remain short of a military agreement.

Toward a Japan-German Agreement to Oppose Communism

The Four Ministers' Conference of October 1936 proposed a Japan-China anti-Communist agreement whose aim was "general prevention of the spread of Communism." From that point forward, a link was forged between a Japan-China anti-Communist agreement aimed at "opposition to Communism," and negotiations on the Japan-Germany Anti-Comintern Pact. Starting in 1935, the Japan-Germany Anti-Comintern Pact was an agreement promoted by Army General Ōshima Hiroshi (military attaché in Germany). The Ministry of Foreign Affairs, though it did not get involved in the negotiation process of the agreement, had a concern that the agreement might undermine cordial relations with the United Kingdom and the Soviet Union. The Ministry, however, was not against it: The purpose of the pact was merely ideological or "opposition to the Comintern" and was simply intended to be an exchange of information, not the sort of thing that would develop into a military agreement. Foreign Minister Arita hoped to use this sort of agreement to improve Japan-China relations, and he was promoting the idea of a trilateral Japan-Germany-China anti-Communist pact. For this reason, he was pursuing the idea of Japan-China negotiations aimed at an anti-Communist pact in parallel with the Japan-Germany treaty negotiations going on in Berlin.

On October 8, Ambassador Kawagoe met with Chiang Kai-shek, and stressed to him the significance of a Japan-China anti-Communist agreement, for the purpose of joint defense against "international Communism." Chiang, however, was not very excited about the idea. While not opposed to the idea of joint defense against Communism, he said his higher priority was to deal with pro-Soviet sentiments within his own borders.

The talks in Nanjing made little progress, but the Berlin talks on the Japan-Germany agreement made great headway, and a draft was initialed in late October. The Ministry of Foreign Affairs was hoping that a trilateral anti-Communism agreement between Japan, Germany, and China would help to improve relations with China, but Japan was able to secure such an agreement only with Germany.

8-5. The Kawagoe–Chiang Kai-shek Talks on October 8, 1936

The Japan-Germany Anti-Comintern Pact, signed in November 1936, was signed not by Germany's foreign ministry, but by the Dienststelle Ribbentrop, a department led by Joachim von Ribbentrop that has been described as Hitler's personal diplomatic corps. The treaty does not bear the signature of Germany's foreign minister.

Among international agreements, there was no precedent for the Japan-Germany Anti-Comintern Pact, the aim of which was to oppose a specified ideology, namely to jointly defend against the activities of the Communist International (Comintern). In truth, however, it was a military pact aimed at the USSR. The treaty negotiations between Military Attaché Ōshima Hiroshi and Ribbentrop clearly advanced as discussions of an anti-Soviet military agreement. In subsequent talks, the military agreement was made into a secret appendix to the main treaty, hidden under the cloak of ideology.

The Anti-Comintern Pact contributed to the souring of Japan's relations with both the Soviet Union and China, and it did great harm by hindering any improvement in relations between Japan and the United Kingdom.

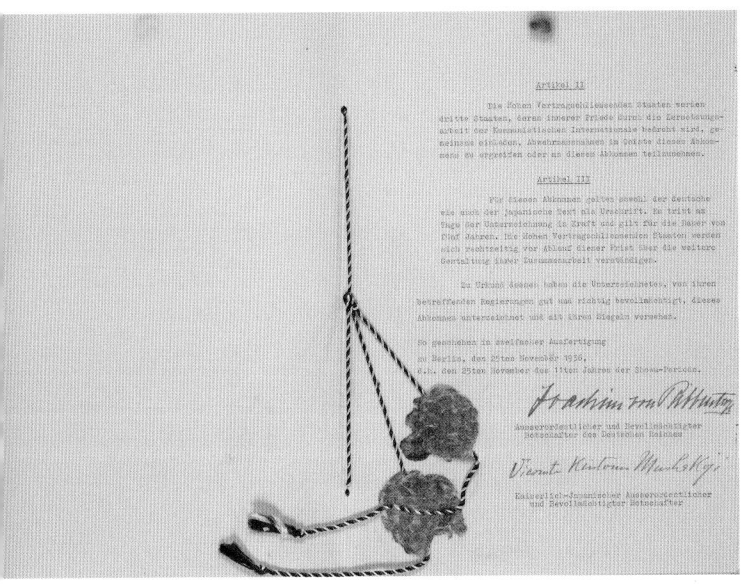

Artikel II

Die Hohen Vertragschliessenden Staaten werden dritte Staaten, deren innerer Friede durch die Zersetzungsarbeit der Kommunistischen Internationale bedroht wird, gemeinsam einladen, Abwehrmassnahmen im Geiste dieses Abkommens zu ergreifen oder an diesem Abkommen teilzunehmen.

Artikel III

Für dieses Abkommen gelten sowohl der deutsche wie auch der japanische Text als Urschrift. Es tritt am Tage der Unterzeichnung in Kraft und gilt für die Dauer von fünf Jahren. Die Hohen Vertragschliessenden Staaten werden sich rechtzeitig vor Ablauf dieser Frist über die weitere Gestaltung ihrer Zusammenarbeit verständigen.

Zu Urkund dessen haben die Unterzeichneten, von ihren betreffenden Regierungen gut und richtig bevollmächtigt, dieses Abkommen unterzeichnet und mit ihren Siegeln versehen.

So geschehen in zweifacher Ausfertigung
zu Berlin, den 25ten November 1936,
d.h. den 25ten November des 11ten Jahres der Showa-Periode.

Ausserordentlicher und Bevollmächtigter
Botschafter des Deutschen Reiches

Kaiserlich-Japanischer Ausserordentlicher
und Bevollmächtigter Botschafter

8-6. Japan-Germany Anti-Comintern Pact

The Xi'an Incident and the Formation of the Anti-Japanese Union Front

In the Xi'an Incident of mid-December 1936, Zhang Xueliang (Chang Hsüeh-liang), commander of the Northeast Army, and General Yang Hucheng of the Northwest Army held Chiang Kai-shek in confinement, demanding that he end China's internal strife and join forces against Japan. As already described, opposition to the Japanese military's North China Buffer State Policy was already active, in the form of the December 9 movement, under the slogan, "Resist Japan and Save the Nation!" All of China was rallying under the cry, "End the Civil War! Fight Japan!" The Communist Party of China, under the August 1 Declaration in 1935, urged the Nationalist Party to join them in a united struggle against Japan. Nonetheless, Chiang held fast to his conviction that it was important to have peace at home before waging war against a foreign power, and he continued his large-scale punitive war against the Chinese Communist Party. While the Northeast Army was on the front lines of the Nationalist government's war against the Chinese Communist Party, however, it lacked the will to fight. In the middle of 1936, the Northeast Army began to seek a cease-fire with the Communists, who intended to build a united front against Japan.

Undeterred, Chiang Kai-shek was getting ready for a final major assault on the Communist Party (Sixth Encirclement Campaign). In early December, he traveled to Xi'an to direct the campaign and put pressure on Zhang Xueliang. In what amounted to a "military uprising," Zhang responded by arresting and imprisoning Chiang in an effort to change his mind. Zhang put forth eight demands, including an end to the civil war, a united front against Japan, and the release of political prisoners. Chiang refused to accede to these demands.

When the Chinese Communist Party learned of the incident, it dispatched Zhou Enlai to Xi'an to mediate the situation and discuss Zhang Xueliang's demands with him. It is said it was Zhou who persuaded Zhang to release Chiang Kai-shek, and convinced Chiang to promise to join the fight against Japan. Chiang denied ever having made such a promise, but regardless, he was able to return to Nanjing and resume the leadership of the Nationalist government. He halted the civil war and greatly advanced the idea of Nationalist / CCP collaboration as a united front against Japan.

Without Chiang Kai-shek and his emergence as a dictator, the united front against Japan would not have been possible. Chiang intensified the sense of urgency with regard to Japan's North China Buffer State Policy. He pressed for the strengthening of China's defense systems against Japan, but he did not shut out the possibility of an accommodation with Japan.

4 Change and Setbacks in China Policy

Changes in China Policy: Satō Becomes Foreign Minister

Early in 1937, observing the atmosphere of national unity and opposition to the civil war in China that followed the Xi'an Incident, the War Guidance Division of Army General Staff Office concluded that inter-faction strife was coming under control, and it issued a paper demanding revisions to the Imperial Diplomatic Guidelines of the previous August. The gist now was to make clear that North China was under the control of the Nationalist government by reining in the North China Buffer State Policy and dissolving the government of East Hebei. Strongly reflecting the ideas of Division Chief Ishiwara Kanji, these new policies were preparations for war with the USSR. For the time being, the idea was to defend Japan against the Soviet Union by developing Manchukuo and improving relations with other countries. The Ministry of the Army was also updating its China policies.

After the Xi'an Incident and the success of the currency reform, the Japanese people's trust in Chiang Kai-shek was rising, and in the latter half of 1936 an attitude of "reappraising China" grew more widespread in the media, bringing internecine strife under control and heading in the direction of unity.

Satō Naotake (1882–1971)

8-7. Satō Naotake

Born in Osaka Prefecture, Satō Naotake was the son of a police officer—and his father's frequent job transfers meant that Naotake spent his youth bouncing from place to place. He graduated from Seisoku Middle School in Tokyo and then enrolled at the Tokyo Higher Commercial School, aiming to make himself a businessman. During his time in school, he was adopted by his uncle, Satō Aimaro (Japan's ambassador to the United States from 1916 to 1918, when he retired and served as an official in the Imperial Household Ministry until he died in 1934). At Aimaro's urging, Naotake sat for the foreign-service examination in 1905 and passed, putting himself in a recruiting cohort that also included career diplomat Saburi Sadao. Satō served his first overseas assignment in Russia. As he went about his diplomatic business, Satō also spent his time learning Russian, French, and social skills over his nearly nine-year Russian stay.

In 1917, he received an appointment to serve as the consul general in Harbin. The Russian Revolution erupted not long after Satō took up his post, and the Japanese government began debating a possible Siberian Expedition. Based on his perceptions of the situation, Satō advised Foreign Minister Motono Ichirō that a large-scale military dispatch would be crucial in both halting the Red Army's eastern advance and keeping the United States out of the fray. The 1920s would see Satō turn himself into a self-professed "international-conference specialist": after attending the first General Assembly of the League of Nations in 1920, he continued to represent Japan at an array of different international gatherings. In 1927, Foreign Minister Shidehara Kijūrō recommended that Satō take over as the head of the Japanese Bureau for the League of Nations Affairs—a significant responsibility that Satō embraced with a dogged zeal. Convinced that holding his ground at the League of Nations would "elevate Japan's standing," Satō brought a tenacious determination to discussions on opium, disarmament, ethnic minorities, and other key contemporary issues.

Japan would gradually establish a strong foothold within the League of Nations, but the Manchurian Incident sparked a steady decline in the trust that Satō had worked so hard to earn from the international community. Serving a concurrent post as Japan's ambassador to Belgium, Satō did what he could to help protect Japan's actions and interests—but before long, Japan was pushed to the point of withdrawal. Before the Manchurian Incident broke out. Satō made a temporary return home to persuade government officials to bolster Japan's standing in the League of Nations. "The Manchuria Problem is bound to come up for discussion, and Japan needs to be ready for when that happens," he told leaders at the Ministry of Foreign Affairs.

At the same time, the Ministry of Foreign Affairs, led by the First Division of the East Asia Bureau (under Division Director Kamimura Shin'ichi), was beginning to rethink its policies on China. The new thinking was to abandon the idea of autonomy for the five provinces of North China, and pivot to an economic plan based on economic cooperation between Japan and China.

In late January 1937, as the Army Central Command and the Ministry of Foreign Affairs began to reshape their policies on China, Hirota Kōki and his cabinet were forced to resign after a slip-up in dealing with the Diet. Hirota's successor as prime minister would be Ugaki Kazushige, the moderates' last chance. However, Ugaki was blocked by the mid-level officers of the army, and it fell to General Hayashi Senjūrō to form a government.

Satō Naotake, ambassador to France, was named foreign minister in the Hayashi cabinet. Satō was an old-timer in diplomatic circles who had spent more than thirty years of his career in other countries, so he was relatively little known at home in Japan. When he joined the cabinet, he appealed to Hayashi for several options: treating China as an equal, seeking to maintain peace with the Soviet Union, and adjusting relations with the United Kingdom. With regard to China, he said, "Now that China is unified, it is no longer the old China. Japan must clearly understand China's new power." Following Satō's new diplomatic direction, early in April the Four Ministers' Conference decided on a revised North China policy that would involve

---

"That means building a solid foundation in the League of Nations. We need to develop a deeper, closer understanding of how the League of Nations functions and reinforce our efforts within the organization." His pleas rang hollow, however; it was as if "the leaders in the Ministry of Foreign Affairs were hearing about the matter for the first time." Japan ended up paying the price for its indifference to Satō, as the Manchurian Incident thrust Japan's response into an unflattering light. What was most unfortunate for Japan was that it was unable to convince the League of Nations of its interests, the goal that Satō was hoping to achieve.

Satō was ready to retire from diplomatic service after serving out a later term as ambassador to France, but Hayashi Senjūrō tapped him to serve as his foreign minister in February 1937. The main text offers a more detailed description of Satō's time in this role, but one point that merits mention here is his decision to abandon the diplomatic strategies of Hirota Kōki and Shigemitsu Mamoru for an entirely new China policy that included terminating Japan's maneuvers in North China and implementing other changes. Another key element of Satō's stint as foreign minister was how he framed the efforts to restore free international trade and open up access to resources as statements of Japan's "right to exist." Satō would not have much time to propel those visions forward, however, as the entire Hayashi cabinet folded in June 1937—just four months after forming—and Satō relinquished the Ministry of Foreign Affairs to Hirota.

Satō was serving as a diplomatic advisor after the war with the United States had broken out. In February 1942, Foreign Minister Tōgō Shigenori asked him to become Japan's ambassador to the Soviet Union. Satō accepted the offer and, through his steady, hardworking efforts to find solutions to issues concerning Japan's rights in North Karafuto (Sakhalin), renewals of fishing treaties, and other pending problems, he worked to keep Japan-Soviet Union relations neutral and prevent the Soviet Union from declaring war on Japan. During Tōgō's second term as foreign minister, Satō's role in directing Japan's Soviet relations took on an even deeper dimension: instead of simply looking to maintain neutrality, he now had the task of trying to work out a favorable peace with the United States and the United Kingdom through the Soviet Union. In Satō's eyes, however, there was no conceivable reason to expect the solidarity linking the United States, the United Kingdom, and the Soviet Union to weaken; putting too much faith in the Soviet Union being willing to help Japan, he said, would be a mistake. He instead argued for a quick peace contingent on Japan's ability to defend and maintain its national polity. He sent the Japanese government a stream of telegrams outlining his reasoning right up to just before the end of the war, and his fears ultimately proved justified. The Soviet Union entered the war against Japan, sealing Japan's defeat.

In Satō's postwar career, he became a member and later president of the House of Councillors. In 1956, he joined Foreign Minister Shigemitsu Mamoru in representing Japan at the 11th Session of the United Nations General Assembly and overseeing Japan's admission to the United Nations.

abandoning the former "North China Five Provinces Autonomy" policy. The core of the approach to China as a whole was to show an attitude of fairness toward the unification movement led by the Nationalist government. The previous year's focus on concluding an anti-Communism pact was out the window.

Still, some tenets of Japan's previous North China policy were not abandoned. Japan wanted to promote its economic plans in North China in pursuit of two main aims: First, strengthening defenses against the Soviet Union; and second, securing natural resources for national defense. At the same time, it wished to consider cooperating with the United States and the United Kingdom for the economic development of North China. Satō had the army and navy ministries working on the problem of eliminating smuggling in East Hebei (see sidebar on page 276) and determining how to replace it.

The Cabinet of Prime Minister Konoe

In mid-March 1937, a diverse group of businesspeople led by Kodama Kenji, the head of Yokohama Specie Bank, Ltd., visited China with the support of the Japanese government. One of the aims of their visit was to make up for lost time in establishing economic cooperation between Japan and China. Leveraged by the currency reform, China's economy was recovering. In 1936–37, countries like Germany, the United Kingdom, and the United States were engaging in economic development such as investing in exports of heavy industrial and chemical products. The Soviet Union was also pursuing closer relations with China. Japan felt isolated and left behind.

During its visit, however, all the group managed to accomplish was to ascertain that the Chinese side was not interested in economic cooperation that did not address the need to adjust diplomatic relations (i.e., political cooperation). In April, after returning to Japan, Kodama submitted a paper to Satō appealing for the dissolution of the East Hebei government and the elimination of smuggling in East Hebei.

The Kwantung Army and the Tianjin Army in China believed Chiang Kai-shek's anti-Japan policy was an immutable part of his political position. They maintained the view that compromise on North China would not weaken his stance against Japan.

Satō ordered Yoshida Shigeru, who at that time was Japan's ambassador to the United Kingdom, to seek UK cooperation on China. He also sought to correct the Japan-Soviet Union relationship, which had chilled due to the Japan-Germany Anti-Comintern Pact.

It would take time to see tangible results in the form of policy changes. In June of that year, before results could be realized, the Hayashi cabinet stepped down. There were some within the Ministry of Foreign Affairs who wanted Satō to stay on in his post, but it was Hirota Kōki who returned to the post of foreign minister in the cabinet of Konoe Fumimaro.

At the outset of the Konoe cabinet, Konoe was welcomed as prime minister by the press, who saw him as "the prime minister for our times." The mid-ranking military officers, who insisted on "revolution within the law," eagerly embraced Konoe due to his political stance of seeking reform rather than preserving the status quo, and his youth—he was just forty-five years old.

CHAPTER 9

War with the United States Begins

9-1. Japanese ambassador Admiral Kichisaburō Nomura (left) and Special Envoy Saburō Kurusu (right) meet US secretary of state Cordell Hull, November 1941

TIMELINE

1937 (Shōwa 12)

July 7	Marco Polo Bridge Incident (Lugou Bridge Incident)
July 11	Local cease-fire agreement takes effect
July 17	Chiang Kai-shek, Mount Lu talks (announced July 19)
July 25	Japanese and Chinese troops clash in Langfang (between Beijing and Tianjin) and again the next day in Beijing's Guanganmen
July 27	Three military divisions from the interior ordered to North China. Tianjin Army begins all-out assault July 28
August 9	Lieutenant Ōyama Isao and one other member of the Naval Landing Forces killed in Shanghai by Chinese security forces (Ōyama Incident)
August 14	Japanese and Chinese forces battle in Shanghai (Second Shanghai Incident), signaling start of full-scale war
October 5	President Roosevelt gives "quarantine speech," likening Japan and Germany to an epidemic
October 6	League of Nations meets, criticizes Japan's military actions
November 2	Start of Trautmann mediation
November 3	Nine Power Treaty Conference opens in Brussels (Japan absent)
December 12	Japanese naval aircraft attack American gunboat USS *Panay* on Yangtze, near Nanjing
December 13	Japanese Central China Area Army takes control of Nanjing (Nanjing Massacre)
December 14	Provisional government of the Republic of China established under supervision of Japanese Northern China Area Army

1938 (Shōwa 13)

January 16	First Konoe Declaration ("non-opposition" [*aite to sezu*] to Nationalist government)
April 1	National Mobilization Law proclaimed
May 12	Germany recognizes Manchukuo
July 11	Battle of Lake Khasan, on Soviet border with Manchukuo (cease-fire agreement on August 11)
July 26	Japanese foreign minister Ugaki meets with British ambassador Craigie
September 29–30	The United Kingdom, Germany, France, Italy reach agreement on German annexation of Sudetenland (Munich Agreement)
October 27	Japanese army occupies three Wuhan cities
November 3	Second Konoe Declaration (New Order in East Asia)
December 20	Wang Zhaoming leaves Chongqing, arrives in Hanoi
December 29	Wang Zhaoming responds to Third Konoe Declaration (good neighbor policy, joint anti-Communism, economic cooperation) of December 22 by writing open letter to Kuomintang leadership urging peace with Japan, which falls on deaf ears

1939 (Shōwa 14)

January 5	Hiranuma Kiichirō cabinet formed
May 11	Battle of Khalkhin Gol (cease-fire agreement on September 15)
June 14	Japanese army blockades British, French settlements in Tianjin
July 22	Arita-Craigie Agreement
July 26	US gives notice of termination of US-Japan Treaty of Commerce and Navigation (effective January 26, 1940)
August 23	Molotov-Ribbentrop Pact (German-Soviet Non-Aggression Pact)
August 30	Abe Nobuyuki cabinet formed
September 1	Germany invades Poland
September 3	Great Britain, France declare war with Germany (outbreak of World War II)
September 4	Abe cabinet declares "non-intervention" in European war

November 4 Foreign Minister Nomura Kichisaburō holds talks with US ambassador Joseph Grew

1940 (Shōwa 15)

January 16 Yonai Mitsumasa cabinet formed

March 30 Wang Zhaoming forms government in Nanjing (Nationalist Government of the Republic of China, or formally, Reorganized National Government of the Republic of China)

May 10 German Army begins invasion of Western Europe

June 14 German Army enters Paris (France surrenders June 22)

June 24 Konoe Fumimaro resigns as head of Privy Council, declares decision to promote new political system movement

July 22 Second Konoe cabinet formed

July 26 Konoe cabinet decides Fundamental National Policy Framework

August 30 Matsuoka-Henry Agreement on northern French Indochina

September 13 Negotiations between Japan, the Netherlands on Dutch East Indies (broken off June 17, 1941)

September 22 Japanese army stationed in northern French Indochina

September 27 Japan, Germany, Italy sign Tripartite Alliance Agreement in Berlin

September 28 US bans exports of scrap iron to Japan

November 30 Wang Zhaoming administration signs Japan-China Basic Relations Treaty

December 29 US president Roosevelt gives "Arsenal of Democracy" speech

1941 (Shōwa 16)

January 31 Cease-fire agreement ends Franco-Thai War

March 12 Foreign Minister Matsuoka departs for visits to Berlin, Moscow (through April 22)

April 13 Soviet-Japanese Neutrality Pact signed in Moscow

April 16 Japan receives the complete version of the "Draft Understanding" between Japan and the US

May 9 Treaty ending Franco-Thai War is signed in Tokyo (Japan signs as mediator)

June 22 German Army begins attack on Soviet Union (German-Soviet War)

July 2 Imperial Council approves "Imperial Policy Frameworks Regarding Developments in the Current Situation"

July 18 Third Konoe cabinet formed

July 25 US freezes Japanese assets, having gained intelligence on July 2 of Imperial Council decision on southern military advance based on decoded messages

July 28 Japanese military stationed in southern French Indochina

August 1 US embargoes oil exports to Japan

August 7 Foreign Minister Toyoda Teijirō proposes summit talks between Konoe, Roosevelt

August 14 US, UK proclaim Atlantic Charter

September 6 Imperial Council approves "Essentials for Executing Imperial Policies"

October 2 Hull rejects idea of summit talks between Konoe and Roosevelt

October 18 Tōjō Hideki cabinet formed

November 5 Imperial Council reapproves "Essentials for Executing Imperial Policies" (Plan A, Plan B)

November 26 US delivers Hull Note

December 1 Imperial Council approves commencement of war on US, UK, the Netherlands

December 7–8 Attack on Pearl Harbor, Hawaii. Hours prior to this, the Japanese army attacks Kota Bharu on the Malayan Peninsula

December 21 Signing of Japan-Thailand Alliance treaty

1 The Second Sino-Japanese War

Gunfire at Marco Polo Bridge

In 1937 in North China, the provinces of Hebei and Chahar were combined under the Hebei-Chahar Political Council, with Song Zheyuan (who was also head of Hebei Province) as chairman. Faced with the pressure of Japan's North China Policy, the Nationalist government established the Hebei-Chahar Political Council as a buffer entity. The Council had a very different character from the East Hebei Autonomous Government. Many members of the Hebei-Chahar Political Council were actually anti-Japanese soldiers. Furthermore, the Tianjin Army harbored a deep mistrust of the 29th Army, which was also led by Song.

Given these local conditions, in April 1936 Japan decided to triple the strength of the Tianjin Army to roughly 5,800 troops, provoking greater mistrust on the China side. This increase in troop strength was aimed at countering Communist Chinese Forces, which had settled in Yenan, Shaanxi Province, after the Long March ended in the fall of 1935, but it also had another aim. The Kwantung Army, which had been implementing the North China State Policy, was to focus on the development of Manchukuo, leaving the Tianjin Army to take care of the North China Policy.

At around 10:30 p.m. on the night of July 7, 1937, the Tianjin Army was on night maneuvers near the Marco Polo Bridge, in Wanping, on the outskirts of Beijing, when they were fired upon twice with live ammunition. To this day, the identity of the assailant is unknown. The incident prompted both armies to intensify their readiness, but they were not yet engaged in battle. Shortly after the incident at Marco Polo Bridge, it was discovered that the whereabouts of one Japanese soldier were unknown

9-2. Japanese army captures Marco Polo Bridge

(he later returned to his unit). The real fighting began only after a third shooting incident in the early morning hours of July 8. Formal negotiations were begun to prevent further spread of hostilities, and a local agreement was reached during the night of July 11. The 29th Army agreed to make an apology, punish the perpetrator, and tighten control over anti-Japanese agitators, in accordance with Japan's demands.

The Konoe Cabinet

At a special meeting on July 8, the cabinet decided on a basic policy of "non-expansion, local resolution," to rein in the army in northeast China. It was cautious about dispatching reinforcements to the scene. At its meeting on the 11th, the cabinet recognized the possibility that the situation could spread and worsen, and it decided to send three divisions from the interior in addition to the Kwantung Army and the Korea Army—although in fact the interior divisions were held in reserve. The cabinet stood by its policy of "non-expansion, local resolution."

Immediately after the decision to send troops was

made on the 11th, Prime Minister Konoe Fumimaro summoned members of the press, as well as business and political leaders, to garner full support for the decision to dispatch troops and to encourage the Nationalist government to show remorse. Konoe did not want the tensions to spread, but he hoped Japan's hard-line posture of sending troops would force the Chinese to make concessions. He believed the situation could be dealt with in a short span of time, and his cabinet expected a localized solution would be reached that would involve only Song Zheyuan and the 29th Army.

In Tianjin, as well, efforts to seek a localized solution continued. On July 19, local troops agreed to a detailed cease-fire agreement that included cracking down on anti-Japanese activity. On the 21st, the Tianjin Army acknowledged the situation had quieted down, and telegraphed Tokyo to urge discretion in dispatching fresh troops. The day before, the Konoe cabinet had reached a decision to send troops from the interior to North China, but with the provision that they would be withdrawn if the situation improved. In the meantime, the army in Tokyo postponed a decision on sending troops.

Chiang Kai-shek, on the other hand, moved his Central Army to the north. His priority, for the moment, was to see a peaceful resolution of the matter, as he was reorganizing internal and external structures to resist Japan. In his address from Mount Lu on July 17 (made public on the 19th), Chiang Kai-shek expressed his expectations for a diplomatic solution, but he declared that if matters came to a head, with no prospect of a resolution, he was prepared to wage war. For the time being, matters had not yet gone that far.

On July 25, Japanese and Chinese troops clashed in Langfang, between Beijing and Tianjin, and again the next day in Beijing's Guanganmen. On the 27th, the Konoe cabinet again decided to send troops from the interior, and their order was

The Undeclared War (1937–41)

Although the clash between Japan and China in July 1937 ended up developing into an all-out military conflict, the countries actually avoided declaring war on each other until the start of the Pacific War in 1941. The Second Sino-Japanese War, therefore, was an "undeclared war."

The Japanese government carefully weighed the pros and cons of elevating its hostilities with China to "war" status, but officials continued to refer to the events only as "incidents" up to the onset of its official war with the United States. One of the reasons Japan refrained from making an official war declaration was that doing so would make the country subject to the US Neutrality Act—which would have exposed Japan to the equivalent of economic sanctions. Another was that Japan was aiming to defeat the Chiang Kai-shek administration and its military; Japan had no real sense that it was fighting China as a whole. Declaring war on China would have thus framed the relationship differently.

Japan was also of the view that elevating the fighting to full-on war would make it more difficult to bring the conflict to a quick resolution. If its struggle with China were to drag on, Japan would also have no realistic way to make sufficient preparations for war against probable future enemies like the Soviet Union, the United Kingdom, and the United States. Hoping to avoid the "war" designation, Japan thus first referred to its hostilities with China as the "North China Incidents," and, after the conflict began to intensify further in September 1937, the "China Incidents."

Another distinctive aspect of the Second Sino-Japanese War was that it saw Japan pursue myriad avenues to peace from start to finish, a reflection of how urgently and anxiously the government was hoping for a quick conclusion to the fighting. Despite Japan's pressing to put the conflict to rest, however, the hostilities raged on for more than eight years and grew even more intense and cutthroat than they would have if Japan had officially declared war. In the end, the Second Sino-Japanese War took a heavy toll—both in terms of the burdens placed on the people and the lives lost—on inhabitants of both countries, with war-ravaged China bearing the brunt of the damage.

9-3. First cabinet of Prime Minister Konoe Fumimaro

enacted. The Tianjin Army began its all-out attack on the 28th, and by the following day it had largely established order in all areas of Beijing and Tianjin north of the Yongding River.

Military Solutions vs. Diplomatic Solutions

Japan and China faced a choice of whether to pursue a military solution or a diplomatic solution. The main proponents of a military solution on the Japan side were the expansionist faction in the army in Tokyo—particularly Army Affairs Division Director Tanaka Shin'ichi and Military Operations Division Chief Mutō Akira—who advocated a "single blow" against the army of the Nationalist government to cause it to change its anti-Japanese stance, a "single blow" to resolve the Japan-China problem.

On the other hand, the main proponents of a diplomatic solution were a group led by Ishii Itarō, director-general of the East Asia Bureau of the Ministry of Foreign Affairs. Ishii first submitted a letter of appeal, to Foreign Minister Hirota Kōki in late July 1937 asking him to have the cabinet do something to keep the situation from becoming more serious. Ishii then contacted Gao Zongwu and others in the diplomatic branch of the Nationalist government, and sought a path to resolution through negotiations with the Nationalist government. Ishii also aimed to maintain a constructive relationship with Ishiwara Kanji, director-general of the military operations department, who was the main advocate of "non-expansion" within the army. Ishiwara and others advocated a localized solution to avoid a protracted war in China, as a lengthy conflict would sap Japan's power, weaken its ability to withstand the threat from the Soviet Union, and open the door for the Soviets to intervene. Similarly, the military plans for North China drawn up by the military operations department were limited in scope to Beijing and Tianjin.

At the end of July, Ishii prepared a position paper setting forth the ministry's view of how best to control the situation in North China, and arguing for the importance of direct negotiations between Japan and China. The aim was to achieve a solution through negotiation with the Nationalist government, recognizing the Chinese central government's claims regarding North China and

The Funatsu Operation

Once the Second Sino-Japanese War broke out, diplomats who favored a resolution via negotiations (East Asia Bureau director-general Ishii Itarō and Gao Zongwu, Republic of China, for example) began looking for a way to resolve the strife as quickly as possible. The Japanese faction, aiming for a diplomatic resolution and adhering to the new policy that previous foreign minister Satō Naotake had implemented a year earlier, wanted to initiate direct negotiations with the Nationalist government contingent on the recognition of the central Chinese government's sovereignty in North China and an agreement that no special regional administration would be established. Japanese officials decided that compelling China to propose a cease-fire was the optimal course of action, and discussions turned to the idea of sending an adept negotiator, capable of talking directly with Chinese representatives, into Nanjing for advance talks. The plan went into motion in early August 1937, when Japan dispatched Gao's friend Funatsu Tatsuichirō to Shanghai.

Funatsu had spent his entire diplomatic career abroad in China, serving as the consul general in Shanghai and Mukden and then as a councillor at the German embassy before retiring in 1926. Leaving active duty did not mean leaving China behind completely, however. Not only did Funatsu maintain a reputation in Japan as one of the country's leading "China specialists" and boast an extensive network of Chinese contacts, but he also served as the president of the Japanese Cotton Mills Association in China. Upon receiving the assignment to handle negotiations in Nanjing, Funatsu shipped out of Tokyo for Shanghai on August 4, 1937. On August 9, Gao paid a visit to Funatsu's residence in Shanghai. Funatsu told Gao that, personally, he was hoping for a peaceful solution to the issue and asked Gao to put himself in contact with Ambassador Kawagoe Shigeru. Funatsu then asked Kawagoe to talk with Gao, but gave him no background information. Kawagoe met with Gao that very night, but the talks made little progress given the lack of input from Funatsu. East Asia Bureau director-general Ishii remembered being outraged at what he assumed to have been Kawagoe simply wresting control over the negotiations from Funatsu. "It's all fine and well that Ambassador Kawagoe made an approach," he wrote in his diary, "but I find it extremely regrettable that he got in Funatsu's way and threw a wrench into the negotiations with Gao." The talks likely left Gao without a clear sense of Japan's true intentions, and the Ōyama Incident—which also occurred later that very August 9—ended up sealing the fate of the fruitless Funatsu operation.

abandoning the idea of a separation with North China, in accordance with what had been the new policy prior to the outbreak of the "series of incidents." Based on these guidelines, Ishii and his colleagues sought an opportunity for direct negotiations with the Nationalist government.

Within the Nationalist government was a diplomatic negotiations faction led by Gao. Gao had attended Kyushu Imperial University, and he became close with Chiang Kai-shek and Wang Zhaoming. Now, as head of the Asia division of the Nationalist government's diplomatic branch, he was the central figure responsible for negotiating with Japan. Advocacy for diplomatic negotiations remained strong even after the Japanese army's all-out attacks at the end of July, and the Nationalist government had not closed the door on the diplomatic route.

Chiang held an urgent news conference on July 29, stating that the "final critical moment" had been reached. Acknowledging that there was no longer any possibility for a localized solution, he said he was ready to fight a war of resistance. The Kuomintang (Nationalist Party) was moving toward joining hands with the Chinese Communist Party to form a united front to fight Japan. The Second United Front, led by the Kuomintang, was formed in late September.

But Wang, Gao, and other senior officials of the Nationalist government had not yet abandoned the possibility of peace. They remained in contact with Ishii, Ishiwara, and others in that group on the Japan side. Their persistence led to the Funatsu operation (see sidebar above).

The Fires of War Move to Shanghai

Once all-out war broke out in North China, the Japanese government directed that the roughly 30,000 inhabitants of the Japanese settlement along the Yangtze River be repatriated to Japan. These Japanese residents gathered in Shanghai, where an atmosphere of emergency prevailed. On August 9, 1937, Lieutenant Ōyama Isao and a sailor from the Japanese Naval Land Forces of the Japanese Naval Land Forces were killed in Shanghai by Chinese troops (Ōyama Incident). Shanghai turned into a tinderbox. Minister of the Navy Yonai Mitsumasa had, up to that point, put his faith in diplomatic solutions, and he had hopes for the Funatsu operation, which was making strides behind the scenes. But this provocative act by the Chinese convinced him that more troops should be sent. He demanded that the cabinet redeploy troops from the interior to Shanghai, and on August 13 this was approved. Battle commenced in Shanghai the same day. On the 15th, the government issued a statement that decisive action "to encourage the Nanjing government to reflect on its behavior and punish the Chinese army for its treachery," could no longer be avoided. On the 17th, the cabinet reached a formal decision to abandon the non-expansion guidelines.

At the same time, Chiang Kai-shek, taking the situation in Shanghai quite seriously, made himself commander of China's land, sea, and air military, and on August 14 he declared all-out war. He hoped the start of open war might prompt the Soviet Union to intervene and motivate other nations to act against Japan, forcing the Japanese military to engage on multiple fronts and undermining its plans to occupy North China. The Nationalist government deployed its most elite troops to defend Shanghai. This force numbered over 700,000, an enormous number of whom would give their lives in battle. The Battle of Shanghai escalated from a localized conflict to real, full-scale war.

North China and Mengjiang

Within the army, a majority favored a military solution and the proactive deployment of troops to address the "series of incidents" in China. In the wider sphere, as well, journalists and political parties subscribing to the military solution fanned the flames of popular opinion using the slogan, "Punish savage China." Rather than trying to rein in military expansion, the Konoe cabinet, seeing an opportunity to break the logjam in China policy, allowed the deployment of large numbers of troops to achieve a swift defeat of Chiang Kai-shek and his government, and the military expanded the scope of its activities in North China and Shanghai. Nonetheless, Ishii and others continued to favor a diplomatic solution, and they advocated continued negotiations with the Nationalist government to reach a solution.

At the end of August 1937, the Japanese Northern China Area Army (an occupying force that comprised the reorganized Tianjin Army) split into two troops in North China and proceeded south to attack the provinces of Hebei, Shanxi, and Shandong. By late October, the Japanese Northern China Area Army controlled all of North China. At the end of 1937, the Provisional Government of the Republic of China was established, supplanting the defunct Hebei-Chahar Political Council. In January 1938, the Provisional Government annexed the East Hebei Autonomous Government, the Henan Autonomous Government, and others.

At the same time, the Kwantung Army had been advancing on Changchiak'ou (Zhangjakou) since August 1937, subduing Chahar and Suiyuan provinces along the way. It set up the puppet governments of Mongukuo, Chinbei, and Chanan. In November, the United Committee of Mengjiang was formed, subsuming all of these smaller regional governments. (In September 1939, all were merged into the Mongukuo United Autonomous Government.)

The "autonomous" puppet governments Japan set up in North China and Inner Mongolia came to be known as the "New China Regime," freed from the power of the Nationalist government. All had Japanese advisors and occupying troops. The main aim of these puppet governments was to exploit important resources.

The Attack on Nanjing

In mid-October 1937, the Army General Staff Office shifted the main focus of the military effort from North China to Shanghai. In early November, the Japanese army launched a surprise attack on Hangzhou Bay. Immediately thereafter, the Japanese Central China Area Army was reorganized under the command of Matsui Iwane. The mandate of these troops, like that of the Northern China Area Army, went beyond the protection of Japanese citizens; it was to "break the fighting spirit of the enemy." The success of Japan's attack on Hangzhou Bay completely altered the military prospects for Shanghai. The Chinese army began to retreat, and in mid-November the Japanese army took over the entire Shanghai area.

Hoping to cut off the enemy's retreat, the Japanese army, in its zeal, decided to attack Nanjing, defying restraints imposed by the Army General Staff Office. With the Trautmann mediation (discussed in greater detail below) in progress, there were those within the Army General Staff Office who argued strongly for caution, for peace negotiations, and a diplomatic solution before an attack on Nanjing. However, it was difficult to arrest the advance, and on December 1 the Central China Area Army was ordered to attack Nanjing. On December 10, the general attack on Nanjing began, and by the 13th the city had fallen.

In taking the city, the Japanese army committed many atrocities, and killed many POWs and non-combatants (Nanjing Incident). In a diary entry dated January 6, 1938, Ishii Itarō, director-general of the East Asia Bureau of the Ministry of Foreign Affairs, wrote: "I have received telegrams from Shanghai reporting atrocities committed by our troops in Nanjing. Looting, rape, unspeakable terror. Ah! Is this how imperial soldiers behave?"

Throughout Japan, people thought of themselves as the "victors" in the occupation of Nanjing. This had a major impact on how the event was processed

9-4. Japanese tank corps destroys Zhonghua Gate in Nanjing

and on the terms for peace. At a meeting at the end of December, the Konoe cabinet decided on a new China policy that would place North China and the Shanghai area under strong Japanese influence, both politically and economically, reflecting the perception that Japan was the victor in this conflict.

In March 1938, the Central China Area Army set up the Reformed Government of the Republic of China to govern central China and to rival the Provisional Government of North China.

The Brussels Conference and the Trautmann Mediation

Chiang Kai-shek then sought to achieve ultimate victory from the strife in China through "internationalization"; that is, by asking the Soviet Union to join the war against Japan following the signing of the Sino-Soviet Non-Aggression Pact (August 1937), and by litigating the situation in North China before the League of Nations (mid-September). At the same time, the basic position of the Japanese government in processing the conflicts in China was to approach them as a bilateral problem, and to eschew the intercession and interference of third-party nations. However, as matters dragged on, Japan also began to entertain the idea of seeking peace through the "amicable good offices" of third-party nations.

The United Kingdom was the first to offer assistance. In mid-September 1937, Sir Robert Craigie, the newly appointed ambassador to Japan, approached Foreign Minister Hirota about the possibilities for intercession. Hirota laid out his specific ideas about peace terms. He wanted to see a demilitarized zone set up in North China, control over anti-Japanese elements, cooperation in fighting Communism, and acquiescence regarding Manchukuo. In essence, particularly in their continued emphasis on "joint anti-Communism," these terms were extensions of Hirota's Three Principles and the Kawagoe-Chiang talks from before the "series of incidents" in China.

9-5. Brussels Conference

At the League of Nations, China's representative, Wellington Koo, called for international sanctions against Japan because of the invasion, but only the USSR was in favor. The matter of the Second Sino-Japanese War was referred to a special committee. The committee prepared a report calling Japan's action a violation of the Nine-Power Treaty, and submitted it to the full Assembly, which called for a meeting of the participant nations of the Nine-Power Treaty (Brussels Conference). The Brussels Conference happened at the request of the United States, which participated even though it was not a member of the League of Nations.

The Roosevelt administration had avoided friction with Japan, but as Japan's war with China intensified it grew increasingly interested in maintaining peace in the Asia-Pacific region through multilateral cooperation. Roosevelt's first step would be a speech in early October in which he characterized Japan and Germany as an "infectious disease" that needed to be kept apart from the community of nations. But when it came to actual sanctions, America took a cautious approach.

Japan feared intervention by Western nations, and a cabinet meeting in late October decided against participation in the Brussels Conference. In the statement regarding that decision, the cabinet described Japan's actions in China as "self-defense measures against provocations from the Chinese side," and reiterated its position that the matter could "only be resolved through direct negotiations between the two nations." At the same time, in late October Foreign Minister Hirota informed ambassadors that Japan was prepared to accept the "amicable good offices" of third-party nations. Only Germany, however, put forward a concrete proposal for peace terms.

The Army General Staff Office responded to Germany's proposals with enthusiasm, and officials from the intelligence section engaged in frequent contact with the German embassy. This interaction was successful, and in late October the peace terms were presented to Oskar Trautmann, Germany's ambassador to China, in Shanghai. Meanwhile, in Tokyo, Foreign Minister Hirota asked German ambassador to Japan Herbert von Dirksen to share with the China side peace terms that were roughly the same as those that had been shown to Craigie. In early November, Trautmann delivered the Japan side's peace terms to Chiang. Chiang, believing that the Brussels Conference then underway would decide on sanctions against Japan, rejected them.

At the Brussels Conference, China pleaded for economic sanctions and material assistance, but most of the participating nations were very cautious, each for their own reasons. In the end, the conference ended in mid-November with no more than a statement criticizing Japan.

Konoe's *Aite to Sezu* Declaration

As the Brussels Conference ended without any tangible action being taken, and as Nationalist China was losing ground in Shanghai, Chiang Kai-shek began to change his thinking. Early in December 1937, through Ambassador Trautmann, Chiang told Japan he was willing to negotiate based on Japan's terms. Hirota avoided responding immediately, however, equivocating that recent changes in the situation required changes in the peace terms. Japan was about to attack Nanjing. In fact, over the objections of East Asia Bureau director-general Ishii and others, the peace terms that were offered to the Chinese side by the end of December contained additional demands, such as the stationing of peacekeeping troops in North China and Inner Mongolia and the establishment of a "special division" in North China. China demanded an explanation of these new conditions, but the Japanese government regarded this as a delaying tactic, and leaned toward rejecting Germany's intervention. The Army General Staff believed the fall of Nanjing would make a good opportunity to end the war on generous terms.

At the same time, within the Nationalist government there was a division of opinion over whether to accept peace with Japan. More than a few leaders sided with Wang Zhaoming in thinking peace was the best idea. In the end, Chiang rejected the German mediation in early January 1938 and set a course to fight a war of resistance. In Japan, the Imperial Council was convened on January 11, at the request of the Army General Staff Office, for the first time since the Russo-Japanese War. But that was hardly the venue for a discussion of how to sweeten the terms for peace. The Army General Staff Office argued to the end in favor of peace through negotiations, but on January 15 the government finally decided to break off talks.

The fall of Nanjing was the best chance to achieve peace between Japan and China, but that opportunity was lost. The Imperial Council decided that if peace was not achieved, Japan could not expect to resolve the situation by talking to Chiang Kai-shek and his regime. Rather, Japan would help the "New China Administration" get off the ground, and either annihilate the Nationalist government or bring it under the control of the New China Administration. This was the context in which Prime Minister Konoe made his *aite to sezu* declaration (also called the First Konoe Declaration) on January 16, which essentially stated that Japan refused to deal with the Nationalist government on an equal basis in negotiations.

Seen from the Chinese side, the *aite to sezu* declaration did not mean the disruption of peace negotiations. Wang Zhaoming and Kung Hsiang-hsi had long advocated diplomatic negotiations, and even Chiang Kai-shek, who had opted for the route of relentless war, left open the possibility of both war and peace. The termination of peace negotiations without thorough discussions still left both the route to war and the route to peace open, with no consensus achieved. In fact, another attempt at peace would arise a half-year later, with Kung as the contact person (the Ugaki-Kung Plan).

Confusion on the Road to Resolution

In late May 1938, Prime Minister Konoe Fumimaro shuffled his cabinet, selecting Ugaki Kazushige as foreign minister and Itagaki Seishirō as minister of the army. His aim was to correct the course he had set with the *aite to sezu* declaration. Ugaki agreed to join the cabinet only on the condition that Japan would not hold to its refusal to deal with the Chiang Kai-shek regime, and that it would open peace talks with the new administration in Chongqing (the new capital of the Nationalist government). In an effort to bring matters in China to a swift resolution, after the cabinet reorganization, in June Konoe replaced the dormant Imperial General Headquarters and Government Liaison Conference with the Five Ministers' Conference (consisting of the prime

9-6. Anti-Japanese slogans displayed during the Second Sino-Japanese War

Konoe Fumimaro (1891–1945)

9-7. Konoe Fumimaro

Konoe Fumimaro, born in Tokyo in October 1891, was the eldest son of the Konoe family. The Konoe were the highest-ranking of the Five Regent Houses, the families with the closest connections to the imperial throne. His father, Atsumaro, was a noble (holding the title of prince) and served as the chairman of the House of Peers before dying at the young age of forty. Fumimaro, whose mother had died shortly after his birth, was only twelve when he lost his father. His younger years were thus a lonely time. As a student, he took an interest in philosophy and made his way through the First Higher School and into the philosophy department at Tokyo Imperial University. He then found a new interest in socialism, which led him to transfer to Kyoto Imperial University to study under Marxist economist Kawakami Hajime. He went on to become a member of the House of Peers in 1916 and, at the age of twenty-seven, published "Ei-Bei hon'i no heiwa-shugi o haisu" (Reject the Pax Anglo-Americana) in the issue of *Nihon oyobi Nihon-jin* (Japan and the Japanese) dated December 15, 1918.

The essay assailed contemporary international society, which Konoe saw as a dichotomy of the "have" countries (which aimed to maintain the status quo) and the "have-not" countries (which aimed to overturn the status quo). He argued that Japan—one of the "have-nots"—should embark on an open campaign to "overturn the status quo" of the Western powers' vested interests. Arguing that "nations which stand to benefit from upholding the status quo call for peace, while nations which stand to benefit from overturning the status quo cry for war," Konoe made an incisive reading of the international politics of the minister, the finance minister, the foreign minister, the army minister, and the navy minister).

Japan's China policy was based on the assumption that Chiang Kai-shek would reject the peace agreement. Japan's aims were to combine the new regimes ("provisional governments," "reformation governments") in the occupied territories of North China and Central China into a central government that could supplant the Nationalist government. Once the new regimes became fully functional, Japan planned to either destroy the Nationalist government or bring it under the authority of the new regimes. The problem was that the fall of Nanjing had brought no visible change to the administration in Chongqing.

Faced with this situation, the Japanese

---

time. He also saw substantial promise in the development of democracy and humanitarianism, praising President Woodrow Wilson's vision of national self-determination and the conceptual foundation of the League of Nations. Konoe also accompanied the Japanese delegation to the Paris Peace Conference, where the peace process struck him as a "restructuring of the world" in the spirit of "justice and humanity." At the same time, the gathering gave Konoe a firsthand glimpse of Wilson's new diplomacy being "trampled by European politicians' obsession with their own realistic interests."

Although Konoe served as the president of his father's Tōa Dōbunkai (East Asia Common Culture Society) and the head of the Tōa Dōbun Shoin (East Asia Cultural College) in Shanghai, his connections with China were relatively sparse. He visited the country only twice and had little in the way of a personal network with key Chinese figures. In the aftermath of the Manchurian Incident, Konoe came out in vocal defense of the Japanese army's actions. In a context where Japan was denied the two basic principles of the freedom of economics and transport and the freedom of immigration, Konoe argued, the "only path to surviving today" amid Japan's struggles with an increasing population was to expand into Manchuria-Mongolia.

Attributing the growing tensions between Japan and China not to Japan's actions but rather to China's lack of understanding, scheming by the Western powers, and communist machinations, Konoe urged China to acknowledge its past shortcomings in relation to the worsening situation. His career continued to develop, eventually culminating in his appointment as prime minister in June 1937. Just a month after forming his first cabinet at the age of forty-five, he found himself confronting a crisis: the Marco Polo Bridge Incident. While Konoe himself was wary of expanding the war effort, he agreed to send troops to North China with the conviction that a hard-line, uncompromising response would prompt China to back down. He would serve as prime minister a total of three times leading up to the war with the United States (June 1937–January 1939, July 1940–July 1941, and July–October 1941), but his inability to bring the Second Sino-Japanese War under control—the preeminent issue during his time in office—has lowered his reputation considerably.

Konoe's approach to foreign relations rested on his belief that solutions to the Second Sino-Japanese War hinged on far-reaching, bold "reforms" that could rescue domestic politics from the "grip of the military." When he formed his second cabinet, he thus set out to initiate an overhaul of domestic politics by forming a new party and fostering a movement to establish a new political system. A new structure took shape in the form of the Imperial Rule Assistance Association (Taisei Yokusankai), which began operations in October 1940, but the organization was more of an apolitical auxiliary body than a full-scale reimagining of the political landscape. Konoe's third cabinet put repairing Japan's relations with the United States high on the priority list. Although he hoped to bring that goal to fruition through his own proposal for a summit conference with President Franklin Roosevelt, the United States would only sit down for talks if Japan agreed to pull out of China—a demand that Konoe was unable to meet.

In February 1945, during the latter stages of the Pacific War, Konoe submitted the so-called Konoe Memorial to the emperor in his capacity as a senior statesman. The report underlined what Konoe saw as the most pressing cause for concern: that Japan's defeat would lead to a communist revolution. In that light, bringing the war to an end was contingent on purging the army of its Soviet-leaning faction. Following Japan's capitulation, a warrant for Konoe's arrest as a suspected war criminal was issued in December 1945. On the morning of the day he was to report to prison, however, he took his own life. His suicide note explained that he found "the idea of being tried as a war criminal in an American court unbearable."

government was divided into two camps: One side, represented by Foreign Minister Ugaki, was carrying on the diplomatic tradition discussed previously. They were more interested in direct negotiations with the Nationalist government than in the rapid establishment of a central government.

In June 1938, Ishii argued in favor of working with the Nationalist government, saying it was not realistic to hope to precipitate Chiang's resignation by combining the emerging administrations to form a new central government, or somehow merging the Nationalist government into provisional and reformation governments. Maintaining that the Nationalist government should be recognized as the rightful government, Ishii recommended to the foreign minister that Japan continue to negotiate with the Nationalist government, and that it initiate peace negotiations before attacking the city of Hankou.

On the other side were those who sought the collapse of the Nationalist government through military action, or through some operation that would result in Chiang's resignation. These opponents of the Nationalist government were represented by Army Minister Itagaki and by the Japanese army leadership in China.

The Five Ministers' Conference took the position that if Chiang were willing to step aside, Japan would allow certain members of his administration to form a new central government. This could create the possibility of limited peace negotiations. The biggest obstacle was the fundamental weakness of the new administrations that were to be responsible for forming the new central government.

The Ugaki Plan and the Idea of Japanese Cooperation with the United Kingdom

Foreign Minister Ugaki Kazushige, who aligned himself with Ishii Itarō's argument in favor of working with the Nationalist government, engaged in several peace initiatives with the Nationalist government. One of these was the Ugaki-Kung Plan, worked out by Ugaki and Nationalist Premier Kung Hsiang-hsi (H. H. Kung). These two men had been brought together by Kung's secretary Qiao Fusan and Japan's consul general in Hong Kong, Nakamura Toyoichi. Nakamura and Qiao met in Hong Kong from late June to September 1938. As instructed by Ugaki, Nakamura was taking a flexible position on peace terms. Ultimately, however, these talks were broken off, as Ugaki came under pressure from anti-Chiang sentiment in Japan that called for the resignation of Chiang Kai-shek.

Ugaki shifted his attention to other routes, in particular contact with Kung through Kayano

Ugaki Kazushige (1868–1956)

9-8. Ugaki Kazushige

After graduating from primary school, Okayama Prefecture native Ugaki Kazushige took a job as an assistant teacher at his alma mater. His aspirations for a military career, however, eventually led him to enroll at the Imperial Military Academy (as part of the institution's first graduating class), continue on to the Army War College, and make two trips to Germany for further study. Over the course of his ensuing career, he served in multiple key army posts and impressed Tanaka Giichi with his performance. That helped pave the way toward even higher posts: Ugaki became vice-minister of the army in 1923 and ascended to army minister the following year, occupying that cabinet position for a total of five years as a member of several Minseitō administrations. An important development that made a name for Army Minister Ugaki was the "Ugaki disarmament" effort, which Ugaki implemented with the assistance of Finance Minister Hamaguchi Osachi and Foreign Minister Shidehara Kijūrō. Ugaki's project aimed to both conform to international calls for disarmament and simultaneously modernize Japan's army equipment. To do so, he set out to eliminate four infantry divisions, streamline personnel, and bring in a variety of new weaponry and equipment. Despite fierce opposition from within the army organization, Ugaki went through with his bold reforms—changes that earned him

Nagatomo. Kayano was an important source of information for Hong Kong consul general Nakamura. He had gone to China immediately after the Marco Polo Bridge Incident on orders from Matsui Iwane, the general in command of the Shanghai expeditionary force, to seek a route to peace. While in Shanghai, Kayano had sought out contact with people from the Nationalist government who were living there, and he grew confident he could initiate direct peace negotiations on terms that were favorable to Japan. When Kayano arrived in Tokyo early in June 1938, he looked up his old acquaintance, retired politician Ogawa Heikichi. Ogawa took a very positive view, and passed the word to Konoe and Ugaki. Ultimately, this led to direct dialogue between Ugaki and Kung. Ugaki wanted direct talks, and he had already dropped the precondition that Chiang step down before peace could be established. He received the approval of the Five Ministers' Conference in late September, and he also made his proposal to the emperor and obtained tacit consent for what was called the Kayano Plan.

But then, at the end of September, Ugaki abruptly resigned. The reasons for his resignation are not clear, but it is possible that his plans for peace through negotiation with the Nationalist

respect for his ability to control the military but also stoked smoldering discontent within military ranks.

Ugaki focused his energies on ensuring the independence of the military (especially the prerogative of the supreme command), but he actually worked most closely not with the hawkish Seiyūkai but rather with the Minseitō, which was critical of the military. It was a bit of a paradoxical balancing act: by eagerly collaborating with a party cabinet as a representative of the military, Ugaki was aiming to prevent critical assaults on military independence—and thereby make the military's political independence and the party-cabinet system function in harmony. When Tanaka Giichi became prime minister and installed a Seiyūkai cabinet, therefore, Ugaki turned down the offer to stay on as army minister. Although he returned to the helm of the Army Ministry in 1929 as part of the Hamaguchi cabinet, he resigned in June 1931 and became governor-general of Korea after his second disarmament effort (military-system reforms) ended in failure.

After the Manchurian Incident, the political situation began to center on harnessing the strength of the parties in forging a "Seiyūkai-Minseitō partnership" that would enable the government to deal with crises both at home and abroad more effectively. If the Seiyūkai and Minseitō were to join hands, Ugaki was the leading candidate for the premiership. From his post in Korea, Ugaki was hoping for that opportunity to come his way—but the Seiyūkai-Minseitō partnership never materialized. Frustrated at the workings of party politics, Ugaki began to align himself with the Research Institute of National Policy and its critical stance on Japan's existing parties. When Hirota Kōki's administration resigned en masse in January 1937, Ugaki received an imperial order to form a cabinet, seemingly making his ascension to the premiership a foregone conclusion. That was when the army stepped in, refusing to endorse anyone to serve as army minister. Lacking an army minister for his cabinet, Ugaki tried to get Lord Keeper of the Privy Seal Yuasa Kurahei to persuade the emperor to name an army minister via imperial order. The plan failed, however, and Ugaki abandoned any hopes of assembling a cabinet. One reason the army was so set on preventing Ugaki from taking over as prime minister was that army officials suspected him of aiding an attempted coup in 1931 (the March Incident), but the more important factor was his past political activity: the army saw Ugaki and his close ties with the Minseitō as having obstructed efforts to expand the military and drive reform policies.

In May 1938, Ugaki became foreign minister and began working to bring the ongoing, deadlocked Second Sino-Japanese War to a conclusion. His attempts to resolve the conflict included enlisting the United Kingdom's help in mediating negotiations and developing overtures for peace, but he resigned suddenly after just under five months in office with nothing to show for his efforts.

Ugaki's skills and knack for action in both military affairs and diplomacy were first-rate, but his successes in shrinking the military during the years of Taishō democracy (1920s) gave him a reputation as a "big gun" in controlling the army (which had fostered momentum for making him prime minister). That association with military reductions brought disappointing results in the "age of reform" in the 1930s, as the army exacted revenge by denying him the opportunity to preside over a cabinet as prime minister.

government lacked support in Japan. Furthermore, he opposed the army's plan for the establishment of the Asia Development Board. Ugaki must have realized that if he stuck to his ideas, the Konoe cabinet would be forced to resign, and the peace process would also collapse.

While he served as foreign minister, Ugaki was also working on the idea of cooperating with the United Kingdom regarding China. The key person in this effort was Ikeda Shigeaki, the new finance minister in the reshuffled Konoe cabinet. Ikeda believed the issues should be resolved through cooperation between Japan and the United Kingdom, imposing on China a "reconciliation" that would be advantageous to Japan, leaving postwar business under the powerful influence of Japan and the United Kingdom. These ideas, which appealed to the elder statesman Saionji Kinmochi and other Anglophiles, became part of the Ugaki Plan. Although Ugaki approached negotiations with British ambassador Craigie, he was intent on negotiations with China and less interested in the United Kingdom's intervention, so the negotiations never got very far.

Ugaki's resignation, however, did not cause the peace process to fall apart. Another process was ascendant: Gao Zongwu's plan to create a new central government in China.

Declaration of a New Order in East Asia

In the fall of 1938, the Army General Staff Office began to carry out two major operations: the Wuhan (Hankou) Operation and the Canton (Guangdong) Operation. With these two campaigns, Japan gained effective control of all the important parts of China, generating expectations that the fall of the Chiang Kai-shek regime was not far off. In late October, the Central China Area Army occupied Hankou. In late September it took decisive action in the South China Campaign and occupied Guangdong. Nonetheless, the Chiang regime, which was sheltering in the provisional capital Chongqing, showed no sign of surrendering. Instead, it focused on a narrower front, and waged a war of attrition. Japan's army in Tokyo responded by deciding on a new direction for how the war would be conducted, and received the approval of the emperor in early December. The army's new goals were to limit the area of actual fighting, stabilize and restore security in the occupied territories, access and exploit natural resources, and transition to a "long-term war of attrition."

On November 3, 1938, the Konoe cabinet issued the Declaration of a New Order in East Asia, also known as the Second Konoe Declaration. Japan defined this as the new international order in East Asia. It declared the promotion of joint construction in Japan, Manchukuo, and China as "unwavering principles of the Empire," and stated that the three nations would move forward together, as equals, in economic cooperation and mutual defense.

One month earlier, in early October, the US government had issued a long memorandum citing examples of discriminatory treatment of Americans, and market monopolization, in China since the Marco Polo Bridge Incident. The memorandum said these were violations of both the open-door policy (giving Japan, the United States, and European nations equal access to Chinese trade) and the 1922 Nine-Power Treaty affirming China's sovereignty as described in the open-door policy, and demanded that improvements be made. Arita Hachirō, who had taken Ugaki's place as foreign minister, disputed these claims, arguing that ideas and principles dating back to before the "series of incidents" in China were no longer applicable to the present or future situation in East Asia. He officially repudiated the Nine-Power Treaty and other international accords. The Declaration of a New Order in East Asia was therefore an expression of the principles informing the new order in East Asia, supplanting the old international order that had been imposed by Western nations.

The confrontation between the United States and Japan regarding the form that the international order should take reached a peak at the end of December 1938, as the United States let Japan know it could not tolerate a "new order" that ignored the open-door policy. However, that confrontation did not lead directly to war. Japan's wartime economic system may have supported the current new order in East Asia, but it was also overwhelmingly dependent on the United States. In other words, there would be no conflict with the United Kingdom or the United States as long as the "New Order in East Asia" was based on an economic open-door policy rather than the pursuit of self-sufficiency.

The Progress of the Gao Zongwu Plan

The Declaration of a New Order in East Asia stated that if the Nationalist government changed its policies on opposition to Japan, its tolerance of Communism, and its personnel lineup, then Japan was prepared to reconsider its refusal to negotiate. Around this time, Gao Zongwu was head of the Asia bureau of the Nationalist government's diplomatic branch. He was a central figure in a newly surfaced plan to install Wang Jingwei as head of the unified central government of the Japan-occupied territories, undermine the Chiang administration, and ultimately to force Chiang Kai-shek to resign and shift his position to one supporting peace with Japan. Proponents of this "Gao Zongwu Plan" included Army Colonel Kagesa Sadaaki and Lieutenant Colonel Imai Takeo on the Japan side, and Gao on the China side, as well as Zhou Fohai (former deputy head of the propaganda department of the Nationalist Party), who was regarded as a close colleague of Wang.

Beginning in mid-November 1938, Gao met regularly with Wang and Japanese officials, including Kagesa, to work on the action plan for extracting Wang from Chongqing and the terms of peace. In late November, a joint document was signed which centered on terms for the garrisoning of Japanese troops. Of particular importance were the troops dedicated to fighting Communism in designated areas of Mengjiang and North China. The Ministry of Foreign Affairs was kept uninformed.

In early December, Kagesa and his colleagues whisked Wang and his associates out of Chongqing and sent them to Hanoi. In concert with that action, on December 22 the Japanese government published the Third Konoe Declaration (a statement by Prime Minister Konoe). The main message of that statement was approval of the Japan-China Cooperation Document. At the end of December, from Hanoi, Wang called for peace with Japan. In an open telegram, he encouraged influential members of the Nationalist Party to leave the Chiang regime. Regarding the peace terms, he stressed that the Japanese army would soon withdraw troops, and that Japanese troops would occupy only limited areas.

Within the Army General Staff Office, progress was being made on a cease-fire agreement based on the situation following the Wuhan Campaign. The terms of this agreement, called "Adjusted Guidelines on the New Japan-China Relationship," were approved by the Imperial Council in November 1938. They listed requirements that were not part of the Third Konoe Declaration or the Japan-China Cooperation Document, including the "divided governance and cooperation principle" adapted to the political situation; security troops stationed in the triangle formed by the cities of Nanjing, Shanghai, and Hangzhou; an economic "strong bond area"—effectively a closed-door policy zone—formed in the lower Yangtze River; and the dispatch of Japanese advisors. These stipulations were harsh, going beyond the terms of the Twenty-One Demands, and they were not shown to the Wang government until the fall of 1939.

Wang's escape from Chongqing was confirmed in January 1939; shortly thereafter, Prime Minister

Konoe's entire cabinet resigned. Even though not many powerful members of the Nationalist Party or anti-Chiang military officials responded to Wang's escape from Chongqing, Gao, Wang, and their associates continued their efforts to form a new central government. In May 1939, on a visit to Japan, Wang himself told Kagesa of the decision to set up a new administration. In early June, this new government was recognized by the Five Ministers' Conference. The Wang regime was well on its way to being recognized, but a growing chorus of people within the Japanese army leadership expressed skepticism about the real capabilities of the new government.

Other Nations Aid China

After the Marco Polo Bridge Incident, it was the Soviet Union that sprang to the aid of China. In August 1937, the Soviet Union entered into a nonaggression pact with the Nationalist government. It also provided weapons, ammunition, and aircraft, and dispatched volunteer troops and groups of military advisors. This assistance made a significant difference in China's ability to defend itself until aid from the United States and the United Kingdom became fully available.

Direct aid from the United States to China began with a US$25 million loan agreement (provision of export credit) at the end of 1938. It took off from there, with the United States becoming the largest donor to China beginning in 1940. The United Kingdom's assistance to China was limited to meeting its moral obligations, but in 1938 it built the Burma Route (completed in December 1938), and moved in the direction of providing loans. In March 1939 it supplied 5 million pounds to help stabilize China's currency.

In these ways, the United States and the United Kingdom began to get serious about assisting in China at the end of 1938, but that did not mean they had hardened their stance on Japan. They stood by the guidelines of Secretary of State Hull, who said the United States would "not stir up trouble with Japan, not withdraw from Asia, not consent to Japan's actions." At the same time, the United Kingdom was increasingly reliant on the United

Arita Hachirō (1884–1965)

9-9. Arita Hachirō

Born in Sado, Niigata Prefecture, Hachirō was adopted into the Arita family shortly after birth. His blood relatives also included prominent personages: his biological older brother was Yamamoto Teijirō, who would go on to become a Seiyūkai member of the House of Representatives and serve in a cabinet. Arita graduated from the First Higher School and Tokyo Imperial University before passing the foreign-service examination in 1909, making his way into service the same year as fellow diplomats Itō Nobufumi and Kurusu Saburō. The following year, he took his first diplomatic appointment at the consulate general in Mukden, which gave way to posts in a variety of locations. Arita also accompanied the Japanese delegation to the Paris Peace Conference. The experience in Paris opened his eyes to weaknesses in Japan's foreign policy structure leading him to form the "Ministry of Foreign Affairs Reform League" with such like-minded ministry members as Shigemitsu Mamoru, Horinouchi Kensuke, and Saitō Hiroshi. As the organization's primary coordinator, Arita worked to coordinate requests for efforts like enhancing and expanding the organization of the Ministry of Foreign Affairs, training ministry personnel, and making open-door arrangements.

Arita later became Japan's consul general in Tianjin in 1925 and director-general of the Asia Bureau under Prime Minister (and, concurrently, Foreign Minister) Tanaka Giichi in 1927, remaining in the latter position through 1930 under subsequent foreign minister Shidehara Kijūrō. Arita was serving as Japan's minister to Austria when the Manchurian Incident occurred, and he weighed in on the situation by sending the government a telegram reprimanding the Kwantung Army for its "reckless" advance into North Manchuria. In May 1932, Arita served as vice-minister under foreign ministers Yoshizawa Kenkichi and Uchida Yasuya (Kōsai). His career then took him back

States with respect to problems in East Asia. That dependence was only magnified when war broke out in Europe in September 1939, and the United Kingdom shifted its focus to its own defense.

The Blockade of the Tianjin Concession: A Crisis in Japan-UK Relations

In June 1939, some influential people sympathetic to Japan were killed inside the British concession.

abroad in 1934, when he became Japan's ambassador to Belgium.

After a stint as ambassador to China, Arita made his way back home in 1936 when Prime Minister Hirota Kōki—who had risen to power in the aftermath of the February 26 Incident—made him his foreign minister. With the military wielding a stronger political influence at home and increasingly tense relations with China, the United States, and the United Kingdom brewing abroad, Arita aimed to mend ties with the major powers around the shared goal of containing the spread of Communism. His past work experience in Europe had made him conscious of the Soviet threat, and his first priority was forging a pact with Germany. As talks about a possible Japan-Germany partnership had already been making progress via the army route, Arita rode that momentum and directed the negotiations toward a pact that would stop short of a military alliance (into a "gray area," as Arita put it). The talks eventually culminated in the Anti-Comintern Pact, which Japan and Germany signed in November 1936. Efforts to conclude a similar anti-Communist agreement with China failed to get off the ground, however. Arita's time atop the Ministry of Foreign Affairs ended with the mass resignation of the Hirota cabinet in February 1937.

With the Second Sino-Japanese War still dragging on, Arita found himself back at the top of the Ministry of Foreign Affairs when Ugaki Kazushige suddenly resigned as foreign minister in October 1938. Shortly after Arita once again assumed the foreign-minister post, Prime Minister Konoe Fumimaro issued his statement on the "New Order in East Asia"—and Arita's chief foreign-relations objective immediately became the completion of the "new order." As the main text notes, Arita informed the United States and the United Kingdom immediately after Konoe's proclamation that it would be "impossible to apply prewar standards and principles in unaltered form toward solutions to present and future situations." Arita was not the first to suggest that the situation in China had simply developed outside the original scope of the Nine-Power Treaty and other international principles; as foreign ministers, Uchida and Hirota had also made the argument that the existing standards no longer applied to the current conditions. What Arita did, however, was appeal directly to the United States and the United Kingdom and demand revisions to the standards. Although he saw the formation of an East Asia–specific, bloc-type regional order as an inevitability in the evolving world economy, he wanted to avoid conflict with the United States and the United Kingdom—two countries with which Japan was economically interdependent. That diplomatic element explains why Arita stayed as far away as possible from forging a military alliance during negotiations with Germany surrounding a possible pact—which the army was pushing hard for in hopes of bolstering the united front against Communism—and held fast to limiting the scope of the tie-up to the Soviet Union. Arita maintained the same resolute stance under the ensuing Hiranuma Kiichirō administration, too. When the Japanese army blockaded British and French concessions in Tianjin in June 1939 and anti-British sentiment continued to rage nationwide, Arita met with British ambassador to Japan Robert Craigie and tried to convince him to see Japan's side of things. Arita ultimately left the Ministry of Foreign Affairs in August 1939, when the signing of the Treaty of Non-Aggression between Germany and the USSR brought negotiations on a Japan-Germany military alliance to a standstill. The diplomatic frustrations prompted the Hiranuma cabinet to resign en masse.

When the war in Europe broke out in September 1939, Japan took a non-interventionist policy and instead tried to devise a resolution to the Second Sino-Japanese War. Arita once again became foreign minister as part of the Yonai Mitsumasa cabinet in January 1940. That spring, with the German army's sweeping conquest of Europe showing no signs of slowing, a chorus of voices in the army and pockets of the political landscape began calling for stronger ties with Germany and Italy and an aggressive southward expansion. Although Arita worried that adopting a hasty southward-advance doctrine might endanger Japan's relations with the United States and the United Kingdom, the surge of support for upending the status quo in league with Germany proved too fervent for the Yonai administration to weather; the cabinet stepped down as a group in July 1940, and Arita was out as foreign minister.

In retaliation, the Japanese Northern China Area Army blockaded the British and French concessions in Tianjin that were the seat of finance and business in North China. The United Kingdom was perceived as hindering Japan's ability to respond to the conflicts in China and establish a new order in East Asia. The blockade of the concessions was an effort to achieve harmonization by resolving the incidents and striking a blow at the government of Chiang Kai-shek. The plan to blockade the concessions began in the summer of 1938, and Japan gradually tightened the net thereafter.

Within the British government, which took the blockade seriously, some wanted to revisit sanctions against Japan, but Prime Minister Neville Chamberlain opted to pursue diplomatic negotiations instead. The Arita-Craigie talks took place in Tokyo against a backdrop of very vocal and widespread protests against the United Kingdom. In late July 1939, the UK made concessions and a compromise was reached. the United Kingdom agreed to accept the status quo in China (i.e., the existence of a state of war), and said it would not obstruct the Japanese military's efforts to maintain security in China. In a political context, accepting the status quo signaled a loss of prestige for the United Kingdom more than an acceptance of Japan's right of belligerency under international law. While China criticized the United Kingdom harshly for this act of appeasement, Japanese prime minister Hiranuma Kiichirō took a highly positive view of the blow against the Chiang administration.

The Anti-British Movement and Japan's War with the United Kingdom

In the long run, there was more behind the Pacific War than just the conflict between Japan and the United States. If one were to look solely at the division between the US insistence on the global principles of open-door policies and free trade on the one side and Japan's aims of building a closed New Order in East Asia on the other, one could very well interpret the Pacific War as a direct offshoot of that fundamental conflict over the optimal international order. However, war with the United States was no easy mission to undertake; Japan obviously had reservations about waging war against a country that it depended on so heavily economically. The prospects of building a New Order in East Asia, too, hinged on Japan's economic interdependence with the United States. What broke those economic bonds was the September 1940 Tripartite Pact (between Germany, Italy, and Japan), which many observers convincingly cite as the actual impetus for the war against the United States.

A broader look at the domestic and international climate shaping Japan's circumstances in the 1930s also shows that Anglo-Japanese relations were actually more fraught with tension than Japan-US relations were. The United Kingdom had maintained a diplomatic stance toward appeasing Japan amid intense Anglo-Japanese trade friction that came to a head in the first half of the decade. However, events in the latter half of the decade exacerbated the animosity between the two. The Second Sino-Japanese War created a specific local concern for the United Kingdom as Japanese military operations threatened British interests south of the Yangtze River, and Japan's proclamations of its intentions to establish a New Order in East Asia in the fall of 1938 fanned anxiety on an even broader scale. Both at home in Japan and abroad, anti-British sentiment ran rampant; the number of voices calling the United Kingdom the biggest barrier to the construction of a new order swelled.

One of the key forces fueling that antagonism was the Greater Asia Association. Committed to a vision of "Pan-Asianism," the Greater Asia Association's movement started in Japan and grew from there—not only inspiring Indian traders (non-resident Indians) who were planning their own anti-British movement from within the British empire but also sweeping through Taiwan, Korea, China, and beyond. By the time of the Arita-Craigie talks in the summer of 1939, the Greater Asia Association's drive had developed into a massive political movement. The Pan-Asian ideology implanted perceptions of an "exploited Asia" and the "exploitative British imperialism" in the public consciousness, stirring a powerful undercurrent that drove the momentum of the Second Sino-Japanese War toward a war between Japan and the United Kingdom. While no clear anti-American movement took shape in Japan, the anti-British movement was intense.

The Death of Saitō Hiroshi and the USS *Astoria*

Saitō Hiroshi (1886–1939) studied at the Gakushūin, where he demonstrated exceptional performance in Chinese classics, and then made his way to Tokyo Imperial University. After graduating in 1910 and entering the Ministry of Foreign Affairs, he took an assignment at the Japanese consulate in Seattle and ended up spending eight years in the United States. There, Saitō honed his command of American English and developed his social skills, forming a personal network in a variety of professional circles along the way. He married musician Nagayo Miyoko, who was the sister-in-law of Inukai Takeru (the son of Prime Minister Inukai Tsuyoshi). Saitō's ensuing career included several trips to major international gatherings: in addition to serving as a member of the Japanese delegation to the Paris Peace Conference in 1919, he was the interpreter and chief secretary for Minister Plenipotentiary Katō Tomosaburō at the Washington Naval Conference. He also served as Japan's consul general in New York, where he drew the attention of Matsudaira Tsuneo, and traveled with the Japanese contingent to the London Naval Conference in 1930. Having built a laudable track record and impressed key figures, Saitō landed a string of high-ranking positions: counselor at the Japanese embassy in Washington, ambassador to the Netherlands, and, at the age of forty-seven, ambassador to the United States.

In 1934, Saitō proposed that Japan and the United States make a joint declaration in hopes of dispelling the American public's qualms about Japan's withdrawal from the naval treaty and restoring the sense of trust that had once bonded the two nations. The idea was to have both countries recognize their responsibilities and interests as "major stabilizing forces" on both sides of the Pacific. While the Department of State rebuffed the suggestion, Saitō took it upon himself to assuage Americans' fears by giving talks on Japan's standpoint and fielding questions from the public across the country. When a Japanese naval aircraft fired on the USS *Panay* in December 1937, Saitō seized the development as a chance to appear on American radio. In using the platform to assure listeners that the attack had been a mistake and that Japan would promise to keep foreigners in Japan-occupied China safe and secure, Saitō was taking matters into his own hands—neither the Ministry of Foreign Affairs in Tokyo nor the Department of State had given him the green light to make such statements on the airwaves.

9-10. Saitō Hiroshi

Saitō soon began to experience a decline in his health, as a lung affliction began to worsen in the summer of 1938. He ultimately withdrew from his official post that winter in hopes of recuperating, but he succumbed to the disease in Washington at the end of February 1939. His funeral took place in Washington. Joseph Ballantine (deputy director of the Office of Far Eastern Affairs in the US Department of State) proposed escorting Saitō's ashes back to Japan aboard the USS *Astoria*, a heavy cruiser in the American fleet; the escort was an honor normally reserved for the death of an incumbent ambassador. While some of Ballantine's colleagues objected to the gesture, a recommendation from Stanley Hornbeck (a political advisor to Secretary of State Cordell Hull) convinced President Franklin Roosevelt to sign off on the idea immediately. Foreign Minister Arita Hachirō thanked the American government for its gesture in a speech to Congress, while Yoshida Shigeru, who had just concluded his time as ambassador to the United Kingdom and made his way back to Japan, sent Ambassador Joseph Grew a letter expressing his gratitude.

Once the USS *Astoria* had brought Saitō's ashes to Yokohama, the Ministry of Foreign Affairs held Saitō's funeral at Honganji Temple in the Tsukiji district of Tokyo. With former prime ministers Konoe Fumimaro and Hirota Kōki in attendance, Foreign Minister Arita called the funeral a testament to the friendship between Japan and the United States, and Ambassador Joseph Grew responded with a moving address of his own. Saitō was the third person to receive a Ministry of Foreign Affairs funeral, after Komura Jutarō and Sugimura Yōtarō.

Richmond Kelly Turner, captain of the USS *Astoria*, met with the emperor to present an official letter on behalf of President Roosevelt. Ongoing disputes over whether or not to strengthen the Anti-Comintern Pact had dampened the mood in Tokyo, however, making the welcoming ceremony for the *Astoria* a subdued affair.

However, just days after the accord between Japan and the United Kingdom, the United States gave notice it would terminate the US-Japan Treaty of Commerce and Navigation on January 26, 1940. In the United States, a lively debate was taking place concerning sanctions on Japan, including economic sanctions, and this influenced President Roosevelt's decision. The United States had not coordinated its action with the United Kingdom, but it was a tangible step toward supporting the United Kingdom's position in East Asia. It wiped out Japan's diplomatic victory, strengthening the United Kingdom's position in the negotiations regarding China, and the agreement reached in Tokyo was rendered worthless. Having won the strong support of the United States, the United Kingdom no longer had any reason to choose to cooperate with Japan.

Negotiations with Germany

With little progress being made toward resolution of the ongoing strife in China, the army embarked on a diplomatic strategy that would make use of the new fluidity in the European situation brought about by the emergence of Nazi Germany. The idea behind this was to try to improve relations with the United States, to strengthen the Mutual Defense Pact with Germany and Italy to fight both the Soviet Union and the United Kingdom, and to restrain the United Kingdom and the Soviet Union. The army saw these as the greatest impediments to dealing with the "series of incidents" that had taken place in China and establishing the new order in East Asia.

On the German side, Joachim von Ribbentrop had become foreign minister in February 1938, and Germany's foreign policy on the Far East was shifting from pro-China to pro-Japan. Negotiations between Japan and Germany began early in 1938, represented by Ribbentrop and Military Attaché Ōshima Hiroshi. When ambassador to Germany Tōgō Shigenori learned of this in July, he asked Foreign Minister

9-11. The signing of the Molotov-Ribbentrop Pact (German-Soviet Non-Aggression Pact)

Ugaki to put a stop to it, but he was not successful. Tōgō feared a Japan-Germany alliance would not prove useful in resolving war with China, and it might even draw Japan into the war in Europe.

Germany's expectations regarding an alliance with Japan had less to do with the Soviet Union than with the United Kingdom and France, which Germany perceived as its main adversaries. The resignation of the Konoe cabinet in January 1939 had come about in part because it could not reconcile the position of the Ministry of Foreign Affairs, which wanted to focus mainly on the Soviet Union, with the position of the army, which wanted to include the United Kingdom and France.

Shortly after the new Hiranuma cabinet was formed, Germany once again formally proposed an alliance, but it was still a military alliance aimed at the United Kingdom and France. Arita Hachirō, who was foreign minister in the Hiranuma cabinet, persuaded the Five Ministers' Conference to approve a proposal for an alliance containing a confidential section that effectively omitted the United Kingdom and France. He sent Itō Nobufumi as special emissary to give direct orders to Ōshima (who had been appointed ambassador to Germany in October 1938) and Shiratori Toshio (ambassador to Italy). The ambassadors concluded Germany would not accept the proposal, and took the unusual step of sending a joint proposal demanding the removal of the confidential section. Arita, dumbfounded, set about trying to get control of the situation; even the emperor warned the two ambassadors they may have exceeded their authority. Arita proposed at the Five Ministers' Conference that the missive from the ambassadors be expunged and the negotiations stopped, but he was unable to achieve consensus due to the opposition of Army Minister Itagaki.

After that, the army and the Ministry of Foreign Affairs continued their back-and-forth about whether to limit the target of the alliance to the Soviet Union, a discussion that was not resolved until August 1939, when Germany and the Soviet Union concluded their own non-aggression pact.

"Complex Mysteries"

From the point of view of the Soviet Union, which was not invited to participate, the Munich talks involving the United Kingdom, France, and Germany that took place in the fall of 1938 could be summarized as the United Kingdom and France trying to redirect the threat presented by Germany toward the Soviet Union. Rather than trying to cooperate with the Soviet Union to neutralize the threat posed by Germany, the United Kingdom and France opted to appease Germany. At that point, the Soviet Union proposed the idea of a trilateral mutual-aid agreement with the United Kingdom and France, but little progress was made. Shut out from

The Question of Whether to Create a Ministry of Trade

In August 1939, the Cabinet Planning Board presented Japan's various ministries with a proposal to create a new "Ministry of Trade" as part of an effort to optimize the administrative structure. The plan would consolidate the Trade Bureau in the Ministry of Foreign Affairs and the trade-related divisions within the Ministry of Finance, the Ministry of Commerce and Industry, and other ministries into a single integrated organization under the control of the minister of trade. The proposal prompted unanimous opposition from every corner of the government; some of the strongest detractors were from the Ministry of Foreign Affairs, which vehemently resisted the prospective reforms on the grounds that it was fundamentally impossible to separate trade from political diplomacy and that the centralization of all foreign-policy elements was vital. A draft amendment managed to secure cabinet approval in early October, and the provisions essentially laid waste to the Ministry of Foreign Affairs' trade policy: in addition to scaling down the Trade Bureau's authority, the draft amendment also gave the minister of trade full rein over appointing and dismissing trade officers. Trade Bureau director-general Matsushima Shikao immediately announced his resignation in protest, with numerous high-ranking officials in the Ministry of Foreign Affairs following suit. Facing the threat of widespread upheaval, the Abe Nobuyuki cabinet ultimately abandoned the plan to establish the Ministry of Trade.

Another point warranting mention is that the Cabinet Planning Board's proposal to effectively consolidate all trade rights into the Ministry of Commerce and Industry's Trade Bureau was a target of criticism by the Ministry of Foreign Affairs, which saw the plan as a ploy to apply import revenues toward funding the expansions that the military wanted. The creation of the Board of Asia Development was a hard pill for the Ministry of Foreign Affairs to swallow, as the new organization robbed the ministry of both its key role in directing Japan's relations with China and its authority over trade diplomacy.

the diplomatic systems of Europe and isolated in its security concerns, the Soviet Union was compelled to change its policy stance toward Germany, and in May 1939 it replaced its foreign minister, Maxim Litvinov, with Vyacheslav Molotov, and embarked on a course of improving relations with Germany.

For the Soviet Union, improving relations with Germany was even connected to the situation in the Far East. In May 1939, the Soviet spy Richard Sorge, in Tokyo, informed Moscow that the military alliance under negotiation between Japan and Germany was aimed at the Soviet Union, and that if war were to break out between Germany and the Soviet Union, Japan would automatically side with Germany. Around the same time, there was a serious battle between the Kwantung Army and Soviet forces at Khalkhin Gol, on the border between Manchukuo and Mongolia. To avoid its worst fear—having to fight wars on both its eastern and western borders at the same time—the Soviet Union needed to conclude a non-aggression pact with Germany. As negotiations between Japan and Germany dragged on, Germany was also negotiating with the Soviet Union in secret, and on August 23 the German-Soviet Non-Aggression Pact was announced. This treaty put an end to the military alliance targeting the Soviet Union that Japan and Germany were pursuing.

The Hiranuma cabinet lodged a protest against the German-Soviet Non-Aggression Pact, saying it violated the 1936 Japan-Germany Anti-Comintern Pact. With that, the cabinet members all resigned. In explaining the cabinet's resignation, Hiranuma said, "The realm of Europe, with its complex mysteries,

Nomura Kichisaburō (1877–1964)

Nomura Kichisaburō was born in Wakayama Prefecture and graduated from the Imperial Naval Academy in 1898. He took up a post in Germany from 1908 to 1911, after which he served in Washington as a naval attaché to the Japanese embassy in the United States during World War I (1914–18). It was during that time in Washington that Nomura would make the acquaintance of future US president Roosevelt and Captain William Pratt (later the United States' chief of naval operations), earning a reputation as a pro-American "navy man." Nomura went on to represent the Japanese navy at the Paris Peace Conference and Washington Conference. After receiving a promotion to vice-chief of the Navy General Staff, Nomura attended the Eastern Conference (Tōhō Kaigi) in 1927 and voiced his support for a diplomatic approach over a military-oriented policy toward China. Firm in his belief that "any compromise is better than war," Nomura worked in a cooperative relationship with Foreign Minister Yoshizawa Kenkichi and led the response to the 1932 Shanghai Incident in his official capacity as Commander of the 3rd Fleet.

Nomura became foreign minister as part of Abe Nobuyuki's cabinet in September 1939 and soon confronted the debate swirling around the contentious issue of creating a Ministry of Trade. While that controversy commanded his attention on the home front, Nomura worked to repair the diplomatic damage that the termination of the US-Japan Treaty of Commerce and Navigation by the United States had dealt to US-Japan relations. He began meeting with US ambassador Joseph Grew in November to float the idea of signing a new commercial treaty and provisional agreement on the conditions of compensating for the losses of American citizens in China and opening the Yangtze River, but the United States was reluctant. In February 1941, Nomura was named Japan's ambassador to the United States and entrusted with negotiations concerning diplomatic relations. He went into the talks that April with onlookers confident that his respectable military deportment would pave the way for a fruitful outcome, but he was unable to prevent the war from breaking out. After the war, Nomura ran a successful campaign for election to the House of Councillors as a member of the Liberal Democratic Party and chaired the party's Research Commission on Foreign Affairs, among several other positions. He died in 1964.

9-12. Nomura Kichisaburō

has a new situation. . . . The policies we had been preparing are no longer valid, and we will have to establish other policies." As for the "other policies" he was contemplating, Hiranuma set aside the problem of reinforcing the Anti-Comintern Pact and embarked once again on an active approach to improving relations with the United States. In a way he was appealing to those both inside and outside Japan; his hope was that Japan would pivot to cooperation with the United States and the United Kingdom rather than rebuilding the alliance with the Axis powers, and that the succeeding cabinet could achieve this.

2 Disruption in Europe and Japanese Diplomacy

The "Non-Intervention" Policy and the Ministry of Trade Issue

After the cabinet of Hiranuma Kiichirō stepped down, the army-backed Abe Nobuyuki formed a cabinet at the end of August. On September 1, 1939, the Second World War began. (Abe initially also served as foreign minister until Nomura Kichisaburō took up the post in late September.) On September 4, the Abe cabinet issued a "declaration of non-intervention" in the war in Europe, which stated, "The Empire will not interfere in the war in Europe; other nations will not interfere in Japan's affairs in China." The statement separated war in China from the war in Europe and expressed a desire to reach localized solutions. It was also a restatement of Japan's longstanding position that it had no desire for other nations, or for the League of Nations, to become involved in the resolution of the situation in China, even in the new international environment.

With the outbreak of war in Europe having diverted the attention of the United Kingdom, France, and the Netherlands—all of which had colonies in Southeast Asia—a prime opportunity for Japan's southward advance doctrine arose. In fact, the middle-ranking navy officers were in favor of a decisive shift in the direction of the southward-advance doctrine, and even within the Ministry of Foreign Affairs the subject of a switch to the southward-advance doctrine was actively discussed, particularly by the Reform Faction. However, Japan's political and military leadership could not reach agreement on such a strategy, which would be equivalent to an intervention in the war in Europe. Quite the contrary, there was active discussion of economic involvement with both the Dutch East Indies and French Indochina.

To achieve localized solutions to Japan's predicaments in China, the Abe cabinet's first priorities were to build the structures needed for prolonged war in China and to strengthen Japan's domestic preparations for war. Within the army, which had effectively made Abe prime minister, the voluntary withdrawal of troops from China was considered as an option to solve the longstanding issues. In the end, the army opted not to withdraw from China, but instead to set up the structures it needed for prolonged warfare. Domestically, Japan proceeded to put auxiliary support systems and supervisory entities into position. Part of this effort was the idea, promoted by the cabinet, to establish a Ministry of Trade that would unilaterally administer trade; this became an issue for Foreign Minister Nomura. (See sidebar on the previous page.)

The Nomura-Grew Talks and the Improvement of Japan–Soviet Union Relations

The immediate external challenges faced by the Abe Nobuyuki cabinet included dealing with the aftermath of the fighting at Khalkhin Gol.

Fortunately, with the changes in the international situation, those conflicts started to settle down, and by mid-September 1939 a cease-fire agreement was reached. Tōgō Shigenori, at that time Japan's ambassador to Moscow, recommended to Foreign Minister Nomura that Japan go one step beyond the cease-fire agreement and conclude the Soviet-Japanese Non-Aggression Pact. However, the Abe cabinet was none too keen on the neutrality pact, wanting first to press for resolution of oil and coal rights in North Karafuto (Sakhalin), as well as the problem of the fishing industry. The cabinet argued that Soviet aid to China should be halted before the pact was concluded. This basic policy mindset remained unchanged in the administration of the next prime minister, Yonai Mitsumasa.

Once the matter of the Ministry of Trade was dealt with, Nomura focused his attentions on addressing the effects of non-treaty status resulting from the termination of the US-Japan Treaty of Commerce and Navigation in July (to take effect in January 1940). As the incidents in China continued, Japan's economy grew increasingly dependent on the United States. Heightened economic sanctions could cripple Japan's wartime economy. When Nomura looked at the occupied areas of China,

Matsuoka Yōsuke (1880–1946)

9-13. Matsuoka Yōsuke

A native of Yamaguchi Prefecture, Matsuoka Yōsuke traveled to the United States with his cousin at the age of twelve after his father's business went bankrupt. Working his way through school stateside, Matsuoka eventually graduated from the University of Oregon law school and made his return to Japan in 1902. He passed the foreign-service examination with top honors in 1904, after which he immediately received an assignment to work at the Japanese consulate general in Shanghai. He also took on a concurrent role as the director of the Foreign Affairs Section for the Office of the Governor-General of Kwantung, a capacity in which he made the close acquaintance of Gotō Shinpei. That connection would help propel Matsuoka to higher-level positions: in 1916, when Matsuoka was a staff secretary at the Japanese embassy in the United States, Gotō recommended him to serve as secretary to Prime Minister Terauchi Masatake. After assuming his cabinet role, Matsuoka made himself an outspoken proponent of an aggressive Siberian Expedition and clashed with caution-minded leaders like Vice-Minister for Foreign Affairs Shidehara Kijūrō. He was also part of the Japanese government's delegation to the Paris Peace Conference, heading up the country's information efforts, and served as the chief of the second division of the Information Department until he retired from the Ministry of Foreign Affairs in 1921. Yamamoto Jōtarō, a Seiyūkai politician, promptly recommended Matsuoka to be a director of the South Manchuria Railway. Matsuoka took the position and set out to implement company reforms. He would leave the South Manchuria Railway for a time, but his absence was only temporary—he made a triumphant return in 1927 as vice president (and later president) under Yamamoto, who by that time had risen to the presidency. Working with Yamamoto, Matsuoka helped forge a secret agreement with Zhang Zuolin that October to authorize the pending construction of five Manchuria–Mongolia railroads. However, Zhang's assassination the following year derailed the plan. In 1929, Matsuoka bid farewell to the South Manchuria Railway, won a seat in the House of Representatives as a member of the Seiyūkai, and spoke out forcefully against Shidehara diplomacy.

Matsuoka later served as Japan's representative at the October 1932 extraordinary general meeting of the League of Nations, which convened to focus mainly on the resolution of the Manchurian Incident. On the official directive of the Japanese government, Matsuoka worked strenuously to keep Japan in the League of Nations—but Japan ended up withdrawing from the organization the following March. Observers in Japan praised Matsuoka in the drama surrounding Japan's exit, commending him for breaking the mold of Japan's conventional "impotent diplomacy"—a pattern of deceptive double-talk and submissive subservience—and acting in the interests of the country's people. On his voyage back from the League of Nations, Matsuoka apparently said, "Withdrawing from the League of Nations does not mean he saw a serious economic crisis stemming from a shortage of capital, with little hope of recovery without the cooperation of other nations. Nomura thus criticized Foreign Minister Arita Hachirō, who had walked away from the Nine-Power Treaty the previous fall, and sent a notice to the United States. Within the government, Nomura argued that the open-door policy should be observed.

In bilateral talks beginning in early November, Ambassador Grew protested the ongoing discriminatory treatment in the occupied territories. As a first step toward carrying out Japan's open-door policy, Nomura proposed opening the lower Yangtze River to ships from third nations, and said he hoped to conclude a tentative agreement before the Treaty of Commerce and Navigation was ended. Nomura tried to reach out to Secretary of State Hull through Japan's ambassador to the US, Horinouchi Kensuke, but the United States did not respond to the idea of a tentative agreement.

Nomura recognized the need for the establishment of a central government in the occupied territories, but he was wary of excessive interference that would threaten the independence of the new government. He was adamant about adhering to the open-door policy, and that exposed him

withdrawing from the world. . . . It is on the premise of truly autonomous diplomacy that true international cooperation should rest." He had not, therefore, abandoned the idea of global cooperation.

Matsuoka made another return to the South Manchuria Railway in 1935, this time as president, but he returned to the political realm in July 1940, when he became foreign minister in Konoe Fumimaro's second cabinet. With hostilities between Germany and the United Kingdom throwing Europe into turmoil, Matsuoka first set out to bring the Second Sino-Japanese War to a conclusion via diplomatic means. The talks with China eventually stalled, however, and Matsuoka turned his attention to developing a "southern expansion doctrine" with an eye to the possibility that Germany might take the United Kingdom. Matsuoka envisioned Japan, Germany, and Italy signing a tripartite military alliance against the United States and the United Kingdom, which would create pressure that Japan could leverage into forging a non-aggression pact with the Soviet Union, thereby securing Japan's northern position, and maintain separation between the Anglo-American side and the Soviets. What worried Matsuoka most was the prospect of straining Japan's relationship with the United States, so he worked to maintain a delicate balance between putting pressure on the United Kingdom but still maintaining solid ties with the United States as he signed the Tripartite Pact, stationed troops in the northern part of French Indochina, coordinated diplomatic relations with the Soviet Union, and addressed a host of other pending issues in quick succession.

While the army and reformist factions in the government were hoping to form a "Quadripartite Entente" by bringing the Soviet Union into the existing Tripartite Pact, that type of grand design was not what Matsuoka had in mind. A variety of factors, including growing tension in German-Soviet relations, made the prospects of a solid Quadripartite Entente unfeasible. Eventually, Germany initiated a major shift in its foreign-policy strategy near the end of 1940: instead of focusing on bringing down the United Kingdom, Germany now had its sights set on toppling the Soviet Union via war. Negotiations for a Japanese-Soviet non-aggression agreement fell short of their aims, only resulting in a neutrality pact, and Japan's southward-advance strategy—originally devised to operate in concert with Germany taking the United Kingdom—thus hit a dead end. With the southward-advance strategy stalled, Matsuoka saw no other option but to cooperate with Germany in vanquishing the Soviet Union, and thus began advocating a hard-line northward-expansion policy.

On the other side was Japan's relations with the United States. Matsuoka took a tough stance at the diplomatic negotiations with the American representatives, confident that the Tripartite Pact would provide him with valuable leverage. However, Prime Minister Konoe was apprehensive about the talks breaking down because of Matsuoka's approach. In mid-July 1941, Konoe dissolved his entire cabinet and then reformed the administration without Matsuoka. Upon learning that Japan and the United States had officially gone to war, Matsuoka supposedly intimated that the Tripartite Pact was the biggest mistake he had ever made. After the war, Matsuoka was arrested on war-crimes charges but died in prison in June 1946 awaiting his trial at the International Military Tribunal for the Far East.

to criticism from the reform faction within the Ministry of Foreign Affairs. This faction of the Ministry of Foreign Affairs argued that termination of the regime based on the Nine-Power Treaty had already been called for, and that Japan had embarked on a course of building a new order in East Asia. From this, there could be no turning back. When the cabinet of Yonai Mitsumasa took over, Arita replaced Nomura, thereby undertaking his third term as foreign minister.

The Wang Zhaoming Regime

The cabinet of Yonai Mitsumasa, which was established in January 1940, embraced a policy of non-intervention in the Great War in Europe, and grappled with several important issues within that framework. One of these was the establishment of a powerful new central government in the occupied territories in China.

In November 1939, secret diplomatic negotiations had begun based on an assumption that Wang Zhaoming would be able to form a new government. The "Adjusted Guidelines on the New Japan-China Relationship" of the year before formed the basis for these negotiations. In these talks, Wang resisted Japan's demands for the withdrawal of Chinese troops and the right to station Japanese troops in China, but in the end, he acquiesced to the harsh terms for peace. In March 1940, the new central government was established, and with this, the Nationalist government returned to Nanjing.

In the new government, Wang was both president of the Executive Yuan and acting chairman of the national government. The Reform Government was abolished, and the provisional government changed its name to the North China Political Council. When the new Nationalist government was established, Secretary of State Hull issued a statement that the US position remained unchanged: that the Nationalist government in Chongqing was the true government of China. Nonetheless, while the geographic footprint of the new central government may have been small, it controlled important cities such as Beijing and Shanghai, and roughly 90 percent of China's revenue from customs tariffs.

The power base of the Wang regime was weak, however. Japan's Army General Staff pursued the possibilities for direct negotiations with Chongqing through a variety of routes, in hopes the Wang regime would be able to join forces with the Chiang Kai-shek regime. In 1940 it explored a route to peace through Soong Tse-liang. This peace plan, surreptitiously known as the "Kiri Plan," was developed in June 1940 based on a promise made by Wang, Chiang, and a representative of Japan to hold cease-fire talks. In mid-June, the Battle of Yichang broke out right at the doorstep of Chongqing. As the latest in the China incidents, this battle for control of Yichang put the most pressure on the Nationalist government in Chongqing. The government in Tokyo and the Japanese army both delayed recognizing the Wang government as they waited to see what the Kiri Plan might achieve.

Steps taken within the framework of "non-intervention" included military and diplomatic efforts focused on cutting off third-party aid to Chiang (that is, material and financial support for the Chongqing government from other nations). The Nationalist government was receiving a large volume of goods via French Indochina, and Japan repeatedly pressured the French government to stop shipments of military equipment. However, these appeals had little effect. At the end of 1939, the Battle of Nanning was fought near the border with French Indochina. This brought pressure on the French government to enter into negotiations, but the administration of French Indochina showed little inclination to cut off the supply routes that were assisting Chiang. The deadlock on the French Indochina situation was broken by the German army's blitzkrieg assault on Western Europe.

The Emergence of Matsuoka Diplomacy

The fall of 1939 was the beginning of the "phony war," with little actual fighting taking place on the western front in Europe. Then, in the spring of 1940, Germany used its blitzkrieg tactics to take Belgium and the Netherlands, followed by France in June. Germany's conquest of Europe helped lead to a resolution of Japan's thorny problem with Chiang's lines of support. In mid-June 1940, the United Kingdom agreed to Japan's demand that the Burma Route be closed for three months, and authorities in French Indochina agreed to stop the shipment of aid to China via that country. France's defeat by Germany provided the answer for whether Japan should deploy soldiers of the Fifth Division, who were idle after the occupation of Nanning, or let them invade French Indochina. At the end of September, the decision was reached to dispatch the troops to the northern part of French Indochina.

In Japan, there was much discussion of an alliance with Germany for the purpose of building a "New World Order" together with that nation. Germany had taken control of European nations that held colonies in Southeast Asia, and this created a power vacuum that also fanned discussion of a hasty southward-advance doctrine. However, the Yonai cabinet, hewing to its policy of non-intervention in the war in Europe, did little to pursue either the southward-advance strategy or an alliance with Germany. This drew withering criticism from the army and from reformist elements. In late July 1940, the cabinet resigned under pressure from the army. The non-intervention policy had hit its limits.

The second Konoe cabinet was formed with the strong backing of the army. Late in July, it decided two important national policies: the cabinet decision on the Fundamental National Policy Framework and the Imperial General Headquarters and Government Liaison Conference decision on the Framework for National Policy Processes in View of Trends in the Global Situation (hereinafter the "Framework for National Policy Processes"). Just before the formation of the cabinet, in a conference at Konoe's private residence in Ogikubo (Ogikubo Meeting), these decisions were agreed by Matsuoka Yōsuke, who was in line to become foreign minister; Tōjō Hideki, who was in line for minister of the army; and Yoshida Zengo, who was in line to remain in office as navy minister.

The Fundamental National Policy Framework stated that the world was "at a major historic turning point," and that Japan's national policy was to build a "New Order for Greater East Asia." With the changes in Japan's domestic political alignments, the new government intended to achieve economic self-reliance, self-sufficiency, and the establishment of a national defense state. In early August, the new foreign minister, Matsuoka, first officially used the

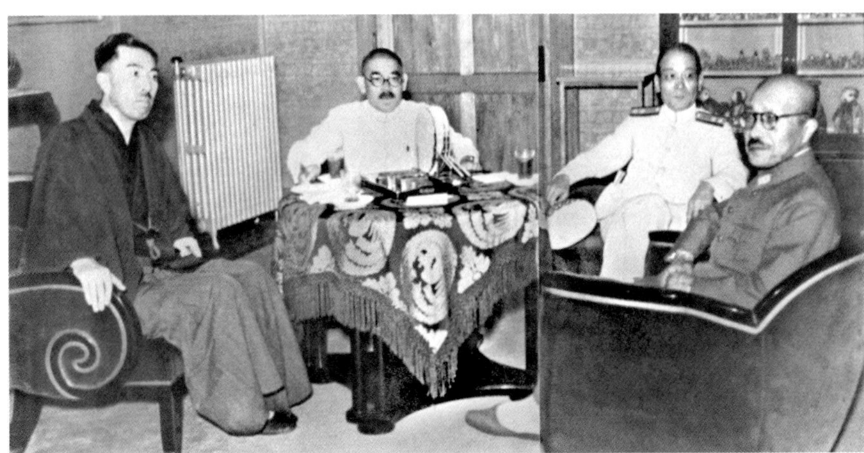

9-14. The Ogikubo Meeting

9-15. German minister of foreign affairs Joachim von Ribbentrop announces the Tripartite Pact

9-16. The signing of the Soviet-Japanese Neutrality Pact

phrase "Greater East Asia Co-Prosperity Sphere." He said this included not just the three East Asian nations of Japan, Manchukuo, and China, but also the Southeast Asia region.

At the same time, beginning in late June, the Army General Staff, among others, began to advance the Framework for National Policy Processes, based on assumptions that Germany would conquer Europe and a new cabinet would be formed to take Yonai's place in Japan. One pillar of this new policy, assuming the United Kingdom itself would be defeated at home, was a military conquest of British territories in the Far East. Of course, this would require that Germany actually conquer the United Kingdom's home territory, and that Japan put an end to the difficulties in China, but it would also be possible for Japan to take military action even if the issues in China were not resolved. There were those within the army who hoped that carrying out the southern military campaign would be a recipe for a successful resolution of the troubles in China. However, it appeared that the United Kingdom's valiant defense of its home island would mean the war in Europe would not come to a quick end. Japan's prospects for militarily attacking British colonies in Asia, such as Hong Kong or Singapore, in response to Germany's actions grew dim.

The Tripartite Alliance and the Soviet-Japanese Neutrality Pact

The diplomatic aspect of the Framework for National Policy Processes was the strengthening of the Tripartite Alliance and the Soviet-Japanese Neutrality Pact. Even after the German-Soviet Non-Aggression Pact, enthusiasm for stronger cooperation with the Axis powers did not fade within the army or the Ministry of Foreign Affairs. The details, however, consisted basically of the idea of mutual toleration of Japan's hegemony in Asia and Germany's hegemony in Europe. Given the German army's conquests in Europe and the resulting changes in the global situation, Japan's main aim was to prevent Germany from extending its influence to the resource-rich regions of Southeast Asia.

The problem for Japan was the extent to which it should promise cooperation to Germany, which was engrossed in war with the United Kingdom. In the army's proposal, Japan promised "to respond, in principle" if asked by Germany to attack Singapore. However, in negotiations with Germany that began in late August 1940, Foreign Minister Matsuoka added the United Kingdom and the United States to the coverage of the alliance, changing it into a military alliance against those two countries, and encountered strong opposition from the navy and the Ministry of Foreign Affairs.

Matsuoka's idea was to create an alliance so powerful it could avert a war with the United States. Germany's idea of a Japanese-German alliance was also aimed at preventing the United States from entering the war in Europe. Consequently, Japan and Germany were in agreement that the main goal of their alliance was to discourage American intervention in the war in Europe and in the disputes in Asia. Matsuoka, however, was still open to the idea of using the power of the Axis alliance to create a Soviet-Japanese Non-Aggression Pact that would ensure Japan's security to the north. The idea behind this was to prepare for a military advance to the south in response to Germany's attack on the United Kingdom.

The navy remained opposed to the Axis to the end, but was willing to approve on the condition that if war broke out between the United States and Germany, room would be left for the navy to make an autonomous decision on the problem of participating in war against the United Kingdom and the United States through an exchange of notes and other diplomatic documents. With that, Germany, Italy, and Japan signed the Tripartite Alliance forming the Axis alliance in Berlin in late September. Even as Matsuoka was emphatic in his view that the significance of the Axis was to prevent war between Japan and the United States, the United States and the United Kingdom were increasing their support for Chiang and expanding economic sanctions on Japan.

In the process of forming the Axis, the Japanese army and the reformist elements proposed the idea of creating a "Four-Nation entente" that would add the Soviet Union to the roster. Matsuoka wanted to use Germany's influence on the Soviet Union to amend the relationship between Japan and the Soviet Union, but it is not clear whether he expressed this idea from the outset.

Since the resolution of the Battle of Khalkhin Gol (September 1939), Japan had tried to adjust diplomatic relations with the Soviets in hopes of limiting Soviet support for the Chongqing regime. As the prospect of a southward advance arose in the summer of 1940, Japan added the goal of ensuring security in the north in preparation. This made mending fences with the USSR even more important.

However, negotiations with the Soviet Union made little headway. Matsuoka and the army wanted to set up something similar to the German-Soviet Non-Aggression Pact, but they had little to offer, and all their efforts since the fall of 1940 to reach some sort of non-aggression agreement were rejected by the Soviets. Matsuoka made a trip to Moscow and Berlin that began in March 1941, and in April he and Stalin signed the Soviet-Japanese Neutrality Pact. However, by the time this pact took effect, the relationship between Germany and the USSR had soured—Hitler had already decided to attack the Soviet Union—and the chances of a German attack on the United Kingdom had faded. These factors effectively crushed Matsuoka's idea of a southern military campaign.

Recognition of the Wang Government: The Possibility of Resolving Issues in China Fades

In the fall of 1940, hopes for peace and an armistice waned. Suspicions grew that the Japanese army's Kiri Plan involving negotiations between Japan, Wang, and Chiang was a plot by the Chinese side to undermine the Wang Zhaoming regime. Moreover, the peace plan backed by Qian Yongming, head of the Zhejiang conglomerate, which was secretly unfolding under the gaze of Foreign Minister Matsuoka, was judged to be sabotage directed against the Wang regime. Having lost all means to achieve peace with the Chiang regime, on November 30, 1940, the Japanese government formally recognized the Wang regime as the Nationalist government in Nanjing and signed the Japan-China Basic Relations Treaty. Honda Kumatarō was named ambassador in December.

The Japan-China Basic Relations Treaty, which was based on the Adjusted Guidelines on the New Japan-China Relationship, aimed for a "good-neighbor relationship" predicated on respect for territory and autonomy and mutual equality. It allowed for Japanese troops to be stationed in Mengjiang and North China in order to fight Communism and ensure security. It also provided for joint development of national defense resources in Mengjiang and North China, and gave Japan priority access to these supplies. Recognition of the Wang regime did not contribute to resolving the longstanding difficulties in China, however. On the contrary, it made the confrontation with the Chongqing regime all the more inevitable, effectively shutting down any path to peace. After Japan recognized the Wang regime, the Framework for Processes for Dealing with the China Incidents (Imperial Council decision) of November 1940 could be no more than a recognition that the primary goal of its China policy was to ensure security in the territories Japan already occupied.

In the fall of 1940, the army believed the only possibility remaining for a resolution of the situation in continental Asia would be a military advance to the south—even at the risk of conflict with other nations—to establish a region that would be self-reliant and self-sufficient over the long term. However, as the United States and the United Kingdom strengthened their ties, and the ABCD (America, Britain, China, and the Dutch) line grew tighter around Japan, Japan could not afford to risk a full-scale military invasion of Southeast Asia. It decided instead to pursue diplomatic negotiations with the Dutch East Indies and French Indochina in hopes of expanding its sphere of influence and exploiting natural resources in those areas. However, the United States and United Kingdom supported Thailand and the Dutch East Indies and acted as a restraint on Japan's ambitions, making expansion to the south through peaceful negotiations impossible.

In hopes of reducing its reliance on the United States for strategic materials such as oil and tin, Japan made an effort to shift its supply to the Dutch East Indies. Intense negotiations began in the fall of 1940, but by 1941 the Dutch were pursuing delaying tactics, with the aid of the United States and the United Kingdom, leaving the negotiations in a precarious state.

3 The Japan-US Talks Collapse

Resolving the Issues in China and Negotiating with the United States

To resolve the issues in China, the best diplomatic route remaining to Japan was to seek peace through the mediation of the United States, and Japan hoped to enter into negotiations with the United States with that aim. In the fall of 1940, Japanese and Americans, mainly civilians, surreptitiously started working toward this goal. In mid-April 1941, ambassador to the US Nomura Kichisaburō informally presented the fruits of those efforts as a "Draft Understanding" (see sidebar on next page). This proposal assumed that the Axis would effectively be rendered powerless, but it did not demand that Japan withdraw from the Axis.

To normalize trade relations between Japan and the United States, the two nations would have to cooperate with one another on access to natural resources in Southeast Asia. Both Prime Minister Konoe Fumimaro and the military welcomed this prospect. The army in particular welcomed the fact that the proposal mentioned the possibility of peaceful intervention in the ongoing problems in China, under certain conditions. However, the Proposal for Japan-US Understanding stipulated that Japan had to accept Hull's Four Principles (respect for territory and sovereignty, non-interference in internal affairs, equality of opportunity, and no changes in the status quo in the Pacific region except through peaceful means) as a precondition of mediation by the United States.

Talks with the United States continued until December, focusing on three main points of

The Curious Case of the "Draft Understanding" between Japan and the United States

In the late fall of 1940, Bishop James Walsh and Father James Drought of the Catholic Foreign Mission Society visited Japan for discussions with Japanese leaders in financial circles, the diplomatic sphere, and other areas. During their stay, the two priests' closest contact was Ikawa Tadao, a director at the Industrial Cooperative Central Bank. Making arrangements behind the scenes on the American side was prominent Democrat and US postmaster general Frank Walker. In January 1941, Walsh and Drought spoke with President Franklin Roosevelt and US secretary of state Cordell Hull about the possibility of a Japan-US peace, earnestly arguing that there was a base of support for a partnership with the United States in Japan, that the Tripartite Pact might become a dead letter, and that there was potential for peace in the Pacific. Ikawa headed to the United States on the priests' heels with specific instructions from Prime Minister Konoe Fumimaro, Military Affairs Bureau director-general Mutō Akira, and others to sound out American leaders on their intentions.

In early March 1941, Ikawa began working with the priests and Walker to formulate a basic proposal (a draft of an agreement in principle) that would lay the foundation for smoothing Japan-US diplomatic relations. Additional help came the following month in the form of Iwakuro Hideo, chief of the Army Ministry's Military Affairs Division, who arrived in the US under the pretext of assisting Ambassador Nomura Kichisaburō and started collaborating on the draft. Ambassador Nomura soon began receiving reports on the proposal, giving the drafting process a semi-official quality. With Iwakuro on board, the basic proposal underwent revisions, culminating in the "Draft Understanding" on April 16. Ambassador Nomura presented the document to Hull, who read the terms and told Nomura that the Draft Understanding would make a suitable basis for initiating conversations if the Japanese government agreed to four principles of international peace: respect for territorial integrity and sovereignty, non-interference in the internal affairs of other countries, equal opportunity, and non-disturbance of the status quo in the Pacific, except as the status quo might be altered by peaceful means. Nomura immediately cabled the Draft Understanding to Konoe.

However, Prime Minister Konoe and the rest of the Japanese government assumed that the document was an American proposal—one that President Roosevelt and Secretary of State Hull had already signed off on—because Ambassador Nomura had appended the cable with a statement that "Secretary Hull has informed me that it is advisable to proceed with the negotiations based on the Draft Understanding between the two nations and asked me to obtain an official directive from the Japanese government." It appears that Ambassador Nomura and Section Chief Iwakuro framed the Draft Understanding as a proposal by the US government so that the Japanese government would be more willing to accept its terms. A key factor behind the ensuing misunderstanding was Ambassador Nomura's failure to clearly inform the Japanese government that any Japan-US conversations would be premised on the four principles Hull had stipulated.

There is reason to doubt, however, that the US government was truly committed to establishing peaceful relations with Japan through negotiations under the terms of the Draft Understanding. For the United States, which was training its focus on the Atlantic theater, the top priorities were bolstering aid to the United Kingdom and preparing for war with Germany. Negotiations with Japan, then, had different dimensions besides just seeking peace: they would also help check Japan's southern expansion and buy some valuable time to prepare for battle with Germany without the distraction of Japan and Asia to deal with. When the Japan-US negotiations began to raise eyebrows among British government officials in late May, Hull reassured British foreign secretary Anthony Eden that the talks were a "measured political maneuver to stall Japanese action and thereby turn the conditions in the Pacific and Mediterranean in the United Kingdom's favor."

The Tokyo Olympics That Never Were

Japan took home its first-ever Olympic gold medals at the Amsterdam Olympics—the ninth Olympic Games—in 1928. Oda Mikio (triple jump) and Tsuruta Yoshiyuki (200-meter breaststroke) captured gold in their events, while Hitomi Kinue won a bronze medal in the women's 800-meter race. When the chairman of the International Amateur Athletic Federation paid a visit to Japan the following year, he met with Inter-University Athletics Union of Japan president Yamamoto Tadaoki, who had led the Japanese Olympic team at the Amsterdam Games, and discussed the possibility of Tokyo hosting the Olympics. Yamamoto passed the idea on to the Tokyo city government and the mayor—and as soon as word began to get around, a frenzy of excitement propelled the bidding process forward. In October 1931, the Tokyo city council unanimously approved a "Proposition on Holding the International Olympic Games" as part of an effort to commemorate the 2,600th anniversary of Japan's founding in 1940. With that, Tokyo city mayor Nagata Hidejirō asked the Ministry of Foreign Affairs to start promoting Tokyo's bid for the 1940 Games by lobbying the International Olympic Committee (IOC) through diplomatic missions abroad.

Japan made the Tokyo bid official at the 1932 Los Angeles Olympics, which came roughly a year after the Manchurian Incident. Questions thus arose about whether the new state of Manchukuo was to field athletes in competition. Embroiled in the controversy was one of the athletes originally slated to represent Manchukuo at the games, Liu Changchun, who fled to North China and decided to represent the Republic of China (as its first Olympic athlete) rather than Manchukuo. The Japanese contingent at the Los Angeles Games, meanwhile, had an impressive showing: the men's swimming squad won gold in five of the six events on the program, and Nanbu Chūhei (triple jump) and Nishi Takeichi (equestrian) topped the podiums in their events as well.

At the 1935 IOC Session, there were three cities vying for the 1940 Games: Tokyo, Rome, and Helsinki. Japan sent Sugimura Yōtarō, the ambassador to Italy, to meet with Italian prime minister Benito Mussolini, and Sugimura successfully persuaded Mussolini to withdraw Rome's bid. The final decision on the host city would not come until the 1936 Berlin Olympics, but the city of Tokyo established a Tokyo City Bid Committee and began making concrete preparations for the games as early as late 1935. The 1936 Olympics were another showcase for Japanese athletes, with the team rivaling its predecessors in terms of performance. Japan took home a total of six gold medals, including Tajima Naoto in the triple jump, Son Kitei (Sohn Kee-chung) in the marathon, and Maehata Hideko—Japan's first female gold medalist—in the women's 200-meter breaststroke.

9-17. The official logo of the 1940 Tokyo Olympics

Japan's success in the global athletic spotlight fueled even more momentum for the Tokyo Olympics, but the Second Sino-Japanese War in 1937 cooled the Olympic fever sweeping the country. As the conflict dragged on, observers both abroad and in Japan began to raise concerns about the upcoming Games taking place in Tokyo. In April 1938, IOC chairman Count Henri de Baillet-Latour visited Japanese ambassador to Belgium Kurusu Saburō. Pointing out that an increasingly protracted war with China would likely lead the United States, the United Kingdom, and numerous other countries to refuse to take part in the Games, de Baillet-Latour recommended that Japan forfeit the Tokyo Olympics. The Japanese government, taking both de Baillet-Latour's argument and domestic opposition to the Games into consideration, decided in July 1938 to forfeit the Tokyo Olympics and notified the organizing committee accordingly. Helsinki took over for Tokyo as host city, but the outbreak of World War II resulted in the cancellation of the Helsinki Games altogether.

1932 Los Angeles Olympics

Gold medals	
Men's triple jump	Nanbu Chūhei
Men's 100 m freestyle	Miyazaki Yasuji
Men's 1500 m freestyle	Kitamura Kusuo
Men's 100 m backstroke	Kiyokawa Masaji
Men's 200 m breaststroke	Tsuruta Yoshiyuki
Men's 800 m relay	Miyazaki Yasuji, Yusa Masanori, Yokoyama Takashi, Toyoda Hisakichi
Equestrian jumping, individual	Nishi Takeichi

1936 Berlin Olympics

Gold medals	
Men's triple jump	Tajima Naoto
Men's marathon	Son Kitei (Sohn Kee-chung)
Men's 1500 m freestyle	Terada Noboru
Men's 200 m breaststroke	Hamuro Tetsuo
Women's 200 m breaststroke	Maehata Hideko
Men's 800 m relay	Yusa Masanori, Sugiura Shigeo, Taguchi Masaharu, Arai Shigeo

contention: non-discriminatory treatment in trade, the problem of whether to apply the obligation of entering into war stipulated in the Axis Pact, and the resolution of the incidents between Japan and China through US intercession. For the first two of these, a route to compromise was possible depending on how the agreement was interpreted. Regarding the resolution of China incidents, however, which was the point Japan was most interested in, the United States would not serve as mediator unless Japan was willing to accept Hull's Four Principles.

The obstacle to progress in this direction was Foreign Minister Matsuoka Yōsuke, who returned to Japan from Berlin and Moscow in late April. He was strongly opposed to the negotiations, seeing the proposal as a betrayal of Germany and Italy. According to Matsuoka, the Draft Understanding might appear to be flexible, but its main aim was to separate Japan from the Axis. Matsuoka felt that, to clarify Japan's obligations to the Axis and the peace terms needed to resolve the issues in China, major changes would have to be made to the Draft Understanding. To avoid third-nation intervention in achieving a resolution, Japan submitted a proposal reflecting Matsuoka's views (May 12 Proposal to the United States). In the section concerning the China incidents, it asked that the United States "accept" the November 1940 Japan-China Basic Relations Treaty and urge the Chiang regime to accept peace.

America's response to this (dated June 21) essentially rejected Japan's proposal: it repudiated the Wang regime, demanded the return of Manchuria to China and the unconditional withdrawal of Japanese troops from China, repudiated Japan's stationing of troops to fight Communism, and insisted on non-discriminatory treatment in trade and commerce. In subsequent talks, America refused to back down from this position. Matsuoka was indignant at this response, saying it treated Japan as "a weak nation, a vassal nation," and recommended that the talks be abandoned.

The German-Soviet War and the Rethinking of National Policy

When war broke out between Germany and the Soviet Union on June 22, 1941, it was a clear indication that the Soviet Union stood in opposition to the Axis powers, ending any wishful thinking about the formation of a four-party entente comprising Japan, Germany, Italy, and the Soviet Union. Matsuoka was aware that the relationship between Germany and the Soviet Union had changed, but he thought the Soviet Union would be willing to make concessions to Japan because Moscow feared Germany's advance.

News of the outbreak of war between Germany and the Soviet Union circulated within the Japanese army in early July, sparking an energetic debate about what Japan should do: attack the Soviet Far East (northward-advance doctrine), in line with Germany's expectations, or make a military move southward (southward-advance doctrine) to pursue the natural resources there while maintaining security in the north. The Army General Staff Office and Foreign Minister Matsuoka were in favor of attacking the Soviet Union, as Germany expected. Matsuoka had advocated the southward-advance doctrine based on the Soviet-Japanese Neutrality Pact, suggesting that Germany's victory seemed to be at hand, and if America could be held at bay for a few months, then the path would naturally open up.

Early in July, the Imperial Council settled on a "Combined North-South Strategy" as a matter of national policy, assuming the war between Germany and the Soviet Union went in Germany's favor. As a preparatory step, the Kwantung Army held special maneuvers to build up its capabilities, and most of Japan's forces on the mainland were secretly moved to Manchukuo. However, the war in the north was called off in early August due to weather conditions in Siberia and the expectation that the war between Germany and the Soviet Union would not end soon.

In mid-July, Prime Minister Konoe dismissed Foreign Minister Matsuoka, who was threatening to break off the Japan-US talks. Konoe and the entire cabinet then resigned and immediately re-formed as the third Konoe government in order to continue negotiations.

The Advance into Southern French Indochina

Negotiations with the Netherlands regarding oil resources were at an impasse, and Japan hoped its advance into French Indochina would instill fear in the Dutch East Indies. One of Japan's aims was to build an airport in Saigon from which it could carry out missions further to the south. To this end, in late July 1941, the Japanese army advanced into southern French Indochina. However, this caused a crisis with the United States. Immediately upon taking office, the new foreign minister Toyoda Teijirō attempted to ease the situation by telling Ambassador Grew that Japan had no intention of expanding beyond French Indochina.

In response to Japan's actions, the United States imposed maximum economic sanctions, freezing Japanese assets in America and blocking all shipments of oil to Japan. The United Kingdom and the Netherlands followed the United States in these measures. However, the United States had not declared war, and neither had Japan. Germany remained the greatest threat to America. Relations between the United States and Germany were extremely bad. German and Italian assets in the United States had already been frozen in June. America's strong measures against Japan were an effort to defeat Japan without fighting, and to stop Japan from making further incursions to the south.

9-18. Imperial Japanese Navy landing force marches through Saigon

From Japan's point of view, however, these maximized economic sanctions were a dire threat to its existence as a nation. By early August, some of the mid-ranking officers of the navy came to think war was unavoidable. This view spread to mid-ranking army officers, along with the idea that Japan should limit diplomatic negotiations and decide to begin war. In this way, a new national policy proposal came before the Imperial Council.

On September 6, the Imperial Council chose the "Essentials for Executing Imperial Policies," setting the deadline for diplomatic negotiations as early October, the completion of war preparations as late October, and the beginning of war as early November. Regarding the China problem, the "detailed paper" on negotiations with the United States described a "firm commitment regarding the stationing of imperial troops."

The Idea of Summit Talks

In August 1941, Prime Minister Konoe indicated his desire to personally deal with Japan's problem with the United States through a summit meeting with President Roosevelt. Such a meeting would be a good way to circumvent the interference of the mid-ranking officers of the army and navy, who were preventing Japan from reconciling its diplomatic relations. Ambassador Grew also regarded Konoe as the only politician who could keep the extremists in the military under control, and he urged his home government not to miss this opportunity.

The Army General Staff Office opposed the idea, however, thinking it would weaken Japan's commitment to the Axis and reverse course in the direction of greater dependence on the United States and the United Kingdom. Army Minister Tōjō Hideki managed to persuade the Army General Staff by saying that if the summit did not happen, Konoe and his cabinet would be forced to resign, resulting in political turmoil in Japan, for which the army would be held responsible.

The government was able to turn its consideration once again to a proposal for a summit meeting with the United States. The Ministry of Foreign Affairs, seeking swift withdrawal of Japan's troops from China, wanted to include strict limits on the places and lengths of time that Japan would station troops abroad, but the army held fast to the idea that Japan would maintain a military presence in North China and Mengjiang. In the end, on September 25 a compromise was reached as far as market-opening measures and equality of opportunity were concerned, to ensure freedom of economic activity, but no compromise was reached on the subject of troops.

Hull Note Shock: Has the Die Been Cast?

On October 2, 1941, US secretary of state Hull gave Nomura a reply to the Japanese government's proposals. This memorandum, a draft of what would be formally submitted as the Hull Note on November 26, reiterated the same four principles that Hull had laid out before, and added that a clear declaration of Japan's intention to withdraw its troops from French Indochina and from China would be required. The memorandum also stated, in part, "This Government has noted the views of the Japanese Government in support of its desire to station troops for an indeterminate period in certain area of China. . . . [T]he inclusion of such a provision in the proposed terms of a peaceful settlement between Japan and China at a time when Japan is in military occupation of large areas in China is open to certain objections." Upon seeing the draft, Ambassador Nomura telegraphed, "The Japan-US negotiations appear to be deadlocked." Senior officials of the Ministry of Foreign Affairs were shocked, but they believed there was still time to negotiate. Efforts were made to seek a compromise with the army regarding stationing of troops and a deadline for troop withdrawal, but the army had decided the time had come to declare war on the United States, pursuant to the Imperial Council decision of September 6.

At the regular cabinet meeting on October 14, Army Minister Tōjō called for the termination of talks, saying, "The troop withdrawal problem is at the heart. . . . To accept the US proposal as-is would spell catastrophe for all that we have achieved in China. It would also endanger Manchukuo. It would also threaten the governing of Korea." Prime Minister Konoe and Foreign Minister Toyoda argued for continuation of diplomatic negotiations, and Navy Minister Oikawa Koshirō deferred to the prime minister. Two days later, the entire Konoe cabinet resigned due to an inability to reach consensus. In July, Konoe had solved his cabinet crisis by forcing out Matsuoka, but this time he was at a loss as to what to do.

Tōjō recommended that Prince Higashikuni succeed Konoe, but instead Tōjō himself became the next prime minister. Lord Keeper of the Privy Seal Kido Kōichi recommended Tōjō for this role because he believed Tōjō was the only person who could control the mid-ranking military officers who were the cause of the army's obstreperousness. On October 18, the Tōjō cabinet was formed, with Tōgō Shigenori as the new foreign minister, simultaneously continuing to serve as minister of the army. When the War Guidance Section learned of the establishment of the Tōjō cabinet, they wrote in their log: "Has the die been cast?" With Army Minister Tōjō, who was

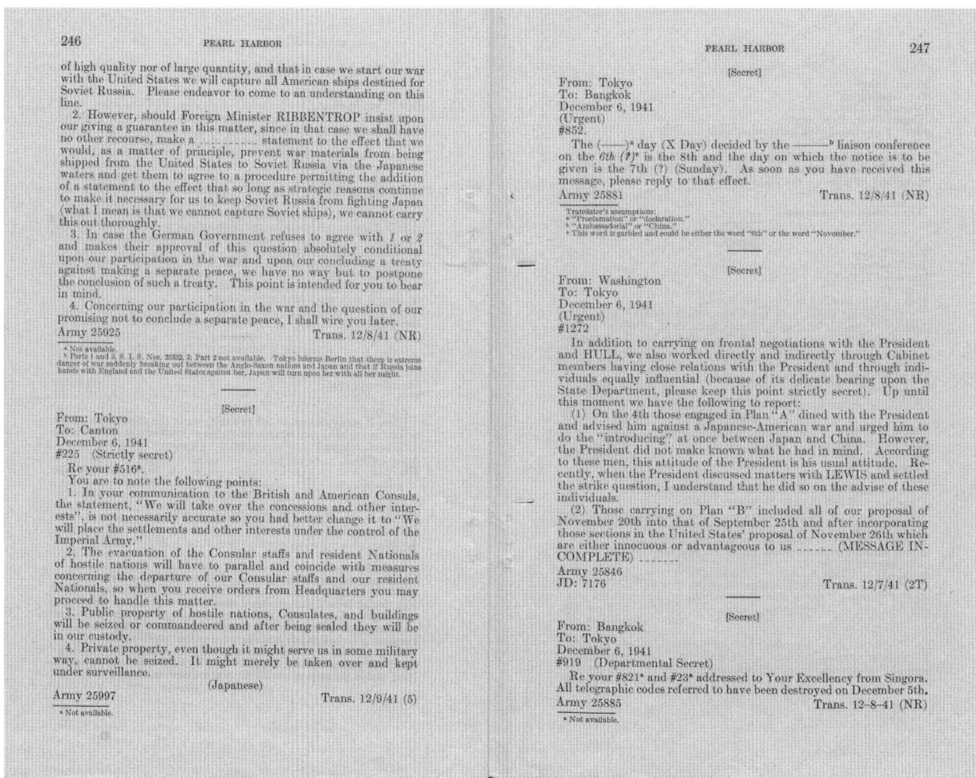

246 PEARL HARBOR

of high quality nor of large quantity, and that in case we start our war with the United States we will capture all American ships destined for Soviet Russia. Please endeavor to come to an understanding on this line.

2. However, should Foreign Minister RIBBENTROP insist upon our giving a guarantee in this matter, since in that case we shall have no other recourse, make a ---------- statement to the effect that we would, as a matter of principle, prevent war materials from being shipped from the United States to Soviet Russia via the Japanese waters and get them to agree to a procedure permitting the addition of a statement to the effect that so long as strategic reasons continue to make it necessary for us to keep Soviet Russia from fighting Japan (what I mean is that we cannot capture Soviet ships), we cannot carry this out thoroughly.

3. In case the German Government refuses to agree with *1* or *2* and makes their approval of this question absolutely conditional upon our participation in the war and upon our concluding a treaty against making a separate peace, we have no way but to postpone the conclusion of such a treaty. This point is intended for you to bear in mind.

4. Concerning our participation in the war and the question of our promising not to conclude a separate peace, I shall wire you later.

Army 25925 Trans. 12/8/41 (NR)

[a] Not available.
[b] Parts 1 and 3, S. I. S. Nos. 25552, 3; Part 2 not available. Tokyo informs Berlin that there is extreme danger of war suddenly breaking out between the Anglo-Saxon nations and Japan and that if Russia joins hands with England and the United States against her, Japan will turn upon her with all her might.

[Secret]

From: Tokyo
To: Canton
December 6, 1941
#225 (Strictly secret)

Re your #516[a].

You are to note the following points:

1. In your communication to the British and American Consuls, the statement, "We will take over the concessions and other interests", is not necessarily accurate so you had better change it to "We will place the settlements and other interests under the control of the Imperial Army."

2. The evacuation of the Consular staffs and resident Nationals of hostile nations will have to parallel and coincide with measures concerning the departure of our Consular staffs and our resident Nationals, so when you receive orders from Headquarters you may proceed to handle this matter.

3. Public property of hostile nations, Consulates, and buildings will be seized or commandeered and after being sealed they will be in our custody.

4. Private property, even though it might serve us in some military way, cannot be seized. It might merely be taken over and kept under surveillance.

(Japanese)

Army 25997 Trans. 12/9/41 (5)

[a] Not available.

PEARL HARBOR 247

[Secret]

From: Tokyo
To: Bangkok
December 6, 1941
(Urgent)
#852.

The (——)[a] day (X Day) decided by the ———[b] liaison conference on the *6th (?)*[c] is the 8th and the day on which the notice is to be given is the 7th (?) (Sunday). As soon as you have received this message, please reply to that effect.

Army 25881 Trans. 12/8/41 (NR)

Translator's assumptions:
[a] "Proclamation" or "declaration."
[b] "Ambassadorial" or "China."
[c] This word is garbled and could be either the word "6th" or the word "November."

[Secret]

From: Washington
To: Tokyo
December 6, 1941
(Urgent)
#1272

In addition to carrying on frontal negotiations with the President and HULL, we also worked directly and indirectly through Cabinet members having close relations with the President and through individuals equally influential (because of its delicate bearing upon the State Department, please keep this point strictly secret). Up until this moment we have the following to report:

(1) On the 4th those engaged in Plan "A" dined with the President and advised him against a Japanese-American war and urged him to do the "introducing" at once between Japan and China. However, the President did not make known what he had in mind. According to these men, this attitude of the President is his usual attitude. Recently, when the President discussed matters with LEWIS and settled the strike question, I understand that he did so on the advise of these individuals.

(2) Those carrying on Plan "B" included all of our proposal of November 20th into that of September 25th and after incorporating those sections in the United States' proposal of November 26th which are either innocuous or advantageous to us ------ (MESSAGE INCOMPLETE) ------.

Army 25846
JD: 7176 Trans. 12/7/41 (2T)

[Secret]

From: Bangkok
To: Tokyo
December 6, 1941
#919 (Departmental Secret)

Re your #821[a] and #23[a] addressed to Your Excellency from Singora. All telegraphic codes referred to have been destroyed on December 5th.

Army 25885 Trans. 12-8-41 (NR)

[a] Not available.

9-19. Japanese diplomatic telegram, December 1941 (deciphered and translated by US)

insistent on Japan's right to maintain a troop presence in China, now also in the role of prime minister, it seemed inevitable that talks with the United States would break down. That night, however, Tōjō was given the emperor's message that the Imperial Council decision of September 6 should be voided.

The mid-ranking army officers overwhelmingly wanted war, and they criticized Prime Minister Tōjō as a "traitor." Tōjō kept the Imperial General Headquarters and Government Liaison Conference in session for days on end for reconsideration of the nation's policies, particularly those related to national resources and mobilization capabilities. On November 5, the Imperial Council decided to pursue both diplomatic negotiations and war preparations until the end of November, and resolved that Japan would go on a war footing in early December if no agreement could be reached. Shimada Shigetarō, who served in the Tōjō cabinet as minister of the navy, was in favor of war, but Tōjō himself and Foreign Minister Tōgō were doing everything they could to reach a diplomatic agreement.

Plan A, Plan B, and the Final Talks

The Imperial Council meeting of November 5, 1941 chose a Plan A (Kō-an) and a Plan B (Otsu-an) for the final negotiations. Plan A was a summation of all the Japanese proposals up to that point, with a little room for concessions and compromise. Particularly with regard to the deployment of troops in China, the areas where troops could be stationed were strictly defined (North China, Mengjiang, and Hainan Island), and a period of roughly twenty-five years was given as a time limit for withdrawal of troops from these areas (in other areas the withdrawal was to be completed within two years).

Plan B was a proposal for a provisional agreement that had been drawn up by Foreign Minister Tōgō in consultation with former ambassador

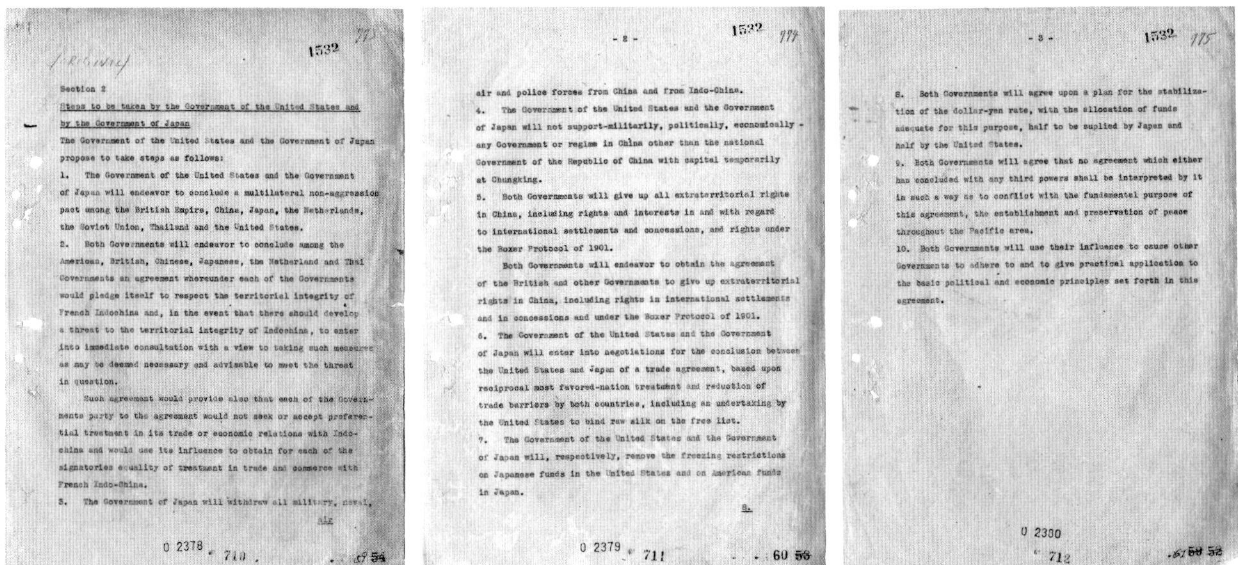

1532

Section 2

Steps to be taken by the Government of the United States and by the Government of Japan

The Government of the United States and the Government of Japan propose to take steps as follows:

1. The Government of the United States and the Government of Japan will endeavor to conclude a multilateral non-aggression pact among the British Empire, China, Japan, the Netherlands, the Soviet Union, Thailand and the United States.

2. Both Governments will endeavor to conclude among the American, British, Chinese, Japanese, the Netherland and Thai Governments an agreement whereunder each of the Governments would pledge itself to respect the territorial integrity of French Indochina and, in the event that there should develop a threat to the territorial integrity of Indochina, to enter into immediate consultation with a view to taking such measures as may be deemed necessary and advisable to meet the threat in question.

Such agreement would provide also that each of the Governments party to the agreement would not seek or accept preferential treatment in its trade or economic relations with Indochina and would use its influence to obtain for each of the signatories equality of treatment in trade and commerce with French Indo-China.

3. The Government of Japan will withdraw all military, naval,

0 2378

\- 2 -

1532

air and police forces from China and from Indo-China.

4. The Government of the United States and the Government of Japan will not support-militarily, politically, economically - any Government or regime in China other than the national Government of the Republic of China with capital temporarily at Chungking.

5. Both Governments will give up all extraterritorial rights in China, including rights and interests in and with regard to international settlements and concessions, and rights under the Boxer Protocol of 1901.

Both Governments will endeavor to obtain the agreement of the British and other Governments to give up extraterritorial rights in China, including rights in international settlements and in concessions and under the Boxer Protocol of 1901.

6. The Government of the United States and the Government of Japan will enter into negotiations for the conclusion between the United States and Japan of a trade agreement, based upon reciprocal most favored-nation treatment and reduction of trade barriers by both countries, including an undertaking by the United States to bind raw silk on the free list.

7. The Government of the United States and the Government of Japan will, respectively, remove the freezing restrictions on Japanese funds in the United States and on American funds in Japan.

0 2379

\- 3 -

1532

8. Both Governments will agree upon a plan for the stabilization of the dollar-yen rate, with the allocation of funds adequate for this purpose, half to be suplied by Japan and half by the United States.

9. Both Governments will agree that no agreement which either has concluded with any third powers shall be interpreted by it in such a way as to conflict with the fundamental purpose of this agreement, the establishment and preservation of peace throughout the Pacific area.

10. Both Governments will use their influence to cause other Governments to adhere to and to give practical application to the basic political and economic principles set forth in this agreement.

0 2380

9-20. The Hull Note

to the UK Yoshida Shigeru and former foreign minister Shidehara Kijūrō. Under this plan, Japan would withdraw its troops from the southern part of French Indochina to the northern part in exchange for a lifting of the embargo on oil shipments to Japan. But it also included a demand that the United States withdraw its support for Chiang.

Both plans were submitted to Secretary Hull on November 20, but Hull had no leeway to approve the presence of Japanese troops in China, in any form, or to agree to end support for Chiang. At the same time, based on Plan B, Hull was backing a proposed provisional plan for partial lifting of the British, American, and Dutch embargo on shipments to Japan in exchange for withdrawal of Japanese troops from the southern part of French Indochina. The United States needed a little more time to complete its preparations for war with Japan. The United States showed this provisional plan to its ambassadors from the United Kingdom, the Netherlands, Australia, and China's Chongqing regime, but China and the United Kingdom rejected it.

From China's perspective, if the United States agreed to compromise on its provisional plan, it would be sacrificing the Chinese people to appease Japan. The British government agreed with China, fearing that a US compromise would have a negative effect on the morale of the Chinese people and the Chinese government.

Hull therefore rejected Japan's Plan B and withdrew his own provisional agreement. On November 26, he handed the document now known as the Hull Note to Nomura as a response to Japan. This note called on Japan to withdraw all its troops from all Chinese territory and all of French Indochina, and to rescind its recognition of all governments in China other than the Chongqing government. It effectively demanded that Japan return to the status quo ante that existed prior to the Manchurian Incident. Upon first reading, Foreign Minister Tōgō said he was "struck by blinding disappointment." At the same time, the mid-level officers of the army saw this development as a "divine grace," because it would result in national unity in Japan. Tōjō and his cabinet viewed it as an ultimatum. On December 1, the entire cabinet attended the meeting of the Imperial Council, which decided that the empire would go to war against the United Kingdom, the United States, and the Netherlands.

The Warning of Impending Hostilities: Shedding Light on the "Sneak Attack"

After Japan made its final decision to declare war on December 1, 1941, the Ministry of Foreign Affairs drafted a final warning of the commencement of hostilities against the United States (an ultimatum) in accordance with international law (the Hague Convention on the Opening of Hostilities). The conclusion of the document explained that Japan had no choice but to terminate negotiations with the United States and that the US government would be responsible for "whatever future events should occur." At the deliberations of the Imperial General Headquarters and Government Liaison Conference concerning the ultimatum on December 4, however, the army and navy authorities in charge of the operation voiced reservations about the conclusion, which they thought the United States might easily interpret as an opening of hostilities. The navy was already preparing for an ambush at Pearl Harbor, while the army was busy gearing up for a surprise attack on Kota Bharu on the Malay Peninsula. Both branches of the military demanded that the Ministry of Foreign Affairs rewrite the end of the ultimatum so that it would not tip Japan's hand and arouse suspicion of a possible ambush.

The Ministry of Foreign Affairs responded by amending the closing to read, "The Japanese Government regrets to have to notify hereby the American Government that, in view of the attitude of the American Government, it can not but consider that it is impossible to reach an agreement through further negotiations." It was a phrasing that only hinted at Japan's intentions to cease negotiations and stopped short of making a formal ultimatum or declaration of war under international law, but Foreign Minister Tōgō explained the conclusion of Japan's diplomatic missions abroad as taking the place of an ultimatum.

Another major issue was when to give the United States notice. To make the ambush a success, Japan wanted to delay the warning as long as possible. On December 6, the Imperial General Headquarters and Government Liaison Conference decided to send the notification at 4:00 a.m. on December 7 (Japan time) and hand-deliver the document to the US president at 3:00 a.m. on December 8 (Japan time). Given the considerable length of the warning (official telegram no. 902), the Ministry of Foreign Affairs broke the message into fourteen parts and began transmission at 8:30 p.m. on December 6 to leave the process some margin for error. By twenty minutes after the calendar turned to December 7, the ministry had finished sending the thirteenth part. At that rate, the transmission of the fourteenth and final part would be complete by around 1:00 a.m., and the Japanese embassy in the United States would have the document in full by around 3:00 p.m. on December 6 (Washington time)—more than twenty hours before the scheduled attack on Pearl Harbor. However, the Ministry of Foreign Affairs held up the concluding statement and the rest of the fourteenth part for a full fifteen hours. Transmission thus began at 4:00 p.m. on December 7 (Japan time), with the Japanese embassy receiving the last installment at around 7:30 a.m. on December 7 (Washington time). It was 2:00 p.m. on December 7, approximately fifty minutes after the surprise attack, that Ambassador Nomura finally hand-delivered the warning to Secretary of State Hull. The British government, meanwhile, received no notification of the invasion of Kota Bharu.

In his speech imploring Congress to declare war on Japan, US president Franklin Roosevelt denounced the notice for arriving more than fifty minutes after the attack on Pearl Harbor and containing "no threat or hint of war or armed attack." Shimoda Takezō (former director-general of the Treaties Bureau and a justice on the Japanese Supreme Court) later said that the warning to the United States failed to meet the requirements of the Hague Convention and thus did not constitute an ultimatum; even if it had made it into American hands by 1:00 p.m. on December 7, the advance notice would still not have made Japan exempt from charges of an underhanded "sneak attack." The Japanese government's process of declaring war, therefore, had two problems: the content of the message and the delay of the message. The delay was what made Pearl Harbor a "sneak attack," an enduring source of bad blood between Japan and the United States.

While the postwar discourse has often attributed the delay in sending the warning to the Japanese embassy in the United States for deciphering and typing the message too slowly, observers have also laid blame at the feet of the Ministry of Foreign Affairs in Japan. Another important factor was the fact that the transmission of the warning's fourteenth segment began fifteen hours after it was originally scheduled, which evidence suggests was largely the result of the army's strategy-making authorities' involvement in not only altering the content of the message but also determining the timing of the transmission. Either way, the heart of the matter was that the embassy in the United States was continually at the mercy of events transpiring in Japan. It hung in the balance as the army and navy put the priority on making the ambush a success while the Ministry of Foreign Affairs put up resistance.

CHAPTER 10

The Pacific War and Wartime Diplomacy

10-1. *The Final Meeting of the Imperial Council* (painting by Shirakawa Ichirō)

TIMELINE

1942 (Shōwa 17)

January 1 Chongqing government (Chiang Kai-shek regime) signs joint declaration of war

January 2 Japanese army occupies Manila

February 15 Japanese army defeats British forces in Singapore

March 9 Japanese army defeats Dutch army in Java

May 1 Japanese army occupies Mandalay, Burma (key milestone for southern campaign)

June 5 Naval battle of Midway begins

October 10 US, UK end unequal treaties with China (Chongqing government) for the first time in 100 years (since 1842 Treaty of Nanjing)

November 1 Establishment of Ministry of Greater East Asia

December 21 Imperial Council sets new China policy (autonomy for Wang Zhaoming regime, etc.)

1943 (Shōwa 18)

January 9 Wang Zhaoming government declares war on US, UK

May 31 Imperial Council decides "Greater East Asia Policy Direction Framework"

August 1 Signing of Alliance Treaty between Japan and Burma

September 8 Unconditional surrender of Italy

September 30 Imperial Council decides "absolute zone of national defense"

October 20 Signing of Alliance Treaty between Japan and the Philippines

October 30 Signing of Alliance Treaty between Japan and the Republic of China with Wang Zhaoming government

November 5–6 Greater East Asia Conference (two days), issuance of joint declaration

November 22–26 US, UK, China leaders meet in Cairo

November 28 US, UK, USSR summit in Tehran (through December 1)

December 1 Cairo Declaration issued

1944 (Shōwa 19)

March 30 Japan, USSR sign memorandum on transfer of rights of natural resources in North Karafuto (Sakhalin)

June 15 US army begins landing on Saipan (July 7 The Japanese army launches the largest banzai charge of the Pacific War)

July 1–22 Bretton Woods Conference

July 22 Koiso Kuniaki cabinet formed

August 21–October 7 Dumbarton Oaks Conference

September 7 Koiso declares "Japan will grant Indonesia's independence in the near future"

October 9 Publication of "Proposals for the Establishment of General International Organization"

October 24–25 Battle of Leyte Gulf (Combined Fleet devastated)

November 6 Stalin, at event commemorating Russian Revolution, criticizes Japan as "aggressor nation"

November 10 Wang Zhaoming dies in hospital in Nagoya

November 24 US B-29s take off from the Mariana Islands for first air raids on Tokyo

1945 (Shōwa 20)

February 4–11	US, UK, USSR hold Yalta Conference, sign Yalta Declaration
March 9	Japanese army military liberation of French Indochina, creating Annam and two other nations
March 10	Great Tokyo Air Raid
April 1	US army begins landing on main island of Okinawa (Battle of Okinawa)
April 5	USSR notifies Japan it will not extend the Soviet-Japanese Neutrality Pact
April 7	Suzuki Kantarō cabinet formed
April 12	US president Roosevelt dies, succeeded by Vice President Truman
April 25	San Francisco Conference (United Nations Conference on International Organization; June 26 signing of UN Charter)
May 7	Germany surrenders
May 14	Supreme Council for the Direction of the War's Executive Committee (Big Six Meeting) agree to end the war, with Soviet Union as mediator
June 3	Hirota-Malik talks begin (through June 29)
June 23	Japanese army ends organized resistance in Okinawa (Okinawa Memorial Day)
July 12	Emperor orders Konoe Fumimaro to send special envoy to Soviet Union
July 16	US successfully tests atomic bomb
July 17	US, UK, USSR summit in Potsdam (through August 2)
July 26	US, UK, China issue Potsdam Declaration (Soviet Union enters war against Japan, joins Potsdam Declaration)
July 28	Prime Minister Suzuki gives "No comment" response to Potsdam Declaration
August 6	Atomic bomb dropped on Hiroshima
August 8	USSR renounces Soviet-Japanese Neutrality Pact, declares war on Japan
August 9	Soviet army invades Manchuria from three directions
August 9	Atomic bomb dropped on Nagasaki
August 10	First imperial decision to conditionally accept Potsdam Declaration
August 14	Second imperial decision to accept Potsdam Declaration; cabinet approves edict ending the war
August 14	Signing of Sino-Soviet Treaty of Friendship and Alliance
August 15	Emperor addresses nation via radio
August 17	Prince Higashikuni cabinet formed
August 17	Sukarno declares independence in Indonesia
August 18	Soviet army lands in Shumshu, Chishima (Kuril) Islands
August 20	Soviet army lands in Maoka, South Sakhalin
August 20	Soviet army occupies Shenyang, Harbin, Changchun, Jilin
August 23	Kwantung Army, Soviet army sign local armistice agreement
August 25	Soviet army occupies all of Sakhalin; by September 5 it occupies Japan's four Northern Territories
September 9	Okamura Yasuji, commander-in-chief of the China Expeditionary Army, surrenders in Nanjing

1 Tōgō's Foreign Policy and the Outbreak of War

"A Cheerful War"

On December 9, 1941 (Shōwa 16), the day after the attack on Pearl Harbor, the writer Itō Sei wrote in his diary: "Today, everyone looks happy, cheerful. Completely different from yesterday."

For Japan, this was the first declaration of war since the war against Germany in World War I. With no effective means to resolve the tensions between Japan and China, many Japanese people had come to believe the United States and the United Kingdom wanted to sap Japan's power and colonize East Asia themselves. They believed this was the cause of Japan's problems on the mainland, and that there was no way to achieve peace and stability in East Asia without driving out the United States and the United Kingdom. The hearts of the Japanese people were cast in a deep shadow of inexpressible sorrow.

The attack on Pearl Harbor did much to dispel this shadow. People believed that war with the United Kingdom and the United States would help solve a lot of Japan's problems, and they were wrapped in a comforting sense of heightened awareness and liberation. The Imperial Edict asserted that the expansion of the Western Powers' economic and military pressure and threats threatened to undermine Japan's yearslong efforts aimed at achieving stability in East Asia, or even the existence of Japan itself, compelling Japan to declare war for its own defense. On December 12, the government passed a resolution declaring that the war would be "known as the Greater East Asia War, including the series of China incidents."

However, the army and navy authorities in charge of the operation did not believe the war would be over in a short period of time. The US was likely to avoid engaging Japan in battle until its naval forces were restored to a level superior to Japan's. Even if Japan's navy desired a decisive battle in the near term, it was unlikely to be able to defeat the United States. Therefore, the prevailing view was that a total, prolonged war was inevitable. If this was the case, the question was how to bring that war toward a conclusion. The key lay in the defeat of the United Kingdom and the Chiang Kai-shek regime; i.e., the Chongqing government.

The thinking was that if Japan could cause the downfall of the United Kingdom and the Chongqing government, which were America's closest allies, by solidifying its foundation for a prolonged

Tōgō Shigenori (1882–1950)

10-2. Tōgō Shigenori

The eldest son of Pak Susong, a Korean potter who had established residence in Kagoshima, Tōgō Shigenori was born Pak Mu-dok. When his father purchased *shizoku* (equivalent to samurai nobility) status in 1886 and took the Tōgō surname, the young Mu-dok became Tōgō Shigenori. Although Tōgō graduated from Tokyo Imperial University with a degree in German literature, his interests lay in the field of diplomacy. He sat for the foreign-service examination in 1912, passed, and spent a considerable stretch of time in Europe on diplomatic service during World War I. He then returned home in 1921 and took charge of Russia-related matters for the Ministry of Foreign Affairs' Europe and America Bureau. In 1923, Tōgō worked with Hirota Kōki, then director-general of the Europe and America Bureau, on establishing stronger diplomatic relations with the Soviet Union, and played a role in bringing the Soviet-Japanese Basic Convention to fruition in 1925. Tōgō took over as director-general of the bureau shortly after Japan's exit from the League of Nations, directing his focus toward stabilizing relations with the Soviet Union through the war by bringing Southeast Asia under its influence, the US might, of its own accord, become unwilling to pursue the war. However, on December 9 the Chongqing government declared war on Japan, and in January 1942 it became the fourth signatory to the Declaration by the United Nations, joining the ranks of the major powers alongside the United States, the United Kingdom, and the Soviet Union. In the absence of any obvious way to topple the Chongqing regime, Japan's large-scale military operations in China would have to be restrained for the duration of the Pacific War apart from "Operation Ichi-Gō" (Operation No. 1) in the second half.

On the other hand, the defeat of the United Kingdom would have to be left up to Germany. The extent of Japan's military cooperation with Germany would be limited to attacks on the Soviet Union in the Far East, if Germany should make such a request. Inside the Army General Staff Office, there were those who were inclined to respond to such a call, but the main assumption was that the first part of the war would focus on regions south of Japan, and that Japan could avoid war with the Soviet Union to the north.

Either way, maintaining the terms of the 1941 Soviet–Japanese Neutrality Pact was a major diplomatic challenge for Japan, and a higher priority than its alliance with Germany. The Soviet Union was the only official route linking the Axis powers with the Allied powers.

Tōgō Shigenori and Shigemitsu Mamoru were the pillars of Japan's wartime foreign policy. Tōgō

---

creation of a Soviet-Japanese non-aggression pact and the purchase of the North Manchuria Railway (Chinese Eastern Railway).

Tōgō would go on to become Japan's ambassador to Germany in October 1937, but his tenure was brief; less than a year later, he received an appointment to serve as ambassador to the Soviet Union—a position he had longed for. While the signing of the Anti-Comintern Pact had exacerbated Soviet-Japanese tensions, Tōgō set to doggedly negotiating a provisional fisheries agreement and settling the Battle of Khalkhin Gol (also known as the Nomonhan Incident). He also tried to bargain his way to a Soviet-Japanese non-aggression pact in 1940 by offering the Soviet Union Japan's oil concessions in the northern part of Karafuto (Sakhalin), but then foreign minister Matsuoka Yōsuke was resistant to the idea due to his focus on building stronger bonds with Germany. Dispirited at what he saw as a missed opportunity, Tōgō left Moscow in October 1940.

A year later, however, he got the chance to take a leading role in shaping Japan's foreign relations: Prime Minister Tōjō Hideki named Tōgō his foreign minister in October 1941 amid a logjam in Japan's negotiations with the United States. The biggest point of contention in the talks was the withdrawal of troops from China, which Tōgō decided to deal with separately. Instead, he drew up a plan to keep the negotiations alive by proposing a provisional arrangement—Plan B (Otsu-an)—under which Japan would pull its troops out of southern French Indochina in exchange for the resumption of petroleum imports from the United States. Secretary of State Hull presented the idea to the United Kingdom and China, seeking their consent to the arrangement, but a Japan-US compromise that would essentially sell China down the river was nowhere close to the realm of possibility. Tōgō would eventually step down as foreign minister in September 1942 due to disagreements with Prime Minister Tōjō over the Ministry of Greater East Asia (see sidebar on page 332).

In April 1945, Tōgō became foreign minister once again at the request of Prime Minister Suzuki Kantarō. His diplomatic policy was unbending: he refused to make direct peace with the United States and instead entreated the Soviet Union to broker a more favorable end to the war. Tōgō's hard-line stance may have reflected the "do-or-die" mentality pervading Japan's domestic discourse of the time, but it would probably be safe to say that his strategy was too roundabout an approach. After the Allies arrived at the Potsdam Declaration, however, Tōgō came out in forceful, unyielding support of a quick end to the war as discussions reached their final stages—and his arguments turned out to be the decisive factor prompting the emperor's official decision to terminate hostilities. At the postwar Tokyo Trials, Tōgō was found guilty of Class-A war crimes and sentenced to twenty years in prison, where he would live out the rest of his life.

had been profoundly shocked by the Hull Note, but even after the war started he remained part of Tōjō Hideki's cabinet. He resigned in September 1942 due to problems at the Ministry of Greater East Asia, but in April 1945 he returned as foreign minister under Prime Minister Suzuki Kantarō.

Shigemitsu, for his part, served as foreign minister from April 1943 to April 1945, succeeding Foreign Minister Tani Masayuki. Both Tōgō and Shigemitsu had served as Japan's ambassador to the Soviet Union, making them well suited to dealing with that nation.

Japan's Soviet Policy and the Problem of German-Soviet Mediation

On New Year's Day in 1942, in an annual speech, Tōgō encouraged officials at the Ministry of Foreign Affairs to research and prepare, saying, "War has come because we were unable to prevent it, but we must make this war end as advantageously to Japan as possible." If the objective was a quick return to peace, the spring of 1942 became that opportunity, as Japan's Southern Campaign wound down. However, following the Southern Campaign and the Imperial General Headquarters and Government Liaison Conference decision of March 1942, the war strategy for both Japan's army and navy, in addition to developing supplies of important natural resources in the occupied territories and securing routes for sea lines of communication, was "maintaining a posture of invincibility, while seeking opportunities and actively pursuing measures." With the portent of deeper penetration of the Pacific region, a rapid peace would not be possible.

Thinking about what outcome of the war would be most advantageous for the Axis powers, assuming

Shigemitsu Mamoru (1887–1957)

The second son of a Sinologist in Ōita Prefecture, Shigemitsu Mamoru studied German law at Tokyo Imperial University, passed the foreign-service examination after graduation, and took a position at the Ministry of Foreign Affairs in 1911 in the same cohort as fellow recruits Ashida Hitoshi and Horinouchi Kensuke. In addition to serving in Germany and the United Kingdom, Shigemitsu was a member of Japan's entourage at the Paris Peace Conference. Shigemitsu would spend the 1920s in China at his own request, faithfully carrying out "Shidehara diplomacy" on the ground. In his tireless efforts to ensure the recognition of China's tariff autonomy and do away with extraterritoriality, Shigemitsu began to see forging a collaborative political and economic partnership with China—which was developing a stronger ethnic self-awareness—as his personal calling. That vision would shape his work as minister to China, too; up until the Manchurian Incident in 1931, Shigemitsu held to the faint hopes of restoring Sino-Japanese bonds through bilateral talks.

10-3. Shigemitsu Mamoru

In 1933, after the tumult of the Manchurian Incident had begun to quiet, Shigemitsu became vice-minister under Foreign Minister Hirota Kōki and set about improving relations with China through ties with "pro-Japanese" factions, in line with Hirota's China policy. Shigemitsu also began to lean toward a more regionalist take on international politics during his time as vice-minister, asserting that the "universal" brand of international order that the League of Nations and Nine-Power Treaty espoused was incompatible with East Asia. Embracing the same basic outlook that would inform the 1934 Amō (Amau) Doctrine, Shigemitsu rejected the idea of the major powers stepping in and interfering with the China issue. For him, the ideal approach centered on Japan and China engaging in direct negotiations. Shigemitsu occupied other high-level capacities in the latter half of the 1930s, becoming ambassador to the Soviet Union in August 1936 and then the United Kingdom in September 1938. From those stations abroad, Shigemitsu would often send the Japanese government telegrams critical of Japan's diplomatic inclinations toward joining forces with the Axis powers.

In early 1942, after hostilities between Japan and China had broken out, Shigemitsu became ambassador to China peace between Japan and the Soviet Union could be maintained, the most desirable possibility would be to induce the Soviet Union to abandon its war with Germany and join the Axis, so Japan and Germany could concentrate on fighting the United States and the United Kingdom. To induce the Soviet Union to abandon its war with Germany, Japan had two options: it could do what it could, diplomatically, to achieve peace between the two countries, or it could act militarily, entering the war against the Soviet Union. In the first option, Japan would work diplomatically to mediate reconciliation between Germany and the Soviet Union. In the second option, the Soviet Union would be under attack from both east and west, leading to its defeat and allowing the Axis powers to achieve an end that would be to their advantage. Japan's government and military had been debating these two options since the outbreak of war between Germany and the Soviet Union. The question was, which option was more realistic?

Of the two options, the military option—going to war with the Soviet Union at Germany's request—would be more difficult for Japan because it would test its capability to fight a war on two fronts, to the north and to the south. In July 1942, the Imperial General Headquarters and Government Liaison Conference decided that, in the current circumstances, Japan would not respond to Germany's request that it go to war against the Soviet Union.

After the war broke out, Japan intermittently pursued the diplomatic route, seeking to intercede for peace between Germany and the Soviet Union and lure the Soviet Union to join the Axis. Tōgō was passionate about working for peace between Germany and the Soviet Union, saying, "Regarding this war, the current diplomatic battle is a struggle

(under the Wang Jingwei regime) and began spearheading what he called a "new policy" in Japan's relations with China. Central to Shigemitsu's approach was the goal of spurring the Nanjing government to autonomy and independence by making the political sphere and the economic environment as free as possible—a major departure from the China policy that Japan had implemented since the Manchurian Incident. In April 1943, Prime Minister Tōjō Hideki made Shigemitsu his foreign minister as the war raged on. In that capacity, Shigemitsu received Tōjō's full backing and also won the support of the emperor in driving a "new Greater East Asia policy" that essentially implemented Japan's new China policy on a broader scale. The new Greater East Asia policy comprised a variety of Asia-related initiatives, most of which took place in 1943, including the Alliance Treaty between Japan and the Republic of China (the culmination of the new China policy); the Alliance Treaty between Japan and Burma and the Alliance Treaty between Japan and the Philippines (which recognized the "independence" of the respective countries); the Greater East Asia Conference (which convened representatives of Japan's "independent" colonies in Tokyo); and the Greater East Asia Joint Declaration, a product of the conference (see the main text for more information).

In August 1944, when the new Koiso Kuniaki cabinet formed, Shigemitsu stayed on as foreign minister on the condition that he could also serve concurrently as minister of Greater East Asia. For Japan's new policy in East Asia to succeed, Shigemitsu knew that he would need to wrest control over Asian diplomacy back from the Ministry of Greater East Asia and return it to the Ministry of Foreign Affairs. Shigemitsu was in a position to do just that, considering that he was heading up both organizations, and he managed to centralize Japan's diplomatic framework for all practical purposes. With that structure in place, Shigemitsu pushed the new Greater East Asia policy into its next phase: fostering self-government and independence in Indonesia, first of all, and liberating French Indochina to independence. A thread running through the various elements of the new Greater East Asia policy was Shigemitsu's vision for the future, which was grounded in the belief that self-determination would be the central theme of the postwar world.

Shigemitsu would also serve as foreign minister in the Hatoyama administration, during which time he helped Japan become admitted into the United Nations.

for the Soviet Union." Throughout the first half of 1942, the army and navy debated the possibilities, and made frequent suggestions for compromise through Germany's ambassador to Japan. What Germany wanted, though, was not Japan's help in pursuing peace, but for Japan to join its war against the Soviet Union.

"Maintaining Peace" in the Japan–Soviet Union Relationship

After the outbreak of the war, Japan's greatest worry with respect to the Soviet Union was the possibility that the Soviet Union would offer the United States a piece of its own territory in the Far East to use as a military base for bombing raids against Japan. In April 1942, Ambassador Satō Naotake met Foreign Minister Vyacheslav Molotov for the first time, seeking fresh assurances about Soviet neutrality and clarification regarding the Soviet stance on this problem. Molotov responded that there was no possibility the Soviet Union would provide a site for a US base, but he did not quell Japan's anxieties entirely. As the US military built up its presence in the northeast Pacific, Japan's suspicions grew deeper. To the very end of the war, however, the Soviet Union never gave the United States a site for a military base.

Ambassador Satō observed that the Soviet Union was focused on maintaining stability in

Sugihara Chiune (1900–86) and the "Visas for Life"

Starting Out as a Russian Specialist

Sugihara Chiune, a native of Gifu Prefecture, moved to Tokyo to study English at Waseda University Higher Normal School. In 1919, while he was enrolled at Waseda, he passed the Ministry of Foreign Affairs scholarship examination. That paid his way to Harbin (in North Manchuria), where he studied Russian and eventually enrolled at the Ministry of Foreign Affairs–controlled School of the Japan-Russia Association (Jp. Nichi-Ro Kyōkai Gakkō; later renamed the Harbin Institute). In 1924, Sugihara received an appointment to serve as a foreign-affairs clerk, and he began his duties at the Japanese consulate in Harbin the following year. His performance on the job drew the attention of Consul General Ōhashi Chūichi, who took Sugihara under his wing and, upon becoming vice-minister of the Manchukuo government's foreign ministry, brought Sugihara along to work under him. Sugihara had a hand in negotiating the purchase of the Chinese Eastern (North Manchuria) Railway and handling other tasks for the Manchukuo administration before returning to the Ministry of Foreign Affairs head office in July 1935. At the end of the following year, Sugihara was named a second-class interpreter at Japan's embassy to the Soviet Union in Moscow—but he was refused the right to take up residence in the country. The Soviet government denied Sugihara's visa and designated him a *persona non grata*, alleging that he had associated with anti-Soviet Russians during his time at the Manchukuo foreign ministry. In the end, Sugihara took a position at the Japanese legation in Finland in August 1937. In two years' time, he would find himself on the move to another post: that of vice-consul at Japan's new consulate in Kaunas, Lithuania.

It was at the end of August 1939 that Sugihara assumed his position in Kaunas, right after the signing of the German-Soviet Non-Aggression Pact—and just a few days before the German army invaded Poland on September 1. The United Kingdom and France then declared war on Germany on September 3, launching World War II. In mid-September, the Soviet Union invaded Poland in accordance with the secret protocol in the German-Soviet Non-Aggression Pact; roughly a month later, Poland would be split between Germany and the Soviet Union. Polish refugees, including many Jews, began streaming north into Lithuania.

Issuing Visas to Refugees

As German forces began their sweeping conquest across Northern and Western Europe in the spring of 1940, the Soviet Union embarked on an initiative to annex the Baltic states. Lithuania was the first target. Leveraging its massive military might and intimidating power, the Soviet Union created the pro-Soviet Socialist Lithuanian Republic in late June and incorporated the new country into the union of Soviet republics in early August. With the threat of Soviet annexation looming, refugees in Lithuania were in danger of losing their safe refuge. The crisis led many to flock to the Japanese consulate in Kaunas, hoping that they could relocate to a third country by way of Japan. To obtain a transit its relationship with Japan. He exploited that by maintaining peace with the USSR, which allowed Japan to focus its energies on its most urgent need: securing and stabilizing the fruits of its Southern Campaign. Consequently, Satō's priority in dealing with the Soviet Union was to steadily seek solutions to the various matters the two countries confronted. Because he was reluctant to intercede in the conflict between the Soviet Union and Germany, for fear of provoking Moscow, he offered the Soviet Union conciliatory terms to resolve outstanding issues such as coal and oil rights in North Karafuto (Sakhalin) and the Fisheries Treaty that had been simmering on the back burner for eight years. Regarding the coal and oil rights in North Sakhalin, when the Neutrality Pact was signed in April 1941, Foreign Minister Matsuoka had given Foreign Minister Molotov a letter promising to resolve "within several months" the problem of the dissolution of coal and oil rights in North Sakhalin. However, there was little forward progress on these issues during Tōgō's time in office.

The Establishment of the Ministry of Greater East Asia: Tōgō's Resignation

A half-year after the war started, Japan had its Asia-Pacific territories in hand; the main problem it faced was how to govern the area it occupied. In March 1942, the government created the Greater

visa, one normally had to have sufficient funds to cover travel expenses and a permit to enter the target third country—but few of the refugees could satisfy the requirements. Sugihara decided to issue the visas to the refugees via "special measures," such as having recipients promise to obtain entry permits to their destination countries, in order to avoid violating the existing directives and ensure that the visas would remain valid. Writing visa after visa, Sugihara rescued scores of Jews and other refugees from a dire situation. The surviving visa list indicates that he issued over 2,100 visas from late July to the end of August—and the actual number may have been higher. Adding in the family members of the visa recipients, the number of people that Sugihara was responsible for saving likely exceeded 6,000.

Sugihara soon found himself on the move after the closure of the consulate in Kaunas, assuming the role of Japan's acting consul general in Nazi-occupied Prague in September 1940. There, too, he apparently issued visas to nearly eighty Jewish refugees. In Kaunas, Sugihara's drive to issue visas was not necessarily an effort to protect recipients from the Nazi threat; in a narrow sense, it would be closer to the truth to say that it was the danger posed by Stalin that he was trying to protect people from during his time in Lithuania. The visas that Sugihara issued in Prague, albeit smaller in scale, served to help people escape the threat of the Nazis.

In 1985, the Israeli government awarded Sugihara with the "Righteous Among the Nations"—the highest honor given to non-Jews who risked their lives to save Jews during the Holocaust.

10-4. Sugihara Chiune

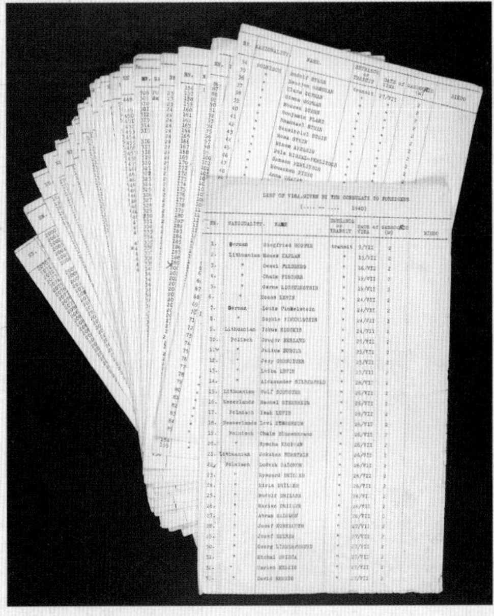
10-5. List of visas issued by Sugihara

The Ministry of Greater East Asia and the Wartime Ministry of Foreign Affairs

As Japan began to occupy larger swathes of Southeast Asia after going to war with the United States, the need emerged for a government body capable of handling the various political and economic matters of the Greater East Asia Co-Prosperity Sphere. That led the army, navy, and Cabinet Planning Board to draw up a proposal in March 1942 for the creation of a "unified governing organization" that would handle political, economic, and cultural concerns in the nations and occupied territories of Greater East Asia, and would ensure the protection of Japanese citizens residing there. In more specific terms, the plan would eliminate the Manchurian Affairs Bureau, the Ministry of Foreign Affairs, the Board of Asia Development, and the Ministry of Colonial Affairs and consolidate all the corresponding tasks into a single ministry. In mid-July, Foreign Minister Tōgō Shigenori met with Prime Minister Tōjō Hideki and voiced his hostility to the idea. "We need to ensure that all matters pertaining to independent nations are the domain of the Ministry of Foreign Affairs," he implored the prime minister. "Whatever new organization the government may establish, it must still see to it that all diplomatic affairs are fully centralized." The Ministry of Foreign Affairs countered the proposal with one of its own: a plan to position the East Asia Bureau and Europe and America Bureau under a "minister of external affairs," with the East Asia Bureau comprising departments for general affairs, China, Manchuria, and the southern region. The official cabinet proposal that Prime Minister Tōjō submitted in late August, however, was the "Ministry of Greater East Asia Proposal"—one that took its major points from the Cabinet Planning Board, along with other suggestions. The cabinet meeting on September 1 turned into a war of words between Tōgō and Tōjō, neither of whom was willing to compromise. Tōgō, unwavering in his conviction that "entrusting matters concerning independent states to any organization other than a diplomatic body is inevitably tantamount to making the nations into vassals, independent in name only," resigned in protest, as did Vice-Minister Nishi Haruhiko. The Ministry of Greater East Asia came into being in November 1942, with Aoki Kazuo serving as its first minister.

The only member of the Privy Council to oppose the new ministry's inauguration was former foreign minister Ishii Kikujirō, who argued that treating countries within the Co-Prosperity Sphere differently from other states was essentially the same as considering them

10-6. The Greater East Asia Conference

"colonies." In response to Ishii's line of reasoning, Prime Minister Tōjō framed the Co-Prosperity Sphere as a type of Confucian patriarchy—a structure in which "sibling" nations needed no diplomatic protocol. It was an apt representation of what the Co-Prosperity Sphere was at that juncture.

The framework for the establishment of the Ministry of Greater East Asia stipulated that its minister's authority would not include "pure diplomacy." Content to keep the definition of "pure diplomacy" intentionally nebulous, the Ministry of Foreign Affairs poured human resources into the new ministry in hopes of centralizing diplomacy for all intents and purposes. In fact, the Ministry of Foreign Affairs sent leading diplomats in to occupy positions at the new ministry, including Yamamoto Kumaichi as vice-minister and Mizuno Itarō as director-general of the Southern Affairs Secretariat. All together, 410 personnel made the switch from the Ministry of Foreign Affairs to the Ministry of Greater East Asia: 97 at the head office and 313 stationed abroad. Despite its presence at the new ministry, however, the Ministry of Foreign Affairs did see its authority shrink. The only organizations left at the head office were the Political Affairs Bureau, the Trade Bureau, the Treaties Bureau, and the Research Bureau; the regional bureaus were no more. In the ministry regime under new foreign minister Tani Masayuki were Vice-Minister Matsumoto Shun'ichi, Political Affairs Bureau director-general Kamimura Shin'ichi, Trade Bureau director Shibusawa Shin'ichi, and Treaties Bureau director-general Andō Yoshirō, forming a team that would remain essentially unchanged through the end of the war.

East Asian Construction Council, headed by Prime Minister Tōjō Hideki, and began to draft the broad outlines of a construction plan. One central theme of this plan was how to create a "colonialism-free Greater East Asia Co-Prosperity Sphere" by overcoming colonialism and the principle of self-determination of peoples. After two months of study, the concept of the Co-Prosperity Sphere, as outlined in the Basic Plan (Basic Items Regarding Construction of Greater East Asia Co-Prosperity Sphere, May 1942), put Japan in the position of "leader nation," responsible for regulating political, economic, and cultural order; interactions with countries outside the sphere were also to be regulated by the leader nation. The plan incorporated traditional Japanese ideas about family and social class, which other Asian nations were to adopt. The countries of Greater East Asia were to accept Japan's instructions as "head of the house"; only then could they be granted "independence" and "self-government." This was different from the Western-style idea of self-determination of peoples, where notions of independence and self-government were tied to the needs of local nationalism.

The Ministry of Greater East Asia was established in November 1942 as an extension of these ideas. (The history leading up to the establishment of the ministry is discussed in the sidebar on the previous page.) The ministry was disparaged as the "Colonial Ministry," and criticized for effectively ending Japan's diplomacy in this area. Prime Minister Tōjō likened its approach to Confucianist patriarchalism; he often said that fraternal nations had no need of diplomatic protocol. This was a fine expression of the idea of the Greater East Asia Co-Prosperity Sphere.

Foreign Minister Tōgō was so strongly opposed to the establishment of the Ministry of Greater East Asia that he resigned in September 1942, to be succeeded by Tani Masayuki. It was not until the tenure of Foreign Minister Shigemitsu that the problems of independence and self-determination in the occupied territories really came to the fore.

The Emergence of a "New China Policy"

As the problem of the Ministry of Greater East Asia faded, the Japanese government began to devise new policies on China that came to be known as the "New China Policy." After Wang Zhaoming's Nationalist regime in Nanjing entered the war in January 1943, siding against the United States and the United Kingdom, Japan began to ease its grip on China, encouraging more autonomy and independence. One background factor at work here was that, in the second half of 1942, the fierce battle at Guadalcanal in the southeastern Pacific had sapped Japan's strength. Particularly on the economic front, Japan decided to give the Nanjing government more leeway in order to lessen its own burden of governance. The Army General Staff Office was a particularly keen supporter of the New China Policy. In addition, the United States and the United Kingdom declared to the Chongqing regime that they would end the unequal treaties (October 10, 1942). Both the Allied nations and Japan were in agreement that abandoning the unequal treaties would be an effective means to "grasp the hearts of the people" and strengthen cooperation in China.

More specifically, Japan's new policy meant a complete reconstruction of Japan's relationship with China, including reversing extraterritoriality and concessions, abandoning the idea of converting North China and Inner Mongolia to "special regions," and embarking on a full-scale reworking of the Japan-China Basic Relations Treaty of 1940 to strengthen the political position of the Nanjing government.

However, the decision to pursue the New China Policy meant giving up many existing advantages, so a good deal of political capital was needed. The chief proponent was Shigemitsu, who was made ambassador to the Nanjing government in January 1942. According to Shigemitsu, to foster the independence and self-determination of the Nanjing government, both political and economic "freedom" would have to be allowed, to the greatest possible extent. If respect for sovereignty and mutual equality could be ensured, the Chongqing regime's pretext for opposition to Japan would vanish, clearing the way for the construction of a foundation for complete peace between the two countries. To that end, Japan would need a "fundamental correction" of its China policies, and a "clearing of mistaken policies." Shigemitsu took pains to explain this way of thinking to Japan's political and military leaders. He won the support of Foreign Minister Tani and Prime Minister Tōjō and even the emperor, and at the end of December 1942 it was brought to the Imperial Council for a decision. Some goals of the new policy, such as greater autonomy and independence for the Nanjing government, and strengthening its political power, were not new, but the new policy was radical in the sense that it set a new course toward tolerating a broad degree of freedom and initiative for the Nationalist government.

Politically, the new policy meant reversing extraterritoriality and concessions. Economically, it meant relaxing control. These reforms began to be implemented in early 1943. However, the effects were limited because in the areas of China ruled by the Nanjing government, the goals and concepts of Japan's new policies were not well understood, institutions on the Japan side squabbled over authority, and the economy was lurching toward crisis. The Chinese people under the rule of the Nanjing government thought the real problem that needed to be solved was the economic pressures stemming from inflation. They felt manipulated by the Japanese military on the one hand and controlled by Japanese merchants on the other. This situation endured until Japan's defeat.

Shigemitsu, however, remained committed to the goals of the new policy, working for the conclusion of a new Japan-China treaty (Alliance Treaty between Japan and the Republic of China) by fully revamping the existing Japan-China Basic Relations Treaty. He continued to work his way into Prime Minister Tōjō's good graces, and in the sudden cabinet reshuffle of April 1943 he was made foreign minister.

2 Foreign Minister Shigemitsu and the Greater East Asia Conference

The "Absolute Zone of National Defense" and the Idea of the Greater East Asia Conference

When Shigemitsu Mamoru joined the cabinet, the tide of the war was turning against Japan in the Southeast and Northeast Pacific, and in Burma. Japan's military had been put on the defensive. For the first time since the war began, the army and the navy were reconsidering their plans for the war. They devised the idea of an "Absolute Zone of National Defense" to shrink Japan's expansive footprint in the Pacific and refocus the war effort on fighting the United States. In a September 1943 decision, the Imperial Council defined the zone of absolute defense to include the Chishima (Kuril) Islands, Ogasawara (Bonin), Micronesia, Western New Guinea, Sunda, and Burma.

An Allied counterattack in the Pacific was expected in the fall of 1943, and the key point of the strategy was to prepare by stabilizing and solidifying Japan's political control of the regions it occupied. Prime Minister Tōjō Hideki decided to hold the Greater East Asia Conference in Tokyo, calling together leaders from throughout "Greater

East Asia," and the Imperial Council approved the idea in May 1943, to solidify Japan's control.

Shigemitsu, on the other hand, raised the goal of concluding a new alliance treaty with the Nanjing government based on the ideas of respect for sovereignty and mutual equality. At the same time, he tried to conclude similar treaties with Thailand and Manchukuo, as well as with Burma and the Philippines, which were scheduled to gain their independence. On the basis of this network of alliances, Shigemitsu intended to create a "Greater East Asia International Organization" made up of several countries that were on equal standing with one another. If Shigemitsu's proposal were followed, the nations of the Greater East Asia Co-Prosperity Sphere (Japan, Manchukuo, China, Thailand, Burma, and the Philippines) would "form a joint organization that would meet either regularly or ad hoc, in Tokyo or elsewhere, and deliberate on matters regarding the course of the war today, or cooperation in peacetime." Based on this concept, Shigemitsu regarded the Greater East Asia Conference as the first step toward the creation of this international organization, and he hoped the conference would issue a joint declaration that would serve as a "Charter for Greater East Asia."

Shigemitsu's motivation for pursuing this idea was to give his personal response to the underlying issues of World War II: achieving independence for ethnic groups and subduing colonialism. His motivation stemmed in part from a desire to disrupt the intervention of the military in foreign relations, which had driven colonialism.

However, Shigemitsu was forced to withdraw these ideas, as they met with a barrage of criticism within Japan, from two perspectives: The first was that the positions of Japan, Manchukuo, and China were not equal to the other three independent nations (Thailand, Burma, and the Philippines); the second was that it would not be desirable to create an institution similar to the League of Nations. People feared that Japan's "leadership rights" would be compromised. In the end, the Greater East Asia Conference became merely the occasion for releasing the Greater East Asia Declaration that was set to become the Charter for Greater East Asia.

10-7. Indonesian president Sukarno visits Japan in 1943

Even so, by the time of the Greater East Asia Conference, three alliance treaties were concluded based on respect for sovereignty and mutual equality. The Alliance Treaty between Japan and the Nanjing Government (October 1943), into which Shigemitsu poured so much of his effort, was a treaty between two equal parties, based on three principles: mutual respect for sovereignty and territory, cooperation on building Greater East Asia, and economic cooperation based on reciprocal benefits. In the protocol attached to the agreement, Japan promised to abandon its right to station troops in China under the protocol concluded when the Boxer Rebellion ended (Boxer Protocol) and withdraw its troops once the war was over. This was largely in line with the demands of the Ministry of Foreign Affairs, but it was not enough to rescue the Nanjing government from the brink of economic collapse, nor was it effective in enticing the Chongqing regime of Chiang Kai-shek to a peace deal.

Around the time the Alliance Treaty between

Japan and the Republic of China was concluded, Japan concluded alliance treaties with Burma (August 1943) and with the Philippines (October 1943), resulting in the "independence" of these two nations and the exchange of ambassadors. Sawada Renzō became Japan's ambassador to Burma, and Murata Shōzō became ambassador to the Philippines.

The Greater East Asia Conference and Japan's New War Aims

In early November 1943, representatives of the independent Asian nations established in places that had been occupied by Japan gathered in Tokyo for the Greater East Asia Conference. Those invited included Prime Minister Zhang Jinghui of Manchukuo, President of the Executive Yuan Wang Zhaoming from Nanjing, Prime Minister Ba Maw of Burma, President José Laurel of the Philippines, and Prince Wan Waithayakon, representing Thailand's prime minister Phibun. Chandra Bose, head of state of the Provisional Government of Free India, also attended.

By gathering these leaders of occupied nations together in Tokyo, Prime Minister Tōjō's aim was to issue a joint statement that would make the case for uniting the peoples of Asia. However, Foreign Minister Shigemitsu and other officials from the Ministry of Foreign Affairs responsible for drafting the joint declaration tried to incorporate new war objectives in the proposal for the joint declaration.

The proposal for the Greater East Asia joint declaration was drafted mainly by the War Aims Research Council, which in August 1943 consisted primarily of Ministry of Foreign Affairs division chiefs led by Treaties Bureau director-general Andō Yoshirō. According to Andō, the declaration was not to be simply wartime propaganda. Greater East Asia had to be "based on principles that anyone would think were objectively fair and just, a singular great basis for maintaining world peace." The proposal was loosely based on the Atlantic Charter of August 1941. It was not easy to reconcile the Atlantic Charter with the idea of a "leader nation." Committee member Sone Eki said, "In the concept of the Co-Prosperity Sphere, the conventional idea of a leader nation is emphasized to an extreme, and that should provoke some reflection."

Among the most important points of

10-8. Greater East Asia Conference

disagreement was the problem of whether the economic system of the Co-Prosperity Sphere should be based on a planned economy or a free economy, particularly where the exploitation of natural resources was concerned. Andō said, "We should loudly proclaim the free access to natural resources." Sone followed this, saying, "If the war ends, it will be necessary to inform the public that complete autarky within the sphere alone is not possible." In the world of scholars and journalists, a closed view of the regional economy predominated, but a majority of the War Aims Research Council favored a more open economic view.

However, in a consultation involving officers from various ministries, there was opposition to "free access to natural resources" to the very end. The navy, in particular, which was responsible for the governance of the important natural resources of Indonesia, regarded free access to natural resources in the occupied territories as "leaving the potential for evil in the future." The Finance Ministry and the Ministry of Greater East Asia supported the navy's position. Consensus was elusive, but "free access to natural resources" eked its way into the draft declaration. Underlying this, it should be noted, was the existence of a definite prospect, as described in the Treaties Bureau's annual report, of a need to "take bold steps to open up East Asia, freeing trade with other countries as much as possible, and promote the introduction of capital and technology after the war," regardless of who won or lost.

The Greater East Asia Joint Declaration of November 6 makes no mention of the construction of the Greater East Asia Co-Prosperity Sphere. Instead, it lists as new objectives of the war (Greater East Asia Construction Plan): (1) respect for self-determination and independence, (2) mutual respect for traditions and expansion of the creativity of ethnic groups, (3) mutually beneficial economic development, (4) elimination of ethnic discrimination, (5) promotion of cultural exchange, and (6) free access to natural resources.

From Foreign Minister Shigemitsu's perspective, the joint declaration had two significant points. First was that "the idea of the New China Policy was expanded to the entire East Asia region, and this would be reflected within Japan, and the military would be set straight." The second, as can be seen in the discussion by the War Aims Research Council, was to reconfigure the objectives of the war to include universal values such as sovereignty, independence, equality, mutual benefit, and liberation, to prepare for the restoration of peace.

In the recollection of Sone, who participated in the drafting of the Greater East Asia Declaration, the aim of the declaration was "an invitation to peace, even though Japan was taking this extremely roundabout route of saying that it does not adhere to the territorial issue of the occupied territories." The declaration incorporated Japan's hopes in the form of a message for peace to the Allies.

However, the New Greater East Asia Policy and the Greater East Asia Declaration, which were effectively an expansion of Japan's New China Policy, failed to have the effect on the Allied nations that Shigemitsu and the Ministry of Foreign Affairs had hoped to achieve. Also, the Greater East Asia Declaration had little success in gaining the cooperation of residents of the occupied territories in procurement of supplies for the war. Particularly in Indonesia, which had not been allowed to participate in the Greater East Asia Conference, mistrust of Japan only increased. For the Greater East Asia Declaration to be more than merely a wartime declaration, it had to outshine the Cairo Declaration that had been issued around the same time. To achieve that end, both domestically and abroad, it had to at least show a concrete aspiration in the form of something like a "Greater East Asia Organization."

Roughly contemporaneous with the Greater East Asia Conference, the Allies were launching a "diplomatic offensive" of their own in the form of a series of conferences: the Cairo Conference, the Tehran Conference, etc. The Cairo Declaration (November

10-9. Chiang Kai-shek, Franklin Roosevelt, and Winston Churchill meet in Cairo

1943), in particular, produced by the United States, United Kingdom, and China, discussed for the first time what the Allied nations would do with Japanese-occupied territories after the war: return Taiwan and the Pescadores (Penghu) Islands to China, stripping Japan of territories it had held since 1914, and granting independence to Korea, among other things. Noting that Chiang Kai-shek was a signatory to the Cairo Declaration, Ambassador Ishii Itarō lamented, "Full peace is now a thousand leagues farther off." In the news coverage of the Cairo Declaration, the Japanese government did not allow the press to report on the territorial issues.

Progress in Japan-Soviet Union Relations

In 1943, the Soviet Union was becoming increasingly strident in its demands that the terms of the Matsuoka Letter (see page 331) be carried out. This set the tone for Japan-Soviet talks in the tenure of Foreign Minister Shigemitsu. In early June 1943, Molotov demanded a clear response from Japan regarding the disposition of rights in North Sakhalin, telling Ambassador Satō Naotake that without the Matsuoka Letter, there would be no neutrality pact. At its June 19 session, the Imperial General Headquarters and Government Liaison Conference discussed proactive solutions for various bilateral issues between Japan and the Soviet Union and reached a decision to sell the rights to North Sakhalin to the Soviet Union for a sum of money. During that session, skepticism was expressed that a transfer without an exchange of real benefit might have major domestic consequences, but Shigemitsu cut that off, saying, "It is imperative that we take this opportunity to advance our friendship with the Soviet Union."

Although Satō entered into negotiations with the Soviet Union to resolve the rights problem, one obstacle was an incident in which ships believed to have been transferred from the United States to the USSR had been detained by Japan's navy. Only after Japanese concessions (unconditional release of the detainees) made resolution of this incident possible did full-scale negotiations begin in the fall of 1943.

In exchange for the rights in North Sakhalin, Japan demanded a sum of money plus 200,000 tons of oil and 100,00 tons of coal for a period of five years after relinquishing the rights. The USSR ignored Japan's demand for cash, and it postponed commitments to supply oil and coal until after the war. Negotiations dragged on into the next year, but in late January 1944, a compromise was reached on a sum of 5 million rubles and 50,000 tons of oil for five years after the war ended. Japan was less than satisfied, but it could at least say it had received something in exchange. The Liaison Conference approved the deal on February 2. Around the same time, agreement was reached on a five-year extension of the problematic fisheries treaty, resolving the operational problems stemming from the erratic provisional treaty.

For Japan's leaders, the resolution of both the

rights issues and the fisheries issues in March 1944 generated expectations of a positive turn in bilateral relations going well beyond the maintenance of neutrality. In Foreign Minister Shigemitsu's view, the resolution of these various issues was meant to drive a wedge into efforts by the United States, the United Kingdom, and the Soviet Union to strengthen their alliance against Japan. Shigemitsu was focused on advancing compromise proposals with the Soviet Union regarding the German-Soviet mediation and the China problem.

Japan sought peace between Germany and the Soviet Union in 1943, making repeated entreaties to both Germany and the Soviet Union; all were spurned. Japan made another appeal to the Soviet Union in the fall of 1944, sending its special envoy charged with interceding between Germany and the Soviet Union, but this, too, was rejected. Ambassador Satō believed such efforts "contradicted the times," and he clashed repeatedly with Shigemitsu on this topic.

The Tōjō Cabinet Falls

In April 1944, Japan set in motion on China's mainland "Operation Ichi-Gō" (Operation No. 1), the largest military campaign in its history. The purpose of this operation, along a 1,500-km front stretching from the Yellow River in Henan Province to the border between Guangdong and French Indochina, was to capture air bases in the southwest of China (Guilin, Liuzhou) from which bombers might reach Japan's main islands. The operation also aimed to establish a transportation network linking China and Korea with the southern natural resources of French Indochina.

The war in the Pacific was also at an important turning point. In June 1944, US forces in the central Pacific were approaching the Mariana Islands, and in early July they captured the island of Saipan in that chain, piercing Japan's "absolute zone of national defense." In the Battle of Imphal, Japanese forces were attempting to attack India from north Burma, but they were repeatedly driven back. As Operation Ichi-Gō went on, the Marianas fell to the Americans, enabling US B-29 long-range bombers to reach the main islands of Japan. Japan was no longer able to prevent air raids on its soil.

As the tide of the war turned against Japan, particularly with the fall of Saipan, the Tōjō cabinet was put in a predicament. Tōjō himself, however, remained both prime minister and minister of the army, with an appointment as chief of the general staff. He was charged with both affairs of state and command of the military. Moreover, with Tōjō's opponents in the political parties and the national legislature reduced to mere figureheads, it was not easy to think about a change of cabinet. Nonetheless, the senior statesmen Okada Keisuke and Konoe Fumimaro, assisted by Lord Keeper of the Privy Seal Kido Kōichi, succeeded in forcing a change of government in late July.

With the fall of Saipan, the Army General Staff was rethinking its entire strategy. In the new strategy, named "Operation Shō-Gō" (Operation Victory), the front line for the defense of Japan contained the main islands of Japan, Okinawa, Taiwan, and the Philippines. The main aim of this new strategy was to defend this line, and particularly the Philippines, against attacks by US forces.

3 The Koiso Cabinet

The Koiso Cabinet and Foreign Minister Shigemitsu's Diplomacy

In late July 1944, Koiso Kuniaki, who had been a general in the army reserve as well as governor-general of Korea, formed a cabinet. The navy had backed Yonai Mitsumasa to become prime minister, but he served as deputy prime minister while also staying on as minister of the navy. Koiso established the Supreme Council for the Direction of the War, replacing the Liaison Conference, in an effort to bring affairs of state and command of the military under a single roof.

To unify management of foreign relations with Asia, Foreign Minister Shigemitsu Mamoru also served as minister for Greater East Asia. In these dual roles, Shigemitsu focused on both self-rule and independence for Indonesia, and liberation and independence for French Indochina. French Indochina and Malaya were the last Western European colonies.

Indonesia (Java) had been primarily under the control of the Japanese navy. In May 1943, as part of the Greater East Asia Policy Direction Framework, Malaya and Indonesia had been designated "Imperial Territories." The government now faced the near-impossible task of moving them out of that designation and in the direction of independence and self-government. Shigemitsu's ideas about independence for Indonesia notwithstanding, the previous administration had done little beyond expanding Indonesia's participation in political affairs. The main obstacle was that the navy, whose primary interest was in exploiting Indonesia's natural resources, opposed any change in the status quo. Even so, the simple "Koiso Statement," which stipulated that Japan would grant Indonesia independence in the future, was announced in September 1944. Nothing specific was said, however, about the timing of that independence or what form it would take.

The road to independence for French Indochina also faced many obstacles. Its parent state, France, was under German occupation, and since the formation of the Axis, Japan had regarded the regime in French Indochina as "friendly," and established an ambassador-level branch there. Since the start of the war, the Japanese government's policy on French Indochina had been one of "maintaining the peace" (i.e., keeping the status quo). In August 1944, however, de Gaulle formed a provisional government in France, compelling Japan, which was allied with the rival Vichy government, to regard French Indochina as a political problem. The establishment of the new de Gaulle government was a crisis for Japan.

The Japanese government and military made urgent preparations for the military liberation of French Indochina, but in December 1944, de Gaulle forged a treaty of alliance with the Soviet Union, adding a new wrinkle to the situation. The problem with the liberation of French Indochina was determining what form of government it should have afterward. Japan's army and the troops in French Indochina wanted to maintain military rule there, but Shigemitsu was strongly opposed. In the end, Shigemitsu and the Ministry of Foreign Affairs, whose goal was to prioritize independence based on the Greater East Asia Declaration, used Japan-Soviet Union relations to win this concession from the army. The army acceded to Shigemitsu's calls for immediate independence not out of some recognition of ethnic self-determination, but rather to prevent any worsening of relations between Japan and the Soviet Union. Allowing French Indochina its own governance was a demonstration of non-aggression toward the Soviet Union. This military liberation of French Indochina was accomplished in March 1945, giving rise to three "independent" nations.

Efforts toward Peace with China

Since the outbreak of war between Japan and the United States, Japan had entrusted to the Nationalist government in Nanjing the task of achieving peace with the Chongqing government. Japan itself played no direct role in the process. At the August and September 1944 sessions of the Supreme Council for the Direction of the War, the Koiso cabinet resolved to unify the Chongqing operation under the authority of the prime minister, with the main objective to be to create an impetus for direct talks to end the war between Japan and China.

In early September 1944, the Supreme Council for the Direction of the War decided the following "Plan for Peace Terms." These were watershed terms for peace that, had they been issued around the time of the outbreak of war between Japan and the United States, might have opened the possibility of peace between Japan and China. They comprised: (1) peace based on a position of complete equality; (2) respect for China's view on peaceful relations between Chongqing and the United States and the United Kingdom; (3) treating relations between Wang Zhaoming and Chiang Kai-shek as a domestic issue; (4) if the United States and United Kingdom withdrew their troops, Japan would withdraw all its troops, and Hong Kong would be returned to China.

These stipulations were delivered to the Nanjing government as terms for peace with Chongqing, but Zhou Fohai and other leaders of the Wang regime hesitated to pass them along to the Chongqing due to vagueness about the return of Manchuria to China (i.e., the elimination of Manchukuo). The text did contain a single line stating that the Ministry of Foreign Affairs "recognized that Manchukuo would ultimately be China's territory," but the final draft of the peace agreement would reflect the view of the army, which was that the status of Manchukuo would not change. Another obstacle to the agreement was that it opposed Japan's existing policy stance of strengthening the Wang regime.

Back in Japan, Foreign Minister Shigemitsu was critical of the final draft of the peace agreement out of consideration for the position of the Wang regime. In the end, the September 1944 decision by the Supreme Council for the Direction of the War showed that Japan's position had been reduced to the point where Japan itself had to propose its own tacit defeat, in the form of Chiang's return to Nanjing to form a unity government, and Japan's complete withdrawal from China. In the aftermath, Japan pursued peace through various routes, but none of them passed through the government in Chongqing.

10-10. The Japanese naval base in Kobe Port in flames after being bombed by US B-29 bombers

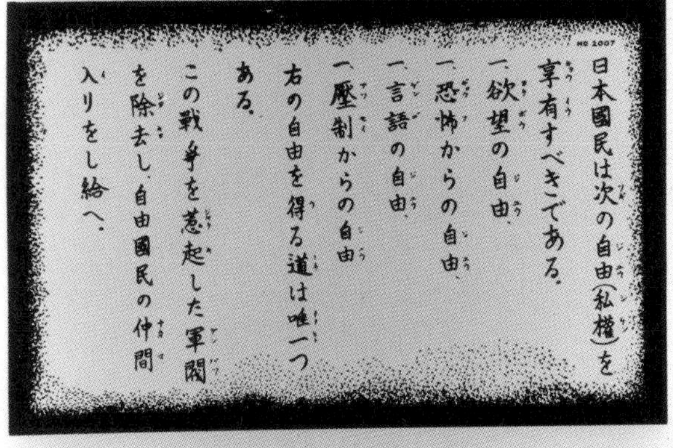

10-11. Leaflets dropped by US forces

Miao Bin's Plan

Amidst all this, the Miao Bin Affair came to light. Miao Bin was deputy head of the Nanjing government's Examination Yuan. He was not part of Wang's inner circle, and secretly he remained in contact with the Chongqing regime. Miao was connected to Koiso through a small group of men: Minister of State Ogata Taketora in Tokyo; Tamura Shinsaku, who had been a correspondent for the *Asahi Shimbun* during Ogata's tenure there, in Shanghai; *Asahi Shimbun* reporter Ōta Teruhiko; and Yamagata Hatsuo, a former army colonel who was a confidant of Koiso. Of this group, Tamura was closest to Miao, and was sympathetic to his ideas for peace.

Over objections from Shigemitsu and others, Koiso met with Miao in Japan in mid-March 1945. Miao's "Proposal for Complete Peace between China and Japan" consisted of the elimination of the Nanjing government, the establishment of a "caretaker government" approved by the Chongqing side, and the start of armistice talks between Japan and China, as represented by the "caretaker government." Miao discussed this plan with Ogata, Koiso, and Prince Higashikuni (supreme commander of the Homeland). At the Supreme Council for the Direction of the War in late March, Koiso made a formal proposal of this plan and requested the council's understanding for its execution. However, Shigemitsu, who was skeptical of the plan from the outset, opposed it to the end. For Shigemitsu, the elimination of the Nanjing government and full withdrawal of Japanese troops were major policy decisions that would first require Japan's "determination to end the war." Without a decision to end the war against the United States and the United Kingdom, no plan for peace with Chongqing that ignored the Nanjing government would be possible. Early in April 1945, Koiso reported to the emperor on the progress of the Miao Bin plan, but the emperor ordered Koiso to send Miao back to China, due to the opposition of the ministers of the army, navy, and foreign affairs. That was the end of the Miao Bin plan, as well as one reason for the collapse of the Koiso cabinet.

The Battle of the Philippines; the Battle of Okinawa

Beginning in the second half of 1944, in both Europe and the Pacific, the Allies were gaining the upper hand in the war. The United States and the Soviet Union intensified their tug-of-war over the shape of the postwar world. In Europe, the main focus was on Eastern Europe, while in the Asia-Pacific region it was on Manchuria after the withdrawal of Japan. As early as the Tehran Conference in November 1943, the Soviet Union had promised to join the war against Japan. At the Yalta Conference in February 1945, Stalin said the Soviet Union would start fighting Japan three months after Germany was defeated. In exchange, he wanted Port Dalian to be opened to international commerce, with priority rights for the USSR. He also wanted leases for Port Arthur and joint Chinese-Soviet operation of the Chinese Eastern and Manchurian railways. The United States and the United Kingdom acceded to these demands. Japan desperately sought information from the Yalta Conference, but it was not able to learn of the secret agreements that were made there.

Amid this international situation, the US military landed on Leyte Island in the Philippines in late October 1944. The Combined Fleet attacked Leyte with all its might, and the Japanese navy was dealt a decisive blow, losing some thirty warships in the Battle of Leyte, marking a clear end for Operation Shō-Gō in January 1945. The commanders of Japan's army and navy decided on a new defensive plan covering the main islands and outlying islands of Japan, Manchukuo, and China, resolving that any US forces entering that perimeter would be destroyed. Part of that plan was to fight a war of attrition on Okinawa, causing as much harm as

10-12. US forces make landing on Okinawa

possible to US forces there before a final all-out defense of the main islands of Japan.

The US navy arrived at the main island of Okinawa from the west on April 1. This was a major force, with over 540,000 personnel on more than 1,300 ships. Japan had 77,000 troops, and mobilized 25,000 Okinawans. By June, 110,000 Japanese troops and 100,000 Okinawans had lost their lives.

4 The Suzuki Cabinet and the End of the War

The Formation of the Suzuki Cabinet

Admiral Suzuki Kantarō was already seventy-seven years old when the emperor summoned him again, this time to serve as prime minister. In his many years as grand chamberlain, Suzuki had learned to do as the emperor wished. This time, that meant bringing a "swift conclusion to the war, as the circumstances warranted." While these were not the emperor's explicit instructions, it was Suzuki's sense of what was expected of him.

Suzuki placed great importance on his cabinet, as the highest public decision-making body in the land, and on the solidarity of its ministers. Suzuki's was unlike the cabinet of Tōjō Hideki, where the prime minister held multiple portfolios. Suzuki's aim was to prevent the collapse of the cabinet due to ministerial resignations or terminations. In fact, to the end, he managed to avoid adding or losing any members in his cabinet. In directing the course of the war, Suzuki's aim was not to exclude discussions on resistance to the bitter end. Rather, by listening intently, he hoped to find an opportunity to end the war while preventing the collapse of the cabinet. Suzuki's top priorities in putting his cabinet together were to retain Yonai Mitsumasa as minister of the navy and to include General Anami Korechika.

In order to include the army's view on the need for resistance to the bitter end, Suzuki wanted to make Anami his army minister, because Anami enjoyed the trust of the mid-ranking army officers. At the same time, he wanted to keep Yonai in the cabinet as a voice

10-13. Suzuki Kantarō

Mourning the Death of Roosevelt

After the death of US president Franklin Roosevelt on April 12, 1945, the Japanese government sent the following public relations instructions to its diplomatic missions abroad: Avoid any personal attacks on Roosevelt; avoid any observations implying that Roosevelt's death might have a direct impact on the American fighting spirit or war strength; and avoid making it sound as if Roosevelt's passing was a victory for Japan. While the government's directives may not have been observed faithfully, they can be read as a message to the United States. Prime Minister Suzuki also issued a statement expressing sorrow at Roosevelt's death to the American public. The gesture rankled the German Ministry of Foreign Affairs, which objected to Japan's extension of condolences to its enemy. The Japanese consulate in Berlin thus found itself having to explain the prime minister's statement by clarifying how the Japanese saw life and death differently from their Western counterparts.

On April 19, German author Thomas Mann, then exiled in the United States, encouraged the German public over the airwaves to see the developments from a different angle.

> German listeners, what do you make of the Japanese Empire's prime minister, Suzuki Kantarō, calling the late president Franklin Roosevelt a "great leader" and expressing his deepest condolences to the American people on behalf of the Japanese? Does it not strike you as a surprising statement? . . . Japan is now engaged in a life-or-death struggle with the United States. A group of power-hungry, feudalistic leaders has dragged Japan into the war. However, Japan has not seen its militarism create the moral ruin or moral paralysis that Nazi national socialism has spawned across the wretched state of Germany. Even now, the Oriental nation of Japan maintains a sense of chivalry and human dignity. Even now, it maintains a reverence toward death and reverence for greatness. Therein lies the difference between the nations of Germany and Japan.

10-14. Atlantic Conference

powerful enough to act as a counterbalance to the army. After the Battle of Leyte, the army wanted to merge with the navy, which had lost many of its most important ships, to become more effective in the war against the United States, but Yonai was vigorously opposed. At the end of April, Suzuki called leaders of the army and navy to his official residence. He lectured them on what it would mean to merge the army and navy for the first time since the founding of Japan's modern armed forces, in hopes of dissuading proponents of the idea. Yonai was to play an extremely important role in the process of bringing the war to an end, but if the army and navy merged, he would lose his leverage to speak.

Foreign Minister Tōgō and Negotiations with the Soviet Union

Tōgō Shigenori returned as foreign minister in Suzuki's cabinet, and his foremost task was to manage the diplomatic dimension of ending the war. More specifically, this meant maintaining Japan's relations with the Soviet Union to prevent them from entering the war against Japan. Just before the Suzuki cabinet was formed (April 7, 1945), the Soviet Union gave notice it would not extend the Neutrality Pact when the agreement ended in a year's time, and offered no assurance it would not enter the war against Japan. The Army General Staff's plan for the defense of Japan's main islands relied on the assumption that the Soviet Union would remain neutral. In late April, the newly appointed deputy chief of the Army General Staff Kawabe Torashirō paid a call on Foreign Minister Tōgō and promised the army's full support in prioritizing the prevention of the Soviet Union's entry into the war against Japan. For his part, Tōgō decided to use this "hope of the army" as leverage for peace with the United Kingdom and America.

Tōgō therefore had to recast negotiations aimed at preventing the Soviet Union from entering the war against Japan, shifting them to peace negotiations with the Soviet Union as intermediary that would require an extreme care. One important reason the army opted to pursue a final battle to defend Japan's main islands was that if Japan "submitted to peace" with the United States and the United Kingdom, it might be forced to accept unconditional surrender, including the destruction of the national polity (*kokutai*) itself. Japan could not enter peace negotiations with the Soviet Union while awaiting battle on the main islands. To "conjure an opportunity for peace" among Japan's top political and military leaders, Tōgō would first have to seek to persuade a meeting of the country's six most elite leaders (referred to hereinafter as the "Big Six": Prime Minister Suzuki, Foreign Minister Tōgō, Army Minister Anami, Navy Minister Yonai, Chief of the Army General Staff Umezu Yoshijirō, and Chief of the Navy General Staff Oikawa Koshirō, who was replaced at the end of May by Toyoda Soemu), without the administrative staff of the Supreme Council for the Direction of the War, and receive approval from the Big Six.

The first meeting of the Big Six began on May 11. On the final day, May 14, they agreed to add a goal for negotiations with the Soviet Union: in addition to the previous goals of having the Soviet Union agree to maintain neutrality and preventing it from entering the war, Japan would ask the Soviet Union to intervene to Japan's advantage when the war ended. This agreement was based on an assumption by the Big Six that the Soviet Union was the only nation that would "guide the process to a reconciliation that would go beyond unconditional surrender."

To entice the Soviet Union to agree to these goals, the Big Six proposed to undo the Treaty of Portsmouth and the Japan-Soviet Basic Treaty, and make several major concessions, including returning South Sakhalin, settling the issue of fishing rights, opening up the Tsugaru Strait, handing over ownership of railways in North Manchuria, and handing over the northern half of the Kuril Islands. In Japan's view, the Soviet Union's main aim was the elimination of the Treaty of Portsmouth, and Japan was prepared to respond to that desire. Further, the Big Six were prepared to maintain the "neutrality" of Korea, and the "independence" of Manchukuo, and to establish a tripartite alliance of Japan, China, and the Soviet Union. The aim here was to improve relations between Japan and the Soviet Union before the end of the war, when Japan anticipated the Soviet Union would emerge as an antagonist of the United States.

At the same time, the Big Six made no progress on the peace terms they should have been preparing to present to the United States and the United Kingdom. Regarding the outlook for Japan's ability to continue fighting the war, which should have been the basis of this discussion, the army leadership and Foreign Minister Tōgō could not agree. Anami, the new minister of the army, disagreed sharply with Foreign Minister Tōgō on this matter. Anami contended, "Japan still occupies a vast expanse of enemy territory, while the enemy holds only a small area of Japanese territory. Terms of peace with the United States and United Kingdom should reflect these basic facts." Tōgō was pessimistic about Japan's ability to continue the war. For a time, the two men were at loggerheads regarding the request to the Soviet Union about interceding on Japan's behalf at the end of the war. Then it was decided that former prime minister Hirota Kōki should sound out the Soviets about their views.

Limiting this discussion to just the Big Six was part of an effort to prevent the peace issue from getting entangled in other domestic matters. The Big Six were hoping to be able to discuss the matter freely, sharing their thoughts on how best to bring the war to an end, removed from the stubborn opposition of the mid-ranking army and navy officers. This effort achieved a certain degree of success. On the other hand, they were focusing narrowly on Moscow, closing off the possibility of direct peace negotiations with the United States and the United Kingdom, or approaching them through a neutral nation such as

Maneuvers to End the War Play Out in Switzerland

The Dulles Operation Grows

As World War II entered its final stages, a variety of maneuvers to make peace with Japan took place in neutral countries in Europe: operations involving Allen Dulles (in Switzerland), Onodera Makoto (Sweden), Widar Bagge (Sweden), and the Holy See (Vatican City) are four prominent examples of clandestine peacemaking discussions. Most of the initiatives aimed to establish a direct peace between Japan and the Western Allies, circumventing the Soviet Union, but they ultimately came up short; conventional arguments have blamed the failures on breakdowns in negotiations, cited opposition by the Japanese government or military leaders as roadblocks, or just dismissed the efforts as trivial embellishments to the narrative surrounding the war's end.

However, recent studies have pointed to one operation that did have a certain impact on Japan's decision to end the war: the activities of an extensive peace network that formed around Allen Dulles, the director of the US Office of Strategic Services (OSS) in Switzerland. The formation started with Friedrich Hack, an anti-Nazi, pro-Japanese German with close ties to the Japanese navy. Hack, then in Zurich, had been in contact with the Naval Attaché Office in Berlin and the OSS since sometime in 1943, but his involvement in end-of-war negotiations took on a deeper layer in the latter half of 1944 as he began to usher various personnel on the Japanese side into Dulles's network of connections. The key figures were Yoshimura Kan and Kitamura Kōjirō, both from the Bank for International Settlements; Kase Shun'ichi, Japan's minister to Switzerland in Bern; and Major-General Okamoto Kiyotomi (formerly the director-general of the intelligence department in the Army General Staff Office, the military attaché to Japan's legation).

Dulles had been close friends with Per Jacobsson, an executive at the Bank for International Settlements, since before the war. The bank was more than just a leading international financial institution; it also functioned as an intelligence organization with considerable information-gathering

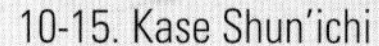

10-15. Kase Shun'ichi

10-16. Friedrich Hack

capacities. By the end of 1944, the various connections linking people around Dulles had coalesced into a Bank for International Settlements group (Jacobsson, Kitamura, and Yoshimura) and a Swiss legation group (Kase and Okamoto) that together formed a communication channel between Japan and the United States. The network expanded again in the spring of 1945, with the additions of Captain Nishihara Ichirō and Commander Fujimura Yoshirō (both of whom had relocated from Berlin to the Naval Attaché Office in Switzerland). Hack was not the driver of the operation to the end the war; rather, he acted as an agent for Dulles's network.

With Germany nearing the point of surrender (which eventually came on May 7, 1945), Dulles began feeling out Japan's conditions for peace by having Hack probe the Kitamura-Yoshimura route and the Minister Kase route for information. In early May, Kase sent Foreign Minister Tōgō Shigenori a private opinion in which he recommended face-to-face peace talks with the United States and the United Kingdom as a better option than Soviet Union–mediated negotiations, and argued that the only condition on Japan's surrender should be the preservation of the emperor system. The key point of interest for Kase, as well as Kitamura and Yoshimura, was whether Japan would be able to retain the emperor system and defend the national polity under the unconditional-surrender policy that President Truman announced in May.

Switzerland or Sweden. At the very least, none of the six actively pursued such an approach.

The Hirota-Malik Talks

Throughout June of 1945, Hirota met continuously with Yakov Malik, the Soviet ambassador to Japan. At their first meetings (June 3–4), Hirota said, "Security in Asia can only be built through the cooperation of the Soviet Union, Japan, and China. Friendly relations between Japan and the Soviet Union are the foundation of that cooperation." This proposal was in line with the consensus by the Big Six that in postwar Asia a tripartite alliance of

"Before the Empire Falls"

In mid-July, Jacobsson, Kitamura, and Yoshimura gathered for a discussion with Minister Kase. Jacobsson then relayed the results of the conversation to Dulles, who left Bern in early June and made contact with Acting Secretary of State Joseph Grew and other officials in Washington. Dulles asked Jacobsson to send a message informing Japan that there was a possibility that the emperor system would be safe if the Japanese government were to accept the terms of unconditional surrender. On July 21, Kase sent Tōgō a wire explaining what Jacobsson and Dulles had discussed and advised Tōgō to begin engaging in direct negotiations with the United States.

At his meeting with Jacobsson, Dulles had emphasized Grew's statement of July 10. Grew had served for several years as the US ambassador to Japan and, along the way, developed a reputation as a Japanophile. After returning home from Japan, Grew had become the US under-secretary of state in November 1944 and served as acting secretary of state in 1945. He joined Dulles in recommending that the Allies' joint statement at the Potsdam Conference expressly guarantee the status of the emperor—but the US government had yet to come to a decision on whether to include that provision. In his statement of July 10, the same statement Dulles mentioned to Jacobsson, Grew stressed, without departing from the scope of Truman's policy, that an unconditional surrender would not mean the extermination or enslavement of the Japanese people.

Meanwhile, a campaign to prompt Japan's surrender was also underway on another front. At the Office of War Information (OWI), which had close connections to the activities of the OSS, an employee by the name of Ellis Zacharias began broadcasting messages from a Washington radio station in May 1945 urging Japan to surrender. The sources of information guiding the "Zacharias broadcasts" were the OSS activities in Switzerland. Zacharias and Grew, using both radio and newspaper outlets, worked tirelessly to reach the Japanese public with the reassurance that accepting an unconditional surrender would not endanger Japan's rights under the Atlantic Charter, its freedom to choose its own form of government, or its territorial integrity.

Grew's views on preserving the emperor system did not find their way into the Potsdam Declaration on July 26. However, Kase reached out to Jacobsson through Yoshimura to confirm that the Potsdam Declaration would not signify the enslavement or extinction of Japan, hold the emperor criminally responsible, or apply the terms of unconditional surrender to any party outside the military. Upon receiving confirmation from Jacobsson, Kase wired an official opinion to Tōgō on July 30. The telegram from Kase explained that the declaration was different from the Allies' demands on Germany: It made no reference to the emperor or national polity, recognized Japan's sovereignty as a nation, and allowed Japan to maintain a "foundation for continuing to live its national life under the national polity for which the Japanese people are willing to die." The wire from Kase was also forwarded to Ambassador Satō Naotake in Moscow. On August 4, Satō, touching on points in Kase's telegram, pleaded with Foreign Minister Tōgō to abandon what he saw to be a fruitless path to peace through the Soviet Union and instead pursue an end to the war based on the Potsdam Declaration before the empire fell.

Although the Dulles operation ultimately failed to bring Japan into direct peace negotiations with the United States and the United Kingdom, it did help prompt the leading peace advocates in Japan—the emperor, Foreign Minister Tōgō, and Lord Keeper of the Privy Seal Kido Kōichi, for example—to make their decision to end the war. It did so by providing a credible answer to the final and most crucial question facing Japan, one that neither the Potsdam Declaration nor the Byrnes Reply made clear: whether the Chrysanthemum Throne would be safe.

Japan, China, and the Soviet Union would have to be built. Malik asked about the details and methods of developing such a relationship, but Hirota responded only that he hoped to see friendship between Japan and the Soviet Union grow, and that China could be pulled into that relationship.

After that, at their meeting on June 22, the Big Six, with the emperor in attendance, confirmed that their agreement of mid-May to ask the Soviet Union to intercede on Japan's behalf in peace negotiations with the United States and the United Kingdom should be implemented. Hirota, however, did not present this as a formal proposal to Malik. No one had been able to figure out what the Soviet Union thought of the idea.

In the end, at the final meeting on June 29, Hirota proposed a Japanese-Soviet Non-Aggression Pact, incorporating the concept of a neutral Manchukuo (from which Japanese troops would withdraw after the war ended), among other ideas, to replace the Neutrality Pact. These ideas were communicated through Malik to Foreign Minister Vyatcheslav Molotov, but his only response was to promise Ambassador Satō Naotake that he would give them "serious consideration."

Clearly, the Soviet side had little interest in talks with Hirota. Around that time, Stalin was close to going to war against Japan. He invited T. V. Soong from the Chongqing regime to visit Moscow, seeking China's understanding regarding the secret agreements made at Yalta. This was part of Stalin's determined plan for going to war against Japan, and circumstances made it unnecessary for him to respond to Japan's idea of a nonaggression pact.

The Debate over a Final Battle on Japan's Main Islands: The Search for Peace

Talks with the Soviet Union were not going well, and Japan was losing the Battle of Okinawa. The army and the reformist bureaucrats were forced to focus on a discussion of whether to engage in a decisive final battle for Japan's main islands. On June 8, led by the army and the cabinet, the Imperial Council decided new guidelines for the direction of the war, emphasizing a successful completion of fighting and a decisive battle for the defense of Japan's main islands. Regarding this final battle, Army General Staff Office declared, "If a strong will to resist the invaders can be inculcated in the Japanese army and the Japanese people, we may be able to gain a favorable opportunity to end the war under relatively positive conditions." Army Minister Anami concurred with this view.

However, there was a wide gap between this view and the "Current Assessment of National Power" that was also approved on June 8 by the Imperial Council. Feeling threatened by that disparity, that very day the Lord Keeper of the Privy Seal, Kido Kōichi, wrote a "Policy Proposal for Controlling the Situation." In that document, viewed from all possible angles, he stressed that Japan was likely to lose its ability to continue to wage war in the second half of 1945, due to the "Current Assessment of National Power" and the potential damage caused by air raids. He concluded that it was time to end the war through an Imperial proclamation. More specifically, rather than direct negotiations with the United States and the United Kingdom, he said it would be best for Japan to negotiate through a mediator (the Soviet Union). Japan's terms, based on an official letter from the emperor, would guarantee independence for the territories it occupied in Asia, abandon its leadership role, and voluntarily withdraw its troops.

The enemy was intent on defeating Japan's military clique, so the "right route" for Japan was for the military to proclaim peace. However, if Kido waited until the right time to persuade the hard-liners, Japan would miss its opportunity. According to information from the Ministry of Foreign Affairs, the Allies, while aiming for the defeat of Japan's military clique, were inclined to

10-17. Mass suicides during the Battle of Okinawa

be relatively generous in their treatment of Japan. In that case, Kido believed it would be possible to pursue a peace that ensured that the national polity would be preserved.

Kido briefed the emperor on this line of thinking, and asked the emperor to consult with the prime minister, the ministers of the army and the navy, and the foreign minister. The emperor responded that Kido should "get started right away." Kido held discussions with the Big Six and brought it up at an official Big Six conference with the emperor in attendance, where it was decided to request the intervention of the Soviet Union with the aim of ending the war. In Tōgō's view, this decision superseded the June 8 decision of the Imperial Council, which leaned toward a final battle for Japan's main islands. Suzuki's view was that Japan should both fight and negotiate. Either way, Kido's plan to persuade the others was meaningful in that the Big Six shared a "Policy Proposal for Controlling the Situation"; that is, in the absence of a possibility of a peace proposal from the military, only a decision by the emperor could bring the war to an end.

However, the Big Six could not reach any decision on compensation for the Soviet Union or specific peace terms with the United States and the United Kingdom.

Sending Konoe to Negotiate as Special Envoy

In late June, Foreign Minister Tōgō decided to give up on the Hirota-Malik talks. As the Potsdam Conference was approaching, Tōgō came to believe the only avenue available was to send someone to Moscow, and he decided former prime minister Konoe Fumimaro should be that person. On July 8, when he was offered Tōgō's suggestion, Konoe demanded that he be sent by order of the emperor, and that he be given carte blanche to begin the negotiations.

In preparation for Konoe's visit, on July 12, Tōgō sent a telegraph to Ambassador Satō suggesting that he inform Molotov about the emperor's message and Konoe's visit to Moscow. The emperor's message, however, was not a direct appeal for peace. The message said that as long as the United States and the United Kingdom insisted on Japan's unconditional surrender, Japan had no choice but to continue fighting to the end. This situation was not the emperor's wish. Rather, he hoped for a "recovery of peace." On July 13 Satō telegraphed Moscow's likely response to Tokyo: from the emperor's message, the Soviet Union understood him to be a "lover of peace," but it did not understand what role he wanted the Soviet Union to play. On July 18, as Satō had feared, the Soviet Union said it could not respond because Konoe's mission was unclear.

On July 20, a conference of the Big Six confirmed that Konoe's mission was to ask Stalin's help to end the war. Even at this point, however, the Big Six were not able to agree on compensation for the Soviet Union or peace terms with the United States and the United Kingdom.

On July 21, Tōgō telegraphed Satō, telling him to communicate the agreement reached by the Big Six the previous day to the Soviet Union, but he had to add a clause stating that "for both internal and external reasons, it is not possible to determine specific conditions" as the Soviet Union desired.

The Potsdam Declaration and the "No Comment" Statement

The Two "No Comment" Reports

The United States, the United Kingdom, and China issued the Potsdam Declaration demanding Japan's surrender on July 26, 1945. Upon receiving the statement, officials at the Ministry of Foreign Affairs took little time in reaching an agreement to accept the terms in principle. The declaration clearly limited the terms of unconditional surrender to the Japanese military, recognized Japanese sovereignty, and made no mention of the emperor system (in terms of the imperial household and the national polity)—three of several points that made ministry leaders receptive to the terms. Foreign Minister Tōgō Shigenori also decided to accept the declaration because he saw the potential for a "conditional peace," and recognized that the declaration was "clearly not a demand for unconditional surrender."

The foremost concern about the terms, however, was that they contained no stipulations whatsoever about whether the emperor system was to remain in place. During the initial drafting stages in the United States, the Potsdam Declaration did contain provisions guaranteeing the survival of the emperor system; Undersecretary of State Grew and fellow Japan experts in the government demanded that the terms allow for the preservation of the system to help stabilize the postwar Japanese occupation. In the end, however, opposition from Secretary of State James Byrnes and the military nixed the corresponding provisions. Easing the conditions on Japan would have meant subverting the unconditional-surrender policy that President Truman had committed to almost immediately after taking office—a virtually impossible act, considering the circumstances.

Foreign Minister Tōgō decided that, rather than immediately accepting the Potsdam Declaration, it would be more prudent to remain noncommittal. That became the official Ministry of Foreign Affairs policy on addressing the declaration, and Prime Minister Suzuki Kantarō concurred. At the cabinet meeting on July 27 and the subsequent gathering of the Supreme War Council, Tōgō and Suzuki worked to quell the military's calls for an outright rejection of the declaration and held the line on refraining from making their intentions clear. They were clinging to the slim thread of hope that the Soviet Union would mediate a favorable peace for Japan, as the Ministry of Foreign Affairs was still talking with the Soviets about dispatching Konoe for negotiations with the Soviet Union, which had not been a party at the Potsdam Declaration. On the morning of July 28, Tōgō thus sent a telegram to Satō Naotake, Japan's ambassador to the Soviet Union, informing him that Japan would wait for the Soviet Union's response before making an official statement on the Potsdam Declaration.

The cabinet members decided at their meeting on July 27 to release the text of the Potsdam Declaration to the general public, save for any provisions that could potentially sap the people's will to fight. Suzuki also took up Tōgō's suggestion to avoid making any statement on the declaration, which meant that the government would be withholding any official comment on the matter. The major newspapers thus ran the edited Potsdam Declaration—minus paragraphs 1 through 4, per the Cabinet Information Bureau's instructions—in their pages the following morning. The papers were free to include their own commentaries on the text. The *Asahi Shimbun*, for example, published its take under the headline, "Government reticent." The imperial government was choosing "to withhold any statement on what it views as a meritless declaration," the article read, and was "resolutely determined to see the war through to a successful end." A similar sentiment informed the editorial in the *Yomiuri Shimbun*. With a headline reading "Ridiculous terms of surrender," the piece observed that the imperial government was "laughing off its enemies' outrageous schemes and instead rousing the people in Japan toward fulfilling the aims of the Greater East Asia War, a self-defensive struggle for Japan's survival."

At the information-sharing session between Imperial General Headquarters and the government on the morning of July 28, the prime minister, ministers of the army and navy, chiefs of staff, and Chief Cabinet Secretary Sakomizu Hisatsune conferred again on how to respond to the declaration. Absent from the discussions was Tōgō, who had other engagements to tend to. Without Tōgō on hand, there was little stopping the military leaders from advancing their arguments for rejecting the Potsdam Declaration—and that afternoon, Prime Minister Suzuki announced that the government's response to the matter would be to "ignore it" (*mokusatsu*); i.e., it would make no comment.

The basic outline for Suzuki's dialogues with the press was the work of Sakomizu and the directors of the military affairs bureaus in both the army and the navy, who worked together to lay out talking points based on a draft by the Cabinet Information Bureau. Sakomizu wanted to add the phrase "for the time being" to the "no comment" statement, but Military Affairs Bureau director-general Yoshizumi Masao of the Ministry of the Army apparently shot the idea down. On the afternoon of July 28, Suzuki fielded questions from reporters in accordance with the outline. The August

30 edition of the *Asahi Shimbun* included the following account of an exchange between the prime minister and a reporter.

> Q: Japan's enemies have recently spread a variety of propaganda on bringing the war to an end. What are your thoughts?
> A: To me, the three-party declaration is little more than a rehash of the Cairo Declaration, and the Japanese government does not see it as a matter of much significance. We have no comment to make on it.

This was not the first time that Japan had said *mokusatsu*, or "no comment," to an Allied declaration; it was the same policy that had defined Japan's response to the Cairo Declaration. The difference was in how the government's response appeared in the press. After the Cairo Conference, Japanese newspapers made no specific mention of the government's "no comment" policy; they simply published an abridged version the statement, minus the portions concerning unrecognized territorial issues, without detailing the government's corresponding statement. In a word, the government's position was just to express no opinion on the declaration. The response to the Potsdam Declaration was essentially a continuation of that basic stance, but military pressure carelessly pushed the *mokusatsu* or "no comment" doctrine out into the open.

The Impact of the "No Comment" Statement

The "no comment" conversation did not actually constitute an official statement to the Allies, which made for complicated implications in the international arena. The Potsdam Declaration was not a formal diplomatic document in accordance with international practices, either; diplomatic authorities in both the United States and the United Kingdom saw the joint statement as a propaganda tool to broadcast at regular intervals. The declaration was apparently a propaganda document in the eyes of President Truman, too, who sent it to the OWI with instructions on how to implement the statement in the propaganda war. When reports of the "no comment" statement emerged, therefore, American and British diplomatic authorities had trouble deciding whether the response represented the Japanese government's final stand on the Potsdam Declaration. A document from the British Foreign Office recommended that if Japan were to issue no other statement apart from its "no comment," the US Department of State and British Foreign Office should discuss the advisability of continuing the repeat propaganda broadcasts as a means of "political war."

Had the declaration been treated as a formal diplomatic document from the start and passed along to the Japanese government via Switzerland, its protecting power, there is no denying that the Allies and Japan may have been able to communicate their respective positions more effectively. Some observers argue that the fact that the Potsdam Declaration "emerged as nothing more than a cog in a diplomatic propaganda campaign and thus failed to create a circuit for Japan-US negotiations" held the parties a step or two back from an opportunity for peace.

In any case, there was essentially no way for Japan to satisfy the Allies without expressing at least some willingness to accept the Potsdam Declaration. Suzuki could maintain the "no comment" line at press conferences—but unless he somehow indicated that Japan was either ready to accept or on its way to accepting the terms, the results would be the same. Given the mood pervading Japan at the time, however, saying even a single word suggesting that Japan might accept the terms was unthinkable. Ultimately, the problems with Suzuki's response to the Potsdam Declaration were not necessarily what determined the Allies' position on Japan. The dropping of the atomic bomb and the Soviet Union's entry into the war were both part of an already existing policy. In a presidential address following the atomic bombing of Japan, President Truman explained the actions by citing Japan's "rejection" of the Potsdam Declaration and alluding to the "no comment" position—but that justification seems to have been made somewhat after the fact.

In terms of what prolonged the war, the biggest factor was the Japanese government's decision to hang its slim hopes on dispatching Konoe as a special envoy to Moscow and stand pat with an unflinching "no-comment" stance in the meantime.

Tōgō's priority, even more than making a decision on the terms, was fulfilling Konoe's "carte blanche." He felt his most urgent task was to get the Soviet Union to allow Japan to send Konoe. On July 25, Ambassador Satō met with Vice-Foreign Minister Rosovsky. Rosovsky said he understood that the Japanese government wanted the Soviet Union to intercede to end the war, but he asked what "tangible proposals" Prince Konoe had. All Satō could do was to stress the importance of Konoe's mission. The next day, the Potsdam Declaration demanding Japan's surrender was released.

The Potsdam Declaration and the "No Comment" Response

With Japan's negotiations with the Soviet Union at a standstill, the Potsdam Declaration was released on July 26. For the Japanese government, which had ventured to send Konoe Fumimaro to Moscow, the fact that Moscow was not a signatory to the Potsdam Declaration offered a glimmer of hope about what the Soviet Union would do next. Confronted with those in the military who wished to deliver an immediate refusal, Suzuki and Foreign Minister Tōgō decided to say nothing for a time. On the morning of July 28, Tōgō telegraphed Ambassador Satō to say Japan would await the Soviet Union's response before responding to the Potsdam Declaration.

However, it was Suzuki himself who broke the idea of saying nothing for the time being. The military's idea of immediate refusal could not be completely contained, and at a news conference on the afternoon of the 28th, Suzuki replied, "No comment" (*mokusatsu*, lit. "ignoring"; see sidebar on previous page). This had not yet been officially communicated to the Allies, but it was effectively perceived as a rejection. While the Allies had already decided on the course they would take, this became the pretext for the Soviet Union's entry into the war and the dropping of the atomic bombs. Suzuki greatly regretted having uttered these words.

The First Imperial Decision

In early August, the Big Six focused their interest on the Soviet response to the problem of the special

10-18. Winston Churchill, Harry S. Truman, and Joseph Stalin in Potsdam, Germany

envoy's mission. Given the Soviet Union's non-participation in the Potsdam Declaration, the Big Six had been increasingly hopeful that the Soviet Union would act "on its own." After the atomic bomb was dropped on Hiroshima on August 6 and the Soviet Union declared war on August 9, Japan's political leaders, who had become more rigid on matters of peace and war, were prompted to take action. The atom bombs were unexpected, but the Soviet Union's entry into the war was not unanticipated. In early August, the view of the Army General Staff Office was that the Soviet Union would make military preparations to enter the war in late August, and that it would actually enter the war in the fall. In late July, the Ministry of the Army had begun studying what diplomatic steps should be taken as the Soviet Union prepared for war. According to research performed immediately before the Soviet Union entered the war, it was Moscow's intention to give Japan an ultimatum, and not to attack without warning. Also, it planned to enter the war "of its own accord," and not as part of the Allied forces.

However, because the Soviet Union joined the Potsdam Declaration just as it entered the war, mediation by the Soviet Union was no longer an option. The only choices remaining for the Big Six were to accept the terms of the Potsdam Declaration, or reject them and continue fighting.

From August 9 to August 14, the ministers were locked in a fractious debate over these choices. "Preserving the national polity" was an absolute condition, but until the emperor made his first decision at the Imperial Council meeting in the early hours of August 10, the main argument revolved around whether to add three more conditions: the voluntary surrender of weapons, having Japan punish its own war criminals, and avoidance of protective occupation. Foreign Minister Tōgō and Navy Minister Yonai favored acceptance with just the one condition of preserving the national polity, but Army Minister Anami, Chief of the Army General Staff Umezu, and Chief of the Navy General Staff Toyoda all favored adding the three additional conditions. Neither side was willing to budge. Suzuki declined to divulge his own opinion until the emperor made his decision.

The emperor chose to employ the "Tōgō proposal," deciding to accept the terms with just the one condition of preserving the national polity. Initially, the telegram of acceptance to the Allies was supposed to include the unilateral declaration, "We accept under the understanding this will not be combined with demands for changes in the supreme authority of the emperor in the governance of Japan," but the Imperial Council decided to add language asking the Allies about their view of the appropriateness of that interpretation.

The Second Imperial Decision

The response received from the Allies on August 12 (the Byrnes Response), particularly the fourth paragraph, stipulated that the ultimate form of the Japanese government "should be established by the freely expressed will of the Japanese people." This was the same language used in paragraph 12 of the Potsdam Declaration. Foreign Minister Tōgō interpreted the fourth paragraph to mean "non-intervention in Japan's internal affairs," effectively ensuring that the national polity would be preserved. But this view clashed with that of President of the Privy Council Hiranuma Kiichirō, Chief of Navy General Staff Toyoda, and Home Minister Abe Genki, who did not see a need to share Japan's affairs of state with the people. Suzuki, who viewed the problem in terms of which option (acceptance of terms, inquiring again about terms, or continuing the war) would present the least risk for the preservation of the national polity, leaned for a time toward inquiring again about the terms.

At the cabinet meeting on the afternoon of the 13th, Suzuki agreed with the Ministry of Foreign Affairs' interpretation of the fourth paragraph, but he said, "Our future concern is the protective occupation and the surrender of arms. We must remember the dangers faced by the Osaka Castle summer campaign. If we fail to take care, we will end up repeating these mistakes." The "Osaka Castle summer campaign" refers to the Siege of Osaka in the seventeenth century, when Tokugawa Ieyasu's garrison broke a promise and filled in the inner moat, thereby wiping out the Toyotomi Clan. Suzuki feared that if, after Japan accepted the terms of the Potsdam Declaration, the Allies were to run roughshod over the condition of preservation of the national polity, Japan would no longer have any means of resisting.

However, Suzuki wagered the preservation of the national polity on the Allies' "benevolence," rather than their "malice." At the meeting, Suzuki suddenly changed his attitude, which had been noncommittal up to that point. He pointedly asked each member of the cabinet for their opinion, and expressed a clear preference for a decision based on the Imperial Decision. He was frantic to prepare the way for the Second Imperial Decision ahead of the next day's Imperial Council meeting.

The meeting began at 10:50 a.m. on August 14. The decision to accept the terms of the Potsdam Declaration was reached, via the Second Imperial Decision, shortly after 11 a.m. The emperor's command made reference to the fourth paragraph of the Byrnes Response: "In the language of this document, I understand that the other party bears significant goodwill. I fully understand why the other party might have some uncertainty, but I have no wish to doubt them. I believe the problem is one of the faith and readiness of the people as a whole." In other words, the emperor was clearly saying he agreed with the interpretation of the Ministry of Foreign Affairs in its belief that the national polity would be preserved. On the afternoon of that day, all members of the cabinet co-signed an imperial edict to end the war, affirming that to do so was the desire of the Japanese people.

The edict included the phrase, "With this, I have managed to preserve the national polity." At the cabinet meeting after the Imperial Council meeting on August 14, Anami said this assertion "was necessary to prevent rebellion within the army." In order to advance, both inside and outside Japan, the smooth demobilization and disarmament of Japan's military, numbering over 3 million spirited troops, it was necessary that the edict include a statement of conviction from the emperor himself—not the government or the people—that the national polity would be preserved.

The "Statement on Ending the War," issued in the names of Anami and Umezu at 6 p.m. on August 14 to Japan's troops abroad, said it was not believed the Potsdam Declaration would harm the national polity, and that it had been accepted through the judgment of the emperor personally. These considerations were effective in ensuring the smooth demobilization and disarmament of the army, and were an important reason why the process of ending the war was accomplished peacefully.

The Significance of the Imperial Decisions

The use of an "imperial decision" as a method of determining national policy should ordinarily be avoided if Japan's system of constitutional monarchy is faithfully adhered to. When he first formed his cabinet, Suzuki expected to bear the full responsibility for soliciting the emperor's sanction, and assisting him, in getting the entire cabinet to agree to end the war before matters went from bad to worse. A decision by the Imperial Council is not the same as an "imperial decision," just as, when the war began, such a decision should be seen as having been made within the framework of the Constitution of the Empire of Japan.

With Japan at the brink of an unprecedented national calamity, when Suzuki asked the emperor for an imperial decision, he was setting aside his responsibility to advise the emperor on state affairs in order to truly reflect the will of the emperor and of the people. This was the only way in which the will of the emperor and of the people could be directly reflected at the Imperial Council as the highest expression of the will of Japan. The truth was that, just like the decision to start the war, politics in Japan had fallen to a point where political decisions were really only serving the needs of a few politicians, rather than truly reflecting the will of the nation, or the happiness of the people. Politics in Japan reflected neither the thinking of the emperor nor of the people.

The emperor had come to accept Suzuki's view on this. Until that point, the emperor went along with the facade that the Imperial Council was a complete formality, and that the emperor had no power to control the council. Believing that neither the national polity nor the people could be saved, the emperor thus tied his fate to Suzuki, who was so close to him.

As would be pointed out in the Imperial Diet after the war, these imperial decisions certainly abrogated the system of serving the emperor, representing the de facto collapse of the Constitution of the Empire of Japan. For Suzuki, this was the moment when control of Japanese politics was returned to the people and the emperor.

Following the Second Imperial Decision, a cabinet meeting was convened at 1 p.m. on August 14. There, all the cabinet members co-signed the "Imperial Edict Ending the War," as an expression of the will of the nation. However, there was an attempted coup, known as the Kyūjō Incident, where Lieutenant Colonel Takeshita Masahiko (Army Minister Anami's brother-in-law) and other military officials of the commissioned field officer class from the Imperial Guard Division and the Eastern Army plotted to take over the palace and detain people there to convince the emperor to change his mind. Beginning on the 13th, the conspirators were in close communication with Army Minister Anami, and pressed him for a decision to go ahead with their plan. Anami, however, after consulting with Chief of the Army General Staff Umezu, decided against it. In the end, Takeshita and his co-conspirators were baffled as to why Anami had refused to resign and had co-signed the edict.

5 Demobilization and Retreat

Internment in Siberia

At noon on August 15, the emperor addressed the nation via the radio, conveying the edict to end the war. This address, which was written to resemble the edict that began the war, was a personal expression by the emperor, to listeners domestic and foreign, that the war with America and the United Kingdom was at an end. As a result, it did not mention the war with China, or the war with the Soviet Union in Manchukuo, Sakhalin, and the Kuril Islands. The Soviet army had entered the war on August 9, and by early September occupied all of the Kuril Islands.

In that short span of time, Stalin abandoned the idea of occupying all of Hokkaido (August 22), but he did begin the forced internment of Japanese prisoners of war. One aim of the proposed occupation of Hokkaido was to access a large number of Japanese laborers in northern Hokkaido. In the forced internment, 600,000 soldiers, mainly from the Kwantung Army, were taken to Siberia, Mongolia, and Central Asia, where they were held as forced labor for a long time; almost 50,000 of them perished. The treatment of the internees was different from one place to another, and some of the places where they were held still bear witness to their presence. In Uzbekistan, for example, the Navoi Theater, built in part by Japanese internees, is still standing.

The last of the internees were returned home with the Soviet-Japanese Joint Declaration of 1956. The transport of Japanese prisoners of war to Soviet territory, and the way they were treated during their internment, constituted violations of the Hague Convention and the Potsdam Declaration. The problem of compensation for these prisoners of war continues to this day.

At the end of the war, there were roughly 3.53 million Japanese soldiers and sailors outside Japan; there were 1.05 million in China alone. For most of the troops in central and southern China, the disarmament process was completed by October 1945. However, in parts of northern China, it took time for Nationalist forces to arrive, and Japanese disarmament was delayed. Well after the August 15 surrender, 7,000 Japanese troops were killed or wounded defending themselves against attacks by Chinese Communist forces. It was not until September 9 that the Japanese military was able to sign an instrument of surrender in Nanjing. During this interval, the Chinese side showed immense generosity to the Japanese forces, encouraging the surrender process as directed by Chiang Kai-shek's August 15 address ("Remember not evil against others," and "Do good to all men.")

In regions governed by the United Kingdom, most members of Japan's southern armies were repatriated by the end of 1946. About 130,000 men were forced to remain in Burma, Thailand, and Malaya for about a year as workers.

10-19. The repatriation ship *Hikawa Maru*

The Failure of "Remaining in Place"

At the end of the war, roughly 3.5 million Japanese civilians were living abroad (490,000 in China; 1.55 million in Manchukuo; 340,000 in Taiwan; 220,000 in Kwantung). As the Allies had issued no general order for the repatriation of civilians, at first the Japanese government was indecisive about what to do. The basic policy was to let Japanese civilians abroad remain where they were. On August 14, Greater East Asia Minister Tōgō Shigenori wrote to diplomats in China and Southeast Asia, "We command residents to remain where they are, as much as they possibly can." This policy was motivated by circumstances in Japan, where the resident population was experiencing short supplies of food and housing. China's great generosity to Japanese civilians was another factor encouraging people to remain where they were. It was not long, however, before that policy failed. Both the United States and China were concerned that Japanese people might maintain their influence on the mainland. The Japanese people living in China were increasingly pessimistic due to the ongoing fighting between Nationalist and Communist forces, as well as the "deep-rooted enmity of the Chinese people." These factors led to the de facto collapse of the "remain in place" policy. The Allies changed course toward quick repatriation of Japanese living abroad.

In all areas other than Soviet-occupied Manchukuo, rapid repatriation began in March 1946, and most Japanese civilians in those areas returned to Japan by the end of the year. The 1.55 million Japanese in Manchukuo, however, suffered great hardships in trying to leave because of the Soviet invasion. Fighting and pillaging continued in that area, and many people fell victim to starvation and mass suicide. The unrest had largely subsided by October, but conditions were terrible in the internment camps, and many lives were lost there. Only when the Soviet military withdrew in May 1946 was it finally possible to begin mass repatriation. Ships left Huludao bound for Maizuru, Sasebo, Hakata, and other ports in Japan. About 1.05 million people were repatriated by August 1948 before the program was terminated. Another 30,000 were repatriated in 1953.

The Good and Bad of Detainee Labor

While repatriation of Japanese residents in China was an urgent problem, some remained in China for various reasons, and how to treat them became a problem. For example, technical and medical personnel stayed behind, at the request of the Nationalist government. During the war, Japan had built manufacturing and medical facilities, as well as a transportation network, that were operated by Japanese people. The skills of these people would be indispensable for the reconstruction of China after the war. In February 1946, the US government decided that all Japanese citizens would be repatriated, but the Chinese side made a strong appeal that Japanese technical personnel be allowed to remain, and so that exception was made. It is estimated that more than 35,000 Japanese people were kept on the mainland under the Nationalist government, and remained even under the Communists after 1949. The number of Japanese nationals remaining in Northeast China (former Manchukuo) under Communist rule was estimated at over 16,700.

In Taiwan, more than 27,000 technical and medical personnel, and their family members, were retained at the request of the Chinese side, but this situation did not endure for long.

More than a few detainees contributed, of their own volition, to the reconstruction of China. In a November 1945 letter to T. V. Soong, head of the Nationalist government's Executive Yuan, Nishikawa Akitsugu of Toyota Bōshoku, which was contributing to the manufacture of the first automatic looms built to Chinese standards, wrote:

> Now that the fighting has ended, today I must think about how to repay your kindness. What we are able to do is to serve China and the people of China through spinning technology. . . . We believe we can open the road to mutual coexistence and plant the seeds of friendly relations between our two peoples by establishing Toyota's spinning technology as part of the reconstruction of China.

* * *

In the immediate aftermath of the war, the situation in East Asia was chaotic. In China, it appeared that the Nationalists, with the help of the United States, would be able to build a government. But the conflict between the Nationalists and the Communists grew more intense, and fighting continued in the northeast (former Manchukuo). In the summer of 1946, the conflict expanded into a true civil war. The Korean Peninsula was divided: Soviet troops occupied the northern half and supported the establishment of a pro-Soviet government under Kim Il-sung, while American troops occupied the southern half and supported the establishment of a pro-US government under Rhee Syngman. In Taiwan, there was conflict between Taiwanese people and Chinese newly arrived from the mainland, culminating in a riot by the Taiwanese in 1947 (February 28 Incident). In occupied Japan, however, there was no reason for people to be aware of the upheaval occurring in East Asia.

CHAPTER 11

The Era of Yoshida Diplomacy:
The San Francisco Peace Treaty

11-1. Prime Minister Yoshida signs the Peace Treaty of San Francisco

TIMELINE

(The People's Republic of China was founded in 1949. After 1949, ROC denotes the Republic of China and PRC denotes the People's Republic of China.)

1945 (Shōwa 20)

August 17 Prince Higashikuni Naruhiko forms cabinet

August 30 General MacArthur, Supreme Commander for the Allied Powers (SCAP), arrives in Atsugi

September 2 Signing of the Instrument of Surrender

September 11 Allied General Headquarters (GHQ) issues arrest warrants for Tōjō Hideki and thirty-eight other war criminals

September 22 US government issues first guidelines for post-surrender Japan

September 27 Emperor Shōwa calls on MacArthur

October 4 GHQ issues memorandum on removal of restrictions on citizens' political and civil rights

October 9 Shidehara Kijūrō cabinet formed

October 11 MacArthur asks Prime Minister Shidehara for Five Major Reforms

November 6 Order to break up zaibatsu industrial groups

December 6 GHQ orders arrest of Konoe Fumimaro, Kido Kōichi, and others; Konoe commits suicide on December 16

December 7 Allied Reparations Commission Representative E. W. Pauley issues interim report

1946 (Shōwa 21)

January 1 Emperor denies his divinity

January 4 Purge of public servants (260 members of Nihon Shinpotō [Japan Progressive Party], thirty from Nihon Jiyūtō [Japan Liberal Party], ten from Shakaitō [Socialist Party], others)

January 19 Charter of International Military Tribunal for the Far East (Tokyo Trials) announced

January 24 MacArthur meets Shidehara

February 1 *Mainichi Shimbun* scoops Matsumoto draft for Constitutional Problems Investigation Committee (Matsumoto Committee)

February 3 GHQ Government Section begins drafting constitution in line with MacArthur's "Three Principles" (emperor as head of state, eliminate ability to wage war, abolition of nobility)

February 13 GHQ Government Section submit draft to Japanese government

February 20 Soviet Union declares occupation of South Karafuto (Sakhalin), Chishima (Kuril) Islands

February 22 Cabinet decides to accept GHQ draft of constitution, publishes it as outline of draft "Bill for Revision of the Imperial Constitution" on March 6

March 5 Former UK prime minister Churchill gives "Iron Curtain" speech

May 3 International Military Tribunal for the Far East (Tokyo Trials) begins

May 22 First Yoshida Shigeru cabinet formed

August 24 Draft Constitution passed by House of Representatives (421 for, 8 against); passed by House of Peers on October 7, takes effect November 3

1947 (Shōwa 22)

March 12 Proclamation of Truman Doctrine

May 24 Katayama Tetsu cabinet formed (first coalition cabinet led by Shakaitō)

June 5 Announcement of Marshall Plan

1948 (Shōwa 23)

January 6 Speech by General Royall (US secretary of the army): Japan as bulwark against totalitarianism

March 1 US State Department head of policy planning George Kennan arrives in Japan

March 10 Ashida Hitoshi cabinet formed

March 15 Establishment of Minshu Jiyūtō (Liberal Democratic Party); main members from Nihon Jiyūtō

June 24 Soviet Union blockades Berlin through May 12 1949

August 15 Republic of Korea established

September 9 Democratic People's Republic of Korea established

October 15 Second Yoshida cabinet formed

November 12 International Military Tribunal for the Far East finds twenty-five guilty, sentences seven to death by hanging

1949 (Shōwa 24)

February 16 Third Yoshida cabinet formed

March 7 US economic advisor Joseph M. Dodge outlines nine points for economic stability (start of "Dodge Line")

April 4 Signing of NATO Agreement

October 1 People's Republic of China established

1950 (Shōwa 25)

February 14 Signing of Sino-Soviet Treaty of Friendship, Alliance and Mutual Assistance

March 1	Establishment of Jiyūtō (Liberal Party); former Minshu Jiyūtō and some former Minshutō (Democratic Party) members join
June 25	Outbreak of Korean War
August 10	National Police Reserve established
October 25	Chinese People's Liberation Army joins Korean War
November 24	US State Dept. issues "Seven Principles of the Peace Treaty with Japan"

1951 (Shōwa 26)

January 25	Presidential envoy John Foster Dulles arrives in Japan, meets with Yoshida
April 11	MacArthur relieved of duty
September 4–8	San Francisco Peace Conference
September 8	Treaty of Peace with Japan (San Francisco Treaty) signed by 49 nations, including Japan; signing of Security Treaty between the United States and Japan ("Kyu-Anpo" Treaty)
October 26	House of Representatives ratifies San Francisco Treaty
December 24	Yoshida sends assurances to Dulles that Japan is at peace with the Nationalist government (ROC/Taiwan)

1952 (Shōwa 27)

January 18	South Korea establishes Syngman Rhee Line
February 15	Start of first talks between South Korea and Japan
February 28	Signing of US-Japan Administrative Agreement
April 1	Start of Government of the Ryūkyū Islands
April 28	San Francisco Treaty takes effect, ROC-Japan Peace Treaty signed
June 1	First Japan-PRC nongovernmental trade agreement signed
June 9	India-Japan peace treaty signed
August 1	National Safety Agency established
September 18	Japan applies to join United Nations; Security Council disapproves due to Soviet Union veto
September 18	Japan joins COCOM (Coordinating Committee on Multilateral Export Controls)
October 30	Fourth Yoshida cabinet formed

1953 (Shōwa 28)

January 20	Republican Dwight D. Eisenhower becomes president of the United States
March 5	Joseph Stalin dies
May 21	Fifth Yoshida cabinet formed
July 27	Signing of Korean Armistice Agreement
September 12	Khrushchev becomes first secretary of Soviet Communist Party
October 1	Signing of Mutual Defense Treaty between US, South Korea
October 5–30	Ikeda-Robertson Talks
October 15	At third round of talks between Japan and South Korea, Kubota praises Japan's colonial governance
October 29	Second Japan-PRC nongovernmental trade agreement signed
December 25	Amami Islands returned to Japan

1954 (Shōwa 29)

March 1	US experimental hydrogen blast on Bikini Atoll; *Daigo Fukuryū Maru* Incident
March 8	Signing of US-Japan Mutual Security Agreement (Mutual Defense Assistance Agreement, etc)
July 1	Start of Japan Defense Agency, Self-Defense Forces
July 21	Signing of armistice agreement in First Indochina War
September 3	PRC military bombards Quemoy (Kinmen), Matsu Islands (First Taiwan Strait Crisis)
September 8	Signing of Southeast Asia Treaty Organization (SEATO) agreement
September 12	Soviet foreign minister Molotov speaks of preparations for normalization of relations with Japan
September 22	Formation of Japan Association for Promotion of International Trade (JAPIT)
September 26	Yoshida visits Europe, US (through November 17)
October 6	Japan decides to join Colombo Plan, aiding mainly British Commonwealth nations
October 12	Sino-Soviet Joint Declaration
November 5	Signing of peace treaty, reparations agreement with Burma

1 Occupation and Reform

The Signing of the Instrument of Surrender

Two days after the war ended, Prince Higashikuni formed a government. His foreign minister was Shigemitsu Mamoru. For quite some time, the biggest issue was the demobilization and repatriation of Japan's military, along with more than three million civilians; Japan also had to make preparations for the arrival of the occupation forces. These tasks required a member of the imperial family to head the government.

On August 30, 1945, Supreme Commander for the Allied Powers (SCAP) MacArthur arrived at Atsugi Airfield. Three days later, on September 2, a ceremony was held aboard the USS *Missouri* in Tokyo Bay for the signing of the Instrument of Surrender. The stars-and-stripes flag used by Admiral Perry in Japan in 1853 hung in a frame on the bulkhead of a gun turret on the *Missouri*.

For a time, people in the United States wanted the emperor himself to sign the Instrument of Surrender, but this idea was abandoned due to British government objections that demands for the emperor's signature would discourage the Japanese military from giving up their arms without a fight.

The signing ceremony began at 9:00 a.m. MacArthur gave a short speech, and then he asked the Japanese delegation to sign the Instrument of

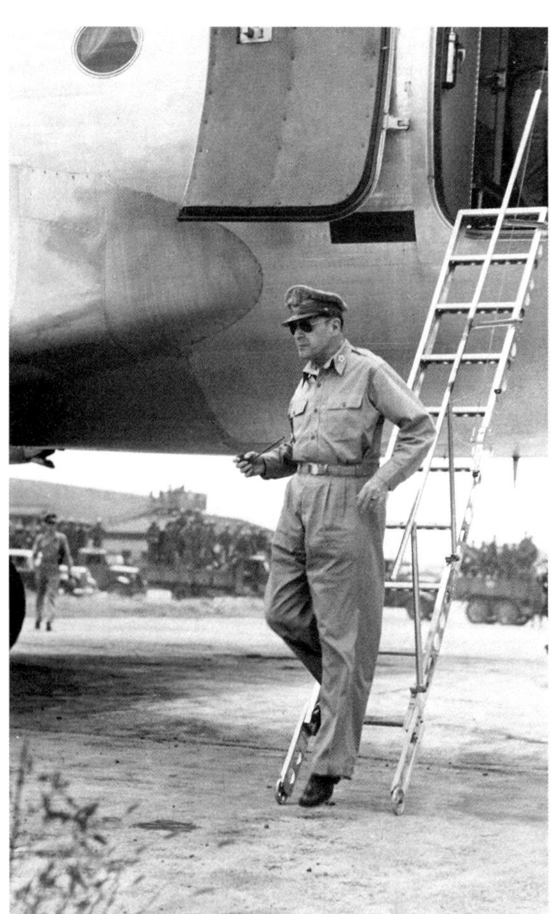

11-2. MacArthur arrives in Atsugi

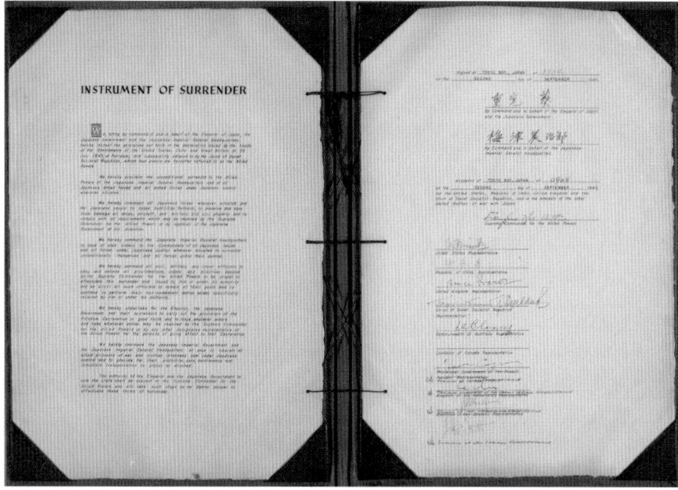

INSTRUMENT OF SURRENDER

11-3. Instrument of Surrender

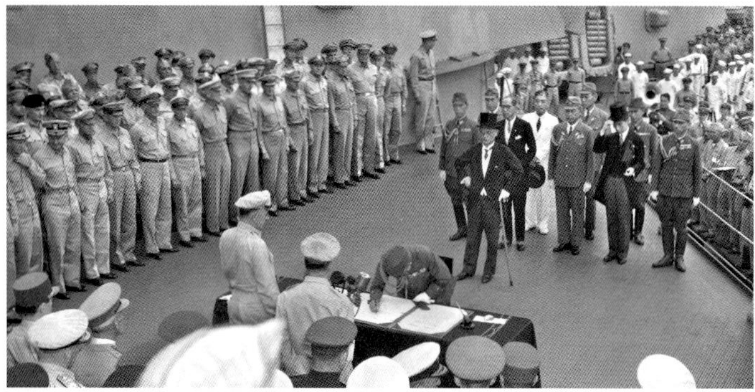

11-4. The signing of the Instrument of Surrender aboard the USS *Missouri*

Surrender. The Japanese side presented a "Power of Attorney" from the emperor himself. Shigemitsu signed as representative of the government, while Umezu Yoshijirō signed as representative of Imperial General Headquarters (High Command). Then MacArthur signed, as representative of the Allied Nations, followed by representatives of the United States, China, the United Kingdom, the Soviet Union, and others. The Instrument of Surrender stated that Japan formally accepted and would faithfully execute the Potsdam Declaration, that the Japanese military surrendered unconditionally, and that the military and the Japanese people would cease all hostilities.

Suspension of Diplomatic Rights

At the time of Japan's surrender, the United States demanded that Japan transfer the assets and official papers of its embassies in six neutral nations to the Allies through the Swiss government. On August 16, Foreign Minister Tōgō Shigenori told Minister to Switzerland Kase Shun'ichi to reject this demand, because it was not part of the Potsdam Declaration.

Japan Faces the Possibility of Direct Military Rule

On the afternoon of September 2, 1945, immediately after the signing ceremony for the Instrument of Surrender, Deputy Chief of Staff Richard Marshall summoned Envoy Suzuki Tadakatsu (director of the Yokohama Liaison Office) and informed him that Allied forces would be occupying Tokyo. He also presented the texts of three decrees that officials were planning to make the following morning. The first decree stated that "all powers of the Imperial Japanese Government, including the executive, legislative and judicial, will henceforth be exercised under my [MacArthur's] authority," making it clear that Japan would be under direct military rule. The second decree said that violators of occupation policy would be tried by a military court, while the third stipulated that military yen currency (Type B military yen) issued by the occupation forces would be legal tender and equivalent to regular yen issued by the Bank of Japan (Bank of Japan notes). Suzuki, shocked, immediately notified the government. Perceiving the three decrees as a potential means of instituting direct military rule, Japanese government leaders convened for an extraordinary cabinet meeting. The cabinet members reached a resolution to request that GHQ cancel the decrees and sent Okazaki Katsuo, chief of the Central Liaison Office, to Yokohama late that very same night in hopes of forestalling them. Okazaki met with Chief of Staff Sutherland and entreated him to stop the decrees from coming out. Sutherland agreed and instructed the occupation units to hold off on issuing the statements.

Through arrangements by Envoy Suzuki, Foreign Minister Shigemitsu also met with MacArthur on the morning of September 3 and implored him not to issue the decrees. Shigemitsu insisted that if GHQ were to issue the decrees directly, the people would lose trust in the Japanese government, which could plunge the political environment into chaos. MacArthur agreed to retract the text of the decrees, saying that the Allies had no intentions of destroying Japan, and assured Shigemitsu that he would go through the Japanese government in implementing any of the provisions in the decree. The following day, Shigemitsu also sat down with Chief of Staff Sutherland and got his word that GHQ would not be using Type B military yen. With the plans for the decrees scrapped, all of the roughly 100,000 posters announcing their terms—already distributed to occupation forces nationwide—were burned, never to be seen by the Japanese public. The effort to thwart the issuance of the decrees might have succeeded, but the fact that military scrip in German marks was already in use in Allied-occupied Germany was one of several factors that led many to feel less than optimistic about the prospects of avoiding direct military rule in Japan. In the end, Japan managed to stave off direct Allied rule thanks to the rapid responses by Foreign Minister Shigemitsu and other officials, for one, and also the sturdy government operations and stable order that enabled Japan to disarm its military in what Chief of Staff Sutherland called a "miraculously" clean, methodical fashion.

11-5. Okazaki Katsuo

That was Tōgō's last official act as foreign minister. The Allies were of no mind to listen to Japan's position on this matter, and in early November 1945 they cut off all of Japan's contacts and communications with foreign governments. Japan lost its diplomatic rights, and all of Japan's embassies in neutral nations were closed. Japan's ability to function in diplomatic relations with other nations was nullified, and the only "diplomacy" it was allowed was interactions with the occupation government.

Although there was still a Ministry of Foreign Affairs in Tokyo, the organization and responsibilities of that bureaucracy were fundamentally changed. Structural reforms carried out in February 1946 merged two core bureaus—the Political Affairs Bureau and the Economic Affairs Bureau—to form the General Affairs Bureau. This ministry now consisted of just four bureaus, which were responsible for treaties and conventions, general affairs, research, and administration, plus the information department (this was revived in January 1946 when the Cabinet Information Bureau was dissolved). This was the era of maximum downsizing of the Ministry of Foreign Affairs.

At the same time, many bureaucrats in the Ministry of Foreign Affairs were transferred to the central and regional offices of the Central Liaison Office, which was formed in late August as an external bureau of the Ministry for Foreign Affairs in order to accommodate the presence of Allied troops. The office was headed by Director-General Okazaki Katsuo (later minister for foreign affairs), and most of the core officials in both the central office and the regional offices were career bureaucrats in the Ministry of Foreign Affairs.

The Start of Occupation Reforms

In its first guidelines for post-surrender Japan dated September 22, 1945, the United States declared that the aim of the occupation was "to insure that Japan will not again become a menace to the United States or to the peace and security of the world." To put it plainly, its objective was the complete demilitarization of Japan.

An earlier draft of that document, prepared in June before Japan's surrender, imagined direct government by the Supreme Commander, but as explicitly stated in the Potsdam Declaration, the role of the occupation forces was indirect; their policies would be executed through the Japanese government. At the same time, occupation authorities retained the right to act directly, asserting they would "make use of the current form of government, but not support it." This problem was highlighted by the *sanfukoku* (three decrees) issue (see sidebar on previous page).

The General Headquarters (GHQ) was established in Tokyo in early October for the purpose of carrying out the policies of the occupation forces. Before that, however, the "Memorandum on Freedom of Speech and the Press" was issued to the Japanese government on September 10. The memorandum forbade criticism of the occupation forces, and not just in newspapers and magazines; it initiated censorship that prohibited criticism of the occupation forces using the mail or electronic communications. The next day, September 11, the occupation forces demonstrated their power by ordering the arrest of Tōjō Hideki and thirty-eight others on suspicion of war crimes.

2 Shidehara, Yoshida, and Postwar Reforms

Japan-Style Democracy

On October 4, 1945, another memorandum on lifting restrictions on citizens' political and civic freedoms was issued. This memo included the dismissal of Yamazaki Iwao as Home Minister. The entire cabinet of Prince Higashikuni resigned the following day, saying it "could not give tacit approval to the dismissal of a minister of the emperor by the occupation forces." Foreign Minister Shigemitsu had already resigned in mid-September following a clash with Chief Cabinet Secretary Ogata Taketora over the problems of the lines of authority for the Central Liaison Office and responsibility for the war. Yoshida Shigeru became Shigemitsu's successor.

Lord Keeper of the Privy Seal Kido Kōichi proposed Foreign Minister Yoshida to succeed Prince Higashikuni as prime minister, but Yoshida nominated Shidehara Kijūrō. Shidehara was the choice for three reasons: the United States did not oppose him, he was not suspected of bearing responsibility for the war, and he was well versed in diplomacy. Shidehara, who was already seventy-three years old, initially turned down the position, but in an audience with the emperor he could see his ruler's anguish, and so he took the job.

The Shidehara cabinet, which got its start in early October, kept Yoshida as foreign minister and added a number of bureaucrats and politicians who had maintained their independence under the wartime regime. The cabinet was unified in its dedication to the reconstruction of Japan. In a news conference following the first meeting of his cabinet, Shidehara made a clear commitment to establishing democracy. More specifically, he said he would "respect the basic rights of citizens in line with the spirit of the Five-Charter Oath with complete restoration of freedom of speech, assembly, and association." This did not imply, however, that there would be any drastic departure from the Constitution of the Empire of Japan (that is, the Meiji Constitution).

The first step in the specific reforms initiated by the Shidehara cabinet was the reform of election laws (December 1945), creating the current system of electoral districts and ensuring that women had the right to vote, among other things. From the perspective of political democratization (expansion of participation in politics), certain aims of modern constitutional law, such as granting the right to vote to all citizens of at least a specified age, were instituted even before the new constitution was put in place.

On October 11, Shidehara had a meeting with MacArthur. MacArthur read a statement demanding the so-called Five Major Reforms (women's suffrage, democratization of education, formation of labor unions, breakup of the zaibatsu, justice-system reform). Shidehara was already at work on some of these, such as the vote for women, with his cabinet, and he promised to take care of the rest.

Shidehara told MacArthur that Japan had been moving in the direction of democracy earlier, but that "toxic forces" had reversed that trend during Japan's occupation of Manchuria. It would not be difficult to move forward again, he said, but rather than American-style democracy, he would prefer to see a "Japanese-style democracy," appropriate to the Japanese environment, that would "reflect the will of the people." MacArthur concurred that this would be the right thing to do.

The Investigation Council for the War

In his policy speech to the eighty-ninth Imperial Diet at the end of November, Shidehara spoke frankly of the causes of Japan's defeat in the Greater East Asia War. He expressed hope that the "great mistake" would not be repeated, and he announced the establishment of an investigation council for the war attached to the cabinet. Shidehara sensed early on the need for such a council, and at the end of October he had the cabinet pass a resolution regarding an "investigation of the causes of the defeat and the true state of affairs." But he had no intention for the results of such an investigation to lead to any assignment of blame. The contemplated scenario was that judgments based on the results of the investigation would be left up to "sound public

Investigation Council for the War: Where Did Japan Go Wrong?

At the end of October 1945, shortly after Japan's surrender, the Shidehara Kijūrō cabinet established the Investigation Council for the Greater East Asia War (later renamed the "Investigation Council for the War" at the direction of GHQ) in order to delineate the "causes and facts of the Greater East Asia War." Shidehara saw the council as such an important body that he himself served as council president alongside his duties as prime minister. To round out the council's leadership, Shidehara appointed Ashida Hitoshi the organization's vice president and made Aoki Tokuzō, a former official in the Ministry of Finance, the council's director-general.

The roster of council members comprised twenty influential figures, including Arisawa Hiromi (economics professor at the University of Tokyo), Ōuchi Hyōe (economics professor at the University of Tokyo), Katayama Tetsu (the former chair of the Socialist Party), Takagi Yasaka (American history professor at the University of Tokyo), Tomizuka Kiyoshi (electrical engineering professor at the University of Tokyo), Saitō Takao (a member of the House of Representatives), Baba Tsunego (president of the *Yomiuri Shimbun*), Yagi Hidetsugu (president of Osaka University and former director-general of the Technology Agency), and Watsuji Tetsurō (philosophy professor at the University of Tokyo). Vice-ministers from all of Japan's governmental ministries also sat on the council as extraordinary members, as did several former military personnel. Within the larger organizational structure were six working groups: teams of members focusing on politics, foreign policy, military affairs, public finance, the economy, thought and culture, and science and technology. The council's official investigative framework came together in the spring of 1946, but the working groups had already launched their own intensive inquiries. Although locating the responsibility for the start of the war was part of the council's scope, the goal of that pursuit was not necessarily to determine who was liable for the outbreak of hostilities, but rather "to prevent Japan from repeating the same grave mistakes in the future."

However, as GHQ would not permit the council to conduct any voluntary independent investigations that might take the place of the Tokyo Trials, the organization ceased operations the following August. It was the first and last time that the Japanese government would conduct a sweeping, comprehensive study of the "Last Great War."

The council produced a plethora of materials spanning fifteen full volumes, which also included the minutes of more than forty council meetings. If one were to take inventory of all the myriad interpretations of how Japan went wrong in the progression toward its involvement in World War II, the minutes of the meetings would be a good starting point—a majority of the explanations appear in those pages. The members evidently debated an array of different questions, delving deep into potential underlying origins of the war. They traced the roots to the Meiji Restoration itself, found problematic elements in the application of the Meiji Constitution, and explored how demilitarization and Taishō democracy in the aftermath of World War I may have sown bitterness in military circles—and thus fueled the military's rise in subsequent years.

Discussions also touched on the Manchurian Incident. Looking at the surrounding events, the council cited the "cooperative cabinet" movement among Japan's political parties and the government's response to the Lytton Report as contributing factors. Another element was the Nationalist government's Northern Expedition, which had threatened the lives and property of Japanese citizens in the areas involved. Had Japan sought the help of the League of Nations in resolving those concerns, the council determined, it would have been possible to avoid the incident. As the members looked at Japan's inability to bring the Second Sino-Japanese War to a close, they reached the conclusion that the government could have arrived at a quick peace, given that the Chinese Nationalist government was also engaged in a civil war with the Communist Party. The points that the members raised all warranted close inspection.

After the council officially disbanded, Shidehara tried to establish a foundation in hopes of keeping the research effort going. GHQ would not allow the investigation to continue in that form, however, so Shidehara instead entrusted all subsequent investigations to Aoki alone. Pouring his energies into that solitary venture, Aoki eventually completed *Taiheiyō sensō zenshi* (The historic background of the Pacific War). Although the volume was more a repository of information than a treatise on the war, as it contained no subjective analysis, Shidehara wrote in his preface to the book, "I believe that this volume provides an ample, convincing basis for compelling future generations to reflect on the war."

opinion," and that what should be done with each of the leaders regarded as "persons responsible" should ultimately be considered on an individual basis. This, it was believed, would be a more effective method than punishment resulting from a domestic trial, which would only sow the seeds of domestic friction.

At the same time, regarding the responsibility of the emperor for the war, in early November Shidehara introduced, and the cabinet passed, a resolution endorsing the view that the decision to begin the Pacific War had been the result of "customs and practices established by the application" of the Meiji Constitution.

At the end of the year, Shidehara was pressed by the need to finalize English wording for a declaration of the emperor's humanity that denied his divinity. The day after that was completed, he collapsed from pneumonia, and did not return to work until late January. The idea of the Declaration of Humanity had come from GHQ, but in reality, it was a collaborative effort by American and Japanese pundits. According to the emperor himself, the heart of the Declaration of Humanity was the Five-Charter Oath of Emperor Meiji at the beginning, starting with "the need to demonstrate that democracy is not something imported."

Toward Revision of the Constitution

After the order for the Five Major Reforms, GHQ issued a series of important orders for the removal of militaristic education and educators. By the end of the year, it was declared that all supports for the system of imperial government had been destroyed. The revision of the Meiji Constitution was the most important of the occupation-era reforms, but the United States was expecting Japan to take this action of its own accord.

In late October 1945, the Shidehara cabinet formed a Constitutional Problems Investigation Committee (Matsumoto Committee), headed by Minister of State Matsumoto Jōji. The Matsumoto Committee, which was advised by Minobe Tatsukichi and others, was made up of the leading constitutional scholars of the day, including Miyazawa Toshiyoshi and Kiyomiya Shirō. It put forward several drafts in 1946, but most remained largely in line with the Meiji Constitution with respect to the emperor's authority to govern the nation.

Constitutional reform proposals drafted by the major political parties of the postwar era shared the same fundamental concept. The January 1946 proposal by the Nihon Jiyūtō (Japan Liberal Party), for example, contained the sentence, "The emperor is the person who controls sovereign rights." These proposals were not sweeping reforms. Items regarding the military were changed, but the heart of the Meiji Constitution, based on Japan's system of constitutional monarchy, remained intact. In fact, these proposals differed little from the constitutional monarchies of Northern European nations such as Norway and Sweden. These prospects, however, would soon change.

The Presentation of the MacArthur Draft

It is a well-known story that early in February 1946, MacArthur, without waiting for the Japanese to complete their draft, ordered the Government Section of GHQ to draft a constitution for Japan that was presented to the Japanese government in mid-February. Foreign Minister Yoshida and others were astonished when they learned that the main points of the Government Section draft included a symbolic emperor, sovereignty resting in the people, and renunciation of war. A majority of Shidehara's cabinet ministers found the Government Section draft difficult to accept. Shidehara paid a call on MacArthur in late February to find out what he truly thought. MacArthur unhesitatingly stated that the fundamental intent of the Government Section draft was to make the emperor the symbol

11-6. Shirasu Jirō

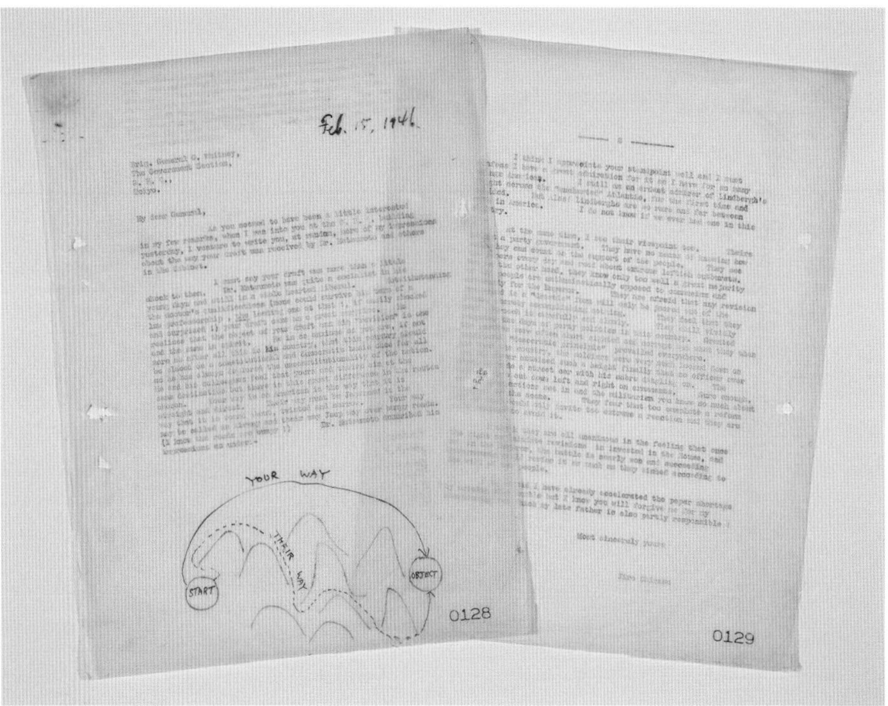

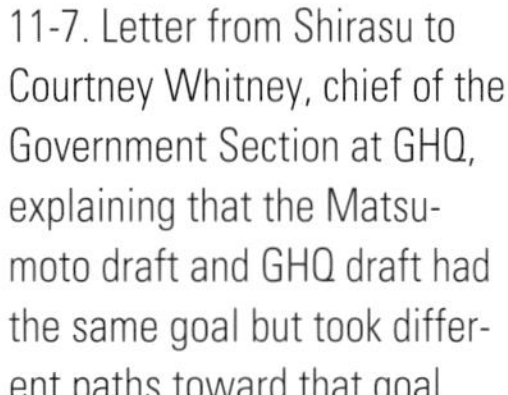

11-7. Letter from Shirasu to Courtney Whitney, chief of the Government Section at GHQ, explaining that the Matsumoto draft and GHQ draft had the same goal but took different paths toward that goal

of the unity of the people and for the nation to renounce war. The Soviet Union in particular, he said, opposed Japan's system of imperial rule.

The Japanese government had no choice but to accept at least the broad outlines of the Government Section draft. In early March, Shidehara and Matsumoto visited the palace to seek the acquiescence of the emperor, after which the cabinet voted to accept the new document. Shidehara told the cabinet, "Given the current circumstances, we have no other avenue." On March 6, an outline of the draft "Bill for Revision of the Imperial Constitution" was published.

Concerns in the Ministry of Foreign Affairs

The ninetieth Imperial Diet, which began in late June, devoted three months to hearings on the bill. While some members expressed admiration for the idealism of Article 9 (renouncing war, not maintaining military forces, repudiating belligerency), the debate bogged down on questions like what sort of international protections there would be for Japan's security, and what military preparations Japan would be allowed to maintain for its own defense. Amid this discussion, the Treaties Bureau issued a written opinion (On the Draft Revised Constitution, April 1946).

"Regarding Article 9 Paragraph 1, Japan has already renounced war in the invasive sense, and it does not permit the maintenance of an army or navy as in Paragraph 2. It should be said that Japan has taken sufficient internal measures to prevent war. There should be no need for Japan to go that step further to 'renounce the right to wage war.'"

The Treaties Bureau asked that one of two corrections be made: either the phrase "renounce the right to wage war" should be excised, or that language be added to the paragraph indicating that in the event of an invasive war, Japan would not recognize the right to wage war. This written opinion was an early version of the Ashida Amendment.

The Treaties Bureau issued another opinion

asserting that Japan's obligations to abide by treaties should be made explicit in the Constitution. In the draft made public in March, this idea was included in Article 93, but was later eliminated in hearings at the House of Representatives. Treaties Bureau Chief Hagiwara Tōru submitted an opinion to Foreign Minister Yoshida and others that Article 93 should be revised again, and in the end the following was added as Article 98, Paragraph 2: "Treaties concluded by Japan, and established international laws and regulations, must be respected, together with this Constitution." This added sentence would come to have great significance in Japan's diplomatic and security policy after independence.

The Coalition Government and the Emergence of the Nihon Jiyūtō (Japan Liberal Party)

In April 1946, in the first general elections to be held after the war, the Nihon Jiyūtō emerged as the victor; its leader, Hatoyama Ichirō, was set to become prime minister. Early in May, however, orders from the GHQ barred Hatoyama from politics. It proved difficult to choose a prime minister from among the other members of the party, so Foreign Minister Yoshida became head of the Nihon Jiyūtō. In late May, the Nihon Jiyūtō and the Nihon Shinpotō (Japan Progressive Party; later the Minshutō [Democratic Party]) formed

The Ashida Amendment

The Bill for Revision of the Imperial Constitution made its way into the House of Representatives in June 1946. After four days of deliberations, lawmakers sent the bill to the Special Committee on Revision of the Imperial Constitution, which was chaired by Ashida Hitoshi. By late July, the Special Committee had completed its work on the bill and developed an official "government proposal" on constitutional revision. The process was not yet complete, however, as the government proposal needed its own amendments—and a new, informal subcommittee thus took shape, with Ashida again serving as the group's leader. When the Special Committee wrapped up its activities in July, the government proposal for a revised Article 9 read as follows:

(1) War, as a sovereign right of the nation, and the threat or use of force, is forever renounced as a means of settling disputes with other nations.
(2) The maintenance of land, sea, and air forces, as well as other war potential, will never be authorized. The right of belligerency of the state will not be recognized.

Discussions on Ashida's subcommittee soon produced a suggestion for an amendment to the government proposal. The prevailing understanding is that the so-called "Ashida Amendment" added the phrase "in order to accomplish the aim of the preceding paragraph" to the beginning of paragraph 2, thereby leaving room to interpret the Article as still allowing Japan to arm itself for the purposes of self-defense. Ashida repeatedly stated that the addition was his own idea and that the "aim of the preceding paragraph" referred to war for the purpose of executing national policy and war as a means of settling international disputes—and thus did not prohibit the use of force for self-defense.

The actual minutes of the committee meetings, which have since come to light, show no evidence of Ashida proposing the "aim of the preceding paragraph" addition himself. However, the records do indicate that he voted in favor of the proposed phrasing.

As soon as GHQ began drafting its version of the constitution, Ashida—a diplomatic historian—saw the connections between the American proposal's renunciation of war and the movement to make war illegal, which eventually fostered the 1928 Treaty for Renunciation of War. He also took it for granted that Japan would have a right of self-defense. During the discussions on the amendment, Ashida pointed out that Article 51 of the Charter of the United Nations recognized nations' right of self-defense and thus argued that, even under the terms of Article 9, Japan would be able to maintain and exercise that right.

a coalition government, with Yoshida as prime minister. Beset by economic crisis and the many reform orders emanating from GHQ, the Yoshida cabinet lasted less than a year, as the Nihon Jiyūtō was defeated by the Shakaitō (Socialist Party) in the election of April 1947.

From the time of the first Yoshida cabinet until the general election of January 1949, no single party won a majority of seats in the House of Representatives. Japan was governed by unstable coalition governments—the cabinets of Katayama Tetsu and Ashida Hitoshi—that were then succeeded by the second Yoshida cabinet; this cabinet was formed by Yoshida's party alone, even though it did not have a majority in the House of Representatives.

During this time, the Nihon Jiyūtō (which later became the Minshu-Jiyūtō [Democratic Liberal Party]) was gaining in strength. From the time of Prime Minister Katayama, the Nihon Jiyūtō was an outspoken critic of a command economy controlled by the national government. Its basic goal was to establish a free economic system to replace Japan's wartime command economy. In the summer of 1947, GHQ allowed Japan to resume external trade, and this worked in favor of the Nihon Jiyūtō. The resumption of trade opened the door to integration in the international economy and the introduction of foreign capital. The Nihon Jiyūtō was able to promote exports as a way of getting Japan's economy back on its feet.

In the general election of January 1949, Yoshida's Minshu-Jiyūtō won in a landslide. Yoshida formed his third cabinet in February, and remained in power for a long time. This political stability became the foundation that allowed Yoshida to chart a new course, shifting the GHQ's "reforms" in the direction of "reconstruction." GHQ itself began to change as well, supporting a more conservative government, rather than a reform-oriented centrist government, and hoping to change its direction.

The third Yoshida cabinet worked with US economic advisor Joseph M. Dodge, who came to Japan to carry out nine principles of economic stability; to reduce the dependence of Japan's economy, which was suffering from severe inflation and stagnant production, on American aid; and to promote exports to create a free market economy. To promote exports, the exchange rate was set at 360 yen per dollar, preparing the way for Japan's reintegration in the global economy. The economic stabilization plan known as the Dodge Line managed to conquer Japan's severe inflation, but it ushered in deflation instead. The economy shrank, unemployment increased, and labor disputes became frequent. What bailed Japan out of these straits was the outbreak of the Korean War.

From Demilitarization to Economic Revival

Beginning around 1946, the standoff between the United States and the Soviet Union grew more overt. Preventing the spread and penetration of Soviet Communism was the foundation of the US postwar global policy, for which Germany in Europe and Japan in Asia came to be seen as regional center points. Under this Cold War framework, the person bearing the main responsibility for Japan policy was George F. Kennan, the director of policy planning at the State Department. When Kennan visited Japan in March 1948, he criticized GHQ for its sudden reforms, and said it was urgent that Japan be strengthened, both economically and socially, so it could stand as a bulwark against Communism for the long term. He also said GHQ should aim to be generous in its reconciliation with Japan, avoiding punitive measures that might keep the nation from becoming economically and politically independent and provoke anti-American feelings.

Based on Kennan's report, the US government shifted the emphasis of its Japan policy away from demilitarization in the direction of economic reconstruction. The most conspicuous aspect of this change was the US policy on reparations for the war. Under the initial US policy, described as

11-8. Children carrying a barrel that was used to transport milk from an aid agency

medium-term reparations (Pauley Reparations), all of Japan's production facilities for aircraft, steel, machine tools, ships, and other industrial properties were to be seized as reparations. Where possible, this equipment was to be transferred elsewhere in Asia for the revitalization of those places. In May 1949, however, the McCoy Declaration ended these confiscations. Satō Eisaku, the chair of the Policy Research Council for the Minshu-Jiyūtō, welcomed the move, saying, "The outlook for Japan's economic reconstruction is now bright." After that, the United States urged other nations to forsake their claims for reparations from Japan in the peace treaty.

3 Peace and Security

The Cold War and "Majority Peace"

Yoshida's foremost goal was the establishment of an "international position of honor" through restoration of independence. In his view, establishing Japan's security was the key to reestablishing the nation's recovery and sovereignty. He viewed the peace treaty and the US-Japan Security Treaty as inseparable from one another. For that reason, he prioritized security over resolving the problems rooted in the war, which were properly part of the peace treaty.

At the end of 1945, the Ministry of Foreign Affairs began quiet research efforts related to the peace treaty. The ministry's initial ideas about peace were quite strict: onerous reparations, prevention of a return to militarism, restrictions on economic activity, establishment of a supervisory body for execution of the treaty, etc. It had to be an "overall peace" agreeable to all countries that had been involved in the war. The United States and the United Kingdom had similar ideas about what the peace efforts would look like.

It was not long, however, before the United States dropped the idea of a "quick peace," and reconciliation started to look less achievable due to the advance of Communism in Asia. In 1948, the Republic of Korea was established on the southern half of the Korean Peninsula, and the Democratic People's Republic of Korea in the north. On the Chinese mainland, the Red Army of the Communist Party gained the upper hand in the civil war, and in October 1949 the People's Republic of China was formed. The Nationalist government of Chiang Kai-shek escaped to Taiwan. These changes enhanced the US need to maintain its occupation forces in Japan; as a result, the chances of a quick peace agreement became more remote.

In the fall of 1949, the United States and the United Kingdom began exploratory moves toward a peace agreement with Japan, and Japan's Ministry of Foreign Affairs made intensive studies of methods and procedures. With China now under Communist control, however, hopes of an "overall peace" seemed difficult, and achieving a quick peace with the free nations became an important option. At some point, this idea became known as "majority peace" (or partial peace, or separate peace). The concept of "majority peace" hinged on the continued

Ashida Hitoshi (1887–1959) and the Ashida Memorandum

The Argument for Rearmament

Born in Kyoto Prefecture, Ashida Hitoshi graduated from Tokyo Imperial University and made his way into the Ministry of Foreign Affairs in 1912. In 1932, after the Manchurian Incident, he suddenly retired from the foreign service and mounted a successful campaign for a seat in the House of Representatives. Ashida would remain in the House of Representatives through the war and into the postwar years, but his tenure met with its share of challenges. The rise of the military during the war years fueled the surge of the one-party system of the Imperial Rule Assistance Political Association, stifling his hopes for effective party politics. In November 1945, after the war had come to an end, Ashida helped found the Nihon Jiyūtō (Japan Liberal Party) with Hatoyama Ichirō as official party leader. He also served under the first Yoshida Shigeru cabinet as chair of the House's Special Committee on Revision of the Imperial Constitution, overseeing discussions on proposals for constitutional revisions (see page 369). In March 1947, he left the Nihon Jiyūtō, formed the Minshutō (Democratic Party), and assumed the directorship of the new party. With the support of GHQ, Ashida aligned the Nihon Minshutō in a coalition with the Shakaitō (Socialist Party) and Kokumin Kyōdōtō (National Cooperative Party) to establish a "centrist" political group. He then ascended into cabinet roles, becoming foreign minister in the Katayama Tetsu administration and later assuming the premiership in a concurrent capacity in March 1948. Ashida's stint as prime minister would be fleeting, however, as his involvement in the Shōwa Denkō graft scandal prompted his resignation after just seven months in office.

11-9. Ashida Hitoshi

Ashida played a relatively small role in the subsequent political processes leading to the formation of the Jimintō (Liberal Democratic Party), but he remained vocal in other capacities. The holder of a doctorate in law and author of the three-volume *Saikin sekai gaikō-shi* (Recent history of global diplomacy; published in 1934), he leveraged his eloquence and copious expertise in diplomatic history and international politics to craft incisive critiques of Yoshida diplomacy and posit an alternative route for Japanese diplomacy: the path to rearmament, an idea that gained traction amid the Korean War.

In the fall of 1950, the UN forces on the ground in Korea were facing an increasingly daunting war situation—and

極秘

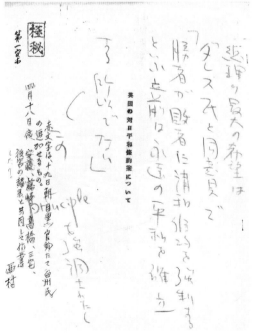

英国の対日平和条約案について

11-10. Overview of the United Kingdom's peace proposal (draft)

presence of US occupation troops to ensure Japan's all-important security. The continued presence of US troops in Japan also became a topic of debate in the United States. For Japan, the idea of US forces having a permanent presence was not easy for the public to accept. It was incompatible with the Constitution; it ran counter to Japan's renunciation of war; and it seemed to shut out the idea of an "overall peace." This was not an option Japan wished to take.

At the same time, Prime Minister Yoshida had to accept the stationing of US troops in order to settle the peace swiftly. The Ashida Memorandum of September 1947 was foremost in his mind, and he was looking for the right opportunity. In May 1950, he sent his trusted confidants Ikeda Hayato (his finance minister) and Shirasu Jirō (former secretary of the Foreign Trade Agency) to Washington, where they the threat of Communism was becoming more and more real for Japan. In hopes of holding off the Communist tide, Ashida began making forceful arguments that the government needed to raise public awareness of the issues through nonpartisan action and bolster Japan's self-defense capabilities. Ashida rooted his argument for rearmament in a deep, nuanced understanding of the ideological currents that had propelled the movement to outlaw war on a global scale in the 1920s. From that vantage point, he asserted that it would be optimal for Japan to play its own part in ensuring collective security through active contributions to the Western Bloc—a proposal that struck a contrast with voices advocating an independent-defense approach. While Ashida understood the reasoning behind the joint Japan-US defense policy that Yoshida favored, he came down hard on arguments against rearmament. Ashida's nonpartisan push for rearmament garnered its share of support, but the drive eventually lost its momentum as the Korean War began to die down.

The Ashida Memorandum

In September 1947, when Ashida was foreign minister and had yet to begin arguing for rearmament in the political realm, he submitted a memorandum to Robert Eichelberger, commander of the Eighth US Army. The "Ashida Memorandum," as it came to be called, was one of the many approaches that the Ministry of Foreign Affairs was exploring in an effort to ensure Japan's national security in the aftermath of the peace agreement. In the memorandum, Ashida recommended a Japan-US treaty that would "establish a special pact with the United States against aggression by a third party and enhance Japan's police force" until the tensions between the United States and the Soviet Union had eased and the United Nations had regained its original functions. In his later years, Yoshida remembered the Ashida Memorandum as having the "same exact conceptual underpinnings as the Japan-US security framework that ultimately took shape."

However, the Ashida Memorandum bore a difference from the eventual US-Japan Security Treaty that was ratified in 1952: it advocated stationing American troops on the Japanese mainland only during emergency situations, a provision that aimed to minimize the American military presence during peacetime and thereby avoid potential claims that the permanent stationing of American personnel constituted an infringement on Japanese sovereignty. In any event, sensitivities to constitutional concerns and popular sentiment made the Ministry of Foreign Affairs hesitant in its work on the Ashida Memorandum; the government did not simply put forth the memorandum as its counter-proposal as it was written.

told his old acquaintance Joseph M. Dodge it would be acceptable for the Japanese government to propose the idea of having US troops stationed in Japan. This proposal was not public or official. It was meant to offer the United States a way out of a jam, giving them some encouragement to pursue the peace process more aggressively by saying that once the peace had been settled, the stationing of US troops would be a focus for both Japan and the United States. But this was no more than one option among many—that is, until the outbreak of the Korean War.

The Debate over Peace

Before the Korean War, when asked in the Diet about the peace problem, Yoshida routinely responded, "A comprehensive settlement would be the best solution. Japan might say it wants an overall peace, or it might say it wants individual settlements, but it is not up to us to decide." It is certainly true that Japan was in no position to dictate to the Allied nations what the terms of the peace should be. Nonetheless, beginning in the second half of 1949, the problem of the form of peace became a central topic of discussion in Japan's Diet and in the public sphere. By 1950, the predominant view, supported by a wide segment of the Japanese people, turned to "overall peace," while opposition to "majority peace" grew.

The concept of overall peace embraced a large number of speculative ideas and expectations. For example, a peace that excluded China and the Soviet Union would shut off Japan's economic relationship with its traditional markets in mainland

China. The argument that this would be a serious obstacle to Japan's economic independence began to carry some weight. In addition, a significant force behind the overwhelming emotional support of the Japanese people for overall peace was the experience of having lost the war, and wanting never again to be caught up in war.

The argument for overall peace became a symbol for both anti-American and anti-government reformists in Japan. At a major convention in January 1950, the Shakaitō proclaimed its "Three Principles of Peace" (overall peace, neutrality, and opposition to military bases), leading other political parties on these issues. Then, in April of that year, the Shakaitō led all opposition parties (with the exception of the Kyōsantō [Communist Party]) in drafting a joint declaration proclaiming perpetual neutrality and overall peace.

The Shock of the Korean War

The Korean War broke out in late June 1950. President Truman regarded North Korea's attack not as an isolated action, but as the start of a meticulously planned major Communist offensive, and he immediately ordered a military response. At the end of June, the decision was reached to deploy the US army and navy, and the four divisions stationed in Japan were moved to the Korean Peninsula. MacArthur, concerned that the defense of Japan would be weakened, ordered the establishment of a National Police Reserve with 75,000 members in early July. Provisions were made for the transportation of troops and military equipment. The National Police Reserve was also permitted to work with UN forces (who were actually US forces) in the manufacture of military goods.

After the start of the Korean War, Prime Minister Yoshida told the Diet that the concepts of overall peace and perpetual neutrality were "unrealistic." In rejecting these ideas, Yoshida said Japan's security would be guaranteed when Japan was welcomed "as a member of the community of free nations." Yoshida threw his influence behind the concept of majority peace and clearly rejected the idea of overall peace—an idea that still lingered within the Ministry of Foreign Affairs—as it involved China and the Soviet Union. Having declared his preference for majority peace, Yoshida asserted that Article 9 of the constitution was not inextricably tied to the idea of "perpetual neutrality." This was his solution to the problem of how Japan could take its place as a member of the community of free nations and still opt to remain unarmed.

On the other hand, for the reformists who regarded overall peace and perpetual neutrality as inseparable, the outbreak of the Korean War meant they had to set this discussion aside for the time being. The opposition parties were agitated. The Shakaitō had provoked the right wing, and had itself fragmented into factions.

The Korean War caused a huge upswing in Japan's economy, which had been suffering from the strengthening of the Dodge Line and the need to balance the government's finances. What might be termed "special demands related to the Korean War" fueled spectacular growth in Japan's exports that swept up all unclaimed inventories and quickly turned Japan's ledger sheet to the black. Corporate activity, which had been stagnating, was brought back to life.

US-Japan Security and the Problem of Rearmament

The Korean War became a proxy war between the United States and China in October 1950, when the Chinese People's Liberation Army entered the fray. At that point, the United States came to rely on Japan for sites for military bases and began to seek Japan's rearmament. By the end of 1950, the tide of the war had definitely turned against the UN forces, and polls showed more than 60 percent of Japanese people favored remilitarization.

In the United States, adjustments were being made to achieve a peace settlement with Japan as soon as possible. John Foster Dulles, the State Department advisor and special envoy charged with resolving the peace problem, proposed "Seven Principles of the Treaty with Japan" (issued in November 1950) as a means for facilitating negotiations with the nations concerned. The principles were all intended to help Japan become part of the freedom camp, including the need for a bilateral Japan-US security agreement; UN trust governance concept for Okinawa and Ogasawara (Bonin); the resolution of territorial issues based on the Cairo Declaration, etc.; and relinquishment of all countries' claims for reparations (i.e., the principle of non-reparation). Dulles made the rounds of Japan's neighboring countries in Asia, hoping to get them to accept the non-reparation principle in particular.

The Japan side, and Treaties Bureau head Nishimura Kumao in particular, prioritized the Japan-US agreement on providing bases and the relationship with the UN. The Japan-US agreement would position the stationing of US troops as a joint bilateral responsibility under Article 51 of the UN Charter (right of collective defense); the language was finalized just before Dulles's visit to Japan. It was expected that this would preserve compatibility with Japan's constitution, and would maintain at least the appearance of equality between the two nations.

Another factor was the response to the problem of rearmament. Yoshida emphatically denied that Japan was rearming. He was worried that the cost of rebuilding military power would add to Japan's economic burden, and he was also concerned about the emotional response of people both in Japan and in neighboring countries who strongly opposed the idea of rebuilding military facilities in Japan. Yoshida was less worried about Communism as a military threat than as a possibility that might infiltrate Japan. The idea was to strengthen Japan's ability to protect public safety, to resist and oppose that threat, to provide sites for bases, and to cooperate with the UN in nonmilitary areas, so that Japan could fulfill its responsibilities to defend the community of free nations. At the same time, Yoshida secretly asked military advisors—mainly former military personnel—to study proposals for rebuilding the military.

Dulles's Visit to Japan: Agreement on the Security Treaty

In January 1951, Dulles's goals for his visit to Japan were settled. First, the United States would assent to the proposed agreement, treating it as an idea from the Japan side. With the sites for maintaining the US bases secured, decisions about rearmament would be next.

When Dulles and his party arrived in Japan in late January, the Japan side presented him with a paper on peace and security issues entitled "Our View." This was Japan's first official response to Dulles's "Seven Principles." Japan's main aims in the area of security were: (1) ensuring its right to self-determination in domestic security and rejecting rearmament; (2) "hoping" for American cooperation in ensuring Japan's external security, with joint decisions to be made under a bilateral Japan-US agreement for that purpose; and (3) maximal response to US demands regarding Okinawa and the Ogasawara Islands for military strategic purposes (government in trust), while still preserving Japan's sovereignty.

The first thing that caught Dulles's eye was Japan's expression of "hope" regarding the stationing of US troops under a bilateral decision. As expressed in Finance Minister Ikeda's proposal of May 1950 (described above), this "hope" had not been communicated officially. It had been difficult for Dulles to gauge Yoshida's true intention, but now he could be confident that the way was clear for the stationing of US troops in Japan.

The problem was rearmament. From the outset,

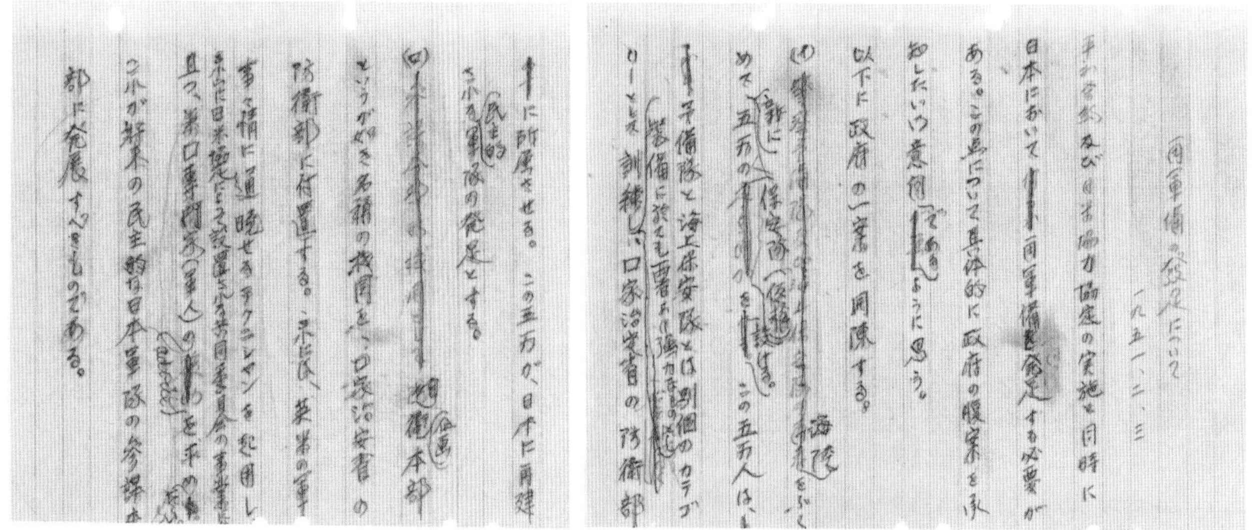

11-11. Draft of the Japanese government's plan regarding Japan's rearmament

Dulles was intent on the rearmament of Japan, but for the reasons discussed earlier, Yoshida rejected the idea. In the end, as of February 3, all Yoshida offered was the same proposal he had already discussed with his military advisors; that is, the idea of creating a "self-defense planning command" that would become the headquarters of a "democratic" military in the future, based on the mustering of a "new, 50,000-member security force including naval and ground forces." From that point on, until Japan achieved independence and recovery, the United States never again mentioned the rearmament problem.

Through a series of conversations, the United States first wanted to make certain of the stationing of US troops; it would then create a plan for the rearmament of Japan. Its only actual promise was a short reference to rearmament in the Preamble to the US-Japan Security Treaty stating that Japan would "increasingly assume responsibility for its own defense against direct and indirect aggression."

At a meeting on February 1, Japan proposed an agreement on providing bases with the US, but the United States did not accept it. In effect, the US proposal of mutual cooperation based on Article 51 of the UN Charter was rejected. The reason was the US Senate's Vandenberg Resolution of 1948, which supported "the association of the United States, by constitutional procedures, with regional or collective arrangements based upon continuous and effective individual or mutual aid." Because Japan was not yet in a position to provide for its own defense, it did not qualify. As Nishimura put it, until the time when a collective defense relationship could be established, the US-Japan Security Treaty would be a makeshift garrisoning agreement constituting "an effort to defend Japan where Japan provides the facilities, and America provides the troops."

After these meetings, the most important change was that at the end of July, the so-called Far East articles were inserted. Until February, the Japan-US draft proposal stated that the purpose of the US troops stationed in Japan was "to contribute to the defense of Japan against external military attacks." From the US military's perspective, however, there was no guarantee that bases in Japan could be used if something like the Korean War happened in the Asian region. To clarify this point, a few words were added specifying that the purpose of the troops was "to maintain international peace and security in the Far East."

4 Territorial Problems

Okinawa, Ogasawara, and "Residual Sovereignty"

The "Seven Principles of the Treaty with Japan" stated that Okinawa and the Ogasawara (Bonin) Islands should be governed as part of a UN trusteeship system. This was the result of consideration for the US military, which wanted exclusive control of Okinawa for reasons of military strategy. The Japanese, however, were concerned that if these territories were governed as part of a trust, Okinawa would be separated from Japan based on the UN Charter. In the January 1951 bilateral meeting, Japan expressed its fervent desire to retain territorial sovereignty. Initially, Dulles refused to listen, saying the matter was settled, but gradually he and the State Department started to come around to the idea of searching for a way to allow Japan to retain sovereignty.

However, the draft peace agreement prepared by the United Kingdom in early April explicitly stated that Japan would give up sovereignty. This problem was on the agenda of a June meeting between the United States and the United Kingdom. In the end, the UK side conceded that a trust government would not require Japan to abandon its rights of sovereignty. As a means of preserving both Japan's sovereignty over Okinawa and America's exclusive control, Dulles envisioned a trust government arrangement under which the United States would be "sole holder of administrative rights," and he wrote this into Article 3 of the peace treaty.

When the peace treaty, including this Article 3, was made public in mid-July, the Japanese government feared it would be criticized. But, having affirmed that Article 3 meant Japan would retain its rights of sovereignty, it made a statement that Japan would retain sovereignty over Okinawa. Dulles confirmed this at the peace conference in September. In this way, the US would exercise the right to administer Okinawa while Japan would retain "residual sovereignty," leaving the door open to the possibility of an eventual return to Japanese control. The significance of Article 3 was that the question of whether or not to make Okinawa a trust government was left up to the United States. In fact, the trusteeship system in Okinawa was never established.

Unresolved Territorial Issues

According to the Cairo Declaration of November 1943 made during World War II by the United States and the United Kingdom, Japan was to recognize Korea's independence and give Taiwan and Penghu to the Republic of China. Under the Yalta Agreement of February 1945, which was signed by the United States, the United Kingdom, and the USSR, South Karafuto (Sakhalin) and the Chishima (Kuril) Islands were to be given to the Soviet Union. Japan's Ministry of Foreign Affairs expected these things to happen. Article 2 of the peace treaty, which dealt with the disposition of territory, stated clearly that Korea should be granted independence, and that all claims to Taiwan, Penghu, South Sakhalin, and the Kurils should be renounced. But it did not specify to which nation they should belong, because the nations to which these territories would presumably be returned were not signatories of the peace treaty.

America's first draft of the peace treaty gave a clear picture of the borders of postwar Japan. Seeking to avert future conflicts, it also showed clearly to which nations the islands Habomai, Shikotan, and Takeshima, for example, would be returned. The questions left unresolved, however, were vulnerable to the aftershocks of the Cold War that washed across Asia.

Of the territories whose recipient nations were unspecified, the most important to Japan was the

Kuril Islands. Japan was to relinquish control of these islands, but exactly which ones was not precisely defined. In his address accepting the peace agreement, Prime Minister Yoshida said South Sakhalin and the Kuril Islands, which Japan had obtained through treaties before World War II, remained occupied by the Soviet Union. He demanded that that islands of Habomai and Shikotan, in particular, be returned to Japan, because they formed an integral part of the geography of Hokkaido.

Another problem was the return of Taiwan and Penghu, which Japan had given up. That is because, by the time of the peace conference, there were "two Chinas": Taiwan, governed by the Nationalists; and the People's Republic of China, governed by the Communist Party in Beijing.

The Position of Taiwan

Dulles thought he would invite both the Beijing government and the Nationalist government to represent "China" at the San Francisco Peace Conference, but then Communist China intervened in the Korean War, causing him to lean heavily in the direction of the Nationalists. The United Kingdom, which had recognized the Beijing government in January 1950, took the position that Beijing should be invited, and that Taiwan should be handed over to

The Yoshida Letter and the Treaty of Peace between the Republic of China and Japan

After holding joint discussions of a peace treaty with Japan in June 1951, the United States and the United Kingdom decided to give Japan the discretion to choose which of the "two Chinas"—the Beijing government (People's Republic of China) or the Taiwanese Nationalist government (Nationalist Government of the Republic of China)—to make peace with. The United States was hoping that Japan would conclude its peace treaty with the Nationalist government, but statements by Prime Minister Yoshida Shigeru gave US officials cause to temper their optimism. With Yoshida emphasizing that he had "never given Mr. [John] Dulles the assurance that we would recognize the Nationalist government," the US government and American senators were apprehensive about how the issue would play out.

Ambassador Dulles was worried that the Treaty of San Francisco might fall apart altogether. A peace agreement between Japan and the Nationalist government was a prerequisite for the US Senate's ratification of the treaty, which had already been signed. In late December 1951, Dulles visited Japan and asked Yoshida to approve a statement indicating that Japan had no interest in concluding a bilateral peace treaty with the Beijing regime. Yoshida agreed, as he indeed had no interest in recognizing the Beijing government for the foreseeable future. The "Yoshida Letter," as it came to be called, was released in mid-January 1952, and the US Congress ratified the Treaty of San Francisco in late March.

Heading up Japan's delegation to conclude the peace treaty with the Nationalist government was Kawada Isao,

11-12. The signing of the Japan–Republic of China peace treaty

an old friend of Yoshida's and a former official at the Ministry of Finance. When the peace negotiations began at the end of January, the Nationalist government adhered to its position that it was representing China (as a whole) in forging a "peace treaty." Japan, on the other hand, argued that the treaty with the Nationalist government would be an agreement with the "Taiwanese government" that would serve to bring the state of war to an official end and resolve a variety of outstanding issues. With the two sides adhering to fundamentally different viewpoints, the negotiations made slow progress. The Nationalist government insisted that the agreement be an official peace treaty, which the delegation saw as a means of preventing Japan from forging closer ties with the Beijing government. The Japanese side was reluctant to assent to the Nationalist government's demands, as treating the agreement as an official peace treaty would mean making peace with a government the Communists. Dulles, however, believing that the US Congress would object, concluded it would not be possible to invite Beijing to the peace conference.

In the end, Article 2 of the peace treaty, as it was affirmed in mid-June, contained only the provisions regarding Japan's abandonment of claims to sovereignty over Taiwan and Penghu, as Dulles had maintained all along. At the same time, regarding the problem of who represented "China," the United States and the United Kingdom had to agree either to invite neither China to the peace conference, or to allow Japan itself to decide, once it was independent, what it wanted to do about China. Japan would be able to choose which of the two "Chinas" to make peace with.

Based on this understanding between the United States and the United Kingdom, Japan chose to sign the Peace Treaty between Japan and the Republic of China with the Nationalist government in Taiwan (see sidebar below).

The San Francisco Peace Conference

The San Francisco Peace Conference was held in early September 1951, with the participation of fifty-two nations, including Japan. The Japanese government was represented by Prime Minister Yoshida and Finance Minister Ikeda, both of whom held

representing "all of China." In the end, however, Japan decided to yield in hopes of forging favorable compromises on other issues.

In relation to the extent to which the treaty would apply, the two sides established in an exchange of notes that the agreement would "be applicable to all the territories which are now, or which may hereafter be, under the control of the government [of the Republic of China]" and thereby avoid any impact on the continent. The issue of reparations was another point of contention, however. While the Nationalist government demanded service reparations, using the Treaty of San Francisco as a model, the Japanese delegation argued that forfeiting Japanese assets in the Republic of China would be enough to cover its reparation obligations. The Nationalist government eventually conceded, agreeing to waive its right to seek reparations in the official protocol (which excluded Japanese assets under Nationalist government control from the scope of the agreement). From that point on, the Japanese government maintained that all the reparation issues between China and Japan had been resolved—a stance that became a target of sharp criticism by Zhou Enlai, the premier of the People's Republic of China, during the 1972 normalization talks between the two countries.

While Japan and the Nationalist government continued their negotiations, the date on which the Treaty of San Francisco would enter into force was fast approaching. The United States, worried that the talks would break down and imperil the Treaty of San Francisco, began urging both Japan and Taiwan to work out a compromise. Complying with the request, Yoshida instructed Kawada's delegation to "take the Nationalist government's wishes into full consideration and work toward achieving an amicable agreement." The two sides still moved slowly, however, taking until April 27—the day before the Treaty of San Francisco took effect—to iron out all the points of dispute and finally arrive at a compromise.

The Japanese government tried to limit the scope of the agreement to the Taiwan region in hopes of leaving room for a potential normalization of diplomatic relations with the Beijing government. In an address to the Diet, Yoshida also explained that the Treaty of Peace between the Republic of China and Japan was an agreement with the "government of Taiwan" and had nothing to do with Beijing. However, the peace treaty also included provisions that one could construe as terms of agreement with China's de jure government—stipulations terminating the state of war and waiving rights to claim reparations, for example—which forced Japan to adopt a legal rhetoric that the treaty was, indeed, with "China" and not specifically the Taiwanese government.

The Beijing government came out in fierce opposition to the Treaty of Peace between the Republic of China and Japan and began heaping rebuke on the Yoshida cabinet. In the end, the treaty led to a sticky situation: the Beijing regime and Nationalist government locked in a thorny dispute, each claiming to be the "one China."

full powers (to negotiate). Japanese political parties also sent representatives, except for the Shakaitō, which opposed the idea of "majority peace."

Talk of "majority peace" aside, it was desirable that a large number of Asian countries that had suffered in the war would participate in the peace conference, and the United States and the United Kingdom worked to persuade them to do so. It had already been decided that China would not be there, and some Southeast Asian countries such as Burma had said they would not participate because they were dissatisfied with the terms of the reparations. India said it did not intend to participate because it believed the peace treaty should be one in which all countries with an interest in maintaining peace in the Far East should be able to take part.

The peace conference, as prepared by the United States and the United Kingdom, was meant to be a venue for participants to sign the peace agreement that had been carefully drafted by those two nations, not a venue for discussion and debate. The representatives of the participating nations made solemn speeches for and against it. Foreign Minister Romulo of the Philippines and Foreign Minister Soebardjo of Indonesia spoke of the tremendous damage their countries had suffered, and pressed for the swift conclusion of a reparations agreement. Yoshida held separate talks with each of these men, and promised Japan would provide fair reparations.

One central focus was the Soviet representative, Andrei Gromyko, and his speech calling for revisions to the draft. Gromyko's proposed revisions included a ban on the stationing of foreign troops in Japan, restrictions on Japan's remilitarization, and a conference of five nations, including the People's Republic of China, to decide the amounts and funding sources of reparations, but these ideas did not receive further deliberation.

In his speech accepting the terms of the peace treaty, Yoshida said, "This treaty is not a treaty of revenge, but rather a document of reconciliation and trust." But he also expressed a few complaints, one of which was the territorial issues. He called for the swift return of the islands to the southwest of Japan to which Japan retained residual sovereign rights. He also stated that South Sakhalin and the Kuril Islands were not territories taken by Japan, and that the islands of Shikotan and Habomai, occupied by the Soviet Union, were an integral part of Hokkaido.

On September 8, representatives of forty-nine

The Treaty of San Francisco and Territorial Issues

The Allies released three agreements concerning territorial and regional issues in the Asia-Pacific region. The first was the Atlantic Charter, which began as a joint statement by the United States and the United Kingdom in August 1941 and later won the support of a larger group of nations via the Declaration by United Nations in January 1942. The Atlantic Charter set forth a set of common Allied principles, including two on territorial matters: no territorial aggrandizement and no territorial changes against the wishes of the peoples concerned.

The next major Allied statement on territorial concerns came in November 1943 with the Cairo Declaration, an agreement between the United States, the United Kingdom, and China. Outlining the Allies' basic approach to the handling of Japanese territories, the Cairo Declaration contained five main provisions: that the Allies (1) coveted no gain for themselves and had no thought of territorial expansion, (2) would strip Japan of all the islands in the Pacific which she had "seized" or occupied since the beginning of the First World War in 1914, (3) would restore all the territories that Japan had "stolen" from the Chinese, such as Manchuria, Formosa, and the Pescadores, (4) would expel Japan from "all other territories which she had taken by violence and greed," and (5) would ensure that "Korea shall become free and independent."

The third was the July 1945 Potsdam Declaration, which Japan eventually accepted as its terms of surrender. Clause 8 of the Potsdam Declaration made mention of territorial matters, saying, "The terms of the Cairo Declaration shall be carried out and Japanese sovereignty shall be limited to the islands of Honshu, Hokkaido, Kyushu, Shikoku and such minor islands as we determine."

countries, including Japan, signed the Treaty of Peace with Japan. The Soviet Union, Poland, and Czechoslovakia were absent and did not sign the document. Japan was subsequently able to normalize relations with countries that did not attend the peace conference by reaching a series of bilateral agreements.

Laos and Cambodia were signatories to the Treaty of San Francisco, but they relinquished the right to make claims. India was not present at the San Francisco conference. In the Treaty of Peace between Japan and India signed in 1952, India gave up its rights to reparations, and it restored Japanese assets in India. Other nations abandoned their claims to reparations, but did not go so far as to return Japanese assets that had been seized. Many in Japan therefore praised the India-Japan peace treaty when the Diet convened to ratify it in June of 1952.

The Signing of the US-Japan Security Treaty

On the evening of September 8, 1951, Yoshida went alone to an army base in the San Francisco suburbs to sign the Security Treaty between Japan and the United States. He had decided to bear the weight of this responsibility personally.

The text of the treaty was one-sided, and not to Japan's advantage. Article 1 stated that US troops in Japan "may be utilized to contribute to . . . the security of Japan against armed attack from without." In other words, Japan would provide the sites for the bases, but the United States was not making a commitment to defend Japan.

Moreover, the treaty contained a clause covering insurrection, saying that at the request of the Japanese government, US troops might be used "to put down large-scale internal riots and disturbances in Japan." This subjected the treaty to criticism for interfering in Japan's internal affairs.

Article 1 also stated that "such forces may be utilized to contribute to the maintenance of international peace and security in the Far East," but the "Far East" was not defined. This opened the door to the danger that Japan might become caught up in military actions by US forces.

When the US-Japan Security Treaty was signed on September 8, Yoshida and US secretary of state Dean Acheson also exchanged notes ensuring that Japan would continue to cooperate with UN forces after the peace treaty was signed. The Korean War

Running through the Allied agreements, rooted in the Atlantic Charter, are two consistent threads: that the Allies were not pursuing territorial expansion and that Japan had taken regions and islands "by violence and greed." As World War II came to an end, then, the Allies positioned those two points as a foundation for ensuring peace and stabilizing the regional order in the postwar Asia-Pacific region.

For these international agreements to have any legally binding power in relation to Japan, the parties would need to sign an official peace treaty. That requirement was met with the conclusion of the Treaty of San Francisco, signed by Japan and forty-eight other countries. Clause 2 of the treaty stipulated that Japan would relinquish Korea, Formosa and the Pescadores, the Kuril Islands, and "that portion of Sakhalin . . . over which Japan acquired sovereignty as a consequence of the Treaty of Portsmouth," among other land and territories, in accordance with the Cairo Declaration and the Potsdam Declaration (which committed to carrying out the terms of the Cairo Declaration).

In the wake of World War II, the legal adjustments to Japan's territorial dynamics thus fell in consistent line with a series of written agreements that began with the Atlantic Charter and culminated in the Treaty of San Francisco. However, the Treaty of San Francisco did not explicitly define what paragraph 8 of the Potsdam Declaration meant by the "minor islands as we [the Allies] determine" to be the part of Japan's sovereign territory. The Chishima (Kuril) Islands, Senkaku Islands, and Takeshima all belonged to that nebulous category.

was becoming entrenched, with US and Chinese forces at loggerheads. The inclusion of the "Far East clause" and securing the right to freely use bases in Japan constituted essential parts of the US military's strategy.

The US-Japan Administrative Agreement and the Problem of Authority

The US-Japan Administrative Agreement followed the security treaty to clarify details of the relationship between the two countries. This administrative agreement was made between governments; they did not require legislative approval, and it could be revised at will.

The administrative agreement specifying the terms under which US troops could be stationed in Japan was negotiated at the end of January 1952 by Assistant Secretary of State Dean Rusk and Minister of State Okazaki Katsuo. As US military personnel came to live alongside ordinary Japanese people, many difficult problems emerged. Under the Allied occupation rules, US troops enjoyed many special rights. The signing of the peace treaty may have changed their status, but attitudes did not change so quickly, and the previous special privileges continued to be honored, at least to some degree, though incremental improvements were made. One issue related to the stationing of US troops was the matter of criminal jurisdiction. The position of the US Senate was that US troops stationed abroad were there because the host country wanted them there; jurisdiction over their crimes should therefore lie with the US side.

Japan's National Safety Agency was established in August 1952 and members of the national police reserve became the National Safety Forces. In connection to this, the Diet began a contentious debate. Of course, Japan's prime minister was the commander-in-chief of Japan's national defense, but if something should happen, would the commander of US forces in Japan be in overall command, or would the Japanese government be? Rusk's position was that, in the event of an enemy action or

The Key Points of the Treaty of San Francisco (The Treaty of Peace with Japan)

The Treaty of San Francisco was signed on September 8, 1951. The main points were as follows:

(1) Territory: Japan renounces all right, title and claim to Korea, Taiwan (Formosa), the Pescadores Islands, Kurile Islands, and South Sakhalin and also recognizes the "independence of Korea," which includes the islands of Jeju Island (Quelpart), Ulleungdo (Port Hamilton), and Ulleungdo (Dagelet). (Article 2)

Japan will concur in any proposal of the United States to the United Nations to place under its trusteeship system, with the United States as the sole administering authority, Nansei Shotō south of 29° north latitude (including the Ryūkyū Islands and the Daitō Islands) [and] Nanpō Shotō . . . (including the Bonin Islands, Rosario Island, and the Volcano Islands). [Note: Although none of the territory was actually placed under the trusteeship system, it was placed under US military control.]

(2) Right of self-defense and security: The Allied Powers for their part recognize that Japan as a sovereign nation possesses the inherent right of individual or collective self-defense referred to in Article 51 of the Charter of the United Nations and that Japan may voluntarily enter into collective security arrangements. (Article 5 [c])

All occupation forces of the Allied Powers shall be withdrawn from Japan as soon as possible after the coming into force of the present Treaty, and in any case not later than ninety days thereafter. Nothing in this provision shall, however, prevent the stationing or retention of foreign armed forces in Japanese territory under or in consequence of any bilateral or multilateral agreements . . . between one or more of the Allied Powers . . . and Japan.

(3) Reparations and claims: The Allied Powers and Japan both relinquish claims arising out of war-related actions. (Articles 14 and 19) Japan will

an imminent threat in the Japan region, the two governments would undertake the necessary joint response. To meet the goals of Article 1 of the security treaty, they would have to confer closely with one another. This would become Article 24 of the administrative agreement, but details of the consultation process were omitted.

Reparations

Under the "Seven Principles of the Treaty with Japan," all Allied nations were to relinquish their claims to reparations. The United States and the United Kingdom, the Netherlands, France, and other major Allied nations were moving toward abandoning their claims to reparations. However, the Philippines and other countries that had suffered significant direct harm from the war were adamantly opposed to giving up such claims. Article 14 of the peace treaty allowed countries that wished to do so to negotiate with Japan for payment of reparations in the form of service.

However, Article 14 also included the principle that the amount of the reparations would depend on Japan's ability to pay. That was because of the lessons of World War I, when reparations were imposed on Germany with no consideration given to its economic circumstances or ability to pay. The harsh demands of reparations destroyed Germany's economy and paved the way for the rise of Nazism.

In the end, four countries negotiated with Japan for reparations: the Philippines, Vietnam, Burma, and Indonesia. These negotiations were arduous, but Burma reached a reparations agreement in 1954, the Philippines in 1956, Indonesia in 1958, and, finally, Vietnam in 1959. Burma was the first to reach such an agreement, but after it saw Japan's agreements with Indonesia and the Philippines, it sought to renegotiate its deal, leading to the economic and technological cooperation agreement of 1963.

The reparations negotiations did not go smoothly. First of all, the amount of reparations sought was enormous. The total initially demanded by these four countries was over US$33 billion, which at

promptly enter into negotiations with Allied Powers so desiring, whose present territories were occupied by Japanese forces and damaged by Japan, with a view to assisting to compensate those countries for the cost of repairing the damage done, by making available the services of the Japanese people in production, salvaging and other work for the Allied Powers in question. (Article 14 [a]) [Note: The treaty established the principle of "service indemnity," a form of reparations that covered the provision of services and labor (and later production) to countries desiring reparations.]

. . . To indemnify those members of the armed forces of the Allied Powers who suffered undue hardships while prisoners of war of Japan, Japan will transfer its assets . . . in countries which were neutral during the war. . . to the International Committee of the Red Cross. (Article 16)

(4) War crimes: Japan accepts the judgments of the International Military Tribunal for the Far East and of other . . . Courts both within and outside Japan, and will carry out the sentences imposed thereby . . . The power to grant clemency, to reduce sentences and to parole with respect to such prisoners [shall be based] on the recommendation of Japan. (Article 11) [Note: In the Japanese translation of the treaty, the phrase "accepts the judgments" was rendered as "*saiban o judaku*," which literally means "accepts the court decisions."]

As a whole, the peace treaty was extremely generous to Japan in comparison to the many other peace agreements that took shape in the twentieth century. The Treaty of Versailles and the Treaty of Peace with Italy (1947), for example, called for substantial reparations, placed stringent limitations on armaments, and included statements attributing war responsibility to the target countries.

that time was more than double Japan's annual gross national product (GNP). Some members of the Diet expressed skepticism that Japan should have to pay any war reparations at all to Indonesia or Vietnam, which had hardly been involved in the war. The Japanese government, however, decided that, rather than trying to determine the reasoning behind some unsettled amount of reparations, it should prioritize mutual economic benefit and development, and work with the industrial and financial world to solve the problem through "economic cooperation."

Economic cooperation meant giving due consideration to certain political aims that were aligned with American ideas. Foremost among these was curbing the penetration and expansion of Communism. In November 1954, on a trip to the United States, Yoshida met with Dulles and proposed the idea that "reparations are a form of investment." He asked for financial cooperation, because if reparations could take the form of cooperation in economic development in Southeast Asia, the penetration of Communism could be halted, "killing two birds with one stone." But Dulles rejected this idea, saying that if America

The Tokyo Trials: What Constitutes a War Crime?

"Crimes against Peace"

The Tokyo Trials (International Military Tribunal for the Far East) began in May 1946 on the basis of the Potsdam Declaration, which stipulated that "stern justice shall be meted out to all war criminals" (Paragraph 10). Japan interpreted "all war criminals" to mean individuals who had abused prisoners or committed similar crimes on the battlefield, and assumed that the trials would take place under existing international laws and regulations, such as the Hague Conventions. Contrary to those expectations, however, the Tokyo Trials marked a departure from the established norm: not only would the tribunal try defendants for "conventional war crimes," but it would also hear arguments on the new legal concepts of "crimes against peace" and "crimes against humanity." The two additional categories of war crimes were less than a year old; the United States, the United Kingdom, France, and the Soviet Union had defined them as part of "civilization's justice" at the London Conference in the summer of 1945. The group created "crimes against humanity" to establish a legal framework for prosecuting German (Nazi) atrocities that extended beyond the scope of international laws and regulations.

11-13. Chief Counsel Joseph Keenan

At the Tokyo Trials, the three types of crimes each corresponded to a different "class" of charges: crimes against peace, or the planning, preparation, or waging of a war of aggression or a "conspiracy" for the accomplishment thereof, were Class A charges. Crimes against humanity, which referred primarily to political or racial victimization (the category to which Nazi atrocities would have belonged), fell into Class C. Class B was for conventional war crimes.

All twenty-eight defendants at the Tokyo Trials were charged with crimes against peace (Class A crimes), and the question of whether the defendants were guilty of "conspiracy"—a key element defining Class A crimes—became the central issue of the court proceedings. In arguing its case, the counsel for the defendants contended that the war had been one of self-defense, and that Japan had had no other choice but to wage war in order to protect itself from the debilitating economic impact of the ABCD (American, British, Chinese, and Dutch) embargo line. The court, however, set its focus on the causal relationship between Japan's war of aggression against China after the Manchurian Incident and its subsequent conflicts with the United States, the United Kingdom, and the Netherlands. Defendant Kido Kōichi (former Lord Keeper of the Privy Seal of Japan) wrote that "the defense's weak point was the connection to the China incidents," as using the "self-defense" argument to rationalize Japan's military invasion of China—especially after the Marco Polo Bridge Incident—was somewhat of a stretch.

The defense also stated that the defendants had simply been carrying out their duties within their respective authority over the course of a given period, making it impossible to hold them individually liable for war crimes on charges of a "conspiracy." According to Nishi Haruhiko (former Japanese ambassador to the United Kingdom), who represented Tōgō Shigenori (former foreign minister) at the Tokyo Trials, "Those who started the Manchurian Incident were also responsible for starting the Greater East Asia War; any were to "cosign" Japan's reparations, then the partner countries would only increase their demands.

Although it was unable to get the United States to provide financial support, Japan prioritized the formation of a basis for economic creation through investment. Most of the reparations (economic cooperation) payments made through Japanese corporations were for electric power development, roads, railways, and other infrastructure in the partner nation, creating a foundation for the entry of Japanese companies. Over time, it became possible to switch the reparations to yen loan credits.

Japan–South Korea Talks and the Syngman Rhee Line

After South Korea, which had been colonized by Japan, was liberated in August 1945, it demanded a seat among the "victorious nations" at the San Francisco Peace Conference. As a signatory to the peace agreement, South Korea should have been accorded the same rights to demand reparations as all other Allied nations. But because it had not fought in the war against Japan, it was not invited to the peace conference. The United States promised to grant

11-14. International Military Tribunal for the Far East

involvement at all meant full liability. It was a line of reasoning that was wholly untenable from a theoretical standpoint."

In the end, the court's majority opinion (November 1948) stated that the Japanese "conspiracy" to establish military, political, and economic control in the Asia-Pacific took root amid the Tanaka Giichi administration in 1928, spurred the invasion of China in 1931, prompted the large-scale invasion of China in 1937, and propelled the opening of hostilities against the United States and the United Kingdom in 1941.

The court found twenty-four of the twenty-five defendants at the time of its ruling (all except for former army general Matsui Iwane) guilty of crimes against peace for their involvement in the general "conspiracy" that arose in 1928. Seven defendants received the death penalty: six former high-ranking army officers, including Doihara Kenji, Itagaki Seishirō, Tōjō Hideki, and Matsui, along with former prime minister Hirota Kōki. No one received a death sentence for being involved in the conspiracy alone, however; also factoring into the sentences were individual acts of aggression and violations of the laws of war with respect to China, the United States, the United Kingdom, and the Soviet Union, for example. Hirota was sentenced to death for his involvement in the general conspiracy and his disregard for duty as prime minister to prevent breaches of the laws of war in the Nanjing Massacre. Matsui, the only one of the twenty-five defendants convicted of a Class B crime, meanwhile, was, like Hirota, found guilty

South Korea treatment "equal to the Allies," but Japanese assets, public and private, on the Korean Peninsula were placed under the administration of the US military, where they were then subject to negotiations between Japan and South Korea (San Francisco Peace Treaty, Article 4).

In mid-February 1952, Japan and South Korea began official discussions aimed at the establishment of bilateral relations. Just before that, however, in mid-January, the South Korean government, in the name of President Rhee Syngman, had unilaterally claimed sovereignty over certain adjacent waters inside the "Syngman Rhee Line." Inside this line was Takeshima, a small group of islands that South Korea should have surrendered in the process of drawing up the peace treaty. The Japanese government lodged a complaint, saying this violated the principle of freedom of the seas, but South Korea continued to seize Japanese fishing boats that ventured across the Syngman Rhee Line. This developed into a dispute over territorial rights to Takeshima that hindered the talks between the two nations.

The Tokyo Trials: What Constitutes a War Crime?

of breaches of duty surrounding the Nanjing Massacre and sentenced to execution.

Sixteen defendants, most of them army personnel, received life sentences, while Tōgō and Shigemitsu Mamoru received definite prison sentences of twenty years and seven years, respectively. None of the defendants were charged with Class C crimes against humanity.

"Civilization's Justice" and "Victors' Justice"

The defense argued that applying an ex post facto law clearly went against the basic legal principle holding that there is "no crime without a law." The court, however, dismissed the defense's argument by saying that giving legal protection to aggressors who had violated ex post facto law also ran against the "principles of justice" at the heart of law itself.

The Allies, acknowledging the allegations of applying ex post facto law, began constructing the concept of "civilization's justice," a legal framework that would transcend the criticisms of their case's legality. The factors prompting the formation of the new approach were twofold: the Axis powers' widespread atrocities and wars of aggression in the 1930s would be difficult to try under the provisions of customary international law, first of all, and the United States—the primary driver of the trials—needed to demonstrate its moral leadership in the spirit of universal "justice" and "civilization" to fortify its position as the preeminent force in the postwar world order.

For US secretary of war Henry Stimson, the architect of the postwar international tribunals, the need for a new legal precedent was a matter of key importance. Rather than exacting revenge on the former Axis powers, Stimson insisted, the proceedings should serve to prevent future wars of aggression by establishing a new legal concept. The Tokyo Trials championed that cause, as the prosecution poured its energies into substantiating the criminality of aggressive wars in the name of "civilization." With these types of political aims at the heart of the proceedings and a lineup of judges from victorious nations, the Tokyo Trials came under fire for being a court of "victor's justice." GHQ political advisor William Sebald, a keen observer of the trial proceedings, later raised the question of whether it was prudent to have used the court process to expose Japan's militaristic past to the country's people. In the context of the overarching occupation policy, however, one can see how the adoption of the new legal concept of "civilization's justice" represented an attempt by the United States to refashion itself as not only a victor but also a peaceful nation that others could cooperate with.

Still, the Japanese government went along with the court proceedings in a methodical, compliant fashion, never challenging the legal basis of the trials head on. Nor was there any evidence of a concerted effort to build a specific, unified strategy on the question of the emperor's war responsibility, the foremost concern for the Japanese side, as counsel determined that presenting the truth of the facts would be enough to prove the emperor's innocence. That decision also likely had at least something to do with the political dynamics between GHQ and the Japanese government, which were coalescing around an agreement that the emperor would be exempt from responsibility. In April 1946, shortly before the trials began, the Far Eastern Commission had already decided that the emperor would not be subject to prosecution—not because the members interpreted the constitution as exempting the monarch from liability, but rather because they wanted to avoid fueling political instability in Japan.

The Treaty of San Francisco and the Tokyo Trials

A remaining question for the Allies was how to position the

As soon as the bilateral talks began, the disposition of Japanese assets in South Korea became a subject of dispute. The South Korean side demanded repayment of wartime debt, saying that the public and private Japanese assets in South Korea were insufficient reparation for its thirty-six years of suffering under Japanese rule. The Japan side retorted that it had claims to its public and private assets in South Korea, and that the Japanese people would not accept losing all of those assets, not to mention having to pay more as well.

Behind these two positions were different perceptions of history and differing views on what had been within or against the law during the colonial period. South Korea took the position that the Japan-Korea Treaty of 1910 was invalid. Japan held that both that treaty and the Japan-Korea agreements before 1910 had been recognized by both the United States and the United Kingdom. Assuming that the Treaty of 1910 was legal, the economic activity of Japanese people on the Korean Peninsula had been right and just. The two sides reached a sort of agreement based

trials, which had taken place under the occupation administration, in the context of the peace treaty with Japan. In the UK drafts of the peace treaty, there were war-responsibility provisions that specifically held the nation of Japan responsible for undertaking a war of aggression. However, the final version of the peace treaty made no explicit reference to war responsibility. Instead, it included provisions on the handling of post-peace judgments, which appeared in Article 11.

The first portion of Article 11 stipulated that Japan "accepts the judgments of the International Military Tribunal for the Far East and of other Allied War Crimes Courts" and "will carry out the sentences imposed thereby." As the text suggests, the Tokyo Trials were just one set of proceedings concerning Japanese war crimes; other military trials (the "Class BC war crimes trials") had also taken place in Yokohama and other locations around Asia. Article 11 obligated the Japanese government to carry out the sentences of all the corresponding trial judgments, a duty that continued to apply after the signing of the peace treaty.

The latter half of Article 11 stated that if the Japanese government sought to take measures that deviated from the Allies' sentences, it would need to secure the approval of the relevant parties through a Japanese "recommendation." The Japanese government was thus responsible for executing the sentences after the peace had been made, but their Allied counterparts held the final authority to issue pardons, reduce sentences, or extend other forms of mercy.

The prevailing thinking behind Article 11 was that it simply served to keep the judgments of the war trials in full force and effect, not necessarily signifying that Japan had accepted the legitimacy of the trials. The question that then arose in Japan was what to do about the sentenced war criminals. At meetings of the Diet concerning the signing of the peace treaty, legislators dealt with virtually innumerable petitions and appeals from citizens seeking the release of war criminals, some of which received parliamentary approval. Grounding their rationale in the contention that the sentenced war criminals were actually victims of the war, the petitions sought to repatriate prisoners being detained abroad, pardon prisoners being held in Japan, or have prisoners' sentences commuted. With calls for the release of war criminals gaining support among both government circles and the general public, a memorandum from the office of the minister of justice in May 1952 explained that the war criminals were not criminals under domestic Japanese law and recast their deaths as "deaths in service of the country" rather than "executions," thereby paving the way for their enshrinement—regardless of the class of the war crimes (A, B, or C)—at Yasukuni Shrine.

Meanwhile, the government set to "recommending" that other countries pardon or parole Japanese war criminals in accordance with Article 11 of the peace treaty, a process that officials took up in earnest. The governments of the other nations were receptive to Japan's recommendations, agreeing to grant releases as a means of facilitating reparation negotiations, stabilizing relations with Japan, or addressing a variety of other factors. By the end of 1958, when the Kishi Nobusuke cabinet was in power, all the war criminals had been released.

While the Diet had to tangle with interpretations of Article 11 again in the second part of the 1980s, as historical issues with China and South Korea came to the fore, the Japanese government has never formally recognized the legitimacy of the International Military Tribunal (or the BC Class trials). Neither, however, has it raised any corresponding objections.

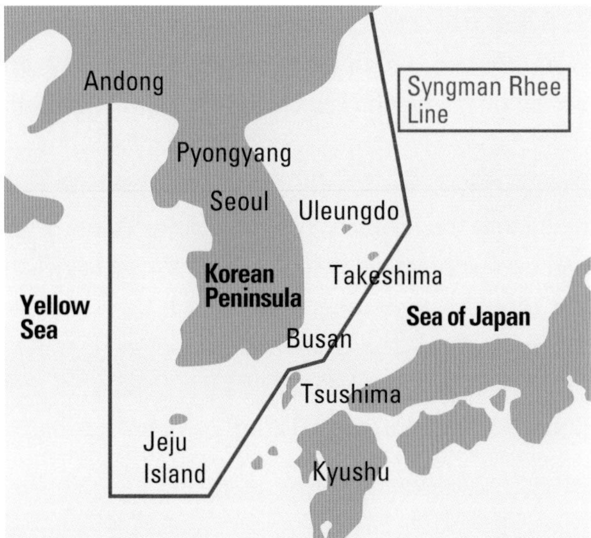

11-15. Syngman Rhee Line

on the idea that the 1910 Treaty was "no longer valid," but this did not solve the problem of claims, and talks were broken off in late April.

At a third round of talks held in October 1953, Japan representative Kubota Kan'ichirō told the South Korea side, "[Japan] developed Korea's economy, spending large sums in subsidies to build railways, harbors, rice fields," which should be seen as part of an exchange (Kubota Statement). This statement was a provocation to the South Koreans, and talks broke down in late October.

Another focus of the Japan–South Korea talks was the legal standing (both in terms of nationality and treatment) of the 600,000 Koreans who remained in Japan after the war. When the peace treaty took effect, Koreans and Taiwanese in Japan lost their Japanese citizenship and became "foreigners." As of the date of the Instrument of Surrender, Koreans and Taiwanese in Japan were permitted to stay in Japan, even without a visa, until such time as the matter was settled in the law. They had to register as foreign nationals. To obtain Japanese citizenship, they would have to become naturalized by following the procedure in the Nationality Act.

5 The End of the Yoshida Cabinet

The Issue of Remilitarization

After the restoration of independence, politics in Japan became less stable, with a broader range of policy options, due to the withdrawal of the occupying troops with their final authority. Not only were government and opposition parties at odds with one another, but within the ruling party, Hatoyama Ichiro and Kishi Nobusuke and other politicians from the wartime era who had been driven from public life came back on the scene, creating new rivalries for Yoshida.

In the general election of 1953, Yoshida failed to win a majority but was able to form a government. Undeterred, he set himself to the most important task of peacetime: remilitarization. In his talks with Dulles in January 1951, Yoshida had committed only to the minimum level of remilitarization. There was no agreement between the United States and Japan regarding the pace or scale of remilitarization.

Negotiations regarding America's external aid began in Tokyo in the summer of 1953 under the Mutual Security Act (MSA, as revised in 1953). Japan needed additional US aid to rebuild its economy, and it hoped to be able to receive more aid in exchange for setting up a minimal defensive force. The United States wanted to promote Japan's remilitarization. It was not long, though, before negotiations ground to a halt. In October, chair of the Policy Research Council of the Jiyūtō Ikeda Hayato traveled to the United States in search of a compromise solution. In talks with Assistant Secretary of State Walter Robertson, the US side asked that Japan build an army of 300,000 troops or more, but Ikeda said he could only commit to up to 180,000. Before traveling to America, Ikeda had persuaded Yoshida to talk with Shigemitsu, who

11-16. Special Envoy Dulles and Prime Minister Yoshida

at that time was head of the Kaishintō (Reform Party), hoping to get him to agree to the idea of the formation of a self-defense force. When the Self-Defense Force was formed, it in fact consisted of 180,000 troops. Ikeda stuck to Yoshida's idea of light armament and maintained a course of prioritizing economic reconstruction.

Southeast Asian Development and the Colombo Plan

In September 1954, Yoshida visited Europe and America. One of his important goals was to ask the United States for support for development in Southeast Asia. Yoshida's cabinet had made export promotion a priority task, but China's conversion to Communism had closed off trade with the mainland. Japan sought a route through Southeast Asia. Economic development of Southeast Asia was also necessary as a means of fending off the influence of Communist China, and America's financial assistance would be indispensable. For this reason, Yoshida set out on his US visit with the hope that the United States might prepare an "Asian Marshall Plan" involving a huge sum of money, but that was not to be.

The second main topic Yoshida wanted to discuss with the leaders of the United States and European nations was the estrangement between China and the Soviet Union. According to Yoshida, Chinese people never did anything that "didn't make sense on an abacus" (i.e., that was not profitable). Free nations might be able to lure Communist China into their camp by driving a wedge between it and the Soviet Union.

The third item was the need for Japan and the United Kingdom to work together on their policy vis-à-vis Communism. From Yoshida's perspective, America's postwar China policy had been a failure, causing China to overreact and pushing it in the direction of Communism. The United Kingdom and Japan knew China better, and had a longer acquaintance. By working together, they could forge a smarter policy on China.

On his trip to Europe and America, Yoshida realized some success with this idea. Japan was able to join in the Colombo Plan, a Commonwealth-centered cooperative plan to aid economic development in South and Southeast Asia (October 1954). Japan's role was limited to the technology area, but this placed several goals within reach. For example, the Colombo Plan would serve as a good platform for Japan to diversify its aid and expand the range of its regional cooperation. Whereas in the first half of the 1950s, Japan focused its aid on South Asia (India, Ceylon), the Colombo Plan covered a greater area of Asia.

When Yoshida returned to Japan from his two-month journey to the United States and Europe, he was greeted by a new anti-Yoshida movement. The Nihon Minshutō (Japan Democratic Party) had been formed, with Hatoyama at the helm, in early December, and in a left/right coalition with the Shakaitō, it submitted a motion of no confidence in the government. Yoshida had no choice but to resign together with his entire cabinet.

Yoshida Shigeru (1878–1967): The "Yoshida Line"

Changing Assessments

11-17. Yoshida Shigeru

Born in Kōchi in 1878, the fifth son of liberal democratic-rights activist Takeuchi Tsuna, Yoshida Shigeru was adopted as a baby by Yokohama-based trader Yoshida Kenzō and inherited a massive fortune at the age of eleven when his adoptive father died. Bouncing from school to school, Yoshida eventually graduated from Tokyo Imperial University with a degree in law in 1906 at the age of twenty-eight. He then made his way into the Ministry of Foreign Affairs in the same group as fellow recruits Hirota Kōki and Hayashi Kyūjirō.

Yoshida spent the bulk of his first two decades at the Ministry of Foreign Affairs in China, serving as Japan's consul general in both Tianjin and Mukden. In line with the Tanaka Giichi cabinet's aims to annex Manchuria-Mongolia from China proper, Yoshida famously refused to back down on the Japanese interests that had been guaranteed by international treaties. For Yoshida, the best path toward maintaining and expanding Japan's interests in China was through a cooperative arrangement with the United Kingdom; he distanced himself from "new diplomacy," instead focusing on a bilateral approach. After the Manchurian Incident, Yoshida was an advocate of Shidehara Kijūrō's push for international cooperation—but his focus was on the United Kingdom. Being sensitive to the Anglo-Japanese relationship as Japan's ambassador in London, Yoshida felt that Japan should focus more on its standing with the United Kingdom than on its US ties, criticized the Axis alliance from beginning to end, and explored the potential for an Anglo-Japanese partnership on China. Although he retired from diplomatic service in 1939, Yoshida was still active in dealing with foreign counterparts; before Japan went to war against the United States, he met several times with US ambassador to Japan Joseph Grew and Foreign Minister Tōgō Shigenori in hopes of averting hostilities. During the war years, Yoshida teamed up with his old friend Konoe Fumimaro and others on furtive attempts to strike a direct peace with the United States and the United Kingdom—efforts that ended up getting him imprisoned by the military police just before the end of the war.

Yoshida saw the defeat in World War II as an opportunity to build a new Japan. Working to bring both foreign investments and new technologies into the country, forge a cooperative relationship with the United States, and prioritize joint defenses over independent defenses, Yoshida set about ushering Japan into the Western world as an independent nation. Assessments of "Yoshida diplomacy," the foreign policies that Yoshida implemented for more than five years, were less than stellar up to the 1960s. The contemporary intellectual climate was not necessary welcome to positive takes on conservative policies, after all. When the politics of leading public servants who had been purged from the government just after the war, such as Shigemitsu Mamoru, Hatoyama Ichirō, and Kishi Nobusuke, had faded and Japan began embarking on its rapid economic growth during the Ikeda Hayato administration, however, observers began to see Yoshida in a different light. Shortly after taking office, Prime Minister Ikeda gave a speech in which he noted the "diplomatic successes of the conservative governments that came before us" and explained that the US-Japan Security Treaty had spurred the Japanese economy forward by entrusting the country's security to an international agreement and thereby minimizing defense expenses. Academic reflections on Yoshida's legacy also painted a more flattering picture. In 1964, Professor Kōsaka Masataka wrote that "the idea that it was the drive of the Japanese people that propelled and supported the country despite poor politics is little more than a myth, a mistaken notion born of the postwar intellectual climate." In Kōsaka's estimation, Yoshida deserved a share of the credit for Japan's economic "boom." By maintaining a tactfully discreet, evasive position between pro-militarization and anti-militarization arguments coming from both sides, Kōsaka asserted, Yoshida made it possible to focus on building domestic and foreign policies around an "econocentric" core that opened doors to prosperity. By the second half of the 1960s, observers had begun referring to three of Yoshida's key tenets—Japan-US security ties (cooperation with the United States), light armament, and a focus on the economy—as the "Yoshida Line." The ensuing decade saw the emergence of the concept of the "Yoshida Doctrine," which attributed a more strategic dimension to Yoshida's policies.

Yoshida's Choices

Observers also began to argue that the successes of the Yoshida Line likely stemmed from Japan's policy of following the United States' lead. The crux of that argument actually rests on two important choices that Yoshida made deliberately. One was his decision to commit Japan's security to the treaty with the United States and allow foreign military personnel to station permanently in Japan—a drastic departure from Japan's prewar approach to national defense, which had adhered to the policy of protecting the country without any outside help. The other was to pursue economic development by promoting exports and attracting foreign capital within the US-led free-trade system. Attempting to secure a foothold in the free-trade framework entailed joining the dollar bloc, which also meant facing a reduction in total trade value—in the 1950s, Japan sent more than 60 percent of its exports to the "sterling bloc" (countries that pegged their currencies to the British pound, many of which were in Southeast Asia).

The Yoshida Line, with its focus on strengthening the economic bonds between Japan and the United States, had its share of critics. Advocates of building a self-sustaining economy criticized Yoshida's policies for making Japan too US-dependent and flooding the country with pointless foreign currency. Yoshida's econocentrism was not just a coincidental product of the times.

The collateral effect of Yoshida's choices, however, was that Japan failed to build stable relationships with its neighbors. On the flip side of the "generous peace," which put Japanese and American interests first, was what some have pointed to as the "absence of Asia" in Yoshida's policies. By essentially ignoring the Asian element, Yoshida's diplomacy glossed over an array of issues that the war had created—and thus made tackling those concerns all the more challenging. Still, Japan worked to fulfill its obligations for war reparations, invested the fruits of its own economic growth in the development of the Asian community, and succeeded in making a sizable impact on the progress of democratization in the region. The implications of the Yoshida Line—a product of the Cold War era—in steering Japan and the rest of the twenty-first-century world are bound to come into question.

Yoshida continued to wield sizable influence after his resignation as prime minister in 1954. Upon his death at the age of eighty-nine, Yoshida became the first postwar prime minister to receive a state funeral.

11-18. Exterior view of the former residence of Yoshida Shigeru

CHAPTER 12

"Autonomous Diplomacy" and Coordinating with the United States

12-1. Ratification of the revised US-Japan Security Treaty

TIMELINE

1954 (Shōwa 29)

March 1	*Daigo Fukuryū Maru* Incident
October 28	Formation of people's conference for restoration of Japan-PRC, Japan–Soviet Union diplomatic relations
November 24	Nihon Minshutō (Japan Democratic Party) founded
December 7	Fifth Yoshida cabinet resigns
December 10	First Hatoyama Ichirō cabinet formed

1955 (Shōwa 30)

January 25	Former Soviet representative in Japan Andrei Ivanovich Dominitski visits Hatoyama's private residence; delivers notes
March 19	Second Hatoyama cabinet formed
April 18–24	Asian-African Conference (Bandung Conference) adopts ten-point declaration
May 4	Third Japan-PRC nongovernmental trade agreement signed
May 14	Signing of Warsaw Pact Treaty
June 1	Japan–Soviet Union negotiations begin in London (through September 21)
July 18–23	Geneva Summit of Big Four leaders
August 29	Foreign Minister Shigemitsu meets US secretary of state Dulles in Washington, suggests revisions to US-Japan Security Treaty ("Kyu-Anpo" Treaty)
October 13	Leftist, Rightist Shakaitō (Socialist Parties) merge to form Nihon Shakaitō (Japan Socialist Party)
November 15	Jiyūtō (Liberal Party) merges with Nihon Minshutō (Japan Democratic Party) (conservative merger) to form Jiyū-Minshutō (Liberal Democratic Party)
November 22	Third Hatoyama cabinet formed

1956 (Shōwa 31)

January 17	Second round of Soviet-Japanese negotiations (through March 20)
February 24	First Secretary Khrushchev of the Soviet Communist Party gives speech denouncing Stalin
April 29	Agriculture Minister Kōno Ichirō visits Moscow for start of fishing negotiations
May 9	Signing of the Reparations Agreement between the Republic of the Philippines and Japan
May 14	Signing of Japanese-Soviet fishery agreement (takes effect December 12)
June 9	Publication of Price Report on Okinawa military base sites; start of island-wide struggles for defense of land
July 26	President Nasser of Egypt declares nationalization of Suez Canal
July 31	Foreign Minister Shigemitsu visits Moscow for start of negotiations on diplomatic relations with Soviet Union; calls for decision on return of two islands on August 12
October 15	Hatoyama visits Moscow for restart of negotiations with USSR
October 19	Signing of the Soviet-Japanese Joint Declaration (effective December 12)
October 23	Hungary Uprising
October 29	Second Middle East War (Suez War)
December 18	UN General Assembly approves admission of Japan
December 23	Ishibashi Tanzan cabinet formed

1957 (Shōwa 32)

January 30	Girard Incident
February 25	First Kishi Nobusuke cabinet fromed
March 25	Treaty of Rome signed, forming European Economic Community (EEC)
April 2–11	First meeting of the Committee for Promotion of ROC-Japan Cooperation

May 20	Japan decides on Basic Policy for Japan's National Defense
May 20	Kishi makes first tour of Southeast Asia, South Asia (through June 4)
June 14	Japan decides on first Defense Buildup Plan
June 16	Kishi visits US, where bilateral statement is issued on June 21 (Kishi-Eisenhower Joint Communiqué heralding a "New Era for US, Japan")
July 6	Signing of Australia-Japan Agreement on Commerce
September 28	Publication of first Diplomatic Bluebook (*Gaikō seisho*)
October 4	Soviet Union succeeds with launch of first satellite, Sputnik
October 4–13	Prime Minister Nehru of India visits Japan
November 18	Kishi makes second tour of Southeast Asia, Oceania (through December 8)

1958 (Shōwa 33)

January 20	Signing of peace treaty, reparations agreement with Indonesia
March 5	Signing of fourth Japan-PRC nongovernmental trade agreement
May 2	Nagasaki Flag Incident (all relations between Japan and PRC severed)
June 12	Second Kishi cabinet formed
August 23	PRC bombards Quemoy (Kinmen) and Matsu Islands (Second Taiwan Strait Crisis)
October 4	Foreign Minister Fujiyama Aiichirō, Ambassador MacArthur begin full negotiations on revision of US-Japan Security Treaty

1959 (Shōwa 34)

February 13	Japan decides Korean residents of Japan permitted to return to North Korea
March 28	Formation of the National Conference for Joint Struggle against Security Treaty Revisions
March 30	In Sunagawa Incident, court declares US bases unconstitutional (Date Judgment)
May 13	Signing of reparations agreement with government of South Vietnam
July 11	Prime Minister Kishi departs on visit to Europe, Central/South America (until August 11)
December 14	Repatriation program for North Koreans (first ship departs from Niigata)

1960 (Shōwa 35)

January 19	Signing of new mutual security treaty between United States and Japan with exchange of notes between Kishi and Herter
January 27	Soviet Union says return of Habomai, Shikotan promised in joint declaration with Japan will not happen unless all foreign troops leave Japanese soil
May 1	US U-2 military aircraft shot down over Soviet Union
May 20	New US-Japan Security Treaty ("Anpo" Treaty) ramrodded through House of Representatives
June 10	Hagerty, press secretary to US president Eisenhower, on visit to Japan, is surrounded by demonstrators, evacuated by helicopter (Hagerty Incident)
June 15	Female college student Kanba Michiko dies as Zengakuren (All-Japan Federation of Students' Self-Governing Associations) occupies Diet, clashes with police
June 16	President Eisenhower's trip to Japan postponed
June 19	New security treaty passes on approval by House of Representatives alone
July 15	Kishi cabinet steps down
July 19	First Ikeda Hayato cabinet formed

1 The Hatoyama Cabinet and "Autonomous Diplomacy"

Negotiations for Restoration of Diplomatic Relations with the Soviet Union: The "1955 System" Is Established

With the Nihon Minshutō (Japan Democratic Party) in charge of government, the Hatoyama cabinet was formed in December 1954. In an address in late January 1955, Hatoyama outlined his policy priorities, stating, "Our biggest challenges . . . are [to achieve] autonomous diplomacy . . . and autonomous reconstruction." He also touched on the subject of revising the Japanese constitution. In the area of diplomacy, thinking mainly of China and the Soviet Union, Hatoyama promised "proactive, autonomous, peaceful foreign relations" aimed at "adjusting relations with countries with which relations have not been restored." The enthusiasm for Hatoyama that swept Japan was a result of the prime minister's emphasis on "autonomy," appealing to the emotional desire for autonomous, independent nationalism that the people held in their hearts.

12-2. The beginning of the Jiyū-Minshutō (Liberal Democratic Party) in 1955

Around the time of the inception of the Hatoyama cabinet, the former Soviet representative to Japan, Andrei Ivanovich Dominitski, reached out directly to Foreign Minister Shigemitsu Mamoru, who spurned his advances. The Soviet Union had declined to sign the Peace Treaty, and in response, Japan had not recognized the Soviet government's legation. Through the mediation of Sugihara Arata, a member of the House of Councillors and a former Foreign Ministry bureaucrat, Dominitski was able to visit Hatoyama secretly at his private residence to deliver a letter saying the Soviet government desired a normalization of diplomatic relations with Japan. Through UN channels, the Foreign Ministry confirmed that this was truly the intent of the Soviet government, and in February the cabinet resolved to begin negotiations.

Actual talks began in June in London. Matsumoto Shun'ichi, member of the House of Councillors and former deputy foreign minister, was fully empowered to negotiate for Japan. The Japan side demanded the return of its Northern Territories that the Soviet Union had occupied at the end of World War II—in other words, South Karafuto (Sakhalin), the Chishima (Kuril) Islands, Habomai, and Shikotan. However, the Soviet side took the position that these matters had been settled by the Yalta Agreement and the Potsdam Declaration. It rejected Japan's claims, saying that Japan should already have abandoned them.

In early August, however, the Soviet ambassador to the United Kingdom, Yakov Malik, said the Soviet Union might be prepared to return Habomai and Shikotan if the conditions were right. Matsumoto hoped to achieve an agreement along these lines, and he checked with Foreign Minister Shigemitsu in Tokyo. Shigemitsu, however, instructed Matsumoto to communicate Japan's position that, while Japan had relinquished its claims to South Sakhalin and the Kuril Islands in the peace treaty, the Southern Kurils (Kunashiri, Etorofu) were not part of the territorial claims that Japan had

12-3. The signing of the Soviet-Japanese Joint Declaration

abandoned under the treaty; rather, they were an inherent part of Japan's territory. In other words, the Soviet Union should return all four islands—Habomai, Shikotan, Kunashiri, and Etorofu—to Japan. In mid-September, the negotiations reached an impasse. At the UN Security Council meeting in December, the Soviet Union vetoed Japan's admission to the United Nations.

While Japan-Soviet Union negotiations were suspended, German chancellor Konrad Adenauer, on a visit to Moscow for quick negotiations, managed to set aside territorial disputes and arrange for the return of 50,000 German prisoners of war. The "Adenauer method" captured the attention of Japan's Ministry of Foreign Affairs.

Around this time, big changes were taking place in domestic politics in Japan. In October 1955, the Leftist and Rightist Shakaitō (Socialist Parties) joined to form the Nihon Shakaitō (Japan Socialist Party). Then, in November, the Nihon Minshutō and the Jiyūtō (Liberal Party) merged to form the Jiyū-Minshutō (Jimintō; Liberal Democratic Party), with Hatoyama becoming the party's first leader in April 1956. With these moves, politics in Japan overcame their earlier instability. The Jimintō held a majority of seats in the House of Representatives, while the Nihon Shakaitō had only half that number. This Jimintō dominance came to be known as the "1955 system," and it persisted until 1993.

However, the merged Jimintō, under Hatoyama, included Jiyūtō members who took a cautious stance on relations with China and the Soviet Union, and the anti-Hatoyama group. As an emergency measure, the Jimintō published its "Rational Adjustments for Japan-Soviet Union Relations." This included a call for the return of all four disputed islands, in line with the policies of the former Jiyūtō.

Restoration of Japanese-Soviet Relations: Japan's Admission to the United Nations

The second round of London talks began in January 1956. The following month, Khrushchev denounced Stalin. Japan hoped the Soviet Union would soften its stance, but by late March the talks were broken off once more. Shigemitsu did not alter his position of the previous year, insisting on the return of the four islands.

At the same time, the Soviet Union unilaterally set up a special maritime zone to limit salmon fishing in northern waters and included the Kuril Islands in this zone. After that, more and more Japanese fishing boats were detained by the Soviet Union, and the repatriation of Japanese detainees in Siberia, which was barely being carried out, was suspended. In response, Hatoyama sent Minister of Agriculture, Forestry and Fisheries Kōno Ichirō to negotiate fishing rights. A fishery treaty was signed, and was to take effect the day Japanese-Soviet relations were restored. The negotiations ended up in line with Soviet expectations, making the normalization of bilateral relations an urgent necessity.

In a third round of discussions, beginning at the end of July in Moscow, Shigemitsu had full authority to negotiate. He focused the negotiations solely on the return of the Southern Kuril Islands, but the Soviets rejected his plea. Khrushchev and Premier

Nikolai Bulganin said directly that the return of Habomai and Shikotan would be their final offer. That caused Shigemitsu to change tack and urge Japan to accept the situation. But Japan's response to this idea was to dig in, and the cabinet did not accept the Soviet proposal.

In mid-August, Shigemitsu traveled to London to attend the conference on the Suez Crisis. There, US secretary of state John Foster Dulles threatened him, saying that if Japan conceded full authority over the Kuril Islands to the Soviet Union, the United States would assert its full authority over Okinawa. When Shigemitsu returned to Japan, he conferred with others about the path forward. He reached a decision to reopen negotiations based on the idea that in the worst case, the territories issue would be shelved, but the state of war would be ended, ambassadors would be exchanged, detainees would be repatriated, the fishery agreement would go into effect, and Japan would get support for its bid to join the United Nations. This was how to restore diplomatic relations, Adenauer-style.

At the final talks in Moscow in October, Hatoyama took part with plenipotentiary powers, despite being ill. The Soviet Union had already been informed of Japan's Adenauer-style strategy, and after several days of talks, the Soviet-Japanese Joint Declaration was signed. The Soviet Union promised to release and repatriate the Japanese detainees it held, and committed to supporting Japan's admission to the United Nations. The joint declaration also stated explicitly that after the conclusion of a peace treaty, the Soviet Union would return Habomai and Shikotan.

In mid-December, on the day the instruments of ratification were exchanged in Tokyo, Japan's admission to the UN was reported by UN headquarters in New York. This was approved December 18 by the UN General Assembly.

Crisis in the Hatoyama Cabinet over Defense Costs

In the allocation of funds for Japan's defense, Japan had agreed to bear part of the cost of hosting US troops. Under the US-Japan Administrative Agreement, Japan was obligated to pay 55.8 billion yen annually. From the time of the Yoshida cabinet,

Hatoyama Ichirō (1883–1959)

Born in Tokyo and educated at Tokyo Imperial University, Hatoyama Ichirō won a seat in the House of Representatives in 1915 as a member of the Seiyūkai. He then went on to serve as chief cabinet secretary under Prime Minister Tanaka Giichi and as minister of education in the Inukai Tsuyoshi and Saitō Makoto cabinets. Around the time he stepped down from the top of the Ministry of Education in 1934, he became a self-appointed "liberal," turned his back on the Imperial Rule Assistance movement, and, after the onset of hostilities with the United States, won a seat in the "Yokusan" election (the 1942 general election that essentially established one-party rule) without a party endorsement. Hatoyama continued his rise in the postwar years, forming the Nihon Jiyūtō (Japan Liberal Party) in November 1945 with Ashida Hitoshi and associates. As party president, Hatoyama led the Nihon Jiyūtō to a majority in the April 1946 general election—but he was forced to concede the premiership to Yoshida Shigeru amid the ensuing purge of public officials. After the lifting of the purge, Hatoyama joined the Jiyūtō (Liberal Party) but took an "anti-Yoshida" stance, arguing for rearmament and the restoration of Japanese-Soviet relations. Opposition to Yoshida gathered momentum and spurred the creation of the Nihon Minshutō (Japan Democratic Party), with Hatoyama appointed party head, in November 1954. When Yoshida resigned a month later, Hatoyama finally secured a clear path to the premiership.

12-4. Hatoyama Ichirō

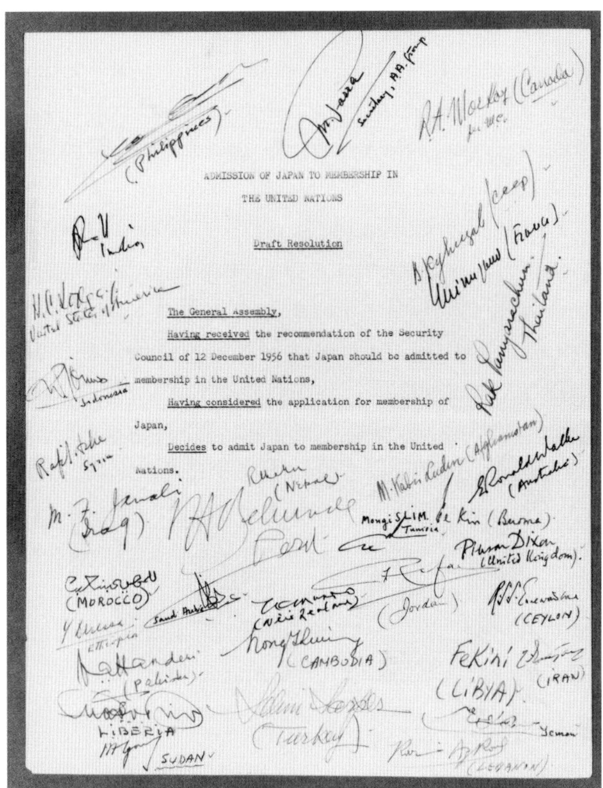

ADMISSION OF JAPAN TO MEMBERSHIP IN THE UNITED NATIONS

Draft Resolution

The General Assembly,

Having received the recommendation of the Security Council of 12 December 1956 that Japan should be admitted to membership in the United Nations,

Having considered the application for membership of Japan,

Decides to admit Japan to membership in the United Nations.

12-5. Document affirming Japan's admission to the United Nations

however, Japan had been trying to reduce this sum. In April 1954, the US side agreed to a 2.5 billion yen reduction, but only for that year. In the general election of February 1955, the governing Nihon Minshutō called for a reduction in Japan's defense payment, promising to spend the savings on housing construction. But that promise became a problem.

Hatoyama was inclined to compromise with China, and did not favor an increase in Japan's defense capabilities. In an effort to manipulate him, the United States ignored his call for a reduction in Japan's defense costs. The Hatoyama cabinet sent Shigemitsu to the United States to probe Washington's thinking, but the United States rejected Japan's plea. The House of Representatives' Foreign Affairs Committee passed a resolution calling the Hatoyama cabinet's efforts a foreign policy failure. The Hatoyama cabinet was in a bind. It told US ambassador John Allison that unless it could reach a compromise with the United States, it would not be able to draw up a budget, and the government would collapse, allowing the Shakaitō to take power. Allison demanded that Japan not engage in talks for a third Japan-China nongovernmental trade agreement.

In early April, the US adopted a new policy with respect to Japan: To allow the stabilization of Japan's politics and the strengthening of its economy to continue unimpeded, it would no longer pressure Japan to increase its defense capabilities. This policy change was reflected in the negotiations regarding the allocation of defense costs, culminating in United States concessions and a compromise solution. The Hatoyama cabinet just managed to draw up a one-trillion yen budget, avoiding a political collapse. As a result, the problem of allocating defense costs helped to stabilize the shaky Japan-US relationship, but at the same time it put the brakes on improving Japan's relationship with China.

Shigemitsu Visits the United States: Security Treaty Revisions Are Considered

The aim of turning the Security Treaty between Japan and the United States into a mutual defense treaty was a clear part of the Nihon Minshutō's policy platform, and also a personal goal for Shigemitsu himself. In preparation for a visit to the United States in the summer of 1955, Shigemitsu asked Treaties Bureau head Shimoda Takezō to draft a proposal for revising the treaty. The Shimoda Draft (Mutual Defense Treaty Draft) was created to be similar to a NATO-style mutual defense treaty with a geographically defined region for joint defense. It would apply to territories of and regions administered by the two nations in the Western Pacific. While limited in geographic scope, the agreement would provide for "undertaking an obligation for sending troops abroad."

The Shimoda Draft also foresaw an eventual

withdrawal of all US troops from Japan. It is not certain whether Hatoyama was aware of the proposal, but it was certainly in line with the policy guidelines calling for Japan to develop defensive capabilities commensurate with its national strength, and for the early withdrawal of US troops from Japan.

When Shigemitsu met Dulles in the United States in August 1955, he commented that in the event of an attack on the US territory of Guam, Japan would confer with the United States about whether it could dispatch troops for its own defense. Dulles responded that he could not see that interpretation of Japan's constitution, and he warned against any rash switch to a mutual defense treaty.

Kishi Nobusuke, who accompanied Shigemitsu as secretary-general of the Nihon Minshutō, took a different stance from Shigemitsu. During the Shigemitsu-Dulles talks and other unofficial meetings, Kishi insisted that a powerful and stable administration—one that would bring stability to the peoples' lives—would be a strong bulwark against Communism. Kishi's thinking was that, rather than hastily revising the security treaty, it would be more important first to consolidate conservative forces and stabilize the economy. This view was favorably received by the US side, and helped propel Kishi to the premiership.

Trade Problems with China

Shortly after becoming prime minister, Hatoyama had expressed a desire to improve relations with Communist China, but Dulles soon sent him a note aimed at curbing that desire. Soon after that, in March 1955, a group of Chinese trade officials arrived in Japan for the signing of the third Japan-China nongovernmental trade agreement and the start of negotiations with the Association for the Promotion of International Trade, among other matters. The main focus points were the establishment of a trade representative office, as stipulated in a memo tied to the second bilateral trade agreement of 1953, and the establishment of direct methods of payment or settlement between the central banks. Both required government approval and helped pave the way to the bilateral agreement.

Hatoyama had made it clear in advance that he was willing to approve the establishment of the trade representative office, but only if it was to be a private entity, not a part of the government. The trade agreement was signed in May, but the trade office, direct payments, and the intergovernmental agreement were all left for future efforts. There was little to distinguish the third agreement from the second. Despite Hatoyama's desire, with the restraints imposed by the US, there were limits to how much Japan could trade with China, and things would have to be built up one layer at a time.

The Asian-African Conference (Bandung Conference)

In April 1955, representatives of twenty-nine nations—mainly emerging nations of Asia and Africa—gathered in Bandung, Indonesia for the Asian-African Conference. This was an unprecedented international assembly representing the emergence of a new force in international politics. The idea for the Bandung Conference had been conceived in the spring of 1954 at the Colombo Conference of leaders of India, Burma, Ceylon, Pakistan, and Indonesia. These five countries, which came to be known as the "Colombo Group," were the standard-bearers for non-alignment in Asia. During the Cold War, in particular, Indonesia felt the threats lapping at its shores, and it relied on this group for solidarity.

China was also invited to participate in the Bandung Conference. China and India had reached agreement on "five principles of peaceful coexistence." These five principles were nothing particularly new; they included tenets like respect for each other's territory and sovereignty and a mutual pledge of nonaggression. But the China-India agreement laid the groundwork for broader support for mutual coexistence of nations with different political systems. At Bandung, the number of principles was increased to ten, with the original five at the core. Some countries, such as Pakistan, were not enthusiastic about China being invited, but they agreed on the condition that Japan also participate as a representative of the group of free nations that were standing up to China.

For Hatoyama and his administration, participation in this conference was an act symbolizing "autonomous diplomacy," in marked contrast to the Yoshida administration and its dependence on the United States. This was an opportunity for Hatoyama to show to those both inside and outside the country that Japan was a "part of Asia." The problem was how to reconcile this with Japan's ongoing coordination and cooperation with the United States. Foreign Minister Shigemitsu welcomed the Bandung Conference in a policy speech, saying, "Asia is Japan's ancestral home. The people of Asia have been liberated from the colonialism of the past, and it is Japan's fervent wish that they develop into free and independent nations." Shigemitsu, however, had his anti-Communist dimension, and his fear of "East Asia turning Red" overpowered his consideration for Asian nationalism.

In the end, to "prevent the conference from being led in an undesirable direction," Shigemitsu told the United States about Japan's plans to participate. Secretary of State Dulles encouraged the idea. While the United States was concerned that this international conference would create an opportunity for China to strengthen its influence in Asia and create a new nonaligned, anti-American bloc, Japan's participation helped to assuage those fears.

The Japanese government's instructions to its delegation, reflecting the US concerns, limited the areas of Japan's active participation to economic cooperation and cultural exchange. This would be the first time since World War II that Japan had participated in a major international conference. Its delegation would be led not by the prime minister or the foreign minister, but by Takasaki Tatsunosuke, head of the Economic Council Agency.

12-6. The Asian-African Conference (Bandung Conference)

At the main conference, which began in mid-April, the Japan delegation focused its attention on economics and culture, as instructed. The "Proposal on Economic Cooperation" set out the adjustments that would be needed in multilateral development plans. These ideas were an extension of concepts dating back to the Yoshida administration, and the Southeast Asian nations that still gave priority to ties with their former colonial rulers were not so enthusiastic about these ideas. In the area of cultural cooperation, Japan proposed an "AA Regional Cultural Prize," among other ideas, but in the end this, too, was put off as a matter for future efforts.

Regardless, Japan's actions at the Bandung Conference took place at the intersection of its identity as part of Asia and its cooperation with the United States. In the final analysis, it furthered neither of these ends; in fact, it was rather passive. Japan was called upon to hammer out a diplomatic posture that would allow it to act at the crossroads of these two dimensions.

The Bandung Conference also represented Japan's

first attempt to interact with China at a ministerial level. Upon meeting Zhou Enlai, Takasaki spoke of his desire to advance the economic relationship between Japan and China, divorced from political issues. He said, "I apologize from my heart for all the trouble my country caused your country during the war." The two men promised to pursue further dialogue, but that commitment was never realized.

2 The Kishi Cabinet and Asia Diplomacy

Kishi's Visit to Southeast Asia and Development Planning

The Hatoyama cabinet stepped down in November 1956, followed in December by the first election of a party president from the Jimintō. Kishi Nobusuke was the favorite, but the campaign came down to a struggle between small factions, and Ministry of International Trade and Industry (MITI) minister Ishibashi Tanzan came out on top, forming his cabinet in December 1956. Ishibashi's main policy aims were to promote Japan's autonomy in diplomatic relations and to expand its economic relationship with China. However, the political footing of his administration was weak. To secure greater stability, he would have had to dissolve the Diet and hold a general election, which required a national campaign. Ishibashi therefore campaigned all over the country. Whether for that reason or some other, in late January 1957 he suffered a stroke, and the following month he had to step down. Kishi was promoted from interim prime minister to prime minister, while simultaneously serving as minister for foreign affairs. All members of Ishibashi's cabinet stayed on.

As prime minister, Kishi's top diplomatic priorities were to achieve greater equality in Japan-US relations and to update the US-Japan Security Treaty. He planned a visit to the United States to pursue these goals. Before going, however, he spent roughly two weeks visiting six nations of Southeast Asia. For Kishi, strengthening relations with Asian nations was a means of paving the way for negotiations with the United States.

The Southeast Asia development fund was a central concept of Kishi's administration. It was

Kishi Nobusuke (1896–1987)

A native of Yamaguchi Prefecture, Kishi Nobusuke graduated from Tokyo Imperial University in 1920 and took a position at the Ministry of Agriculture and Commerce. He later served in the Ministry of Commerce and Industry before retiring from service in 1936, after which he made his way to Manchuria and became the vice-director of Manchukuo's Ministry of Industry. Kishi was appointed to the Tōjō Hideki administration in 1941, serving as minister of commerce and industry from 1941 to 1943, and was charged with war crimes after the war. Upon his eventual release in 1952, Kishi joined forces with Shigemitsu Mamoru and other politicians to establish the Japan Reconstruction League, for which he served as chairman, and won election to the House of Representatives the following year. He was also one of the founding members of the Nihon Minshutō (Japan Democratic Party), along with Hatoyama Ichirō and associates, serving as the party's secretary-general and bolstering Japan's conservative bloc. Kishi's climb up the political ranks continued, as he became foreign minister under Ishibashi Tanzan at the end of 1956, ascended to the premiership the following February, and remained in office through July 1960.

12-7. Kishi Nobusuke

The Speech Envisioning a "Bridge between East and West"

In December 1956, Japan finally became a member of the United Nations. It was on that occasion, at the UN General Assembly on December 18, that Foreign Minister Shigemitsu Mamoru gave what would later be referred to as the "bridge between East and West" speech. The address contained many revealing glimpses of how Shigemitsu conceived of international politics.

One of the themes he addressed was nationalism. "Nationalism thrived in Eastern Europe after the First World War and has risen in the Arab and Asian regions since the Second World War," Shigemitsu noted. "It is a natural process in the liberation of mankind," he explained, saying that he believed the sentiment "should be fostered with understanding, but . . . should avoid running into excesses or into extreme nationalism." That basic idea, together with his argument that open, UN-driven initiatives for resource development would build "a firm basis for peace and justice," captures the essence of Shigemitsu's perspective on international politics with a focus on the opening of resources throughout the world.

At the end of his speech, Shigemitsu delivered a clear description of what he believed Japan's role would be in the global community: "The substance of Japan's political, economic, and cultural life is the product of the fusion within the last century of the civilizations of the Orient and the Occident. In a way, Japan may well be regarded as a bridge between the East and the West."

In this vision that Shigemitsu proclaimed with a sense of pride, Japan's role was not to span the gap between the clashing poles of the Cold War. Rather, he had a different, dual role in mind: Japan as a bridge between Western civilization and Asian civilization, on the one hand, and Japan as a bridge between the developed world and the developing world on the other. For the Ministry of Foreign Affairs, the "bridge" metaphor oriented Japan in a coordinating, mediating position between the West and Asia, where neutralist stances and anti-colonial movements were gaining steam. The core idea was that if Asian nationalism were to begin verging on extremism, Japan would embody a consistent diplomatic policy by offering benevolent advice and promoting mutual understanding. In the realm of Japanese foreign affairs, then, efforts to reconcile the North-South problem (the preponderance of developed countries in the northern parts of the world versus the tendency of countries in the southern parts to be undeveloped) with respect to the nationalist context took on enormous importance. Officials figured that Japan's extensive experience with Asian nationalism could help moderate nationalist sentiments in the region. With this awareness, the vision of a "bridge between East and West" became a diplomatic concept.

"Japan's mission," Prime Minister Kishi Nobusuke declared, "is to restrain emerging Asian countries from hurtling toward radical extremes in the name of semi-colonialism and help them develop in harmony with the West. It is through this policy that we aim to eliminate the dangers of rampant nationalism." That sense of responsibility, which established the foundation for the Kishi administration's relations with Southeast Asia, shaped Japan's initiatives to benefit the free world—an approach that the Western community, including the United States, supported well into the 1960s.

feared that Asian nations, having attained political independence but still being economically weak, would be led down the road to Communism. To prevent that by linking Asian nations together and fostering overall economic development, a framework for economic cooperation was needed. All Japanese prime ministers since Yoshida had been focused on this problem. The concept of a development fund was based on the assumption that the United States would provide funding. It had been proposed several times during the Yoshida and Hatoyama administrations, with only minor changes distinguishing the different proposals, but each time it was rejected by both the United States and by the nations of Asia. Kishi took up the issue again, feeling pressured by the possibility that Southeast Asian nations might come under the sway of China's economic influence.

On his second tour of Southeast Asia, in November and December of 1957, Kishi persisted in focusing on the idea of a Southeast Asia development fund. No matter how much Japan wanted to push for comprehensive regional cooperation, the Southeast Asian nations continued to show a strong preference for bilateral aid, holding fast to a deep mistrust of Japan. They could not get past their concerns that the economy of the region would take second place in a system of cooperation led by Japan. The US view mattered as well, but the United States was unable to support Japan's comprehensive approach, which would certainly involve enormous sums of money.

Nehru and Sukarno

On Kishi's two trips through Southeast Asia, his main focus points were India and Indonesia. On his first visit, all eyes were on his meeting with Prime Minister Nehru of India, because of Nehru's non-aligned stance. Nehru did not agree with the idea of a development fund, viewing it as just a variation

Kishi Nobusuke and Asian Studies

In late August 1957, Prime Minister Kishi met with a group of Asia scholars and made the following remarks about "establishing a field of Asian studies."

> If Japan is to assist in building a new Asia, it will not be able to make any valuable contribution toward that cause if it neglects to study and understand Asia. We must first establish a "framework for Asian studies." Japan was once the world's premier force in Asian studies. Westerners used to come to Japan for insights into Asia. Given the current state of the discipline, however, Japan must now redouble its efforts to further its expertise in a field that has remained forgotten for far too long.

Kishi's drive to follow through on that pursuit led him to fund a variety of Asian-research programs, the core of which was the Asian Affairs Research Society. The group was the brainchild of Fujisaki Nobuyuki, a former employee in the Manchukuo administration, who launched the organization with a group of like-minded colleagues in 1951 to help meet what he felt to be an "urgent need" for studies pertaining to Asia. Rallying around Fujisaki's call were the likes of Itagaki Yoichi, a student of Akamatsu Kaname who had long been hoping for a resumption of Asian research activity; Hara Kakuten, a researcher on the Economic Stabilization Board; and Ōkita Saburō, another Economic Stabilization Board researcher. In securing its funding, the group received a pledge of financial assistance from Kishi himself, who had just reentered the political field after the lifting of the public-official purge. He also took charge of procuring funding for the group, and advised the organization to become an incorporated entity.

The Asian Affairs Research Society would eventually become the official research wing of the larger Asia Society, which originated in 1954. While the Asia Society's founding purpose was to handle reparations to countries in such a way that would "avoid making economic cooperation appear to be a form of economic aggression on the part of Japan," Kishi saw the organization as more than just a means of dealing with reparation obligations—in his eyes, the Asia Society represented a vital foundation for Asian diplomacy that would "harness the ingenuity of the private sector into fruitful people's diplomacy between Japan and the nations of Asia." The Asia Society ultimately folded in 1958, but its legacy continued on in the activities of the Institute of Developing Economies (which inherited the group's research division) and the Overseas Technical Cooperation Agency (now the Japan International Cooperation Agency), which took up the Asia Society's economic and technical aid programs.

Of all the Asia Society's different projects, the activities of the research division merit special mention. Not only was the research division responsible for numerous publications and research tours abroad, but it also sent research teams on a variety of missions, organized public lectures, sponsored a host of seminars, and engaged in awareness and publicity initiatives. The Asia Society's research division also had an official journal, *Ajia mondai* (Asian Affairs; 1952–58), which dated back to the days of the Asian Affairs Research Society. Though primarily policy-oriented in its content, the publication devoted space to exploratory reports on potential targets for economic assistance and dealt with a variety of themes; topics ranged from agricultural issues and possible joint markets to nationalism, political frameworks, and plans for economic development. The journal's contributing authors were an impressively diverse group of experts from academia, government circles, the business world, international organizations, and journalism, highlighting how the field of Asian studies had developed a sprawling scholarly network.

on other forms of US assistance. After Kishi and Nehru spoke, however, Kishi expressed his gratitude for the signing of the momentous Treaty of Peace between Japan and India, and for the position taken by Justice Pal in the Tokyo Trials, where Pal had held that the Japanese defendants were not guilty. Nehru responded by holding a welcome party and telling the assembled crowd that Japan's victory in the Russo-Japanese War had had a major impact on India's independence movement.

In October 1957, at Kishi's invitation, Nehru traveled to Japan, where he visited Hiroshima and made an anti-nuclear speech. Unlike Yoshida and Hatoyama, Kishi opposed nuclear testing by the United States and the United Kingdom. In his meeting with Nehru, the two men spoke of Indo-Japanese cooperation to ban nuclear testing.

Kishi also responded to India's requests for yen-denominated loans. The loan to India in 1958 was the first yen-denominated loan Japan made in the postwar period, and loans to South Vietnam and Pakistan soon followed. Yen loans were reputed to be a means of promoting exports, but they also marked the start of economic cooperation offered voluntarily by the Japanese government, unlike reparations, which were obligatory.

When Kishi visited Indonesia in late November, in a single meeting with President Sukarno he achieved a breakthrough in long-stalled negotiations regarding payment of reparations. This move was a political decision by Kishi, made without approval from the cabinet. Foreign Minister Fujiyama Aiichirō traveled to Indonesia the following January for the signing of the reparations agreement and the peace treaty. By that time, however, the Sukarno administration, under attack from separatists in Sumatra, was on the verge of collapse. The United States, worried about Communist advances, leaned toward supporting the separatists, and Japan, which was aligned with the United States, had to choose whether to support Sukarno.

The Kishi cabinet concluded it would be to Japan's benefit if Sukarno could unify Indonesia under his rule, so Japanese policy steered a course of strengthening the foundations of Sukarno's administration by quickly concluding the reparations agreement and moving steadily toward the payment of reparations. April 1958 brought the ratification of the reparations agreement, the economic cooperation agreement, and the peace treaty. For the Japanese government, these treaties and agreements represented a way to ensure political and economic stability in Indonesia while preventing it from leaving the "free world." After that, Japan continued to support Sukarno right up until the September 30th Movement in 1965.

12-8. Prime Minister Nehru of India visits Japan

Japan's Relations with China and South Korea Reach an Impasse

Progress was made in resolving the reparations issue, but headway was slow on other adjustments to relations with China and South Korea. From the moment he took office, Kishi was intent on finding a route to a breakthrough in relations with South Korea. By the end of 1957, after the outrage caused by Kubota Kan'ichirō's remarks regarding Korea in

The Three Principles of Japanese Diplomacy

In September 1957, the Ministry of Foreign Affairs issued its first postwar Diplomatic Bluebook (*Gaikō seisho*), officially titled *Waga gaikō no kinkyō* (Recent developments in Japanese foreign relations). The document laid out "three principles for diplomatic activity": (1) conforming to a United Nations–centric doctrine, (2) cooperating with free nations, and (3) maintaining Japan's position as a member of the Asian community. None of the three principles was particularly new, however. In November 1952, shortly after Japan regained its independence, Prime Minister Yoshida Shigeru cast his vision for the country's international role as "working together with the United Nations and democracies across the globe to maintain world peace . . . and, above all, contributing to fuller peace and stability in Asia." Essentially, Yoshida made cooperation and collaboration with three partners—the UN, the Western Bloc, and Asia—the guiding tenets for Japanese diplomacy. According to Kuriyama Takakazu, former vice-minister for foreign affairs, the element tying the three principles together was international cooperation; that approach grew out of Japan's remorse for the self-righteous "unilateral diplomacy" that had colored the years leading up to World War II.

The three principles have taken on different connotations as Japan saw its standing in the international arena improve. While Japan has continually maintained its collaborative relationship with the United Nations, elevating its position within the UN has become an increasingly important focal point. In its partnerships with the Western world, Japan's core objective has gone from pursuing the common interest of containing the Communist Bloc to cooperating with Western industrialized nations. The principle of collaborating with Asia, too, has assumed a slightly different shade of meaning: instead of putting the priority on fostering stability and prosperity in Asia, Japan has started to focus more intently on blazing trails for regional collaboration across the Asia-Pacific region.

For former ambassador to the United Nations Saitō Shizuo, who helped formulate the three principles, the policy "enabled Japan to balance a UN-centric focus and a collaborative relationship with the West by acting as a bridge in the context of the North-South problem." Wedged between the neutrality-focused Asian zone and the Western

1953 and efforts to impose claims on South Korea had been cleared out of the way, he succeeded in reopening dialogue between Japan and South Korea. At the same time, there were large numbers of Koreans in Japan who wished to return to North Korea, and in February 1959 the Kishi cabinet voted to allow them to do so for humanitarian reasons. The first repatriation ship left Niigata in December 1959. Over time, more than 90,000 Koreans and their Japanese spouses left for North Korea. South Korea objected to this, and talks between Japan and South Korea broke off again in 1960.

In September 1957, talks concerning a fourth Japan-China nongovernmental trade agreement opened in Beijing. Problems arose regarding the opening of trade representative offices in each nation and the fingerprinting of individuals connected to a planned trade fair for Chinese goods. After Japan was forced to make concessions, such as exempting such individuals from fingerprinting, the fourth trade agreement was signed in March 1958. However, Taiwan and the United States objected to the agreement, which they said elevated the trade representative offices to the status of embassies, giving diplomatic privileges to staff, and gave de facto national recognition to China. Kishi wrote to Chiang Kai-shek, stating that the agreement did not recognize China as a nation, granted no special rights to China's trade representative office, and did not allow the display of China's flag.

In May 1958, the "Nagasaki Flag Incident" occurred, in which a drunken Japanese man tore down a five-starred red flag of China on display at a show of Chinese goods in a department store in Nagasaki. Though the man was punished for obstruction of commerce, removal of signs, and defamation, China was incensed that he had not been charged with damaging its national symbol. China decided there would be no further interaction with Japan, ruling out even trade and cultural exchanges.

Bloc, Japan's role was to buffer friction and ease tension.

A good example of the "bridge" concept in practice was Japan's response to the Suez Crisis, which began when the Egyptian government announced in 1956 that it would be nationalizing the Suez Canal. The resulting standoff pitted the West, which demanded that the canal remain an international property, against Arab nationalism—and the tensions appeared increasingly likely to break out into a full-blown war. Japan, which was on the verge of joining the United Nations, decided to try to reconcile the mounting clash through UN channels. The attempt came to nothing in the end, as Israel, the United Kingdom, and France launched a joint military operation in Egypt at the end of October. However, it did exemplify Japan's aim of "bridging the gap" as an intermediary between emerging nationalism and the West, ultimately serving to protect Western interests.

Japan's response to the issue of China's representation in the United Nations, meanwhile, revealed that the three principles were fraught with contradictions when it came to the UN-centric policy. The Kishi Nobusuke cabinet's approach to the situation was to "address the Communist China issue in line with the UN policy"—but the United Nations when Japan joined was home to a growing number of countries that recognized Communist China but not Taiwan, with a host of newly independent states driving the count up. For the Ministry of Foreign Affairs, the situation presented an important choice. Aligning with the United States and holding fast to a flat-out refusal to admit China to the United Nations—or not recognize China at all, for that matter—may have fallen largely in line with Japan's core policies, but it was not necessarily the most advisable approach. Another viable option was to adopt a "two-China" policy under which Japan would both ensure Taiwan's security and keep the path to recognizing China open.

Whatever the case, the growing presence of emerging Asian and African countries in the United Nations made the contradictions between Japan's UN-centric stance and collaborative ties with the Western Bloc all the more apparent. The three principles were absent from the third edition of the Diplomatic Bluebook and have remained so since.

3 Pursuing Equality between the United States and Japan

The Girard Incident

At the end of January 1957, just before the start of the Kishi administration, a US soldier on a base in Sōmagahara, Gunma Prefecture, shot and killed a Japanese woman who was picking up shell casings. This event, which came to be known as the Girard Incident, fanned the flames of anti-base sentiments that had sprung up in various places across the country, such as the Sunagawa Struggle opposing the expansion of the Tachikawa Base the previous fall. The anti-base movement was aimed directly at the "inequity" of the security treaty and the administrative agreement. In Okinawa, opposition to US bases had been heating up since 1956, with island-wide struggles taking place to defend land that was being bought up for use as bases.

Given these movements within Japan, people in the US government and the US embassy began to worry that Japan was leaving the community of free nations to join the non-aligned group. The establishment of the conservative Jimintō did nothing to allay fears that Japan was drifting toward non-alignment. The only effective means of dispelling these fears would be to rewrite or readjust the security treaty so that it would enhance the standing of the conservative administration.

Kishi's Visit to the United States and the Joint Japan-US Statement

At the end of May, before Kishi's visit to the United States, his cabinet approved the Basic Policy for Japan's National Defense, and then in June it passed the first "Defense Buildup Plan."

The former discusses Japan's support for the United Nations, its high degree of respect for patriotism, and its dependence on its bilateral security agreement with the United States, saying Japan would "gradually assemble effective defensive capabilities, as much as it needs for its own defense." Based on that document, the Defense Buildup Plan represented Japan's first stipulation of a medium-term self-defense plan, including amassing a 180,000-member Ground Self-Defense Force in three years, beginning in 1958.

Proclaiming a "new era for the US and Japan" as his slogan, Kishi traveled in mid-June to the United States, where he met with President Eisenhower and Secretary of State Dulles. He made clear his support for the existing security treaty, but said he hoped for a reformulation of that treaty to reflect the growth of Japan's own self-defense capabilities and the possibility of Japan's participation in collective security efforts by the United Nations. His proposed key points of such a revision included the establishment of a mechanism for prior consultation regarding the use of US bases in Japan, the inclusion of some sort of expiry date for the treaty, and the return of

The Issue of Banning Nuclear Testing

The Aftermath of the *Daigo Fukuryū Maru* Incident

The American hydrogen bomb test at Bikini Atoll in the South Pacific on March 1, 1954, exposed the crew of the *Daigo Fukuryū Maru*, a Japanese vessel that was operating nearby, to substantial amounts of radiation, and ultimately led to the death of Kuboyama Aikichi, the boat's captain. The incident proved to be a powerful catalyst for the movement to prohibit atomic and hydrogen bombs. One campaign against nuclear arms started out as a signature-collecting drive by the "Sugi-no-Ko Kai" (Children of the Cedars), a book club based in Suginami, Tokyo, and proceeded to grow into a massive movement; with physicist Yukawa Hideki and others furthering and popularizing the cause, the initiative eventually gathered over twenty million signatures. The Japan Council against Atomic and Hydrogen Bombs (Gensuikyō) also formed in 1955, adding to an increasingly anti-nuclear public discourse that transcended party lines and sectarian affiliations.

In tandem with the growing antagonism against US bases in Japan, the anti-nuclear movement cultivated "anti-American sentiment" throughout the country—and it was enough to get Washington to take notice. In May 1954, US ambassador to Japan John Allison warned the US government that Japan was gradually moving toward a "neutralist" or "pacifist" position; although it was far from the dominant discourse, the shift signified a change that could pull the country toward an anti-American stance. Taking that cautionary advice and recognizing other factors pointing to a need for action, the US government began reworking its policy on Japan in the spring of 1955. The resulting "New Look" on Japan stipulated that bolstering Japan-US relations and preventing Japan from leaning toward neutrality would require an effort to help stabilize the Japanese political environment through the formation of a moderate conservative bloc.

Inconsistent Policy on Nuclear Weapons

The surging anti-nuclear movement among the general public did not, however, translate directly into an anti-nuclear foreign policy. Having just entrusted the country's safety to the protective shield of the American "nuclear umbrella" under the US-Japan Security Treaty before its revision, the Japanese government was in no feasible position to demand that the United States or other countries with nuclear capabilities put an end to their nuclear testing. Foreign Minister Okazaki Katsuo actually advocated for nuclear testing in an address to the Diet in April 1954, explaining that the current peace arrangement rested on a "balance of power" and that nuclear testing was essential to the defense of the free world.

After the resignation of the Yoshida Shigeru cabinet, however, the Shakaitō and like-minded reformist factions spearheaded several successful efforts to pass parliamentary resolutions seeking bans or suspensions of nuclear testing. The Japanese government echoed that shift, too, by calling for a halt to nuclear testing on the international stage. In February 1956, the "Resolution Demanding a Ban on Atomic and Hydrogen Bomb Testing" passed both houses of the Diet. The government then sent the resolution to the United Kingdom, which was planning to go ahead with a hydrogen bomb test. The anti-nuclear stance was a particularly powerful element of Japanese diplomacy under the administration of Prime Minister Kishi Nobusuke, whose

Okinawa and Ogasawara (Bonin) to Japanese rule within ten years, among other items. Kishi had informed Ambassador MacArthur of these items prior to his visit, and the United States received these ideas favorably, but concrete discussions were not held. Agreement was reached, however, on the establishment of the Japan-United States Security Consultative Committee. The visit produced a joint Japan-US statement in which the United States welcomed Japan's Defense Buildup Plan, and even touched upon the idea of a speedy withdrawal of US ground troops. As Dulles was disinclined to take up the issue of the return of Okinawa and Ogasawara at that time, the joint statement merely reaffirmed the US position that "Japan retained latent sovereignty over the islands."

Fujiyama Joins the Cabinet: Kishi's Decision

In July 1957, after his trip to the United States, Kishi reshuffled his cabinet, replacing all the ministers to create a lineup that was more to his liking. For the position of foreign minister, he chose his old friend,

focus in foregrounding Japan's opposition to testing had to do with his aims of wresting leadership of the anti-nuclear movement back from the reformists and giving the Jimintō a broader base of domestic support.

Japan also solidified its position as a leading anti-nuclear voice in the global community. At its General Assembly in November 1961, the United Nations passed the "Declaration on the prohibition of the use of nuclear and thermonuclear weapons"—and Japan was the only nation in the Western bloc to vote in favor of the measure. In the late 1950s to the early 1960s, a litany of resolutions championing bans on nuclear testing and the use of nuclear weapons was passed with support from across the political spectrum. However, the 1961 vote would be the first and last time that the Japanese government endorsed a UN resolution banning nuclear weapons amid the Cold War. As the Jimintō regime established a stable foundation, the number of opposition parties proliferated, and schisms began to develop in the movement against nuclear weapons. The movement began to see its effect on discussions of nuclear disarmament and nonproliferation diplomacy diminish. Gradually, the Japanese government shifted its focus from achieving the ideal of nuclear abolition to pursuing a more realistic approach with an emphasis on its role in nuclear deterrence.

The Peaceful Use of Nuclear Power

On the other hand, the government took up the task of developing Japan's nuclear-energy capabilities, making a clear distinction between the "peaceful use" and "military use" of atomic power. Propelling that effort forward was the Atomic Energy Basic Act, which passed in December 1955. Article 2 of that law stipulated that Japan would limit its use of nuclear power to peaceful purposes, effectively establishing what would become one of Japan's three non-nuclear principles—the "non-production of nuclear weapons."

12-9. The *Daigo Fukuryū Maru*, contaminated by US atomic tests on Bikini Atoll business leader Fujiyama Aiichirō. It would not be until May 1958, however, after a House of Representatives election and the formation of his second cabinet, that Kishi would really grapple with the problem of revising the US-Japan Security Treaty.

During this interval, early in 1958, Ambassador MacArthur moved before the Japan side did, and advised Dulles regarding the proposed new treaty modeled on mutual aid. To prevent Japan from going down the path of non-alignment, MacArthur argued that the security treaty should be revised, and that Japan should be treated as a full and equal partner like any other US ally. Late in August, MacArthur met with Kishi and Fujiyama and proposed two options: either leave the security treaty as it was and resolve differences through side agreements; or revise the existing agreement as much as possible within the framework of Japan's current constitution. Kishi expressed a preference for a major revision, responding, "A fundamental reworking [of the treaty] would spark a major debate in the Diet. But I think such a debate would be a good thing." Passing the agreement through a harsh debate process would, he felt, "put Japan-US relations on a firm foundation for a very long time."

For the Ministry of Foreign Affairs, which envisioned "side agreements" that would avoid a debate in the Diet, this was a surprising decision.

Start of Revision Negotiations

Negotiations to revise the US-Japan Security Treaty began in October 1958 in Tokyo. The US side presented a draft of a new treaty, along with a proposal for prior consultation. (See sidebar below.)

One point of contention in the proposed new treaty was the geographic scope of the Japan-US joint defense zone. In the US draft, the joint defense zone included "US territories in the Pacific region." In a literal interpretation of "mutual aid," if the US

Prior Consultation and the Secret Japan-US Agreement

In the fall of 1958, Japan and the United States began negotiating revisions to their security treaty. Throughout the talks, the Japanese side continually underscored the need for "prior consultation" between the parties in two sets of circumstances. First were cases where the United States was to use US bases in Japan for purposes other than the defense of Japan; for Japan, prior consultation would make it possible to avoid the risk of being "entangled" in a war against its wishes. The second set of circumstances involved the deployment or introduction of nuclear weapons into Japan. If the United States was indeed committed to considering the "special sensitivities of the Japanese people regarding nuclear weapons," a framework for prior consultation was an obvious necessity. With lawmakers in the Diet wrangling over the two issues even before the negotiations began, the Ministry of Foreign Affairs was hoping to reach some kind of agreement with the United States on the matter.

The negotiations thus progressed along two tracks: defining what the actual terms of the new security treaty would be and deciding how to create a structure for prior consultation. While the Japanese side premised its proposal on ensuring prior consultation for the two sets of circumstances via an exchange of notes for public release, the US side was hoping for a confidential agreement; that way, there would be no concerns about a prior consultation potentially denying the US military the ability to depart from its bases or introduce nuclear weapons in an emergency situation. The delegations went back and forth over the terms, trying to make adjustments that would bring about a satisfactory result. Ultimately, the two sides finalized the "Kishi-Herter Exchange of Notes" (January 1960), which stipulated that both of the cases described above would be subject to prior consultation, and also signed two undisclosed (confidential) documents on situations that would not require prior consultation. Foreign Minister Fujiyama Aiichirō and Ambassador Douglas MacArthur signed the two confidential documents in January 1960.

One was the "Korea Minutes," an agreement that allowed for the US military to take immediate action from its Japanese bases without the need for prior consultation with Japan in the event of an "emergency" on the Korean territory of Guam, for example, were attacked, this would be recognized as a threat to Japan's peace and security, and Japan would be obliged to provide support for the US military. However, for Japan to dispatch troops to Guam would clearly be an instance of sending troops abroad, which would certainly be a violation of its constitution, even if it were an exercise of Japan's right to collective defense. Until this point in time, Japan's government had interpreted the constitution to mean that the exercise of the right to collective defense was not permitted. But Ambassador MacArthur added the restrictive words "in accordance with constitutional procedures," explaining that Japan was not expected to do anything that was unconstitutional. The Japanese negotiators, however, were certain that the idea of sending troops abroad would subject the government to criticism in the Diet, and therefore asked that the draft be rewritten to define the geographic scope of the joint defense zone as "areas under the administration of Japan."

12-10. Fujiyama Aiichirō

In the first US draft, Okinawa and Ogasawara were included in the geographic scope, and Kishi and Fujiyama agreed to this. They later realized, however, that the inclusion of Okinawa and Ogasawara might trigger calls for the return of these islands to Japanese administration. Moreover, the cabinet had already been shaken by public backlash to the revision of the Police Duties Execution Act at the end of 1958, and there were fears this issue could be used by those who opposed Kishi. Because of these considerations, Okinawa and Ogasawara were taken out of the draft.

Aiming for a swift signing of the new treaty, in February 1959 Foreign Minister Fujiyama published

Peninsula. The other was the "Record of Discussion," which made the "introduction" of nuclear weapons into Japan subject to prior consultation and also stipulated that the terms would not affect "present procedures regarding the deployment of United States armed forces and their equipment into Japan and those for the entry of United States military aircraft and the entry into Japanese waters and ports by United States naval vessels."

The "Record of Discussion" was unclear about whether naval vessels carrying nuclear weapons into a Japanese port would be subject to prior consultation. On the Japanese side, the understanding was that the prior-consultation rule would apply, considering that operations of that kind would constitute an "introduction" of nuclear weapons into Japan. The Americans, on the other hand, interpreted the agreement to mean that the entry of ships or aircraft carrying nuclear weapons into Japan would not require prior consultation as long as they were just making "temporary stops" or passing through. While those diverging interpretations would come to light through various events and developments over the years, such as the entry of a nuclear-powered submarine into a Japanese port and the 1974 La Rocque testimony (Rear Admiral Gene La Rocque's statement to Congress saying that ships carrying nuclear weapons had not unloaded those weapons before entering Japan's ports), neither government attempted to reconcile their differences of opinion. The US government adopted a "Neither Confirm nor Deny" (NCND) policy on the presence or absence of its nuclear weapons abroad to maximize its arsenal's deterrence. Meanwhile, the Japanese government remained silent on the interpretations of the two undisclosed documents to avoid compromising the NCND policy or thrusting its long-held three non-nuclear principles back into public debate.

With virtually every transfer of power in the Japanese government, lawmakers in the Diet demanded that leaders confirm whether the two confidential documents were actually real. It was not until the Minshutō (Democratic Party of Japan) administration took over in 2010 that the Japanese government finally confirmed their existence—but by that time, well after the end of the Cold War, the terms were essentially void.

his own personal draft version. This was virtually identical to the revised treaty that would be signed. Fujiyama's version had four salient points: first, the scope was defined as areas under Japanese administration, which excluded Okinawa and Ogasawara; second, the role of US troops in the defense of Japan was clarified; third, the use, deployment, and readiness of US troops in Japan were specified as matters for bilateral consultation; and fourth, the treaty would be given a term of ten years.

From that point forward, however, the negotiations became rocky. First of all, Fujiyama had to show consideration for anti-Kishi members within the Jimintō who wanted to see revisions of the administrative agreement, and so he asked the US side what could be done about that. From the outset, US and Japanese diplomats had affirmed that the administrative agreement would not be renegotiated, so the US side expressed strong displeasure. In the end, revisions were made, in line with Japan's requirements, out of consideration for the political position of the Kishi government. The revised administrative agreement took effect simultaneously with the new security treaty, positioned as agreements governing the status of US troops in Japan.

The Signing of the New Security Treaty: Japanese Relations with the Soviet Union

The rise of a movement opposed to the revision of the treaty hampered the progress of negotiations. The Nihon Shakaitō (Japan Socialist Party) was at the core of this opposition, as it stated clearly at its special convention in November 1958. The Nihon Shakaitō's aim was to nullify the security treaty and establish a security system based on agreements involving four nations: the United States, the USSR, China, and Japan. In March of the following year a coalition of more than 100 groups, led by the Shakaitō and the Sōhyō (Japan General Council of Trade Unions), joined to form the National Conference for Joint Struggle against Security Treaty Revisions, the group that led the movement going forward. The essence of the opposition's criticism was that the treaty represented a threat to world peace because it cast China and the Soviet Union as enemies, and that Japan's tolerance of US bases carried the threat that Japan would become embroiled in US military conflicts in the Far East.

In these circumstances, in January 1960 Prime Minister Kishi led a group of Japanese officials with plenipotentiary powers to Washington, where they signed the new security treaty and a Status of Forces Agreement replacing the administrative agreement, and exchanged notes on prior consultation. Dulles, who had created the original security treaty, had passed away the year before, and Secretary of State Christian A. Herter signed for the United States side.

The new security treaty committed the United States to defend Japanese territory against external armed attacks, with the geographic scope defined as "territories under the administration of Japan." In the event of an armed attack on the United States within this geographic area, Japan was committed to treating this as a "common danger" and taking defensive action (Article 5). The treaty reiterated that the United States was allowed to use "facilities and areas in Japan" (i.e., bases) to maintain the defense of Japan as well as the peace and security of the Far East (Article 6).

In addition, in the event of a threat such as that described in Article 5, provision was made for prior consultation at the request of either party (Article 4). Regarding the prior consultation provided under Article 4, under the terms of auxiliary documents that were exchanged, prior consultation was required whenever US troops were deployed from Japan-administered territories to other locations, or in the event of any other major changes in US military deployment or equipment.

The "domestic conflict clause" of the older version

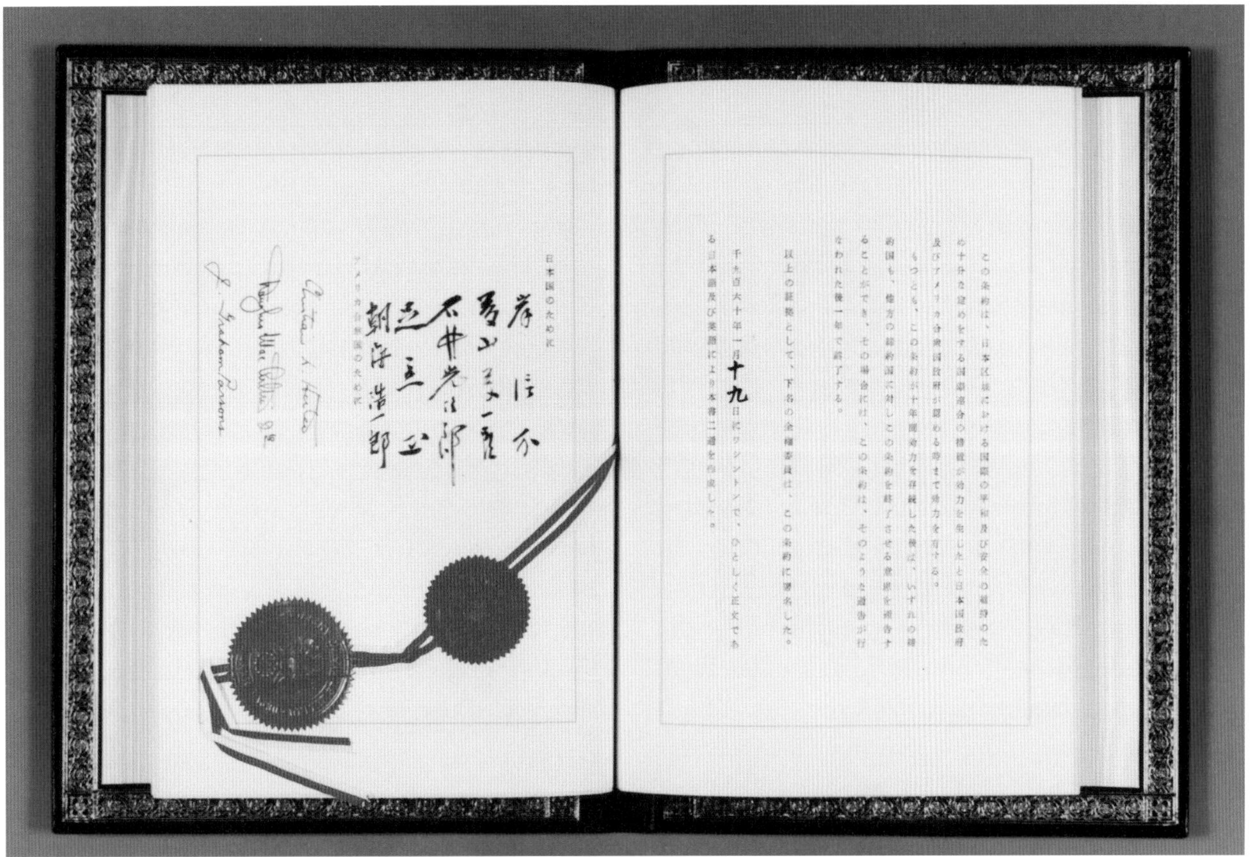

12-11. Treaty of Mutual Cooperation and Security between the United States and Japan (signature page)

of the treaty, which allowed the deployment of US troops to quell domestic conflicts or disturbances in Japan, was removed, and a new clause promoting economic cooperation was inserted (Article 2). The treaty was given a ten-year term of expiration, and could be canceled with a one-year advance notice. It also made explicit reference to the rights and obligations of the parties under the Charter of the United Nations regarding collective defense, a subject of particularly keen interest for the Foreign Ministry.

The new security treaty represented no change to the basic structure of the older version of the agreement—Japan provided the bases, and the United States protected the Far East, including Japan—but it was one step closer to being the defense treaty based on mutual equality that the Foreign Ministry desired, and it was accomplished without changing Japan's constitution.

In late January 1960, the Soviet Union objected strenuously to the new treaty, and said that as long as foreign troops remained on Japanese soil, it would not give back the islands of Habomai and Shikotan, as promised in the Soviet-Japanese Joint Declaration. After that, peace-treaty negotiations between Japan and the Soviet Union ground to a halt, but progress was made in private-sector economic interaction, and in 1965 the first Japanese government economic delegation traveled to the USSR. A series of Siberia development projects ensued, beginning the following year. For some time, Japanese-Soviet relations remained characterized by a sharp divide between politics and economics.

Anti-Anpo Protests

After the new security treaty (known in Japan as the Anpo Jōyaku, or the Anpo treaty) was signed, it was submitted in February 1960 to a regular session of the Diet. The main debate took place within the special security committee in the House of Representatives. There were no new points of contention, but the deliberations soon became deadlocked. The opposition parties remained recalcitrant, but the Jimintō, taking them by surprise, broke off deliberations and extended the Diet session. On May 20, the Jimintō placed the various bills associated with the new security treaty on the agenda on an emergency basis and forced their passage. Twenty-eight Jimintō Diet members were absent for the vote, including Kōno Ichirō, Miki Takeo, Ishibashi Tanzan, and Matsumura Kenzō.

After the steamrolling, opposition Diet members boycotted the Diet, and deliberations in the House of Councillors were suspended. Sit-in demonstrations were held in the Diet and surrounding the prime minister's residence, growing increasingly raucous. In early June, the Sōhyō held a general strike involving 5.6 million people, demanding that the Kishi cabinet step down. The anti-Anpo protest movement had shifted its focus to forcing the resignation of the "reactionary" politician Kishi and his colleagues, and "protecting the system of parliamentary democracy."

In 1960, President Dwight D. Eisenhower was to become the first sitting US president to visit Japan. The visit was intended to mark the 100th anniversary of friendship between the two nations. On June 10, however, Eisenhower's press secretary, James Hagerty, in Japan to prepare for Eisenhower's visit, was in a car that was surrounded by demonstrators, and ended up having to be rescued by US military helicopter. That did not stop Eisenhower from taking off from Washington. (The initial plan had been for Eisenhower to visit the Soviet Union first, and then Japan, but on May 1 a US U-2 spy plane was shot down over the Soviet Union, and Eisenhower's stop in the Soviet Union was cancelled.) Security preparations for Eisenhower's visit to Japan went so far as to include consideration of security operations by the Defense Agency and Self-Defense Forces. On June 15, student demonstrators led by the Zengakuren (All-Japan Federation of Students' Self-Governing Associations) forced their way into the Diet building, where they clashed with police; University of Tokyo student Kanba Michiko lost her life in the melee.

Given the chaos surrounding the Diet, Kishi decided to cancel Eisenhower's visit to mainland Japan (Eisenhower did visit Okinawa on June 19, however, and encountered demonstrators there). At the same time, Kishi became firmly resolved that his entire cabinet would resign after the automatic approval of the new treaty in the upper house.

12-12. Anti-Anpo demonstration

CHAPTER 13

Diplomacy during the Period of Rapid Economic Growth: Ikeda and Satō

13-1. Satō Eisaku and Ikeda Hayato

TIMELINE

1960 (Shōwa 35)

October 12	Assassination of Shakaitō (Japan Socialist Party) chairman Asanuma Inejirō
November 8	Democrat John F. Kennedy elected president of US
December 8	Second Ikeda cabinet formed
December 27	Cabinet approves Income Doubling Plan

1961 (Shōwa 36)

April 19	US ambassador to Japan Edwin Reischauer arrives in Japan
June 20	Ikeda meets Kennedy in Washington, DC
August 14–22	First Deputy Premier Anastas Mikoyan of the USSR visits Japan
August 15–September 4	Trade fair for Soviet industrial and commercial companies opens in Tokyo's Harumi district

1962 (Shōwa 37)

April 5–26	Soviet industrial mission arrives in Japan
August 8–26	Economic mission led by Kawai Yoshinari visits USSR
October 22–28	US naval blockade of Cuba (Cuban Missile Crisis)
November 4–24	Ikeda visits seven nations in Europe
November 9	Liao Chengzhi and Takasaki Tatsunosuke sign LT Trade Agreement on Japan-PRC trade
November 12	Foreign Minister Ōhira meets Kim Jong-pil, head of the Korean Central Intelligence Agency (KCIA), and broad agreement is reached on claims problem (Ōhira-Kim Memo)

1963 (Shōwa 38)

August 5	Partial Nuclear Test Ban Treaty (PTBT) signed by US, UK, and USSR
October 7	PRC interpreter Zhou Hongqing (Shū Kōkei) asks for asylum in Soviet Union
December 9	Third Ikeda cabinet formed

1964 (Shōwa 39)

April 1	Japan becomes an International Monetary Fund (IMF) "Article 8 nation"
April 28	Japan joins Organization for Economic Cooperation and Development (OECD)
May 7	Former prime minister Yoshida sends letter to Chiang Qun (Chang Ch'ün), secretary-general to the president of the Republic of China (second Yoshida letter)
August 2	Tonkin Gulf Incident (US destroyer attacked by North Vietnamese torpedo boats) revealed
August 11	Japan decides first round of US$500,000 aid for South Vietnam
October 10–24	Olympic Games held in Tokyo
October 15	Soviet Communist Party first secretary Khrushchev dismissed; succeeded by Leonid Brezhnev
October 16	PRC's first successful nuclear-bomb test
November 9	First Satō Eisaku cabinet formed
November 12	US nuclear submarine makes first port call in Sasebo

1965 (Shōwa 40)

January 13	Satō visits US, meets President Lyndon Johnson
February 7	US begins bombing of North Vietnam
March 8	US military begins direct intervention in Vietnam
June 22	Signing of Treaty on Basic Relations between Japan and the Republic of Korea; signing of Agreement Concerning the Settlement of Problems in Regard to Property and Claims and Economic Cooperation
August 19	Satō becomes first Japanese prime minister to visit Okinawa since World War II
September 30	September 30th Movement (failed coup d'état) in Indonesia

1966 (Shōwa 41)

April 6–7	First Ministerial Conference for the Economic Development of Southeast Asia held in Tokyo
May 16	Start of Cultural Revolution in PRC
November 24	Asian Development Bank (ADB) inaugural meeting held in Tokyo

1967 (Shōwa 42)

February 17	Second Satō cabinet formed
April 21	Satō proclaims Three Principles on Arms Exports in Diet
June 17	PRC's first successful hydrogen bomb test
July 20–25	Foreign Minister Miki visits USSR for first Japanese-Soviet regular consultations
September 20	Satō visits Southeast Asia (through September 30)
October 8–21	Satō's second visit to Southeast Asia and Oceania
October 20	Former prime minister Yoshida Shigeru dies (state funeral held October 31)
November 15	Japan-US summit (agreement to return Okinawa "within a few years")

1968 (Shōwa 43)

January 19	US nuclear aircraft carrier *Enterprise* port call in Sasebo
January 30	Satō formally proclaims Three Non-Nuclear Principles in Diet
March 6	Japan-PRC LT trade becomes "memorandum trade"
March 31	US president Johnson declares end to bombing of North Vietnam
April 5	Signing of agreement to return Ogasawara (Bonin), effective June 26
July 1	UN opens Treaty on the Non-Proliferation of Nuclear Weapons (NPT) for signing
August 20	Prague Spring

1969 (Shōwa 44)

March 2	PRC-Soviet Union military clash at Zhenbao Island (Damansky Island)
March 10	Satō declares negotiating stance for return of Okinawa: "nuclear-free, homeland-level status"
July 20	Apollo 11 moon landing
July 25	US president Nixon proclaims Guam Doctrine
November 21	Joint statement by Satō and Nixon (agreement to extend security treaty, return of Okinawa in 1972)
November 26	Satō reiterates Three Non-Nuclear Principles, declares Japan will bar import of nuclear devices, even in the event of a contingency

1970 (Shōwa 45)

January 14	Third Satō cabinet formed
February 3	Japan signs Treaty on the Non-Proliferation of Nuclear Weapons (NPT)
April 19	Zhou Enlai explains Four Principles on trade with Japan to Japanese trade delegation
June 23	Treaty of Mutual Cooperation and Security between the United States and Japan automatically extended
October 13	PRC, Canada establish diplomatic relations (November 6, Italy)
October 20	Publication of first *Bōei hakusho* annual white paper

1971 (Shōwa 46)

April 10	At table-tennis tournament in Nagoya, US team is invited to PRC (Ping-Pong Diplomacy)
June 17	Signing of Okinawa Reversion Agreement
July 9	US presidential advisor Kissinger secretly visits PRC
December 30	PRC Ministry of Foreign Affairs declares sovereignty over Senkaku Islands

1 Economic Growth and Japan's Diplomacy

After achieving independence, from 1953 until the first oil crisis of 1973 Japan showed virtually unbroken economic growth. Over this twenty-year period, growth averaged nearly 10 percent per year, and real gross national product tripled, an astounding record. The 1960s, in particular, were the golden age of the free-trade system, supported by the overwhelming economic power of the United States. Japan was able to participate in this free-trade system unimpeded by burdens, benefiting from the actively open markets and technology of the US economy and cheap imports of energy resources.

In the midst of this rich international environment, private-sector activity became the engine of growth, through active imports of foreign technology, technical innovation, and capital investment. The conditions provided by stable, conservative government must also be acknowledged. The long-lived administrations of Ikeda Hayato and Satō Eisaku in the 1960s coincided with the period of Japan's economic growth.

Ikeda and Economic Diplomacy

The Ikeda cabinet that began in July 1960 gave a fresh impression. There were no holdovers from the previous administration, and it had Nakayama Masa, Japan's first female cabinet-level official. In a speech shortly after he took office, Ikeda mentioned "the diplomatic successes of preceding conservative administrations." He stressed the effectiveness of the "Anpo system." With the Treaty of Mutual Cooperation and Security between the United States and Japan (the Anpo treaty) taking care of Japan's safety and security, Japan had achieved economic development with a minimal level of defense expenditures. This was the hallmark of the "Yoshida Line": a conservative government based on the policy principles of the security treaty with the US, a focus on economic development, and low levels of militarization (see sidebar on pages 390–91). To realize the goal of doubling the national income, increasing exports was the most important challenge. In that regard, focusing on the economy was the centerpiece of Ikeda's diplomacy.

In the eyes of the US government, the fuss about the security treaty represented a crisis of democracy in Japan. However, the Jimintō (Liberal Democratic

Ikeda Hayato (1899–1965)

Born in Hiroshima Prefecture, Ikeda Hayato joined the Ministry of Finance in 1925 after graduating from Kyoto Imperial University. He eventually went on to serve as the director-general of the Tokyo Local Finance Bureau, the director-general of the Tax Bureau, and in 1947, vice-minister in the first Yoshida Shigeru cabinet. He retired from the post in 1948 and secured a seat in the House of Representatives the following year. When Yoshida formed his third cabinet, he named Ikeda—still just a first-year representative—his minister of finance, a sign of the promise Ikeda showed. After the 1955 *hoshu gōdō* (conservative merger), Ikeda went on to serve in a variety of roles, including minister of finance and minister of international trade and industry, and eventually ascended to the premiership in July 1960. In that capacity, he worked to propel economic growth, to put Japan on equal footing with the rest of the Western bloc, and to explore a unique role for the country in the Asian community. The 1964 Tokyo Olympics marked a triumphant flourish to Ikeda's career, bringing one of his strongest aspirations to fruition, but failing health forced him to step down as prime minister and hand the reins over to Satō Eisaku. Ikeda passed away a year later in 1965.

13-2. Ikeda Hayato

Party) won the elections of November 1960, and calm was restored in Japan-US relations. Kennedy was inaugurated in 1961, and embraced a policy of "equal partnership" in relations with Japan. It is said that this was at the suggestion of Edwin Reischauer, the new ambassador to Japan. According to John Emmerson, deputy chief of mission for the US Embassy to Japan, there was still concern about Japan moving into the non-aligned camp. To keep it in the "free world," it should be invited to play an equal role. In response, Prime Minister Ikeda made becoming a powerful member of the "free nations" camp a target of his diplomatic efforts.

In June 1961 Ikeda visited the United States. President Kennedy invited him to meet on his private yacht on the Potomac River. They talked there, on the yacht, and agreed to set up the Joint Japan-US Committee on Trade and Economic Affairs, which would meet annually. The first meeting, in November 1961 in Hakone, was attended by nearly half of the US cabinet members. Only a few were left behind in Washington—a rare event in postwar US diplomatic relations.

In November 1962, immediately after the Cuban Missile Crisis, Ikeda visited Europe. The purpose of his visit was to convince Western European nations to stop applying Article 35 of the General Agreement on Tariffs and Trade (GATT) to Japan, which was resulting in trade discrimination. He was successful in this goal, first signing the Anglo-Japanese Treaty of Commerce and Navigation, which was soon followed by agreements with other Western European nations.

Ikeda was also able to set in motion the process for Japan to join the Organization for Economic Cooperation and Development (OECD). European

Satō Eisaku (1901–75)

Hailing from Yamaguchi Prefecture, Satō Eisaku was born the younger brother of Kishi Nobusuke, who was five years his senior. Satō obtained a degree from Tokyo Imperial University, landed a position at the Ministry of Railways in 1924, and spent the next twenty-three years forging a career as a railway bureaucrat before entering the political sphere. After the end of World War II, Satō became the director-general of the Railways General Bureau in 1946 and then vice-minister of transport the following year. The year after that, he retired from ministerial service and joined the Minshu-Jiyūtō (Democratic Liberal Party). He then began his rise through Japan's political ranks, even securing an appointment to serve as chief cabinet secretary in the second Yoshida Shigeru cabinet despite not having a seat in parliament at the time. Yoshida evidently saw plenty of promise in Satō. After winning a seat in parliament in the 1949 general election, Satō served in a string of ministerial positions: minister of transport and minister of construction in the third and fourth Yoshida cabinets, respectively, as well as minister of finance and other positions under Prime Minister Kishi. Having become a prominent political force, Satō eventually began vying with Ikeda Hayato for party leadership and the post of prime minister. Although Ikeda reached the premiership first, Satō took over the position when Ikeda stepped down for health reasons in 1964—and subsequently embarked on one of the longest uninterrupted prime-ministerial tenures in Japanese history, at a full seven years and eight months. Although the Vietnam War (1965–75) put limits on what the Satō cabinet could do in terms of foreign relations, Satō worked to normalize relations with South Korea, propel development in Southeast Asia, and establish Japan's non-nuclear policy, to name just three of many different efforts. Most importantly, he led the way in a united, government-wide effort to bring Okinawa, which had been a vital component of the United States' Far East strategy, back under Japanese administration. Satō saw Okinawa's reversion through to fruition in May 1972 and resigned two months later. His central role in establishing Japan's Three Non-Nuclear Principles, among other accomplishments, earned him the 1974 Nobel Peace Prize.

13-3. Satō Eisaku

13-4. President Kennedy and Prime Minister Ikeda

nations responded favorably, and Japan joined the OECD in 1964. Joining the OECD meant Japan was a member of the "advanced nations club," but at the same time, with the freeing of capital flows, it was also compelled to free its trade and capital. In fact, Japan was making steady progress in liberalizing imports of foreign goods. In 1967, the Satō cabinet decided to allow the free movement of capital.

With the United States, Japan, and Europe working together as three pillars, the "free nations" camp became stronger. Ikeda discussed with all the heads of government the need to fight back against Communism. All the leaders, particularly President Charles de Gaulle of France, welcomed Ikeda's message of the "three pillars" of Japan, the United States, and Europe working together. In this way, Ikeda drew Japan closer to the United States, and also moved in the direction of working with Western Europe. Japan began to participate in the global marketplace based on free trade, alongside the United States and Europe, placing itself in a good position to strengthen its efforts to increase trade.

Trading with the Communist Bloc: Advances and Limitations

Restoring Japan's trade with China, which had been broken off during the Kishi era, was the biggest Asian diplomatic issue facing Ikeda. Shortly after the Ikeda administration began, China hammered out a new version of Three Principles of Trade, aiming for a restoration of amicable trade relations. At the same time, however, the "two Chinas" problem remained a political dilemma, as Japan had to deal with both mainland China and Taiwan. In the 1960s, a series of newly independent nations joined the United Nations. The Republic of China (Taiwan) had been a permanent member of the Security Council since the UN was founded, but its position was threatened by the possibility of the People's Republic of China joining. Officials within the Ministry of Foreign Affairs gave thought to the idea that "both Chinas" could be members of the UN, but in the end, cooperating with the United States, Ikeda stuck with the idea of supporting the continued membership of the Nationalist government in Taiwan.

In 1962, businessman Okazaki Kaheita proposed to mainland China a politically neutral kind of trade that would be different from "friendship trade." China accepted this proposal, and in the fall of 1962, Takasaki Tatsunosuke of the Jimintō visited China, following in the footsteps of Matsumura Kenzō, who had led a mission to Beijing in 1961. The five-year Liao-Takasaki (LT) trade agreement was signed in November of that year. Both domestically and abroad, Ikeda advocated for the separation of politics and economics. While superficially his contribution may have appeared slight, in fact he was engaged in prior consultations and information exchange through both Matsumura and Takasaki. The political significance of trade with China was more important to Ikeda than the material benefit. He left open the possibility of mainland China's recognition in the future.

The Nationalist government in Taiwan objected to Ikeda's China policies, and was particularly offended by two events. First, in August 1963, the Japanese government approved financing from the Export-Import Bank of Japan for a deferred payment export contract for a vinylon plant to be built in China under the LT Trade Agreement. Then, in October, the Zhou Hongqing (Shū Kōkei) Incident occurred, in which Chinese interpreter Zhou Hongqing, accompanying a group visiting Japan, took refuge in the Soviet embassy. He wanted asylum, but kept changing his mind about where he wanted to go. In the end, the government decided to send him back to China. Taiwan's Nationalist government objected strenuously to these two developments, going so far as to threaten to break off relations with Japan. This galvanized the pro-Taiwan members of the Jimintō. In February 1964, concerned about intra-party strife, Ikeda asked Yoshida Shigeru to visit Taiwan to smooth the situation. Yoshida met three times with Chiang Kai-shek, and managed to assuage the Nationalist government's loss of faith in Japan. One result of this was the "Yoshida Letter" of May 1964, promising that the funds from the Export-Import Bank of Japan for the export of the plant to China would not be released before the end of the year.

As for the USSR, the Soviet posture toward Japan at that time was basically limited to criticism of the new US-Japan Security Treaty. Given the standoff between China and the Soviet Union, as well as the economic stagnation occurring at that time, it seemed that attention would gradually shift to the idea of economic cooperation. In August 1962, a large economic mission was sent to the Soviet Union, led by Kawai Yoshinari, president of Komatsu Ltd. The mission succeeded in concluding agreements on export contracts for ships and imports of lumber from Sakhalin. Due to concerns about the US response to these agreements, the Keidanren (Japan Business Federation) made a public statement that it had no connection to this trade mission. Positioning the mission as purely a private-sector exchange forestalled any pushback from the United States. In May 1964, a high-level delegation led by First Deputy Premier Anastas Mikoyan visited Japan at the invitation of the National Legislature. This group was warmly received, with both sides offering initiatives for the expansion of trade, and several major deals were concluded. For the sake of civility, Prime Minister Ikeda met with Mikoyan, but out of deference to China and the United States, their discussion did not go beyond formalities.

The Japan–South Korea Agreement: The Ōhira-Kim Memo

The 1961 coup d'état in South Korea that brought Park Chung-hee to power served as an impetus for dialogue between Japan and South Korea, which had been stalled up to that point. Park showed interest in receiving economic assistance and improving relations with Japan. However, a significant divide still separated South Korea from Japan, based on South Korean claims rooted in past colonial history, and these differences were not easy to resolve.

In July 1962, Foreign Minister Ōhira Masayoshi, who had recently joined the reshuffled cabinet, began working on a way to sort out this

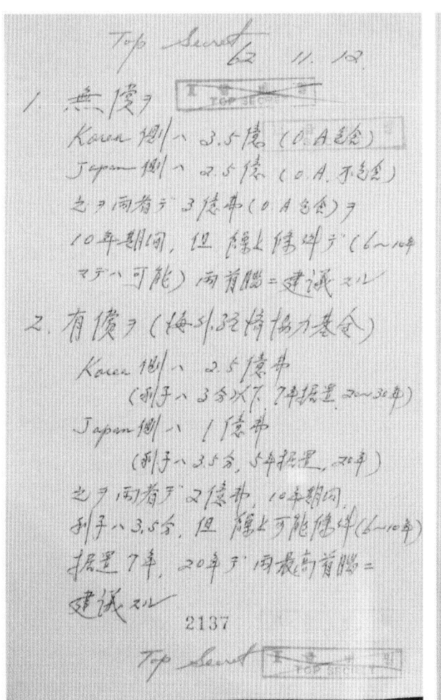
Top Secret 62. 11. 12
1. 無償ヲ
Korea側ハ 3.5億（O.A.含）
Japan側ハ 2.5億（O.A.不含）
之ヲ両者デ3億弗（O.A.含）ヲ
10年期間，但 繰上ゲ可能（6〜10年マデハ可能）両首脳ニ建議スル
2. 有償ヲ（海外経済協力基金）
Korea側ハ 2.5億弗
（利子ハ3分以下 7年据置 20〜30年）
Japan側ハ 1億弗
（利子ハ3.5分, 5年据置, 20年）
之ヲ両者デ2億弗, 10年期間,
利子ハ3.5分, 但 繰上可能條件(6〜10年)
据置7年, 20年デ両最高首脳ニ
建議スル
2137
Top Secret

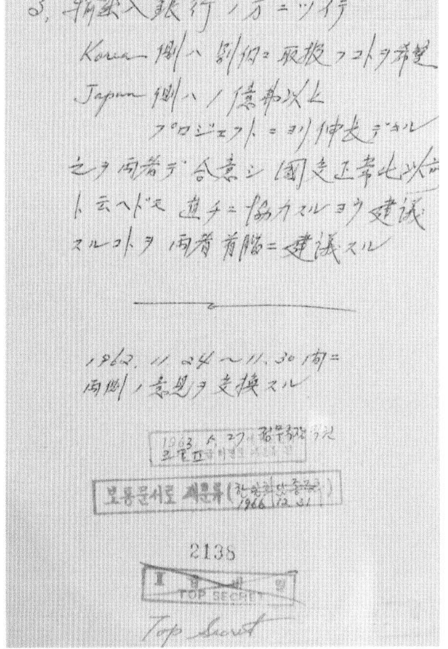
Top Secret
3. 輸出入銀行ノ方ニツイテ
Korea側ハ 別個ニ取扱フコトヲ希望
Japan側ハ 1億弗以上
プロジェクトニヨリ伸長デキル
之ヲ両者デ合意シ国交正常化以前ニデモ早期ニ協力スルヨウ建議スルコトヲ両首脳ニ建議スル
1962. 11. 24〜11. 30 間ニ
両側ノ意見ヲ交換スル
2136
TOP SECRET
Top Secret

13-5. The Ōhira-Kim Memo

situation. In November, he met in Japan with Kim Jong-pil, head of the Korean Central Intelligence Agency (KCIA), and the two men agreed on the broad outlines of what became known as the Ōhira-Kim Memo. This memo included US$300 million in grants, $200 million in yen-denominated loans, and $100 million in private-sector credits as settlement for the South Korean claims. Although this solution took the form of economic aid, its aim was to bolster South Korea's anti-Communist resolve through economic development. Such an agreement would be difficult to conclude, however, without the tacit approval of the United States. Furthermore, Ikeda was less than enthusiastic about a speedy resolution of the Japan–South Korea negotiations due to the financial burdens it would impose. Domestic unrest in South Korea also contributed to slowing subsequent negotiations to a crawl.

Southeast Asia and Economic Cooperation

Throughout the 1950s, Japan was busy resolving its reparations problems with countries in Southeast Asia. In the 1960s, Southeast Asia displaced South Asia as an important platform for Japan's economic cooperation. Corporations also began to turn their attentions away from South Asia's India and Pakistan in the direction of Burma (Myanmar) and points eastward in Southeast Asia. Amid this expansion of Japan's economic assistance, the Overseas Economic Cooperation Fund was initiated. This was meant to take the place of the Southeast Asia Development Fund concept that had been tried and abandoned during the Kishi administration, the objective being to provide capital and funding to development undertakings in developing nations.

However, the Ministry of Finance, which put priority on balancing the government budget, was less than enthusiastic about providing aid to developing nations, and the idea did not move ahead. It was the Satō cabinet, in 1965, that would pass Japan's first unbalanced budget of the postwar period, doubling the budget for economic assistance and issuing government bonds to make up the gap.

At the same time, in Europe, economic regionalism was gathering steam, as the European Economic Community (EEC) was founded in 1958, followed by the European Free Trade Association (EFTA) in 1960. Against this background, Japan proclaimed the idea of "open regionalism." Ikeda promoted the idea of an "Organization of Asian Economic Cooperation" (OAEC) to promote increased trade within Asia. This effort, however, collapsed in the face of pushback from those within Japan who opposed trade liberalization and tighter government budgets.

While progress on the idea of regional cooperation may have been impeded, Ikeda and Ōhira took a more targeted approach, advocating economic cooperation with countries where it seemed doable, based on the idea of preventing the spread of Communist China's influence to neighboring countries. Japan decided to steer a policy course to prevent nationalism among Asian nations from joining hands with Communism and becoming extreme, to strengthen domestic development systems and steer them in the direction of cooperation with the West.

In 1962, the aim of Ikeda's foreign policy was to resolve the thorny "special yen problem" with Thailand through economic cooperation. During the war, Thailand had maintained a "special yen" account in the Bank of Japan to which it received payments for supplies procured in Thailand for Japanese troops. Japan therefore owed Thailand money. The first economic cooperation treaty signed had specified that Japan would repay 5.4 million yen in sterling, and would extend 9.6 billion yen in loans. However, Thailand demurred at borrowing money from its own debtor and demanded to renegotiate. Ikeda's solution was to extend the

9.6 billion yen as grants, rather than loans, over a period of eight years. In Burma, meanwhile, a new military government had just taken power through a coup d'état. To prevent that country from moving closer to China, Ikeda proposed a conciliatory measure of additional reparations, which had been a cause of concern. Both these moves related to Southeast Asia were intended to apply pressure in terms of the "inter-system competition" with Communist China through economic means. The same was true of Japan's ongoing support for the regional power, Indonesia.

The Indonesian Confrontation and Ikeda's Resignation

Throughout the 1960s, the United States relied on Japan to guide the nations of Asia in toeing a moderate line. This was directed mainly at Indonesia, which was gripped by anti-colonialism and had strong misgivings about Europe and the United States, causing concern it might be swayed by the influence of Communist China. Ever since the resolution of the reparations issue, there were strong expectations that Japan, which had been able to build good relations with Indonesia, would keep it and other Asian nations in line.

Japan tried hard to live up to those expectations by mediating the military conflict between Indonesia and Malaysia (1963–66). In early 1964, Ikeda submitted to concerned nations a mediation proposal drafted by Vice-Foreign Minister Ōda Takio, whom Sukarno trusted deeply. The proposal called for the withdrawal of Indonesian troops from the disputed regions of Sabah and Sarawak in Malaysia and a referendum of the citizens there. US attorney general Robert Kennedy also made a mediation proposal at around the same time regarding Sukarno's growing friendship with China. Ikeda's intent was to coordinate with Kennedy to divert Sukarno from military action and set him on a course of building his own nation's economy. However, this scheme failed, and the United States ended up terminating all aid to Indonesia.

In January 1965, Indonesia withdrew from the United Nations and aligned itself more closely with China. Japan continued to support Sukarno, and the following cabinet, under Satō, sent Jimintō vice president Kawashima Shōjirō to Indonesia to attempt further mediation.

During this period, in July 1964 Ikeda was reelected head of the Jimintō, but he fell ill, and in late October, after overseeing the success of the Olympics, he stepped down, recommending Satō Eisaku as his successor.

The Satō Cabinet and the Vietnam War

The Satō cabinet, which got its start in November 1964, retained all the ministers of the preceding Ikeda cabinet, including Foreign Minister Shiina Etsusaburō. Most diplomatic policies carried on as they had in Ikeda's day, but one new area of concern was China's successful nuclear-bomb test, which had taken place in mid-October. In January 1965, Satō traveled to the United States, where he met with President Lyndon B. Johnson. Johnson explained that United States would use its nuclear deterrent force to defend Japan, and he warned

13-6. From left to right: US ambassador Reischauer, Vice President Hubert H. Humphrey, Prime Minister Satō Eisaku and Foreign Minister Shiina Etsusaburō

Japan against developing nuclear weapons of its own. This was likely in response to the fact that, in December 1964, Satō had spoken positively about nuclear weapons in a meeting with Ambassador Reischauer.

In February 1965, shortly after Satō's visit, the United States began its campaign of bombing North Vietnam. The following month, it sent its first ground troops to Vietnam. The United States sent over 500,000 troops, basing its engagement in the conflict on the "domino theory" that the loss of South Vietnam would lead other Asian nations—including Japan—to turn to Communism.

Prime Minister Satō expressed support for the Johnson administration's intent to protect the "independence and security" of South Vietnam. However, he declined to provide direct support for the Vietnam War policy. In April 1965, President Johnson gave a speech in Baltimore in which he pledged US$1 billion to build regional cooperative systems for the development of Southeast Asia. Johnson's idea was multi-faceted: he hoped to prevent the spread of Communism in Southeast Asia while encouraging regional efforts that would lighten America's burden.

For its part, Japan's Ministry of Foreign Affairs forged an "Asia Peace Plan" that included a wide range of joint proposals for the economic development of Asia. The ministry's intention was to pursue peace in Vietnam through a shared plan that would include China and North Vietnam. To make this idea easy for others to accept, the ministry limited the role of the United States in its proposal. Satō, however, declined to pursue this plan for financial reasons. In 1965, Japan slipped into an economic recession.

The Asian Development Bank and the Ministerial Conference for the Economic Development of Southeast Asia

As an alternative plan for peace in Asia, the Ministry of Foreign Affairs proposed the idea of thinking ahead, beyond the end of the war, to build a platform for social and economic development, limiting its aid tied directly to the Vietnam War to a scale that would not disrupt the relationship with the United States. More specifically, this meant the concepts of the Asian Development Bank (ADB) and the Ministerial Conference for the Economic Development of Southeast Asia. These ideas garnered US approval. The Japanese government was particularly enthused about the establishment of the ADB, which would help realize the concepts of sound banking and commercial lending. These institutions would help encourage the efforts of Southeast Asian nations themselves, and Japan's funding burden would not be overly large.

At the same time, the Ministerial Conference for the Economic Development of Southeast Asia was proposed as a practical multilateral aid scheme that would be a step removed from political interests. It would be a way to "prime the pump" for aid from the United States. The US welcomed this idea as well, expecting that it would allow for policy coordination with Japan in the area of Southeast Asian development, as well as mutually complementary roles.

The first Ministerial Conference for the Economic Development of Southeast Asia was held in 1966. With eight countries participating, the conference focused on gradual economic development and regional cooperation, primarily in agricultural projects. However, most of the projects stalled because the participating countries were unable to establish a common position with respect to the Vietnam War. The ADB, too, began operations in 1966. Rather than being an aid organization, it was intended to encourage efforts in the target nations to establish healthy banking practices on a commercial basis, and then to provide templates for aid policies later.

After the September 30, 1965 coup d'état in Indonesia, Japan continued its policy of support for Indonesia, now ruled by the Suharto regime. To process the large debt left from the preceding

Sukarno government, in 1966 Japan helped Indonesia issue bonds through the Inter-Governmental Group on Indonesia (IGGI). The IGGI became an important means for Indonesia to receive assistance from advanced nations, and Japan played a key role in this program.

The Vietnam Peace Plan

For the Satō cabinet, the idea that, after the Vietnam War, the United States could withdraw completely from Southeast Asia opened the door for China to increase its influence in the region. This would harm prospects for stability in Asia. Satō hoped the United States would work urgently for peace, but at the same time he intended for Japan to pursue peace in Vietnam on its own, while still coordinating with the United States.

Diplomatic efforts to achieve peace in Vietnam were taking place on an international scale, and Japan's initiatives should be understood in that context. The opportunity came during the December 1965 pause in the bombing of North Vietnam. In January 1966, Foreign Minister Shiina traveled to Moscow and tried to persuade Soviet foreign minister Andrey Gromyko that a continuation of the Vietnam War would benefit only China, and that it would be in the best interests of the Soviet Union to apply pressure on Hanoi to get them to come to the peace table. Gromyko responded that Japan should call on the United States to end the war.

With the understanding of the United States, Miki Takeo, who had joined the Satō cabinet as foreign minister in December 1966, visited heads of state of the Soviet Union and Eastern Europe in late July 1967, asking that North Vietnam come to the bargaining table if the United States agreed to stop the bombing. However, the leaders of the Soviet Union and Eastern Europe were not very interested in mediating peace, and Miki's effort was unsuccessful.

The Signing of the Treaty on Basic Relations between Japan and the Republic of Korea

After the Ōhira-Kim Memo, relations between Japan and South Korea did not make much progress. This prompted the United States to intervene in an effort to get talks between the two East Asian nations going again. Rapprochement between Japan and South Korea was needed both to drum up support for the Vietnam War among free nations and to reduce the burden on the United States. America's strategy was to promise to continue its aid to South Korea while attempting to persuade it to soften its stance toward Japan. At the same time, the United States pressured Japan to issue a public, cabinet-level apology. In February 1965, at the urging of US ambassador Reischauer, Foreign Minister Shiina visited South Korea and made a public apology for Japan's colonial rule. This statement, later known as the Shiina Declaration, was the first public apology by a cabinet-level Japanese official for the colonial rule of Korea.

Shiina had prepared a draft of the basic statement, which was signed provisionally in late February. The joint statement included the words "regrettable" and "reflection." Shortly thereafter, South Korean foreign minister Lee Dong-won visited Tokyo, and an agreement was reached to increase private-sector credits to over US$300 million. South Korea called this "funds for claims on Japan."

13-7. Signing of the Treaty on Basic Relations between Japan and the Republic of Korea and associated agreements

The "Unlawful Occupation" of Takeshima

The Roots of the Takeshima Issue

From the early seventeenth century onward, Takeshima (Dokdo) was both a navigational guide for Japanese sailors heading for Utsuryōtō (Ulleungdo) and a bustling site for hunting sea lions and catching abalone. After Japan's cabinet passed a resolution in January 1905 incorporating Takeshima into Shimane Prefecture, the government added Takeshima to the State Land Register and began charging fees for the use of state land on an ongoing basis.

Japan maintained effective control over Takeshima through the end of the Pacific War, but the Supreme Commander for the Allied Powers Instruction Note (SCAPIN) 677 in January 1946 named Utsuryōtō (Ulleungdo), Saishūtō (Jeju), and Takeshima as territories to be excluded from Japan's administrative authority. When the Allies later drew the "MacArthur Line" that June, Takeshima lay outside the zone where Japanese fishing vessels could operate. With the postwar environment prompting alterations to Japan's territory and administrative scope, South Korea began to claim that Takeshima was now separate from Japan and therefore South Korean territory.

However, the Allied documents on the matters were clear about their ambiguity, in a sense: SCAPIN-677 stipulated that it should not be interpreted as an "ultimate determination" of the Allies, first of all, and the memorandum establishing the MacArthur Line emphasized that it was not a final Allied decision on national jurisdiction, international boundaries, or fishing rights. The actual final decision eventually came in September 1951, with the signing of the peace treaty. Article 2 of the agreement differed from Directive 677, stipulating that "Japan, recognizing the independence of Korea, renounces all right, title and claim to Korea, including the islands of Quelpart [Saishūtō/Jeju], Port Hamilton [Komuntō/Geomundo], and Dagelet [Utsuryōtō/Ulleungdo]." Takeshima was no longer part of the territory that Japan was to forfeit. During the drafting of the peace treaty, the Korean government demanded that the US government specify Takeshima as one of the territories to be released from Japanese control under the provisions of Article 2. The US State Department declined, however, on the grounds that Takeshima had never actually been part of Korea, nor had Korea ever staked a claim to the territory.

In January 1952, following the signing of the San Francisco Peace Treaty, the South Korean government announced the "Syngman Rhee Line." The territorial demarcation was a unilateral move that incorporated Takeshima into the nation's territory—an "unlawful occupation" in the context of international law. In the ensuing years, Japan–South Korea relations would grow increasingly testy as the Korean government continued to seize Japanese fishing vessels operating on the inside of the Syngman Rhee line.

Negotiations on Normalization and the Takeshima Issue

Over the course of negotiations regarding normalization between Japan and South Korea, the Takeshima issue came up for discussion during two meetings between Foreign Minister Ōhira Masayoshi and the head of the Korean Central Intelligence Agency, Kim Jong-pil, in the fall of 1962, when the Park Chung-hee regime was in power. Representatives of the Park administration voiced their hopes of delaying discussions of the Dokdo situation until after the normalization negotiations were complete. For the Japanese side, though, the issue needed to be part of the negotiations—the matter was so pressing, the delegation maintained, that Japan was fully prepared to bring the case to the International Court of Justice.

The Japanese contingent, adhering to its threat of battling South Korea in the International Court of Justice, eventually determined that trying to reach an agreement on the Takeshima issue via negotiations was a futile endeavor. To leave room for possible discussions on the territorial disagreement via an "Exchange of Notes . . . Concerning the Settlement of Disputes," the Japanese side argued that the

The South Korean government used these funds as a foundation for its economic development, making large investments in places like Posco Steel. It asked Japan for additional money for long-term projects such as modernization of agriculture, electrification of railways, and construction of subways. South Korea's resulting economic growth was dubbed the "Miracle on the Han River."

The Treaty on Basic Relations between Japan and the Republic of Korea, which was formally signed in June 1965, stipulated that the Japan-Korea Annexation Treaty of 1910 and the preceding older treaty were "already null and void," and also stated that the Republic of Korea was the only legal government on the Korean Peninsula. The treaty further stipulated that the promised economic aid

13-8. Takeshima

notes should cover "all disputes between the two nations, including the dispute concerning Takeshima." The final version of the document was less explicit, however; the text stipulated that the "two Governments shall settle disputes between the two countries primarily through diplomatic channels," a rendering that reflected the Korean position.

Whether or not "disputes between the two countries" actually include the Takeshima issue remains a point of contention, with Japan and Korea still reading the terms of the notes differently. However, recently disclosed Korean diplomatic records suggest that the two nations had a type of tacit agreement not to object to one another's divergent interpretations.

The relatively reserved attitudes on both sides of the table during negotiations on normalization may have been what made the 1965 Treaty on Basic Relations between Japan and the Republic of Korea possible. After the normalization talks wrapped up, neither Japan nor Korea attached much weight to the Takeshima issue. Meanwhile, progress on solutions to outstanding fishing issues has been steady, as the two sides have handled the fishing situation and territorial disputes as separate matters. Japan has periodically issued statements through the Ministry of Foreign Affairs declaring Takeshima to be Japanese territory, but the South Korean government has simply let the announcements pass with little in the way of a reaction. Instead, South Korea has focused more on establishing "peaceful effective control" via measures to designate Takeshima a nature reserve and build pier facilities, among other efforts. Japan's reactions to the South Korean initiatives involving Takeshima have been relatively subdued, as well—the government has done little more than lodge protests against the various projects.

The days of mutual restraint may be numbered, however. President Lee Myung-bak's directive to land on Takeshima in August 2012 emboldened South Korean politicians to advocate action, a shift that could amplify the tensions.

Calling "Peaceful Management" into Question

At the core of the Takeshima conflict is South Korea's persistent claim that Takeshima was "first sacrificed in the course of the forcible colonization . . . by Imperial Japan," a position that has remained consistent since the 1950s. The incorporation of Takeshima into Japanese territory in 1905 came right before the signing of the Japan-Korea Treaty of 1905, which served to make Korea a protectorate of Imperial Japan. From the South Korean perspective, then, the annexation of Takeshima represented the first step of the "colonization process"—and everything that Japan has done since has thus been a continuation of its invasion of South Korea, not a continuation of territorial control within the bounds of international law.

Even if Japan were to admit to an "illegal" colonial occupation of Takeshima, however, Korea would need to prove that it had effective control over Takeshima prior to Japan's incorporation in order to refute Japan's claim of "inherent territory" argument.

(US$300 million in grants, $200 million in loans, etc., as discussed above) "completely and finally" settled South Korea's claims against Japan. The treaty also settled the legal status of South Koreans in Japan by defining the scope of their rights to permanent residence, among other things.

Both sides also signed an "exchange of notes regarding settlement of disputes," which the Japan side regarded as the formula for settlement of the Takeshima problem. While it was never brought up in a series of discussions, this had been agreed to in the Ōhira-Kim talks in the fall of 1962.

Later, the legislatures of both nations ratified the new treaty, and diplomatic relations were formally set up, with the establishment of embassies in the two countries. The long and difficult negotiating process of restoring relations involved a total of 1,200 meetings taking place since the start in October 1951.

Winter Comes for Japan-China Relations

In 1964, under the Satō administration, Japan began making yen loans to the Nationalist government in Taiwan. Taiwan's economy had been supported by US aid, but those funds were waning, so Taiwan relied increasingly on Japan. With the progress of the normalization of diplomatic relations with South Korea, it appeared to mainland China that Japan, Taiwan, and South Korea were forming an anti-Communist bloc of resistance. The inevitable worsening of relations between Japan and China manifested itself in the form of problems with financing the export of an industrial plant to China by the Export-Import Bank of Japan. Under the terms of the 1962 Liao-Takasaki (LT) Agreement, Chinese purchases of industrial plants were to be financed partly through medium-term credits from the Japan Export-Import Bank.

Prime Minister Satō felt that approval of the financing in this case would help move Japan-China relations forward. On the other hand, declining to finance the deal through the bank would show deference to Taiwan and the pro-Taiwan faction within the Jimintō, both of which opposed approval. He dithered on the dilemma of "two Chinas," and in March 1965 he reached a decision not to utilize the Export-Import Bank of Japan financing. The government of mainland China soon began to harshly criticize the Satō administration, characterizing its actions as a revival of Japanese militarism.

Communist China's criticism of Japan was taking place in the context of its staunch anti-Americanism, the deepening confrontation between the United States and China over the bombing of North Vietnam, and the September 30 coup in Indonesia, which had wiped out the Communist Party there. The destruction of Indonesia's Communist Party, which had been deepening its ties to China, stole the wind from the sails of the "export of revolution" in Asia. Amid these external crises, in the spring of

Staking a Claim to the Senkaku Islands

The Absence of a Territorial Dispute

It was in January 1895 that the Japanese government incorporated the Senkaku Islands (called the Diaoyu Islands in Chinese) into the country's territory via a cabinet resolution. Through a bevy of field surveys, the government had found that the island was not only uninhabited but also uncontrolled by any other nation. In terms of international law, the incorporation was a legitimate measure in conformance with the "principle of occupation" (prior occupation of a "terra nullius").

The Japanese government then decided to lease the newly government-owned Senkaku Islands to Naha businessman Koga Tatsushirō, list the islands in its State Land Register, and send in administration officials to tour the territory, establishing a framework of peaceful management in the process. In the wake of the Pacific War, however, control changed hands: the Senkaku Islands were in the Nansei island group, over which the United States assumed administrative control. The fate of the islands hung in the balance in the meantime. As the official peace treaty began to take shape, the Japanese government worked to convince the Americans to define the Senkaku Islands as a part of the Nansei Islands and not one of the territories that it would need to relinquish. The Allies eventually accepted the Japanese proposal. Article 2 of the Treaty of San Francisco required Japan to forfeit control of "Formosa and the Pescadores," and the Senkaku Islands were not mentioned in the stipulations.

Japan regained its administrative rights to the Senkaku Islands when the Okinawa Reversion Agreement took effect in May 1972. The months prior had seen controversy over the islands erupt, however. In mid-June 1971, just before the signing of the Okinawa Reversion Agreement, the Republic of China (Taiwanese) government issued a statement that "the islets belong to Taiwan Province and constitute part of the territory of the Republic of China." The government of the People's Republic of China made its own statement through the Ministry of Foreign Affairs in December that year, claiming that the Senkaku Islands were "affiliated islands" of

1966 Mao Zedong embarked on his "Cultural Revolution," sweeping away the forces of "revisionism" in China and paralyzing China's diplomatic activities.

For Satō, China's development of nuclear weapons was a much bigger concern than the Cultural Revolution. In 1966, China began to deploy medium-distance ballistic missiles mounted with nuclear warheads. The following year, China conducted its first successful test of a hydrogen bomb. These developments increased the importance of the US "nuclear umbrella" (enhanced nuclear deterrence), which was the main reason Satō placed such high priority on coordination with the United States.

As the LT Trade Agreement was approaching its expiration in 1968, the deepening mutual mistrust between Japan and China cast a pall over negotiations on private-sector trade between the two nations. The LT Trade Agreement was recast as "memorandum trade," with the agreement set up for renewal on an annual basis. The Japan-China relationship was headed for a chilly, wintry phase.

2 The Agreement between Japan and the United States of America Concerning the Ryūkyū Islands and the Daitō Islands

Resolving to Restore the Homeland

No previous administration had taken a straightforward, front-door approach to asking that Okinawa and Ogasawara (Bonin) be returned to Japan. As the US military grew more deeply involved in the Vietnam War, the strategic importance of Okinawa to the United States increased, which seemed to make the idea of the return of Okinawa more remote. At the same time, opposition party Diet

Taiwan and thus that including the islands among the territories subject to reversion under the Okinawa Reversion Agreement constituted a "violation of China's territorial sovereignty." One of the factors prompting the claims was the recent discovery of promising oil reserves in the East China Sea, which had sparked a flurry of anticipation about the possibility of tapping the seafloor resources.

The disputed claims to the Senkaku Islands did not come up for discussion during the negotiations to normalize relations between Japan and China in September 1972, however. Before the negotiations began, the Ministry of Foreign Affairs had already made it clear that "the government of Japan . . . will not discuss the territorial sovereignty of the Senkaku Islands with any country" because it was "an indisputable fact that the Senkaku Islands are part of Japanese territory." The territorial dispute, in other words, was nonexistent.

Nationalizing the Islands

In late October 1978, Chinese vice premier Deng Xiaoping visited Japan to exchange the instruments of ratification for the Treaty of Peace and Friendship between Japan and the People's Republic of China. During his meeting with Prime Minister Fukuda Takeo, Deng became the first top Chinese official to suggest "shelving" the issue surrounding the Senkaku Islands, saying, "Our generation is not wise

13-9. The Senkaku Islands

Staking a Claim to the Senkaku Islands

enough to find common language on this question. Our next generation will certainly be wiser. They will find a solution acceptable for all." Prime Minister Fukuda refrained from making any comments on the matter. Although no direct dialogue concerning the islands took place during the negotiations, the talks with China made it clear to the Japanese government that the two countries had different takes on the Senkaku situation. Knowing that it would need to be even more careful about maintaining peaceful management of the islands to ensure its position of effective control, Japan adopted a more cautious policy that limited the placement of structures on the islands and curtailed the numbers of civilians making landfall.

The Senkaku Islands remained under peaceful management for several years, into the 1980s, until China abruptly and unilaterally declared the islands to be part of its territory via new domestic legislation—the Territorial Sea Law—in 1992. While the law had no international implications and thus no direct impact on Japan's sovereignty over the islands, it marked the beginning of China's efforts to change the conventional assumptions itself.

In September 2012, the Noda Yoshihiko cabinet transferred the Senkaku Islands from civilian ownership to national ownership under the Japanese Civil Code, citing the country's "peaceable and stable maintenance and management." The move by the government was an attempt to prevent Tokyo governor Ishihara Shintarō from purchasing the islands himself and launching initiatives to develop a site for a port and erect a lighthouse, a turn of events that would have represented

members were constantly deriding the government for its timidity. "Give Okinawa Back" was a slogan more for opposition parties and for Okinawans than it was for the government.

Satō had been concerned with the political issue of how to achieve the return of Okinawa and Ogasawara since his time as minister of international trade and industry in the Ikeda cabinet. He expressed his determination on his first visit to Okinawa as prime minister in August 1965 in a speech at Naha Airport in which he stated, "Until Okinawa is returned to Japan the postwar period has not ended." The Prime Minister's Office had worked together with the North American Affairs Bureau (the name had been changed from "American Affairs Bureau" in May 1965) of the Ministry of Foreign Affairs to scrupulously plan both Satō's Okinawa visit and the speech.

In his speech, Satō spoke of the atmosphere between Japan and the United States, and said that while the time was not yet right to broach the subject of returning Okinawa to Japan with the United States, it was the right moment to discuss the topic domestically. In public debate, there was lively discussion of Japan's administrative rights over education in Okinawa, although this was a separate matter. In a talk in Ōtsu in January 1967, Satō proposed that the return of Okinawa to Japan should happen fully at a single point in time, rather than through a gradual process.

Japan and the United States had begun working-level talks on this matter, but the crucial issue was what would happen with the military bases. While the Japanese government wished to resolve the issue of the bases within the framework of the current security treaty, the United States wanted to retain free use of the bases outside that framework. Somehow, the two sides had to get past this impasse. For the United States, retaining the function of the Okinawa bases was pivotal to the entire return process. Japan could not satisfy that aim while still hewing to its own desire for "homeland-level status" for Okinawa. For the Japanese government, "homeland-level status" meant that post-return Okinawa would be covered by the security treaty and its requirement for "prior consultation" (see sidebar on page 410–11).

Diplomats on both sides strove to make a special arrangement between Japan and the United States. Consideration was given to guaranteeing that the United States could continue to use the bases freely, but the concept of prior consultation had already been approved by the Diet, and creating an exception would clearly open the government to the kind of "change in the conventional assumptions" that both Japan and China were apprehensive about. China, deeming the Japanese government's ownership transfer a "nationalization" of the islands, condemned Japan for violating the existing understanding that the island dispute had been "shelved," defying international order, and infringing on Chinese sovereignty. The shift in ownership has left the waters around the dispute murky—and increasingly choppy. As more and more Chinese government vessels began making their way into the contiguous zone and trespassing into Japanese territory for the sake of provocation, Sino-Japanese relations continued to deteriorate.

harsh criticism in the legislature. In August 1967, senior officials of the Ministry of Foreign Affairs proposed such an exception to Satō, but he was not interested. What he had in mind was to encourage progress in the negotiations to set a date on which Okinawa would be returned to Japan.

Despite criticism from North American Affairs Bureau director-general Tōgō Fumihiko, when Satō met President Johnson again, in November 1967, he asked him, "Wouldn't it be possible to set a date for the return within the next two or three years?" Around that time, the United States was suffering an unprecedented deficit of international payments due to the costs of the Vietnam War, and it was in difficult negotiations with West Germany and other Western nations. Johnson replied that he wanted Japan to increase its aid to other Asian nations and provide additional capital for the ADB. He also asked Japan for US$500 million in "balance-of-payments cooperation" (medium-term bonds). Satō gave the most noncommittal response possible to these demands. In the meantime, regarding the joint declaration, he succeeded in reaching a clear agreement that the return would take place within two or three years.

Satō and the Ministry of Foreign Affairs aimed to reach an agreement on the return of Okinawa in 1969. In March of that year, Satō gave a speech in the Diet that made clear that his aims were "nuclear-free, homeland-level status." Satō had already publicly expressed his support for the Three Non-Nuclear Principles (see sidebar on the next page). Based on that position, he now made clear his expectation that, when administration of Okinawa reverted to Japan, all nuclear weapons would be removed.

The Problem of Nuclear Weapons Removal

In the main round of negotiations, which began between Satō and US president Richard Nixon in May 1969, the United States' goal was to maintain unfettered access to the bases. The United States indicated its willingness to negotiate the removal of nuclear weapons. Observing this, the Ministry of Foreign Affairs decided to focus first on the former so that it could at least reach agreement on prior consultation and put in place a curb on deployment. In other words, in the joint Japan-US statement planned for November, Prime Minister Satō would be able to say that the security of the Republic of Korea "was essential to Japan's own security." In a speech made after the agreement was completed, Satō said that in the event of an armed attack on South Korea, if combat operations were to be organized, Japan would "decide its stance quickly and positively based on prior consultation."

The final point of contention was the problem of the removal of nuclear weapons. The United States feared that once its nuclear weapons were removed after control of Okinawa reverted to Japan, the Three Non-Nuclear Principles would be applied, and the requirement of prior consultation might prevent nuclear weapons from being brought back into Okinawa or stored there, if that was necessary. To the bitter end, the US side avoided any official discussion of this topic. The Japan side prepared a joint statement that included a stipulation that reversion would be carried out "without harming the position of the US government regarding prior consultation," but the United States had not responded to this by the time of the meeting between the two leaders. At the summit meeting on November 19, however, Satō and Nixon came to an interpretation for the joint statement that was closely in line with the Japanese proposal, promising at least the removal of nuclear weapons and prior consultation in cases where they would have to be brought back in. For Tōgō and others, this was an unanticipated result.

The final joint statement released by Nixon and Satō on November 21 stated that administration of Okinawa would revert to Japan three years hence, in 1972. The return of Okinawa was thus settled at last in spite of all the opposing factors. The background reason for this was that Satō's secret envoy Wakaizumi Kei and Nixon's national security advisor Henry Kissinger had prepared a secret "agreed minute" guaranteeing the United States the right to bring in or transit with nuclear weapons in the event of an emergency. Satō and Nixon signed this agreement in a back room after the summit. Without that "agreed minute," the joint statement might not have been possible. At the very least, it was clearly needed to persuade the US military.

For Satō, accepting the "agreed minute," meant making an exception to the Three Non-Nuclear Principles that had just been adopted. It is said that before Satō met Nixon, he impulsively divulged his opinion that the third of the non-nuclear principles—not to allow nuclear weapons to be brought into Japan—had been a regrettable mistake. Regardless, Satō took sole responsibility for the secret agreement, and he alone signed it; with that act, the talks were brought to a close.

In a speech (discussed earlier) given shortly after that joint statement, Satō said South Korea's security was "essential" to Japan's own security, and

The Three Non-Nuclear Principles

Central to Japan's security policy are the "Three Non-Nuclear Principles": That Japan will not possess, nor produce, nor permit the introduction of nuclear weapons. Two of the principles—non-possession and non-production—essentially took shape via the 1955 passage of the Atomic Energy Basic Act, which stipulated that the "utilization of nuclear energy shall be limited to peaceful purposes" (Article 2). The other principle, "not permitting the introduction of nuclear weapons," had established firm roots in government policy by the early 1960s.

The non-introduction principle was a bit ambiguous in practice, however. A number of incidents that appeared to run against the principle, including the entry of an American warship carrying nuclear weapons into a Japanese port and the docking of the USS *Enterprise*—a nuclear-powered aircraft carrier—at Sasebo in January 1968, inflamed anti-nuclear sentiment among the general public and made the third principle an object of constant scrutiny. The issue came to a head during the Okinawa reversion negotiations in the late 1960s, as the American side was leery about applying the non-introduction policy in effect on the Japanese mainland to Okinawa; doing so, the US delegation felt, would encumber the United States' Far East strategy.

At the end of January 1968, Prime Minister Satō Eisaku clarified Japan's position. Responding to questions in the Diet, Satō established that "making a clear-cut distinction between the use of nuclear weapons and the peaceful use of nuclear energy is of chief importance" and then proceeded to outline four nuclear policies: maintaining the Three Non-Nuclear Principles; using atomic energy in a peaceful manner; promoting nuclear disarmament via international cooperation; and relying on the US nuclear umbrella (for nuclear deterrence). According to Wakaizumi Kei (a professor at Kyoto Sangyo University), who was then an advisor to Satō, maintaining the Three Non-Nuclear Principles (the first of the four policies) was contingent on the other three policies. Put simply, the only way for Japan to uphold its Three Non-Nuclear Principles—a critical bottleneck for the Okinawa reversion talks—was through US nuclear deterrence. By linking those two policy components together, the government was aiming to chart a clearer path forward for its negotiations with the United States regarding Okinawa. The "Basic Guidelines on Nuclear Policy," which the Jimintō announced in March 1968, indeed spelled the connection out in clear terms by stating that relying on nuclear deterrence was a precondition for upholding the Three Non-Nuclear Principles.

The Ogasawara Reversion Agreement

The Ogasawara (Bonin) Islands, comprising Chichijima, Hahajima, and Iwo Jima (Iō-tō), were incorporated into Japan under an agreement between the Meiji government and the Western powers in 1876 (see chapter 1). The islands' native inhabitants gained Japanese nationality, and by 1882, all foreigners living on the islands had also received the same. In the years following Japan's annexation of the islands, the government ramped up colonization efforts to settle the territories, established a local sugar industry, and cultivated the land for vegetable farming, efforts that proved successful. In the 1930s, construction projects established military fortifications on the islands, including airfields for Japanese planes on the Iwo Islands. In 1944, near the end of the Pacific War, the Japanese government evacuated roughly seven thousand islanders to the mainland and also conscripted approximately eight hundred male inhabitants between the ages of sixteen and sixty into military service. The majority of the conscripted soldiers died in the harrowing ground battle on Iwo Jima.

After the war, the US military occupied the Ogasawara Islands and refused to allow former inhabitants to return, save for the roughly 130 residents of Western descent. The islands gradually lost their strategic value to the United States, however, and the US government agreed to return the administrative rights to the Ogasawara Islands to Japan during the Satō-Johnson talks in 1967. In April of the following year, the two countries signed the Ogasawara Reversion Agreement to formalize the reinstatement and allow residents to return. While the terms of the agreement finally put Chichijima and Hahajima back under direct Japanese jurisdiction, the fate of Iwo Jima was slightly different. The US military handed authority over the island to the Japan Self-Defense Forces, but barred former residents from returning home. It is said that this was due to a secret agreement between Japan and the United States permitting the US military to continue bringing nuclear weapons onto the island after the reversion was complete.

In March 1969, Satō thus laid out a policy of Okinawa being returned to Japan as a territory with "nuclear-free, homeland-level" status, an approach that ultimately received official approval via the Satō-Nixon talks that November. The domestic debate over the issue was far from over, however, as questions about the introduction of nuclear weapons and base reductions during sessions for the ratification of the Okinawa Reversion Agreement in November 1971 sparked an imbroglio among lawmakers. Although the Jimintō had continually avoided passing a Diet resolution on the Three Non-Nuclear Principles, the parliamentary discord created enough pressure to elicit a compromise. In the end, the government weathered the storm by agreeing to pass a Diet resolution on adherence to the Three Non-Nuclear Principles and the reduction of bases on Okinawa.

In 1992, after the Cold War came to an end, the United States began removing tactical nuclear weapons from its warships—a development that enhanced the effectiveness of the non-introduction principle. Despite that change, Japan's reliance on US nuclear deterrence remained an important component of Japanese security; the policy appeared in the country's National Defense Program Guidelines in both 1995 and 2004.

That commitment to American deterrence has steered Japan's actions on the international stage as well. The 2017 UN Treaty on the Prohibition of Nuclear Weapons, for example, echoed the exact same points as Japan's Three Non-Nuclear Principles—but Japan, despite voicing its support for the idea of eliminating nuclear weapons, declined to sign the agreement due to concerns that it might undermine the legitimacy of US nuclear deterrence.

The first official government statement to hint at the three principles in the Diet was likely made on May 18, 1967, when then director-general of the Defense Agency Masuda Kaneshichi noted, during a meeting of the House of Councillors Committee on Cabinet, "Since the Kishi administration, the government has firmly maintained the rigorous policy of not producing, possessing, or introducing nuclear weapons." On December 11, 1967, Prime Minister Satō also told the House of Representatives Committee on Budget that Japan would "adhere to the three principles on nuclear weapons" in its approach to the introduction of nuclear weapons to the Ogasawara (Bonin) Islands.

The Treaty on the Non-Proliferation of Nuclear Weapons (NPT) and Japan

Countries around the world began to develop nuclear power for peaceful purposes in the late 1950s, leading to the spread of nuclear materials and technologies that could theoretically power nuclear weapons. As the resources became more widely available, the possibility of an increase in the number of "have" countries (countries with nuclear capabilities) also grew. When China conducted a successful nuclear-bomb test in 1964, the need to contain nuclear proliferation became a pressing issue for the international community. Under a resolution by the United Nations General Assembly, the Eighteen-Nation Committee on Disarmament (ENDC) launched into negotiations on a nonproliferation treaty in 1966. The goal was to recognize five nuclear-weapon states—the United States, the United Kingdom, France, the Soviet Union, and China—and safeguard against the emergence of any other new "haves."

Although Japan was not a member of the ENDC, the United States strongly encouraged the country to join the effort. The ENDC had already deemed Japan to be a "potential" nuclear-weapon state with the technical and economic resources to manufacture nuclear weapons, and Prime Minister Satō Eisaku had also hinted to US ambassador to Japan Edwin Reischauer that Japan was a potential "have" in late 1964.

To help dispel international worries about its nuclear capabilities, Japan worked to make its position as a "non-nuclear state" clear through statements to the United Nations. Aiming to ensure proper equity and balance with respect to the obligations on haves and have-nots, Japan argued for the disarmament of nuclear-weapon states, the sharing of technologies and information pertaining to the peaceful use of nuclear energy, and the need to protect non-nuclear states via UN resolutions and other security measures. The call for sharing information on nuclear energy also included a demand that all signatories be required to implement safeguards against the diversion of nuclear materials intended for peaceful purposes toward military use.

The draft of the treaty incorporated many of Japan's suggestions. Deeming the draft to be in line with its aims, the Japanese government approved a resolution commending the treaty, which the UN General Assembly adopted in April 1968. The UN opened the resulting Treaty on the Non-Proliferation of Nuclear Weapons (NPT) for signature that July, and Japan officially signed it in February 1970. However, it was not until 1976 that the Japanese government actually ratified the agreement; opposition to what some saw as the treaty's discriminatory nature, along with debates over the pros and cons of developing nuclear weapons, were cause for hesitation. By ratifying the NPT, Japan not only made an official declaration of its non-nuclear-weapon policy but also obligated itself to the entire international community not to produce or possess nuclear weapons. Japan has stressed the importance of the NPT framework ever since, and has played a central role in supporting international disarmament and promoting nonproliferation policy. These principles, upheld by the pillars of nuclear disarmament, nonproliferation (of weapons of mass destruction), and the peaceful use of atomic energy, remained sturdy for decades—until suspicions of North Korean nuclear tests in the 1990s began to shake the foundation.

that the security of Taiwan was "an important factor." He also expressed his intention to cooperate with America's Far East strategy. These statements became known as the "South Korea clause" and the "Taiwan clause" of the Japan-US alliance. The point, of course, was that the safety and security of South Korea and Taiwan would be immediately affected if the reversion of Okinawa were to lessen the functioning of the bases there. These nations were paying close attention, as they were very concerned about the outcome of the negotiations, but in the end they felt somewhat reassured.

The Signing of the Okinawa Reversion Agreement

Soon after Satō returned to Japan in late November 1969, he visited the grave of Yoshida Shigeru in Aoyama Cemetery. Yoshida had been unable to accomplish the reversion of Okinawa to Japan in his lifetime, and Satō wished to stand before his grave and assure him that that task had been achieved.

In June 1970, the Treaty of Mutual Cooperation and Security between the United States and Japan (called the "Anpo Treaty" in Japan) was

The Mystifying "Secret Agreements" on Okinawa

Japan's negotiations with the United States on the reversion of Okinawa are rumored to have generated several "secret agreements," four of which have gained particular attention.

(1) Satō-Nixon Agreed Minute to Joint Communiqué (November 1969, "Agreed Minute"): First, the US president required Japan's assurance that the United States would have the right to reintroduce nuclear weapons to Okinawa with prior consultation in the event of a "great emergency." The prime minister recognized the US government's requirements in a time of emergency and would meet said requirements without delay upon prior consultation. Technically, the Satō-Nixon joint statement would have taken shape with or without the Agreed Minute; it would be difficult to conclude that the secret agreement was a precondition for the end result. However, the real significance of the Agreed Minute was its role in convincing the US military: the second half of the document includes a passage indicating that the United States would require the maintenance of existing nuclear storage locations and the use of base facilities in Kadena, Henoko, and Naha, among other sites. The requests must have been made on behalf of the US military, as the US government would not normally have made such specific demands otherwise.

(2) Summation of Discussion (June 1971): This agreement between Japan and the United States stipulated that Japan would cover the restoration costs for US base land (roughly US$4 million). A portion of the records detailing the corresponding negotiations was eventually leaked, setting off the commotion over the "Nishiyama Incident" (where Nishiyama Takichi, the *Mainichi Shimbun* reporter who uncovered the secret pact, was sued for obtaining information via fraudulent means).

(3) Japan-US agreement memo on Japan's burden of expense for VOA relocation (June 1971): In this document, the Japanese government promised to bear the relocation expenses (US$16 million) for the Voice of America (VOA; a radio station run by the US government that broadcasts internationally).

(4) Kashiwagi-Jurich memorandum of understanding on currency conversion and other economic and fiscal-policy matters (December 1969).

The original copy of secret agreement (1) was confirmed in late 2009 to have been in the possession of the Satō family, but the Ministry of Foreign Affairs has no record of the document; no officials from the Ministry of Foreign Affairs who were on duty at the time knew of the agreement's existence, either. Whether the document was passed along, and what effective force the agreement had, remains largely unknown.

Agreements (2), (3), and (4) have been confirmed to exist in the United States (but not in Japan). The legitimacy of documents (2) and (3) as official "agreements," however, is uncertain; they bear only the initials of American Affairs Bureau director-general Yoshino Bunroku, which means that they never received approval from the foreign minister either before or after the fact. Having never made their way through the formal chain of command, therefore, the agreements are flimsy in terms of their reliability as records of diplomatic agreements between the two countries.

In any case, Japan found itself on the hook to a considerable extent for resolving the issues subject to secret agreements (2) and (3)—a result of the United States' determination to "return Okinawa without incurring any expenses" and its resulting insistence that Japan take up the full financial burden of the process.

Secret agreement (4) was a memorandum outlining an understanding between Kashiwagi Yūsuke (vice-minister of finance for international affairs at the Ministry of Finance) and Anthony Jurich (an advisor in the US Treasury Department). Negotiations on the financial and economic aspects of the Okinawa issue took place separately from talks involving the Ministry of Foreign Affairs: the Japanese Ministry of Finance and the US Department of the Treasury sat down at the negotiating table in September 1969 and reached a consensus before the Satō-Nixon joint statement came out. The fourth secret agreement outlined that understanding, which was a detailed collection of various complex provisions. One of the key points was an agreement by which Japan would deposit US dollars recovered via currency conversion in a non-interest-bearing account at the Federal Reserve Bank; the funds would remain on deposit for at least twenty-five years, so that they would not be a liability for either Japan or the United States.

13-10. Yara Chōbyō (left), chief executive of the government of the Ryūkyū Islands, visits Foreign Minister Aichi Kiichi (right)

due to expire. All over Japan, there was opposition to the treaty, mainly from college students and from the Sōhyō (General Council of Trade Unions of Japan). Diet approval was not required for the renewal of the treaty this time, however, so the disruptions of a decade earlier would not be repeated. The government did issue a statement about the automatic renewal.

At the same time, looking ahead to the reversion of Okinawa in 1972, as discussed in the joint statement, the government grappled with the urgent tasks of preparing for the event and drafting the actual agreement. This was a major undertaking. At a stroke, a region with one million inhabitants would be returned to Japanese administration. This was no task for the Ministry of Foreign Affairs alone. It would require the cooperation of ten or more government ministries and agencies. There was a mountain of work to be done: How would currency be converted? How would the costs of the reversion be borne? How would the United States bases be downsized and administered?

The negotiations between Japan and the United States were difficult. The United States wanted to spend as little as possible on the reversion, so it lobbied to push the post-reversion financial burden, including the costs of maintaining the bases, onto Japan. The US government's finances were in shambles at that point, with a burgeoning international deficit, so it was important for the United States not to spend money on the reversion. It also viewed minimizing spending on the reversion as key to maintaining a steady global policy and stability in the free world. All of this was an important part of the US strategy for defending the dollar.

Detailed negotiations regarding these problems were brought to a conclusion, capped by a cabinet decision, and then the Okinawa Reversion Agreement was signed in mid-June 1971. As the negotiations were winding down and it became clear that most of the bases would remain as they were, Okinawa was gripped by a feeling of disappointment, and the growing opposition to the reversion treaty culminated in a general strike.

Against this background, the Okinawa Reversion Agreement was signed in parallel ceremonies in Tokyo and Washington, DC, on June 17. Nixon,

13-11. Ceremony commemorating the return of Okinawa to Japan

who had been unable to resolve the textiles dispute between Japan and the United States, did not attend the signing. While paying tribute to the efforts of Foreign Minister Aichi Kiichi and Prime Minister Satō, Yara Chōbyō, chief executive of the government of the Ryūkyū Islands, chose not to attend the signing of the agreement, which left many bases as they were, contrary to the wishes of the Okinawan people.

The Okinawa Reversion Agreement faced a steep path to ratification in the Diet. The government hoped to get approval by the time of the Japan-US summit meeting scheduled for January 1972, but opposition parties dug in their heels, and major demonstrations all around the Diet building shut down the business of the national legislature. Senior Jimintō leaders strove to regain control of the situation through a Diet package that would combine the Three Non-Nuclear Principles with the Okinawa Reversion Agreement. Up to that point, the Jimintō had opposed a Diet resolution on the Three Non-Nuclear Principles, but they negotiated with the centrist Kōmeitō and the Minshatō (Democratic Socialist Party) to get the reversion treaty ratified. At the end of 1971, a package of bills related to reversion were passed all together by the Lower House in regular session.

In May 1972, twenty-seven years of US military rule over Okinawa came to an end. Having succeeded in this accomplishment, Satō stepped down the following month.

The Japan-US Textile Trade Conflict

The tussle between Japan and the United States over the textile trade had its roots in a campaign promise made by Richard Nixon during his 1968 run for the presidency. In an appeal to the textile industry in the American South, a favorable constituency, Nixon vowed to restrict textile imports from Japan, South Korea, Taiwan, and other nations. Nixon attempted to follow through on that promise after entering the White House, demanding that Japan and the other target countries impose voluntary export restraints on textiles. These countries' respective textile industries came out in strong opposition to the requests; in the end, it took four years to sort the issue out. The back and forth between Japan and the United States was so prolonged, in fact, that it spanned the terms of three successive ministers of international trade and industry (Ōhira Masayoshi, Miyazawa Kiichi, and Tanaka Kakuei) and went through three different American negotiators.

The deadlock was due to the United States' pressing demands for voluntary restraints on US-bound exports conflicting with Japan's claims that voluntary export restrictions deviated from the General Agreement on Tariffs and Trades (GATT) free-trade doctrine. Neither side was willing to let its respective domestic industries down. Japan was fully prepared to file a formal complaint with GATT participants, in fact. During the Japan-US Summit in November 1969, leaders had discussed the textile situation along with the reversion of Okinawa. At that time, Prime Minister Satō Eisaku agreed to Kissinger's proposal for voluntary restraints on exports to the United States, and assured the US delegation that he would bring the conflict to a resolution. Playing a vital role in laying the ground for the agreement was Wakaizumi Kei, who scrambled behind the scenes to reconfirm the arrangements with Kissinger and eventually arrive at a commitment. However, Satō kept silent on the pledge after returning to Japan and never even told the minister of international trade and industry—the official with jurisdiction over the matter-about his assurance to the United States. Rumor circulated that Japan was preparing to make a "textile-Okinawa trade-off."

Satō met with President Nixon again in the fall of 1970, a year after their initial talks. Although the two sides reaffirmed their friendly ties and agreed to resume talks on the textile issue, they never came close to finding a promising approach to a solution. The situation was finally resolved by Minister of International Trade and Industry Tanaka, who worked out an arrangement in which the Japanese textile industry would implement voluntary export restraints in exchange for massive subsidies from the Japanese government. Miyazawa, Tanaka's predecessor in the negotiations as minister of international trade and industry, later offered some insight on the subsidy solution in an interview. "It all worked out because Mr. Tanaka was a politician," he said, "and I wasn't."

CHAPTER 14

The Liabilities of Being a "Great Economic Power"

14-1. World leaders gather for the Tokyo Summit

TIMELINE

1971 (Shōwa 46)

July 15	US president Nixon announces he will visit PRC by May 1972 (First Nixon Shock)
August 15	President Nixon suspends gold/dollar convertibility (to protect the dollar), announces 10 percent tariffs on imports (Second Nixon Shock)
September 27	Emperor visits Europe (through October 14)
October 25	UN votes to expel ROC and to invite PRC to join

1972 (Shōwa 47)

January 3	Signing of Japan-US Textile Accord
February 21–28	Nixon visits PRC, US-China Joint Communiqué
May 15	Administrative rights of Okinawa returned
May 26	US, USSR sign Strategic Arms Limitation Talks (SALT) Agreement
July 7	First Tanaka Kakuei cabinet formed
September 29	Signing of PRC-Japan Joint Communiqué
December 22	Second Tanaka cabinet formed

1973 (Shōwa 48)

January 27	Vietnam peace agreement signed in Paris
February 14	Shift to a floating exchange rate system
August 8	Kim Dae-jung is kidnapped in Japan
September 21	Japan and North Vietnam establish diplomatic relations
October 6	Outbreak of Fourth Middle East War, First Oil Crisis
October 7–10	Tanaka visits USSR (first Japan-USSR summit in seventeen years)
December 10	Deputy Prime Minister Miki Takeo visits Middle East as special envoy
December 25	OAPEC (Organization of Arab Petroleum Exporting Countries) designates Japan a "friendly nation"

1974 (Shōwa 49)

January 7–17	Tanaka visits five Southeast Asian nations; met by anti-Japanese demonstrations in Bangkok and Jakarta
April 20	Signing of Japan-China civil aviation agreement
August 9	President Nixon resigns, succeeded by Gerald Ford
November 18	Ford becomes first US president to visit Japan while in office
December 9	Miki Takeo cabinet formed

1975 (Shōwa 50)

April 5	ROC president Chiang Kai-shek dies
April 30	Fall of Saigon (end of Vietnam War)
September 30	Emperor visits US (through October 14)
November 15	First summit of leaders of advanced nations

1976 (Shōwa 51)

January 8	PRC premier Zhou Enlai dies
July 2	Unification of Vietnam
July 27	Lockheed Incident results in arrest of former prime minister Tanaka
September 9	Mao Zedong dies; Hua Guofeng becomes party chairman on October 7
October 29	Japan decides on National Defense Program Guidelines
November 5	Japan decides on guideline for defense expenditures at 1 percent of GNP
December 24	Fukuda Takeo cabinet formed

1977 (Shōwa 52)

January 20	Democrat James Carter inaugurated as US president
August 18	Cultural Revolution in PRC ends
August 18	Fukuda visits Southeast Asia; in Manila he announces three diplomatic principles for Southeast Asia (Fukuda Doctrine)

1978 (Shōwa 53)

July 16–17	Fourth summit of advanced nations (Bonn Summit)
August 12	Signing of Treaty of Peace and Friendship between Japan and the People's Republic of China
December 7	First Ōhira Masayoshi cabinet formed
December 25	Vietnamese army invades Cambodia

1979 (Shōwa 54)

January 1	US, PRC establish diplomatic relations
January 7	International oil producers decide to reduce oil supplies to Japan (Second Oil Crisis)
February 17	Outbreak of Sino-Vietnamese War
June 18	US, USSR sign SALT II Agreement
June 28–29	Fifth summit of advanced nations (Tokyo Summit)
October 26	Assassination of South Korean President Park Chung-hee
November 4	US embassy staff taken hostage in Iran
November 9	Second Ōhira cabinet formed
December 5–9	Ōhira visits China, promises first yen loan to Deng Xiaoping
December 27	Soviet Union invades Afghanistan

1980 (Shōwa 55)

January 15	Ōhira visits Oceania, proclaims Pacific Basin Cooperation Concept
April 25	Japan announces it will not participate in Moscow Olympics
June 12	Prime Minister Ōhira dies suddenly
June 22–23	Venice Summit
July 17	Suzuki Zenkō cabinet formed
September 22	Outbreak Iran-Iraq War
November 4	Republican Ronald Reagan elected US president

1982 (Shōwa 57)

July 26	China lodges objections regarding Japanese history textbooks
August 26	Chief Cabinet Secretary Miyazawa Kiichi announces Japan position on China's textbook complaints ("Japan will . . . make corrections at the Government's responsibility")
November 27	First Nakasone Yasuhiro cabinet formed

1983 (Shōwa 58)

January 11–12	Nakasone visits South Korea, promises President Chun Doo-hwan $4 billion in economic aid
January 17–20	Nakasone visits US; in American newspaper interview, describes Japan as "unsinkable aircraft carrier"
May 28–30	Williamsburg Summit
September 1	USSR fighter plane shoots down Korean Airlines passenger plane over Sakhalin
December 26	Second Nakasone cabinet formed

1984 (Shōwa 59)

September 6	South Korean President Chun Doo-hwan visits Japan; at state dinner at the Imperial Palace, emperor expresses regret for "unfortunate past"

1985 (Shōwa 60)

March 11	Mikhail Gorbachev becomes general secretary of the Soviet Communist Party
August 15	Nakasone makes official visit to Yasukuni Shrine
September 22	Finance ministers and central bank heads from five advanced nations (G5) reach agreement to correct overvaluation of dollar (Plaza Accord)

1986 (Shōwa 61)

April 7	Advisory Group on Economic Restructuring issues Maekawa Report
April 26	Chernobyl nuclear accident in USSR
May 4–6	Tokyo Summit
July 22	Third Nakasone cabinet formed
September 8	Fujio Masayuki dismissed as Minister of Education for controversial remarks on Japanese colonial rule in South Korea
September 15	Start of GATT (General Agreement on Tariffs and Trade) Uruguay Round

1987 (Shōwa 62)

January 24	Japan decides to discard 1 percent of GNP guideline for defense budget
February 22	G7 Louvre Accord on currency stabilization
November 6	Takeshita Noboru cabinet formed
November 29	Korean Airlines Bombing Incident
December 8	US, USSR sign Intermediate-Range Nuclear Forces (INF) Treaty

1988 (Shōwa 63)

May 4	In London, Takeshita announces "international cooperation scheme"
June 20	Compromise reached in negotiations to liberalize imports of beef, oranges

1989 (Shōwa 64/Heisei 1)

January 7	Emperor Shōwa dies, succeeded by son Akihito; Heisei Era begins
April 5	Vietnam announces unconditional withdrawal from Cambodia
May 15–18	General Secretary Gorbachev visits PRC, first Chinese-Soviet rapprochement in thirty years
June 3	Uno Sōsuke cabinet formed
June 4	Tiananmen Square Incident in China
August 9	First Kaifu Toshiki cabinet formed
November 6	Establishment of APEC (Asia Pacific Economic Cooperation)
November 9	Opening of border between East and West Germany (destruction of Berlin Wall)
December 3	General Secretary Gorbachev meets President Bush in Malta (end of Cold War)

1 The Nixon Shocks and the Normalization of Japan-China Relations

The End of Postwar Diplomacy

One year before the cabinet of Satō Eisaku stepped down, Japan faced unprecedented changes in international relations. For one thing, in mid-July 1971, President Nixon suddenly announced that he would visit China. This marked a huge shift from the Cold War between the United States and China that had endured since the outbreak of the Korean War. Washington did not inform Tokyo of this warming of relations until shortly before the joint communiqué. Up to that point, concerning the problem of who should represent China in the United Nations, the US had consistently supported Taiwan, and Japan had aligned itself with that US position. Opposition parties in Japan were vocal in their criticism of Satō on this policy. The position of the pro-Taiwan faction within the Jimintō (Liberal Democratic Party) was weakened, and in the blink of an eye a growing number of people, both inside and outside the Diet, were calling for change in Japan's relationship with China. Prime Minister Satō and Foreign Minister Fukuda Takeo hurried to gather information about China, but foremost in their mind was the need to secure the position of Taiwan in the Western camp. They were in no hurry to increase contact with China.

14-2. Richard Nixon shaking hands with Mao Zedong in China

In October 1971, however, on the basis of a resolution introduced by Albania, the Republic of China was expelled from the United Nations and the People's Republic of China was admitted. The reversal of fortunes between Taiwan and mainland China in the United Nations settled the question of Taiwan relations in Japan, and the Ministry of Foreign Affairs began to move forward to explore how to sever relations with Taiwan and establish relations with China. The normalization of relations between Japan and China, and the problem of what to do about Taiwan, would be left for the administration of Tanaka Kakuei.

In mid-August 1971, Japan was struck by another Nixon Shock. Nixon took new measures to defend the value of the dollar, including a temporary suspension of dollar-gold convertibility. This move portended the demise of the Bretton Woods system that had helped maintain order in the international financial system since the end of World War II. Particularly since the 1960s, America's external liabilities far exceeded its reserves of gold. This undermined public faith in the gold-backed dollar, threatening a crisis for the system of fixed exchange rates. Even so, at the end of 1971, advanced nations entered into the Smithsonian Agreement, agreeing to maintain the system of fixed exchange rates, at least for the time being.

The reason for the two Nixon Shocks was, above all, America's military intervention in Vietnam, which had sapped its relative national power. America was the principal creator and defender of the world order, but it was now in the process of unwinding its excessive intervention in international affairs. To achieve this, it was asking other nations of the free world to bear more of the burden, in terms of both the economy and security. The Guam Doctrine, announced in 1969, presaged America's gradual withdrawal from Vietnam. It called upon America's allies to strengthen their own efforts. Japan, in particular, bore "a great responsibility for the peaceful development of the region," it said.

Japan's foreign policy, directly confronting these sorts of international developments, would achieve normalization of relations with China, which was the final challenge of the postwar period. Japanese diplomacy would be freed from the long succession of bilateral diplomacy that was characterized by postwar settlements, allowing it to expand its horizons. Japan was expected to contribute to stability in the Asian region and to coordinate multilaterally with other advanced nations in dealing with the new issues facing the world.

What Made Japan-China Rapprochement Possible?

In early July 1972, after the first meeting of the Tanaka cabinet, both Tanaka Kakuei and Foreign Minister Ōhira Masayoshi took an ambitious stance regarding the normalization of Japan's relations with China. During a visit to China by a delegation from the conservative Kōmeitō party in July the previous year, China had said three conditions had to be recognized for the normalization of the bilateral relationship: First, that the People's Republic of China was the only government representing the people of China (One China); second, that Taiwan was a part of China; and third, that the Treaty of Peace between the Republic of China and Japan (Treaty of 1952) was null and void. The second and third points were problematical, because they were connected with the status of Taiwan.

Tanaka Kakuei (1918–93)

Born in the Kariwa district of Niigata Prefecture, Tanaka Kakuei made his way to Tokyo at the age of fifteen after graduating from his hometown's higher elementary school. In the capital, he worked a variety of jobs by day and took part-time classes at night. He founded the Tanaka Civil Engineering Company in 1943 and, after the war, ran a successful general-election campaign for a seat in the House of Representatives in 1947. At the age of twenty-eight, he had become a lawmaker. Tanaka received his first cabinet assignment under Prime Minister Kishi Nobusuke in 1957, serving as minister of posts and telecommunications. He would continue to serve in different high-level positions, including that of minister of international trade and industry as part of the Satō Eisaku cabinet in 1971. In that capacity, he finally brought an end to the Japan-US textile-trade conflict that had been festering for a full four years.

Around that same time, Tanaka began gathering significant political momentum within the Jimintō. Rousing support around his calls to "reform the Japanese archipelago" with a firm emphasis on domestic affairs, he bested several rivals to become party president, and rose to the premiership in 1972. Amid shifting tides in the waters of international affairs, from the Sino-American rapprochement process to the global oil crisis, Tanaka saw Japan through to normalizing its relations with China—thanks in part to close friend and foreign minister Ōhira Masayoshi—and managed to convince the Soviet Union to recognize the presence of "unresolved problems left over since World War II" during ongoing peace-treaty negotiations at the 1973 Japan-Soviet Union Summit. When the oil crisis hit after his return from the Soviet Union, Tanaka outlined his "Arab-friendly" policy plan to help secure oil supplies. That dilemma also led Tanaka to take considerable interest in diversifying and decentralizing Japan's energy sources, which he pursued by making trips to Europe and Southeast Asia to sign an array of agreements for joint-development projects. Tanaka ultimately stepped down in December 1974, however, before his efforts could materialize.

14-3. Tanaka Kakuei

In late July 1972, Kōmeitō leader Takeiri Yoshikatsu returned from a meeting with Chinese premier Zhou Enlai with a proposal for a joint bilateral statement. This statement included the three conditions, but it did not mention the US-Japan Security Treaty, and it made no claims for reparations from Japan. The statement was vague on the matter of the treatment of Taiwan, but there were hints that working-level relations could be maintained even if official relations were broken off. This "Takeiri Memo" encouraged Tanaka and Ōhira to visit China. In late August, Tanaka and Ōhira traveled to Hawai'i, where they gained President Nixon's understanding that Japan would normalize relations with China. Jimintō vice president Shiina Etsusaburō was sent to Taiwan to explain Japan's position. In late September, Tanaka and Ōhira flew to Beijing.

In the Beijing negotiations, the Japan side was prepared to agree to break off relations with Taiwan, but found it difficult to say that the Treaty of 1952 was null and void. In the end, together with the joint communiqué, Foreign Minister Ōhira reached a compromise by declaring that the Treaty of 1952 was "at an end." The "two Chinas" problem that was causing such angst for Japan was solved by ending the Treaty of 1952, which allowed Japan to maintain working relations with Taiwan at the private-sector level.

Regarding the problem of reparations, Premier Zhou sharply criticized Japan's legal argument, saying, "We cannot simply accept the idea that [reparations] are unnecessary just because Chiang Kai-shek said so. That is an affront to us." At the same time, however, he did not reject the idea of forgoing reparations demands. In the Treaty of 1952, the Nationalist government had already abandoned its rights to claim reparations. In the end, the joint communiqué used the expression "claims" in place of "claims rights," thereby respecting both points of view. At the same time, the joint communiqué included Japan's expression of a "keen sense of responsibility and deep regret" for its past actions. China's relinquishment of reparations demands was matched with Japan's apology.

This cleared the way for the Sino-Japanese joint communiqué of September 29. Japan and China had not had formal diplomatic relations for over twenty years, but they were able to reach a compromise after brief negotiations. That was because of the strong popular desire on both sides for normalization, careful preparation by the foreign ninistries, and the leadership of the top officials. In addition, as China grew more entrenched in its standoff with the Soviet Union, it feared a warming of relations between Japan and the USSR; this was a strong motivating factor in the negotiations. For China, the normalization of relations with Japan was an extension of the rapprochement between China and the United States and an important element of its international strategy vis-à-vis the Soviet Union.

In the sense that diplomatic solutions had been found for both Japan-China and Japan-US relations, the normalization of Japan-China relations was a major success for Japan's postwar foreign policy, but it made the restoration of good relations with the Soviet Union less likely.

Relations with Taiwan: Breaking Off and Continuing

The Nationalist government in Taiwan was quick to announce the breaking off of diplomatic relations with Japan, but it was equally quick to work with Japan in considering how to maintain working-level relations and cultural exchanges. As early as December 1972, the Japan-Taiwan Exchange Association opened in Taipei, and the Atō Kankei Kyōkai (East Asia Relations Association) opened in Tokyo, allowing cultural exchange to continue even after diplomatic relations were broken off.

The next issue would be the signing of the Treaty of Peace and Friendship between Japan and China.

14-4. The first Japan-China Summit

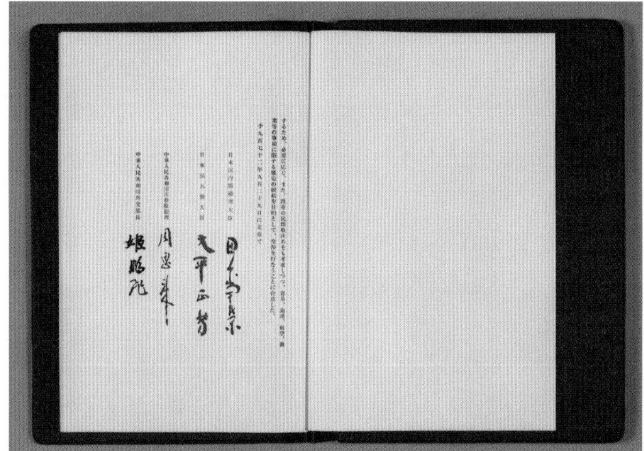

14-5. The signed Japan-China Joint Communiqué

The normalization of relations took the form of an intergovernmental joint declaration, which did not require Diet approval, but China wanted to see a peace treaty that would require ratification by the legislature. Initially, it was expected that the Treaty of Peace and Friendship could be put together in a short time, but it actually took another six years.

During that time, under the terms of the joint communiqué, Japan and China continued negotiations for working-level agreements in four areas: trade, marine transport, air transport, and fishing. The air transport negotiations were particularly difficult. The main sticking point—and the cause of numerous revisions to the text—was how to handle air traffic between Japan and Taiwan. In the end, in the compromise reached at the topmost level, routes between Japan and Taiwan were maintained as private-sector affairs. CAAC (PRC) flights were permitted to fly into Narita Airport, while China Airlines (Taiwan) could serve Haneda. The Japan-China civil aviation agreement was signed in April 1974. Taiwan, however, was incensed, and terminated China Airlines service to and from Japan. It was not until the next year that Japan-Taiwan relations were restored to the point that these airline services could resume.

Prime Minister Tanaka Visits Moscow

For the Soviet Union, the Japan-China rapprochement was a provocation, but the Soviet Union needed Japan's economic cooperation. In late 1972 it sent signals to Japan that it wished to improve relations. The Ministry of Foreign Affairs, bypassing the prime minister and the foreign minister, sought a political discussion with General Secretary Brezhnev, the top leader. Tanaka and Brezhnev met for three days in October 1973. The joint declaration stated that the negotiations for a peace treaty were continuing, and at the insistence of the Japan side, it referred to "several unresolved postwar problems," at least hinting at the existence of a territorial dispute. After that, however, the Soviet Union returned to acting as if there were no territorial dispute.

2 The Search for Cooperation among Advanced Nations

The Oil Crisis

With the outbreak of the Fourth Middle East War in October 1973, six Persian Gulf nations belonging to OPEC (Organization of the Petroleum-Exporting Countries) decided on a major increase in the price of crude oil. Then in November, OAPEC (Organization of Arab Petroleum-Exporting Countries) stopped all oil exports to the United States and the Netherlands, as these countries pursued pro-Israel policies, and reduced oil supplies to "unfriendly nations," including Japan. The *Nihon Keizai Shimbun* sounded the alarm: "Following on the heels of the big increase in crude oil prices, OAPEC's decision to cut oil supplies will rattle the foundations of Japan's existence, as we depend on foreign sources for 99.7 percent of our oil resources." For Japan, which had no interest in a drawn-out war in the Middle East, and which had coordinated its policies with the United States to ensure peaceful trade relations, being designated an unfriendly, pro-Israel country by the Arab nations came as a shock.

14-6. Discussions during the oil crisis

Secretary of State Henry Kissinger, who was coordinating the response of oil-consuming nations to the change in the Arab world's oil strategy, arrived in Japan in November. Prime Minister Tanaka stressed how dependent Japan was on oil from the Middle East, and sought Kissinger's approval of a shift in Japan's policy, telling him that Japan would have to seek friendlier ties with Arab nations unless the US offered alternative supplies of oil. The chief cabinet secretary gave a speech in late November in which he announced the Japanese government's "Arab-friendly" policy, saying, "Given the current situation, we have to rethink our relationship with Israel."

Early in December, Deputy Prime Minister Miki Takeo visited eight countries in the Middle East, explaining Japan's Middle East policy, including economic assistance and cooperation in establishing peace in the region. Arab nations responded positively to this gesture by Japan. In late December OAPEC designated Japan a "friendly nation" and made clear it would supply Japan with the oil needed.

Resource Diplomacy and International Cooperation

After the Third Middle East War in 1967, the Ministry of Foreign Affairs had taken measures to make the stability of Japan's oil supply a priority diplomatic issue. Some Japanese politicians took a strong interest in this problem, including Nakasone Yasuhiro and Tanaka Kakuei, who had both served as ministers of international trade and industry. As OPEC and the major international oil companies concluded several agreements that were favorable to oil-producing nations in the 1970s, the Ministry of Foreign Affairs defined the basic guidelines for resource diplomacy, aimed at securing a stable supply of oil by participating in the planning of agreements between oil-consuming nations, as conceived by the OECD (Organization for Economic Cooperation and Development). At the same time, based on the idea of growing closer to the oil-producing nations, some politicians were of a strong, persistent opinion that Japan's Middle East policy should be "neutral, but leaning toward the Arab side."

Nonetheless, for Japan's resource diplomacy, the oil crisis was not unexpected. From a long-term perspective, the problem was how to build stable relationships between oil-producing and oil-consuming nations. As the basic direction of Japanese policy prior to the oil crisis had been based on the idea of cooperation among oil-consuming nations, Japan looked forward to the thirteen-nation energy conference organized by Kissinger in February 1974. While America's stance was defined by its strong antagonism toward oil producers, Japan wanted to work with other oil-consuming nations to bring about a harmonious solution. Japan worked hard to realize the idea of an International Energy Agency (IEA) within the OECD.

Summit Participation

The Tanaka cabinet was forced to resign in December 1974 due to a financial scandal, and Miki Takeo took over as prime minister. Under Miki, Japan faced the same unprecedented issues of economic

Miki Takeo (1907–88)

After graduating from Meiji University in 1937, Tokushima Prefecture native Miki Takeo took his university degree and set off to undertake more studies in the United States and Europe. Several years later, thirty-year-old Miki won a seat in the House of Representatives—a position he would maintain for nearly fifty years. He eventually earned an appointment to the position of foreign minister as part of the Satō Eisaku cabinet and, as Japan's diplomatic lead, formulated an "Asia-Pacific collaboration" policy in 1966 to chart a path for Japan's role in addressing the North-South Divide. Seeing Japan as a "bridge," Miki eloquently verbalized his vision of his country "championing the fight against Asia's North-South Divide across the entire breadth of the Asia-Pacific community." He became prime minister in December 1974. Major developments during Miki's tenure in the premiership included his talks with US president Gerald Ford in August 1975, which led to an agreement to deliberate on effective implementation of the US-Japan Security Treaty, and a cabinet resolution in October 1976 to limit the defense budget to 1 percent of Japan's GNP in the National Defense Program Guidelines.

14-7. Miki Takeo

Miki also attended the first G6 ("Group of Six") Summit in 1975. Although he tried to convince the other representatives to address the North-South Divide, the issue never made it onto the agenda. The diplomatic concerns facing Miki's administration proved to be challenging, and progress on two key issues—the Treaty of Peace and Friendship between Japan and the People's Republic of China and peace-treaty negotiations with the Soviet Union—was negligible. Despite the lack of action on those fronts, Miki did orient Japan to focus on the ASEAN community and essentially set the course for the country's future approach to relations with Southeast Asia. Controversy marred the latter half of Miki's administration, however, as the Lockheed bribery scandals came to light and inflamed the political situation. The ensuing uproar over culpability for the scandal prompted in-party fighting and brought Diet operations to a halt, shunting diplomacy to the back burner. In the end, Miki's only trips abroad as prime minister were the 1975 G6 Summit and a visit to the United States.

diplomacy as it had under his predecessor: how would Japan, as an advanced Western nation, deal with the Nixon Shock and the oil crisis that had disrupted the international economic order for the first time since World War II?

With regard to international currencies, advanced nations signed off on the Smithsonian Agreement at the end of 1971, but by 1973 its future was in doubt. Japan and European nations were moving to systems of floating exchange rates, meaning that international transactions were increasingly unstable. Maintaining the stability of the international economic order by keeping exchange rates in international transactions stable would require collective, multilateral action. Because of the oil crisis, advanced nations were suffering from both inflation and economic stagnation at the same time: serious "stagflation." Leaders of advanced nations organized

Summit Meetings and Japan

The first G6 Summit took place in Rambouillet, a suburb of Paris, in 1975. Coloring the backdrop of the gathering were several economic predicaments that the oil crisis had foisted upon the Western world, including a recession of unprecedented scale and considerable instability in exchange rates. With American economic dominance starting to show cracks in its foundation, the other major powers knew that they would need to work together to maintain international monetary stability. France spearheaded that collaborative effort, calling on West Germany, the United States, the United Kingdom, Italy, and Japan to unite for discussions on how to steady the situation. In time, the group developed into a platform for openly exchanging views and building trust among top-level leaders. The aim was to enable the world's foremost developed countries to bolster the United States and keep the international economic structure going. The changes of the times had made that coordination crucial: by the 1970s, it was virtually impossible for any single country to correct problems in areas like currency, energy, and trade imbalance on its own.

Canada joined the gathering for the second Summit, making the group the "G7." Changes continued in the ensuing decades. The third Summit marked the introduction of an unofficial (extraordinary) member, the president of the European Commission, and Russia eventually made its way into the fold after the Cold War. That created the "G8," which had thus become less a consortium of "Western industrialized nations" and more a gathering of the leading global powers (which is also why the organization called itself the "meeting of major powers"). The G8 has since gone back to its G7 incarnation, as the members suspended Russia's status after it annexed Ukraine's Crimean Peninsula in 2014.

One important outcome of the first Summit was an agreement between the United States and France on international monetary stability, which paved the way for the conclusion of the official agreement the following year. From the late 1970s into the 1980s, the group engaged in talks on topics ranging from country-specific ceilings on oil imports (at the 1979 Tokyo Summit), macroeconomic-policy coordination among the member states, and multilateral surveillance of economic operations—with the members agreeing to monitor one another's economic activity on a mutual basis.

Japan began taking a more proactive approach to the Summits starting with the meeting in London in 1977 (the third G7 gathering), around the time that the international community began embracing the "locomotive theory" that viewed the United States, Germany, and Japan as the primary drivers for the world economy. The three "locomotives" needed to chug along in the same direction, of course, so coordination was key. In addition to sorting out how the three engines would work together, another issue was how to balance out the economic effects. As the locomotives would undoubtedly enjoy skyrocketing trade surpluses, countries around the world called on the three nations to expand their respective domestic demand in order to reduce the imbalance.

At the 1978 Summit in Bonn, the G7 members asked Japan and West Germany to set their real growth targets to 7 percent for the year. West Germany put up a resistance to the request, but Prime Minister Fukuda Takeo made it clear that pulling out of the recession would require cross-border cooperation. Firm in his commitment to the "locomotive theory," Fukuda pledged to the international community that Japan would adhere to the 7 percent growth target. It was that international promise, along with the high hopes that countries around the world were placing in Japan, that drove Fukuda into another (yet unsuccessful) run for the Jimintō presidency.

At the 1979 G7 Summit in Tokyo (the group's fifth gathering), the main topic for discussion was how to deal with a summit in November 1975 in Rambouillet, under France's leadership, to seek a solution to the problem.

Japan was the only Asian nation to be invited, and Prime Minister Miki went as its representative. Miki went prepared to speak about his favorite issue, the North-South Divide affecting support by advanced nations for developing nations. While the North-South Divide was an important topic, this particular summit had no room for peripheral discussions. Nonetheless, participation in this summit, as well as in the thirteen-nation energy conference, signaled the arrival of new opportunities for Japan to address global issues through policy coordination with advanced Western nations, along with an expansion of Japan's diplomatic horizons. Japan's participation in the 1972 United Nations Conference on the Human Environment held a similar significance.

OPEC's decision to hike the prices of crude oil. With the "second oil crisis" bubbling, the developed countries moved to counter the price increase via import restrictions. At the G7, France proposed that it set control targets for six years down the road and then instructed the other countries to set their own targets accordingly. The approach put Japan in a bind: going along with the French proposal would leave the Japanese economy in the lurch, but rejecting the proposal would throw a wrench into the collaborative arrangement among the developed nations. The dilemma vexed the Ōhira Masayoshi cabinet—but a helpful, more flexible alternative proposal by the United States gave Japan what it needed to navigate the situation.

Taking part in the Summit gatherings effectively expanded the horizons of Japanese diplomacy from a bilateral approach to a multilateral perspective. At the same time, that larger, more active role in global affairs required Japan to be accountable for its actions in the international sphere by embodying a clear, consistent approach and demonstrating its guidelines for action to the global community.

The 1997 Asian financial crisis showed how an economic crisis in one specific country could immediately trigger a global breakdown, regardless of whether the underlying source of the problem came from a developing country or a developed nation. The nature of the problem had begun to exceed what Summit meetings could handle.

Discussions of global economic issues have thus moved from Summit meetings to more specialized, diverse settings. Organizations like the Finance Ministers and Central Bank Governors Meeting, which the G7 members agreed to establish at the Tokyo Summit in 1986, and the G20 Summit (Group of Twenty Summit on Financial Markets and the World Economy), which originated in the immediate aftermath of the 2008 global financial crisis, have shouldered that responsibility.

At the G7 Ise-Shima Summit in May 2016, Prime Minister Abe Shinzō announced that Japan would be providing a total of US$6 billion in support of human-resource development programs for roughly 20,000 people to aid in the stabilization of the Middle East and North Africa—part of an effort to halt the spread of extremism and thus strengthen overall energy security. Abe also promised to accept Syrian students for study in Japan as a means of contributing to Syria's recovery.

The countries making up the G20 Summit account for roughly 80 percent of the world's total GDP and two-thirds of the global population. A key force in the power structure is China, especially in terms of steering the world's monetary policy. The question of whether the G20 can globalize and oversee the world economy effectively will hinge on China's involvement.

The G20 has abided by an anti-protectionist philosophy, one that has helped the international community overcome numerous currency crises—but that approach lost some of its stability after Donald Trump moved into the White House.

14-8. First summit of the world's leading industrialized nations in 1975

The UN Conference on the Human Environment was a gathering of over a hundred nations, the first international conference to take up comprehensive discussion of several problems concerning the "human environment." Regarding the positioning of environmental issues, advanced nations tended to emphasize the problems of environmental pollution, in contrast to developing nations' emphasis on economic development. Japan, with its priorities on environmental pollution policy, felt somewhat isolated. Its policies on whaling were also out of step, as other nations no longer regarded mammals as natural resources. On the other hand, Japan was successful in its efforts to portray atmospheric nuclear tests as a problem of cross-border radiation pollution, and thus to include a ban on such tests in the environmental declaration.

3 The Fukuda and Ōhira Cabinets

The End of the Vietnam War and Recognition of North Vietnam

The Vietnam peace agreement was reached in January 1973 with the signing of the Paris Peace Accords, and the US military began its withdrawal. The Vietnam War was finally at an end. Japan's Ministry of Foreign Affairs had already played a major role in the postwar restoration of Indochina, and it was in contact with North Vietnam from around the time of the establishment of the Tanaka cabinet, simply as a reminder of Japan's existence. Japan established diplomatic relations with North Vietnam in September 1973, shortly after Western nations did so. Japan could not accept, however, the idea of recognizing the Provisional Revolutionary

Fukuda Takeo (1905–95)

Fukuda Takeo, a native of Gunma Prefecture, took a position at the Ministry of Finance upon graduating from Tokyo Imperial University in 1929. After a stint in London, he landed at the Budget Bureau. Fukuda proceeded to develop a career at that bureau, working as a financial advisor for Wang Jingwei's Republic of China (a rival of Chiang Kai-shek's Nationalist government in eastern China) and eventually becoming director-general of the Budget Bureau in 1947—but his involvement in the Shōwa Denkō graft scandal forced him out. After retiring from ministerial service, he ran for office in the 1952, won a seat, and joined the Jiyūto the following year. Instead of aligning himself with Ikeda Hayato, one of his predecessors at the Ministry of Finance, Fukuda followed the lead of Kishi Nobusuke, who had made his way back into the political sphere after the lifting of the Allies' purge. In 1962, after Kishi's cabinet had folded, Fukuda took up the cause of his former mentor's faction by forming the Tōfū Sasshin Renmei (Party Renovation Alliance) and mounting concerted criticism of what he saw as Ikeda's "materialistic" approach driven by economic growth.

14-9. Fukuda Takeo

Fukuda served as an economic minister in successive administrations, starting with the Satō Eisaku cabinet and continuing through to Miki Takeo's premiership, and played a vital role in bringing the early 1970s economic crisis (sky-rocketing prices) under control. Having impressed plenty of leaders with his performance, Fukuda emerged as a promising heir apparent to the Kishi-Satō brothers. He would have to wait for some time to become prime minister, however. It was not until the end of 1976—after prime ministers Tanaka Kakuei and Miki Takeo had come and gone—that Fukuda finally got a chance to assemble a cabinet and set right to work on implementing his long-held vision of Japan as a "peaceful power." The ultimate goal was to nurture world peace through the economic power Japan had amassed. Determined to avoid following the path of a military power, Fukuda put economic cooperation and "communion" at the

Government of the Republic of South Vietnam, or North Vietnam's demands for reparations, so in fact there continued to be little if any interaction between Japan and those governments.

However, when Saigon fell in April 1975, and Vietnam was unified under the leadership of the North, and then Laos and Cambodia began to turn toward Communism, in October 1975 the cabinet of Miki Takeo agreed to give North Vietnam 13.5 billion yen in grants, and to exchange ambassadors. After the unification of the North and the South, Japan continued its support for Vietnam in an effort to prevent the country from becoming overly dependent on China and the Soviet Union. This was the diplomatic initiative expected by the United States, which had lost its own influence over Indochina.

At the same time, as the United States and China, which had been the main adversaries in the Cold War in Asia, moved toward normal relations, regional cooperative entities that had been strongly under the influence of US Cold War policy, such as the Japan-led Ministerial Conference for the Economic Development of Southeast Asia (SEAMCED), and the strongly anti-Communist ASPAC (Asian and Pacific Council), began to curtail their activities. SEATO (Southeast Asia Treaty Organization), the military organization for collective defense, also ended its activities in 1975. In its place, ASEAN (Association of Southeast Asian Nations), which had formed in 1967, became more prominent. ASEAN comprised five nations of Southeast Asia (Indonesia, Malaysia, Thailand, the Philippines, and Singapore), which worked together to block intervention by powerful nations from outside the region and to pursue regional autonomy in both economics and politics. It was with the Miki cabinet that Japan first came to prioritize its relationship with ASEAN.

heart of his policies. In that same spirit, Fukuda drove the creation of the Japan Foundation—a fund that served to infuse Japanese diplomacy with a stronger emphasis on human resources and cultural exchange.

The Fukuda Doctrine, which Fukuda articulated during a visit to Southeast Asia in August 1977, captured his "peaceful power" ideal in concrete terms: "expanding Japan's diplomatic foundation" by tackling the Asian community's various post–Vietnam War issues without adhering strictly to the bilateral framework of Japan-US relations. Out of that context, the larger, broader idea of "omnidirectional foreign policy" was formed. Japan's efforts to sign the Treaty of Peace and Friendship between Japan and the People's Republic of China and take a proactive approach to the Soviet Union both had their roots in the "peaceful power" policy—but both failed to come to full fruition. Fukuda had to relinquish power after losing the election for party leadership in December 1978, but he continued to chair the InterAction Council of Former Heads of State and Government and work on international issues ranging from the environment to energy.

The Fukuda Doctrine

In December 1976, Fukuda Takeo took over from Miki as prime minister. Fukuda took it upon himself to raise Japan's profile by expanding the parameters of Japan's foreign policy. He wanted to change Japanese diplomacy, not in a passive way, but by working on a wide variety of regional issues. Southeast Asia, where the presence of the United States had been greatly diminished, was the perfect platform.

In August 1977, Fukuda embarked on a tour of all five ASEAN nations. He gave a speech in Manila where he made clear Japan's support for ASEAN, expressing Japan's position in terms of three principles: (1) Japan would seek peace, not positioning itself as a military power. (2) Japan would seek to build "heart-to-heart" relationships of mutual trust with Southeast Asian nations. (3) Japan would work for peace and stability throughout the region by fostering mutual trust between ASEAN and the nations of Indochina.

Item (1) was meant to counter concerns about Japanese military expansion like what had occurred before World War II. Item (2) was aimed at easing frictions that might arise as a result of Japan's increased economic engagement. By calling for "heart-to-heart mutual understanding," Fukuda was trying to revive the idea of the Japan Foundation, which he had first floated during his time as foreign minister in the Satō cabinet.

Fukuda had not forgotten Prime Minister Tanaka's visit to Southeast Asia in January 1974, when he was met with loud anti-Japanese demonstrations and riots in Thailand and Indonesia. Some believed these anti-Japanese riots were meant as criticisms of military dictatorships and the influx of foreign capital, and simply took aim at Japan. But the Ministry of Foreign Affairs concluded there were also problems with the way Japan conducted its private-sector-led economic penetration and economic cooperation.

The most significant aspect of the Fukuda Doctrine was its forthright statement of support for ASEAN and building peaceful coexistence between ASEAN and the three Socialist nations of Indochina. Japan's Diplomatic Bluebook recorded this as "Japan's first active diplomatic posture of the postwar period."

The question of whether the three Indochinese nations that had just embarked on a socialist course would be able to coexist peacefully with ASEAN could only be answered by Vietnam, which was emerging as the most powerful nation of the region. By continuing its support for Vietnam, Japan hoped to lessen Vietnam's dependence on China and the USSR, encouraging it to tread a path toward greater autonomy and independence. The Ministry of Foreign Affairs concluded that if active support for Vietnam could help lead that country to a stance of cooperation with Western nations, in the long term that might contribute to the realization of peaceful coexistence between ASEAN and Vietnam.

If, however, the conflict between China and the Soviet Union were to spread to Southeast Asia and take hold there, the conditions needed for peaceful coexistence between ASEAN and Indochina as visualized by the Ministry of Foreign Affairs would be lost. Vietnam was at odds with Cambodia's Pol Pot regime, and in late December 1978, just after it signed a treaty of friendship and cooperation with the Soviet Union, it invaded Cambodia and installed a pro-Vietnam government. In February 1979, China, which was allied with the Pol Pot regime, attacked Vietnam (Sino-Vietnamese War). This set off a civil conflict in Cambodia that would last for thirteen years. Cambodia became the stage for a complex international conflict reflecting interests specific to the region as well as the conflicts between the United States, China, and the Soviet Union, making the idea of peaceful coexistence between ASEAN and the nations of Indochina seem even more remote.

At the same time, Japan and the ASEAN countries grew even closer to one another, with Japan providing large amounts of Official Development Assistance (ODA) and Japanese companies rapidly increasing their investments and their presence. All of this formed a strong foundation for a "development system" whose priority was the economic development of the ASEAN nations.

Japan-China Treaty of Peace and Friendship: Yen Loans to China

The Miki cabinet, with Miyazawa Kiichi serving as foreign minister, showed a strong desire to improve relations with both China and the Soviet Union, but little progress was made. In 1976, Zhou Enlai died, and Mao Zedong passed away soon after. Deng Xiaoping succeeded Zhou in taking responsibility for foreign affairs, but Japan-China relations were paralyzed as machinations by the Gang of Four disrupted China's internal politics.

Deng was out of favor for a time, but took control again in the summer of 1977, successfully stabilizing China's external relations and returning to a course of positive progress in restoring relations with Japan. Prime Minister Fukuda prevailed over the still-powerful members of the Jimintō who advocated caution, and managed to return to negotiations of the peace and friendship treaty the following year. In the new negotiations, an "anti-hegemony clause" became an issue, even though China had not made any fuss about it at the time of the joint communiqué. Japan wanted to insert a clause about third parties that would downplay the anti-Soviet aspects and make clear that the treaty was not intended to have any impact on third parties. In the end, China accepted this. The Treaty of Peace and Friendship between Japan and the People's Republic of China was signed in August

14-10. The ratification of the Treaty of Peace and Friendship between Japan and the People's Republic of China

Ōhira Masayoshi (1910–80)

A native of Kagawa Prefecture and graduate of Tokyo University of Commerce, Ōhira Masayoshi joined the Ministry of Finance in 1936 and quickly found himself on assignment to the Board of Asia Development. Following a stint in China, Ōhira made a return to the Ministry of Finance prior to Japan's defeat in WWII. He decided to retire in 1951 and sought a seat in the following year's election for the House of Representatives, a campaign that proved successful. As one of Ikeda Hayato's closest advisors, Ōhira flourished in the political realm and landed the position of chief cabinet secretary when Ikeda took over as prime minister in 1960. He also served as foreign minister in two cabinets, focusing on restoring diplomatic ties with neighboring nations: under Ikeda, Ōhira pushed forward progress in the negotiations on normalizing relations between Japan and South Korea, and under Tanaka Kakuei, his efforts culminated with the normalization of relations between Japan and China. Ōhira rose to the premiership in late 1978, succeeding Fukuda Takeo. As prime minister, Ōhira saw Japan in an excellent position to stake out a larger presence in the global arena as the United States' military and economic might showed signs of waning. For Japan, an emergent "economic powerhouse" in Ōhira's eyes, there were two key roles to play in the contemporary context. He translated those roles into policy visions. One was the "Pacific Basin Cooperation Concept"—an open, diverse partnership with the aim of enhancing stability and development in both the Pacific (Japan, the United States, Canada, and Australia) and Asia. The vision not only covered mutual economic development but also attached a great deal of importance to cultural exchange and mutual understanding. In 1980, Japan took the first step toward realizing Ōhira's vision by forging an agreement with Australia on economic development in the Pacific region (see page 454).

14-11. Ōhira Masayoshi

Ōhira also envisioned "comprehensive security." Perceiving the increasingly interdependent global society as a "single collective," Ōhira sought to frame Japan's international affairs, economy, and culture as elements with connections to the country's security. Essentially, he painted "security" in broad strokes—the security of the country meant protecting the lives and livelihoods of the people from threats, which included not only military dangers but also food shortages, energy shortages, national disasters, and other potentially dire circumstances. In those ideas, one could see the outlines of a National Security Council that would direct the country's approach to comprehensive security. Ōhira never got to see his policy ideals get past the "vision" stage during the course of his life, which ended suddenly in June 1980, but his idea of the proper direction for Japan was largely what laid the groundwork and forged the structure for future deliberations on Japan's foreign relations and security policies.

1978 in Beijing by Chinese foreign minister Huang Hua and Foreign Minister Sonoda Sunao. The Treaty of Peace and Friendship contained nothing that was not already in the joint communiqué of 1972, but it became an important building block of Japan-China-US cooperation against Soviet military buildup.

Deng visited Japan in October 1978 for the exchange of instruments of ratification for the treaty. He showed great interest in visiting factories across Japan, and he was enthralled to ride on the Shinkansen bullet train. Japan was a powerful model of development for China, which at that time was following Deng's policy course, steering in the direction of "reform and opening." China was clearly facing a shortage of the capital it would need to truly build its economy.

In December 1978, shortly after Deng's visit to Japan, Ōhira Masayoshi, who had served as foreign minister in the Tanaka cabinet, took office as prime minister. In September 1979, Ōhira received a formal request from China for economic assistance, and he made the decision to make yen loans to China. However, there were several concerns regarding such loans. One possible complication was that the focus of Japan's economic cooperation efforts seemed to be shifting away from ASEAN in favor of China. Ōhira expounded three principles to address this, one of which was to set balance with the nations of ASEAN as a condition for yen loans. The other two principles were a ban on military cooperation and a ban on market monopolies (coordination with Europe and the United States).

In December 1979, Ōhira visited Beijing and announced the first six projects to be financed by yen loans, including harbor infrastructure, railways, and hydroelectric power. That marked the start of Japan's ODA to China. The long-term goal was to support the economic development of China and to encourage its government to cooperate with the West.

The Pacific Basin Concept

In his inaugural address in December 1978, Prime Minister Ōhira announced the "Pacific Basin Cooperation Concept," and followed up in March by forming the Pacific Basin Cooperation Study Group to consider specific policies. Recognizing the issues that had arisen in the free-trade system, the goals stated in the study group's report were "to shape free and open mutual interdependence," and to secure support from advanced nations for the efforts of developing nations. At the same time, if economic interdependence were to grow deeper, in this region, with its rich diversity of ethnicities and cultures, there was a risk that frictions and conflicts would increase. The group therefore also argued for the promotion of cultural exchanges to encourage mutual understanding.

Another aim was to work with Australia to draw America into the multilateral coordination. Through a January 1980 agreement with Australian prime minister Malcom Fraser, Ōhira's idea gave rise to the private-sector Pacific Economic Cooperation Council (PECC), to explore the possibilities for economic cooperation. PECC's activities ultimately laid the foundation for the creation of APEC (Asia-Pacific Economic Cooperation) in 1989.

In matters of national security, Ōhira saw a diversity of threats—not just military threats—from which the Japanese people needed to be protected. He therefore espoused the idea of "comprehensive security," establishing a framework for future discussion (see sidebar on the previous page).

The New Cold War

Détente (easing of tensions) between the United States and the USSR went downhill as Soviet military expansion and influence spread around the world in the second half of the 1970s. That picture changed completely with the Soviet invasion of

Afghanistan in December 1979. This marked the start of a "New Cold War." Prime Minister Ōhira reiterated his call for coordination with the United States, reminding people that Japan was a "Western nation." In the early 1980s, he set limits on cultural exchanges with the USSR, and decided that Japan would join the boycott of the Moscow Summer Olympics. That was Japan's first strategic sanction.

Following Ōhira's untimely death in June of 1980, Suzuki Zenkō became prime minister. Pressed to resolve trade frictions in economic relations with the United States, he took it upon himself to strengthen political relations. In May 1981, Prime Minister Suzuki met President Ronald Reagan. The two issued a joint statement, saying, "The alliance between the United States and Japan is built upon their shared values of democracy and liberty." This was the first time that the word "alliance" appeared in a joint statement between the two countries.

4 The Nakasone and Takeshita Cabinets

The "Japan-US Alliance" Takes Hold

In November 1982, Nakasone Yasuhiro formed his new cabinet, and the following January he visited South Korea, delivering part of his Seoul remarks in Korean. This was the first official visit by a Japanese prime minister to South Korea since World War II. Nakasone built a close relationship with President Chun Doo-hwan, and Japan provided a total of US$4 billion in aid to resolve troublesome issues surrounding economic cooperation. South Korea had demanded a large amount of economic assistance, citing the "division of roles" mentioned in the Japan-US joint statement and asserting that Seoul was shouldering a large measure of Japan's defense burden by standing up to North Korea.

Shortly after his visit to South Korea, Nakasone visited the United States and met with Reagan. Where earlier Japanese administrations had refused to respond to US demands for Japanese weapons technology, citing the three principles on arms exports, before his trip to the United States Nakasone had stated that he saw no problem with this kind of technological cooperation because the United States was an "ally." The United States greatly appreciated this shift in Japan's policy. The joint declaration spoke clearly of the Japan-US "alliance." At a breakfast with the chief executive of the *Washington Post*, according to reports in English-language newspapers, Nakasone said the Japanese archipelago represented "a strong defense, like an unsinkable aircraft carrier" against a major attack by the Soviet Union. This statement caused a great deal of controversy in Japan, but Nakasone was unmoved.

Nakasone built a relationship of trust with Reagan, ushering in the "Ron-Yasu" era of US-Japan relations. At the Williamsburg Summit in May 1983, one major point of contention was the Pershing II missiles that the United States proposed to deploy in Europe as a defense against Soviet SS-20 medium-range missiles. While France and West

14-12. US president Reagan visits Japan

The Issue of History Textbooks

In 1982, a decade after Japan and China had normalized their relations, a new diplomatic crisis drained whatever celebratory mood the ten-year anniversary of renewed Sino-Japanese ties might have brought. A furor began to erupt on June 26, when major Japanese newspapers ran articles reporting that the Ministry of Education had made revisions to Japan's high-school history textbooks: the updated descriptions of the Sino-Japanese war cast Japan's actions in the conflict as "advances" or "attacks" instead of the customary "aggression." Although the articles may not have been completely factual, as they incorrectly claimed that the revisions had been specifically ordered, it was undeniable that certain "opinions on improvements" from the Ministry had resulted in some textbook companies substituting "advances" for "aggression." Whatever the case, the Chinese government came out with a statement a month later lambasting the Ministry of Education for "falsifying the history of Japan's militarism invading China" and demanding that officials address the corresponding errors in the approved textbooks. The South Korean government also objected to textbook passages on Japan's colonial administration, but China was more forceful in its calls for corrective action.

When Japan made it clear that it would not be acquiescing to China's protests, China and South Korea responded with even more outrage—and the resulting unease in the countries' relations complicated Prime Minister Suzuki Zenkō's scheduled visit to China in September. The Japanese government decided to try to remedy the situation by making an official statement. In late August, Chief Cabinet Secretary Miyazawa Kiichi said that "from the perspective of building friendship and goodwill with neighboring countries, Japan will pay due attention to these criticisms and make corrections at the Government's responsibility." In line with the "Miyazawa statement," the Ministry of Education changed its official policies in November 1982. The ministry adopted a new authorization criterion for history textbooks—the "Neighboring Country Clause," which required textbooks to "give the necessary consideration to international understanding and international harmony in their treatment of modern and contemporary historical events involving neighboring Asian countries."

Another volatile development emerged in May 1986. The *Asahi Shimbun* broke a story about a textbook called *Shinpen Nihon-shi* (A new edition of Japanese history), the work of a group that saw the Japanese government's 1982 response (the Miyazawa statement) as "weak," before the textbook screeners had completed their assessment of the text. When China and South Korea got wind of the

Germany were reluctant to allow the deployment of the US missiles, Nakasone took Reagan's side, contending that the Western nations should stand together as a way to draw the Soviet Union to the negotiating table. Nakasone's position played an important role in shaping the final agreement. In the joint statement, the nations participating in the summit said, "The security of our countries is indivisible and must be approached on a global basis." This meant the Soviet Union had to restrict its deployment of missiles in Asia.

In September 1983, an incident occurred where a Soviet fighter jet over Sakhalin shot down a Korean Airlines passenger plane bound for Seoul. Nakasone made the decision to release the communications records from the Soviet fighter that had been intercepted by the Self-Defense Forces, and share them with the UN Security Council. The Soviets acknowledged the facts of the attack, and the US Senate unanimously approved a resolution thanking Japan for its actions. Reagan visited Japan in November that year, becoming the first sitting US president to address the Diet. He talked about Soviet military expansion, and said (in Japanese), "Japanese-American friendship is forever."

The Plaza Accord

Like preceding administrations, the Nakasone cabinet had to deal with the problem of the imbalance in Japan-US trade. In response to US demands that Japan open its markets, Nakasone took a variety of measures, but the impact was limited. Up to that point, for reasons related to the free market and international prestige, the Reagan administration had allowed the dollar's value to story, which told how the textbook tended to justify Japan's foreign aggression and paint Japan as a victim, both countries came out in vehement opposition. China took particular umbrage with the textbook's ambiguity about the "war of aggression," and the Nakasone Yasuhiro cabinet responded by subjecting the textbook to partial revisions. On the domestic scene in Japan, meanwhile, some voices charged that China and South Korea were infringing on Japan's sovereignty and interfering with the country's internal affairs. The Chinese government, though not necessarily satisfied with Japan's response, made no further demands for revisions.

In the 1920s, the League of Nations had created the International Committee on Intellectual Cooperation and tasked it with addressing textbooks. The organization knew that if a country's government chose to teach "convenient" history and skew the content to reflect well on the nation in question, students could very well end up harboring unfounded prejudices or enmity toward other countries—circumstances that could also prepare citizens for war on a psychological level. The International Committee on Intellectual Cooperation thus held thorough discussions of history textbooks with members from multiple countries present, aiming to eliminate any content that might misrepresent or lead to serious misunderstandings of other countries.

A Japanese project in a similar vein, the "Keimeikai" (a fledgling teachers' union), made it known that it was doing away with all textbooks that cultivated animosity toward other nations and compiling an international history textbook. The Keimeikai movement would eventually peter out in the mid-1930s as the world's major powers accused the initiative of violating textbook sovereignty and meddling in domestic affairs. Worth noting, however, is that the 1929 report by the International Committee on Intellectual Cooperation was based on the guiding principle that a style of historical education that conceived of Europe as a single entity, not a collection of separate entities, would aid European unification.

In the mid-1980s, the Japanese Diet also discussed cultivating conversations about the textbook issue when members of the Jimintō submitted a proposal to "hold roundtable discussions between private citizens from Japan and South Korea, as well as private citizens from Japan and China, to foster frank, heart-to-heart dialogue." That idea eventually took real shape in the 1990s, as scholars from Japan, China, and South Korea began coming together to develop shared textbooks at the private-sector level.

remain high, but it finally decided some correction was needed. In September 1985, the US government convened a meeting of finance ministers and heads of central banks from the Group of Five advanced nations (the United States, the United Kingdom, France, Germany, and Japan). Their aims were to lower the value of the dollar to a level that better reflected economic realities, to restore the international competitiveness of US industry, and to put the brakes on the worsening of the US balance of payments. The other four nations shared the concern that increasing imbalances in global trade could destabilize the world economy, so they reached an agreement—the Plaza Accord—for international cooperation to adjust economic policies and intervene in markets to correct the high value of the dollar.

The dollar's value fell swiftly in response to the Plaza Accord, but this did not have the desired effect of correcting trade imbalances. As a consequence, the yen rose to unprecedented heights. As the strong yen became an established fact, Japan greatly increased its overseas direct investment, especially in South Korea, Taiwan, and the ASEAN group. This became a major engine of economic development in Asia. Japan also increased direct investment in Europe and America, expanding its local production, and this helped to relieve trade frictions. At the same time, Japan also increased its investments in properties and acquired many companies synonymous with the United States. This caused Japan to be perceived as a threat.

Nakasone decided it was his urgent mission to change Japan's policy course to put greater emphasis on international coordination. He decided to do so by shifting Japan's economy toward greater

Japan-US Trade Friction: The Pros and Cons of "External Pressure"

From "Voluntary Restraints" to Open Markets

The United States boasted overwhelming competitiveness in a host of industrial sectors after World War II came to an end, but that edge eventually began to dull. The postwar decades saw import volumes overtake exports in everything from textiles in the 1950s and iron and steel in the 1960s to home appliances and cars in the 1970s and cutting-edge technologies in the 1980s. Over the course of those changes, the United States gradually sank into an international trade deficit. As the United States eventually became the world's biggest debtor nation in 1985, Japan became the globe's top creditor—and the Japan-US trade imbalance became an increasingly gaping divide.

The textile industry was one of the sectors where lagging American competitiveness in international markets was most apparent. In the 1950s, a massive stream of low-priced Japanese cotton goods made its way into the American market. The US textile industry appealed to the government for assistance in fending off the influx, and the US government responded by demanding that Japan place voluntary restraints on its exports. Japan agreed, promising to limit the volume of cotton products leaving the country for the United States, and signed the Japan-US Agreement on Cotton Products in 1957 to formalize the arrangement. The countries then followed a similar process for regulating Japanese exports of wool, synthetic-fiber products, and later iron and steel to the United States; voluntary restraints gradually became the go-to solution for Japan-US trade conflict.

The United States' once-mighty economic dominance began a relatively significant decline in the latter half of the 1960s, which led the US government to step up its pressure in seeking stiffer voluntary restraints—and, as a result, Japan-US relations began to suffer on a broader diplomatic scope. The Japan-US textile trade conflict, which erupted in the second half of 1969, was at the center of that discord. Out of the negotiations to rectify the situation came the 1972 Japan-US Textile Agreement, which ended up affecting the trade of textile goods on a global level through various quantitative limits, and put the textile trade outside the scope of the GATT framework for liberalizing world trade.

In the 1980s, the United States adopted a different stance on the issue. Instead of the "defensive" approach of limiting Japanese exports to the United States through voluntary restraints on the part of Japan, the United States mounted more "offensive" tactics that centered on urging Japan to open and expand its markets through larger import quotas so that American products would have more opportunities to establish a foothold in Japan. The strategy not only applied to textiles, but also covered agricultural products like beef and oranges, cutting-edge technologies, and more.

The issue of liberalizing imports of beef and oranges had been a pending concern since 1978. Japan headed into the corresponding negotiations with the hopes of resolving the issue via a gradual expansion of import quotas, but the talks ultimately stalled. Frustrated with the lack of progress, the United States decided to appeal to the GATT in 1988. The Japanese government, under the Takeshita Noboru cabinet, favored finding a bilateral solution over battling the United States in the GATT framework—but the import-quota system itself was soon on the chopping block. To mitigate the impact of the quota system's demise, the Japanese government started pumping investments (subsidies) into rationalization and modernization efforts in the agricultural sector.

Solving the issues surrounding the opening of the Japanese market was by no means an easy task. Japan's pledge to open up and expand its market did not guarantee that the volume of American exports to Japan would grow and correct the trade imbalance as intended, and the trade gap did, indeed, remain. While the closed nature of the Japanese market was partially responsible for that outcome, a number of other circumstances on the US side—the country's budget deficit, declining industrial competitiveness, and inadequate export efforts—were also contributing factors.

Japan-Bashing and the Structural Impediments Initiative

In the early months of 1985, Prime Minister Nakasone Yasuhiro made a visit to the United States and reached an agreement with President Ronald Reagan to adopt a new approach to their negotiations: Market-Oriented, Sector-Selective (MOSS) talks. The new method would bring relevant ministry and government officials from the two sides together in separate, direct dialogues on specific topics in four target areas that the United States excelled in—electronics, telecommunications, pharmaceutical products, and forest products—to identify key issues and bring down barriers to entry into the Japanese market. While the MOSS talks resulted in some progress, they failed to root out the problems at the core of the Japan-US trade imbalance. Still, they did address the existing Japanese systems and practices that were hindering imports; the negotiations were a healthy form of external pressure, a push to correct long-standing impediments. Japan was eager to see the changes through, too. In that sense, the MOSS talks were a precursor to the later Structural Impediments Initiative.

The biggest point of contention was what to do about semiconductors. In the late 1970s, US semiconductor trade had fallen into a deficit—and Japan's share of the market ballooned in turn. The American government, pressured by congressional lobbyists from semiconductor-related industries to make the domestic market more closed and prevent dumping, demanded that Japan make a significant increase in the share of foreign-made semiconductors in its domestic market. In the end, the two sides reached the Japan-US Semiconductor Agreement in 1986, which included provisions for the US requests. The following year, however, the United States imposed sanctions on Japan for not holding up its end of the bargain. The US government contended that Japan had failed to ensure that foreign companies would have a 20 percent share of the Japanese market, which tied into a provision in an accompanying document stipulating that foreign producers would have at least a 20 percent share in Japan's semiconductor market in five years' time. The Japanese side countered, arguing that presetting a specific market-share level for a given party went against the principles of free competition. It also argued that the terms in the document accompanying the agreement were not an official government promise but simply an indication that it would strive to meet the American requirements. Japan eventually made a concession in the Second Japan-US Semiconductor Agreement (1991), which moved the 20 percent provision out of the accompanying document and into the main text of the pact, but it refused to back down from its position that the stipulation was a non-binding target.

In the meantime, in 1987 both chambers of the US Congress passed a resolution to sanction Japan through tax measures on the grounds that Japan had violated the Semiconductor Agreement. The executive branch thus proceeded to levy a 100 percent tariff on a variety of Japanese products, including small color TVs and computers. Nakasone reached out to Reagan with several ideas for resolving the deepening impasse, but he never received a favorable answer.

An attempt at easing the trade friction came with the Japan-US Structural Impediments Initiative, which began in September 1989 during the earliest days of the Kaifu Toshiki cabinet. Aiming to tackle the Japanese economic systems, land-taxation systems, and business practices that observers saw as possible causes of the trade strife, the far-reaching Structural Impediments Initiative was essentially a test run for "remodeling Japan" through external pressure. The experiment proved successful in some respects. For example, it sparked momentum for a complete overhaul of the legal structures that had long been protecting retailers by shutting mass marketers out of competition—a change that enjoyed support among members of the Japanese public who were hoping to see the country finally abandon outdated norms and pursue deregulation.

However, the United States' trade deficit with Japan persisted after the Cold War. The various measures Japan took to open up its markets failed to make much of a difference. With the United States hinting that it might invoke the "Super 301" provision (Section 301 of the 1988 Omnibus Foreign Trade and Competitiveness Act, which served to strengthen retaliatory action against unfair foreign measures and practices that went against American trade interests), the pressure to find a solution to the trade-imbalance quandary was mounting.

Under the Clinton administration, the US government pushed Japan with sustained requests to accept "numerical targets" that would determine how much of the Japanese market US-made automobiles and car parts could stake a claim to. Those numerical targets proved to be a sticking point for years, as talks between Japan and the United States slogged acrimoniously along through multiple Japanese cabinets—beginning with the Miyazawa-Clinton talks in 1993 and dragging on through the Hosokawa Morihiro and Hashimoto Ryūtarō administrations. The economic friction would eventually cool, however, as agreements on cars, car parts, and financial services finally came to fruition in 1995; an agreement on insurance took shape the following year. While the trade imbalance remained after Japan and the United States arrived at the agreements, the ensuing American economic rebound and the faltering of the Japanese economy helped turn the heat of the conflict down.

reliance on domestic demand and less on foreign demand. In 1985 he initiated the Advisory Group on Economic Restructuring (Maekawa Commission). The Maekawa Report, which recommended that Japan alter the structure of its economy to one driven more by domestic demand, was published in April 1986, just before the Tokyo Summit, and helped dampen criticism of Japan at the summit.

A Brief Honeymoon Period for China and South Korea

In March 1984, Nakasone visited China. One main issue was a second round of yen loans. To bolster China's modernization efforts, Japan had decided on an increase of 470 billion yen over a seven-year period. General Secretary Hu Yaobang expressed gratitude for Japan's economic assistance. "China will never forget your generosity and friendship," he said. Japan-China relations were said to be "the best since the war."

President Chun Doo-hwan visited Japan in September 1984, the first South Korean president to do so. At a formal banquet for Chun, the emperor expressed regret for Japan's colonial rule. Chun showed his appreciation for the emperor's remarks by saying, "Fair weather follows rain." At a luncheon the following day, Nakasone voiced his "deep regrets" for the "great suffering" of the South Korean people. The Ministry of Foreign Affairs described President Chun's visit to Japan as "the completion of the process of normalization of relations that began in 1965," and said bilateral relations had entered an "era of maturity."

Visits to Yasukuni and the Problem of History

On August 15, 1985, the fortieth anniversary of the end of World War II, Nakasone visited Yasukuni Shrine, the first postwar prime minister to do so. For Nakasone, this official visit, together with the abandonment of the 1 percent of GNP limit on defense spending, were tangible targets of a program for a "final accounting of postwar politics." Until that point, the visits by cabinet members to Yasukuni were essentially a domestic issue. The government (Cabinet Legislation Bureau) determined that Nakasone's trip to the shrine would be constitutional as long as it was not overtly religious. However, it invited an unanticipated reaction from China.

The *People's Daily*, noting that Class-A war criminals were venerated at Yasukuni Shrine, sharply criticized the prime minister's official visit, saying it "muddies the nature of and responsibility for the war." There were many student demonstrations criticizing the Japanese government for reviving militarism. In China's view, the prime minister's official visit to Yasukuni Shrine, where former prime minister Tōjō Hideki and others responsible for the war of aggression were enshrined, was an affirmation of the war of aggression and an evasion of responsibility. At the same time, the *People's Daily* wrote that "the Chinese government has consistently maintained a position of strictly distinguishing between the small number of Japanese people who support militarist elements and the broad range of the Japanese people." According to

14-13. Prime Minister Nakasone makes an official visit to Yasukuni Shrine

this division of responsibility, Class B and Class C war criminals should be grouped with the victims of war, and should be treated differently from the Class A war criminals who bore primary responsibility for the war of aggression.

The Japanese government found itself at a loss for how to respond, and for ten years after Nakasone's time Japanese prime ministers avoided visiting Yasukuni Shrine, whether officially or privately. Chief Cabinet Secretary Gotōda Masaharu

Nakasone Yasuhiro (1918–2019) and Japan as an "International State"

Nakasone Yasuhiro, who died at the age of 101 in 2019, was born in Takasaki, Gunma Prefecture. After obtaining a degree from Tokyo Imperial University, he joined the Home Ministry in 1941 but quickly shifted gears: he decided to pursue his naval aspirations and eventually became a commissioned officer and paymaster in the Imperial Navy. The onset of the war between Japan and the United States promptly thrust him into action. Serving in a naval convoy, Nakasone witnessed relentless bombings and heated gunfire on Mindanao and Borneo, and saw legions of his fellow soldiers—ordinary citizens of "pure, genuine patriotism"—die for the Japanese cause. That "patriotism among the general public," Nakasone remembered, "is what spurred me to become a politician." In the wake of Japan's defeat, Nakasone ran for election in 1947 as a member of the Minshutō (Democratic Party) and won a seat in the House of Representatives. His victory at the age of just twenty-eight made him, along with Tanaka Kakuei, one of the two youngest elected lawmakers in the country. Nakasone spoke out vocally against Yoshida Shigeru's brand of diplomacy, criticizing the approach as an "obsessive preoccupation with the United States" that threatened to undermine Japan's spirit of independence, and underscored the need for the creation of a self-defense force and an equal mutual defense treaty. Another point of emphasis for Nakasone was the peaceful use of nuclear energy, which led him to play an active role in formulating the 1955 Atomic Energy Basic Act.

Under the third Satō Eisaku administration, Nakasone became the director-general of the Defense Agency on his own initiative and set out to bring his vision of "autonomous defense" to fruition. He tried to reorient the 1957 "Basic Policy on National Defense" as a supplement to the Japan-US security arrangement, but pushback from the opposition parties and a lack of cabinet coordination brought his efforts to a standstill. From that point onward, Nakasone began taking a more pragmatic approach to policy. Just before the oil crisis hit, he visited the Middle East as minister of international trade and industry under Prime Minister Tanaka and brought a dire concern—that Japan's access to oil resources might be at risk—to the fore. He eventually ascended to the premiership in November 1982 and remained in the position all the way through November 1987, assembling a team of some of the best minds in the political sphere to establish a "top-down" style of leadership that drove a string of successes in both diplomacy and security. Although Nakasone was a staunch advocate of making official visits to Yasukuni Shrine, he was mindful of the implications that the practice had on the international scene. While he normally insisted on visiting the shrine, Nakasone admitted at a Diet session in February 1983 that Japan's past war against China had been a "war of aggression" and refrained from paying his respects at Yasukuni Shrine in deference to Hu Yaobang's views. In that context, Nakasone demonstrated quite a balanced stance.

14-14. Nakasone Yasuhiro

He also recognized the importance of forging bonds of trust with leaders from around the world and made "summit diplomacy" a centerpiece of his foreign relations, putting his vision of "Japan as an international state" into practice. That philosophy is evident in an address that he gave to the Diet in September 1986:

> If Japan is to be a truly influential member of the international community, it is essential that we not seem to simply reap the benefits of international peace and prosperity but that we bear our fair share of the burden and contribute to the international good. The true meaning of my call for making Japan an international state lies in having Japan act responsibly for world peace and prosperity as it grows from a nation in the world to a nation at one with the world and to a nation contributing to the international community.

expressed the view that, because Japan had accepted the judgment of the Tokyo War Crimes Tribunal under the San Francisco Peace Treaty, "the feelings of the counterparty [concerned about official shrine visits] cannot be ignored." With this, he was able to persuade cabinet members and other powerful Jimintō opinion leaders to stop shrine visits, both official and private.

Stagnation in Relations with the Soviet Union

In the Soviet Union, Gorbachev, with his "new thinking" about diplomacy, became general secretary in March 1985. Nakasone lost no time in going to visit Moscow to try to build a new relationship, but he found the task difficult. Still, Foreign Minister Shevardnadze, who had taken the place of Gromyko, visited Japan in January 1986 to reopen regular bilateral talks after an eight-year hiatus. The same pattern prevailed. Foreign Minister Abe Shintarō would ask the Soviet Union to reduce its military, and the Soviets would respond they needed the military because of the existence of US bases in Japan and the surrounding area. Despite this, and the ongoing territorial dispute, they agreed to a regular series of meetings between foreign ministers.

Gorbachev switched his stance to favor dialogue with the West, and there were hopes that this would lead to a new phase with regard to Japan as well. But the conservative faction within the Soviet Union put up strong resistance, and in the end a renewal of Japanese-Soviet relations would have to wait until after the collapse of the Soviet Union itself.

The "Ron-Yasu Charter"

The Jimintō won the general election of July 1986 with a record 304 seats. In September, as prime minister, Nakasone made the decision to join the studies for the US-led Strategic Defense Initiative (SDI). The following January he scrapped the guideline that Japan's defense spending should not exceed 1 percent of GNP.

In 1987, Japan-US trade frictions heated up, as there were disputes over the selection of the next Japanese fighter plane (FSX), and Toshiba Machine Co. was found to have committed COCOM (Coordinating Committee for Multilateral Export Controls) violations. These events fueled "Japan bashing," most notably in the US Congress. In March, both the Senate and the House of Representatives voted unanimously to impose trade sanctions on Japan for violations of the 1986 semiconductor agreement, accusing Japan of "dumping" its semiconductors on world markets. As a result, the Reagan administration imposed unreasonable 100 percent tariffs on Japanese products such as small color televisions and computers. In April 1987, Nakasone prepared for a summit meeting with Reagan, with proposals for a mammoth stimulus package, big plans for government procurement, and other economic measures, but he did not receive a favorable response.

He had another opportunity to speak with Reagan at the UN General Assembly in September that year. It was their twelfth summit meeting. Reagan thanked Nakasone, because in the five years of the Nakasone administration, the world's view of Japan had changed in significant ways. At this, their final meeting, the two men issued a statement celebrating their genuine personal connection, the "Ron-Yasu Charter," in which they praised their joint contributions to the strengthening of the friendship and trust between Japan and the United States, Reagan's role in solidifying the Western alliance, and Nakasone's success in raising the profile of Japan. Regarding the problem of economic frictions, which showed no signs of easing, the two leaders sent a message that these should be resolved constructively.

The Kōkaryō Dormitory Issue and the "Man above the Clouds" Controversy

The Kōkaryō Dormitory, a residence for students from the Republic of China (Taiwan) in the Sakyō Ward of Kyoto, became the official property of the Republic of China at the end of 1952. However, most of the students living at the facility aligned with the Chinese Communist Party and ignored the Republic of China's administrative authority over their home in Japan. In September 1967, the Republic of China decided to do something about the situation: in the name of its embassy in Japan, it filed a lawsuit with the Kyoto District Court to evict the boarders. The legal motion became an international issue in September 1972, while the proceedings were taking place, when the Japanese government recognized the Beijing government as the "sole legal government of China" in a joint communiqué with China—and thus severed its diplomatic relations with the Republic of China.

The situation created two legal disputes. First was the question of whether the government of the Republic of China could still be a party to the legal proceedings in Japanese court even though Japan no longer recognized it as a government. Second was the question of whether the ownership of the Kōkaryō Dormitory would switch hands from the Republic of China to the Beijing government. The first hearing, in September 1977, found that the Republic of China would retain its admissibility as a party in court but dismissed the plaintiff's claim, ruling that the Beijing government was the rightful owner of the Kōkaryō Dormitory. However, the legal proceedings were far from over. The subsequent appeal went to the Osaka High Court, which ruled in the plaintiff's favor. In February 1987, the court officially changed the name of the plaintiff to "Taiwan," recognized Taiwan's eligibility as a party to the proceedings and its ownership of the Kōkaryō Dormitory, and turned down the defendant's appeal. The Chinese government had urged the Japanese government to be careful about the political implications of the ruling, anticipating that Taiwan would win its appeal in Osaka, and indeed, the High Court's decision resulted in a protest from Beijing. Claiming that the ruling effectively recognized "two Chinas," the Chinese government argued that Japan had violated the People's Republic of China–Japan Joint Communiqué and the Treaty of Peace and Friendship between Japan and the People's Republic of China.

The Japanese government insisted that it was unable to do anything about the Kōkaryō Dormitory decision due to the separation of powers among its three branches of government, but China dismissed Japan's reasoning and kept up its protests of the decision into the following month. When Kōmeitō chairman Yano Jun'ya made a visit to China in June, Deng Xiaoping himself told Yano that the situation in Japan—which had also reached a cabinet resolution to do away with the stipulation capping defense spending at 1 percent of the GNP—was fanning concerns that Japan might be looking to enhance its military and resurrect its militarism. He also told Yano to see to it that Japan would take care of the Kōkaryō Dormitory dispute, voicing his suggestion that Prime Minister Nakasone Yasuhiro resolve the problem. Another topic of discussion between Deng and Yano was the Japan-China trade imbalance. Deng noted that, even though Japan owed more debt to China than any other country did, China had never sought war reparations from Japan during negotiations to restore diplomatic relations between the two nations. Considering the situation, Deng said, Japan should do more to contribute to China's economic development.

An official in the Ministry of Foreign Affairs responded to Deng's remarks at a press gathering that day, saying that Chairman Deng had "become a man above the clouds" and that "anyone who gets old gets hard-headed . . . Japan should not swing between hope and fear over what Chinese leaders say." In Japanese, a "man above the clouds" connoted a high-ranking official who had removed himself from worldly affairs—but in China, the phrase was translated as "senile old man." The statement provoked a fierce backlash from China, instantly inflaming Sino-Japanese tension.

At odds, Japan and China again engaged in a standoff over the Kōkaryō Dormitory issue at their regular ministerial meeting in June 1987. Japan contended that the controversy was a legal issue at its core, while China saw it as a matter of principle. Despite the ongoing friction, Japan remained eager to see its third package of yen loans to China through. Animosity on the Chinese side gradually cooled, too, as China began to suppress its criticism of Japan after the Nakasone cabinet's resignation in November 1987. Furthermore, the situation had no impact on Prime Minister Takeshita Noboru's visit to China the following year.

The Takeshita Cabinet and the Idea of International Cooperation

In October 1987, Nakasone named Takeshita Noboru, who had served a long time as finance minister, to succeed him as prime minister. Takeshita formed his cabinet in November under the slogan, "Japan serves the world."

Takeshita's "International Cooperation Initiative" had three components: (1) Strengthening cooperation for the purpose of peace, (2) strengthening economic cooperation, and (3) promoting international cultural exchange. One tangible sign of (1) was Takeshita's address to the UN Special Session on Disarmament in June 1988. In that speech, Takeshita discussed how to promote political dialogue to lay the foundations for peace, how to contribute to activities to prevent conflict, personal contributions to activities to maintain peace, and support for refugees, among other topics. These ideas would take tangible form in the 1990s as Japan's foreign policy embarked on a fresh course for its initiatives. Beginning in the summer of 1988, the Ministry of Foreign Affairs assigned one official to join the UN Good Offices Mission in Afghanistan/Pakistan (UNGOMAP) and another to the UN Iran/Iraq Military Observer Group (UNIIMOG). Although only two people were sent, it was Japan's first step toward contributing personnel to operations such as these.

Specific policies related to (2) included improvements in the quantity and quality of ODA. The new target was US$50 billion, double the level of the preceding five years. With this new goal, in the 1990s Japan became the world's largest provider of economic aid.

This expansion of ODA was exemplified by the third round of yen loans to China, the centerpiece of Takeshita's visit there in August 1988. The funds were used to support reform and opening measures promoted by the new general secretary, Zhao Ziyang. Takeshita also promised to support efforts to preserve archaeological sites at Dunhuang.

As the emperor's health declined, the prime minister refrained from traveling abroad from September 1988 until after the emperor's death in January 1989. For a week around the funeral in late February 1989, representatives of over 190 nations and international organizations paid condolence calls, making it the largest occasion of its kind in the twentieth century.

In June 1989, the Recruit scandal caused great public mistrust in politics, forcing Prime Minister Takeshita to step down. His successor, Uno Sōsuke, took office in June, but the Jimintō suffered a major defeat in the Upper House election in July, so the Uno cabinet was short-lived. Uno's successor was Kaifu Toshiki.

14-15. Funeral procession of Emperor Shōwa

CHAPTER 15

The Post–Cold War Era

15-1. US president George W. Bush and Prime Minister Koizumi at a bilateral summit

TIMELINE

1990 (Heisei 2)

August 2 Iraq invades Kuwait; start of Gulf Crisis
August 30 Japan decides to provide US$1 billion support for Gulf Crisis ($13 billion by following January)
October 3 Unification of Germany

1991 (Heisei 3)

January 17 Coalition forces invade Iraq, start of Gulf War
April 24 Japan decides to send Maritime Self-Defense Force troops to Persian Gulf
November 5 Miyazawa Kiichi forms cabinet
December 25 Dissolution of Soviet Union

1992 (Heisei 4)

June 15 Peacekeeping Operations (PKO) Cooperation Act enacted. Self-Defense Force units sent to Cambodia PKO on September 17
October 23–28 Emperor Akihito visits China

1993 (Heisei 5)

January 20 US president Clinton inaugurated
March 12 North Korea announces withdrawal from Nuclear Non-Proliferation Treaty (NPT)
May 29 North Korea launches Nodong-1 missile into Sea of Japan
August 4 Chief Cabinet Secretary Kōno makes statement on comfort-women issue
August 9 Hosokawa Morihiro cabinet formed (end of "1955 System")

1994 (Heisei 6)

April 28 Hata Tsutomu cabinet formed
June 13 North Korea announces withdrawal from International Atomic Energy Agency (IAEA)
June 30 Murayama Tomiichi cabinet formed
July 20 In Diet, Prime Minister Murayama declares intention to firmly maintain Security Treaty, says Self-Defense Forces (SDF) are constitutional

1995 (Heisei 7)

January 17 Great Hanshin-Awaji Earthquake
June 9 Resolution to Renew the Determination for Peace on the Basis of Lessons Learned from History (*fusen ketsugi*)
August 15 Murayama Statement marking fiftieth anniversary of the end of World War II
August 15 Fundraising advertisements for Asian Women's Fund placed in major newspapers
September 4 Okinawa rape incident

1996 (Heisei 8)

January 11 First Hashimoto Ryūtarō cabinet formed
March 8 China conducts missile launch tests in Taiwan Strait (Taiwan Strait Crisis)
April 12 Japan, US announce agreement on return of Air Station Futenma
April 17 Hashimoto meets US president Clinton; redefining Japan-US alliance announced
November 7 Second Hashimoto cabinet formed

1997 (Heisei 9)

November 1–2 Hashimoto visits Russia, meets President Yeltsin (Krasnoyarsk Agreement)

1998 (Heisei 10)

April 18–19 President Yeltsin visits Japan, meets Hashimoto in Kawana
July 30 Obuchi Keizō cabinet formed
August 31 North Korea test launches Taepodong-1 ballistic missile
October 7–10 South Korean president Kim Dae-jung visits Japan as state guest; Japan–Republic of Korea Joint Declaration
November 25 PRC president Jiang Zemin visits Japan; Japan-China Joint Declaration

1999 (Heisei 11)

May 24 1997 Guidelines for Japan-US Defense Cooperation-related laws enacted

2000 (Heisei 12)

April 5 First Mori Yoshirō cabinet formed
July 4 Second Mori cabinet formed
July 21–23 Kyushu-Okinawa Summit

2001 (Heisei 13)

January 20 US president George W. Bush inaugurated
April 26 First Koizumi Jun'ichirō cabinet formed
September 11 September 11 attacks in US
October 7 US, UK invade Afghanistan
October 29 Anti-Terrorism Special Measures Law enacted; Maritime Self-Defense Forces conduct refueling exercise in Indian Ocean in late November

2002 (Heisei 14)

September 17 Koizumi visits North Korea, signs Japan–North Korea Pyongyang Declaration

2003 (Heisei 15)

January 10 North Korea announces withdrawal from Nuclear Non-Proliferation Treaty
March 20 Coalition led by US, UK, invades Iraq (Iraq War)
June 6 Three contingency-related laws enacted
July 26 Special Measures Law for Humanitarian and Reconstruction Assistance in Iraq enacted
November 19 Second Koizumi cabinet formed

2004 (Heisei 16)

May 22	Koizumi visits North Korea again; accompanies family members of abduction victims back to Japan
June 14	Seven contingency-related laws enacted
August 13	US helicopter crashes on campus of Okinawa International University

2005 (Heisei 17)

September 21	Third Koizumi cabinet formed
December 12–14	First East Asia Summit (EAS)

2006 (Heisei 18)

August 15	Koizumi makes official visit to Yasukuni Shrine on End-of-War Memorial Day
September 26	First Abe Shinzō cabinet formed
October 8	Abe visits China (Japan-China Joint News Conference)
October 9	North Korea announces successful underground test of nuclear device

2007 (Heisei 19)

April 11-13	PRC Premier Wen Jiabao visits Japan
September 26	Fukuda Yasuo cabinet formed
December 27–30	Fukuda visits China

2008 (Heisei 20)

January 11	New Terrorism Special Measures Act (limited to two years) enacted
May 6–10	PRC president Hu Jintao visits Japan; joint statement highlights comprehensive promotion of strategic, mutually beneficial relationship
June 18	Japan-China agreement on gas field exploration in East China Sea
September 15	Collapse of Lehman Brothers sets off global financial crisis
September 24	Asō Tarō cabinet formed

2009 (Heisei 21)

January 20	US president Barack Obama inaugurated
April 5	North Korean missile passes over Japan to land in Pacific Ocean
May 25	North Korea conducts second underground nuclear test
September 16	Hatoyama Yukio cabinet formed

2010 (Heisei 22)

May 23	Hatoyama abandons effort to move Air Station Futenma out of Okinawa
June 8	Kan Naoto cabinet formed
August 10	Kan releases statement on 100th anniversary of Japan's annexation of Korea
September 7	Chinese fishing boat collides with Japan Coast Guard patrol vessels near Senkaku Islands

2011 (Heisei 23)

March 11	Great East Japan Earthquake
September 2	Noda Yoshihiko cabinet formed

2012 (Heisei 24)

April 11	Kim Jong-un becomes first secretary of Workers' Party of Korea
April 16	Governor Ishihara announces Tokyo's intention to purchase Senkaku Islands
August 10	South Korean president Lee Myung-bak visits Takeshima (Dokdo)
September 11	Noda decides Senkaku Islands to be "nationalized"
December 26	Second Abe cabinet formed

2013 (Heisei 25)

November 23	PRC establishes Air Defense Identification Zone (ADIZ) in East China Sea
December 4	Japan establishes National Security Council

2014 (Heisei 26)

March 18	Russia annexes Crimea from Ukraine
July 1	Japan decides to allow limited actions in collective self-defense
December 24	Third Abe cabinet formed

2015 (Heisei 27)

August 14	Abe releases statement marking the 70th anniversary of end of World War II
December 28	Japan-South Korea agreement regarding comfort women

2016 (Heisei 28)

May 27	US president Obama visits Hiroshima

2017 (Heisei 29)

January 20	US president Donald Trump inaugurated
July 29	North Korea launches intercontinental ballistic missile
November 1	Fourth Abe cabinet formed

2018 (Heisei 30)

April 27	Inter-Korea Summit (Kim Jong-un, Moon Jae-in); Panmunjon Declaration
June 12	First meeting of leaders of US and North Korea (Trump, Kim Jong-un)
October 25	Abe makes first official visit to PRC in seven years
November 14	Japan-Russia Summit (accelerating progress toward peace treaty based on 1956 Declaration)

2019 (Heisei 31)

February 27	Second US-North Korea Summit

1 The End of the Cold War Brings Changes to Japanese Diplomacy

The Cold War Ends: Political Destabilization Follows

The year 1989 was one of unprecedented change in international relations. First came democratic reforms in Eastern Europe, followed in November by the unification of East and West Germany and the fall of the Berlin Wall. In December, President George H. W. Bush met Soviet chairman Gorbachev in Malta and declared the end of the Cold War. Bush and Gorbachev also made headway in reconciling their two nations and reducing their stockpiles of nuclear weapons. At the end of 1991, the Soviet Union itself collapsed.

The end of the Cold War between the United States and the USSR did not have the same kind of impact on Japanese diplomacy as the shock of the rapprochement between the United States and China in the early 1970s had had, but two changes occurred in matters of security. The first was the elimination of the Soviet threat, which had endured for decades. The second was that, while the chance of a major war may have diminished, the chances of multiple regional conflicts increased. In other words, Japan's security environment became extremely unstable and opaque.

On the economic front, however, the Japan-US trade frictions that had plagued Japan's cabinets since the 1980s eased in the mid-1990s. Trade imbalances continued, but economic recovery in the United States and sluggishness in Japan served to reduce the friction.

Japan was on the "winning side" of the Cold War, but as the phrase "lost decade" indicates, its economy slowed down and political instability was difficult to overcome. In 1993, the Jimintō (Liberal Democratic Party) lost its right to govern, and the "1955 System" that had endured for thirty-eight years came to a (temporary) end. Hosokawa Morihiro formed a coalition government—the first ever not to include members from the Jimintō. The Jimintō was able to make a comeback in June 1994, building a coalition government with the Nihon Shakaitō (Japan Socialist Party) and the Shintō Sakigake (New Harbinger Party), headed by Shakaitō chairman Murayama Tomiichi. After that, until the election of Koizumi Jun'ichirō in 2001, the nation was governed by a series of short-lived administrations under prime ministers Hashimoto Ryūtarō, Obuchi Keizō, and Mori Yoshirō. Japan had fifteen prime ministers between the cabinet of Kaifu Toshiki, which started in 1989, and the 2006 cabinet of Abe Shinzō.

During that time, the Japan-US alliance may have been shaken, but it managed to grow deeper. Prime Minister Fukuda Yasuo regarded the Japan-US alliance as the "commonly held property" of the entire Asia-Pacific region. He viewed it as a stability mechanism that reduced risks in commerce and trade within the region. In fact, that sense of the alliance was taking hold.

15-2. The fall of the Berlin Wall

The Effect of the Gulf War on Global Security

In early August 1990, Iraq suddenly invaded and annexed Kuwait. In November, the United Nations Security Council, deciding Iraq was not inclined to withdraw, voted to allow the exercise of military force. In January 1991, a coalition of forces led by the United States quickly overpowered Iraq and liberated Kuwait by the end of February. This was the first Gulf War.

The conflict was a matter of international security, but one that posed no direct threat to the security of Japan. What contribution should Japan make? It was the Kaifu cabinet that had to deal with this new kind of problem. Beginning around the time of the push into Iraq, President Bush asked Prime Minister Kaifu to send minesweepers and transport ships. At the end of August 1990, Kaifu announced that Japan would provide the coalition forces with transportation and material support, medical help, and financial support. He also sought ways for the Self-Defense Forces to make a personnel contribution in the form of backup logistics. Japan quickly drafted a bill that would allow it to support UN peacekeeping operations (PKO), but the preparations with respect to other domestic laws that would allow the dispatch of SDF troops were insufficient. Debate in the Diet bogged down and in November 1990 the bill was abandoned.

In the end, Japan's cooperation was limited to US$13 billion in financial support—an enormous amount exceeding that provided by Germany. The funds from Japan, which were raised through tax increases, covered a large share of the costs of the US military activity. After the war ended, Japan participated in minesweeping efforts in the Persian Gulf, and its performance was praised by experts from many nations.

However, this contribution was regarded as insufficient. In the US, in particular, Japan was criticized, and Japan-US relations deteriorated for a time. The reaction of the world to Japan's Gulf War response was a setback for Japan's diplomacy and left the nation traumatized.

Peacekeeping Operations in Cambodia

International criticism that Japan's response in the Gulf War had been insufficient soon had its impact on politics in Japan. Debate raged both inside and outside the Diet regarding what Japan could do to support international security. At the heart of this debate was the problem of Japan's participation in UN peacekeeping activities.

It was just at that point that the civil war in Cambodia, which had been going on for more than ten years, began to wind down. Vietnam withdrew its forces from Cambodia in 1989, and other factors underlying the civil war—disputes between superpowers, conflicts among the four factions within Cambodia—were also easing. An international conference was held in Paris in October 1991 in search of a peace agreement that would represent a comprehensive political solution. During this time, Japan was playing an active role in the peace process and in the restoration of Cambodia. The United Nations Transitional Authority in Cambodia (UNTAC) was in charge of carrying out the Paris Peace Agreement. Akashi Yasushi, then UN under-secretary-general, was named head of UNTAC; he began serving in that role in March 1992.

15-3. Minesweepers at work in the Persian Gulf

The cabinet of Miyazawa Kiichi made progress crafting a new bill that would allow members of Japan's SDF to take part in UN peacekeeping activities. The Act on Cooperation for United Nations Peacekeeping Operations and Other Operations was passed in June 1992 through the cooperation of the Jimintō, the Minshatō (Democratic Socialist Party), and the Kōmeitō. Peace in Cambodia was not just about Cambodia. It was of great significance for the democratization of politics throughout Asia, stabilization of international relations, and regional economic cooperation.

Based on a strict interpretation of Japan's constitution, the scope of the SDF's actual activities was severely circumscribed. For a time, the SDF was frozen out of participation in the main PKO operations—cease-fire monitoring, surrender of arms, etc.—where there was a real possibility of involvement in violence, and in effect it was allowed only to provide logistical support. Even so, Japan was able to send 1,200 SDF personnel to Cambodia for one year from September 1992 under the PKO Cooperation Act, mainly to build infrastructure for UNTAC.

This was a successful result, not just because it represented a comeback from the "diplomatic defeat" of Japan's activities in the Gulf War, but because it represented Japan coming one step closer to a goal it had held since the start of the Fukuda Doctrine; that is, stability in Southeast Asia through coexistence with Indochina and the ASEAN group. Japan continued its participation in PKO activities after that, and public support is regularly over 70 percent, according to polls conducted by the Prime Minister's Office (and, beginning in 2001, the Cabinet Office).

The Cambodia PKO: Making "Personnel Contributions" to International Security

The United Nations has worked to help keep or restore the peace in conflict zones across the globe through peacekeeping operations (PKOs) that UN member states participate in on a voluntary basis. While the PKOs during the Cold War centered on dispatches of military personnel, in the years since the end of the Cold War countries have offered a diversity of different resources—not just military personnel, but also administrative officials, police officers, and election specialists, to name a few—to aid with post-conflict reconstruction assistance, electoral assistance, refugee measures, and other initiatives.

After joining the UN, Japan was asked several times to contribute personnel to UN PKOs. The Ministry of Foreign Affairs tried time and time again to figure out a way of putting together an organized dispatch consisting primarily of self-defense forces, but officials were never even able to round up a team of civilians. The difficulties stemmed from vexing questions about how Japan should be involved in international security, a debate that divided opinions both within the Diet and among the public. Mustering the "political will" to propel Japan's PKO efforts forward was a challenge.

Progress eventually came in 1988, when Prime Minister Takeshita Noboru outlined the "International Cooperation Initiative" that involved sending personnel abroad on missions (see page 462). With that "Takeshita Initiative" established, the government began putting the pieces in place for potential Japanese involvement in a PKO. When the Gulf War broke out in 1990, the time had come for Japan to put that framework in practice. After several legislative twists and turns, the Act on Cooperation for United Nations Peacekeeping Operations and Other Operations took effect in 1992 and made it possible for Japan to contribute its self-defense forces to PKOs. The biggest issue was making sure that the involvement of Japanese peacekeeping forces was in compliance with the Japanese constitution. The government managed to work its way through that concern by setting forth "five principles" of Japan's participation in UN PKOs.

In the spring of 1992, Japan sent a 600-member engineering unit, 60 cease-fire observers, 75 civilian police officers, and 41 electoral observers to Cambodia to join the United Nations Transitional Authority in Cambodia (UNTAC), which had formed as a result of the Paris Peace Accords.

The Cambodia peace process eventually culminated in May 1993, when the country successfully held a general election with a voter turnout of nearly 90 percent. In a statement praising the outcome, Prime Minister Miyazawa Kiichi congratulated the "true victors" of the effort: the "people of Cambodia."

During this time, however, a civilian police officer from

Responding to "Situations in the Areas Surrounding Japan"

In March 1993, North Korea, which was making progress in extracting plutonium from spent fuel rods for its "nuclear research" (i.e., nuclear weapons development), objected to inspections by the International Atomic Energy Agency (IAEA), and declared it would withdraw from the Nuclear Non-Proliferation Treaty (NPT). Early in 1994, US forces in Japan began preparations for military action to stop this "nuclear research," and war seemed more likely than at any time since the Korean War. For Japan, the Gulf War had seemed far away, but this crisis was much closer to home. The nuclear situation with North Korea had revealed a problem: the Treaty of Mutual Cooperation and Security between the United States and Japan had no operating rules to prepare for an emergency on the Korean Peninsula, and it did not clarify the degree of Japan's involvement in military cooperation.

Around that time, the Japanese and US governments were making progress in adjusting the positioning of the US-Japanese security arrangements, which were based on the US-Japan Security Treaty of 1960, to the post–Cold War security environment. The crisis in North Korea had a major impact on this process, speeding up the drive to revise the security arrangements and enhance their credibility. The results of this process, referred to as the "redefinition" of the security arrangements, were reflected in the Japan-US Joint Declaration on Security given by President Bill Clinton and Prime Minister Hashimoto Ryūtarō in April 1996.

This joint declaration indicated that, with the threat of the Soviet Union gone, the purpose of

Japan was killed in the line of duty in Cambodia. Voices calling for the withdrawal of the country's PKO personnel grew louder and louder, but Miyazawa decided to keep the personnel on the ground and task Japan's SDF engineering battalions with keeping civilians safe. Although strict limits on the use of weapons elevated the risk level for the engineering battalions, the personnel did their part as members of the UNTAC effort and gained the trust of fellow participants.

After the UN PKO withdrew from Cambodia, the Cambodian government and the UN found themselves in a disagreement over the creation of a war-crimes tribunal. The Cambodian government wanted the court to be domestic, while the UN insisted on an international tribunal. Japan intervened, guiding the two sides to a compromise that involved establishing a domestic court with foreign judges. Japan's contributions to the Cambodian PKO, therefore, went beyond just dispatching personnel. By also mediating international disagreements and assisting with peace overtures, Japan took a far-reaching, policy-oriented role in the initiative—and that opened the door to a new age in Japanese diplomacy.

The Japanese government's PKO policy has evolved since then, especially since the terrorist attacks in the United States on September 11, 2001. In addition to focusing on efforts to facilitate the peace process, offer humanitarian support, and provide reconstruction assistance, the government has rooted its policy in "sustaining peace" in the interest of human security.

To date, Japan has contributed a total of 12,500 people to twenty-seven PKOs (as of December 31, 2017). Recent efforts include the UN's mission in South Sudan, where Japanese engineering battalions helped drive infrastructure development and other projects from 2012 to 2017.

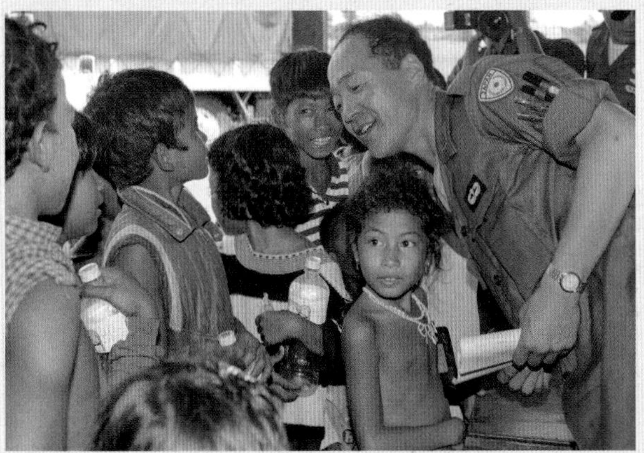

15-4. The UN PKO in Cambodia

Miyazawa Kiichi (1919–2007)

Tokyo native Miyazawa Kiichi graduated from Tokyo Imperial University and proceeded to join the Ministry of Finance in 1942. The years prior to the start of his ministerial career were formative, especially in terms of his international outlook. In 1939, he headed to the United States as one of Japan's delegates to the Japan-America Student Conference. The experience was a bit of a shock for Miyazawa, who quickly found that the English he had learned in Japan was virtually useless in practice. He thus began pouring his energies into teaching himself English, an earnest effort that eventually gave him what many called the best English of anyone in the Japanese political sphere.

Miyazawa left the Ministry of Finance in 1952 and then made his way into politics by securing a seat in the House of Councillors with an endorsement from Ikeda Hayato, whom he served as a close advisor during the Ikeda-Robertson talks and Ikeda-Kennedy talks. In 1962, Miyazawa became director-general of the Economic Planning Agency at the age of forty-two. He went on to occupy a variety of high-level positions after Ikeda's death, including minister of trade and industry under Prime Minister Satō Eisaku and foreign minister in the Miki Takeo cabinet. Soft-spoken and partial to liberal ideals, Miyazawa soon began to draw attention as a potentially promising "new leader" for the Jimintō. The ways of factional politics always irked Miyazawa, however; his aversion to making bold grabs for power via sectarian wheeling and dealing slowed his rise, and it was not until he was seventy-three years old that he finally secured an appointment as prime minister.

As his approach to the textile-trade conflict with the United States (when he was minister of trade and industry) and his response to economic friction (as prime minister) showed, Miyazawa expected the United States to take a politically correct stance on international matters—a natural reflection of its identity as a developed nation with a commitment to upholding freedom and democracy, in Miyazawa's eyes. That explains much of why Miyazawa was particularly critical of the United States when it deviated from GATT rules or took any other unfair actions that contradicted its identity. When it came to Asia, on the other hand, Miyazawa took a different approach; he consistently showed a willingness to reach out to victims of Japan's past actions in Asia, exemplified by his handling of the comfort-women issue.

15-5. Miyazawa Kiichi

Miyazawa diplomacy was instrumental in paving the way for Japan to pledge self-defense forces toward UN peacekeeping operations in Cambodia. The groundwork took shape with the 1992 passage of the Act on Cooperation for United Nations Peacekeeping Operations and Other Operations (the "PKO Cooperation Act"), which Miyazawa brought to fruition despite pushback from opposition parties and questions about the law's constitutionality. When the killing of a Japanese civilian police officer who had been in Cambodia on election-observation duty stoked calls for Japan to pull out of the mission, Miyazawa stood his ground and decided to keep Japan's personnel in place—for him, that continuing presence was integral to maintaining Japan's international credibility and fulfilling the purpose of the PKO. Miyazawa remained a force in politics even after he resigned from the premiership in August 1993, as prime ministers Obuchi Keizō and Mori Yoshirō both selected him to serve as their finance minister. Miyazawa died at his home in June 2007. In accordance with his wishes, his family has declined to accept any decorations on his behalf.

the security treaty was to prepare for new kinds of threats, such as terrorism and weapons of mass destruction, in addition to traditional military threats. The essence of the declaration was the revisions made to the 1978 guidelines for Japan-US defense cooperation. Making the need for these revisions even more urgent was the Third Taiwan Strait Crisis, in which the United States sent an aircraft carrier to the Taiwan Strait in response to missile tests conducted by China in August 1995 and again in March 1996, ahead of the first presidential election in Taiwan.

The key changes in the new guidelines published in September 1997 had to do with the responses to incidents in areas surrounding Japan that might have a major impact on the peace and security of Japan. The old guidelines only went so far as to clarify cooperation between Japan's SDF and the

15-6. The signing of the Japan-US Joint Declaration on Security

US military should something happen in Japan. The new guidelines established a framework for cooperation and joint action if something should happen on the Korean Peninsula, even if there was no direct attack on Japan. The Hashimoto cabinet expressed the view that situations in the areas surrounding Japan were not a matter of geography; rather, what mattered was the nature of the situation. The cabinet maintained "strategic ambiguity" on the question of whether the Taiwan Strait was included in "the areas surrounding Japan," and stepped down before the question could be resolved. Under the Obuchi cabinet, which followed, the Jimintō was defeated in the Upper House election, resulting in a divided Diet. Later, however, it was able to draft the Act on Measures to Ensure the Peace and Security of Japan in Perilous Situations in Areas Surrounding Japan and other bills related to the guidelines.

The redefinition of the Japan-US alliance required tackling the difficult issue of how to apply the security arrangements to a new post–Cold War international environment without altering either the US-Japan Security Treaty or the constitution.

The Problem of Moving Futenma

In September 1995 came an incident of the kind that could not help but upset the Japan-US alliance: the sexual assault of a young girl by US servicemen. Repeated instances of this kind of tragic event had caused a large group of Okinawan people to organize in opposition to the burden of military bases in the prefecture. Within two months of the incident, the governments of Japan and the United States formed a Special Action Committee on Okinawa (SACO) to deal with the question of how best to restructure and consolidate the bases in Okinawa.

Based on SACO's deliberations, the US government was inclined to return the aging Marine Corps Air Station Futenma, which is located in an urban area, to Japan, and thus to calm the situation in Okinawa and promote the redefinition of Japan-US security. The United States told Japan in March 1996 it would consider this possibility, and sought consultations with Japan aimed at setting the terms and conditions for the return of the base. In mid-April, Prime Minister Hashimoto and Ambassador Walter Mondale held a news conference to announce the return of the Futenma base. Among the conditions for the return of the base were the construction of a new helicopter port and the transfer of some functions to Kadena Airfield.

In November 1997, SACO issued a final report on agreements for the return of eleven US military facilities in Okinawa and operational improvements to the Status of Forces Agreement. Left unspecified, however, was any detail about what would have been the main event: the location and size of a facility that might take the place of Air Station Futenma (whether in Okinawa or elsewhere). Ever since that time, Japan and the United States have continued their search for the ideal alternative that would allow for the return of the Futenma base and lessen the burden on Okinawa. The current proposal, from 2006, is to build it on reclaimed land offshore of Henoko, in Nago City.

Human Security

The Human Development Report (HDR), published by the UN Development Programme (UNDP) in

15-7. US Air Station Futenma

1994, posited that security is a matter of protecting individual people, rather than nations, from threats and shortages. Japan's government showed strong interest in the problem of "human security." Prime Minister Obuchi Keizō was particularly passionate about this.

Obuchi had been interested in this area—for example, the removal of anti-personnel land mines—since his stint as foreign minister. In March 1997, the Japanese government convened a conference in Tokyo on the subject of anti-personnel land mines and took a central role in formulating guidelines for land-mine removal, technological development, and support for victims. Ultimately, this led to the signing of the Anti-Personnel Mine Ban Convention (Ottawa Treaty) at the end of that year. Prime Minister Obuchi took the initiative to create the Trust Fund for Human Security, describing it as a response to "all manner of threats to human survival, livelihood, and dignity."

At the Millennium Summit in September 2000, Obuchi's successor as prime minister, Mori Yoshirō, stated that Japan viewed human security as a pillar of diplomacy, and with Africa in mind proposed the establishment of an international panel to promote international efforts to address this problem. The Commission on Human Security was established in January of the following year, under the direction of former UN High Commissioner for Refugees Ogata Sadako, together with UN Secretary-General Kofi Annan.

"Human security" became part of Japan's diplomacy when it was added as one of the basic guidelines of development aid under the "ODA Charter," as revised in 2003.

"Open Regionalism" in the Asia-Pacific

Despite the absence of a systemic framework, trade and investment in the Asia-Pacific region grew rapidly throughout the 1980s, boosting rapid economic growth. At the same time, there were major problems; namely, trade imbalances and a high degree of dependence on the US market. To secure sustained growth and expansion of trade, a venue was needed for intergovernmental adjustments. This led to the formation of the Asia-Pacific Economic Cooperation (APEC) in 1989. In some respects, this was also a counter-initiative to the market consolidation that was happening in Europe. With the Japan-US economic relationship embroiled in trade frictions, Japan, along with Australia, took an active role in the founding of APEC in hopes of building a regional framework for stable relations. As of 2017, APEC counted twenty-one countries and territories among its members.

The philosophy of "open regionalism" adopted by APEC has also been the principle of Japan's economic diplomacy since the 1950s, based on global rules of freedom and non-discrimination supporting the GATT/WTO system. APEC's efforts to liberalize multilateral trade emphasized the initiatives of participating nations and did not possess the binding power of negotiated agreements, so their progress was disappointing. Participating nations broadened their trade policy options through bilateral and regional free-trade agreements (FTAs) that conformed to their own national interests. The market consolidation of the European Union (EU) and the North America

Obuchi Keizō (1937–2000)

Born in Gunma Prefecture, Obuchi Keizō graduated from Tokyo Metropolitan Kita High School and then went on to enroll in the Faculty of Literature at Waseda University in 1958. His father, Mitsuhei—who had just won reelection to the House of Representatives—died suddenly after Obuchi had begun his collegiate studies. Obuchi decided to follow in his father's footsteps and become a politician. In 1962, he enrolled in the Waseda University Graduate School of Political Science. The following year, he embarked on a solo trip to see the world: beginning with a sojourn in Okinawa, Obuchi made his way to thirty-eight countries across the globe. One stop was Washington, DC, where he visited the office of US attorney general Robert Kennedy and asked if he could speak with the attorney general himself. Kennedy obliged, and Obuchi was struck by the welcoming, accommodating courtesy that a man of that stature was willing to show a mere graduate student from Japan. That fall, Obuchi ran in the general election for Gunma's third district seat in the House of Representatives (a multi-seat constituency) against heavyweight politicians Fukuda Takeo and Nakasone Yasuhiro, along with two big-name candidates from the Shakaitō. Obuchi emerged victorious, becoming a lawmaker at just twenty-six years of age. He was also a "graduate-student lawmaker"—a rarity in constitutional politics. His first cabinet appointment came in 1979, when Prime Minister Ōhira tapped him to be the director-general of the Prime Minister's Office and the director-general of the Okinawa Development Agency. In November 1987, Obuchi became the chief cabinet secretary for the Takeshita cabinet and worked with Takeshita to make the Prime Minister's Office more "open" and in tune with the voices of the people. He also helped usher Japan into the Heisei era after the passing of Emperor Shōwa in early January 1989.

15-8. Obuchi Keizō

Later, as foreign minister in the Hashimoto cabinet, Obuchi worked hard to bring the Anti-Personnel Mine Ban Convention (Ottawa Treaty) to fruition and fended off detractors from both the domestic and international spheres to sign the agreement. The passage of the ban was a sign of what was to become Japan's firm commitment to "human security," a new dimension of international security. Obuchi became prime minister in July 1998 and, that fall, welcomed both South Korean president Kim Dae-jung and Chinese general secretary Jiang Zemin for meetings in Japan. The summit with Kim led to the groundbreaking Japan–Republic of Korea Joint Declaration (A New Japan–Republic of Korea Partnership towards the Twenty-First Century; see page 480).

Japan was to host the 2000 G8 summit, and Obuchi decided to hold the gathering in Okinawa. Not only had he visited Okinawa several times since his days as a student, but he also had profound sympathies for the wartime events that had taken place on the islands. Obuchi would not see the gathering for himself, however. In April 2000, just before the summit was to convene, he suffered a stroke that ultimately proved fatal, and died at the age of sixty-two. Obuchi's untimely passing cut short his effort to chart a new path of "wealth and virtue" for Japan as the country headed into the twenty-first century.

Former prime minister Murayama Tomiichi eulogized Obuchi in the Diet, saying, "Mr. Obuchi was a man of the people, always listening to their voices, seeing things through their eyes, and sharing in their carefree spirit." Murayama repeatedly referred to Obuchi's humble, unpretentious personality, which he saw as the reason that "Obuchi resonated so strongly with the public."

Free Trade Agreement (NAFTA) were the starting points for regionalism in trade.

Until the late 1990s Japan had emphasized trade policy based on global rules, and had been unenthusiastic about FTAs, but at that point it began to shift course in the direction of FTAs. The White Paper on International Economy and Trade 2000 made strengthening the GATT/WTO system one of its basic tenets, stating for the first time that the government's basic policy was to aim for a "multi-tiered trade policy" through a combination of regional cooperation (regionalism) in East Asia and bilateral trade relationships. In 2002, Japan concluded an Economic Partnership Agreement (EPA), its first FTA, with Singapore. In addition to expanding free trade, EPAs like this one aim to build cooperative relations by creating rules across a wide expanse, from investment to the movement of people, and in some cases may expand the possibilities for acceptance of foreign workers in certain capacities, and easing other domestic regulations. The use of EPAs is expected to increase.

In the realm of international finance, following the Asia financial crisis of 1997, Japan drove the regional framework that allowed East Asian nations to lend each other the foreign currencies they needed to withstand the currency/financial crisis. In 2000 it built regional financial cooperation (Chiang Mai Initiative).

The dynamic development within the Asia-Pacific region, which deepened economic interdependence and advanced real economic integration—helped boost the idea of regional cooperation in the 1990s. Two groups that were essential in that respect were the cooperative framework of ASEAN Plus Three (Japan, China, South Korea) that formed after the currency crisis and the ASEAN Regional Forum (ARF) that was established in 1994. Japan played a major role in the establishment of the ARF, in the form of "coordinated security." This was a new form of security mechanism—a cooperative entity aimed at averting conflict and building trust primarily among ASEAN nations.

China and Japan after the Tiananmen Square Incident

Prompted by the death of reformist leader Hu Yaobang, a pro-democracy movement of students and citizens surged in China in April 1989. In early June, China's leadership imposed martial law in Beijing, and in what became known as the Tiananmen Square Incident, security troops used military force to clear student demonstrators from Tiananmen Square.

Western nations sharply criticized China's actions, and Prime Minister Uno Sōsuke's cabinet announced a freeze on ODA. However, immediately after the incident at the Summit of the Arch, while other Western nations emphasized human

15-9. The Tiananmen Square Incident

rights, Japan's government expressed expectations that the road to reform and opening would be maintained, and said isolating China would serve no one's interests. In the end, Japan's viewpoint was incorporated into the joint communiqué. The fundamentals of Japan's policy toward China were to avoid driving China out of the international community and to support its efforts to reform. In August 1991, Prime Minister Kaifu Toshiki became the first leader of an advanced "Western" nation to visit China after the Tiananmen Square Incident. There he spoke again of his hopes for reform and opening. In November, the decision was made to lift the freeze on yen loans.

Amid this pressure from Western nations for democratization, China faced a choice: whether to continue its reforms and opening efforts, aiming for a return to the international community, or whether to further strengthen its closed systems. In 1992, Deng Xiaoping chose the former course, and the National Congress of the Chinese Communist Party formally declared the "socialist market economy." It chose to strengthen the foundations of its systems through active participation in a market economy. This decision would attract investment from around the world that fueled a period when China's annual economic growth would exceed 10 percent.

In October 1992, the emperor visited China to commemorate the twentieth anniversary of the normalization of diplomatic relations, in accordance with the wishes of General Secretary Jiang Zemin. At the evening banquet, the emperor acknowledged Japan's aggressions in the context of the long-shared history of the two nations, saying, "In the long history of relationships between our two countries, there was an unfortunate period in which my country inflicted great suffering on the people of China. About this I feel deep sadness."

For Japan, the emperor's words were a kind of punctuation mark for postwar Japan-China relations. China, however, passed its own Territorial Sea Law in February 1992, claiming that the South China Sea was Chinese territory. It also claimed as its own the Senkaku Islands, which are part of Japanese territory. This caused a bit of a stir, but due to internal political difficulties in Japan, its significance was overlooked.

China was perplexed when the Jimintō was forced out of power in 1993, bringing to an end the 1955 System. In a news conference, Prime Minister Hosokawa Morihiro, who was head of a coalition government, described the Sino-Japanese War as a "war of aggression." In his policy speech to the Diet, Hosokawa expressed deep remorse and apology for "acts of aggression" in the past; his words were welcomed by China. In 1995, the fiftieth anniversary

The Murayama Statement

Prime Minister Murayama Tomiichi (1924–) gave a statement in 1995 to commemorate the anniversary of the end of World War II ("On the occasion of the 50th anniversary of the war's end"). Central to the message were Murayama's expressions of "deep remorse" and "heartfelt apology" for the suffering that Japan's "colonial rule and aggression" had caused the peoples of other Asian countries.

Discussions of the need for official inquiries into Japan's past wars and colonial rule had come up several times in the Diet and other settings, but a consistent position on the topics never coalesced due to the government's dogged avoidance of pursuing an official review. The government's explanations of historical issues were thus wildly inconsistent, a situation that stirred a downward spiral of verbal gaffes and apologies by cabinet members and other key government officials. Prime ministers expressed apologies or regrets from time to time, but their words often came off as insincere. The Murayama Statement, however, was no passing gesture of remorse or stopgap salve. The Prime Minister's Office and the Ministry of Foreign Affairs carefully drafted the statement together to establish a clear, consistent government position, and the result received official approval via a cabinet resolution. The goal was to lay a solid foundation, one that would persist through potential future changes in the political guard.

The statement may not have fully unified the divergent historical takes in the domestic consciousness, but it at least firmed up the shaky, vacillating historical awareness that had characterized prior government declarations. As a result, the statement also put restraints on what top government officials said in relation to the topics. Cabinet members, at the very least, stopped making remarks suggesting that it was a "matter of perspective" whether or not the Pacific War had been a war of aggression. The government's position reflected a mindset common to Japan's various administrations during the first half of the 1990s—a determination to come to grips with the damage that Japan had done to the countries of Asia—as the Cold War thawed and Jimintō politics wavered.

15-10. Murayama Tomiichi

Prime Minister Koizumi Jun'ichirō, who was adamant about making official visits to Yasukuni Shrine, was also faithful to the Murayama Statement on historical issues. The statement that he made on his first prime-ministerial visit to the shrine, his speech at the Asian-African Summit in April 2005, and his words on the sixtieth anniversary of the war's end later that year all echoed the thrust of the Murayama Statement. In addition to forming the basis for announcements by future prime ministers, Murayama's words also resonated with neighboring nations and laid the foundation for the 1998 Japan-Republic of Korea Joint Declaration (A New Japan-Republic of Korea Partnership towards the Twenty-First Century).

of the end of World War II, the Murayama cabinet released the Murayama Statement (see sidebar on the previous page). With these events, it may have seemed that the historical problems between Japan and China were drawing to a close. However, around that time China began to strengthen its "patriotism education" as preparation for opening to the outside—educational materials that hammered home the lesson that the war of resistance to Japan was a just war. The media in China reported widely on this, and in the ensuing turmoil the message of the Murayama Statement was lost.

The Comfort-Women Issue

A pro-democracy movement emerged in South Korean politics in the latter half of the 1980s. In 1987, President Roh Tae-woo gave a speech on democratization (the June 29 Declaration), which led to direct elections for the presidency. In February 1990, Roh traveled to Japan and met with Prime Minister Kaifu, who said, "I would like to take the opportunity here to humbly reflect upon how the people of the Korean Peninsula went through unbearable pain and sorrow as a result of

The Comfort-Women Issue and the Asian Women's Fund

The existence of "comfort women" in the wartime Asia-Pacific region has been common knowledge for quite some time, but it had long been taken to read as private entities assembling groups of women and providing them to "comfort stations" at military posts, where the women would offer sexual services to troops. That prevailing understanding began to change in the late 1980s, however, as women's organizations argued more forcefully and vocally that the recruitment had been forcible coercion. Calls for justice gained momentum, and former comfort women in South Korea eventually filed lawsuits in the Tokyo District Court in December 1991 seeking a formal apology and indemnification. The issue turned into a diplomatic crisis between Japan and South Korea.

The Miyazawa Kiichi cabinet took the situation very seriously. When information emerged in early 1992 indicating with a high degree of certainty that the military had been involved in the recruitment of comfort women, Prime Minister Miyazawa made repeated expressions of "remorse and regret" to South Korea during an official visit to the country in mid-January and promised to launch a full investigation into the matter. The government published the final results of its investigation that July. However, the report indicated that the examination had failed to turn up any hard evidence indicating that members of the military had forcibly taken women by violent means. South Korea demanded that the Japanese government continue to probe the facts of the case and take action accordingly, and the Miyazawa cabinet responded by ordering an exhaustive investigation. After the inquiry was complete and Japan and South Korea had exchanged views to come up with a statement agreeable to both sides, Chief Cabinet Secretary Kōno Yōhei issued an official statement in August 1993. The text made it clear that "the Korean Peninsula was under Japanese rule in those days, and their recruitment, transfer, control, etc., were conducted generally against their will, through coaxing, coercion, etc.," a point of particular emphasis on the South Korean side. The South Korean government then made an official comment, saying that the Kōno statement "admitted the generally coercive nature of the recruitment, transfer, control, etc. of comfort women for military personnel."

The first administration to explore avenues for expressing Japan's "feelings of remorse and regret" in a more concrete way was the Murayama Tomiichi cabinet, which formed in 1994. To fulfill Japan's responsibility from a "moral standpoint," the Murayama cabinet focused on encouraging the "wide participation of people." That effort led to the creation of the "Asian Peace and Friendship Foundation for Women" (Asian Women's Fund), a national fund drawing on donations from the public and operating with government support, in July 1995.

The fund was not the answer some groups were looking for. Citizens' organizations and political parties that had been demanding direct state reparations slammed the whole concept behind the fund, arguing that the government was using it to skirt state responsibility. However, the government would likely not have been able to make state reparations even if it had tried to. Going through with state reparations (i.e., treasury payments) would have put Japan at the risk of violating legal frameworks like the Treaty of San Francisco, which specifically stipulated that both the our country's actions during a certain period in the past and to express that we are sorry." At a welcome banquet for Roh, the emperor also expressed "deep regret." President Roh said the heart of the history problem had been resolved, and indicated that Korea was ready to focus on the future of the relationship.

During the tenure of the next Japanese prime minister, Miyazawa Kiichi, however, this result was overshadowed by the emergence of the comfort-women problem as a diplomatic issue between Japan and South Korea (see sidebar below). As a result of the democratization of South Korean politics, and particularly as citizens' groups came to exercise influence over politics, women's groups were increasingly vocal in taking up the issue of the comfort women, which had never been recognized up to that point. Japan's government was at a loss for how to respond.

Within the legal frameworks of the San Francisco Peace Treaty and the Treaty on Basic Relations between Japan and the Republic of Korea, Prime Minister Miyazawa wanted to do what was morally right. Believing some sort of "atonement"

Allies and Japan would waive their rights to claims for losses and damages (including compensation to individuals), as well as the Agreement on the Settlement of Problems concerning Property and Claims and on Economic Cooperation between Japan and the Republic of Korea.

The project driving the Asian Women's Fund had three central elements: to pay former comfort women "atonement money" in the amount of 2 million yen per person; to issue a letter of apology from the Japanese prime minister; and to implement Japanese government-funded projects offering medical and welfare support. The fund amassed over 600 million yen in donations by the time it dissolved in 2007, but progress on the first two parts of the organization's aims was a struggle. Although the South Korean government was initially on board with the fund's basic approach, a South Korean regime change altered the course of the process. The Kim Dae-jung administration, which assumed power in 1998, took a negative stance on the fund's aims, and many former South Korean comfort women began refusing to accept the fund's "atonement money." Facing major roadblocks, the Asian Women's Fund had no choice but to suspend its projects in South Korea in 1999. The fund's activities were not all for naught, however, as the initiatives for the Philippines, Indonesia, the Netherlands, and Taiwan received positive assessments and resulted in certain measures of success.

The fund's projects failed to resolve the comfort-women issue between Japan and South Korea. As the problem became an increasingly high-profile humanitarian and human-rights concern at a global level, people began demanding a fuller legal response that went beyond

15-11. Japan and South Korea reach an agreement on "comfort women"

whatever advances the fund could make. Public awareness of the comfort-women issue continued to grow in the 2000s, too, as monuments and statues commemorating the women's stories began to appear in the United States and South Korea.

Japan and South Korea eventually came to a compromise. At a meeting in December 2015, the two countries' foreign ministers agreed to an arrangement by which the South Korean government would establish a foundation for the support of former comfort women and the Japanese government would contribute funds toward the foundation. With the announcement of the agreement, the two sides confirmed that the comfort-women issue had been "resolved finally and irreversibly" and that both governments would refrain from criticizing each other over the issue in the international community.

was needed, the first thing he did was to order a government investigation of the comfort-women issue. Based on the results of this investigation, the Miyazawa cabinet acknowledged the role played by Japan's military, and in August 1993 it issued the "Kōno Statement." In this statement, Chief Cabinet Secretary Kōno Yōhei promised to think about how best to express Japan's apologies and feelings of regret to the former comfort women. The Murayama cabinet, which began in 1994, gave Japan's repentance tangible form in the Asian Women's Fund. (See sidebar on the previous page.)

Kanemaru Visits North Korea

In the wave of economic development and democratization in Asia, North Korea was left behind. In September 1990, a delegation led by former deputy prime minister Kanemaru Shin and Shakaitō deputy chairman Tanabe Makoto went to Pyongyang. In 1988, Roh Tae-woo said, "South Korea aims to establish better relations with China and the Soviet Union. If North Korea is aiming to improve relations with Japan and the United States, we will cooperate." That is what led to the Kanemaru delegation to North Korea.

Kanemaru held a long meeting with President Kim Il-sung, apologized for the unhappy past, and expressed his regrets. North Korea asked for governmental negotiations aimed at normalizing relations between Japan and North Korea. This was a change of direction for North Korea, which until that point had opposed such a move, maintaining that Japan having bilateral relations with both North and South Korea would solidify the division between the two. However, the joint statement of the three parties—the Jimintō, the Shakaitō, and the Workers' Party of Korea—was hampered by the problem of "postwar atonement." North Korea demanded compensation not just for the period of Japan's colonial rule, but also for the absence of diplomatic relations in the postwar period. The joint declaration included a reference to postwar compensation as well as a call for the early normalization of diplomatic relations between Japan and North Korea. Following the joint declaration, government-level negotiations began, but they were broken off due to suspicions regarding North Korea's nuclear development program and the abduction of Japanese citizens.

Joint Declarations as Kim Dae-jung and Jiang Zemin Visit Japan

Following his election as president of the Republic of Korea in December of 1997, Kim Dae-jung showed a strong desire to improve relations with Japan. Hoping to complete a "full accounting of the past," he took a positive view of Japan's peaceful development in the postwar period, and actively sought to end South Korea's censorship of Japanese culture. In October 1998, Kim arrived in Japan for a state visit and met with Prime Minister Obuchi. The two leaders issued a Japan–Republic of Korea joint declaration titled "A New Japan–Republic of Korea Partnership towards the Twenty-First Century." In this joint declaration, using language quoted directly from the 1995 Murayama Statement, the Japanese government apologized to the South Korean people for colonial rule, and the South Korean side expressed its sincere acceptance of that apology.

Further, the joint declaration affirmed that the two nations shared unshakable values of democracy and liberty, as well as political and economic systems based on these values. While the declaration contained no showy flourishes, it was a groundbreaking statement of the relationship between postwar Japan and the Republic of Korea. Kim emphasized the future potential of the relationship between the two nations, going so far as to say that if Japan offered a clear apology for its colonial rule during this visit, South Korea would not raise issues of history again. This exchange seemed to mark the end of any rekindling of historical issues between Japan and South Korea.

General Secretary Jiang Zemin of China followed up with a state visit to Japan in November 1998. In discussions, the Chinese side insisted that the word "apology" should be included in the joint statement, because "deep remorse and heartfelt apology" had been included in the Obuchi-Kim joint declaration. The Japan side, however, demurred, saying Japan had already apologized in the Japan-China Joint Communiqué of 1972 and in the Murayama Statement, and that the emperor's statement regarding historical problems during his 1992 visit to China should stand as the final word on the subject. In welcoming remarks at an evening banquet at the palace, the emperor made no mention of the past war, but Jiang harshly criticized Japan's militarism and external expansionism. In the end, both Jiang and Obuchi declined to sign the joint declaration; in a rare occurrence, the joint declaration was issued without their signatures.

Amid these circumstances, Jiang made repeated statements about issues of history. In a speech at Waseda University, he harshly criticized Japan's past aggression. It seemed, however, that Jiang's harsh words about historical issues had been, to some degree, his personal opinion. After his visit, Japan-China relations did not worsen. China later took a favorable view of both the regularization of Japan–China–South Korea summits and Obuchi's idea of ASEAN Plus Three (Japan, China, South Korea) as a consultative framework.

15-12. The Japan–South Korea Joint Declaration

15-13. Chinese general secretary Jiang Zemin visits Japan

Japan-Russia Relations in the Yeltsin Era

After the Cold War, relations between Japan and the Soviet Union (Russia) were volatile. In April 1991, Gorbachev, the last leader of the Soviet Union, visited Japan and signed a joint communiqué with Prime Minister Kaifu. This joint communiqué documents the consultations that took place regarding the peace treaty, including a solution for the territorial issue, and it mentions the four disputed northern islands—Habomai, Shikotan, Kunashiri, and Etorofu—by name. At the end of that year, the Soviet Union was dissolved, and the Russian Federation, consisting of fifteen independent states, took its place. Yeltsin seized control and became president.

Yeltsin's foreign policy was to befriend the West. In March 1992, Foreign Minister Kozyrev visited Japan, where he held an unofficial meeting with Foreign Minister Watanabe Michio. The two men discussed a proposal aimed at a resolution of the problem of the four islands: Habomai and Shikotan would be transferred to Japan, a peace treaty would be concluded, and then negotiations regarding Kunashiri and Etorofu would continue. The Japan side, however, believing the assurances regarding the transfer of Kunashiri and Etorofu were insufficient, did not view this plan as a sound basis for negotiations. There were plans for Yeltsin to visit Japan, but he canceled shortly before the trip was to take place, citing Japan's demands for the return of all four islands as a single group.

When Yeltsin did visit Japan in October 1993, he and Prime Minister Hosokawa issued the Tokyo Declaration, saying they would resolve the problem of the return of the four islands and conclude a peace treaty. The declaration was basically a restatement of the agreement documented in the Kaifu-Gorbachev Joint Communiqué. Around this time, the primary concerns of the Russian leadership were economic development and the stabilization of domestic politics. Japan's policy priorities with respect to Russia were to support its reforms and to resolve the territorial problem. Progress was also made on the security dialogue and technical cooperation in the operation of a market economy.

Has the Issue of the Northern Territories Been Resolved?

The Origins of the Dispute

The four islands at the southern end of the Chishima (Kuril) Islands (Habomai, Shikotan, Kunashiri, and Etorofu) have never officially been the territory of any other nation besides Japan. In the Tokugawa era, the islands were under the jurisdiction of the Matsumae domain (and occasionally under direct bakufu control); after the Meiji Restoration, they were part of the Hokkaido administrative district.

These islands, collectively referred to as the "Four Northern Islands," have been subject to several agreements over the years. One was the 1855 Treaty of Peace and Amity between Japan and Russia. Not only did the treaty establish diplomatic relations between Japan and Russia, but it also defined the border between the two countries as passing between the islands of Etorofu and Uruppu. The agreement stipulated that Etorofu and everything south of it belonged to Japan, while Uruppu and everything north of it were the possessions of Russia. Under international law, therefore, the Four Northern Islands were clearly Japanese territories. The treaty did not define any borders partitioning Karafuto (Sakhalin), as the island was home to residents of both countries.

The next Russo-Japanese agreement with implications for the Northern Territories was the Treaty for the Exchange of Sakhalin for the Kurile Islands, which the countries signed in 1875. As a result of the treaty, Japan ceded its rights to Sakhalin (in full) in exchange for Russia's rights to the Kuril Islands. The terms of the treaty defined the Kuril Islands as comprising eighteen islands: from Shumushu in the north to Uruppu in the south. In effect, the treaty established that the Four Northern Islands were not part of the Kuril Islands. After the Russo-Japanese War, Japan also gained control over South Sakhalin via the terms of the Treaty of Portsmouth.

In August 1945, during the closing stages of World War II, the Soviet Union broke the Soviet-Japanese Neutrality Pact and declared war on Japan. By September 4, the Soviet Union had unilaterally occupied South Sakhalin, the Kuril Islands, and the Four Northern Islands. Thus began the dispute over the Northern Territories.

Article 2 of the Treaty of San Francisco required Japan to renounce its rights to the Kuril Islands and South Sakhalin. In his address announcing Japan's acceptance of the terms, Prime Minister Yoshida Shigeru informed the global community that the four northern islands were not part of the territories that Japan was to relinquish under the treaty's provisions. The proclamation obviously caused discontent in the Soviet Union. Roundly criticizing Yoshida for failing to acknowledge the Soviet Union's sovereignty over the Kuril Islands and South Sakhalin, the Soviet delegate to the gathering refused to sign the peace treaty.

The territorial dispute was one of the focal points of the Japan-Soviet Union negotiations that began in 1955, but the sides failed to come to a consensus on the matter. An agreement of sorts came about the following year, however, through a joint declaration by Japan and the Soviet Union. The statement stipulated that negotiations for the conclusion of a peace treaty would continue after the countries restored diplomatic relations and that the Soviet Union would transfer Habomai and Shikotan to Japan after the conclusion of a Japanese-Soviet peace treaty. Despite the arrangements, the Soviet Union refused to negotiate a peace treaty in accordance with the declaration on the grounds that the "territorial dispute had already been resolved." It was not until 1972 that the Soviet Union finally agreed to begin negotiating a peace accord.

In November 1997, after Yeltsin's reelection, he met Prime Minister Hashimoto in Krasnoyarsk, where they boldly agreed to conclude a peace treaty by the year 2000. They also agreed on the Hashimoto-Yeltsin Plan, which paved the way for the development of Japan-Russia economic cooperation. At the APEC summit in late November, Hashimoto was instrumental in including Russia in APEC in 1998. His aim was to promote Russia as a player in the Asia-Pacific region, as a curb on China.

At his second meeting with Yeltsin, in Kawana, Izu in April 1998, Hashimoto presented the Kawana Proposal: that the peace treaty would draw the border between Japan and Russia to the north of the Four Northern Islands, and that "for now"—until a separate agreement was reached—Japan would recognize Russia's administration as legal. Yeltsin expressed interest in this proposal, but at

The Yalta Agreement and the Divide between Japan and Russia

The Soviet Union based its occupation of the Four Northern Islands on the February 1945 Yalta Agreement, a pact between the United States, the United Kingdom, and the Soviet Union that determined the conditions under which the Soviet Union would declare war on Japan as part of the Allied effort. The agreement stipulated that South Sakhalin would be "returned" and the Kuril Islands "handed over" to the Soviet Union as a means of restoring to the Soviet Union its "former rights . . . violated [by Japan]" in the Russo-Japanese War.

Japan only learned of the secret Yalta Agreement in February 1946, after the war, when the Soviet government made its provisions public—and there was no way Japan would have known about it up to that point. There were only three Allied agreements that Japan became aware of during World War II: the Atlantic Charter (August 1941), the Cairo Declaration (November 1943), and the Potsdam Declaration (July 1945), all of which were widely publicized and accepted by the Soviet Union. Two common threads running through all three of these international pacts together were the Allies' mutual commitment to seek "no aggrandizement, territorial or other" and stripping Japan of the areas and islands that it had "taken by violence and greed."

In the context of those basic principles, the Four Northern Islands (Southern Kuril Islands) had never officially been Russian territory; the Soviet Union unilaterally occupied the islands after Japan's surrender in August 1945. Therefore, the four islands should be "returned" to Japan, not "handed over" to Russia. Japan had also obtained the rights to the Kuril Islands via the Treaty of Peace and Amity between Japan and Russia and Treaty for the Exchange of Sakhalin for the Kurile Islands, not through "violence and greed." Even the Yalta Agreement appeared to recognize the historical factors behind the sovereignty issue, as the provisions employed different phrasing for the Soviet Union's reclamation: "handing over" the Kuril Islands but "returning" South Sakhalin, which Japan had acquired under the Treaty of Portsmouth.

The Soviet Union ultimately put its pledge of territorial non-aggrandizement behind its top priority: recovering its lost territory on South Sakhalin and the Kuril Islands, as Stalin's declaration of victory over Japan (September 3, 1945) made clear. Since the turn of the twenty-first century, top Russian officials have asserted that the Four Northern Islands are part of Russia's dominion, legitimately obtained as a result of World War II. As the territorial dispute widens the chasm between Japan and Russia, the only way to bridge the gap will be multifaceted Russo-Japanese cooperation.

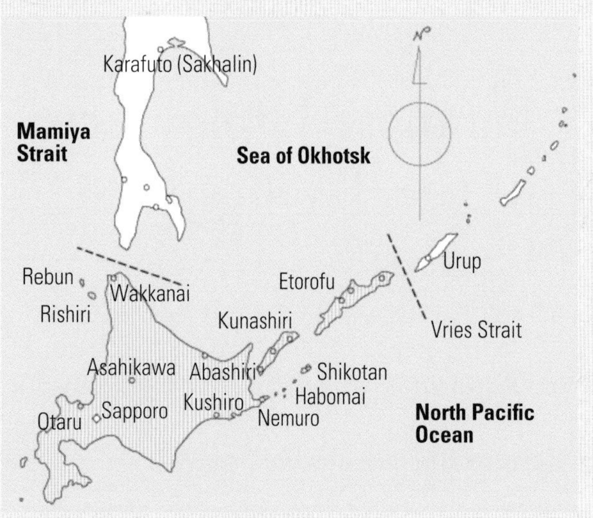

15-14. Map showing the Northern Territories

15-15. President Yeltsin and Prime Minister Hosokawa sign the Tokyo Declaration

the recommendation of his entourage, he decided to take it home to study it.

In response to the Kawana Proposal, in November 1998 Yeltsin offered two points to Prime Minister Obuchi when he visited Moscow: First, that a treaty should precede any redrawing of the border, establishing a special legal system for the realization of joint economic activity on the Four Northern Islands; and second, that separate negotiations should continue regarding the border between the two nations. It is believed that this proposal was the reference point for later Japan-Russia negotiations during the second Abe cabinet.

2 Japanese Diplomacy in the Twenty-First Century

The Dynamism of Koizumi Diplomacy

The Koizumi Cabinet and the Iraq War

The coordinated terrorist attacks that struck the United States in September 2001 (September 11 attacks) gave a jolt to Japanese diplomacy, which had been languishing at a crossroads. The George W. Bush administration set out to war, first against Afghanistan, then Iraq. On September 19, just a few days after the September 11 attacks, the Koizumi cabinet proclaimed its support for the War on Terror, outlining seven specific kinds of support the SDF was prepared to offer, including transport, supply, and intelligence. Prime Minister Koizumi visited the site of the World Trade Center in New York in late September. He met with President Bush, and briefed him on Japan's support measures.

However, when it became apparent that the Act on Measures to Ensure the Peace and Security of Japan in Perilous Situations in Areas Surrounding Japan and other existing laws did not address the idea of sending JSDF troops to provide backup logistics for the War on Terror, by the end of October Japan passed the Anti-Terrorism Special Measures Law with unusual speed, based on the UN Security Council resolution denouncing international terrorism. The process was led by the Prime Minister's Office, and its unprecedented speed was made possible by the Hashimoto administration's July 1999 revisions to the Cabinet Act, which clarified the authority of the prime minister to propose legislation and strengthened the powers of the Cabinet Secretariat, which acts as an advisory body to the prime minister. As early as late November, Maritime Self-Defense Force ships were able to set

15-16. JSDF troops in Samawah

sail for the Indian Ocean to serve as fueling vessels for coalition forces.

In March 2003, the United States went to war against Iraq, based on assertions that Iraq possessed weapons of mass destruction and had refused unconditional inspections, in violation of UN Security Council resolutions. When the "coalition of the willing"—mainly the United States and the United Kingdom–quickly took control of Baghdad and succeeded in subduing Iraq's conventional forces (President Bush declared the end of major combat operations in Iraq in May), the Koizumi cabinet attempted to pass legislation to support reconstruction in Iraq. The main point of contention, once again, was the idea of sending JSDF troops. The government drafted a proposal that would send JSDF troops, but only to areas where there was no active conflict. The widely held view, shared by the centrist Minshutō (Democratic Party of Japan), was that, while the idea of reconstruction support was good, it would be difficult to find "non-conflict areas," due to the worsening political situation in Iraq. Ultimately, the Special Measures Law for Humanitarian and Reconstruction Assistance in Iraq was passed in July, and Prime Minister Koizumi decided in December to send JSDF troops. In the interim, however, two Japanese diplomats in Iraq were shot and killed in November. Although combat operations had technically ended, Koizumi had to reach his decision to send JSDF troops under the stress of knowing that some of them might be sacrificed. In January 2004, Ground Self-Defence Force troops were sent to Samawah, a "non-combat zone." They remained there until 2006, doing reconstruction support work, without a single casualty being reported.

During that time, the Koizumi government, while heeding the Act on Measures to Ensure the Peace and Security of Japan in Perilous Situations in Areas Surrounding Japan and the new 1997 guidelines, among other things, took a step forward to enact contingency legislation that had long been sought by the Defense Agency by passing three contingency-related laws in June 2003, and the Civil Protection Law and others the following year. The most basic of these, the Armed Attack Situation Response Law (the Law for Peace and Independence of Japan and Maintenance of the Nation and the People's Security in Armed Attack Situations etc.), established the government's authority to take strong action in the event of a contingency (or war). This law stipulates that the prime minister has the authority to direct the heads of local municipal entities, as well as executive power to protect and defend the people.

The Jimintō suffered a major defeat in the House of Councillors election of July 2007, and the opposition Minshutō took control of the Upper House, resulting in what came to be called the "twisted Diet." After the first Abe administration, the cabinet of Fukuda Yasuo was unable to extend the life of the Anti-Terrorism Special Measures Law, which had been time-limited when the law was first passed. When the law expired in November, the Maritime SDF fueling vessels were brought back from the Indian Ocean. In 2008 a new law focused specifically on fueling support was passed, and Maritime SDF fueling operations in the Indian Ocean were allowed to resume.

Disruptions in Japan's Relations with China and South Korea: "Cold Politics, Hot Economy"

Prime Minister Koizumi pledged he would always mark End-of-War Memorial Day with an official visit to Yasukuni Shrine, and in August 2001 he made the first of what would eventually be six visits while in office. For several years, he avoided the August 15 date, but on his final official visit, in 2006, he went on August 15, the first prime minister in twenty-one years—since Nakasone Yasuhiro—to do so. Koizumi's first visit was anticipated, so diplomatic authorities scheduled his visit to China early, to contain the damage.

Koizumi traveled to China in October 2001, visiting the Marco Polo Bridge and other historic sites and expressing his "heartfelt apologies and feelings of regret." In his meeting with Jiang Zemin, Koizumi explained the reasons for his visits to Yasukuni Shrine, saying forthrightly he went "to renounce war and show sympathy for those who died in the war." Beginning with Koizumi's second lightning visit, however, the Chinese government criticized the visits harshly and repeatedly, saying they were hurting the feelings of the people of the nations harmed by the war.

Prime Minister Koizumi, while standing firm on the subject of visits to Yasukuni Shrine, remained faithful to the 1995 Murayama Statement acknowledging the harm done by Japan's actions during the war with respect to external statements concerning historical problems. In his speech at the Asian-African Summit in April 2005, and in his remarks marking the sixtieth anniversary of the end of World War II that same year, Koizumi closely followed the content of the Murayama Statement.

When Koizumi met Jiang's successor, Hu Jintao, in May 2003, Hu said merely that he took "history as a mirror, and [looked] toward the future," and that he looked forward to the stable development of Japan-China relations. Koizumi responded that, by strengthening bilateral cooperation, the two nations could contribute together to development and friendship in Asia. However, improvement in Japan-China relations did not gain momentum. In the spring of 2005, a movement emerged in China opposed to selecting Japan as a permanent member of the UN Security Council, and in April of that year large anti-Japan demonstrations were held in Beijing.

Economic interaction between Japan and China continued to grow, however, and in 2004 China surpassed the United States as Japan's largest trading partner. Japan-China relations in the Koizumi era were described as "cold politics, hot economy": political relations may have been chilly, but economic relations were quite warm.

After Prime Minister Koizumi's 2001 visit to China, he went to South Korea, where he visited historical sites, including the site of the prison where pro-independence activists had been held during the colonial period (Seodaemun Independence Park). In his summit meeting with President Kim Dae-jung, Koizumi expressed his "remorse and apology." The two leaders agreed to promote joint research regarding history textbooks in their two nations. In the spring of that year, new issues with history textbooks had emerged, but President Kim's attitude toward Japan had been cautious and restrained. Public opinion in South Korea, however, had escalated, and the government had begun to take steps toward returning to censorship of Japanese culture. Exchanges in various forms continued to be suspended or canceled at the local and private-sector level.

Amid these circumstances, the Japan–Republic of Korea joint history research agreed to by

15-17. The signing of the Japan–North Korea Pyongyang Declaration

Koizumi and Kim, and later Japan-China joint history research (2006–09) became an experiment in new historical rapprochement aimed at calming and depoliticizing historical frictions.

Japan–North Korea Pyongyang Declaration

At the end of August 2002, it was announced that Koizumi would visit North Korea. Negotiations that diplomatic officials in Japan and North Korea had been holding behind closed doors for over a year began to bear fruit. Koizumi and his entourage made the visit as a day trip in mid-September. The day before, US president George W. Bush had sent a message urging caution on nuclear development.

Prime Minister Koizumi met with Defense Commission chairman Kim Jong-il, but just before the summit meeting was scheduled to begin, information was delivered regarding the results of an investigation regarding abductees (eight dead). Koizumi objected strenuously, and demanded a clear apology. North Korea acknowledged the existence of the abductees, and promised that those who survived would be allowed to return to Japan, and that the truth would be investigated.

In the deliberations leading up to the Japan–North Korea Pyongyang Declaration, the North Korea side sought economic cooperation and conformance to the Murayama Statement rather than compensation. The declaration included statements on normalization of diplomatic relations, the Japan side's "keen sense of reflection and heartfelt apology" regarding the past, economic cooperation after normalization, North Korea's expression of regret for "pending questions regarding the lives and safety of Japanese people," and observance of international agreements on nuclear technology and missiles.

In October 2002, five abductees returned to Japan, and their family members returned to Japan in May 2004. After that, however, no further progress was made regarding the problem of abductees. Shortly after Koizumi's visit to North Korea, the Japanese government had begun to try to persuade the US government to hold direct negotiations with North Korea on nuclear issues. Finally, a new round of Six-Party Talks began in August 2003. In September 2005, the Six-Party Talks issued a joint statement agreeing on a framework for a comprehensive solution, including verifiable denuclearization of North Korea, normalization of relations with Japan and the United States, and economic cooperation. The abductee problem was also included as part of the comprehensive solution. The statement set the course for the resolution of outstanding issues and the normalization of diplomatic relations based on the Pyongyang Declaration. However, the problem of nuclear development has hindered progress in resolving these issues.

Aiming for a "Strategic Mutual Relationship"

Prime Minister Abe Shinzō, who was particularly keen on restoring relations with China, visited China in October 2006, shortly after assuming office. The visit was hailed as an "ice-breaking trip," the first visit to China by a Japanese prime minister in five years. At the urging of diplomatic officials on both sides, no statements about visits to Yasukuni Shrine were made. The joint statement with Hu Jintao stated that Japan and China should be aiming for a "mutually beneficial relationship based on common strategic interests." This meant a relationship exploring common interests and future-oriented regional issues, rather than the problems of the past. Regarding historical problems, the statement represented a turn to a posture focusing on Japan's peaceful development in the postwar period, rather than the wartime era.

Premier Wen Jiabao visited Japan in April 2007. In the Diet, Wen said the Chinese government and the Chinese people greatly appreciated the many times the Japanese government and Japanese leaders had publicly acknowledged Japan's aggression, and expressed their feelings of regret and apology to the victim nations. Wen recognized the support China had received from the Japanese government and the Japanese people for its reforms, opening, and modernization. "The Chinese people will never forget this," he said. Such acknowledgement of Japan's support on the part of China was unprecedented.

In December 2007, the next prime minister, Fukuda Yasuo, visited China, and was made to feel extraordinarily welcome. Hu hosted the welcome banquet, the first given by China's top leaders for a Japanese prime minister since Nakasone Yasuhiro. Around the time of Fukuda's trip to China, Japan decided to grant a final large yen-denominated infrastructure loan (loan fund cooperation) for China. The Koizumi cabinet had said that Japan would no longer make new infrastructure loans to China after the Beijing Olympics were held. All official development assistance (ODA) to China ended in FY2018.

Hu arrived for a state visit to Japan in May 2008. He signed a joint declaration proclaiming comprehensive progress toward a relationship of strategic mutual benefit. While the Japan side stated China's development represented great opportunities for the international community, the China side expressed great appreciation for Japan's progress as a peaceful nation in the postwar period. As tangible measures to deepen strategic mutual benefit, the document promised cooperation on global issues including energy, environment, investment, development of resources in the East China Sea, climate change, poverty, and infectious diseases. Prime Minister Fukuda said this marked the first time Japan and China had succeeded in transcending bilateral issues to embrace global issues.

It was not long, however, before something happened to dampen the mood of high-level reconciliation. Early in 2008, several Japanese families who ate frozen dumplings made in China suffered from food poisoning, and this developed into an issue affecting bilateral relations.

Japan-Russia Relations in the Putin Era

The starting point for Japan-Russia relations in the era of President Vladimir Putin came in March 2001, when Putin met Prime Minister Mori Yoshirō for a summit in Irkutsk. With the Japanese-Soviet Joint Declaration of 1956 as starting point, the two nations were still striving for a peace treaty. With the joint statement issued in Irkutsk, Japan-Russia relations should have found a fresh start. But under the Koizumi administration, Japan's Russia policy floundered, and little progress was made.

Koizumi visited Russia in January 2003, hoping to begin anew. He signed a joint statement concerning the adoption of an action plan, affirming issues in various areas and demonstrating efforts at improving relations, but the document fell short with respect to tangible actions. Putin visited Japan in November 2005 and signed twelve different agreements, but none of them said anything about the territorial issue or the peace treaty. At the same time, Russia issued a "Social Economic Development Plan" for the Kuril Islands, including the Northern Territories, aiming for population growth and economic development in the Kuril Islands.

Successes and Failures of the Three Democratic Party Cabinets

In the general election of August 2009, the Minshutō won 308 seats, marking the first real

15-18. The Hatoyama administration attestation ceremony

change of government in Japan since the end of World War II. By the time the Jimintō returned to power in the general election of November 2012, there would be three Minshutō prime ministers: Hatoyama Yukio, Kan Naoto, and Noda Yoshihiko. As far as foreign policy was concerned, the Minshutō manifesto put top priority on "equality and closeness" in Japan-US relations, but each of these Minshutō administrations had a different character.

Prime Minister Hatoyama, who took office in September 2009, came up with the idea of the East Asian Community, and he created new opportunities to promote the idea, for example by jointly chairing the Bali Democracy Forum. Consensus within Hatoyama's own party was lacking, however, because the concept, if not outright anti-American, appeared to aim at putting greater distance between Japan and the United States, and the idea did not get off the ground. Pertaining to the important Japan-US relationship, Prime Minister Hatoyama declared a goal of moving the Futenma airbase "at least outside Okinawa." While this proposal was being considered, public opinion in Okinawa leaned heavily against moving the base within the prefecture. The Hatoyama cabinet, unable to come up with a concrete proposal, lost the trust of the US government, and was compelled to step down.

In September 2010, shortly after Kan, Hatoyama's successor, formed his cabinet, a Chinese fishing vessel operating illegally in the vicinity of the Senkaku Islands struck Japan Coast Guard patrol vessels. Prosecutors decided to release the Chinese captain without charging him, but the incident caused a chill in Japan-China relations. Some people questioned his release, and the leak of information related to the case compounded the problem.

Just before this incident, in September, the Kan cabinet issued a statement marking the hundredth anniversary of Japan's annexation of Korea that included an apology to the Republic of Korea. The content of this statement was similar to the Murayama Statement, but it specified South Korea. Kan's statement was an expression of Japan's desire to build a future-oriented relationship with South Korea, and included the return of cultural properties (mainly books, including the "Uigwe" chronicles of the Joseon dynasty) that had been appropriated during the time Japan ruled Korea. In August 2012, however, Lee Myung-bak took the decisive step of becoming the first South Korean president to visit Takeshima. To resolve the territorial dispute, Foreign

15-19. Operation Tomodachi

Minister Genba Kōichirō proposed to South Korea that the matter be referred to the International Court of Justice, but South Korea rejected this, as it had done in 1954 and again in 1964.

Although the Minshutō had established their government heralding "close and equal Japan-US relations," the reality reflected little improvement to speak of. Occurring shortly after the second reshuffle of the Kan cabinet, however, the Great East Japan Earthquake of March 2011 in a certain sense served as a true test of the mettle of the Japan-US alliance.

By the end of April, the United States had mobilized 24,000 soldiers who were mainly based in Japan in an assistance effort dubbed "Operation Tomodachi." Through its actions, the United States justified its presence to nearby nations.

Response to Emerging China

In September 2011, the newly elected Japanese prime minister Noda visited China. Seeking to further deepen the strategic mutually beneficial relationship between the two nations, he proposed a strengthening of bilateral cooperation on global issues. In 2012, however, he confronted a more serious problem: the "nationalization" of the Senkaku Islands.

In April 2012, Tokyo governor Ishihara Shintarō announced that the Metropolis of Tokyo planned to purchase the Senkaku Islands (Uotsuri and two other islands). Concerned that the "peaceful management" of the Senkakus might be disrupted, Noda and his cabinet decided that the national government should purchase the islands from their current owner, and did so in mid-September. China objected, calling this a "change in the current situation" (i.e., a challenge to the postwar international order). Anti-Japan demonstrations in China grew rancorous and some turned violent. Provocations such as incursions by Chinese government ships in Japan's maritime territory became more frequent.

The foreign-policy options of the three Minshutō cabinets all differed from those of their predecessors, but they were lacking in consistency and stability. One reason for this was that they were too driven by political considerations, leading the cabinets to eschew cooperation with the collective expertise of the bureaucracy. At the same time, there were more than a few issues worthy of attention in the areas of national security and international cooperation. One of these was the formulation of new National Defense Program Guidelines in 2010. Reflecting concerns about China's provocations in the Nansei Islands, these new guidelines introduced the concept of "dynamic defensive force" aimed at flexible deployment of SDF forces in the area surrounding Japan. Twenty years after the end of the Cold War, Japan was finally updating its basic defense force concept. In December 2011, the chief cabinet secretary announced the easing of Japan's three principles on arms exports and their related policy guidelines. Then, in January 2012, Japan sent a large SDF engineering battalion to South Sudan to support the peacekeeping mission there.

15-20. Japan–China–South Korea Summit

Focusing on the emergence of China and the changing balance of power, the Noda cabinet's foreign minister, Genba Kōichirō, set consistent goals of writing new rules conforming with international law, and "creating open, multilayered networks" with the United States, the Republic of Korea, Australia, India, ASEAN, and others, to form a new order in the Asia-Pacific region. The Chairman's Statement issued at the 2011 East Asia Summit mentioned the possibility of an Expanded ASEAN Maritime Forum. The response to the emergence of China from this perspective was to be followed up by the Abe administration.

When the Hatoyama administration was formed, Okada Katsuya, who served as foreign minister, made it his mission to resolve the problem of the "secret agreement" between Japan and the United States. For nearly fifty years, Japanese governments had repeatedly told the Diet that no such agreement existed, generating pointless debate in the Diet and hampering the operations of Japan-US diplomacy. Okada formed a panel of officials from the Ministry of Foreign Affairs (MOFA) and outside experts to conduct a thorough investigation. They released their findings in March 2010. Okada wrote new rules for MOFA to enforce the "thirty-year rule" on disclosure of diplomatic records. Active disclosure of diplomatic records is the driving force for both internal and external understanding of diplomatic activities.

3 The Second Abe Cabinet and Expansion of the Diplomatic Horizon

Indo-Pacific Strategy

When Prime Minister Abe was returned to the premiership in December 2012, he showed his readiness to prioritize working with nations that shared the values of freedom and democracy, the rule of law, and fundamental human rights. Also known as "values-oriented diplomacy," this idea was the brainchild of Asō Tarō, who had served as foreign minister in the first Abe cabinet, propounding the "arc of freedom and prosperity." As Japan was a forerunner among non-Western nations in embracing these "universal values," the idea was to contribute to peace and stability among nations pursuing "freedom and prosperity."

Cooperation with India and Australia was a particularly high priority. Japan issued joint statements on security with both these nations under the administrations of Abe and Asō. This developed into the Abe cabinet's goal of a "free and open Indo-Pacific strategy." Regarding this strategy, in August 2016 Prime Minister Abe said, "Japan bears the responsibility of fostering the confluence of the Pacific and Indian Oceans and of Asia and Africa into a place that values freedom, the rule of law, and the market economy, free from force or coercion, and making it prosperous."

This statement by Abe reflects an awareness of the powerful emergence of China. China was building up its military, and was less than open about doing so. In the East China Sea, it continued to send its government vessels into Japanese waters near the Senkaku Islands, and it continued its unilateral exploitation of natural resources in exclusive economic zones and maritime regions that remained undefined in continental-shelf boundary documentation.

At the same time, in Japan–South Korea relations, in December 2015 Foreign Minister Kishida Fumio and Foreign Affairs Minister Yoon Byung-se (Yun Byung-se) reached a long-awaited agreement on the comfort- women issue. The South Korean government agreed to establish a foundation for the support of former comfort women, and Japan agreed to provide funding for it. This would represent a "final and irreversible" solution to this problem. The two governments agreed to refrain from mutual criticism in the UN and other bodies of the international community. The Reconciliation and Healing Foundation was set up in July 2016, and the Japanese government funded it with one billion yen.

15-21. Russian president Vladimir Putin and Prime Minister Abe Shinzō

Toward "Joint Economic Activities" on the Four Northern Islands

Prime Minister Abe made an official visit to Russia in April 2013, and signed a joint statement with President Putin. It was the first visit to Russia by a Japanese prime minister in ten years. The joint statement reaffirmed the agreement that "final solutions" to the problems that had been identified at the time of Prime Minister Koizumi's visit would be found, "leading to the conclusion of a peace treaty."

The annexation of the Crimean Peninsula in March 2014 chilled Russia's relations with Europe and the United States, but had a limited effect on Russia's relations with Japan. When Abe met Putin at the end of 2016, both remained focused on solving the problem of the peace treaty, showing sincere determination. They agreed to begin consultations aimed at "joint economic activities" on the four Northern Islands, and they made specific project proposals.

Apart from the peace treaty and the territorial problem, Japan and Russia were in agreement in several areas, including efforts aimed at stabilization of the East Asia region such as denuclearization of the Korean Peninsula and confidence-building measures, as well as international terrorism, cybercrime, piracy, illegal arms exports, and other "new threats." These issues had been discussed at bilateral summit meetings since 2007, and foreign and defense ministerial consultations ("2+2" ministerial meetings) were held on a regular basis.

"Heisei Opening of the Nation"

In February 2013, the Abe cabinet formally announced Japan would join the Trans-Pacific Partnership (TPP). The TPP was meant to be more than just a free-trade agreement. It was intended as a new kind of rule-writing entity that would function across the Pacific region to remove barriers to services and investment, protect intellectual property, and incorporate mechanisms to prevent state-owned enterprises from dominating private-sector enterprises.

Japan was already steering toward promotion of multi-layered trade rules combining bilateral free-trade agreements (FTA) and economic partnership agreements (EPA); by the end of 2017 it had signed and implemented sixteen EPAs with twenty nations. However, these EPAs were not as ambitious as the TPP in terms of the areas covered and their degree of freedom. The Kan Naoto administration, which was invited to participate in these negotiations, called them the "Heisei opening of the nation," and sought ways to participate in them, but the magnitude of the hurdles to be overcome was daunting.

In the end, twelve nations participated in the TPP negotiations, and the pact was signed in February 2016. This created a new economic zone that was both free and fair. Under the new rules, Japanese companies would be able to leap into overseas markets, accelerate their efforts to take active part in growth markets, and strengthen the foundations of Japan's economy. The TPP agreement also contributed to security and stability in the Asia-Pacific region by strengthening the rule of law in the economic sphere, among nations that shared basic values.

In January 2017 the Trump administration announced that the US would withdraw from the TPP, but in March 2018 eleven nations signed the new TPP11 Agreement (Comprehensive and Progressive Agreement for Trans-Pacific Partnership, or CPTPP). Japan played a central role in the creation of the CPTPP, sending a powerful message as a "flag-bearer for freedom" fighting against protectionism.

In 2018, after negotiations that lasted five years, Japan and the EU signed the Japan-EU Economic Partnership Agreement (EPA). This created a new free economic zone comprising about 30 percent of global GDP and about 40 percent of trade. Hopes are high that, together with the CPTPP, this will become a catalyst for growth strategy, as well as an important propulsive force.

15-22. Demonstrators protest Japan's exercise of its right to collective self-defense

Approval for Limited Exercise of the Right to Collective Self-Defense

In the meantime, as the emergence of China and North Korea's series of nuclear experiments made the security environment more difficult, the Abe administration looked for new ways to allow the exercise of the right to self-defense so as to enhance the deterrent power of the Japan-US alliance. It accomplished this by taking a different view of Article 9 of the Constitution. As a result, in July 2014 the cabinet passed a resolution allowing the exercise of the right to collective self-defense, but only in "existential crises," if certain conditions were fulfilled. Among the ruling and opposition parties, some favored the right to individual self-defense, or the right to police actions, but the majority of the ruling party endorsed the idea of limiting the exercise of the right of collective self-defense, saying this was compatible with the government's interpretation.

Based on this cabinet resolution, new legislation for peace and security was passed in September 2015 and took effect in March 2016. This legislation comprised a package of ten revised existing laws, plus the International Peace Support Act, allowing Japan to provide backup logistical support for military actions in other nations. This would enable Japanese troops on a peacekeeping mission to use arms to protect NGOs and other civilians in the area, and to provide defensive support for US warships even at normal times. In November 2016, Japan sent troops whose mission included the use of arms to support the peacekeeping operation in South Sudan. These troops returned home in May 2017 without ever engaging in combat.

The new policies accelerated coordination with the United States for the Guidelines for Japan-US Defense Cooperation published in April 2015. The content was wide-ranging, covering extensive Japan-US cooperative systems for support logistics; cooperation for peace and security globally, but particularly in the Asia-Pacific region; cooperation on outer space and cyberspace; and international cooperation in peacekeeping activities, humanitarian support, maritime safety, and support for

15-23. Address by Barack Obama, first sitting US president to visit Hiroshima

capacity-building. This marked a big change from the Act on Measures to Ensure the Peace and Security of Japan in Perilous Situations in Areas Surrounding Japan, based on the previous guidelines of 1997, which limited Japan's actions to naval transport of personnel and equipment in international waters in support of US military activities outside the region.

What is Meant by "Proactive Contributor to Peace"?

In December 2013, the Abe cabinet established the National Security Council (NSC) as a Japanese control center for matters of defense and security. This was an idea Abe had stood behind since his first term in office, but had been unable to realize because of the change of government. In the same month, the cabinet and the NSC formulated a comprehensive National Security Strategy (NSS) to cover both diplomacy and defense strategy for a period of roughly a decade.

The basic philosophy of this NSS was to remake Japan as a "proactive contributor to peace," through international cooperation. The concept of "proactive contributor to peace" did not suddenly appear out of thin air. Throughout the postwar period, Japan had contributed to peace and prosperity in Asia through its peace constitution, its three non-nuclear principles, and its overseas development activities. It had also helped to resolve global issues through UN peacekeeping operations. Furthermore, Japan had upheld the idea of human security by contributing assistance to impoverished nations and helping with nation-building in countries torn by civil war. Being a "proactive contributor to peace" could only mean strengthening these kinds of initiatives further, and expanding these efforts.

The NSS represented guidelines for the kind of foreign-policy strategy Japan ought to pursue in the face of the changing balance of power, particularly the emergence of China, and the diversification of threats in the changing post–Cold War security environment. The plan could be summarized as encouraging Japan to amplify its efforts on each of three levels of security: first, its own efforts; second, cooperation with allies; and third, cooperation with the international community. Particular priority was placed on the third level—cooperation and contribution to efforts by the international community to resolve issues on a global scale.

These wide-ranging, multi-layered security initiatives were already covered by revisions to the most recent National Defense Program Guidelines, and were also reflected in the Official Development Assistance (ODA) guidelines contained in the Development Cooperation Charter (February 2015). There were strong expectations of a close connection between assistance to developing nations and security and national interests.

ODA: Self-Help Efforts and Human-Resource Development

Background and Initial Development

The history of Japan's foreign-aid policy began in October 1954, when Japan joined the Colombo Plan (an organization of countries in the British Commonwealth and elsewhere that aimed to provide development assistance to the Asia-Pacific region). To this day, Japan commemorates October 6—the day it became part of the group—as "International Cooperation Day." While Japan's contributions under the Colombo Plan were limited to areas like technical assistance and trainee instruction, the Colombo Plan essentially represented the starting point for the focus on human-resource development that has played a central role in Japan's foreign-aid policy since.

The basic ODA framework began to come together in the 1960s, with the creation of the Overseas Economic Cooperation Fund (OECF) in 1961 and the establishment of the Japan International Cooperation Agency (JICA) in 1962. Japan's trade balance trended positive in the mid-1960s, which gave the country room to expand its aid policy as a member of the OECD. Most of the aid went toward ODA as a means of paying war reparations to Southeast Asian nations, however.

A turning point came in the 1970s. After the 1973 oil crisis, Japan directed more and more ODA funding to the Middle East to help ensure stable supplies of valuable resources. Japan also considered stabilizing and developing the Asia-Pacific region to be one of its international obligations as a developed nation. In light of those needs and aims, the Fukuda Takeo cabinet set doubling the country's ODA contributions over the next five years as Japan's First Medium-Term Target in 1977. That spurred an enormous increase in Japan's foreign-aid expenditures, most of which went to the Asian community. ODA-driven infrastructure work helped nurture development and energize economic growth—and that economic growth was crucial in bringing peace and stability to the region.

The scale of Japan's ODA continued to swell after the Plaza Accord: the total amount in 1989 was US$9 billion, a sum that pushed Japan past the United States (US$7.6 billion) to become the world's top ODA contributor. China was an important factor in that growth. Japan began issuing low-interest yen loans to China in 1979, and the amount of ODA heading to China soon rose to the level of assistance bound for the ASEAN community. In time, however, the conditions changed; with the Tiananmen Square Incident and China's economic boom having altered the landscape, the Japanese government reworked its policy on ODA to China and discontinued yen loans for major infrastructural development (loan assistance) in 2007. The focus shifted to different forms of contributions on a more limited scope: Japan provided China with access to medical experts, technical assistance, and small grant aids to build schools, for example, but those packages also came to an end in FY2018. All in all, Japan's total ODA provisions to China since 1979 come to 3.65 trillion yen, the highest amount of any donor—outstripping Germany, the United Kingdom, and the United States.

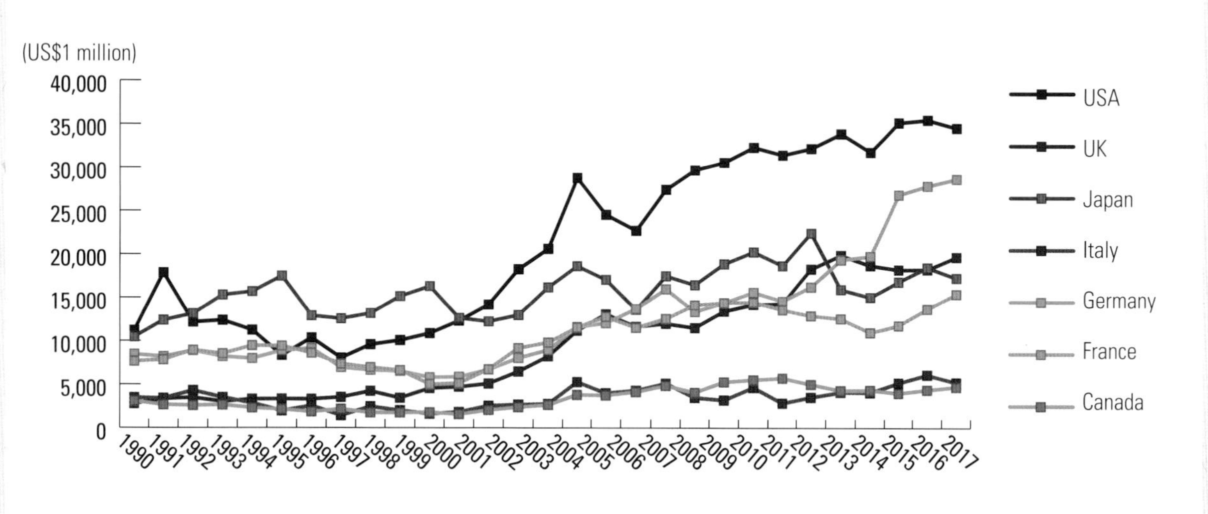

15-24. ODA from major donor nations

ODA: Self-Help Efforts and Human-Resource Development

The Distinguishing Features of Japanese ODA

One of the defining characteristics of Japan's ODA policy has been its clear objective of fostering economic development in Asia through infrastructure development, a strategy that reflects how Japan itself went through the modernization process. Another key feature is the principle of "self-help." Valuing the autonomy of the recipient countries, Japan structures its loans so that beneficiaries need to repay both the principal and the interest on the package. This approach has enabled efficient development across Asia, as recipient governments know that they need to make efficient use of the funding in order to generate profits that exceed their repayment obligations. Third, Japan has also focused on human-resource development by sending teams of specialists into recipient countries for training programs. One notable past participant in a program funded by Japanese ODA was Indonesian president Yudhoyono, who took part in a JICA-sponsored seminar on economic development.

In February 2015, the government established its ODA Charter ("Development Cooperation Charter") to lay out core guidelines on foreign aid. The terms of the charter steered away from the conventional approach to development assistance, which entailed OECD member countries providing unilateral aid, and made "public-private partnership" a new major focus. The climate surrounding the foreign-aid policy has continued to evolve, as well. Following the establishment of the National Security Strategy in 2013, the scope of the target areas requiring ODA has expanded from emergency humanitarian assistance and peacebuilding support to include virtually the entire spectrum of international-security issues. Infectious diseases, major natural disasters, and cross-border threats have entered the picture, as have medium- to long-term concerns about social vulnerabilities arising from climate change. Today, some are calling for Japan's development assistance to embrace the idea of "human security"—a broad, overarching concept that encompasses "freedom from fear," "human dignity," expanded rights for women, and more.

At the heart of the NSS was the idea that Japan's national interests would be best served by maintaining, defending, and expanding the international order based on the "universal values" (liberty, democracy, human rights, and the rule of law). Japan would share these universal values and put priority on working together with countries and regions that also abide by them.

Japan may be an "economic power," but politically it has no special rights or position within the international community like those enjoyed by the permanent members of the UN Security Council. It is not able to maintain its own security or national interests without the perennial support and cooperation of a large number of nations.

In an August 2015 statement marking the seventieth anniversary of the end of World War II, Abe echoed the Murayama Statement, adding his own reflections on an apology for the war. Then he said, "We must not let our children, grandchildren, and even further generations to come, who have nothing to do with that war, be predestined to apologize." That could only be an expression of Abe's determination, backed by history, not to create a situation where future generations would be obligated to apologize again. Effort would be needed to prevent such a development, but even more than that, it would require the building of friendly relations of mutual trust with as many countries as possible throughout the world.

4 A New Era of Hope and Insecurity

Cold War Redux: China Leaps Forward

In the final years of the Heisei era (2018–19), the international environment found itself facing unprecedented turmoil.

At the international political level, a freeze in

US-Russia relations had continued since Russia's annexation of the Crimean Peninsula in 2014. In October 2018, the United States declared its withdrawal from the Intermediate-Range Nuclear Forces (INF) Treaty it had signed with the Soviet Union in 1987. As reasons, the United States cited Russia's development of new kinds of missiles in violation of the INF, and the increase in the nuclear weapons capabilities of China, which was not bound by the INF. During the Cold War, a great network of arms control and disarmament systems had arisen through the conclusion of multiple disarmament and nuclear arms reduction treaties, and the INF stood at the center of that. This arms control system was now collapsing. The new, 2011 US-Russia START (Strategic Arms Reduction Treaty) agreement will not expire until 2021, but its future appears to be in danger. At this point, there is no method for controlling arms, including nuclear weapons, that could take the place of these two treaties.

In July 2017 the UN adopted a treaty banning nuclear weapons (the Treaty on the Prohibition of Nuclear Weapons). Japan stood alongside the nuclear-weapon states in not supporting that treaty. While Japan shares the goal of abolishing nuclear weapons, as stated in the treaty, it still needs the United States to maintain its nuclear deterrence in the current security environment. At the same time, Japan is seeking to serve as a bridge between the nations that support the treaty and the nations that possess nuclear weapons. Given the current lack of progress in efforts to abolish nuclear weapons, fears that the powerful nations will once again resume their race to develop nuclear arms would not be misplaced.

At the same time, at the level of international economics, beginning in the spring of 2018, the United States and China began a trade war, with tit-for-tat imposition of tariffs on imports of each other's goods, generating growing speculation that global trade would shrink. The United States was not just seeking to shrink its trade deficits with China, but to address other issues, such as protection of intellectual property, an end to forced transfer of technology, cyber-attacks, and non-tariff barriers. The US demands may also extend to the kinds of domestic systemic reforms in China that Japan had experienced in past periods of trade friction with the United States.

It goes without saying that the cause of this political and economic turmoil at the global level lay with the economic advance of China. Through reform and opening, China, with its 1.3 billion people, was now open to investment from the world, as both a factory and a marketplace. In the early years of the twenty-first century, the United States accounted for 32 percent of the world's GDP, eight times as much as China. Now, the United States is only 24 percent of world GDP, just 50 percent more than China. Japan's GDP has slipped from 13 percent of global GDP to 6 percent.

China, which is now the world's largest manufacturing and trading nation, has been advancing its Belt and Road Initiative since 2013, promoting trade along the "Silk Road Economic Belt," extending to Central Asia, the Middle East, and Europe. Many nations along this Belt and Road route are benefiting from support for construction of infrastructure such as railways, roads, and harbors. They may also be coming under China's political and military influence.

"Permanent Peace" on the Korean Peninsula?

The situation on the Korean Peninsula was also very volatile. Around the time of the Pyeongchang Olympics in February 2018, North Korea actively pursued dialogue with South Korea, even indicating it would be responsive to calls for its denuclearization. At the end of April, Workers' Party of Korea chairman Kim Jong-un and South Korean president Moon Jae-in held a summit meeting. In their joint declaration, the two nations proclaimed their intention to achieve "through complete denuclearization, a nuclear-free Korean Peninsula." The two Koreas also pledged to restart four-party talks that would include the United States and China; to declare an end to the Korean War, which had technically been suspended under an armistice agreement; and to realize a "permanent and solid peace regime."

Chairman Kim met President Trump for a summit meeting in June. Although the United States had not received a promise of "complete and irreversible" denuclearization, Chairman Kim appeared to show strong resolve for denuclearization, as indicated in his New Year's address for 2019. The United States and North Korea held a second summit in late February 2019, without reaching any agreement, but consultations between the two nations continued.

The Korean Peninsula has been plagued by foreign interference since before the First Sino-Japanese War. If the diplomatic process leads toward denuclearization, a formal end to the Korean War, unification of North and South, and the withdrawal of US troops, the curtain will fall on the final act of the Cold War, and peace will come to the Korean Peninsula. That hope has not yet been ruled out.

Japan-Russia Relations: Is a Peace Treaty Forthcoming?

With respect to bilateral relations since the start of the second Abe administration, Japan-US relations had remained stable, Japan-China relations had improved, and Japan-Russia relations were starting to show signs of a resolution of the territorial dispute.

In mid-November 2018—at the twenty-fifth meeting between Abe and Putin, counting those that took place in the first Abe administration—Japan and Russia agreed to accelerate negotiations based on the 1956 Japanese-Soviet Joint Declaration, which called for the islands of Habomai and Shikotan to be handed over to Japan after the two nations signed a peace treaty. This problem had already lingered for much of the postwar period, and the two leaders showed they had no wish to kick it down the road to future generations. They shared a strong desire to put an end to the matter. Their near-term goal was to make certain the two islands were returned to Japan.

For Russia, however, the issue of the Northern Territories is not just a dispute over a national border; the territories came into Russia's possession as a result of World War II. A great gap separates Russia from Japan, which is still asserting its sovereignty over four islands. One of Russia's concerns is the possibility that, if it returns two of the islands, the United States will set up a military base there. When the 1960 US-Japan Security Treaty was signed, the Soviet Union made withdrawal of US troops from Japan a condition for the return of two islands. Despite economic and natural resources development, Japan-Russia relations cannot foresee the direction political relations will take.

Shaking up the "1965 System"

In Japan-South Korea relations, the foundation that was laid by the 1965 normalization of relations has been rattled. The Supreme Court of Korea heard a case filed by South Korean plaintiffs who had been used as forced labor during the war; they demanded compensation from Japanese corporations. At the end of November 2018, the court ruled in favor of the plaintiffs and ordered that they be compensated. The court stated that the mobilization of Koreans during the war had been an inhumane and illegal action by Japanese corporations, tied to Japan's war of aggression and illegal colonial rule over the Korean Peninsula.

For the Japanese government, whose position was that the 1965 Claims Settlement and Economic Cooperation Agreement between Japan and the Republic of Korea had "completely and finally"

15-25. The Charlevoix Summit (June 2018)

settled South Korean claims—whether on the part of government or private individuals—this ruling threatened to destabilize international law and disrupt the legal basis of Japan-South Korea relations. From the South Korean perspective, individuals' claims had not been expunged. Moreover, the categorization of colonial rule as an "illegal action" came as a major shock to Japan.

The legal evaluation of Japanese rule over South Korea was one reason why the establishment of diplomatic relations had taken such a long time. The South Korean side claimed the 1910 Japan-Korea Annexation Treaty was illegal, while the Japan side maintained that it was legal. In the end, the negotiations dragged on for fifteen years, and agreement was reached on a statement that the 1910 treaty was "already null and void." That language represented the distilled wisdom of the two sides—but now even that wisdom was "already null and void." The Reconciliation and Healing Foundation set up under the December 2015 Agreement on Comfort Women between Japan and the Republic of Korea (see sidebar on page 491) was also disbanded. The reconciliation that had been achieved between governments did not bring reconciliation between different interpretations of history, or between the peoples of the two nations.

Challenges to Liberalism

At the Charlevoix G7 Summit in June 2018, agreement was reached on a joint declaration proclaiming a "fight against protectionism," but President Trump refused to sign it. In December, at the G20 Summit in Argentina, language denouncing protectionism was removed from the Leaders' Declaration for the first time. Anti-protectionism had been a core concept of the G20.

For Japan, and for the world, the most worrisome possibility is that the liberal international order, of which the United States has been the main driver, might collapse. The national interests the United States has pursued were never limited to its own interests in a narrow sense; the US has pursued the ideas of democracy and the republic. At the root of American diplomacy has always been a broad definition of its national interests—encompassing the view that the interests of its friends and allies, and indeed of the entire free world, are America's interests. The United States' tilt toward protectionism in trade and its withdrawal from TPP, as well as its withdrawal from other multilateral agreements such as the UN Framework Convention on Climate Change, certainly represent a crisis for the liberal international order.

However, it is unlikely that the United States will simply drop its longstanding principles of protecting the security of its friends and allied nations, maintaining free trade, standing up for democracy and market economies as well as human rights and the rule of law, and become just "an ordinary superpower." For the United States, with its power, to act like "an ordinary superpower" would mean a tremendous loss of its own national interests.

Japan, caught in the narrow space between the United States and China, will find it challenging to steer the right diplomatic course, but above all it must work to strengthen the functioning of the Japan-US alliance, by bearing its share of the costs of that alliance as the US demands. Meanwhile, the basic conditions that Japanese diplomacy has relied upon—politically, democracy; economically, market economics and free trade; legally, the rule of law on an international scale—should be shared with other like-minded countries, and efforts should be united in tackling global issues. The concept of a "free and open Indo-Pacific," which Japan has propounded for years, is a first step in achieving this.

Activating the UN

Since the end of the Cold War, one phenomenon worthy of attention has been the activation of the UN. The world itself has changed since the Cold War ended. When the UN was founded, the world's population was 2.5 billion. At the time of writing it is 7.5 billion. The world economy is now global. Trade by developing nations has grown rapidly, and the size of the market has quintupled since the Cold War ended. As all this was happening, global issues also exploded.

The UN is the only international entity in a position to deal with this state of affairs. It plays a central role by creating models and shaping legislation not just for disarmament and arms control, but in a wide range of areas including human rights, human security, space, development, the environment, climate change, and disaster management.

As part of these efforts, the UN adopted the Sustainable Development Goals (SDGs) in 2015. These SDGs are intended to achieve a world where economic growth, resolution of societal problems, and environmental protection are achieved and balanced well. One key aspect of the SDGs is the call for active participation by citizens and corporations. In 2018, Japan established the SDGs Promotion Headquarters, consisting of all members of the cabinet, to work with citizens (NGOs), corporations, and other stakeholders on matters of health and disaster management.

The activation of the UN shows that conflicts and estrangement between superpowers, as seen in the rekindling of nuclear arms races and trade wars, need not mean the disintegration of the community of nations.

Bibliography

In the process of writing this book, the author referred to more than 450 works, but most of the titles are in Japanese and are therefore omitted here. Readers of English may find two items of particular interest; both were created as projects of the Japan Association of International Relations (JAIR), and they provide a good deal of valuable information.

The first work is Asada Sadao (ed.), *Japan and the World, 1853–1952: A Bibliographic Guide to Japanese Scholarship in Foreign Relations* (New York: Columbia University Press, 1989).

This volume introduces and analyzes the most important texts pertaining to Japanese diplomacy (both books and papers, in Japanese and in English) and related materals that were published up to 1986, using the following chronological categories:

1. End of Edo period to end of Russo-Japanese War (1853–1905)
2. Post–Russo-Japanese War to Manchurian Incident (1905–1931)
3. Manchurian Incident to Second Sino-Japanese War (1931–1937)
4. Second Sino-Japanese War to start of Pacific War (1937–1941)
5. Pacific War (1941–1945)
6. Allied Occupation of Japan to San Francisco Peace Treaty (1945–1952)

The book includes the following essays: "Introduction: An Overview," "Guide to Documents, Archives, Encyclopedias, and Reference Works," "Japanese Foreign Policy 1931–1945," and "Notes on Basic Sources, 1931–1945."

The second reference is Asada Sadao (ed.), *International Studies in Japan: A Bibliographic Guide* (Tokyo: Japan Association of International Relations, 1988).

This volume, which, like the first, was published as a JAIR project, introduces the literature on Japanese diplomacy subsequent to the San Francisco Peace Treaty. The book provides a well-balanced overview of the scholarly research, mainly in the Japanese language, on diplomatic issues between Japan and major nations up to the mid-1980s. It includes the essays "An Overview of International Studies in Japan," "Japanese-American Relations since 1952," "Postwar Sino-Japanese Relations," and "Postwar Soviet-Japanese Relations."

These two books do a good job of surveying the literature up to the mid-1980s. A great many books and articles about Japanese diplomacy have been published since that time. There have also been many publications that challenge the traditional view of Japan's diplomatic history centering on negotiations between nations. In many ways, this book, *One Hundred Fifty Years of Japanese Foreign Relations*, is based on research done since the mid-1980s; unfortunately, however, no English-language survey of those works has yet been published.

List of Illustrations

No.	Name	Credit
1-1.	Depiction of the challenges faced aboard the *Kanrin Maru*	Diplomatic Archives of the Ministry of Foreign Affairs of Japan
1-2.	Commodore Matthew C. Perry	Yokohama Archives of History
1-3.	"A North American: Portrait of Perry" (woodblock print by unknown artist)	Kurofunekan
1-4.	*First Landing at Gorahama* (print by Wilhelm Heine/Eliphalet M. Brown Jr.)	International Research Center for Japanese Studies
1-5.	The delivery of the letter from the US president to the magistrate of Uraga	*Narrative of the Expedition of an American Squadron to the China Seas and Japan, Performed in the years 1852, 1853, and 1854, under the Command of Commodore M. C. Perry, United States Navy, by Order of the Government of the United States*
1-6.	Diplomatic message from President Fillmore	University of Tsukuba Library
1-7.	The USS *Susquehanna*	Yokohama Archives of History
1-8.	Tanabe Taichi	National Diet Library
1-9.	Japan-US Amity Treaty (copy of signed treaty)	US National Archives
1-10.	Yevfimiy Putyatin	Heda Shipbuilding & Local Data Museum
1-11.	Yokoi Shōnan	Fukui City History Museum, the Lord Shungaku Memorial Library
1-12.	*The Russian Putyatin Mission* (painting by Kishi Magodayū)	Toyo Bunko
1-13.	A model of the *Heda*	Heda Shipbuilding & Local Data Museum
1-14.	Townsend Harris goes to Edo	Kurofunekan
1-15.	Townsend Harris	Takano Norio
1-16.	Japan-US Treaty of Amity and Commerce	Diplomatic Archives of the Ministry of Foreign Affairs of Japan
1-17.	Tokugawa Yoshinobu (Keiki)	Public domain
1-18.	Tokugawa Nariaki	Kyoto University Rare Materials Digital Archive
1-19.	Members of the 1860 mission to the United States visit the Washington Navy Yard	National Diet Library
1-20.	Gold watch with likeness (not visible in photograph) of President Buchanan	Diplomatic Archives of the Ministry of Foreign Affairs of Japan
1-21.	Iwase Tadanari	*Abe Masahiro jiseki*, courtesy of Shitaragahara Historical Museum
1-22.	Kawaji Toshiakira	Takano Norio
1-23.	Mizuno Tadanori	Public domain
1-24.	Tsutsui Masanori	Takano Norio
1-25.	Harry Parkes	Public domain
1-26.	Ernest Satow	Yokohama Archives of History
1-27.	A *bakumatsu*-era passport	Diplomatic Archives of the Ministry of Foreign Affairs of Japan
1-28.	The occupation of the Shimonoseki battery	Yokohama Archives of History
1-29.	Fukuzawa Yukichi	Diplomatic Archives of the Ministry of Foreign Affairs of Japan
1-30.	Fukuchi Gen'ichirō	Diplomatic Archives of the Ministry of Foreign Affairs of Japan
1-31.	First view of the Ogasawara Islands	Diplomatic Archives of the Ministry of Foreign Affairs of Japan
1-32.	Ikeda Nagaoki (Chōhatsu)	Public domain
1-33.	Sakamoto Ryōma	National Diet Library
1-34.	Oguri Tadamasa	National Diet Library
1-35.	Tokugawa Akitake	National Diet Library

No.	Name	Credit
2-1.	From left to right, front row: Itō Hirobumi, Ōkuma Shigenobu, Nakai Hiromu. Back row: Inoue Kaoru, Kuse Jisaku	National Diet Library
2-2.	*The Emperor Receives Foreign Ministers* (painting by Hiroshima Kōho)	Meiji Memorial Picture Gallery
2-3.	Terashima Munenori	Diplomatic Archives of the Ministry of Foreign Affairs of Japan
2-4.	Samejima Naonobu	Diplomatic Archives of the Ministry of Foreign Affairs of Japan
2-5.	Mori Arinori	National Diet Library
2-6.	Henry Willard Denison	Diplomatic Archives of the Ministry of Foreign Affairs of Japan
2-7.	Alexander von Siebold	Siebold Memorial Museum
2-8.	The first Ministry of Foreign Affairs building	Diplomatic Archives of the Ministry of Foreign Affairs of Japan
2-9.	Ōkubo Toshimichi	National Diet Library
2-10.	Kido Takayoshi	National Diet Library
2-11.	*The Iwakura Mission to America and Europe* (painting by Yamaguchi Hōshun)	Meiji Memorial Picture Gallery
2-12.	Iwakura Mission, from left to right: Kido Takayoshi, Yamaguchi Masuka, Iwakura Tomomi, Itō Hirobumi, and Ōkubo Toshimichi	Kyodo News
2-13.	Leaders of the Japanese expeditionary force with Taiwanese aborigines	Internet Archive
2-14.	Enomoto Takeaki	Diplomatic Archives of the Ministry of Foreign Affairs of Japan
2-15.	Kuroda Kiyotaka	Cabinet Public Relations Office
2-16.	Treaty for the Exchange of Sakhalin for the Kurile Islands (instrument of ratification)	Diplomatic Archives of the Ministry of Foreign Affairs of Japan
2-17.	Borders based on the Treaty for the Exchange of Sakhalin for the Kurile Islands (1875)	Ministry of Foreign Affairs of Japan
2-18.	Hanabusa Yoshimoto	National Diet Library
2-19.	"Fishing" (cartoon by Georges Ferdinand Bigot)	Kawasaki City Museum
2-20.	"A Glimpse of Dignitaries Dancing" (woodblock print by Yōshū Chikanobu)	Gift of the Aoki Endowment for Japanese Arts and Cultures
2-21.	*Conference on the Revision of Treaties* (painting by Ueno Kōichi of the 1882 joint conference chaired by Inoue)	Meiji Memorial Picture Gallery
2-22.	Japan-Hawaii Immigration Convention of 1886 (signed treaty)	Diplomatic Archives of the Ministry of Foreign Affairs of Japan
2-23.	The *Normanton* Incident (cartoon by Georges Ferdinand Bigot)	Kawasaki City Museum
2-24.	Ōkuma Shigenobu	Diplomatic Archives of the Ministry of Foreign Affairs of Japan
2-25.	*Promulgation of the Constitution* (painting by Wada Eisaku)	Meiji Memorial Picture Gallery
2-26.	Aoki Shūzō	Diplomatic Archives of the Ministry of Foreign Affairs of Japan
2-27.	The sword used in the Ōtsu Incident; a handkerchief stained with Czar Nicholas's blood	The Museum of Shiga Prefecture Biwako-Bunkakan
2-28.	Anglo-Japanese Treaty of Commerce and Navigation	Diplomatic Archives of the Ministry of Foreign Affairs of Japan
2-29.	Itō Hirobumi	Diplomatic Archives of the Ministry of Foreign Affairs of Japan
2-30.	Inoue Kaoru	Diplomatic Archives of the Ministry of Foreign Affairs of Japan
3-1.	*Declaration of War with Russia* (painting by Yoshida Shigeru)	Meiji Memorial Picture Gallery
3-2.	"News from Korea: An Account of a Skirmish" (woodblock print by unknown artist)	British Library/Uniphoto Press
3-3.	Mutsu Munemitsu	Diplomatic Archives of the Ministry of Foreign Affairs of Japan
3-4.	"The Occupation of Port Arthur by Japanese Forces" (woodblock print by Yōsai Nobukazu)	British Library/Uniphoto Press
3-5.	"The Japanese Naval Attack on Weihaiwei" (woodblock print by unknown artist)	British Library/Uniphoto Press
3-6.	*Peace Conference at Shimonoseki* (painting by Nagatochi Hideta)	Meiji Memorial Picture Gallery
3-7.	Nishi Tokujirō	Diplomatic Archives of the Ministry of Foreign Affairs of Japan
3-8.	Motono Ichirō	Diplomatic Archives of the Ministry of Foreign Affairs of Japan

No.	Name	Credit
3-9.	The Peking Protocol	Diplomatic Archives of the Ministry of Foreign Affairs of Japan
3-10.	The United Kingdom stirs conflict between Japan and Russia (cartoon by Georges Ferdinand Bigot)	Bijutsudōjinsha
3-11.	First Anglo-Japanese Alliance (signed treaty)	Diplomatic Archives of the Ministry of Foreign Affairs of Japan
3-12.	Hayashi Tadasu	Diplomatic Archives of the Ministry of Foreign Affairs of Japan
3-13.	Komura Jutarō	Diplomatic Archives of the Ministry of Foreign Affairs of Japan
3-14.	*The Surrender of Port Arthur* (painting by Arai Rokuo)	Meiji Memorial Picture Gallery
3-15.	*The Scene of the Bridge on* Mikasa (painting by Tōjō Shōtarō)	Memorial Ship MIKASA
3-16.	Japan-Russia Treaty of Peace (Treaty of Portsmouth) instrument of ratification	Diplomatic Archives of the Ministry of Foreign Affairs of Japan
3-17.	Kaneko Kentarō	National Diet Library
3-18.	Portsmouth Peace Conference	Diplomatic Archives of the Ministry of Foreign Affairs of Japan
3-19.	Yamagata Aritomo	Cabinet Public Relations Office
3-20.	Katsura Tarō	Cabinet Public Relations Office
3-21.	Borders based on the Treaty of Portsmouth (1905)	Ministry of Foreign Affairs of Japan
3-22.	*Demarcation of Saghalin [Sakhalin] Frontier* (painting by Yasuda Minoru)	Meiji Memorial Picture Gallery
3-23.	Peace Palace, the Hague	Diplomatic Archives of the Ministry of Foreign Affairs of Japan
3-24.	Tapestries in the Japanese Room of the Peace Palace	Diplomatic Archives of the Ministry of Foreign Affairs of Japan
3-25.	Russo-Japanese Agreement of 1907 (signed treaty)	Diplomatic Archives of the Ministry of Foreign Affairs of Japan
3-26.	Kurino Shin'ichirō	National Diet Library
3-27.	"People, the Exhausted Horse" (cartoon by unknown artist)	Bijutsudōjinsha
3-28.	Ōkuma and Resident-General of Korea Itō	Tokyo Puck
3-29.	Citizens listening to a performance by German prisoners of war (POW Camp in Bandō, Tokushima Prefecture)	The Naruto German House
4-1.	Treaties related to South Manchuria and eastern Inner Mongolia (instruments of ratification)	Diplomatic Archives of the Ministry of Foreign Affairs of Japan
4-2.	Yamaza Enjirō	National Diet Library
4-3.	Ijūin Hikokichi	Diplomatic Archives of the Ministry of Foreign Affairs of Japan
4-4.	Saionji Kinmochi	Diplomatic Archives of the Ministry of Foreign Affairs of Japan
4-5.	Headquarters of the South Manchuria Railway Company	National Diet Library
4-6.	Uchida Yasuya	Diplomatic Archives of the Ministry of Foreign Affairs of Japan
4-7.	Japanese troops enter Tsingtao (Qingdao)	Kyodo News
4-8.	Katō Takaaki	Diplomatic Archives of the Ministry of Foreign Affairs of Japan
4-9.	Leaflet calling for Chinese resolve in the face of Japan's demands	Diplomatic Archives of the Ministry of Foreign Affairs of Japan
4-10.	Terauchi Masatake	Diplomatic Archives of the Ministry of Foreign Affairs of Japan
4-11.	Ishii Kikujirō	Diplomatic Archives of the Ministry of Foreign Affairs of Japan
4-12.	The Lansing-Ishii Agreement	Diplomatic Archives of the Ministry of Foreign Affairs of Japan
4-13.	Ishii Kikujirō and Robert Lansing	Library of Congress
4-14.	"As to Japanese Exclusion." Illustration by Frank A. Nankivell showing a group of "undesirables" dressed in kimono and pretending to be Japanese immigrants	Library of Congress
4-15.	Chinda Sutemi	Diplomatic Archives of the Ministry of Foreign Affairs of Japan
4-16.	The 1909 geopolitical analysis *The Valor of Ignorance* by Homer Lea	Internet Archive
5-1.	Plenipotentiaries present at the signing of the Treaty of Versailles	The Mainichi Newspapers
5-2.	Hara Takashi (Kei)	Diplomatic Archives of the Ministry of Foreign Affairs of Japan
5-3.	Makino Nobuaki	Diplomatic Archives of the Ministry of Foreign Affairs of Japan
5-4.	Japanese delegates to the Paris Peace Conference	Diplomatic Archives of the Ministry of Foreign Affairs of Japan

No.	Name	Credit
5-5.	The Paris Peace Conference	Diplomatic Archives of the Ministry of Foreign Affairs of Japan
5-6.	League of Nations headquarters	United Nations Archives at Geneva
5-7.	Yoshizawa Kenkichi	Diplomatic Archives of the Ministry of Foreign Affairs of Japan
5-8.	Nitobe Inazō	Diplomatic Archives of the Ministry of Foreign Affairs of Japan
5-9.	Sugimura Yōtarō	Diplomatic Archives of the Ministry of Foreign Affairs of Japan
5-10.	Itō Miyoji	National Diet Library
5-11.	Crown Prince Hirohito visits Europe	Kyodo News
5-12.	Troops sent to Siberia	Kyodo News
5-13.	Rice Riots, August 1918	The Asahi Shimbun
5-14.	Gotō and Joffe	Goto Shinpei Memorial Hall
6-1.	National representatives at the Washington Naval Conference	The Asahi Shimbun
6-2.	First day of the Washington Naval Conference	The Asahi Shimbun
6-3.	Japanese delegation to the Washington Naval Conference	Diplomatic Archives of the Ministry of Foreign Affairs of Japan
6-4.	Shidehara Kijūrō	Cabinet Public Relations Office
6-5.	Tung Wen College, Shanghai	Public domain
6-6.	Poster promoting emigration from Japan to South America	Diplomatic Archives of the Ministry of Foreign Affairs of Japan
6-7.	The signing of the Soviet-Japanese Basic Convention	The Asahi Shimbun
6-8.	Document signed by Yoshizawa and Karakhan	Diplomatic Archives of the Ministry of Foreign Affairs of Japan
6-9.	Tanaka Giichi	Cabinet Public Relations Office
6-10.	The bombing of the train carrying Zhang Zuolin	The Asahi Shimbun
6-11.	Obata Yūkichi	Diplomatic Archives of the Ministry of Foreign Affairs of Japan
6-12.	The London Naval Conference	The Asahi Shimbun
6-13.	Takahashi Korekiyo	Cabinet Public Relations Office
6-14.	Inoue Junnosuke	National Diet Library
7-1.	Official photo following the coronation of the emperor of Manchukuo	The Asahi Shimbun
7-2.	September 18 History Museum, Shenyang, Liaoning Province	Kyodo News
7-3.	The Japanese army enters Qiqihar	The Asahi Shimbun
7-4.	The Shanghai Incident (January 28 Incident)	Kyodo News
7-5.	The installation of the Puyi administration	The Mainichi Newspapers
7-6.	Fengtian (Mukden) Station in former Manchuria	Public domain
7-7.	The Lytton Commission	Kyodo News
7-8.	Matsuoka Yōsuke addresses the Assembly of the League of Nations	The Asahi Shimbun
8-1.	The signing of the Japan-Germany Anti-Comintern Pact	Diplomatic Archives of the Ministry of Foreign Affairs of Japan
8-2.	Hirota Kōki	Diplomatic Archives of the Ministry of Foreign Affairs of Japan
8-3.	The railway system in Northern Manchuria and Mongolia	Reprinted from Kitaoka Shinichi, From Party Politics to Militarism in Japan, 1924–1941 (Boulder, CO: Lynne Rienner Publishers, 2021)
8-4.	The February 26 Incident	Kyodo News
8-5.	The Kawagoe–Chiang Kai-shek Talks on October 8, 1936	The Asahi Shimbun
8-6.	Japan-Germany Anti-Comintern Pact	Diplomatic Archives of the Ministry of Foreign Affairs of Japan
8-7.	Satō Naotake	Diplomatic Archives of the Ministry of Foreign Affairs of Japan
9-1.	Japanese ambassador Admiral Kichisaburō Nomura (left) and Special Envoy Saburō Kurusu (right) meet US secretary of state Cordell Hull, November 1941	Public domain
9-2.	Japanese army captures Marco Polo Bridge	The Asahi Shimbun
9-3.	First cabinet of Prime Minister Konoe Fumimaro	Kyodo News
9-4.	Japanese tank corps destroys Zhonghua Gate in Nanjing	Kyodo News
9-5.	Brussels Conference	Diplomatic Archives of the Ministry of Foreign Affairs of Japan

No.	Name	Credit
9-6.	Anti-Japanese slogans displayed during the Second Sino-Japanese War	The Asahi Shimbun
9-7.	Konoe Fumimaro	Cabinet Public Relations Office
9-8.	Ugaki Kazushige	Diplomatic Archives of the Ministry of Foreign Affairs of Japan
9-9.	Arita Hachirō	Diplomatic Archives of the Ministry of Foreign Affairs of Japan
9-10.	Saitō Hiroshi	Diplomatic Archives of the Ministry of Foreign Affairs of Japan
9-11.	The signing of the Molotov-Ribbentrop Pact (German-Soviet Non-Aggression Pact)	The Mainichi Newspapers
9-12.	Nomura Kichisaburō	Diplomatic Archives of the Ministry of Foreign Affairs of Japan
9-13.	Matsuoka Yōsuke	Diplomatic Archives of the Ministry of Foreign Affairs of Japan
9-14.	The Ogikubo Meeting	Kyodo News
9-15.	German minister of foreign affairs Joachim von Ribbentrop announces the Tripartite Pact	The Asahi Shimbun
9-16.	The signing of the Soviet-Japanese Neutrality Pact	Kyodo News
9-17.	The official logo of the 1940 Tokyo Olympics	Diplomatic Archives of the Ministry of Foreign Affairs of Japan
9-18.	Imperial Japanese Navy landing force marches through Saigon	Diplomatic Archives of the Ministry of Foreign Affairs of Japan
9-19.	Japanese diplomatic telegram, December 1941 (deciphered and translated by US)	US National Archives
9-20.	The Hull Note	Diplomatic Archives of the Ministry of Foreign Affairs of Japan
10-1.	*The Final Meeting of the Imperial Council* (painting by Shirakawa Ichirō)	Suzuki Kantaro Memorial Hall
10-2.	Tōgō Shigenori	Diplomatic Archives of the Ministry of Foreign Affairs of Japan
10-3.	Shigemitsu Mamoru	Diplomatic Archives of the Ministry of Foreign Affairs of Japan
10-4.	Sugihara Chiune	Diplomatic Archives of the Ministry of Foreign Affairs of Japan
10-5.	List of visas issued by Sugihara	Diplomatic Archives of the Ministry of Foreign Affairs of Japan
10-6.	The Greater East Asia Conference	National Archives of Japan
10-7.	Indonesian president Sukarno visits Japan in 1943	The Asahi Shimbun
10-8.	Greater East Asia Conference	Kyodo News
10-9.	Chiang Kai-shek, Franklin Roosevelt, and Winston Churchill meet in Cairo	Franklin D. Roosevelt Presidential Library and Museum
10-10.	The Japanese naval base in Kobe Port in flames after being bombed by US B-29 bombers	Kyodo News
10-11.	Leaflets dropped by US forces	The Asahi Shimbun
10-12.	US forces make landing on Okinawa	United States National Archives
10-13.	Suzuki Kantarō	Takano Norio
10-14.	Atlantic Conference	Naval History and Heritage Command
10-15.	Kase Shun'ichi	Diplomatic Archives of the Ministry of Foreign Affairs of Japan
10-16.	Friedrich Hack	The Asahi Shimbun
10-17.	Mass suicides during the Battle of Okinawa	Photo by US Armed Forces
10-18.	Winston Churchill, Harry S. Truman, and Joseph Stalin in Potsdam, Germany	The Harry S. Truman Library and Museum
10-19.	The repatriation ship *Hikawa Maru*	Nakajima Saburosuke to Asobu-Kai (a volunteer organization based in Kanagawa, Japan)
11-1.	Prime Minister Yoshida signs the Peace Treaty of San Francisco	Diplomatic Archives of the Ministry of Foreign Affairs of Japan
11-2.	MacArthur arrives in Atsugi	Kyodo News
11-3.	Instrument of Surrender	Diplomatic Archives of the Ministry of Foreign Affairs of Japan
11-4.	The signing of the Instrument of Surrender aboard the USS *Missouri*	Kyodo News
11-5.	Okazaki Katsuo	Diplomatic Archives of the Ministry of Foreign Affairs of Japan
11-6.	Shirasu Jirō	Diplomatic Archives of the Ministry of Foreign Affairs of Japan

No.	Name	Credit
11-7.	Letter from Shirasu to Courtney Whitney, chief of the Government Section at GHQ, explaining that the Matsumoto draft and GHQ draft had the same goal but took different paths toward that goal	Diplomatic Archives of the Ministry of Foreign Affairs of Japan
11-8.	Children carrying a barrel that was used to transport milk from an aid agency	The Archives of the American Friends Service Committee
11-9.	Ashida Hitoshi	Cabinet Public Relations Office
11-10.	Overview of the United Kingdom's peace proposal (draft)	Diplomatic Archives of the Ministry of Foreign Affairs of Japan
11-11.	Draft of the Japanese government's plan regarding Japan's rearmament	Diplomatic Archives of the Ministry of Foreign Affairs of Japan
11-12.	The signing of the Japan–Republic of China peace treaty	Taipei Guest House
11-13.	Chief Counsel Joseph Keenan	Diplomatic Archives of the Ministry of Foreign Affairs of Japan
11-14.	International Military Tribunal for the Far East	Kyodo News
11-15.	Syngman Rhee Line	The Ministry of Foreign Affairs of Japan website was referenced for the production of this map. https://www.mofa.go.jp/a_o/na/takeshima/page1we_000064.html
11-16.	Special Envoy Dulles and Prime Minister Yoshida	Kyodo News
11-17.	Yoshida Shigeru	Takano Norio
11-18.	Exterior view of the former residence of Yoshida Shigeru	Oiso Municipal Museum
12-1.	Ratification of the revised US-Japan Security Treaty	Kyodo News
12-2.	The beginning of the Jiyū-Minshutō (Liberal Democratic Party) in 1955	The Asahi Shimbun
12-3.	The signing of the Soviet-Japanese Joint Declaration	TASS/Kyodo News
12-4.	Hatoyama Ichirō	Cabinet Public Relations Office
12-5.	Document affirming Japan's admission to the United Nations	Ministry of Foreign Affairs of Japan
12-6.	The Asian-African Conference (Bandung Conference)	Kyodo News
12-7.	Kishi Nobusuke	Cabinet Public Relations Office
12-8.	Prime Minister Nehru of India visits Japan	Kyodo News
12-9.	The *Daigo Fukuryū Maru*, contaminated by US atomic tests on Bikini Atoll	Kyodo News
12-10.	Fujiyama Aiichirō	Diplomatic Archives of the Ministry of Foreign Affairs of Japan
12-11.	Treaty of Mutual Cooperation and Security between the United States and Japan (signature page)	Ministry of Foreign Affairs of Japan
12-12.	Anti-Anpo demonstration	Kyodo News
13-1.	Satō Eisaku and Ikeda Hayato	The Asahi Shimbun
13-2.	Ikeda Hayato	Cabinet Public Relations Office
13-3.	Satō Eisaku	Cabinet Public Relations Office
13-4.	President Kennedy and Prime Minister Ikeda	UPI/Kyodo News
13-5.	The Ōhira-Kim Memo	The Diplomatic Archives of the Ministry of Foreign Affairs of Korea
13-6.	From left to right: US ambassador Reischauer, Vice President Hubert H. Humphrey, Prime Minister Satō Eisaku and Foreign Minister Shiina Etsusaburō	Kyodo News
13-7.	Signing of the Treaty on Basic Relations between Japan and the Republic of Korea and associated agreements	National Archives of Korea
13-8.	Takeshima	Kyodo News
13-9.	The Senkaku Islands	Kyodo News
13-10.	Yara Chōbyō (left), chief executive of the government of the Ryūkyū Islands, visits Foreign Minister Aichi Kiichi (right)	Kyodo News
13-11.	Ceremony commemorating the return of Okinawa to Japan	Kyodo News
14-1.	World leaders gather for the Tokyo Summit	Kyodo News
14-2.	Richard Nixon shaking hands with Mao Zedong in China	UPI/Kyodo News
14-3.	Tanaka Kakuei	Cabinet Public Relations Office

No.	Name	Credit
14-4.	The first Japan-China Summit	Kyodo News
14-5.	The signed Japan-China Joint Communiqué	Ministry of Foreign Affairs of Japan
14-6.	Discussions during the oil crisis	UPI/Kyodo News
14-7.	Miki Takeo	Cabinet Public Relations Office
14-8.	First summit of the world's leading industrialized nations in 1975	UPI/Kyodo News
14-9.	Fukuda Takeo	Cabinet Public Relations Office
14-10.	The ratification of the Treaty of Peace and Friendship between Japan and the People's Republic of China	Diplomatic Archives of the Ministry of Foreign Affairs of Japan
14-11.	Ōhira Masayoshi	Cabinet Public Relations Office
14-12.	US president Reagan visits Japan	Diplomatic Archives of the Ministry of Foreign Affairs of Japan
14-13.	Prime Minister Nakasone makes an official visit to Yasukuni Shrine	Kyodo News
14-14.	Nakasone Yasuhiro	Cabinet Public Relations Office
14-15.	Funeral procession of Emperor Shōwa	Kyodo News
15-1.	US president George W. Bush and Prime Minister Koizumi at a bilateral summit	Kyodo News
15-2.	The fall of the Berlin Wall	Reuters/Kyodo News
15-3.	Minesweepers at work in the Persian Gulf	Japan Maritime Self-Defense Force (JMSDF)
15-4.	The UN PKO in Cambodia	Kyodo News
15-5.	Miyazawa Kiichi	Cabinet Public Relations Office
15-6.	The signing of the Japan-US Joint Declaration on Security	Ministry of Foreign Affairs of Japan website https://www.mofa.go.jp/region/n-america/us/security/security.html
15-7.	US Air Station Futenma	Kyodo News
15-8.	Obuchi Keizō	Cabinet Public Relations Office
15-9.	The Tiananmen Square Incident	Reuters/Kyodo News
15-10.	Murayama Tomiichi	Cabinet Public Relations Office
15-11.	Japan and South Korea reach an agreement on "comfort women"	Ministry of Foreign Affairs of Japan Website https://www.mofa.go.jp/a_o/na/kr/page4e_000364.html
15-12.	The Japan–South Korea Joint Declaration	Kyodo News
15-13.	Chinese general secretary Jiang Zemin visits Japan	Prime Minister's Office of Japan
15-14.	Map showing the Northern Territories	The Ministry of Foreign Affairs of Japan website was referenced for the production of this map. https://www.mofa.go.jp/territory/
15-15.	President Yeltsin and Prime Minister Hosokawa sign the Tokyo Declaration	Ministry of Foreign Affairs of Japan
15-16.	JSDF troops in Samawah	Kyodo News
15-17.	The signing of the Japan–North Korea Pyongyang Declaration	Kyodo News
15-18.	The Hatoyama administration attestation ceremony	Kyodo News
15-19.	Operation Tomodachi	Kyodo News
15-20.	Japan–China–South Korea Summit	Prime Minister's Office of Japan
15-21.	Russian president Vladimir Putin and Prime Minister Abe Shinzō	Kyodo News
15-22.	Demonstrators protest Japan's exercise of its right to collective self-defense	Kyodo News
15-23.	Address by Barack Obama, first sitting US president to visit Hiroshima	News media representative photograph
15-24.	ODA from major donor nations	The Ministry of Foreign Affairs of Japan website was referenced for the production of this map. https://www.mofa.go.jp/policy/oda/summary/1999/d_g3_01.html
15-25.	The Charlevoix Summit (June 2018)	UPI/Newscom/Kyodo News Images

Index by Subject

Note: Page numbers in *italics* refer to sidebar articles.

E

F

O

P

Q

S

U

X

Y

Z

Index of Names

I

J

K

L

S

About the Author

Professor Hatano Sumio (b. 1947) is director-general of the Japan Center for Asian Historical Records (JACAR) at the National Archives of Japan. He is head of the editorial committee for the Ministry of Foreign Affairs' *Nihon gaikō bunsho* (Documents on Japanese Foreign Policy) and is also a professor emeritus at the University of Tsukuba with a specialization in Japanese political and diplomatic history.

After obtaining his doctorate degree from Keio University Graduate School of Law, he became a research fellow at the National Institute for Defense Studies (NIDS). At the University of Tsukuba, he held the posts of professor, vice president, and head of the library. He has also held other academic posts, including as a researcher at Harvard University.

His other works include *Bakuryō-tachi no Shinjuwan* (The staff officers' Pearl Harbor; Asahi Shimbunsha); *Kokka to rekishi* (The Japanese nation and history; Chūōkōron-Shinsha); *Rekishi toshite no Nichi-Bei anpojōyaku* (The history of the US-Japan Security Treaty; Iwanami Shoten); and *Saishō Suzuki Kantarō no ketsudan* (The decision by Prime Minister Suzuki Kantarō; Iwanami Shoten). In addition, he was co-editor of the six-volume series *Nihon no gaikō* (Japanese diplomacy; Iwanami Shoten) as well as *Nit-Chū sensō wa naze okitano ka* (Why did the Second Sino-Japanese War happen?; Chūōkōron-Shinsha), among others. His book *Taiheiyō sensō to Ajia gaikō* (University of Tokyo Press) is available in English as *The Pacific War and Japan's Diplomacy in Asia* (JPIC).

About the Translators

Carl Freire (preface, ch. 1–7) is a translator based in Tokyo. A graduate of Oberlin College and the University of Michigan, he pursued doctoral studies in modern Japanese history at the University of California, Berkeley. He has also worked as a journalist in Osaka and Tokyo. He previously translated Nakamura Tetsu's *Ten, tomo ni ari*, available in English as *Providence Was with Us* (JPIC).

Terry Gallagher (ch. 8–15) has been an independent translator for over twenty years. A graduate of Brown University, he also worked as a journalist in Tokyo, Bonn, and New York. His previous title for JPIC was *The Remarkable History of Japan-US Relations* by Kōsaka Masataka. His translation of *Self-Reference ENGINE* by Akutagawa Prize winner Enjō Tō received the Japan-US Friendship Commission Prize for the Translation of Japanese Literature and the Philip K. Dick Award Special Citation.

Tom Kain (sidebars) is a US-born translator who lives in Saitama. After graduating from St. John's University (MN), he taught English in Okinawa and then completed a master's degree in Japanese studies at Sophia University (Tokyo). He now translates Japanese to English, works on programming for NHK (Japan's public broadcaster), and teaches English at the university level. His previous translation work includes *The Legacy of Kano Jigoro* (JPIC).

About the Editorial Supervisor

Hamaoka Takayuki is assistant director of the Diplomatic Archive of Ministry of Foreign Affairs of Japan. He completed his Master's degree in Area Studies at Tsukuba University. He is now a member of the editorial staff for *Nihon gaikō bunsho* (Documents on Japanese Foreign Policy), a compilation of historical records held by the Ministry of Foreign Affairs first published in 1936.

（英文版）日本外交の150年：幕末・維新から平成まで

One Hundred Fifty Years of Japanese Foreign Relations : From 1868 to 2018

2022年8月29日　第1刷発行

編著者　波多野澄雄
企　画　一般社団法人日本外交協会
訳　者　カール・フレイレ、テリー・ギャラガー、トム・ケイン
英訳監修　浜岡鷹行
発行所　一般財団法人出版文化産業振興財団
〒101-0051 東京都千代田区神田神保町2-2-30
電話　03-5211-7283
ホームページ　https://www.jpic.or.jp/

印刷・製本所　公和印刷株式会社

定価はカバーに表示してあります。

Printed in Japan
softcover ISBN 978-4-86658-173-6
ebook (ePub) ISBN 978-4-86658-185-9